THE SETTLEMENT OF DISPUTES IN INTERNATIONAL LAW

Institutions and Procedures

John Collier
Fellow of Trinity Hall, Cambridge

and

Vaughan Lowe
Fellow of Corpus Christi College, Cambridge

OXFORD
UNIVERSITY PRESS

OXFORD
UNIVERSITY PRESS

Great Clarendon Street, Oxford OX2 6DP

Oxford University Press is a department of the University of Oxford.
It furthers the University's objective of excellence in research, scholarship,
and education by publishing worldwide in

Oxford New York

Auckland Cape Town Dar es Salaam Hong Kong Karachi Kuala Lumpur
Madrid Melbourne Mexico City Nairobi New Delhi Shanghai Taipei Toronto

With offices in

Argentina Austria Brazil Chile Czech Republic France Greece
Guatemala Hungary Italy Japan South Korea Poland Portugal
Singapore Switzerland Thailand Turkey Ukraine Vietnam

Oxford is a registered trade mark of Oxford University Press
in the UK and in certain other countries

Published in the United States
by Oxford University Press Inc., New York

British Library Cataloguing in Publication Data

Data available

Library of Congress Cataloging in Publication Data
Collier, John G. (John Greenwood)
The settlement of disputes in international law: institutions
and procedures/John Collier and Vaughan Lowe.
p. cm.
Includes index.
1. Dispute resolution (Law). 2. Arbitration and award.
3. Pacifc settlement of international disputes.
I. Lowe, Vaughan, 1952- . II. Title.
K2390.C65 1999 341.5′2—dc21 99–16148

ISBN 0-19-825669-8 (Hbk)
ISBN 10: 0-19-829927-3 (Pbk) ISBN 13: 978-0-19-829927-1

9 10 8

Typeset by Hope Services (Abingdon) Ltd.
Printed in Great Britain
on acid-free paper by
Biddles Ltd., King's Lynn, Norfolk

THE SETTLEMENT OF DISPUTES IN INTERNATIONAL LAW

PREFACE

This book has the modest aim of introducing readers to some of the main processes for the settlement of international disputes. The range of such processes is so wide that comprehensiveness is impossible in a short monograph intended, as is this one, as a basis for the teaching of international law. We have concentrated on the most important processes for the handling of international legal disputes, and have sought in the coverage of those processes, and in the selection of documents in the Appendices, to complement rather than duplicate existing texts. Our thanks are due to Oxford University Press for their help and encouragement in the production of this book.

J.G.C.
A.V.L.

Cambridge
January 1999

CONTENTS

Table of Abbreviations   xiii

Table of Cases   xvii

1. **Introduction**   1

   1. Conflict, disputes and the Law   1

   2. The range of dispute settlement procedures   5

   3. Justiciability   10

PART ONE: INSTITUTIONS

2. **Methods of Settlement of Disputes: The Basic Framework**   19

   1. Introduction   19

   2. Negotiation   20

   3. Inquiry and fact finding   24

   4. Mediation and good offices   27

   5. Conciliation   29

   6. Arbitration   31
     6.1 The Permanent Court of Arbitration   35
     6.2 The use of arbitration in recent times   38

   7. Dispute Settlement Mechanisms and other developments   39

   8. New directions? Iraq and the UN Compensation Commission   41

3. **International Commercial Arbitration**   45

   1. Introduction   45

   2. Arbitration rules   46
     2.1 The ICC Rules   47
     2.2 The UNCITRAL Rules   50

   3. National arbitration laws   51
     3.1 The UNCITRAL Model Law   53

4. International agreements on arbitration 54

5. Concluding remarks 58

4. Mixed Arbitrations 59

1. The International Centre for the Settlement of Investment Disputes
(ICSID) 59
   1.1 The ICSID framework 60
       1.1.1 Organs 60
       1.1.2 Jurisdiction 61
       1.1.3 Submission to ICSID jurisdiction 62
       1.1.4 Parties to disputes 64
   1.2 ICSID procedure 68
       1.2.1 Conciliation 68
       1.2.2 Arbitration 69
       1.2.3 Enforcement of ICSID awards 73

2. The Iran-US Claims Tribunal 73
   2.1 The Hostages Crisis 74
   2.2 The Algiers Accords 75
   2.3 The Iran-US Claims Tribunal 76
       2.3.1 Claims of nationals 77
       2.3.2 Official claims 81
       2.3.3 Interpretative cases 81
       2.3.4 Applicable law 82
       2.3.5 Enforcement of Iran-US Claims Tribunal Awards 82

5. Dispute Settlement in the Law of the Sea 84

1. Introduction 84

2. The International Tribunal for the Law of the Sea 87

3. The International Court of Justice 90

4. Annex VII arbitral tribunals 90

5. Annex VIII special arbitral tribunals 91

6. General provisions 92

6. The Settlement of International Economic Disputes 96

1. The GATT and WTO systems 96
   1.1 The GATT system 96
   1.2 The WTO system 99

2. Regional trade dispute settlement systems 104
   2.1 The EU system 105
   2.2 COMESA—the Common Market for Eastern and Southern Africa 107
   2.3 ECOWAS—the Economic Community of West African States 109

2.4 Other African economic organisations 110
2.5 NAFTA—the North American Free Trade Agreement 111
2.6 Mercosur—Mercado Común del Sur/the Southern Common Market 116

3. International financial disputes 117
3.1 The IMF 117
3.2 The World Bank 119
3.3 The Multilateral Investment Guarantee Agency (MIGA) 121

4. Concluding remarks 123

7. **The International Court of Justice** **124**

1. Participation 125

2. Composition of the Court and election of judges: Dismissal 126

3. Sittings: Chambers 127

4. Disqualification of judges 129

5. *Ad hoc* judges 130

6. President; Vice-President; Registrar; Seat 131

7. Competence and jurisdiction in contentious cases 132
7.1 All cases which the parties refer to the Court 133
7.2 Matters specially provided for in the UN Charter 135
7.3 *Forum prorogatum* 136
7.4 Treaties or conventions in force 137
7.5 'Transferred' jurisdiction 139
7.6 The Optional Clause 140
7.6.1 The character of the relationships created by a declaration 140
7.6.2 Reservations 141
7.6.2.1 Domestic jurisdiction 143
7.6.2.2 'Automatic' reservations 143
7.6.2.3 Limitation of jurisdiction to certain categories of case 146
7.6.2.4 Time limitations 146
7.6.2.5 'Multilateral treaty' reservations 148
7.6.2.6 Resort to other means of peaceful settlement 149
7.6.3 Condition of reciprocity 150
7.6.4 Withdrawal or termination of declaration 152
7.6.5 Variation of the terms of a declaration 153
7.6.6 'Transferred' declarations 153
7.6.7 The Optional Clause: Summary 154

8. Admissibility 155
8.1 Hypothetical nature of the case 156
8.2 The case has become 'moot' 157
8.3 Lack of interest in the subject matter 157
8.4 Legal interest of a third State 158
8.5 Other examples 161

9. Intervention   162
   9.1 Construction of a convention   163
   9.2 An interest of a legal nature   164

10. Interim (provisional) measures of protection   168
   10.1 Jurisdiction   169
   10.2 The exercise of discretion   171
   10.3 The scope of interim measures   173
   10.4 Relationship to the claim on the merits   174
   10.5 Enforcement of interim measures   174

11. Procedure of the Court   175

12. Effect of judgments   177

13. Enforcement of judgments   178

14. Interpretation and revision of judgments   179

15. Non-appearance   180

16. Advisory Opinions   182

PART TWO: PROCEDURE

8. The Arbitral Process   **189**

1. Introduction   190

2. Admissibility   191
   2.1 Nationality of claims   191
   2.2 Exhaustion of local remedies   195

3. Submission to jurisdiction   198
   3.1 Written agreement   200
   3.2 Existing or future differences   201
   3.3 Defined legal relationship   202
   3.4 Arbitrability   202
   3.5 Capacity   204
   3.6 Validity   206

4. Who is covered by the arbitration agreement?   207

5. Third parties: Intervention and joinder   208

6. Contents of the arbitration agreement   210

7. Arbitration clauses and submission agreements   212

8. The autonomy of the arbitration clause   212

9. Refusal to arbitrate and the denial of justice   216

10. Establishment and procedure of arbitral tribunals   218

	10.1 Time limits	218
	10.2 Appointment of arbitrators	219
	10.3 Challenge to and disqualification of arbitrators	222
11.	Powers and duties of arbitrators	223
12.	The authority of truncated tribunals	225
13.	Challenges to the tribunal's jurisdiction	227
14.	*Lex arbitri*	229
15.	Delocalisation	232
16.	Procedure	235
17.	Applicable law	239
18.	Remedies	248
	18.1 Interim measures	248
	18.2 Final remedies	250
19.	The award	253
20.	Challenges to awards	257
21.	Effects of the award	261
22.	Enforcement of judgments and awards	263
	22.1 The New York Convention	266
	22.2 State immunity	270

APPENDICES

Appendix 1. Manila Declaration on the Peaceful Settlement of International Disputes — 279

Appendix 2. Hague Convention on the Pacific Settlement of Disputes, 1907 — 285

Appendix 3. ICSID Convention — 302

Appendix 4. UNCITRAL Arbitration Rules — 319

Appendix 5. UNCITRAL Model Law — 334

Appendix 6. Statute of the International Court of Justice — 346

Appendix 7. Rules of the International Court of Justice — 359

Index — 391

TABLE OF ABBREVIATIONS

AJICL	*African Journal of International & Comparative Law*
AJIL	*American Journal of International Law*
BFSP	*British and Foreign State Papers*
BISD	(GATT) *Basic Instruments and Selected Documents*
BYIL	*British Yearbook of International Law*
Cd.	Command Paper (UK)
CLJ	*Cambridge Law Journal*
Cmd.	Command Paper (UK)
Cmnd.	Command Paper (UK)
CSCE	Conference on Security and Co-operation in Europe
CYIL	*Canadian Yearbook of International Law*
DUSPIL	*Digest of United States Practice in International Law*
ECHR	European Court of Human Rights; publications of the European Court of Human Rights
FAO	(UN) Food and Agriculture Organization
Fifty Years of the ICJ	V. Lowe and M. Fitzmaurice (eds.), *Fifty Years of the International Court of Justice* (Cambridge, 1996)
FILJ	(ICSID Review) *Foreign Investment Law Journal*
GA	(United Nations) General Assembly
HCR	J. B. Scott, *The Hague Court Reports*, First Series (New York, 1916); Second Series (New York, 1932)
HR	Hague Academy of International Law, *Recueil des cours*
IBRD	International Bank for Reconstruction and Development
ICC	International Chamber of Commerce
ICC Arbitral Awards	*ICC Arbitral Awards 1974–85* (S. Jarvin and Y. Derains. Deventer, 1990); *1986–90* (S. Jarvin, Y. Derains and J. J. Arnaldez. Paris, 1994); *1991–95* (J. J. Arnaldez, Y. Derains and D. Hascher. Paris, 1997)
ICLQ	*International and Comparative Law Quarterly*
ICSID	International Centre for the Settlement of Investment Disputes
ILC	International Law Commission

ILM	*International Legal Materials*
ILQ	*International Law Quarterly*
ILR	*International Law Reports*
IMO	International Maritime Organization
Int. ALR	*International Arbitration Law Review*
IOC	(UNESCO) Intergovernmental Oceanographic Commission
Iran-US CTR	*Iran-United States Claims Tribunal Reports*
JBL	*Journal of Business Law*
Lapradelle–Politis	A. de Lapradelle and N. Politis, *Receuil des arbitrages internationaux*, vol. 1 (Paris, 1905), vol. 2 (Paris, 1924), vol. 3 (Paris, 1954)
LCIA	London Court of International Arbitration
LMCLQ	*Lloyds Maritime and Commercial Law Quarterly*
LNTS	*League of Nations Treaty Series*
Merrills	J. G. Merrills, *International Dispute Settlement*, 3rd edn. (Cambridge, 1998)
Moore, *Int. Arb.*	Moore, *History and Digest of the International Arbitrations to which the United States has been a Party*, 6 vols. (Washington, DC, 1898)
Neth. Tid. IL	*Nederlands tijdschrift voor internationaal recht*
OAU	Organization of African Unity
Oppenheim	Sir R. Jennings and Sir A. Watts, *Oppenheim's International Law, Vol. 1, Peace*, 9th edn. (Harlow, 1992)
OSCE	Organization for Security and Co-operation in Europe
PCA	Permanent Court of Arbitration
PCIJ	Permanent Court of International Justice; publications of the PCIJ
Proc. ASIL	*Proceedings of the American Society of International Law*
Redfern & Hunter	A. Redfern and M. Hunter, *Law and Practice of International Commercial Arbitration*, 2nd edn. (London, 1991)
Rubino-Sammartano	M. Rubino-Sammartano, *International Arbitration Law* (Deventer, 1990)
SC	(United Nations) Security Council
UKTS	*United Kingdom Treaty Series*
UMA	Union de Maghreb Arabe
UN	United Nations
UNCITRAL	United Nations Commission on International Trade Law

UNEP	UN Environment Programme
UNESCO	UN Education, Scientific and Cultural Organization
UN Handbook	United Nations *Handbook on the Peaceful Settlement of Disputes* (New York, 1992)
UNRIAA	*United Nations Reports of International Arbitral Awards*
UNTS	*United Nations Treaty Series*
Y'bk. Int. Env. Law	*Yearbook of International Environmental Law*
Zamora & Brand	S. Zamora and R. A. Brand (eds.), *Basic Documents of International Economic Law,* 2 vols. (Chicago, 1990)
ZAORV	*Zeitschrift für ausländisches öffentliches Recht und Völkerrecht*

TABLE OF CASES

A/1 (Security Account) (1983) 1 *Iran-US CTR* 189, (1983) 22 *ILM* 591 81

A/2 (1982) 1 *Iran-US CTR* 101 77

A/15 (Excess Iranian Funds) (1986) 12 *Iran-US CTR* 40, (1987) 26 *ILM*
  1562 81

A/18 (1984) 5 *Iran-US CTR* 251, 428 .... 80, 81, 190, 192

A/21 (1987) 14 *Iran-US CTR* 324 82

Abu Dhabi arbitration (1951), see *Petroleum Development Ltd.* v. *Sheikh of
  Abu Dhabi*

Abu Dhabi Gas Liquefaction Co. Ltd. v. *Eastern Bechtel Corp.* [1982] 2 Lloyd's
  Rep. 425, (1982) 21 *ILM* 1057 .... 210, 220

ADGAS, see *Abu Dhabi Gas Liquefaction Co. Ltd.* v. *Eastern Bechtel Corp.*

Adriano Gardella v. *Ivory Coast* (1977) 1 *ICSID Reports* 283 .... 70, 71

Aegean Sea Continental Shelf case.
  Provisional measures, ICJ Rep. 1976, 3......................170, 171, 172
  Judgment, ICJ Rep. 1978, 3......................21

Aerial Incident of 27 July 1955 (Israel v. *Bulgaria)*, ICJ Rep. 1959, 127 .... 139, 154

AGIP S.p.A. v. *The Government of the People's Republic of the Congo* (1979) 1
  ICSID Reports 306, (1982) 21 *ILM* 726 .... 11, 70

Air Transport Agreement arbitration (*USA* v. *France*) (1963), 16 *UNRIAA* 5;
  38 *ILR* 182 38

Air Transport Agreement arbitration (*USA* v. *Italy*) (1965), 16 *UNRIAA* 81;
  45 *ILR* 393 38

Air Transport Agreement arbitration (*USA* v. *France*) (1978), 18 *UNRIAA* 417;
  54 *ILR* 304 38

Alabama claims (1872), (1871), Moore, *Int. Arb.*, vol. 1, 496 .... 32, 33

Alcoa Minerals of Jamaica, Inc. v. *The Government of Jamaica* (1975) 1 *ICSID
  Reports* 296n, 4 *Yearbook Commercial Arbitration* 206 (1979) 62, 243

Alcom Ltd. v. *Republic of Colombia* [1984] AC 580, 74 *ILR* 170 272

Ambatielos arbitration, (1956) 23 *ILR* 306 .... 196, 219

*Amco Asia Corporation, Pan American Development Limited and P. T. Amco
  Indonesia* v. *Republic of Indonesia*.
  Jurisdiction I, 1983, 1 *ICSID Reports* 377, (1984) 23 *ILM* 351,
    89 *ILR* 379......................63, 66, 67, 68, 72, 194, 207
  Provisional measures, 1983, 1 *ICSID Reports* 410; 89 *ILR* 402;
    (1985) 24 *ILM* 365......................72
  Merits I, 1984, 1 *ICSID Reports* 413; 89 *ILR* 405; (1985) 24 *ILM* 1022......................72
  Annulment, 1986, 1 *ICSID Reports* 509; 89 *ILR* 514;
    (1986) 25 *ILM* 1439 ....71, 72, 258

Jurisdiction II, 1988, 1 *ICSID Reports* 543; 89 *ILR* 552;
  (1988) 27 *ILM* 1281 ....72, 261, 262
Merits II and rectification, 1990, 1 *ICSID Reports* 569, 638, (1991) 118 *Journal de*
  droit international 172; 89 *ILR* 580 .... 71, 72
American Cyanamid Ltd. v. *Ethicon* [1975] 1 All ER 504 168
American Manufacturing & Trading, Inc. v. *Republic of Zaire* (1997) 36 *ILM*
  1531 .... 70, 71
AMINOIL, see *Government of Kuwait* v. *American Independent Oil Company*
Amin Rasheed Shipping Corporation v. *Kuwait Insurance Co.,*
  [1984] AC 50 243
Amoco International Finance Corp. v. *Iran* (1987) 83 *ILR* 501 252
Anglo-French Continental Shelf arbitration
  Award, 1977/8, 54 *ILR* 6, (1979) 18 *ILM* 397 38
  Interpretation, 1979, 54 *ILR* 139, (1979) 18 *ILM* 462....................................179, 256
Anglo-Iranian Oil Company case
  Provisional measures ICJ Rep. 1951, 89..169, 170, 171
  Preliminary objection, ICJ Rep. 1952, 93 .... 129, 146, 196, 213
Anglo-Norwegian Fisheries case, ICJ Rep. 1951, 116 85
Appeal Relating to the Jurisdiction of the Council of the International Civil
  Aviation Organisation, ICJ Rep. 1972, 46 .... 138, 153, 213
Applicability of the Obligation to Arbitrate under Section 21 of the United
  Nations Headquarters Agreement of 26 June 1947, ICJ Rep. 1988, 12 .... 11, 12
Application of the Convention on the Prevention and Punishment of the Crime of
  Genocide (Bosnia and Herzegovina v. *Yugoslavia)*
  Provisional measures, ICJ Rep. 1993, 3, 325...9, 172
    ICJ Rep. 1993, 325 ....175, 263
  Preliminary objections, ICJ Rep. 1996, 595 11
Arab African Energy Corporation Ltd. v. *Olieproduktion Nederland BV* [1983]
  2 Lloyd's Rep. 419 259
Aramco, see *Saudi Arabia* v. *Arabian American Oil Co.*
Arbitral Award of 31 July 1989, (Guinea-Bissau/Senegal)
  Provisional measures, ICJ Rep. 1990, 64 ....94, 173
  Judgment, ICJ Rep. 1991, 53 .... 94, 149, 173, 238, 257
Arbitral Award Made by the King of Spain on 23 December 1906
  (Honduras v. *Nicaragua)*, ICJ Rep. 1960, 192 .... 238, 257
Asian Agricultural Products Ltd. v. *Democratic Socialist Republic of Sri Lanka,*
  4 *ICSID Reports* 245, (1991) 30 *ILM* 57 .... 63, 64
Asylum case *(Colombia/Peru)*
  Judgment, ICJ Rep. 1950, 266 ....15, 163, 179
  Request for interpretation, ICJ Rep. 1950, 395 179
Atlantic Triton
  Award, 1986. 3 *ICSID Reports* 13 ....69, 250
  French courts, 1984, 1986, 3 *ICSID Reports* 3, 10 .... 69, 250
Attorney-General v. *Mobil Oil NZ Ltd.* (1987) 4 *ICSID Reports* 117 69
Australian Subsidy on Ammonium Sulphate (1950) 2 *BISD* 188 (1952) 99

Bananas, see *Regime for the Importation, Sale and Distribution of Bananas*

Bank Mellat v. *Helliniki Techniki SA*, [1984] QB 291 .... 233, 249

Barcelona Traction case (*Belgium* v. *Spain*)

Preliminary objections, ICJ Rep. 1964, 6 ....138, 140, 154

Second Phase, ICJ Rep. 1970, 3 .... 7, 80, 158, 193

Beagle Channel arbitration (*Argentina/Chile*, 1978), 52 *ILR* 39; (1978) 17

ILM 634, 738 and (1985) 24 *ILM* 1 .... 28, 38, 218, 237

Behring Sea Fur Seal arbitration (1893), Moore, *Int. Arb.*, vol. 1, 935 .... 33, 236

Belilos (1988) ECHR Ser. A, No. 132 144

Bendore-Derozzi v. *Iran* (1984) 6 *Iran-US CTR* 130 78

Benincasa v. *Dentalkit Srl.*, Case C–269/95, [1998] All ER (EC) 135 214

Bentelerv. Belgium (1983), (1984) 1 *Journal of International Arbitration* 184,

(1985) *European Commercial Cases* 101 205

Benvenuti & Bonfant, see *S.A.R.L. Benvenuti & Bonfant* v. *Government of the*

People's Republic of the Congo

Birch Shipping Corp. v. *Embassy of the United Republic of Tanzania*, 507 F

Supp. 311 (1980), 63 *ILR* 524 413

Border and Transborder Armed Actions (*Nicaragua* v. *Honduras*)

Provisional measures, ICJ Rep. 1988, 9 15

Jurisdiction and admissibility, ICJ Rep. 1988, 69 162

Bosnian Genocide case, see *Application of the Convention on the Prevention and*

Punishment of the Crime of Genocide (*Bosnia and Herzegovina* v. *Yugoslavia*)

BP Exploration Co. (Libya) Ltd v. *Government of Libyan Arab Republic* (1973)

53 *ILR* 297 .... 39, 231, 233, 251

Breard, see *Case concerning the Vienna Convention on Consular Relations*

(*Paraguay* v. *USA*)

Bremer Vulkan Schiffbau und Maschinenfabrik v. *South India Shipping Corp.*

Ltd. [1981] AC 909 .... 215, 218

British Claims in the Spanish Zone of Morocco (1925) 2 *UNRIAA* 615. 14

British Guiana—Venezuela Boundary case (1899) 92 *BFSP* 160 33

Buraimi Oasis arbitration (1955) 223, 227

Buttes Gas and Oil Co. v. *Hammer* [1982] AC 888 .... 16, 202

Cameroon v. *Nigeria*, see *Land and Maritime Boundary between Cameroon and Nigeria*

Canevaro case (1912) 11 *UNRIAA* 397 36

Carl Zeiss Stiftung v. *Rayner & Keeler (no. 2)* [1967] 1 AC 853 178

Carvalho v. *Hull Blyth (Angola) Ltd.* [1979] 1 WLR 1278 80

Case concerning the Vienna Convention on Consular Relations (*Paraguay* v.

USA), ICJ Rep. 1998 .... 133, 170, 171

Certain Expenses of the United Nations, ICJ Rep. 1962, 151 185

Certain German Interests in Polish Upper Silesia, Merits, 1926, PCIJ, Ser. A,

No. 7 .... 177, 237

Certain Norwegian Loans, ICJ Rep. 1957, 9 .... 141, 142, 143, 144, 151

Certain Phosphate Lands in Nauru (*Nauru* v. *Australia*). Preliminary objections,

ICJ Rep. 1992, 240... 149, 156, 159, 161

Chaco conciliation (Bolivia/Paraguay, 1929) 28, 30

Channel Continental Shelf arbitration (*France/UK*, 1978), see *Anglo-French Continental Shelf Arbitration*

Channel Tunnel Group Ltd. v. *Balfour Beatty Construction Ltd.* [1992] QB 656, [1993] AC 334 .... 230, 249

Chevreau case (1931) 2 *UNRIAA* 1113 37

Chorzów Factory, see *Factory at Chorzów*

Chorzów Factory (Interpretation), see *Interpretation of Judgments Nos. 7 and 8 (Factory at Chorzów)*

Chromalloy Aeroservices case, 939 F Supp. 907 (DDC, 1996) 270

City of Tokyo 5% Loan (1960) 29 *ILR* 11 30

Commission v. *France*, Case 26/69, (1970) ECR 565 14

Commission v. *Italy*, Case 7/61, 7 Rec. 633 14

Compagnie du Port, des Quais et des Entrepôts de Beyrouth and Société Radio-Orient (France v. *Lebanon)*, ICJ Rep. 1960, 186 .... 196, 217

Constitution of the Maritime Safety Committee of the Inter-Governmental Maritime Consultative Organization (IMCO), Advisory Opinion, ICJ Rep. 1960, 150 183

Continental Shelf (Libyan Arab Jamahiriya/Malta)
 Application for permission to intervene, ICJ Rep. 1984, 3.............135, 165, 166, 167
 Judgment, ICJ Rep. 1985, 13 133

Continental Shelf (Tunisia/Libyan Arab Jamahiriya)
 Application for permission to intervene, ICJ Rep. 1981, 3 ....165, 166, 167
 Judgment, ICJ Rep. 1982, 18 ....133, 179, 239
 Application for revision and interpretation, ICJ Rep. 1985, 192 179

Corfu Channel case (*UK* v. *Albania*)
 Preliminary objection, ICJ Rep. 1947–48, 15...136, 200
 Merits, ICJ Rep. 1949, 4 .... 251, 262, 263

Czarnikow v. *Roth, Schmidt & Co.* [1922] 2 KB 478 247

Dallal v. *Bank Mellat* [1986] QB 441 .... 83, 235

Dames and Moore v. *Reagan*, 453 US 654 (1981) 75

Delimitation of the Maritime Boundary in the Gulf of Maine Area (Canada/United States of America)
 Constitution of Chamber, 1982 ICJ Rep. 3 .... 9, 128
 Judgment, ICJ Rep. 1984, 246 ....9, 84, 128, 133

Deutsche Schachtbau- und Tiefbohrgesellschaft mbH v. *R'As al-Khaimah National Oil Co. (RAKOIL)* [1990] 1 AC 295 244

Difference Relating to Immunity from Legal Process of a Special Rapporteur of the Commission on Human Rights, ICJ Rep. 1998, 423 183

Diverted Cargoes Arbitration (*Greece* v. *UK*) (1955) 12 *UNRIAA* 53; 53 *ILR* 825.........38

Dogger Bank inquiry (1904), *HCR*, First Series, 413, 614; (1907) 2 *AJIL* 929 25

Dow Chemical et al. v. *Isover Saint Gobain*, see *ICC Case No. 4131*

Dutco (*Siemens AG and BKMI Industrienlagen GmbH* v. *Dutco Consortium Construction Co.*) (French Cour de Cassation, 1992) 210, 221

E-Systems, Inc. v. *Iran* (1983) 2 *Iran-US CTR* 57 224
East Timor case (*Portugal* v. *Australia*), ICJ Rep. 1995, 90 .... 7, 12, 24, 135, 160
Economy Forms Corp. v. *Iran* (1983) 3 *Iran-US CTR* 42 81
Effect of Awards of Compensation Made by the United Nations Administrative
   Tribunal, ICJ Rep. 1954, 7 129
Electricité de Beyrouth Company (*France* v. *Lebanon*), ICJ Rep. 1954, 107 107
Electricity Company of Sofia and Bulgaria, 1939, PCIJ, Ser. A/B, No. 77,
   64 .... 141, 147, 150, 151, 168
Elettronica Sicula SpA (ELSI) (*USA* v. *Italy*)
   Constitution of Chamber, ICJ Rep. 1987, 3 128
   Judgment, ICJ Rep. 1989, 15 .... 128, 129, 155, 194, 196, 197
Elf Aquitaine Iran v. *National Iranian Oil Co.,* 1982, (1986) 11 *Yearbook*
   Commercial Arbitration 97 .... 198, 205, 214
ELSI, see *Elettronica Sicula SpA (ELSI)* (*USA* v. *Italy*)
Esphahanian v. *Bank Tejarat* (1983) 2 *Iran-US CTR* 157 .... 80, 192
Esso/BHP v. *Plowman* (1995) 183 *CLR* 10 262

Factory at Chorzów case
   Jurisdiction, PCIJ. Ser. A, No. 9 (1927) 168
   Interpretation of Judgments No. 7 and 8, PCIJ Ser. A,
      No. 13 (1927) 177, 250, 262
   Merits, 1928, PCIJ, Ser. A, No. 17 (1928) 177, 251
Finnish Shipowners (1934) 3 *UNRIAA* 1479 196
Fisheries Jurisdiction case (*United Kingdom* v. *Iceland*)
   Provisional Measures, ICJ Rep. 1972, 12 170
   Jurisdiction, ICJ Rep. 1973, 3 .... 139, 157, 175, 213
   Merits, ICJ Rep. 1974, 3 .... 180, 263
Flegenheimer (1958) 25 *ILR* 91 192
Flexi-Van Leasing, Inc. v. *Iran* (1982) 70 *ILR* 496 195
Foster v. *Driscoll* [1921] 1 KB 470 241
Franco-US Air Transport Services Agreement arbitration (1963)
   38 *ILR* 182 236
Free Zones of Upper Savoy and the District of Gex, PCIJ, Ser. A/B, No. 46 237
Frontier Dispute (Burkina Faso/Republic of Mali), ICJ Rep. 1986,
   554 .... 13, 128, 129, 133

Gabčíkovo-Nagymaros Project (Hungary/Slovakia), ICJ Rep. 1997, 3 133
General Motors Corp. v. *Iran* (1983) 3 *I-USCTR* 1 195
Georges Pinson (1924) 5 *UNRIAA* 325 236
Golpira v. *Government of Iran* (1983) 2 *Iran-US CTR* 171 80
Gotaverken (1981) 30 *ICLQ* 358 232
Gould, see *Ministry of Defence of Iran* v. *Gould Inc.*
Government of Kuwait v. *American Independent Oil Company (AMINOIL)*
   (1982) 66 *ILR* 519, (1982) 21 *ILM* 976 .... 242, 245, 246
Great Belt, see *Passage through the Great Belt* (*Finland* v. *Denmark*)

Grimm v. *Iran* (1983) 2 *Iran-US CTR* 78 78

Guinea-Bissau/Senegal, see *Arbitral Award of 31 July 1989*

Gulf of Maine case, see *Delimitation of the Maritime Boundary in the Gulf of Maine Area (Canada/United States of America)*

Haddadi v. *US* (1985) 8 *Iran-US CTR* 20 78

Haji-Bagherpour v. *US* (1983) 2 *Iran-US CTR* 38 79

Halliburton Co. v. *Doreen/IMCO* (1982) 1 *Iran-US CTR* 242 80

Haya de la Torre (Colombia v. *Peru)*, ICJ Rep. 1951, 71 .... 15, 163

Headquarters Agreement, see *Applicability of the Obligation to Arbitrate under Section 21 of the United Nations Headquarters Agreement of 26 June 1947*

Heathrow Airport User Charges arbitration (*UK/US*, 1992) 102 *ILR* 216; (1994) 88 *AJIL* 739 38

Heyman v. *Darwins Ltd.* [1942] AC 356 .... 139, 215

Hiscox v. *Outhwaite* [1992] 1 AC 56 268

Hoffland Honey Co. v. *NIOC* (1983) 2 *Iran-US CTR* 41 78

Holiday Inns SA, Occidental Petroleum et al. v. *Government of Morocco* (1980) 51 *BYIL* 123, reprinted in 1 *ICSID Reports* 645 .... 66, 207, 223

Hostages case, see *United States Diplomatic and Consular Staff in Tehran (USA* v. *Iran)*

ICAO Council case, see *Appeal Relating to the Jurisdiction of the Council of the International Civil Aviation Organisation*

ICC Case No. 1512 (1975), 1 *Yearbook Commercial Arbitration* 128 240

ICC Case No. 1704, *Clunet* 1978, 977 208

ICC Case No. 2321 (1974), *ICC Arbitral Awards 1974–85* 8 220

ICC Case No. 2626, *Clunet* 1978, 981 208

ICC Case No. 4131, Dow Chemical et al. v. *Isover Saint Gobain* (1984) 9 *Yearbook Commercial Arbitration* 131 207

ICC Case No. 4381, *Clunet* 1986, 1106 206

ICC Case No. 4402 (1983) 8 *Yearbook Commercial Arbitration* 204, (1984) 9 *Yearbook Commercial Arbitration* 138 .... 207, 215, 228

ICC Case No. 5832 (1988), *ICC Arbitral Awards 1986–94* 352 205

ICC Case No. 6162 (1992) 17 *Yearbook Commercial Arbitration* 153 205

ICC Case No. 6719 (1991), *ICC Arbitral Awards 1991–1995* 567 247

Imperial Japanese 4% Loan (1955) 29 *ILR* 4 30

Interhandel case

    Provisional measures, ICJ Rep. 1957, 105 170

    Preliminary objections, ICJ Rep. 1959, 6 .... 142, 143, 144, 145, 146, 147, 150, 156, 196

Interpretation of Article 3, Paragraph 2, of the Treaty of Lausanne (Frontier Between Turkey and Iraq), 1925, Advisory Opinion, PCIJ, Ser. B, No.12 183

Interpretation of Peace Treaties with Bulgaria, Hungary and Romania

    First Phase, ICJ Rep. 1950, 65 .... 10, 11, 34, 183, 227

Second Phase, ICJ Rep. 1950, 221 .... 10, 34, 227
Interpretation of the Agreement of 25 March 1951 between the WHO and Egypt
    (WHO Regional Headquarters), Advisory Opinion, ICJ Rep. 1980, 73 183
Ipitrade International SA v. *Federal Republic of Nigeria*, 465 F Supp. 824
    (1978) 272
Iran Aircraft Industries v. *Avco Corp.*, 980 F 2d 141 (2d Cir. 1992) 83, 268
Iranian Customs v. *US, Case B/3* (1985) 8 *Iran-US CTR* 89 81
Ireland v. *United Kingdom* (1978) Eur. Court HR, Ser. A, vol. 25, at 62 13
Isaiah v. *Bank Mellat* (1983) 2 *Iran-US CTR* 232 78

Jan Mayen conciliation (Iceland/Norway, 1981) 62 *ILR* 108, (1981) 20 *ILM*
    797 30
Janred Properties Ltd. v. *ENIT* [1989] 2 All ER 444 205
Japanese House Tax (1905) 11 *UNRIAA* 51 36
Jay Treaty commissions (1794) 32
Judgments of the Administrative Tribunal of the ILO upon Complaints Made
    against UNESCO, Advisory Opinion, ICJ Rep. 1956, 77 183

Kaiser Bauxite Company v. *The Government of Jamaica* (1975) 1 *ICSID Reports*
    296 .... 61, 62, 70
Kasikili/Sedudu Island (Botswana/Namibia), ICJ Rep. 1998, 6 133
Kimberley-Clark Corp. v. *Bank Markazi* (1983) 2 *Iran-US CTR* 334 78
Klöckner Industrie-Anlagen GmbH, Klöckner Belge SA and Klöckner
    Handelmaatshappij BV v. *United Republic of Cameroon and Société*
    Cameroonaise des Engrais, ad hoc Committee Decision of 3 May 1985, 2
    ICSID Reports 95 .... 71, 72, 258

Lac Lanoux arbitration (*France* v. *Spain*) (1957) 24 *ILR* 101 23
Land and Maritime Boundary between Cameroon and Nigeria (*Cameroon* v.
    Nigeria), ICJ Rep. 1998, 275 .... 22, 137, 152, 159, 198
Land, Island and Maritime Frontier Dispute (*El Salvador/Honduras:*
    Nicaragua intervening)
    Constitution of Chamber, ICJ Rep. 1987, 10 128
    Application to intervene, ICJ Rep. 1990, 3 .... 128, 129
    Application to intervene, ICJ Rep. 1990, 92 .... 128, 159, 166, 167
    Judgment, ICJ Rep. 1992, 351 168
Legal Consequences for States of the Continued Presence of South Africa in
    Namibia (South West Africa) notwithstanding Security Council Resolution
    276 (1970), Advisory Opinion, ICJ Rep. 1971, 16 .... 130, 131, 183, 184, 185
Legality of the Threat or Use of Nuclear Weapons (1996) ICJ
    Rep. 66, 226 .... 14, 23, 182
Lena Goldfields (1930), (1950) 36 *Cornell Law Quarterly* 44 .... 60, 214, 226, 244
Letelier and Moffitt inquiry (1992) 88 *ILR* 727; (1993) *ILM* 1 25
Libya/Malta Continental Shelf case, see *Continental Shelf (Libyan Arab*
    Jamahiriya/Malta)

Libyan American Oil Co. (LIAMCO) v. *Government of the Libyan Arab Republic*
Award, 1977, 62 *ILR* 140, (1981) 20 *ILM* 1 ....198, 205, 214, 240, 269
French court, 1979, 106 *Journal de droit international* 859 (1979) 272, 273
Swedish court, 1980, 62 *ILR* 225, 20 *ILM* 893 ....272, 273
Swiss court, 1980, 62 *ILR* 228, (1981) 20 *ILM* 151 ....272, 273
US court, 482 F Supp. 1175 (1980), 62 *ILR* 220, (1981)
20 *ILM* 161 ....269, 272, 273
Lockerbie case, see *Questions of Interpretation and Application of the 1971*
Montreal Convention arising from the Aerial Incident at Lockerbie (Libyan
Arab Jamahiriya v. *United Kingdom) (Libyan Arab Jamahiriya* v. *United*
States of America)
Lonrho Ltd. v. *Shell Petroleum Company and British Petroleum Ltd.* (1979) 4
Yearbook Commercial Arbitration 320 202
Losinger case (1936) PCIJ, Ser. A/B, No. 67; PCIJ Rep., Ser. C, No. 78 ...... 196, 214, 216

'*Macao Sardine*' case (1987) 3 *Arbitration International* 79 209
Management of Alcan v. *Ircable Corp.* (1983) 2 *I-USCTR* 294 195
Marine Contractors Inc. v. *Shell Petroleum Development Co. of Nigeria Ltd.*
[1984] 2 Lloyd's Rep. 77 259
Mariposa Development Company (1933) 6 *UNRIAA* 338 12
Maritime Delimitation and Territorial Questions between Qatar and Bahrain.
Jurisdiction and Admissibility, ICJ Rep. 1994, 112; ICJ Rep. 1995, 6 .... 134, 135
Maritime International Nominees Establishment v. *Government of the Republic*
of Guinea, Case No. ARB/84/4
Award of 6 January 1988, 4 *ICSID Reports* 54 ....64, 69
Belgian court, 1985, 4 *ICSID Reports* 32, (1985) 24 *ILM* 1639 69
Swiss court, 1986, 4 *ICSID Reports* 35, (1987) 26 *ILM* 382 69
ad hoc Committee Decision of 22 December 1989, 4 *ICSID Reports* 79 ...... 72, 73, 258
Mastrobuono v. *Shearson Lehman Hutton, Inc.* 115 S Ct. 1212 (1995) 252
Mavrommatis Jerusalem Concessions, 1925, PCIJ, Ser. A , No. 5 .... 136, 237
Mavrommatis Palestine Concessions, 1924, PCIJ Ser. A, No. 2 .... 10, 20
Mergé (1955) 22 *ILR* 443 192
Metalclad Corporation v. *United Mexican States* (Case ARB(AF)/97/1) 62
Mexican Eagle Company case (1938) Cmd. 5758 193
Military and Paramilitary Activities in and against Nicaragua (Nicaragua v.
United States of America)
Provisional measures, ICJ Rep. 1984, 169...170, 172, 175
Intervention, ICJ Rep. 1984, 215...163, 164
Jurisdiction and admissibility, ICJ Rep. 1984, 392 ....15, 21, 138, 141, 142, 144,
146, 148, 151, 152, 153, 154, 155, 159, 161, 173, 175
Merits, ICJ Rep. 1986, 14 .... 148, 170, 180, 181, 263
MINE v. *Guinea*, see *Maritime International Nominees Establishment* v.
Government of the Republic of Guinea
Ministry of Defence of Iran v. *Gould Inc.* (1988) 82 *AJIL* 591 82
Minquiers and Ecrehos, ICJ Rep. 1953, 47 133

Mitsubishi Motors Corp. v. *Soler Chrysler-Plymouth Inc.*, 473 US 614, 105
S Ct. 3346, 87 L Ed.2d. 444 (1985); (1985) 24 *ILM* 1064 203
Monetary Gold Removed from Rome, ICJ Rep. 1954, 19 .... 132, 135, 158, 159,
160, 161, 165, 167
Mortensen v. *Peters* (1906) SLT 227 85
Muscat Dhows arbitration (1905) 11 *UNRIAA* 83 36
M/V *Saiga* (1998) 110 *ILR* 736, (1998) 37 *ILM* 360 .... 89, 90, 237

Namibia, see *Legal Consequences for States of the Continued Presence of South
Africa in Namibia (South West Africa) notwithstanding Security Council
Resolution 276 (1970)*
Nationality Decrees Issued in Tunis and Morocco, 1923, PCIJ Ser. B, No. 4 .... 15, 183
Nauru, see *Certain Phosphate Lands in Nauru (Nauru* v. *Australia)*
Naviera Amazonica Peruana SA v. *Campania Internacional de Seguros de Peru*
[1988] 1 Lloyd's Rep. 116 234
Navigation Maritime Bulgare (Bulgaria) v. *P. T. Nizwar (Indonesia),* 1984,
(1986) 11 *Yearbook Commercial Arbitration* 508 267
Netherlands Measures of Suspension of Obligations to the United States (1952)
BISD 1st Supp. 32 (1953) 98
Nicaragua v. *Honduras,* see *Border and Transborder Armed Actions (Nicaragua*
v. *Costa Rica) (Nicaragua* v. *Honduras)*
Nicaragua v. *US,* see *Military and Paramilitary Activities in and against
Nicaragua (Nicaragua* v. *United States of America)*
Norsolor, see *Société Pabalk Ticaret Sirketi* v. *Société anon. Norsolor*
North American Dredging Company (1926) 4 *UNRIAA* 2, (1926) 20 *AJIL* 800 197
North Atlantic Coast Fisheries arbitration (1910) 11 *UNRIAA* 167 .... 36, 85
North Eastern Boundary case, *Lapradelle–Politis,* vol. 1, 355 257
Northern Cameroons (Cameroons v. *United Kingdom)* ICJ Rep. 1963, 15 .... 13, 156, 168
North Sea Continental Shelf cases, ICJ Rep. 1969, 3 .... 20, 22, 31
Norwegian Loans, see *Certain Norwegian Loans*
Nottebohm case
Preliminary objection, ICJ Rep. 1953, 111...152
Second phase, ICJ Rep. 1955, 4 192
Nuclear Tests (Australia v. *France; New Zealand* v. *France)*
Provisional measures, ICJ Rep. 1973, 99, 135...170, 171, 175
Application to intervene, ICJ Rep. 1973, 320, 324 164
Judgment, ICJ Rep. 1974, 253, 457 ....13, 137, 141, 155, 157, 164, 165, 180

Oil Platforms (Iran v. *USA).* Preliminary objection, ICJ Rep. 1986, 803 .... 133, 138
Orinoco Steamship Company case (1910) 10 *UNRIAA* 184 262
Orion Compania Espanola de Seguros v. *Belfort Maatschappij* [1962] 2 Lloyd's
Rep. 257 244

Palena arbitration (1967) 16 *UNRIAA* 109 38
Panama Canal Tolls controversy,1912–1913 12

Panevezys-Saldutiskis Railway case (1939) PCIJ Ser. A/B, No. 76 192

Parker, 4 RIAA 39 (1926) 195

Parsons & Whittemore Overseas Co., Inc. v. *Société Générale de l'Industrie du
    Papier* 508 F 2d 969 (2d Cir. 1974), (1975) 14 *ILM* 504 .... 238, 269

Passage through the Great Belt (*Finland* v. *Denmark*). Provisional measures,
    ICJ Rep. 1991, 12. 1992 Order, ICJ Rep. 1992, 348 .... 170, 171, 174, 255

Paul Smith v. *H & S Holdings Inc.* [1992] 2 Lloyd's Rep. 127 229

Peace Treaties case, see *Interpretation of Peace Treaties with Bulgaria, Hungary
    and Romania*

Petroleum Development (Trucial Coast) Ltd. v. *Sheikh of Abu Dhabi* (1951) 18
    ILR 122, (1952) 1 *ICLQ* 247 .... 60, 215

Phosphates in Morocco case, 1938, PCIJ Ser. A/B No. 74 .... 12, 147

Pious Fund of the Californias case (1902) 9 *UNRIAA* 1, *HCR* (1916), 1 .... 36, 262

Pomeroy v. *Iran* (1983) 2 *Iran-US CTR* 372 194

Portendick claims (1843) Moore, *Int. Arb.*, vol. 5, 4937 32

Pyramids arbitration, 3 *ICSID Reports* 45, 79, 96; (1983) 22 *ILM* 752. ICSID
    proceedings, 3 *ICSID Reports* 101; (1993) 32 *ILM* 933 207

Qatar/Bahrain, see *Maritime Delimitation and Territorial Questions between
    Qatar and Bahrain*

*Questions of Interpretation and Application of the 1971 Montreal Convention
    arising from the Aerial Incident at Lockerbie (Libyan Arab Jamahiriya* v.
    United Kingdom) (Libyan Arab Jamahiriya v. *United States of America)
    (Provisional Measures)* ICJ Rep. 1992, 3, 114 .... 16, 133, 173

Railway Traffic between Lithuania and Poland, PCIJ Ser. A/B, No. 42, 108 23

Rainbow Warrior arbitration (*New Zealand* v. *France*) (1990) 82 *ILR* 499 38

RAKOIL, see *Deutsche Schachtbau- und Tiefbohrgesellschaft mbH* v. *R'As
    al-Khaimah National Oil Co.*

Rann of Kutch (India/Pakistan, 1968), (1968) 7 *ILM* 633 .... 28, 38

Raygo Wagner Equipment Co. v. *Star Line Iran Co.* (1982) 1 *Iran-US CTR* 411 81

Red Crusader inquiry (1962) 35 *ILR* 485, *Contemporary Practice of the United
    Kingdom in the Field of International Law*, 1962(2), 50 26

Regazzoni v. *K. C. Sethia (1944) Ltd.* [1958] AC 301 241

Regime for the Importation, Sale and Distribution of Bananas (1997), (1998) 37
    ILM 243 104

Republic of Somalia v. *Woodhouse, Drake and Carey (Suisse) S.A.* [1993] Q.B. 54 193

*Request for an Examination of the Situation in accordance with Paragraph 63 of
    the Court's 1974 Judgment in the Nuclear Tests Case (New Zealand* v. *France),
    ICJ Rep. 1995, 288 .... 133, 171

Revere Copper v. *OPIC* (1978) 56 *ILR* 258, (1978) 17 *ILM* 1321 246

Rexnord Inc. v. *Iran* (1983) 2 *Iran-US CTR* 6 81

Right of Passage over Indian Territory
    Preliminary objections, ICJ Rep. 1957, 125 .... 141, 150, 153
    Merits, ICJ Rep. 1960, 6...148

Rights of Minorities in Polish Upper Silesia (Minority Schools), 1928, PCIJ, Ser.
A, No. 15 136
Rights of Nationals of the United States of America in Morocco, ICJ Rep. 1952,
176 262
Robert Azinian and others v. *United Mexican States* (Case ARB(AF)/97/2) 62
Rossell NV v. *Oriental Shipping (UK) Ltd.* [1991] 2 Lloyd's Rep. 625 268
Russian Indemnity case (1912) (Russia v. Turkey) 11 *UNRIAA* 421 36

Saghi v. *Iran* (1987) 14 *Iran-US CTR* 3 80
Saiga, see M/V *Saiga*
San Juan de Fuca case (1871) Moore, *Int. Arb.*, vol. 1, 229 32
Sapphire International Petroleum Ltd. v. *National Iranian Oil Co.* (1963) 35
ILR 136, (1964) 13 *ICLQ* 1011 .... 60, 231, 240, 243, 244, 247
S.A.R.L. Benvenuti & Bonfant v. *Government of the People's Republic of the
Congo* (1980) 1 *ICSID Reports* 335, (1982) 21 *ILM* 740 70
Saudi Arabia v. *Arabian American Oil Co.* (Aramco) (1958)
27 *ILR* 117 ....39, 60, 233, 244, 250
Savarkar case (1911) 11 *UNRIAA* 243 36
SEDITEX Engineering Beratungsgesellschaft für die Textilindustrie mbH v.
Government of the Democratic Republic of Madagascar ICSID Case No.
CONC/82/1 (1982) 68
SEEE v. *World Bank, Yugoslavia and France* (1985) 82 *ILR* 59 231
Serbian Loans, 1920, PCIJ, Ser. A, No. 20 242
SGTM/EPIDC, see *Société des Grands Travaux de Marseille* v. *East Pakistan
Industrial Development Corporation*
Société Commercial de Belgique case, PCIJ Ser. A/B, No. 78 (1939);
9 *ILR* 521 263
Société des Grands Travaux de Marseille v. *East Pakistan Industrial Development
Corporation* (1980) 5 *Yearbook Commercial Arbitration* 177 .... 208, 215, 216
Société Eurodif v. *Iran*, 111 *Clunet* 598 (1984) 272
Société Pabalk Ticaret Sirketi v. *Société anon. Norsolor*
Austrian court, 1982, (1984) 9 *Yearbook Commercial Arbitration* 159 244
French court, 1984, (1986) 11 *Yearbook Commercial Arbitration* 484 270
Socobel v. *The Greek State* PCIJ Ser. A/B, No. 78, 9 *ILR* 521. Belgian court, 1951,
18 *ILR* 3 .... 179, 264
Solel Boneh International v. *Uganda*, (1975) *Journal de droit international* 938 217
South West Africa cases (*Ethiopia, Liberia* v. *South Africa*)
Preliminary objections, 1962 ICJ Rep. 319 ....10, 11, 21, 22
1965 Orders, ICJ Rep. 1965, 3, 9 ....130, 139
Second phase, ICJ Rep. 1966, 6 .... 130, 150, 157, 262
Spain/Canada Fisheries Jurisdiction, ICJ Rep. 1998, 432 .... 84, 133, 146, 237
Sperry Corp. v. *US* 853 F 2d. 904, (1989) 86 *AJIL* 86 82
SPP(ME) Ltd. and SPP Ltd. v. *Egypt*, Decision of 14 April 1988, 3 *ICSID
Reports* 131, (1983) 22 *ILM*, 1048 63
S.S. 'Wimbledon' case, 1923, PCIJ, Ser A, No. 1 164

Starrett Housing Corp. v. *Iran* (1983) 4 *Iran-US CTR* 122, (1984) 23 *ILM* 1091 78

Status of Eastern Carelia, 1923, PCIJ, Ser. B, No. 5 .... 183, 184

'*Superfund*' report, see *United States Taxes on Petroleum and Certain Imported Substances*

Taba arbitration (1988) 20 *UNRIAA* 3, 80 *ILR* 224 38

Tagliaferro (1903) 10 *UNRIAA* 592 219

Tavignano (1912), *HCR* First Series 413, 614..25

Territorial Dispute (*Libyan Arab Jamahiriya/Chad*), ICJ Rep. 1994, 6 133

Tesoro Petroleum Corporation v. *Government of Trinidad and Tobago* (1985) 68

Texaco Overseas Petroleum Co. (TOPCO) and California Asiatic Oil Co. v.
    Libya (Preliminary Award, 1975. Merits, 1977) 53 *ILR* 389, (1978) 17
    ILM 1 .... 7, 39

Textron Inc. v. *Iran* (1981) 6 *Iran-US CTR* 328 75

The Sennar (no. 2) [1986] 1 WLR 490 178

Trail Smelter arbitration (*USA* v. *Canada*, 1941) 3 *UNRIAA* 1938 262

Trial of Pakistani Prisoners of War, ICJ Rep. 1973, 328 .... 175, 180

Tubantia (1922), HCR, Second Series, 135..25

Tunisia/Libya Continental Shelf case, see *Continental Shelf* (*Tunisia/Libyan
    Arab Jamahiriya*)

Ultra Systems Inc. v. *Iran* (1983) 2 *Iran-US CTR* 100 79

Umpire cases (1857), Moore, *Int. Arb.*, vol. 2, 1396 238

Union of India v. *McDonnell Douglas Corp.* [1993] Lloyd's Rep. 48 234

United States Diplomatic and Consular Staff in Tehran (*USA* v. *Iran*), ICJ Rep.
    1980, 3 .... 9, 15, 16, 23, 74, 77, 133, 138, 146, 175, 180, 237, 251, 263

United States Taxes on Petroleum and Certain Imported Substances (1988) BISD,
    34th Supp. 136 at 156–8 (1988) 27 *ILM* 1596 99

Uruguayan Complaints (1962) 11 *BISD* 95 (1963) 99

Vacuum Salt Products Limited v. *Government of the Republic of Ghana*, Award
    of 16 February 1994, 4 *ICSID Reports* 320 .... 67, 194

Venezuela Preferential Claims (1904) 6 *UNRIAA* 99 36

Vita Food Products Inc. v. *Unus Shipping Co. Ltd.* [1939] AC 277 242

Wal-Wal arbitration (1935) 29 *AJIL* 690; 3 *UNRIAA* 1657 .... 235, 237

Westacre Investments Inc. v. *Jugoimport-SPDR Holding Co. Ltd.* [1998] 3 WLR
    770, [1998] 4 All ER 570, affd. (1999) *The Times* 25 May (C.A.) 269

Western Sahara, Advisory Opinion, ICJ Rep. 1975, 12 .... 131, 183, 184, 185

Westland Helicopters Ltd. v. *Arab Organization for Industrialisation, United
    Arab Emirates, Saudi Arabia, Qatar, Egypt and the Arab-British Helicopter
    Co.* (1984) 23 *ILM* 1071. Annulment Proceedings, 1988, (1989) 28 *ILM* 687 208

Westland Helicopters Ltd. v. *Arab Organisation for Industrialisation* [1995] 2
    All ER 387 208

Whitworth Street Estates (Manchester) Ltd. v. *James Miller & Partners Ltd.*
    [1970] AC 583 (HL) 230

1

INTRODUCTION

1. Conflict, disputes and the Law   1

2. The range of dispute settlement procedures   5

3. Justiciability   10

1. Conflict, disputes and the Law

There is a widespread assumption that in a successful legal system disputes should be avoided, or at least resolved quickly and peacefully. That is not the premise from which this book proceeds. Rather, it is assumed that disputes—or, more strictly, the conflicts from which disputes emerge—are not wholly undesirable but have certain valuable characteristics, and that the proper function of law is to manage, rather than to suppress or resolve, conflict. A second premise is that recourse to law in dispute settlement is invariably an optional procedure, chosen because it offers certain short- or long-term benefits to one or more of the parties to the dispute. In this introductory chapter, these premises are explained and explored.

First, disputes should be distinguished from conflicts. In this book the term 'conflict' is used to signify a general state of hostility between the parties, and the term 'dispute' to signify a specific disagreement relating to a question of rights or interests in which the parties proceed by way of claims, counter-claims, denials and so on. Conflicts are often unfocused, and particular disputes arising from them are often perceived to be as much the result as the cause of the conflict. Conflicts can rarely, if ever, be resolved by the settling of the particular disputes which appear to constitute them: the feelings of hostility almost inevitably survive the settlement of the disputes. For example, the immediate crisis arising from the detention of United States' diplomatic and consular staff in the United States' embassy compound in Tehran was solved by the release of the hostages and corresponding concessions made by the United States; but the condition of general hostility between the United States and Iran remained more than a decade later. The specific dispute over the hostages was resolved, but not the conflict.

1

Conflict is by no means without benefit; nor are disputes. The existence of international conflict is invariably a sign that the existing order is not satisfactorily accommodating the interests of every one of the members of the international community. Conflict aims to secure adjustments to that order. In that sense, conflict is necessary for the development of any society. Disputes focus upon particular aspects of that order; and their successful resolution leads either to the confirmation and entrenchment of old rules or to the weakening and eventual replacement of old rules by new. International conflict led, for example, to the refinement of new rules on expropriation of alien property and maritime jurisdiction, on war crimes, and sovereign immunity, just as clearly as successive disputes have seen the confirmation of basic rules such as *pacta sunt servanda*, diplomatic immunity, and the territoriality of enforcement jurisdiction.

This book is primarily concerned with disputes rather than conflicts. It pays relatively little attention to the procedures for avoiding, managing and resolving conflict. Much effort is, quite rightly, being put into the development of techniques for the avoidance and management of conflict. These include, for example, prior notification and consultation requirements; duties to publish and circulate information and to carry out various kinds of impact assessments before engaging in activities; and schemes for the promotion of joint activities and studies of problems. Much has been written on these techniques elsewhere.[1] We concentrate on the techniques for handling conflicts that arise despite these preventive methods.

While there may be an element of truth in the view that law is part of the social superstructure built on the bedrock of economic relations, the converse is also true, and in this context more significant. International law provides the conceptual framework in which the international community and international relations are seen and understood. The ideas of the State, of frontiers, of sovereignty and independence, of nationality, and war, peace and neutrality, are all given clarity and precision as legal concepts. So are the vehicles of international relations: contracts, treaties, diplomatic exchanges and so on. The existence within the Foreign Ministries and other key departments of practically every State in the world of a cadre of lawyers both reflects and entrenches the role of international law. Those officials have a common language. Great numbers of them were trained in international law in universities, in Western and Eastern Europe, the Americas and elsewhere, which follow broadly the same approach to the subject, whatever might be the differences in the critique to which they subject it and in the substantive rules followed within the region. To those officials must be added the large numbers of lawyers handling international law issues in law firms and in the

---

[1] See F. L. Kirgis, *Prior Consultation in International Law* (Charlottesville, Virginia, 1983); B. G. Ramcharan, *The International Law and Practice of Early-warning and Preventive Diplomacy: the emerging global watch* (Dordrecht, 1991); P. Sands, *Principles of international environmental law* (Manchester, 1995), Part Three.

legal departments of corporations around the world. For all these people international law is a kind of lingua franca—a language in which relations between them, and the States and corporations that they represent, can be conducted. Indeed, lawyers commonly find that their view of the world has much more in common with that of lawyers from other countries than it has with the views of politicians in their own countries.

Law is, then, fundamental to the understanding of the world and the conduct of international relations. However, recourse to legal processes for the adjustment of conflicts and settlement of disputes is optional. This point needs to be stressed because there is a tendency to transpose to the international setting a rather crude conception of municipal legal systems, as systems where the law is systematically and inescapably enforced against individuals. But that is a misconception of the role of law in municipal systems, and hopelessly wide of the mark in relation to the international legal system. Law is *chosen* as the framework within which to resolve disputes when it is advantageous to use that framework. A domestic analogy may serve to make the point.

A teacher may lend a book to a student. The book is not returned, and the teacher asks for it back. If it is still not returned, despite increasingly urgent informal requests, he might write to the student on headed paper. By doing so he might imply, or might expressly state, that within the University the lender is a Faculty member and the borrower is a student, bound by university regulations on good conduct and so on. The request remains the same; but shifting it into the University context by means of such signals has the effect of suggesting that the teacher regards the University as in some sense party to the argument, and on his side. If that fails the teacher may turn the ratchet further, and invoke formal University disciplinary procedures. This will force the University to take a stand; and if the teacher is right in his view that the regulations are on his side, the University will stand on his side. That, in turn, may lead bystanders to shy away from taking the part of the student. They may believe that a community needs rules, and that rules should be obeyed; or they may have lent the student books, and fear for their return; or they may simply fear being branded by the authorities as collaborators with the student. In these ways, the shift into the University context increases the teacher's power as against the student. Moreover, the context of the dispute is redefined. The student may previously have argued that he needed the book for an essay, whereas the teacher had no urgent need for it, or perhaps had a second copy. Such moral arguments are powerful in the straight request/ refusal context; but they lose much force, and may be regarded as relevant only to the mitigation of any punishment, in the disciplinary context.

If these steps fail, the teacher may hint at the possibility of civil legal action, or of turning the matter over to the police as a case of theft. This, too, may be done by the use of language. The mere use of a term such as 'tortious liability' or 'theft' in exchanges with the student is enough to indicate the change of context. If police or court action is taken, the context is again redefined. The moral arguments become totally irrelevant to the question of guilt on a theft charge. Support from bystanders is likely to ebb still further when the police become involved. And the teacher's power is immeasurably increased by having the police and the courts on his side.

This analogy, which holds broadly true on the international plane, contains a number of lessons. First, recourse to the legal mechanisms is optional. The dispute could have remained, as the overwhelming majority of disputes, domestic, national and international, remain, on the simple request—refusal—negotiation level. Secondly, the shift into a legal context is signalled by a simple use of language: no more is required. Thirdly, that shift can be made by either party to the dispute, without the need for the co-operation of the other.

Here a distinction between national and international law does exist. In national law, as a serviceable generalisation, it can be said that the teacher has a right, and accordingly has the power, to insist upon the involvement of the university authorities, the police and the courts. No international tribunal has compulsory jurisdiction; and even the discussion of an international dispute (let alone the taking of action to resolve it) by an organisation such as the United Nations is a discretionary matter. States need to lobby and persuade in order to have the matter taken up. While the co-operation of the other party is not needed to shift the context, the co-operation of the members of the organisation is. And if it is desired to refer the matter for judicial settlement in an international tribunal, that reference can only be made with the agreement, in some form or other, of both disputing States. At that point (but not until that point) the analogy breaks down.

There is frequently a battle for the control of language, and through it of the context of dispute settlement, in the early stages of international disputes. The events surrounding the Iraqi invasion of Kuwait in 1990 provide a good example. In the days immediately following the 'annexation' of Kuwait, Iraq attempted to defend its action in the Security Council on historical, political and moral grounds. The States which most immediately opposed the Iraqi action rapidly invoked the language of law, referring to the invasion of Kuwait as a violation of Kuwait's sovereignty and frontiers, a breach of the UN Charter, and so on. As Iraq's opponents won the struggle for language, it became increasingly difficult for any State to take Iraq's side: it is one thing to sympathise with a State's historic claims to an area of border territory, but quite another to defend a clear breach of the prohibition on the threat or use of force by a State. The historical, political and moral arguments had no relevance to the question of the violation of the law.

The Iraq/Kuwait illustration points up the fourth and fifth lessons of the analogy: that the shift imposes limitations upon the kind of arguments which can be made by each party in defence of its actions; and that the shift into the legal context increases the power of one party to the dispute at the expense of the other.

The domestic analogy can be pressed one stage further. If the detention of the book does go before a university tribunal or a court, then whatever the outcome of the proceedings the authority of the tribunal or court is likely to be enhanced. Similarly, whatever rules are applied by the tribunal or court, the authority of those rules is also likely to be enhanced. The mere fact that the tribunal and the rule are used gives them greater prominence, and makes their existence more of a factor in the calculations of members of the community. Furthermore, the decision of the tribunal or court is not the end of the matter. It is said that something like 80 per cent of English court judgments are neither complied with voluntarily, nor enforced in their entirety. The judgment becomes merely one further stage in the dispute settlement process; and the dispute is usually finally resolved by a negotiated settlement based on the judgment. This fact, which implies that criticisms of international law based on its lack of an effective enforcement machinery are based upon a misapprehension of the way in which municipal legal systems operate, needs to be borne constantly in mind.

The points made above must not be allowed to obscure the fact that most international disputes are not handled through formal machinery, whether that be the United Nations or an international tribunal. Most are adjusted by negotiation. We will turn shortly to the question of the justiciability of disputes and see that by no means all disputes are even suitable for resolution by the application of law. Even of those that are so suitable, only a very small proportion are put before judicial tribunals. And of that small proportion, much the greater part goes before municipal courts. The mass of municipal case law on matters such as sovereign and diplomatic immunity, the status of foreign States and governments, maritime jurisdiction, and so on is a clear reflection of the fact that international law is most commonly applied by judges in their own national courts.

2. The range of dispute settlement procedures

This book focuses upon the range of dispute settlement procedures available for the settlement of general international legal disputes. By 'general international legal disputes' we mean disputes between two States, or between a State (or its government) and a 'non-State entity', such as a private commercial corporation, or an international organisation. It is not concerned with the litigation of international disputes in municipal courts, although those courts play a prominent and immensely important role in international dispute settlement. Nor, for the most part, is this book concerned with political arrangements for the adjustment of international conflict, or with the great number of special systems established for the settlement of particular categories of legal disputes. The political systems include not only the United Nations and the institutionalised negotiation systems of bodies such as NATO, but also the more complex schemes established by the OSCE and the OAU. While the instruments establishing those schemes have characteristics which appear to mark them out as 'legal' rather than 'political' procedures, they have not yet been employed to any significant degree as procedures for the settlement of disputes by the application of rules of law. Readers are referred elsewhere for detailed discussion of these mechanisms.[2] Nor do we discuss the international criminal courts established for the Former Yugoslavia and for Rwanda, because they are concerned with the application of criminal law sanctions, rather than the adjustment of international disputes.

The arrangements for the settlement of legal disputes in particular fields include a wide range of systems, such as the Court of Justice of the European Communities[3] and the European Court of Human Rights.[4] Most such tribunals operate on broadly the same principles as the international tribunals discussed in this book. Indeed, some of the tribunals, such as the arbitral tribunals envisaged by the 1982 United Nations Law of the Sea Convention, and those more recently devised by the World Intellectual Property Organization,[5] are to apply the very same rules as are discussed here in the context of other tribunals. But the many specialised systems do not, for the most part, receive detailed consideration here because there are many texts that do discuss them in detail and in the context of the substantive rules that they apply. We have generally tried to supplement, rather than duplicate, the treatment of dispute settlement in current texts.

The dispute settlement procedures that we survey here include negotiation, mediation and conciliation, fact-finding inquiries, arbitration, and the International Court of Justice. Quintessentially inter-State procedures, such as references to the International Court of Justice, are juxtaposed with characteristically 'private', non-State procedures such as international commercial arbitration. The main

---

[2] On the OSCE see D. McGoldrick, 'The Conference on Security and Co-operation in Europe (CSCE) after the Helsinki 1992 Conference' (1993) 42 *ICLQ* 411; CSCE, Stockholm Decision on Peaceful Settlement of Disputes including the Convention on Conciliation and Arbitration within the CSCE, 15 December 1992 (1993) 32 *ILM* 551. On the OAU see T. Maluwa, 'The Peaceful Settlement of African Disputes' (1989) 38 *ICLQ* 299; Declaration of the Assembly of Heads of State and Government on the Establishment within the OAU of a Mechanism for Conflict Prevention, Management and Resolution (1994) 6 *AJICL* 158. And see generally, J. G. Collier, 'The International Court and the peaceful settlement of disputes', in V. Lowe and M. Fitzmaurice (eds.), *Fifty Years of the International Court of Justice* (Cambridge, 1996) (hereafter, *Fifty Years of the ICJ*), 364.

[3] See T. C. Hartley, *The Foundations of European Community Law*, 3rd edn. (Oxford, 1994).

[4] See S. Davidson, *Human Rights* (Buckingham, 1993), chapter 5; D. J. Harris, M. O'Boyle and C. Warbrick, *Law of the European Convention on Human Rights* (London, 1996).

[5] See the WIPO Mediation, Arbitration and Expedited Arbitration Rules (1995) 34 *ILM* 559.

reason for this is that it corresponds to the practical realities of international dispute settlement.

Many, perhaps most, international disputes that are submitted to settlement processes involving some form of third-party adjudication, are commercial; and most of these disputes derive from the terms of contracts between States and private corporations. If the dispute concerns the manner in which the State has treated the corporation, the same facts may form the basis of a claim that the State has breached the contract, and also of a claim that the State is responsible for a violation of public international law. The 'contract' action would typically be litigated in an arbitral tribunal by the parties to the contract (the corporation and the State); the 'public international law' action might be taken up by the corporation's national State and pursued through the inter-State procedures available in the international legal system.[6]

The choice between an action based on the contract and an action for a breach of international law is by no means always free. As will be seen, very significant constraints are imposed by the rule on exhaustion of local remedies; and the mere breach of the contract may not, as such, amount to a violation of international law at all. But the different procedures do operate side by side in contemporary international law. At various stages those involved have a choice as to how to proceed. The State and the corporation, as parties to the contract, can decide whether or not to provide in the contract for the arbitration of disputes arising from it. If they have so provided, and the arbitration does not proceed in a satisfactory manner—perhaps the State party refuses to take part, or to comply with the award, or the award is regarded as wholly misconceived in law—the question of further action before an international tribunal may arise. In that case the corporation's national State will become involved. It, and the other State in the dispute, will have a wide choice of procedures available to them, ranging (to borrow the terminology of article 33 of the UN Charter) across 'negotiation, enquiry, mediation, conciliation, arbitration, judicial settlement, resort to regional agencies or arrangements, or other peaceful means of their own choice'.

There is in one sense a progression evident in that list as it moves from negotiation to the International Court. The processes tend to become more formal. The extent to which third parties are involved in settling the dispute between the parties increases. The law, which can be almost entirely disregarded in negotiated settlements,[7] comes to take an increasingly determinative role in structuring the

---

[6] Consider, for example, what approaches could have been taken on the basis of the facts in the *Barcelona Traction* (ICJ Rep. 1970, 3), *ELSI* (ICJ Rep. 1989, 15) and *Texaco* ((1977) 53 *ILR* 389) cases.

[7] The parties cannot, of course, agree to violate rules of *jus cogens*. But it may be difficult for a third party to raise the question of such a violation before any tribunal: see the *East Timor* case, ICJ Rep. 1995, 90, at 101–2.

settlement—although, as has been said, the Law is always present as an invisible third party, even in negotiations; and the disputing parties' perceptions of the strength of their respective legal arguments is a major factor influencing the outcome of the negotiations or the decision to move from negotiation to some other form of dispute settlement.

On the other hand, the tendency to think of the various settlement procedures as a pyramid up which States climb, from the base of negotiations to the apex of the International Court of Justice, is quite wrong. The various forms of settlement procedure are not stages through which the parties must progress, any more than a garage mechanic 'progresses' through the spanners, hammers, screwdrivers and other tools at his disposal. They are alternatives, from which the parties involved choose the procedure most likely to yield a satisfactory result.

The question of what is a 'satisfactory' result varies from context to context and according to the interests of the parties to the dispute.[8] For example, there has been a long-running dispute between the USA and other States over the limits of US legislative jurisdiction in matters of commerce. Claims to regulate cartels outside the USA, exports of goods from outside the USA to third States, and transactions by foreign subsidiaries of US corporations, have all led to sharp judicial and diplomatic exchanges between authorities in the USA and elsewhere. But, whatever the international legality of the US jurisdictional claims, foreign businesses tend to comply with them. They need to do so in order to be able to trade with the USA without becoming enmeshed in litigation there. Foreign States oppose the encroachment upon their sovereignty implicit (as they see it) in the US claims; the foreign businesses tend to be more tolerant of the substantive law, and to demand only that it be clear, so that they can adjust their behaviour to it.

In this case, governments and businesses have different perspectives on the dispute. Moreover, governments, which deal with each other across the whole spectrum of international relations—trade, aid, immigration, defence, technical co-operation, etc.—commonly desire the ability to be flexible in handling a dispute. A jurisdictional dispute might be pursued vigorously on one occasion, whereas a similar dispute might be quietly forgotten on another if it threatens to upset, say, important trade talks. Governments therefore tend to have a preference for dispute settlement procedures over which they retain the greatest measure of control, whereas businesses are more likely to see advantages in a clear, decisive ruling on a disputed point from an impartial, authoritative tribunal. Indeed, if the governmental interests at stake are important, the risk of an adverse ruling by the tribunal—and both parties may fear an adverse ruling—becomes a very powerful argument against using a prominent international tribunal to settle the dispute. It

---

[8] See A. V. Lowe, 'Ends and means in the settlement of international disputes over jurisdiction' (1985) 11 *Review of International Studies* 183.

may be thought better, for example, for a government to leave jurisdictional disputes to be handled by lower municipal courts, from whose decisions a government can distance itself (and whose decisions are frequently pragmatic accommodations of the particular facts of the case), rather than to try to have the fundamental rules and principles concerning jurisdiction clarified by an international tribunal.

There are exceptions. Sometimes States will decide quickly to refer a matter to the International Court. That was done by the USA in the *Hostages* case.[9] No negotiated settlement appeared possible and the USA had nothing to lose by going to the Court: on the contrary, it stood to strengthen its position by placing the dispute squarely in a legal context and securing an authoritative ruling from the Court. Similarly, the reference of the *Bosnian Genocide* case[10] to the Court may be seen as a use of the Court to inject urgency into a situation where a settlement was being sought concurrently by negotiation, mediation, conciliation and military force. In both examples, judgments were not sought from the International Court as ends in themselves but rather as elements in a much broader strategy for the resolution of the crises of which the disputes formed but a small part.

A rather different exception to the principle that governments prefer to avoid judicial settlement procedures is exemplified by the *Gulf of Maine* case.[11] The disputed maritime boundary between Canada and the USA was a matter of very great local importance and concern, but of little national (and negligible international) significance. Neither government could back down or compromise without appearing to sell its constituents short. But by going to the Court each government could argue unrestrainedly in favour of its national position, without tempering the argument in a search for a compromise. Whichever side won, both Governments knew that they would be able to demonstrate to their domestic constituencies that they had fought the case hard but that, as good international citizens, they were obliged to abide by the Court's ruling. International tribunals can be an expedient way of breaking a negotiating impasse in situations where a government's freedom to negotiate is constrained by domestic considerations.

The discretionary nature of the decision to have recourse to formal legal processes, on this view, underlines the optional nature of recourse to law. This has been the traditional approach to international dispute settlement procedures, the necessity for consent to any particular procedure being regarded as an almost axiomatic principle. But the situation is changing. It is increasingly the case that acceptance of a particular procedure for the settlement of disputes is regarded as an integral part of the parcel of rights and duties that make up the status of membership of a

---

[9] ICJ Rep. 1980, 3.
[10] ICJ Rep. 1993, 3, at 325.
[11] ICJ Rep. 1984, 256.

particular community. The European Community epitomises this development. It is unthinkable that a State should adhere to the substantive obligations of membership of the Community without at the same time accepting the obligation to have disputes arising from them adjudicated by the Community's Court of Justice. The Court has, indeed, been given (or, at least, has assumed) a central role in the development of substantive Community law; and it is impossible to think of the substantive rules without accepting that the Court is one of the primary sources of those rules as they are applied in particular cases. This shift from dispute settlement procedures as an optional, functional supplement to instruments establishing substantive obligations, towards a position in which the procedures are an essential and indispensable element of the structure of specific international regimes, is still in its early stages. But the direction in which the law is moving is unmistakable.[12]

3. Justiciability

It was mentioned above that not all disputes are suitable for judicial settlement. To be suitable, the dispute must be justiciable. A dispute is said to be justiciable if, first, a specific disagreement exists, and secondly, that disagreement is of a kind which can be resolved by the application of rules of law by judicial (including arbitral) processes. These elements are reflected in the classic definition given by the Permanent Court of International Justice in the *Mavrommatis* case: 'A dispute is a disagreement on a point of law or fact, a conflict of legal views or of interests between two persons.'[13]

The existence of the dispute may seem an unproblematic question, but it is not. It may happen that one party denies that a dispute exists. For instance, in the *Peace Treaties* case,[14] complaints had been made by the United Kingdom and United States of America that Bulgaria, Hungary and Romania were failing to comply with certain human rights obligations imposed upon them by the Peace Treaties concluded at the end of World War II. But when it was claimed that these complaints evidenced the existence of a dispute which, under the terms of the Peace Treaties, could be referred to arbitration, Bulgaria, Hungary and Romania argued that there was no dispute in existence. In its Advisory Opinion the International Court, however, noting that 'the two sides hold clearly opposite views concerning the question of the performance or non-performance of certain treaty obliga-

---

[12] See M. T. A. Brus, *Third Party Dispute Settlement in an Interdependent World* (Dordrecht, 1995), *passim*.

[13] (1924) PCIJ Ser. A, No. 2, 11. The reference to 'a conflict of interests' is unfortunate. A mere conflict of interests, without more, does not constitute a dispute, as the Court recognised in the *South West Africa* case, ICJ Rep. 1962, 319 at 328

[14] ICJ Rep. 1950, 65 (First Phase), 221 (Second Phase).

tions', concluded that 'international disputes have arisen', and asserted that 'whether there exists an international dispute is a matter for objective determination'.[15]

A rather fuller statement of the principle was subsequently given by the International Court in the *South West Africa* cases:

> ... it is not sufficient for one party to a contentious case to assert that a dispute exists with the other party. A mere assertion is not sufficient to prove the existence of a dispute any more than a mere denial of the existence of the dispute proves its non-existence. Nor is it adequate to show that the interests of the two parties to such a case are in conflict. It must be shown that the claim of one party is positively opposed by the other.[16]

The final point in that passage, concerning the positive opposition of claims, was considered further by the International Court in the *Tunisia-Libya Continental Shelf (Revision)* case, in which the lack of any requirement of formality in the presentation of the opposing views was stressed,[17] and also in the *Headquarters Agreement* case.[18] The latter case arose from the threatened closure of the PLO mission to the UN in New York. The USA had enacted the Anti-Terrorism Act 1987, which provided *inter alia* for the closure of that PLO mission. The Secretary-General of the UN argued that a dispute had arisen between the UN and the United States, concerning the interpretation of the provisions of the Headquarters Agreement concluded by the UN and the United States, relating to the rights of such missions: and he requested arbitration of the dispute, as provided for in the Headquarters Agreement. The US Government rejected his request on the ground that, because the legal validity of the Anti-Terrorism Act was being litigated in US courts, arbitration was not 'appropriate or timely'. It argued that because the Act had not been implemented by action against the PLO mission in New York, and because the United States Government had therefore not taken up a firm position on the compatibility with the Headquarters Agreement of any such enforcement action, no dispute had yet arisen. The Secretary-General took the view that, in the absence of adequate assurances that the Anti-Terrorism Act would not be enforced against the PLO mission in New York, the dispute existed from the moment that the Act became law.

The International Court found that there was a dispute in existence:

> ... where one party to a treaty protests against the behaviour or decisions of another party, and claims that such behaviour or decision constitutes a breach of the treaty,

---

[15] ICJ Rep. 1950, 65, at 74. The dictum was applied in the *Case concerning Application of the Convention on the Prevention and Punishment of the Crime of Genocide (Preliminary Objections)* case, ICJ Rep. 1996, 595, at 614.

[16] ICJ Rep. 1962, 319, at 328. Cf., the *AGIP/Congo* arbitration (1979) 1 *ICSID Reports* 306, at 317, (1982) 21 *ILM* 726, at 730.

[17] ICJ Rep. 1985, 192.

[18] ICJ Rep. 1988, 12.

the mere fact that the party accused does not advance any argument to justify its conduct under international law does not prevent the opposing attitude of the parties from giving rise to a dispute concerning the application of the treaty . . .

. . .While the existence of a dispute does presuppose a claim arising out of the behaviour of or a decision by one of the parties, it in no way requires that any contested decision must already have been carried into effect. What is more, a dispute may arise even if the party in question gives an assurance that no measure of execution will be taken until ordered by decision of the domestic courts.[19]

The passages quoted above were all employed as part of an argument supporting the finding that a dispute existed, despite arguments to the contrary.[20] This tendency is so marked that it might be thought that a more accurate characterisation of the practice of international tribunals would be to say that there is a rebuttable presumption that a dispute exists if one party so asserts in the context of the reference of the putative dispute to the tribunal—and, it should be stressed, without prejudice to the question whether or not there exists some other preliminary objection or jurisdictional defect which deprives the tribunal of jurisdiction.[21] If that is indeed so, it by no means follows that the attempts to define the various aspects of a dispute are without point. They remain relevant to the question *when* a dispute arises.

This question may be crucial, notably in cases where the jurisdiction of the tribunal is confined to disputes arising before or after specified dates. For example, the passage quoted from the *Headquarters Agreement* case illustrates the proposition that disputes concerning the compatibility of national legislation with international treaty obligations may come into existence at the time of the enactment of the legislation, rather than at the time that powers of legislation are actually exercised.[22] It should, however, be noted that the better view is that this principle applies only to cases based on injuries inflicted directly by one State on another. Where the wrong is indirect, and the claim is based upon an injury to an individual, the dispute does not arise until the law is enforced against that individual. Thus, in the *Mariposa Development Company* case the Panama–US General Claims Commission, in order to establish its jurisdiction, had to determine the date at which a dispute, arising from the application of Panamanian expropriation legislation to a US company, had come into existence. It held that the dispute

---

[19] ICJ Rep. 1988, 12, at 28, 30.
[20] See the passage in the *East Timor* case, ICJ Rep. 1995, 90, at 99.
[21] There are exceptional cases of agreements which establish procedures, separate from the tribunal with jurisdiction over the merits of a claim, for ruling upon the justiciability or arbitrability of a dispute. See, for instance, the US–UK 'Knox Treaty' of 1911, article III (referring such questions to a joint high commission of inquiry: 5 *AJIL Supp.* 255 (1911)).
[22] Cf., e.g. the *Phosphates in Morocco* case, PCIJ Ser. A/B No. 74 (1938), 25, in which the Court's jurisdiction turned on this question; and the *Panama Canal Tolls* controversy of 1912–13, Lord McNair, *The Law of Treaties* (Oxford, 1961), 547–9.

came into existence not when the legislation was enacted but only when it was enforced.[23]

Thus far we have been concerned with the task of establishing that a dispute has come into existence. In the case of most (but not all) tribunals a further aspect of this precondition of justiciability is that the dispute remains in existence up to the point that the judgment or award is given. To put it another way, most tribunals will refuse to give rulings on disputes that are hypothetical or have become moot.[24] As Judge Fitzmaurice put it in the *Northern Cameroons* case:

> courts of law are not there to make legal pronouncements *in abstracto* . . . They are there to protect existing and current legal rights, to secure compliance with existing and current legal obligations, to afford concrete reparation if a wrong has been committed, or to give rulings in relation to an existing and concrete legal situation.[25]

The cessation of the dispute will, of course, ordinarily lead the parties not to submit the case to the tribunal at all or to withdraw it if the case has already been submitted. But where one or both parties wishes to press ahead with the case, mootness is a ground for a refusal to render a judgment. Perhaps the most celebrated, if not the most convincing, application of this principle is the *Nuclear Tests* case. Australia and New Zealand had sought from the Court a declaration that French atmospheric nuclear testing in the Pacific was not consistent with international law. Before the Court gave its judgment France, which did not appear before the Court, announced that it was ceasing such testing. By a chain of reasoning which appears as strained on matters of fact as it does on matters of law,[26] the Court found that France had by its unilateral declarations entered into a legally binding commitment to cease testing, and that the case had accordingly become moot. The Court therefore refrained from giving a ruling on the merits of the case.[27]

A different approach is sometimes taken by certain tribunals, notably the European Court of Human Rights and the Court of Justice of the European Communities. In the case of *Ireland* v. *United Kingdom* the European Court of Human Rights said that its function was 'not only to decide those cases brought before [it], but, more generally, to elucidate, safeguard and develop the rules instituted by the Convention'.[28] Accordingly, the Court proceeded to rule upon the compatibility of interrogation techniques employed by United Kingdom forces in Northern Ireland, notwithstanding the fact that the United Kingdom had, before

---

[23] (1933) 6 *UNRIAA* 338, at 341.
[24] See further chapter seven, 156.
[25] ICJ Rep. 1963, 15, at 117 (Separate Opinion).
[26] See the opinions of Judges Onyeama, Dillard, Jiménez de Arechaga and Waldock, ICJ Rep. 1974, 253, 272; A. P. Rubin, 'The International Legal Effects of Unilateral Declarations' (1977) 71 *AJIL* 1. The Court appears to have pulled back from this position: see the comments on unilateral declarations in the *Frontier Dispute* case, ICJ Rep. 1986, 554, at 572–4.
[27] ICJ Rep. 1974, 253.
[28] (1978) Eur. Court HR, Ser. A, vol. 25, at 62.

the Court hearing, given an unqualified undertaking to abandon those techniques and had argued that the case was consequently moot. Similarly, in cases where there is a sufficient Community interest in declaring the law, the Court of Justice of the European Communities will proceed to give a ruling in a case that has become moot. This might be so, for example, where the European Commission seeks a ruling from the Court in a case which has itself become moot, but where the ruling would govern a number of similar cases pending before the Commission.[29] The common factor motivating the attitude of these tribunals is the responsibility which they have assumed for the rapid development of the ground rules of the legal system of which they are a part, in order that the system might operate as quickly as possible as the day-to-day framework within which the Member States act. The International Court, and, even more, arbitral tribunals, do not see themselves as having the same crucial role in the promotion of a legal system: they consider their function to be essentially confined to the settlement of existing disputes.[30]

We turn now to the second element of justiciability. In order to be justiciable it is not only necessary that the disagreement should have hardened into a dispute; it is also necessary that the dispute should be capable of solution by the application of judicial processes, and susceptible of a decision upon the basis of law.[31] In other words, the dispute must be (or be capable of being treated as) a *legal* dispute, to which the tribunal can apply rules and principles of law so as to decide the dispute.[32]

Attempts have been made to specify the classes of dispute which are 'legal' and so justiciable, drawing up a calendar of causes of action.[33] Such attempts are useful as reflections upon trends in current practice, but they can have no a priori validity. There are two main reasons for this. First, international law is constantly developing, and matters formerly outside its scope may come in time to be regulated by

---

[29] See, e.g., Case 26/69 *Commission* v. *France* (1970) ECR 565. In earlier cases the Court was even more ready to rule on moot cases: see, e. g., Case 7/61 *Commission* v. *Italy*, 7 Rec. 633.

[30] The Advisory jurisdiction of the ICJ and other tribunals is an exception in this respect.

[31] See *British Claims in the Spanish Zone of Morocco* (1925) 2 *UNRIAA* 615, where Judge Huber made a Report on the Notion of Arbitrability, under the terms of an arbitration agreement made between Great Britain and Spain on 29 May 1923. Arbitrability and justiciability were essentially interchangeable terms, in his view.

[32] There is no possibility of a *non liquet*. If the dispute is a legal dispute, the tribunal must decide it according to the law. This is, at least, the rule in contentious proceedings. As Judge Higgins pointed out in her dissenting opinion in the Advisory Opinion of the International Court of Justice on the *Legality of the Threat or Use of Nuclear Weapons*, ICJ Rep. 1996, 226, at 583–4, 591–2, the doctrine of *non liquet* appears not to have been applied in these advisory proceedings.

[33] See, e.g., I. Brownlie, 'The Justiciability of Disputes and Issues in International Relations' (1967) 42 *BYIL* 123, and *System of the Law of Nations: State Responsibility, Part I* (Oxford, 1983), Chs. I–V. Cf., J. G. Merrills, 'The Role and Limits of International Adjudication', in W. E. Butler (ed.), *International Law and the International System* (Dordrecht, 1987), 169; H. Mosler, 'The Area of Justiciability', in J. Makarczyk (ed.), *Essays in International Law in Honour of Judge Manfred Lachs* (The Hague, 1984), 409.

rules of international law.[34] Secondly, the rights and obligations which international tribunals are required to adjudicate upon are not limited to those entailed by the rules of conduct which international law imposes upon States. As will be seen,[35] the rights and obligations may arise under a system of municipal law, or be specifically undertaken by the parties. Again, the parties may be bound by obligations that do not form a part of international law *stricto sensu*.

While it is not possible to draw up an exhaustive list of the kinds of disputes that are legal disputes, it is quite clear that some disputes are not legal. The *Haya de la Torre* case illustrates this point. The International Court had decided, in the *Asylum* case,[36] that the grant of asylum by Colombia to Haya de la Torre in its embassy in Peru was unlawful. The Court was then asked to determine how that unlawful asylum should be brought to an end. It refused to do so, saying that it was 'unable to give any practical advice as to the various courses which might be followed with a view to terminating the asylum, since, by doing so, it would depart from its judicial function'.[37] It was the fact that the question was purely political, and entirely without legal content, which produced that decision.

The mere fact that political issues surround a legal dispute will not prevent a tribunal from ruling on the legal aspects of the dispute. Thus, when Iran argued that the dispute arising from the detention of the US diplomatic and consular staff in the US embassy compound in Tehran, which underlay the US application to the International Court in the *Hostages* case, was only 'a marginal and secondary aspect of the overall problem' which had arisen from twenty-five years of US intervention in Iran, and an aspect which could not be considered in isolation from that context, the Court was not persuaded. It noted that 'legal disputes between sovereign States by their very nature are likely to occur in political contexts and often form only one element in a wider and longstanding political dispute between the States concerned', and firmly rejected the view that 'because a legal dispute submitted to the Court is only one aspect of a political dispute, the Court should decline to resolve for the parties the legal question at issue between them'.[38]

This willingness to separate the legal and non-legal aspects of a dispute is evident also in the principle that the concurrent pursuit of other, typically political,

---

[34] The changing limits of domestic jurisdiction show this clearly. See, e.g., *Nationality Decrees in Tunis and Morocco* (1923) PCIJ Ser. B, No. 4, at 24; G. G. Shinkaretskaya, 'Content and Limits of "Domaine Reservée" ', in G. Tunkin and R. Wulfrom (eds.), *International Law and Municipal Law* (Berlin, 1988), 121.

[35] Below, chapter eight, 239.

[36] ICJ Rep. 1950, 266.

[37] ICJ Rep. 1951, 71, at 83. The result, but not the reasoning, is similar to a declaration of *non liquet*. The finding here is that the matter is not regulated by law: *non liquet* implies that the matter is regulated by law but the Court cannot determine what the law is. See also the *South West Africa* cases *(Second Phase)*, ICJ Rep. 1966, 6 at 250 (Tanaka), 546 (Jessup).

[38] ICJ Rep. 1980, 3, at 20. Cf. *Nicaragua* v. *US (Jurisdiction and Admissibility)*, ICJ Rep. 1984, 392 at 439; *Nicaragua* v. *Honduras*, ICJ Rep. 1988, 69 at 91.

dispute settlement procedures is no obstacle to a judicial tribunal proceeding to hear and determine a case. This point was prominent in the *Hostages* case, where the Security Council was considering the dispute concurrently with the International Court,[39] and in the *Nicaragua* v. *US* case, where it was argued that the International Court proceedings would interfere with the Contadora peace process.[40] In neither case did the Court refrain from the exercise of its judicial function. Perhaps the most extreme example of the logic of this separation of functions, and the clearest demonstration of the dangers which it entails, is to be found in the *Lockerbie* case.[41] While that case, brought against the United Kingdom and United States by Libya, was before the International Court the respondent States promoted the passage of a binding resolution through the Security Council, which decisively altered the legal position of the applicant State. It may be that in such circumstances the concurrent use of Security Council procedures does not entirely preclude the continuation of the judicial process: but there must come a point when the use of the Security Council to alter the rights and duties of the parties during the course of the judicial proceedings threatens to undermine the Rule of Law, and to that extent it is difficult to deny that the concurrent pursuit of non-judicial remedies may hamper the work of a judicial tribunal.

Justiciability is an aspect of the focusing of a disagreement or clash of interests into a concrete dispute, capable of resolution by a judicial process on the basis of law. Disputes that do not have those characteristics ought not to be submitted to judicial procedures;[42] and if they are so submitted, a preliminary objection by one of the parties ought to result in the dismissal of the case by the tribunal. It is with justiciability in this general sense that we have been concerned. However, it is important to note that, in the context of international commercial arbitration, the concept may operate at a different level. Even if the dispute is justiciable according to the criteria discussed above, the provisions of one of the municipal legal systems governing the various aspects of the arbitral process may stipulate that certain categories of dispute must be submitted to the courts, and may not be settled by arbitration. For instance, it might be stipulated that patent disputes are not arbitrable, but must be submitted to the national courts. We return to this question of the limits of arbitrability under national laws below, in Part Two.

In Part One, we outline the main procedures that have been adopted for the settlement of international disputes.

---

[39] ICJ Rep. 1980, 3, at 21.

[40] ICJ Rep. 1984, 392 at 440.

[41] ICJ Rep. 1992, 3. See V. Lowe, 'Lockerbie—changing the rules during the game', [1992] 51 *CLJ* 408.

[42] But those that do have these characteristics should be accepted by courts and decided by them, even if the subject matter is embarrassing. See the decision of the House of Lords in *Buttes Gas and Oil Co.* v. *Hammer* [1982] AC 888.

PART ONE:

INSTITUTIONS

2

METHODS OF SETTLEMENT OF DISPUTES: THE BASIC FRAMEWORK

1. Introduction	19
2. Negotiation	20
3. Inquiry and fact finding	24
4. Mediation and good offices	27
5. Conciliation	29
6. Arbitration	31
6.1 The Permanent Court of Arbitration	35
6.2 The use of arbitration in recent times	38
7. Dispute Settlement Mechanisms and other developments	39
8. New directions? Iraq and the UN Compensation Commission	41

1. Introduction

One of the purposes of the United Nations, set out in article 1(1) of the Charter is 'to bring about by peaceful means, and in conformity with the principles of justice and international law, adjustment or settlement of international disputes or situations which might lead to a breach of the peace'. Among the principles in accordance with which the Organization and its members are to act in pursuit of such purpose are that all members are to 'refrain in their international relations from the threat or use of force against the territorial integrity or political independence of any State, or in any other manner inconsistent with the Purposes of the United Nations' (article 2(4)), and that they 'shall settle their international disputes by peaceful means in such a manner that international peace and security, and justice, are not endangered' (article 2(3)).

These purposes and principles are reflected in Chapter VI of the Charter, which deals with the powers of the Security Council and the General Assembly in respect of the Pacific Settlement of Disputes, as it is termed there. Article 33 enunciates the basic obligation of States, as follows:

> 1. The parties to any dispute, the continuance of which is likely to endanger the maintenance of international peace and security, shall, first, seek a solution by nego-tiation, enquiry, mediation, conciliation, arbitration, judicial settlement, resort to regional agencies or arrangements, or other peaceful means of their own choice.
> 2. The Security Council shall, when it deems necessary, call upon the parties to set-tle their dispute by such means.

This was repeated by the General Assembly of the United Nations in its Declaration of the Principles of International Law concerning Friendly Relations and Co-operation between States of 24 October 1970,[1] and amplified in the Manila Declaration on the Peaceful Settlement of International Disputes of 15 November 1982.[2]

Some of the methods of settlement of disputes referred to in article 33(1) of the Statute will now be discussed.[3]

2. Negotiation[4]

Negotiation (which includes consultation and the exchange of views) is the means by which the large majority of international disputes are settled.[5] In the *North Sea Continental Shelf* cases (1969), the International Court of Justice said that 'there is no need to insist upon the fundamental character of this method of settlement'.[6] In the *Mavrommatis Palestine Concessions* case (1924)[7] the Permanent Court also observed that this is the chief method by which States settle their disputes, whether these arise out of their state interests or in respect of claims by their nationals, and said that 'before a dispute can be made the subject of an action at law, its subject-matter should have been defined by diplomatic negotiations'. However, the existence of active negotiations does not preclude the resort to other

---

[1] GA Res. 2625 (xxv), Annex, reproduced in I. Brownlie, *Basic Documents in International Law*, 4th edn. (Oxford, 1995), 36 and (1970) 9 *ILM* 1292.

[2] GA Res. 37/10, (1982) 21 *ILM* 449.

[3] A useful overview of the main methods of peaceful settlement is to be found in the United Nations *Handbook on the Peaceful Settlement of Disputes* (New York, 1992), and in *Merrills*. See also M. W. Janis (ed.), *International courts for the twenty-first century* (Dordrecht, 1992); G. Guillaume, 'The Future of International Judicial Institutions' (1995) 44 *ICLQ* 848.

[4] C. M. Fombad, 'Consultation and Negotiation in the Pacific Settlement of International Disputes' (1989) 1 *AJICL* 707; F. C. Iklé, *How Nations Negotiate* (New York, 1964); S. L. Kass, 'Obligatory Negotiations in International Organizations' (1965) 3 *CYIL* 36; A. Lall, *Modern International Negotiation* (New York, 1966); P. J. I. M. de Waart, *The Element of Negotiation in the Pacific Settlement of Disputes* (The Hague, 1973).

[5] United Nations *Handbook on the Peaceful Settlement of Disputes* (New York, 1992), 9–24.

[6] ICJ Rep. 1969, 3 at 48.

[7] PCIJ, Ser. A, No. 2, 11–15.

settlement procedures, including judicial settlement, as was pointed out by the ICJ in the *Aegean Sea* (1978)[8] and *Nicaragua* v. *US* (1984)[9] cases. In other words, there is no general rule of international law requiring that negotiations be exhausted before a settlement may be sought by some other procedure.

Negotiations, or in some cases 'consultations', are sometimes referred to in treaties as an obligation of prior consultation before action is taken,[10] sometimes as a means of settlement,[11] and sometimes as a preliminary to resort to other means of settlement.[12] In the form of 'exchanges of views' they are referred to, for example, in the UN Convention on the Law of the Sea 1982, article 283.[13] On occasion, a treaty may make it obligatory to carry out negotiations, consultation or exchanges of views, as in the Agreement Governing the Activities of States on the Moon and other Celestial Bodies 1979 article XV paragraph 1,[14] the provision of the UN Convention on the Law of the Sea referred to above, and the Antarctic Treaty 1959 article VIII paragraph 2.[15] Certain treaties, such as the Revised General Act for the Settlement of Disputes 1949, the International Maritime Organisation Convention 1946, and the UN Convention on the Law of the Sea 1982 make the obligation to resort to third party means of settlement conditional on the failure of negotiations.[16]

Rather than appearing as a dispute settlement provision at the end of a treaty whose primary purpose is to provide for the substantive regulation of some area of the law, the duty to engage in negotiation in specified circumstances has itself sometimes been made the subject of a treaty. The bilateral agreements made by the United States concerning the avoidance of jurisdictional conflicts in the enforcement of antitrust laws are examples, which also illustrate the fact that negotiation, when coupled with a duty of prior notification or consultation, can play an important role in the prevention, as well as the resolution, of disputes.[17]

---

[8] ICJ Rep. 1978, 3.

[9] ICJ Rep. 1984, 392, 440.

[10] See, e.g., the NATO Agreement, 4 April 1949, art. 4, 34 *UNTS* 243. See further F. L. Kirgis, *Prior Consultation in International Law* (Charlottesville, Va.,1983).

[11] See, e.g., the Mexico–US Convention for the Recovery and Return of Stolen Vehicles and Aircraft 1981, art. VIII, (1981) 20 *ILM* 711.

[12] See, e.g., the Treaty Concerning the Establishment of the Republic of Cyprus 1960, art. 10, 382 *UNTS* 10.

[13] (1982) 21 *ILM* 1261.

[14] UN Doc. A/34/12 November 1979. GA Res. 34/68, 5 December 1979, (1979) 18 *ILM* 1434.

[15] 402 *UNTS* 71 (1961).

[16] On this kind of condition see the *South West Africa* cases, ICJ Rep. 1962, 319.

[17] The texts of the agreements are reprinted as follows: US–Australia 1982, (1982) 21 *ILM* 702; US–Federal Republic of Germany 1976, *DUSPIL 1976*, 479; US–Canada 1969, (1969) 8 *ILM* 1305; US–Canada 1984, (1984) 23 *ILM* 275; US–Canada 1995, (1996) 35 *ILM* 319; US–EEC 1991, [1991] *CMLRep.* 823; US–EEC 1998, (1998) 37 *ILM* 1070. For similar provisions see the OECD Council Decisions concerning multinational enterprises, (1976) 15 *ILM* 977 and (1979) 18 *ILM* 1171. Such provisions are common in bilateral treaties of friendship, commerce and navigation: see, e.g., US–Italy, 79 *UNTS* 171, art. XVIII (1948); US–Japan, 206 *UNTS* 143, art. XVIII

It is sometimes said that an obligation to enter into negotiations may be imposed by judicial decisions, as with the obligation to negotiate so as to effect a delimitation of continental shelf boundaries between neighbouring States according to equitable principles, adverted to by the ICJ in the *North Sea Continental Shelf* cases (1969)[18] or the mutual obligation of States to undertake negotiations in good faith for an equitable solution of their differences, mentioned by the same Court in the *Fisheries Jurisdiction* cases.[19] Such statements are, indeed, particularly common in respect of disputes over shared resources. It is arguable that in these cases the Court was referring to an obligation which exists under general international law and was not claiming a right to impose one itself. However, in the *Case concerning Land and Maritime Boundary between Cameroon and Nigeria*, the International Court held that there is no general requirement in international law to exhaust negotiations before a dispute is taken before a tribunal.[20] Any obligation to enter into negotiations would, therefore, have a very limited scope, amounting to little more than the need to negotiate rather than pursue non-peaceful means, and to negotiate in order to define the precise point at issue between the parties.

Negotiations may be bilateral or multilateral, depending on the number of parties to the dispute. In modern times, of course, they are frequently pursued collectively, a conspicuous example being in the United Nations, where the parties may have the assistance of a third party, such as the Secretary-General.[21]

States have sometimes formalised negotiations, establishing permanent commissions to deal with any problems that might arise from time to time in a given field. Several commissions have been established for the settlement by negotiation of problems, such as those concerning pollution and the use of boundary waters, that may arise in frontier areas. Perhaps the best known is the Canada–US International Joint Commission, originally established under the 1909 Treaty Relating to Boundary Waters and Questions Arising along the Boundary,[22] but with a remit subsequently extended by other agreements, such as the 1991 US–Canada Air Quality Agreement.[23] The International Joint Commission in fact may serve both as a forum for negotiation and for the quasi-judicial settlement of disputes by majority decision. In cases where the Commission is equally divided over an issue, after the International Joint Commission has reported the

---

(1953); US–Pakistan, 404 *UNTS* 259, art. XVIII (1959), and cf., M. M. Whiteman, *Digest of International Law*, vol. 6 (Washington DC, 1968), 149–50.

[18] ICJ Rep. 1969, 3.
[19] ICJ Rep. 1974, 3.
[20] *Case concerning Land and Maritime Boundary between Cameroon and Nigeria*, ICJ Rep. 1998 275 (Judgment of 11 June 1998), para. 56.
[21] See the *South West Africa* cases, ICJ Rep.1962, 319.
[22] For text see 36 *Stat.* 2448.
[23] (1991) 2 *Y'bk. Int. Env. Law* 679.

divergent views to the Canadian and US Governments the matter is referred to an umpire for final decision.[24] Joint commissions have also been established in other areas.[25]

The obligation to enter into negotiations cannot delay legal proceedings if one party refuses to negotiate, as the International Court pointed out in respect of the Iranian refusal to negotiate with the United States as required by the Vienna Convention on Diplomatic Relations 1961 in the *Hostages* case (1980).[26] Where the parties are under an obligation to negotiate, said the Permanent Court in the case concerning *Railway Traffic between Lithuania and Poland*,[27] they are under an obligation 'not only to enter into negotiations but also to pursue them as far as possible with a view to concluding agreements', though they are not obliged actually to reach agreement.[28] A failure to fulfil the duty to negotiate, for example by the unjustified breaking off of discussions or abnormal delays or disregard of agreed procedures, may result in the imposition of sanctions, just as is the case in the event of a breach of any other rule of international law.[29]

In recent years much attention has been given to the mechanisms of negotiation, now enjoying an elevated status as a form of 'Alternative Dispute Resolution' or 'ADR' (that is, alternative to judicial settlement). Projects such as the Harvard Law School Program on Negotiation have drawn on practical experience and theoretical insights from fields such as game theory in order to develop both strategies for improving the chances of success in negotiations and a framework within which the dynamics of negotiation can be analysed and understood.[30]

One particular form of negotiated solution to international disputes deserves particular mention, and that is the lump sum settlement.[31] In this process a State negotiates a settlement of claims that it presents on behalf of a number—often a

---

[24] Boundary Waters Treaty, 1909, art. X. The umpire is chosen by the two States, in accordance with the procedure in art. XLV of the 1907 Hague Convention for the Pacific Settlement of International Disputes. On the operation of the International Joint Commission see M. Cohen, 'The regime of boundary waters: the Canadian-United States experience' (1975) 146 *HR* 219; id. (1974) 68 *Proc. ASIL* 236–9; C. R. Ross (1974) 68 *Proc. ASIL* 229–36.

[25] See, e.g., the 1959 Finland–Norway–USSR Agreement concerning Lake Inari, 346 *UNTS* 192.

[26] *United States Diplomatic and Consular Staff in Tehran*, ICJ Rep. 1980, 3.

[27] PCIJ, Ser. A/B no. 42, at 116 (1931).

[28] However, in its Advisory Opinion on the *Legality of the Threat or Use of Nuclear Weapons* the International Court spoke of the obligation of States to pursue negotiations for nuclear disarmament and to bring them to successful completion: ICJ Rep. 1996, 226, at 263–4.

[29] *Lac Lanoux* (France v. Spain, 1957) 24 *ILR* 101, at 127–8.

[30] Among the influential studies in this field are H. Raiffa, *The Art and Science of Negotiation* (Cambridge, Mass., 1982); A. Plantey, *La negociation internationale: principes et methodes*, 2nd edn. (Paris, 1994). See also C. Bühring-Uhle, *Arbitration and Mediation in International Business* (The Hague, 1996).

[31] See R. B. Lillich and B. H. Weston, *International Claims: Their Settlement by Lump Sum Agreements* (Charlottesville, 1975); id., 'Lump Sum Agreements: Their Continuing Contribution to the Law of International Claims' (1988) 82 *AJIL* 69.

very large number—of individuals and corporations who have its nationality. The State first gathers evidence that enables it to estimate the total value of such claims. This is often obtained by public announcements requiring the registration of claims against the foreign State within set time limits. It then proceeds to negotiate with the State against which the claims are made. Agreement is reached on a global sum, payable in full settlement of all the claims. That sum is then available for distribution between the claimants. At this stage there is commonly a further process in which claimants must provide full proof of their losses to a claims commission established in the State which has negotiated the settlement on their behalf, which determines the amount of each claim that is eligible for compensation. In the United Kingdom this function is discharged by the Foreign Compensation Commission,[32] in the United States by the Foreign Claims Settlement Commission,[33] and in France by the *commissions de répartitions*,[34] for example. Once the total amount of eligible claims is known, the lump sum is distributed between them pro rata. Lump sum settlements have been common after, for example, large-scale expropriations of alien property on the coming to power of Communist regimes in Eastern Europe.

In conclusion, it is important to remember that the parties are free to negotiate on any terms they wish, and may exclude the application of rules of international law which might bind them, except for those of *jus cogens*.[35]

3. Inquiry and fact finding

This method of settlement, as its name suggests, does not involve the investigation or application of rules of law.[36] If the dispute is a factual one, inquiry may itself settle it; if it has any legal content, inquiry may help to do so. The function of an inquiry, in the words of article 9 of the Hague Convention for the Pacific Settlement of Disputes 1907, is 'to facilitate a solution of . . . disputes by elucidating the facts by means of an impartial and conscientious investigation'. (This envisages that a third party should carry out an inquiry, but a dispute may be settled by the finding of the true facts by one party which is accepted by the other.)

---

[32] See S. W. Magnus, 'The Foreign Compensation Commission' (1988) 37 *ICLQ* 975; C. J. Warbrick, 'Lump-Sum Settlements' (1988) 37 *ICLQ* 1010; R. B. Lillich, *International Claims: Postwar British Practice* (Syracuse, 1967).

[33] See R. B. Lillich, *International Claims: Their Adjudication by National Commissions* (Syracuse, 1962).

[34] See B. Weston, *International Claims: Postwar French Practice* (Syracuse, 1971).

[35] Though it may be difficult for third parties to overturn agreements made in violation of rules of *jus cogens*: see the *East Timor* case, ICJ Rep. 1995, 90.

[36] For a full study see N. Bar-Yaacov, *The Handling of Disputes by Means of Inquiry* (1974). See also the *UN Handbook*, 24–33, and *Merrills*, chapter 3.

Inquiry is obviously of assistance in combination with negotiation, mediation, good offices and conciliation.

International Commissions of Inquiry are provided for in the Hague Convention 1907,[37] which repeated and expanded upon provisions set out in its predecessor, the Hague Convention of 1899.[38] The 1899 provisions were a consequence of the case of the *Maine*, a US warship which mysteriously blew up in Havana harbour, thus providing the excuse for the Spanish-American War of 1898. Several commissions of inquiry were set up under the Hague Conventions, perhaps the most celebrated being that which was set up (after French mediation) under the 1899 Convention and investigated the *Dogger Bank* incident of 1904,[39] when the Russian Baltic Fleet, on its way to what proved to be its watery grave at Tsushima during the Russo-Japanese War, fired on the Hull trawler fleet which was fishing on the Dogger Bank in the North Sea. The report of the Commission was accepted by Russia and the United Kingdom and closed the incident, which had at one stage threatened to bring the United Kingdom into the war against Russia. The *Dogger Bank* inquiry expended a considerable proportion of its time on settling the Commission's procedure. In an attempt to avert such difficulties, the 1907 Convention expanded the six articles (9–14) of the 1899 Convention concerned with inquiries to twenty-eight articles (9–36), to include more detailed procedural provisions.

Treaties have often provided for fact finding or inquiry. Commissions based on the Hague model were also envisaged in the Bryan Treaties of 1913–14 between the United States and other States, and in other treaties of about the same date.[40] Long dormant, the Bryan treaty provisions were activated by the United States in the case of *Letelier and Moffit*, which arose out of the assassination of Orlando Letelier and Ronni Moffit in Washington DC in 1976. It was alleged that the assassinations were the work of Chilean intelligence officers. While denying responsibility, Chile was prepared to make an *ex gratia* payment equivalent to the amount that would have been payable had its liability been established. A Commission was established under the 1914 US–Chile Bryan–Suárez Mujica

---

[37] *UKTS* 6 (1971) Cmd. 4575, arts. 9–36.

[38] *UKTS* 9 (1901) Cd. 798, arts. 9–14.

[39] See the Anglo–Russian Agreement of 1904, *UKTS* 13 (1904), Cd. 2328, 97 *BFSP* 77; and for the Report, J. B. Scott *The Hague Court Reports*, First Series (New York, 1916), 404, and (1907) 2 *AJIL* 929. See also the *Tavignano* case, 1912, J. B. Scott, *The Hague Court Reports*, First Series (New York, 1916), 413, 614 and the *Tubantia* case, 1922, ibid. Second Series (New York, 1932) 135.

[40] Treaties entered into by the United States before the First World War, such as the Taft (Knox) Treaties with Great Britain and France, provided for joint commissions of inquiry. These treaties never came into operation. The UN Convention on the Law of the Sea 1982 makes provision for an inquiry procedure whose findings of fact are in most cases to be considered final by the parties to the dispute. See chapter five below.

treaty[41] solely to determine that quantum. The incident was settled on the basis of the Commission's report.[42]

Other, *ad hoc* commissions, are exemplified by the one created by agreement by the United Kingdom and Denmark to investigate certain incidents involving the British trawler 'Red Crusader' when it was stopped by a Danish marine protection vessel in 1960.[43]

International organisations have frequently used inquiries or fact finding. The League of Nations did so in seven cases, including the Aaland Islands dispute between Finland and Sweden in 1921 and the Mosul case between Great Britain and Turkey. Organs of the United Nations have done likewise. For example, the Security Council sent a fact-finding mission to the Seychelles in 1981[44] to investigate the involvement of mercenaries in an invasion, and in 1984 the Secretary-General investigated the use of chemical weapons in the Gulf War between Iran and Iraq.[45] Other international organisations also employ inquiries. The International Labour Organisation's Constitution, article 26, provides for them. In 1983 the Council of the International Civil Aviation Organisation set up an inquiry by its Secretary-General into the destruction of Korean Airlines Boeing 747 and an inquiry into another case in 1988.

The General Assembly has, over the years, set considerable store on fact finding in the field of the maintenance of international peace and security. It passed a resolution on fact finding in 1963[46] on the question, based on reports of studies undertaken by the Secretary-General, and another in which it requested the Secretary-General to prepare a register of experts in legal and other fields who could be employed in fact finding.[47] In its Declaration on the Prevention and Removal of Disputes and Situations which may threaten International Peace and Security (1988), the General Assembly established a Special Committee on the Charter and on the Strengthening of the Role of the Organization, from whose report it derived a Resolution and Declaration on Fact-Finding by the UN on 9 December 1991[48] whose wide dissemination was urged by the General Assembly.

---

[41] 14 *US Treaty Series* 621.

[42] For the agreement to refer the matter to the Commission see (1992) 30 *ILM* 422. For the Report of the Commission see 88 *ILR* 727, (1993) 31 *ILM* 1. Cf. (1989) 83 *AJIL* 352.

[43] See Anglo-Danish Exchange of Notes, 15 November 1961, *UKTS* 118 (1961) Cmnd. 1575. For an account of the Report, which contained opinions on law as well as findings of fact, see *Contemporary Practice of the United Kingdom in the Field of International Law*, 1962 (2), 50–3; cf. 35 *ILR* 485.

[44] SC Res. 496 (1981).

[45] SC Res. 598 (1987).

[46] GA Res. 1967 (XVIII). An earlier (1949) attempt to promote the use of Panels for Inquiry and Conciliation, in GA Res. 268 (III), remained a dead letter.

[47] GA Res. 2329 (XXII). The register was issued in September 1968, but seems to have fallen into disuse.

[48] GA Res. 46/59, (1992) 31 *ILM* 235.

The Declaration defines fact finding as:

> any activity designed to obtain detailed knowledge of the relevant facts of any dispute or situation which the competent United Nations organs need in order to exercise effectively their functions in relation to the maintenance of international peace and security.

It urges the use of fact-finding missions, subject, in general, to the consent of a State to whose territory it is to be sent. It emphasises that the Security Council, the General Assembly and the Secretary-General may employ fact-finding missions, the General Assembly or Security Council giving preference to the Secretary-General in deciding to whom to entrust the conduct of a mission. The Security Council may authorise the sending of a fact-finding mission to the territory of a State without that State's consent, as it did when it created a commission for the on-site inspection of the Iraqi weapons programme at the end of the Gulf War in 1991, but generally the consent of the State in question will be required. There will arise considerable practical and legal difficulties if the territorial State refuses to co-operate.[49]

4. Mediation and good offices

In some disputes the degree of animosity between the parties is so great that direct negotiations are unlikely to be an effective approach to a settlement. The intervention of a third party who assumes the task of 'reconciling the opposing claims and appeasing the feelings of resentment which may have arisen between the States at variance', as article 4 of the 1899 Hague Convention puts it, may greatly facilitate settlement of the dispute. Some distinguish between mediation and good offices.[50] Mediation is the participation of a third State or States, a disinterested individual or an organ of the United Nations with the disputing States, in an attempt to reconcile the claims of the contending parties and to advance proposals aimed at a compromise solution. The distinction between mediation and good offices is sometimes taken to be that whereas in the former the mediator takes active steps of his or its own, good offices consist of action taken by a third party to bring about, or initiate, or cause to be continued, negotiations, without the third party actively participating in the discussion of the dispute. Mediation and good offices are, however, very similar, and the terms are usually employed indifferently rather than as labels for distinct approaches to dispute settlement. The

---

[49] SC Res. 687(c) para. 8 (3 April 1991), the 'cease-fire resolution'. For the text see (1991) 30 *ILM* 846; and see C. Gray, 'After the cease-fire: Iraq, the Security Council, and the use of force' (1994) 65 *BYIL* 135 at 152–7.

[50] See, e.g., *Merrills*, 27.

Hague Conventions of 1899 and 1907 do not differentiate between them,[51] and article 33(1) of the UN Charter does not specifically mention good offices. Sometimes, however, both are mentioned and apparently treated as distinct, as in the Pact of Bogota 1948.[52]

Mediation, and sometimes good offices, are identified as approaches to dispute settlement in treaties other than those already mentioned, such as the Pact of the League of Arab States, the Charter of the Organization of African Unity 1964, and the Antarctic Treaty of 1959. Among disputes which were settled by joint mediation was the Chaco War between Bolivia and Paraguay, by Argentina, Brazil, Chile, Peru, the United States and Uruguay between 1935 and 1937. As to individual mediation, an example of a case which was highly sensitive politically and which was eventually settled by mediation was the Beagle Channel dispute over the ownership of certain islands in the entrance to the Channel, between Chile and Argentina. This was the subject in 1977 of an arbitral award in favour of Chile by a tribunal of five judges of the International Court of Justice.[53] This award was totally unacceptable politically to Argentina. Eventually, in 1984, the mediation of the Pope, which was not based on law, was successful in settling the dispute.[54]

Individual States frequently make offers to afford good offices or mediation, as in the disputes between India and Pakistan over the Rann of Kutch, 1955 and Kashmir, 1965, where the United Kingdom[55] and the USSR respectively so acted. Algeria acted as mediator between the United States and Iran to bring about an end to the hostages crisis in 1980.[56]

Both the General Assembly and the Security Council of the United Nations are competent to recommend the use of good offices or mediation by a Member State or an agency or to offer their own services. The United Nations used its good offices in the Indonesian (1947) and Palestine (1966) crises, for instance. The Secretary-General of the United Nations has frequently offered or performed

---

[51] Arts. 2–8 of both the 1899 and 1907 Conventions. For good offices, see *UN Handbook*, 33–40, and for mediation see ibid. 40–5. See also *Merrills*, chapter 2, and G. P. McGinley, 'Ordering a savage society: a study of international disputes and a proposal for achieving their peaceful resolution' (1984) 25 *Harvard International Law Journal* 43.

[52] American Treaty on Pacific Settlement, arts. IX–XIV, 30 *UNTS* 55. Good Offices and Mediation are also mentioned separately in the Manila Declaration 1982, GA Res. 37/10, para. 5, and in GA Res. 45/51 (1988).   [53] (1978) 17 *ILM* 634.

[54] (1985) 24 *ILM* 7 and ibid. 10 (for the Treaty of Peace and Friendship between the two States). Cf. G. R. Moncayo, 'La mediation pontificale dans l'affaire du Canal Beagle' (1993) 242 *HR* 197.

[55] For an account of this by the late Lord Wilson, former British Prime Minister, see *The Labour Government 1964–70: A Personal Record* (London, 1971), 112 reproduced in M. Dixon and R. McCorquodale, *Cases and Materials on International Law*, 2nd edn. (London, 1995), 600–1.

[56] On the Iran-US Claims Tribunal, see further below, chapter four, pp. 73–83. For other examples of mediation and good offices see, e.g., *DUSPIL 1979*, 1686–724 (Nicaragua / USA; Egypt / Israel); S. Touval and I. W. Zartmann (eds.), *International Mediation in Theory and Practice* (Boulder, Colorado, 1985).

good offices,[57] as for example in Cyprus, from 1964, Kampuchea, 1989 and Afghanistan, 1988. During the Falklands 'war' between the United Kingdom and Argentina in 1982, the UN Secretary-General offered his good offices, and the US Secretary of State, Alexander Haig, offered to mediate.[58]

Mediation and good offices require the consent and co-operation of the disputing States in order to function. Any proposals from a mediator require the acceptance of those States, since such proposals are not of themselves binding.

Mediation is also practised in the context of mixed disputes (and, indeed, purely private disputes). As in the case of negotiation, it is attracting increasing attention and is the subject of increasingly sophisticated analysis, particularly in relation to the potential of arbitrators to enhance the utility of arbitration by assuming a more active role—in essence, acting as mediators.[59]

5. Conciliation

Conciliation is a method of settling a dispute which combines the characteristics of inquiry and mediation.[60] A dispute may be referred to a person or commission whose task is to make an impartial elucidation of the facts and to put forward proposals for a settlement, which do not have the binding character of an award or a judgment.[61] It has been described as 'intervention in the settlement of an international dispute by a body having no political authority of its own, but enjoying the confidence of the parties to the dispute, with the task of investigating every aspect of the dispute and of proposing a solution which is not binding on the parties'.[62] It is also useful when the main issues in dispute are legal ones but the parties want an equitable solution.

There have been, and are, multilateral treaties providing for conciliation. Conciliation commissions were provided for in a number of treaties made after the First World War, of which the France–Switzerland Agreement of 6 April 1925 was

---

[57] For an explanation by the Secretary-General of the function of good offices as a part of his responsibilities see the *UN Handbook* 35–6.

[58] See L. Freedman and V. Gamba-Stonehouse, *Signals of War: The Falklands Conflict of 1982* (London, 1990), especially chapters 12–18. For a full account of another individual mediation, in the dispute over the break-up of the East African Community, see V. H. Umbricht, *Multilateral Mediation: practical experiences and lessons* (Dordrecht, 1989). Dr Umbricht played an active role, in many ways closer to that of a conciliator than a mediator.

[59] For an excellent introduction to the theory and the literature see C. Bühring-Uhle, *Arbitration and Mediation in International Business* (The Hague, 1996).

[60] See the *UN Handbook*, 45–55; *Merrills*, chapter 4.

[61] Prior to the revision of the institutional structure of the European Human Rights regime, this was the function of the European Commission on Human Rights in cases where it accepted a complaint made to it of a breach of the European Convention on Human Rights (art. 28(b)).

[62] J.-P. Cot, *International Conciliation* (London, 1972), 9.

perhaps the most influential.[63] In 1922, the League of Nations adopted a resolution encouraging States to submit their disputes to conciliation commissions.[64] Conciliation machinery was provided for in the Geneva General Act for the Pacific Settlement of Disputes 1928 (revised in 1949)[65] and the European Convention for the Peaceful Settlement of Disputes 1957.[66] It is also provided for in, for example, the Pact of Bogota 1948,[67] the Protocol to the Charter of the Organization of African Unity 1964,[68] and in the Agreement of the Organisation of Eastern Caribbean States 1981.[69] Among multilateral conventions dealing with particular legal topics which contain provisions mentioning conciliation are the Vienna Conventions on the Law of Treaties, 1969,[70] and on the Succession of States in Respect of Treaties 1978,[71] and the UN Convention on the Law of the Sea 1982.[72] It is frequently adopted for the settlement of trade disputes.[73] Conciliation is sometimes laid down as an alternative to arbitration in bilateral treaties, such as those between Sweden and Chile, 1920[74] (where conciliation was an optional alternative to inquiry), Germany and Switzerland, 1921,[75] and the France–Switzerland treaty of 1925 mentioned above, which created permanent Boards or Commissions of conciliation. Switzerland also concluded such a treaty with the United Kingdom in 1965.[76]

An individual may act as conciliator, or the function may be performed by a commission. Among disputes dealt with by commissions may be mentioned the *Chaco* case (1929), the Franco-Siamese Border case (1947) (in accordance with the 1928 General Act), the Belgian-Danish dispute concerning Danish ships evacuated from Antwerp (1952), disputes between France and Italy, and France and Switzerland (1955), and the Norwegian-Icelandic dispute which gave rise to the *Jan Mayen* Award (1981).[77]

---

[63] See N. Bar-Yaacov, *The Handling of International Disputes by Means of Inquiry* (London, 1974), 120–5. The provisions in the France–Switzerland Agreement appear to have been used as a model for the provisions in the Locarno Treaties concluded by Germany with Belgium, France, Czechoslovakia and Poland in 1925, designed for the maintenance of peace and security, and the settlement of disputes of a political nature.

[64] League of Nations, Records of the Third Assembly, Text of Debates, 199.

[65] 93 *LNTS* 343 (General Act), 71 *UNTS* 102 (Revised General Act). At their peak 22 States were parties to the General Act and 7 to the Revised General Act.

[66] 320 *UNTS* 244.

[67] 30 *UNTS* 55.

[68] (1964) 3 *ILM* 116.

[69] (1981) 20 *ILM* 1166.

[70] 1115 *UNTS* 331, (1969) 8 *ILM* 679: arts. 65, 66, Annex.

[71] (1978) 17 *ILM* 1488, (1978) 72 *AJIL* 971. Cf. R. Lavalle, 'The Dispute Settlement Provisions of the Vienna Convention on Succession of States in Respect of Treaties' (1979) 73 *AJIL* 407.

[72] See below, chapter five, p. 93.

[73] See below, chapter six, pp. 100, 111.

[74] 4 *LNTS* 273.

[75] 12 *LNTS* 281.

[76] *UKTS* 42 (1967); Cmnd. 3285.

[77] For the *Jan Mayen* conciliation see (1981) 20 *ILM* 797; 62 *ILR* 108. See also *Re Imperial Japanese 4% Loan*, 29 *ILR* 4, *Re City of Tokyo 5% Loan*, ibid. 11.

In this last case, which resolved a dispute over continental shelf rights, the Commission observed that, although a conciliation commission is not bound to apply rules of law, it may take them into account in its report. It said that 'the Conciliation Commission shall not act as a court of law. Its function is to make recommendations to the two governments which in the unanimous opinion of the Commission will lead to acceptable and equitable solution of the problems involved.' But it did examine state practice and decisions of courts, including that of the ICJ in the *North Sea Continental Shelf* cases.[78]

The General Assembly of the United Nations, which may itself appoint commissions to effect conciliation,[79] adopted and circulated to Member States draft rules for the Conciliation of Disputes between States in 1990.[80] These rules deal with the initiation of conciliation proceedings, the number of conciliators (either a sole conciliator or a commission of three or five members) and their appointment, and set out detailed provisions concerning the conduct of the conciliation proceedings. The Permanent Court of Arbitration has also adopted Optional Rules for Conciliation (1996), which may be used by States making use of its facilities,[81] as may the conciliation rules adopted by UNCITRAL in 1980 for use in disputes arising in the context of international commercial relations.[82]

6. Arbitration

Since many aspects of the topic will be dealt with in detail later, arbitration will be summarised here.[83] Arbitration is the name given to the determination of a difference between States (or between a State and a non-State entity) through a legal decision of one or more arbitrators and an umpire, or of a tribunal other than the International Court of Justice or other permanent tribunal. The arbitration may be concerned with one particular matter, such as a boundary; there are many examples of such an arbitration. Or it may be concerned with the claims of nationals of either of the two States against the other State; there are also many examples of such arbitrations. One of the most recent is the Iran–US Claims Tribunal, created in 1981 as part of the settlement of the Hostages crisis, which

---

[78] ICJ Rep. 1969, 3.

[79] See the UN Charter, arts. 10, 14, 36; and see the *UN Handbook* 48.

[80] (1991) 30 *ILM* 229. Adopted as UN GA res. A/50/50 (1996).

[81] The 1996 Rules are published in PCA, *Basic Documents: conventions, rules, model clauses and guidelines* (The Hague, 1998) and also at http://www.law.cornell.edu/icj/pca/eng/home.htm. The PCA had previously adopted provisions concerning conciliation, and concerning conciliation followed by arbitration, in its Rules of Arbitration and Conciliation for Settlement of International Disputes between two Parties of which one only is a State (1962).

[82] Annexed to UN GA Res. 35/52, 4 December 1980. Available at http://www.un.or.at/uncitral/en-index.htm.

[83] See further below, chapter eight; and see *UN Handbook*, 55–65. See also P. Chapal, *L'arbitrabilité des différends internationaux* (Paris, 1967).

has been sitting at the Hague since then and has rendered numerous awards. This Tribunal is discussed later in this work.[84] Another important distinction is that between *ad hoc* arbitration, for the settlement of a particular dispute, and institutionalised arbitration, for the settlement of a class of disputes, such as that of the International Centre for the Settlement of Investment Disputes (ICSID):[85] both kinds of arbitration are examined in this book.

Arbitration as an institution of international law, though it has a long pedigree,[86] developed in a recognisable form only during the latter part of the nineteenth century. The origins of modern arbitration are usually dated from the Treaty of Amity, Commerce and Navigation (the 'Jay Treaty') of 1794, which set up, *inter alia*, mixed tribunals consisting of an equal number of members appointed by each of the two States, with an umpire in the event of disagreement, to consider claims by the nationals of Great Britain and the United States.[87] The Jay Treaty commissions decided many claims by awards expressly applying legal principles. During the first half of the nineteenth century, however, the practice of rendering unreasoned awards persisted, particularly in cases where a foreign sovereign was designated as the arbitrator.[88] Moreover, there was still a widespread view that 'arbitral commissions' were essentially extensions of diplomacy, with the State-appointed arbitrators negotiating a solution with the aid of the neutral umpire, who served a function akin to that of a mediator. What proved to be the decisive step towards the typically modern form of arbitration, with a tribunal reaching by an essentially judicial process a reasoned decision clearly based on law, was taken by the United States and Great Britain in the 1871 Washington Treaty.[89] That treaty established a collegiate tribunal to arbitrate the *Alabama* claims (1872), in which the United States sought compensation for the losses inflicted upon the Union side during the American Civil War by the warship *Alabama*, supplied to the Confederacy by British shipbuilders in breach of Britain's international legal duty of neutrality. The *Alabama* claims tribunal was heralded as a great success, and its example was followed in subsequent disputes, such as the *Behring Sea Fur*

---

[84] See below, chapter four, pp.78–83.

[85] See below, chapter four, pp. 59–73.

[86] See J. H. Ralston, *International Arbitration from Athens to Locarno* (London, 1929); and cf. A. M. Stuyt, *Survey of International Arbitrations 1794–1989*, 3rd edn. (Dordrecht, 1990) for a list of arbitrations with full citations.

[87] For the Jay Treaty see 1 *BFSP* 784. Similar claims tribunals were set up to hear claims of nationals of the two States in 1853, 1871, and 1910. For a short historical account of arbitration after 1794, see J. L. Simpson and H. Fox, *International Arbitration* (London, 1959), Chapter 1, 1–17.

[88] e.g., the *Portendick* claims (1843, Mixed Arbitral Commission), Moore, *Int. Arb.*, vol. 5, 4937, and the *San Juan de Fuca* case (1871, Emperor of Germany), ibid., vol. 1, 229.

[89] For the treaty see 61 *BFSP* 40. See further J. G. Wetter, *The International Arbitral Process*, vol. 1 (New York, 1979), 27–173. For the award see Moore, *Int. Arb.*, vol. 1, 496.

Seal case (1893), and the *British Guiana-Venezuela Boundary* dispute (1897), among others.[90]

The work of the *Alabama* claims tribunal inspired the States represented at the 1899 Hague Peace Conference, convened by the Tsar of Russia in an attempt to find ways of reducing the risks of armed conflict in Europe,[91] to adopt a Convention on dispute settlement in which arbitration, along with mediation, played a central role. The relevant provisions of the 1899 Hague Convention, and its 1907 revision, are outlined below, where we discuss the Permanent Court of Arbitration.

Arbitration was seen as a move away from the power-based system of negotiated settlements towards a more principled system. It is, in the broadest terms, an attempt to bring the Rule of Law into international relations and to replace the use of force with the routine of litigation. But arbitration is a system distinct from litigation. Arbitration is similar to judicial settlement in the International Court of Justice and comparable international tribunals in that an arbitral award is in principle binding on the parties and that, unless the parties stipulate otherwise, it is based upon rules of international law. Arbitration does, however, differ from judicial settlement of disputes in several ways. The arbitration agreement, usually termed the '*compromis d'arbitrage*', may well permit of settlement on extra-legal principles (this is true to some extent of judicial settlement since article 36(2) of the Statute of the ICJ permits that court to decide the case *ex aequo et bono* if the parties agree, but this has never been done).[92] Or the *compromis* may lay down the rules by which the tribunal is to decide the case. Thus, the Treaty of Washington 1871,[93] article 6, laid down the 'Three Rules of Washington' on the duties of neutral powers in time of war, which were to be applied by the arbitral tribunal and which imposed a higher duty on neutrals than those which were generally accepted at the time the American Civil War was being fought and the events underlying the claims took place: they were the basis of the award against Great Britain in the *Alabama* claims (1872). Further, the tribunal consists of persons selected by the States parties[94] and is usually created to deal with a particular dispute or class of disputes, whereas the ICJ is permanent and can deal with any kinds

---

[90] For an analytical discussion of the arbitrations referred to in this paragraph see G. Schwarzenberger, *International Law as applied by International Courts and Tribunals*, vol. IV (London, 1986), Part I, 1–94.

[91] Twenty-six governments, representing around 90 per cent of the world's population and territory, attended the 1899 conference.

[92] For discussion of the *compromis* in the *Tunisia/Libya Continental Shelf* case, ICJ Rep. 1982, 18, which appeared to empower the Court to decide the case on a basis other than that of existing rules of international law, see further chapter eight, p. 239.

[93] 61 *BFSP* 40.

[94] In two senses, this is to some extent true of judicial settlement. For the right of parties to a case before the ICJ to appoint an *ad hoc* judge, and for their role in the selection of a Chamber of the Court, see below, chapter seven, pp. 130 and 128, respectively.

of disputes which involve international law. An arbitration is usually held in private and the award may remain unpublished if the parties so desire; the ICJ must generally hold its hearings in public,[95] and all its judgments are published. One disadvantage is that the parties to an arbitration have to pay the arbitrators and the tribunal's registrar and other officials and meet other expenses of the arbitration, thus making it more expensive than judicial settlement, for the parties do not have to make any of these payments in the case of the ICJ.[96]

In 1949, the Secretary-General of the United Nations submitted to the International Law Commission ('ILC') a 'Survey of International Law in Relation to the work of Codification of the Commission'. Included in the topics that were thought worthy of consideration by the ILC was arbitral procedure.[97] In its deliberations the ILC took cognisance of the decision of the ICJ in the *Peace Treaties* Advisory Opinion (1950).[98] In that case, the Court was concerned with an arbitration agreement contained in the Peace Treaties with Hungary, Romania and Bulgaria which provided, *inter alia*, that each party was to appoint an arbitral commissioner, and failing their agreement on the appointment of a third commissioner, who was to be a national of a third country, the Secretary-General of the United Nations was to appoint such person on the request of either party. The Court held that the Secretary-General could not appoint the third commissioner where one party had refused to appoint its commissioner. Thus, a refusal by one State to appoint its commissioner could prevent arbitration taking place. The need to prevent the frustration by such devices of commitments made by States to arbitrate disputes was a major concern of the ILC.

The ILC produced a draft Convention in 1953. Having discussed it, the General Assembly of the United Nations adjourned further discussion until 1955. It then referred the draft back to the ILC, instructing it to report back, but not before 1958.[99] In view of the evident lack of enthusiasm with which its efforts had been received, the ILC decided to abandon the draft Convention and downgraded it to a set of optional Model Rules on Arbitral Procedure which was adopted by the General Assembly in 1958.[100] The Rules had no binding force of their own but

---

[95] Unless the Court decides or unless the parties demand that the public be not admitted: Statute of the ICJ, art. 46.

[96] The expenses of the Court are borne by the United Nations in such a manner as is decided by the General Assembly: ibid., art. 33. For the salaries, allowances and compensation payable to the judges and registrar and their pensions see ibid., art. 32.

[97] UN Doc. A/CN/4/1 Rev. 1(1949).

[98] See *Yearbook of the ILC*, 1953(i) 325. The *Peace Treaties* case is reported at ICJ Rep. 1950, 65, 221.

[99] UN GA Res. 989(X), 14 December 1955; cf., the Report of the Commission to the General Assembly, *Yearbook of the ILC*, 1958(ii) 80, paras. 10–15.

[100] UN GA Res. 1262 (XIII), 14 November 1958; and *Yearbook of the ILC*, 1958(ii) 80. See further K. S. Carlston, 'Draft Convention on Arbitral Procedure of the ILC' (1954) 48 *AJIL* 296; M. Bos, 'The ILC's Draft Convention on Arbitral Procedure in the General Assembly of the UN' (1956) 3 *Neth. Tid.* 234.

could be adopted by parties to a dispute. The Rules deal with the determination of the existence of a dispute and of the scope of the undertaking to arbitrate, the *compromis*, the constitution of the tribunal[101] and its powers, including the power to adjudge its own competence and interpret the *compromis*, the law to be applied (in the absence of agreement between the parties)[102] and its procedure, a prohibition on a finding of *non liquet*, the deliberations of the tribunal and its award (adopting majority voting and permitting separate opinions). The award must be reasoned and is binding: it constitutes the definitive settlement of the dispute. This is somewhat modified, however, by the authority given to the tribunal to rectify, interpret, or revise the award, and ultimately by the possibility of referring such matters to the International Court of Justice, which also has the power to annul the award for serious procedural errors or want of jurisdiction in the tribunal.[103] If these Model Rules had been adopted by and became binding on the parties to a dispute, obstructive tactics, such as those employed in the *Peace Treaties* case, could not have prevented the arbitration proceeding and producing a binding award. In practice, however, the Model Rules seem to have had little impact.

6.1 The Permanent Court of Arbitration

The advantages of arbitration, along with good offices and mediation and inquiry, were recognised at the Hague Peace Conference 1899, which sought to facilitate its use as a means of settling international disputes and avoiding recourse to the use of force.[104] By Hague Convention I for the Pacific Settlement of Disputes ('the 1899 Hague Convention'),[105] which was amended by Convention I of 1907 ('the 1907 Hague Convention')[106] the Conference created the Permanent Court of Arbitration ('PCA'). It has often been said that it is neither permanent nor a court nor, itself, does it arbitrate.

---

[101] Art. 3 contains a provision designed to close the 'gap' revealed in the *Peace Treaties* case: *Yearbook of the ILC,* 1958(ii) 80, at 83–4.

[102] Art. 10 lists the 'sources' of law that are listed in art. 38 of the Statute of the International Court of Justice: *Yearbook of the ILC,* 1958(ii) 80, at 84.

[103] Arts. 31–8: *Yearbook of the ILC,* 1958(ii) 80, at 86.

[104] For background documents see W. Evans Darby, *International Tribunals,* 4th edn. (London, 1904), which contains accounts of schemes and projects for international arbitration from classical times. See also J. B. Scott, *The Hague Conventions and Declarations of 1899 and 1907* (New York, 1915).

[105] PCA, *Basic Documents: conventions, rules, model clauses and guidelines* (The Hague, 1998), 3; 91 *BFSP* 970; *UKTS* 9 (1901).

[106] PCA, *Basic Documents: conventions, rules, model clauses and guidelines* (The Hague, 1998), 17; *UKTS* 6 (1971), Cmnd. 4575. The texts of the 1899 and 1907 Conventions set out in a comparative manner are to be found in J. B. Scott, *The Hague Conventions and Declarations of 1899 and 1907* (New York, 1915), 41–88. The text of a draft Convention relative to the creation of a Judicial Arbitration Court, annexed to a Vœu of the 1907 Conference, is included in ibid., 31–40: it may be regarded as a precursor of the Statute of the Permanent Court of International Justice.

The seat of the PCA is at The Hague, in the same building as the International Court. The PCA consists of an International Bureau which functions as a registry for the arbitration tribunals, which are created on an *ad hoc* basis by the parties to disputes to hear particular cases.[107] This is its only permanent organ. There is also a Permanent Administrative Council which exercises administrative control over the bureau and which consists of the diplomatic agents of the States Parties to the Convention accredited to The Hague and the Netherlands Minister of Foreign Affairs.[108] In so far as the Permanent Court of Arbitration, as such, has a basis as an institution for arbitration, it is the panel of persons nominated by the contracting States.[109] The States which wish to have recourse to the court for settlement of a dispute may select arbitrators from those whose names are on this panel.[110] The 1899 and 1907 Hague Conventions deal with good offices and mediation and with International Commissions of Inquiry as well as with arbitration. As regards the latter, they lay down detailed rules governing the arbitration procedure (articles 51–85 of the 1907 Convention). These rules deal with, *inter alia*, the *compromis* and its settlement, the number of arbitrators, and the seat and language of the arbitration. They divide the procedure into two distinct phases: 'pleadings' and 'oral discussions', and regulate these. They provide for majority voting, the requirement for reasons in the award, the effect of the award, and its interpretation and revision. Articles 86–90, first included in 1907, lay down brief rules for arbitration by summary procedure, in which the proceedings, except for evidence of witnesses and experts, are entirely in writing. These rules have never been used.

The heyday of the Permanent Court of Arbitration was in the years before World War I. Among the arbitrations under its auspices to which the United Kingdom was a party were the *Venezuelan Preferential Claims* (1904),[111] *Japanese House Tax* (1905),[112] *Muscat Dhows* (1905),[113] *North Atlantic Coast Fisheries* (1910),[114] and *Savarkar* (1911)[115] cases. Other well-known cases include the *Pious Funds of the Californias* (1902),[116] *Canevaro* (1912),[117] and *Russian Indemnity* (1912)[118] cases. After the creation of the Permanent Court of International Justice in 1923, the PCA fell into relative disuse, though it was occasionally resorted to, as by the

---

[107] 1907 Hague Convention, arts. 43, 45.

[108] 1907 Hague Convention, art. 49.

[109] 1907 Hague Convention, art. 44. These must be persons of known competency in questions of international law, of the highest moral reputation.

[110] This does not prejudice their right to select other persons to sit on the tribunal: ibid., arts. 42, 45, though, if they do so, the parties have no *right* to use the facilities of the PCA.

[111] 6 *UNRIAA* 99.

[112] 11 *UNRIAA* 51.

[113] 11 *UNRIAA* 83.

[114] 11 *UNRIAA* 167.

[115] 11 *UNRIAA* 243.

[116] Mexico v. USA, 9 *UNRIAA* 1.

[117] Italy v. Peru, 11 *UNRIAA* 397.

[118] Russia v. Turkey, 11 *UNRIAA* 421.

United Kingdom in the *Chevreau* case (1931).[119] It heard a total of twenty cases. No inter-State cases have been referred to the Court, as such, since 1932, although its facilities have often been used for *ad hoc* arbitrations.

The Permanent Court of Arbitration still exists. Proposals are made from time to time to revive the use of the Court;[120] and during the 1990s the International Bureau concerned itself with the elaboration of model rules for use in the settlement of disputes, issuing a series of revised Optional Rules, to encourage greater use of its facilities[121]—an enterprise that the PCA began in 1962 when it opened its doors to mixed (State/non-State) arbitrations.[122] The 1992 optional rules for inter-State arbitration, for example, were based on the UNCITRAL Arbitration Rules, which had been designed for use in commercial arbitration. The optional rules adapt those UNCITRAL Rules so as to reflect the public international law character of disputes between States, to indicate the role of the Secretary-General and International Bureau of the Permanent Court of Arbitration and the relationship of the rules with those of the Hague Conventions of 1899 and 1907, and to provide freedom for the parties to choose a tribunal of one, three or five persons.[123]

Perhaps the most important exercise of the formal powers of the Permanent Court of Arbitration these days is in practice the part it plays in the nominations to fill the office of judge of the International Court of Justice.[124] Nonetheless, it has considerable practical importance in a less formal manner. It has placed staff and facilities at the disposal of arbitral tribunals formed otherwise than under the Hague Conventions: for example the Secretary-General of the PCA was designated as the functionary under the Iran-United States Claims Tribunal who was to designate the appointing authority[125] for membership of that Tribunal; and staff and

---

[119] 2 *UNRIAA* 1113.

[120] See, e.g., *The Permanent Court of Arbitration—New Directions*, published by the International Bureau of the PCA in 1991, which contains the suggestions of a Working Group on the revitalisation of the PCA.

[121] The Optional Rules concern: Arbitrating Disputes between Two States (1992); Arbitrating Disputes between Two Parties of which only one is a State (1993); Arbitration involving International Organizations (1996); Arbitrations between International Organizations and Private Parties (1996); and Conciliation (1996). All are reprinted in PCA, *Basic Documents: conventions, rules, model clauses and guidelines* (The Hague, 1998), and available at http://www.law.cornell.edu/icj/pca/eng/home.htm.

[122] See the 1962 PCA Rules of Arbitration and Conciliation for the Settlement of International Disputes Between Two Parties of which Only One is a State (1963) 57 *AJIL* 500. On the *Sudan/Turriff* arbitration utilising those rules, see A. Redfern and M. Hunter, *Law and Practice of International Commercial Arbitration*, 2nd edn. (London, 1991), (hereafter, *Redfern & Hunter*), 46–7, 172. The 1962 Rules were replaced by new rules in 1993: see PCA, *Basic Documents: conventions, rules, model clauses and guidelines* (The Hague, 1998), 69.

[123] The 1992 Rules are reprinted in PCA, *Basic Documents: conventions, rules, model clauses and guidelines* (The Hague, 1998), and (1993) 432 *ILM* 572.

[124] Statute of the ICJ, art. 5(1): see chapter seven, p. 127, below.

[125] On the role of appointing authorities, see chapter eight, p. 220, below.

accommodation were provided by the PCA for the Tribunal which dealt with the US/UK Arbitration concerning Heathrow Airport User Charges, which sat from 1989 to 1992.[126]

6.2 The use of arbitration in recent times

Since the end of the First World War, typical inter-State arbitrations have been less frequent than they previously were. One of the reasons for this is, of course, the establishment of the Permanent Court of International Justice and its successor, the International Court of Justice, which are permanent institutions for the judicial settlement of disputes. However, although the Permanent Court of Arbitration has not, as we have seen, had any inter-State cases referred to it for over sixty years, some important controversies have been dealt with by *ad hoc* arbitration during those years. These include territorial disputes, such as the *Rann of Kutch* arbitration (India v. Pakistan) (1968),[127] the *Palena* (1967)[128] and *Beagle Channel* (1978)[129] cases between Chile and Argentina, the *Channel Continental Shelf* arbitration (France v. United Kingdom) (1978),[130] and the *Taba* arbitration (Egypt v. Israel) (1988).[131] Several cases were concerned with the interpretation of treaties, such as the *Air Transport Agreement* arbitration (USA v. France) (1963),[132] that of the same name between the USA and Italy (1965),[133] and the *Air Transport Services* arbitration (USA v. France) (1978).[134] Other notable arbitrations were those which concerned the *Diverted Cargoes* (Greece v. United Kingdom) (1955)[135] and the *Rainbow Warrior* (New Zealand v. France) (1990).[136]

The most notable feature of arbitration in the last sixty years, however, does not concern inter-State arbitration at all. It concerns arbitrations 'between two parties, only one of which is a State', to borrow the words of the relevant set of PCA Optional Rules—that is, mixed arbitrations. Sixty years ago, if a dispute arose between a company and a State over, say, a concession granted to the company, if that dispute was pursued through formal procedures on the international plane, it would most likely have been presented as a claim by the national State of the corporation (exercising its right of diplomatic protection) against the host State of

---

[126] For the award in this case, dated 30 November 1992, see 102 *ILR* 216; (1994) 88 *AJIL* 739–44.

[127] 17 *UNRIAA* 1, 50 *ILR* 2, (1968) 7 *ILM* 633; and see M. G. Untawale, 'The Kutch-Sind Dispute: A Case Study in International Arbitration' (1974) 23 *ICLQ* 818.

[128] 16 *UNRIAA* 109.

[129] 52 *ILR* 39; (1978) 17 *ILM* 634, 738 and (1985) 24 *ILM* 1.

[130] 18 *UNRIAA* 3; 54 *ILR* 6; (1979) 18 *ILM* 397.

[131] 20 *UNRIAA* 3; 80 *ILR* 224.

[132] 16 *UNRIAA* 5; 38 *ILR* 182.

[133] 16 *UNRIAA* 81; 45 *ILR* 393.

[134] 18 *UNRIAA* 417; 54 *ILR* 304.

[135] 12 *UNRIAA* 53; 53 *ILR* 825.

[136] 82 *ILR* 499. See also 74 *ILR* 241 for an earlier phase of this dispute.

the investment. It would have been an inter-State dispute. It has become common for such cases to be presented, not by the national State of the company, but by the company itself, in its own name, against the State, before an international arbitral tribunal. Hence such well-known cases as *Texaco* v. *Libya*,[137] *BP* v. *Libya*,[138] and (to take a converse case) *Saudi Arabia* v. *Aramco*.[139] This depends, of course, upon the agreement of the State and the company to submit disputes to such a tribunal; but such agreement is increasingly common. As will be seen, such agreements are often to be found in concession agreements; and they also appear in international treaties such as the European Energy Charter and the Law of the Sea Convention, which provide for international commercial arbitration of mixed disputes as a part of the basic framework of international dispute settlement.[140] International law has also evolved a number of institutions in different fields specifically designed to deal with mixed disputes: the Iran-US Claims Tribunal and ICSID, discussed below, and certain human rights bodies, such as the European Court of Human Rights, are the most prominent examples.

7. Dispute Settlement Mechanisms and other developments

In recent years, there have been created two 'Mechanisms' for the Peaceful Settlement of Disputes. The first of these was created by the Conference (now Organization) on Security and Co-operation in Europe (OSCE). The OSCE process was initiated at the Helsinki Conference in 1975, and elaborated at several follow-up meetings.[141] At a meeting at Valletta in 1991, the Member States adopted a report on Principles for Dispute Settlement and Provisions for a CSCE Procedure for Peaceful Settlement of Disputes.[142] The Valletta provisions were modified at a meeting at Stockholm in 1992.[143] The Principles, which emphasise dispute prevention and management as much as settlement, require, *inter alia*, that the participating States will endeavour to reach a rapid and equitable solution of their disputes on the basis of international law, using the methods already discussed in this chapter. If they cannot settle the dispute among themselves they are

---

[137] (1977) 53 *ILR* 389.

[138] (1973) 53 *ILR* 297.

[139] (1958) 27 *ILR* 117.

[140] See chapter four, p. 63, below. See also the work of the Institut de Droit International on arbitration between States and foreign enterprises, (1989) 63(i) *Annuaire de l'Institut de Droit International* 31–204 and ibid., (1990) 63(ii), 121–221, 324–31.

[141] For accounts of developments in the OSCE process from the third such meeting (Vienna, 1986–9) to 1990, see D. McGoldrick (1990) 39 *ICLQ* 923, and from 1990 to the fourth meeting (Helsinki, 1992), D. McGoldrick (1993) 42 *ICLQ* 411, especially 429–30. See also K. Oellers-Frahm, 'The mandatory component in the CSCE dispute settlement system', in M. W. Janis (ed.), *International Courts for the Twenty First Century* (Dordrecht, 1992), 195.

[142] The text is to be found in (1991) 30 *ILM* 382.

[143] See (1993) 32 *ILM* 55.

to try to agree upon a suitable settlement procedure and, in the context of the OSCE Procedure, accept the mandatory involvement of a third party when a dispute cannot be settled by other peaceful means.

The OSCE Procedure itself involves the establishment of an OSCE Dispute Settlement Mechanism, consisting of one or more persons from a register of qualified candidates, at the request of one of the parties to the dispute. The Mechanism cannot be established or continued if one of the parties to the dispute considers that it should not be established or continued because the dispute affects its territorial integrity, national defence, title to sovereignty over land territory, or competing claims with regard to jurisdiction over other areas. The chief function of the Mechanism is to give its comments or advice regarding the inception or resumption of negotiations among the parties or as to which dispute settlement procedure or procedures they might adopt. The parties may agree to authorise the Mechanism to conduct a process of fact finding or entrust some other persons or bodies to do this, to request it to undertake or organise any expert function in regard to the subject matter of the dispute, or to accept any comment or advice of the Mechanism as binding.

At the 1992 Stockholm Meeting, the OSCE opened for signature a Convention on Conciliation and Arbitration within the OSCE and made provision for an OSCE Conciliation Commission to complement the Valletta Procedure. This Commission is to have jurisdiction if the parties to a dispute agree or if one party has declared that it will accept, on condition of reciprocity, conciliation by the Commission for disputes between it and other OSCE participating States. The OSCE also agreed on provisions for 'directed' conciliation, by which its Council of Ministers or Committee of Senior Officials may direct any two participating States to seek conciliation of their dispute; this conciliation may take place under the Convention or be undertaken by the OSCE Conciliation Commission.[144]

The second Mechanism was established by the Organization of African Unity's Assembly of Heads of States and Governments at its Cairo meeting in 1993. The Declaration which created it provides for a central administration and states that it functions at the level of Heads of State. The Declaration, compared with the OSCE's provisions, lacks specificity.[145]

---

[144] The texts of the Convention, the Conciliation Commission Provisions and those for Directed Conciliation are contained in Annexes 2, 3 and 4 to the OSCE Stockholm decision: see (1993) 32 *ILM* 557, 568 and 570 respectively.

[145] For the text of the Declaration on the Establishment within the OAU of a Mechanism for Conflict Prevention, Management and Resolution, see (1994) 6 *AJICL* 158 (1994). See M.-C. D. Wembou, 'A propos du nouveau mécanisme de l'OUA sur les conflits' (1993) 5 *AJICL* 725.

8. New directions? Iraq and the UN Compensation Commission

The list of dispute settlement mechanisms in article 33 of the UN Charter is by no means exhaustive; and the development of new approaches to dispute settlement continues. Prominent among the most notable recent innovations is the United Nations Compensation Commission.[146] After Iraq had been expelled by military force from Kuwait following its invasion of that country in August 1990, the United Nations Security Council adopted a resolution under Chapter VII of the Charter setting out the broad lines of a framework for the settlement of claims against Iraq arising from its invasion. That resolution, Resolution 687 (1991),[147] is remarkable, as is the scheme which was established to implement it.

The Resolution contained a number of determinations which might be thought to belong more properly to the judicial sphere. For example, it decided[148] that Iraq was liable for losses resulting from its unlawful invasion and occupation of Kuwait and that Iraqi statements made since 2 August 1990 repudiating its foreign debt are null and void. The difficult questions to which such quasi-judicial determinations by the Security Council give rise are canvassed elsewhere.[149] Here we are concerned with the procedure for the settlement of the claims against Iraq. In Resolution 687 the Security Council decided to create a Fund to pay compensation for claims for 'any direct loss, damage, including environmental damage and the depletion of natural resources, or injury to foreign Governments, nationals and corporations, as a result of Iraq's unlawful invasion and occupation of Kuwait'.

The Fund, known as the UN Compensation Fund, and the claims mechanism were established shortly afterwards,[150] in accordance with recommendations contained in a report[151] by the UN Secretary-General. The Fund is constituted by a

---

[146] See the UNCC web site <http://www.unog.ch/uncc/>. See also R. B. Lillich (ed.), *The United Nations Compensation Commission* (Irvington, NY, 1995); B. G. Affaki, 'The United Nations Compensation Commission: a new era in claims settlement?' (1993) 10(3) *Journal of International Arbitration* 21; J. R. Crook, 'The United Nations Compensation Commission—A New Structure to Enforce State Responsibility' (1993) 87 *AJIL* 144; R. Bettauer, 'The United Nations Compensation Commission—Developments Since October 1992' (1995) 89 *AJIL* 416; V. Heiskanen and R. O'Brien, 'UN Compensation Commission Panel Sets Precedents on Government Claims' (1998) 92 *AJIL* 339; R. P. Alford, 'Well Blowout Control Claim' (1998) 92 *AJIL* 287.

[147] This and other texts are conveniently reproduced in M. Weller (ed.), *Iraq and Kuwait: The Hostilities and their Aftermath* (Cambridge, 1993). Resolution 687 appears at p. 8.

[148] The term is significant, because *decisions* of the Security Council are binding on Member States under art. 25 of the Charter.

[149] See E. Lauterpacht, *Aspects of the Administration of International Justice* (Cambridge, 1991), 37–48.

[150] See Resolution 692 (1991); in M. Weller (ed.), *Iraq and Kuwait: The Hostilities and their Aftermath* (Cambridge, 1993), 13.

[151] UN Doc. S/22559, 2 May 1991; M. Weller (ed.), *Iraq and Kuwait: The Hostilities and their Aftermath* (Cambridge, 1993), 537.

30 per cent levy on the proceeds of Iraqi oil sales authorised by the UN,[152] and, although it initially proved difficult to secure Iraq's co-operation in this respect,[153] the Fund began receiving around $100 million per month in December 1996, and has made substantial payments to claimants.[154] Claims against it are administered by the United Nations Compensation Commission, which is a subsidiary body of the Security Council. The Commission sits in Geneva. It has a fifteen-member Governing Council, composed of the representatives of the current members of the Security Council at any given time, and a secretariat. At its heart lies the body of commissioners. The commissioners, who sit in three-member panels, are experts in fields such as law, accountancy, insurance and environmental damage assessment, appointed by the Governing Council on the nomination of the UN Secretary-General, and serving in their personal capacities. The commissioners are chosen with due regard for the need for geographical representation, professional qualifications, experience and integrity. The panels operate within guidelines laid down in Decisions of the Governing Council.[155]

The nature of the Commission is specific and unusual. The Secretary-General's report commented upon it thus:

> The Commission is not a court or an arbitral tribunal before which parties appear; it is a political organ that performs an essentially fact-finding function of examining claims, verifying their validity, evaluating losses, assessing payments and resolving disputed claims. It is only in this last respect that a quasi-judicial function may be involved. Given the nature of the Commission, it is all the more important that some element of due process be built into the procedure. It will be the function of the commissioners to provide this element.[156]

That statement is more prescriptive than descriptive. On the face of it, the process that the commissioners were to administer was quite plainly judicial. A claimant would present a claim alleging that Iraq was responsible for losses that it suffered; the commissioners would decide if the claim is made out. But pragmatism dictated that the procedures adopted by the commissioners should depart significantly from those normally associated with judicial determinations.

The key factor was the number of claims anticipated. The Secretary-General had anticipated the filing of tens of thousands of individual claims.[157] In fact, around

---

[152] UN Doc. S/AC.26/1991/6, 23 October 1991; M. Weller (ed.), *Iraq and Kuwait: The Hostilities and their Aftermath* (Cambridge, 1993), 545.

[153] See 9(12) *International Arbitration Report* (December 1994), 12, and 10(12) *International Arbitration Report* (December 1995), 14.

[154] See http://www.unog.ch/uncc/fund.htm.

[155] Decisions 1–40, along with other key instruments, are reprinted in *ILR* vol.109. Other Decisions appear at < http://www.unog.ch/uncc/decision.htm>.

[156] UN Doc. S/22559, 2 May 1991, para. 20; M. Weller (ed.), *Iraq and Kuwait: The Hostilities and their Aftermath* (Cambridge, 1993), 539.

[157] UN Doc. S/22559, 2 May 1991, para. 21; M. Weller (ed.), *Iraq and Kuwait: The Hostilities and their Aftermath* (Cambridge, 1993), 540.

2.6 million claims, from over 100 States, were submitted, including claims submitted by around one million Egyptian workers for wages deposited in Iraqi banks but not transferred to the workers' families.[158] The claims had a total value of around $250 billion. Such a caseload could not be handled according to normal judicial procedures by a single tribunal, and some means of expediting the process had to be found. This was achieved, in essence, by dispensing with the judicial hearing stage, and by the computerisation of much of the routine handling of the smaller individual claims.

Under the Provisional Rules adopted by the UN Compensation Commission,[159] claims may be submitted by international organisations and governments on their own behalf, and by governments on behalf of their own individual and corporate nationals and of residents; but if companies cannot persuade their national government to submit their claims, they may do so in their own name, although it is necessary to explain the government's refusal.[160] The Secretariat makes a preliminary assessment of claims in order to determine whether they contain all the necessary documentation,[161] and the claims are then transmitted to the panels of commissioners, which meet in private. Although there is provision for hearings to be held in unusually large or complex cases, the normal procedure involves no hearings: the panels reach their decisions on the basis of the papers submitted with the claim.[162] The decisions take the form of recommendations to the Governing Council, which may review and adjust the amount of compensation recommended: there is no appeal from the decisions of the Governing Council.[163] As of mid-1998, some 2.5 million claims (including the consolidated claim on behalf of the Egyptian workers) had been reviewed by UNCC panels, and a total of over US$7 billion in compensation had been awarded.[164] The claimants receive payments in instalments, as monies flow into the compensation fund, although some of the smaller individual claims have been met in full.

The UN Compensation Commission represents an approach to international claims similar in some respects to the 'national' phase of lump sum settlements, when claims are presented to national claims commissions. There is no argument over liability: the essential determination of Iraq's liability had been taken by the Security Council before the Compensation Commission was established. And

---

[158] 10(4) *International Arbitration Report* (April 1995), 12. And see the decision of the Compensation Commission on jurisdiction in the *Egyptian Workers* case: UN Doc. S/AC.26/1995/R.20/Rev.1, 12 October 1995.

[159] UN Doc. S/AC.26/1992/10, 26 June 1992; M. Weller (ed.), *Iraq and Kuwait: The Hostilities and their Aftermath* (Cambridge, 1993), 553. The Rules are also reprinted in (1992) 31 *ILM* 1053.

[160] Provisional Rules, art. 5.

[161] Provisional Rules, art. 14.

[162] Provisional Rules, art. 36.

[163] Provisional Rules, art. 40.

[164] For reports of the decisions of the panels see 109 *ILR* 1–551; (1995) 34 *ILM* 235, (1996) 35 *ILM* 939, (1997) 36 *ILM* 1279, and (1998) 37 *ILM* 897.

Iraq has little opportunity to raise legal arguments to contest claims for losses substantiated by clear evidence.[165] Perhaps as a result of the unequivocal condemnation of Iraq by the UN, and of the scale of the expected claims, it was considered appropriate to abandon the judicial approach. In any event, the work of the Commission breaks new ground. It establishes that there can be individualised compensation for losses arising from international wars, and offers a valuable alternative model to the much cruder treatment of reparations which has followed previous wars.

We deal in later chapters with other tribunals, such as the International Court of Justice, ICSID tribunals, and the International Tribunal for the Law of the Sea.[166] These tribunals have an importance, and an interest, which demands that they be treated separately. Before turning to them, we step aside from the classical, inter-State procedures for dispute settlement and examine in the next chapter the institution of international commercial arbitration. Though designed initially for arbitrations between private parties, international commercial arbitration is one of the dominant influences on the current development of international dispute settlement systems.

---

[165] M. E. Schneider, 'How fair and efficient is the United Nations Compensation Commission system? A model to emulate?' (1998) 15(1) *Journal of International Arbitration* 15.

[166] On the range of international tribunals see, e.g., G. Abi-Saab, 'The International Court as a world court', in *Fifty Years of the ICJ*, 3.

3

INTERNATIONAL COMMERCIAL ARBITRATION

1. Introduction   45

2. Arbitration rules   46
   2.1 The ICC Rules   47
   2.2 The UNCITRAL Rules   50

3. National arbitration laws   51
   3.1 The UNCITRAL Model Law   53

4. International agreements on arbitration   54

5. Concluding remarks   58

1. Introduction

Commercial arbitration[1] has a long history: it predates the existence of organised systems of States' courts.[2] Arbitration is a natural extension of the informal practice of traders calling upon a respected colleague to express a view on disputes between them. Where the courts might appear remote, rigid, and slow and expensive in their procedures and the judges might seem unversed in the ways of commerce and the law, insensitive and ill adapted to the exigencies of commercial life, arbitrators offered an attractive alternative. They were originally drawn from the same commercial community as the traders, often experienced in the trade, capable of offering practical suggestions for the settlement of the dispute and of doing

---

[1] For helpful introductions see R. Bernstein and D. Wood, *Handbook of Arbitration Practice*, 3rd edn. (London, 1998); Ph. Fouchard, E. Gaillard, B. Goldman, *Traité de l'arbitrage commercial international* (Paris, 1996). For texts of current instruments, international and national, see the massive compilation by E. E. Bergsten, *International Commercial Arbitration* (New York, 1991, looseleaf) (hereafter, *Bergsten*). See also the Parker School of Foreign and Comparative Law, *Commercial arbitration: an international bibliography* (Irvington, NY, 1993).

[2] See D. Roebuck, 'Sources for the History of Arbitration' (1998) 14 *Arbitration International* 237.

so informally, quickly, and cheaply.[3] These advantages of arbitration were magnified in disputes between traders in different countries.

Three problems impeded the development of arbitration as a widespread form of dispute settlement in commercial matters. First, the necessity for prescribing procedures to ensure the orderly conduct of the arbitration demanded increasingly complicated agreements between the parties on the procedural rules for the process. Secondly, no trader could be forced to accept arbitration. The process depended at every point upon the co-operation of the disputing parties. Equally, awards made by arbitrators did not of themselves carry any provision for enforcement against an unwilling defendant. For arbitration to be recognised as an alternative form of dispute settlement, coexisting with the courts, it was necessary that it be supported by national laws. And thirdly, for arbitration to be an effective form of international dispute settlement it was necessary that there should be an agreement between States on the manner in which each State's legal system would treat foreign arbitrations. These three problems have been addressed by the drafting of institutional arbitration rules, national legislation on arbitration, and international conventions on arbitration; and these we consider in turn.

2. Arbitration rules

International commercial arbitration can be conducted on the basis of *ad hoc* rules agreed for each particular arbitration, but the drafting of such rules represents a potentially lengthy and troublesome preliminary to the settlement of the dispute which necessarily falls for completion at a time when relations between the parties are likely to be strained. It is clearly preferable to have predetermined rules to which the parties can swiftly and easily resort. Many institutions, in countries throughout the world, have drafted sets of rules for the conduct of arbitrations, in the hope of attracting lucrative arbitration business to their centres. Among them are the American Arbitration Association, the Euro-Arab Chambers of Commerce, the London Court of International Arbitration (LCIA),[4] the Netherlands Arbitration Institute, the Stockholm Chamber of Commerce, and the former USSR Chamber of Commerce and Industry.[5] It is not possible to discuss each of these in detail; and the rules are in any event very much alike. In this

---

[3] See M. Mustill, 'Arbitration: history and background' (1989) 6 *Journal of International Arbitration* 43; *Redfern & Hunter*, chs. 1, 2; Symposium on International Commercial Arbitration (1995) 30(1) *Texas International Law Journal* 1–221.

[4] For the LCIA 1998 Rules see (1998) 37 *ILM* 669.

[5] A convenient compilation of the rules of these bodies is appended to *Redfern & Hunter*, 531–707. A fuller and more up-to-date collection is H. Smit and V. Pechota, *Arbitration Rules— International Institutions* (London, 1997) and H. Smit and V. Pechota, *Arbitration Rules—National Institutions* (London, 1998, loose-leaf). Most commercial arbitration centres now maintain their own web sites. A convenient place to start is <http://www.internationaladr.com/iir.htm>.

chapter attention will be focused on two systems which have been used extensively in practice, and which illustrate the main variations in arbitration structures: the International Chamber of Commerce (ICC) Rules and the UNCITRAL Rules.

2.1 The ICC Rules

The ICC was founded in 1919 and has its headquarters in Paris. Thousands of arbitrations have been conducted under its rules. The ICC arbitration system is of particular interest because of the manner in which arbitrations are supervised by the ICC International Court of Arbitration.

The International Court of Arbitration is one of the two permanent institutions of the ICC, along with its Secretariat. Both are based in Paris. The function of the ICC Court is to ensure the application of the ICC Rules of Conciliation and Arbitration in the procedures conducted under ICC auspices.[6] Its members are appointed by the various National Committees of the ICC, and its chairman and other officers are chosen by the ICC Council.[7]

Parties may agree to ICC arbitration by the inclusion of a submission clause in their contract, drafted along the following lines:

> All disputes arising out of or in connection with the present contract shall be finally settled under the Rules of Arbitration of the International Chamber of Commerce by one or more arbitrators appointed in accordance with the said Rules.

If a dispute arises either party may apply to the Secretariat of the ICC Court to initiate conciliation or arbitration. Conciliation is optional, and can proceed only if the other party agrees.[8] Arbitration, which may follow unsuccessful attempts at conciliation, is obligatory if the parties have agreed to it. The request for arbitration must set out details of the parties and state the claimant's case, and include the relevant agreements and documentation which will serve clearly to establish the circumstances of the case.[9] The defendant has thirty days to respond, and to enter a defence and any counter-claim or to contest the existence of ICC jurisdiction.[10] If the defendant does not accept that the ICC has jurisdiction, the ICC Court decides whether or not the documents submitted establish prima facie the existence of a valid agreement to arbitrate. If they do not, the claimant is informed

---

[6] Statutes of the International Court of Arbitration, art. 1, (1997) 36 *ILM* 1615. See R. H. Smit, 'An inside view of the ICC Court' (1994) 10 *Arbitration International* 53; J. Paulsson, 'Vicarious hypochondria and institutional arbitration' (1990) 6 *Arbitration International* 226; M. A. Calvo, 'The new ICC Rules of Arbitration—substantial and procedural changes' (1997) 14 *Journal of International Arbitration* 41.

[7] Statutes of the International Court of Arbitration, arts. 2, 3.

[8] ICC Rules of Optional Conciliation (1988), arts. 1–8; <http://www.iccwbo.org/arb/28. htm>.

[9] ICC Rules of Arbitration (1998), art. 4, (1997) 36 *ILM* 1604.

[10] Ibid., arts. 5, 6.

that the arbitration cannot proceed: if they do, the arbitration proceeds without prejudice to the jurisdictional challenge, and the arbitral tribunal takes the definitive decision on the existence of its own jurisdiction.[11]

The parties may choose the tribunal. The claimant should specify the number of arbitrators, and its nominees, in the original request for arbitration. If the parties do not agree on the number of arbitrators the ICC Court appoints a sole arbitrator, unless it thinks the case warrants a three-person tribunal. The parties may agree upon a sole arbitrator; or, in the case of three-person tribunals, may nominate one arbitrator each, the third being appointed (or confirmed, if chosen by the parties) by the ICC Court. Where appointments or nominations are not made in this way, the ICC Court makes the appointment after consulting an appropriate National Committee of the ICC.[12] The arbitrators chosen by the ICC have in the past been predominantly Western European, although in recent years an increasing number of North American, North African and Middle Eastern arbitrators have been appointed. This is partly a reflection of the place in which the arbitration is to be conducted, which may have been agreed by the parties even if they were unable to agree upon the numbers or names of the arbitrators. Where no place has been chosen, the ICC Court fixes it.[13] Most ICC arbitrations take place in Western Europe, and in France, Switzerland and the UK in particular. As we shall see,[14] because of the effect of the place of arbitration upon the law governing the arbitral proceedings, the choice of location can be crucial.

The tribunal begins its work by drawing up, within two months of its receipt of the claimant's request and defendant's answer, terms of reference which specify the parties and summarise their claims, define the issues falling for determination, set out particulars of the rules of procedure, time limits, and so on. This document is signed by the tribunal and the parties and sent to the ICC Court. Clear agreement on the precise scope of the arbitration at this stage avoids many potential difficulties during the arbitration and at later stages when the enforcement of the arbitral award is sought. If, however, one of the parties refuses to participate in drawing up the terms of reference or to sign them, the ICC Court may approve the terms as long as it is satisfied that the tribunal has prima facie jurisdiction.[15]

The rules governing the actual arbitration proceedings, dealing with matters such as the language of the proceedings, the submission of evidence, and time limits, are prescribed by the ICC Rules of Arbitration or, if they are not, are determined by the parties or, if they cannot agree, by the tribunal.[16] The whole procedure is

---

[11] ICC Rules of Arbitration (1998), art. 6.
[12] Ibid., art. 9.
[13] Ibid., art. 14.
[14] See chapter eight, p. 209, below.
[15] ICC Rules of Arbitration (1998), art. 18.
[16] Ibid., art. 15.

designed to ensure that the arbitration cannot be frustrated by the refusal of one party to co-operate: the tribunal is empowered to proceed with the arbitration if a party is absent without valid excuse.[17] The law governing the merits of the dispute may also be determined by the parties; and if they do not agree it is determined by the tribunal, which is directed to apply the rules of law it determines to be appropriate.[18]

One of the peculiarities of the ICC system is that the tribunal does not submit its award directly to the parties. The Rules require that the tribunal submit the draft award first to the ICC Court, which scrutinises it in order to remove all possible obstacles to the enforceability of the award.[19] The role of the Court is limited: article 27 of the Rules of Arbitration states that:

> . . . The Court may lay down modifications as to the form of the award and, without affecting the Arbitral Tribunal's liberty of decision, may also draw its attention to points of substance. No award shall be rendered by the Arbitral Tribunal until it has been approved by the Court as to its form.

The concern with form arises from the fact that some national laws lay down conditions with which arbitral awards must comply, and that a failure to comply with them may render the award unenforceable in the courts of the State where the arbitration took place or elsewhere. For example, the law may require that the award should contain certain details, such as the names and addresses of all arbitrators and parties, the date and place of the rendering of the award, and reasons for the decision,[20] and other details such as the domicile of the parties and the names of the parties' attorneys;[21] or the law may require that the award be signed by all the arbitrators, and not merely by the chairman. The ICC Court checks that any such requirements are met by the draft award.[22] It is sometimes difficult to distinguish between form and substance when a legal requirement that an award be 'reasoned' is in question: the inept or erroneous application of the substantive law to the merits of the dispute might be considered so egregious as to amount to a failure to 'reason' the award. And here the respective roles of the tribunal and the ICC Court can become blurred, giving rise to fears that the Court is interfering with the tribunal's decision. Nonetheless, the prior scrutiny by the Court is a valuable precaution which should ensure the validity and enforceability of the final award.

---

[17] Ibid., arts. 6(2), 6(3), 18(3).
[18] Ibid., art. 17.
[19] Ibid., art. 27.
[20] See, e.g., Netherlands Arbitration Act 1986, art. 1057; *Redfern & Hunter*, 774.
[21] See, e.g., French Code of Civil Procedure, art. 1472; *Redfern & Hunter*, 756.
[22] See W. L. Craig, W. W. Park and J. Paulsson, *International Chamber of Commerce Arbitration*, 2nd edn. (Dobbs Ferry, NY, 1984, loose-leaf), Pt. III, paras. 20.01–20.02.

2.2 The UNCITRAL Rules

UNCITRAL, the United Nations Commission on International Trade Law, was established in 1966 to harmonise and unify the laws of international trade. It was requested to draft a set of arbitration rules which could be adopted in *ad hoc* arbitrations to provide a sound procedure and ensure that the arbitral award would meet the conditions prescribed in courts where the recognition or enforcement of the award might be sought. UNCITRAL was seen as well placed to produce a 'neutral' set of rules, acceptable to States and parties from all regions and of all political complexions, including those who might harbour suspicions that ICC and other rules prepared by Western arbitration institutions were somehow coloured by their capitalist origins. The UNCITRAL Arbitration Rules were adopted in 1976,[23] and, as a result of their employment by regional arbitration centres in Cairo, Kuala Lumpur and elsewhere, and in modified form by the Iran-US Claims Tribunal, they have been well tried and tested in practice.[24]

The UNCITRAL Rules are similar in many respects to the ICC Rules, although they are more detailed on certain procedural matters. The differences between the two systems derive chiefly from the fact that the UNCITRAL system, unlike the ICC, has no permanent institutions to supervise the arbitration process. So, for instance, UNCITRAL arbitration is initiated by the claimant giving notice, containing broadly the same details as are required for the initial requests addressed by claimants to the ICC, to the defendant.[25] If the parties are unable to agree upon a sole arbitrator, or in the case of three-person arbitrators if one party refuses to nominate an arbitrator or if the party-nominated arbitrators are unable to agree upon a third arbitrator to preside over the tribunal, then either party may apply to the Secretary-General of the Permanent Court of Arbitration[26] for the designation of an appointing authority: the appointing authority will then appoint the missing arbitrators, having made such consultations as it sees fit.[27] The Rules provide for challenges to and removal of arbitrators, with the appointing authority acting as arbiter,[28] in the place of the ICC Court under the ICC system.[29]

---

[23] (1976) 15 *ILM* 701; <http://www.un.or.at/uncitral/en-index.htm>. UNCITRAL also adopted a set of Conciliation Rules, in 1980: see (1981) 20 *ILM* 301.

[24] See I. I. Dore, *Arbitration and conciliation under the UNCITRAL rules: a textual analysis* (Dordrecht, 1986); I. I. Dore, *The UNCITRAL Framework for Arbitration in Contemporary Perspective* (London, 1993); S. A. Baker and M. D. Davis, *The UNCITRAL Arbitration Rules in Practice. The Experience of the Iran-United States Claims Tribunal* (Deventer, 1992); J. J. van Hof, *Commentary on the UNCITRAL arbitration rules: the application by the Iran-U.S. claims tribunal* (Deventer, 1991).

[25] UNCITRAL Arbitration Rules (1976), art. 3.

[26] See chapter two, p. 37, above.

[27] UNCITRAL Arbitration Rules (1976), arts. 5–8. The President of the Netherlands Supreme Court acted as appointing authority for the Iran-US Claims Tribunal.

[28] UNCITRAL Arbitration Rules (1976), arts. 9–13.

[29] ICC Rules of Arbitration (1998), art. 11.

The tribunal conducts the proceedings as it considers appropriate, subject to the UNCITRAL Rules and the duty to treat the parties with equality and to give them full opportunity to present their cases at each stage,[30] and to any mandatory provisions of the law applicable to the arbitration.[31] Unless the parties agree on the question, the tribunal determines where it will sit.[32] As in the ICC Rules, the parties may choose the law applicable to the merits of the dispute, failing which the tribunal will determine the appropriate applicable law.[33]

One significant difference between the UNCITRAL and ICC systems concerns the rendering of awards by three-person tribunals. Both systems permit majority awards,[34] but whereas the ICC Rules provide that where there is no majority (i.e., where each of the three arbitrators has a different opinion) the award shall be rendered by the chairman of the tribunal alone,[35] the UNCITRAL Rules contain no such provision[36] and will therefore tend in controversial cases to produce awards which represent a compromise between the views of the arbitrators. On the other hand, the UNCITRAL Rules allow the presiding arbitrator to decide questions of procedure on his own where there is no majority on the question in the tribunal. Helpful as this provision generally is, it may sometimes be difficult to distinguish between questions of procedure and substance.[37]

3. National arbitration laws

Arbitration rules resolve questions concerning the conduct of arbitrations as between the parties and the tribunal. They cannot bind States' courts. To integrate arbitrations into the regular State legal system it is necessary for there to be domestic legislation governing the relationship between arbitral tribunals and the courts. That legislation may deal with a wide range of matters. It may stipulate the circumstances in which courts must refuse to hear cases which the parties have validly contracted to submit to arbitration. Operating as the *lex arbitri*—the law governing the conduct of the arbitration[38]—it prescribes rules to be applied in the

---

[30] UNCITRAL Arbitration Rules (1976), art. 15.

[31] Ibid., art. 1(2). See further, chapter eight, pp. 229–35 below.

[32] UNCITRAL Arbitration Rules (1976), art. 16.

[33] Ibid., art. 33.

[34] And although their rules do not expressly state it, both systems in fact admit separate and dissenting opinions.

[35] ICC Rules of Arbitration (1998), art. 25.

[36] UNCITRAL Arbitration Rules (1976), art. 31.

[37] Ibid., art. 31(2). Is the choice of the place of arbitration, which may entail the application of provisions of the law of that place as the *lex arbitri*, a procedural or substantive question? See *Redfern & Hunter*, 498; P. Sanders, 'Commentary on UNCITRAL Arbitration Rules' (1997) 2 *Yearbook Commercial Arbitration* 172, 194.

[38] The *lex arbitri* is usually the law of the place where the arbitration is conducted or has its seat. See further chapter eight, p. 229, below.

absence of agreement between the parties concerning the establishment and conduct of the arbitration and minimum procedural rules to be observed in arbitral proceedings, and may empower the courts to assist the arbitral tribunal by, for example, compelling the giving of evidence by third parties or issuing *Mareva* (or 'freezing') injunctions,[39] or removing or appointing arbitrators. It may permit the courts to review and quash an award on the application of one of the parties. And it may provide for the recognition and enforcement[40] of domestic and foreign arbitral awards through the courts.

Both the extent of legislative intervention and regulation, and the details of the law, vary from State to State; but in recent years there has been a marked tendency in the States where most international arbitrations take place to reduce the occasions for intervention in the arbitral process. For example, under the 1950 Arbitration Act in the UK it was possible for a party to compel an arbitrator to submit questions of law for determination by the English courts, and for the courts to set aside arbitral awards because of errors of law or fact apparent on the face of the record. This degree of potential intervention from the courts became increasingly unacceptable to those involved in international arbitration.[41] The Arbitration Act 1979, which was enacted so as to bring English law more closely in line with the demands of litigators, greatly reduced the scope for intervention by enabling parties to international arbitrations to make agreements excluding the possibility of recourse to the courts.[42] Then, in 1996, a further step in this direction was taken by the enactment of the Arbitration Act 1996, which brings English law closer to the terms of the UNCITRAL Model Law, which we consider next.[43]

---

[39] See below, chapter eight, p. 249.

[40] See further, chapter eight, p. 265.

[41] See J. M. H. Hunter, 'Arbitration procedure in England: past, present and future' (1985) 1 *Arbitration International* 82; Lord Hacking, 'Where We Are Now . . .' (1985) 1 *Journal of International Arbitration* 9.

[42] See A. Samuel, 'The 1979 Arbitration Act' (1985) 2(4) *Journal of International Arbitration* 53. For similar developments in France see G. Delaume, 'International Arbitration under French Law' (1982) 37 *Arbitration Journal* 38; W. L. Craig, W. W. Park and J. Paulsson, 'French codification of a legal framework for international commercial arbitration: the decree of May 12, 1981' (1982) 7 *Yearbook Commercial Arbitration* 407.

[43] See F. Davidson, 'The New Arbitration Act—A Model Law?' [1997] *JBL* 101; W. W. Park, 'The interaction of courts and arbitrators in England: the 1996 Act as a model for the United States?' [1998] *Int. ALR* 54. And see the Reports of the Departmental Advisory Committee on the Arbitration Bill, reproduced in (1997) 13 *Arbitration International* 275, 317. Strictly, as the Act does not affect Scots law, we should not refer to it as a 'UK' Act; but given the international focus of this text, it is convenient to do so.

3.1 The UNCITRAL Model Law

The desirability of harmonising the wide disparities in national legislation, particularly in relation to the recognition and enforcement of arbitral awards,[44] led to the drafting of the UNCITRAL Model Law on International Commercial Arbitration in 1985.[45] This has served as a model for new legislation in many States.[46] The Model Law is designed to harmonise with both the UNCITRAL Arbitration Rules and the 1958 New York Convention on the Recognition and Enforcement of Foreign Arbitral Awards, which we consider below. It is, therefore, a convenient text to examine in order to understand the role and the typical provisions of national laws on international arbitration.

The Model Law seeks to strike a proper balance between, on the one hand, the will of the parties and the principle of party autonomy, and, on the other hand, the right of the State where the arbitration is held to regulate dispute settlement within its territory. It aims to be a complete code on the subject: article 5 states

[44] See the UNCITRAL Reports, 'Study on the application and interpretation of the Convention on the Recognition and Enforcement of Foreign Arbitral Awards', UN Doc. A/CN.9/168, and 'Possible features of a model law on international commercial arbitration', UN Doc. A/CN.9/207; G. Herrmann, 'The UNCITRAL Model Law—its background, salient features and prospects' (1985) 1 *Arbitration International* 6, and 'The UNCITRAL Model Law on International Commercial Arbitration: introduction and general provision', in P. Šarcevic (ed.), *Essays on International Commercial Arbitration* (London, 1989), 3.

[45] UN Doc. A/40/17, annex 1, (1985) 24 *ILM* 1302. See P. Sanders (ed.), *UNCITRAL's Project for a Model Law on International Commercial Arbitration: International Council for Commercial Arbitration Congress series no. 2* (The Hague, 1984); H. M. Holtzmann and J. E. Neuhaus, *A Guide to the UNCITRAL Model Law on International Commercial Arbitration: legislative history and commentary* (Deventer, 1989); A. Broches, *Commentary on the UNCITRAL Model Law on International Commercial Arbitration* (Deventer, 1990).

[46] P. Sanders, 'Unity and diversity in the adoption of the Model Law' (1995) *Arbitration International* 1. Cf. A. Broches, '1985 UNCITRAL Model Law on International Commercial Arbitration: an exercise in international legislation' (1987) 18 *Netherlands Yearbook of International Law* 3. For convenient access to much national legislation see <http://www.internationaladr.com/e. htm#A>. Other main sources are E. E. Bergsten, *International Commercial Arbitration* (New York, 1991, loose-leaf) (hereafter, *Int. Comm. Arb.*),and the *Yearbook Commercial Arbitration*. The latter also includes the texts of some national decisions on the UNCITRAL Model Law. Some laws are reprinted in *Redfern & Hunter*. Recent examples include the laws of Brazil, (1997) 36 *ILM* 1562; China, (1995) 34 *ILM* 1650, and cf. C. Dejun, M. J. Moser and W. Shengchang, *International Arbitration in the People's Republic of China* (Hong Kong, 1995); Germany, (1998) 37 *ILM* 790, and (1998) 14 *Arbitration International* 1 (with commentaries, ibid., 19–89); and the UK, (1997) 36 *ILM* 155. See also M. I. M. Aboul-Enein, 'Reflections on the new Egyptian law on arbitration' (1995) 11 *Arbitration International* 75; F. S. Nariman, 'India's new arbitration law' [1998] *Int. ALR* 181; D. Williams, 'New Zealand—the new Arbitration Act' [1998] *Int. ALR* 214; J. Seif, 'The new International Commercial Arbitration Act of Iran—towards harmony with the UNCITRAL Model Law' (1998) 15(2) *Journal of International Arbitration* 5, and M. Jafarian and M. Rezaeian, 'The new law on international commercial arbitration in Iran' (1998) 15(3) *Journal of International Arbitration* 31; J. L. Siqueiros, 'Mexican arbitration: the new statute' (1995) 30 *Texas International Law Journal* 227; M. de Boisséson, 'The [sc. United Kingdom] Arbitration Act 1996 and the new ICC Rules 1998: a comparative approach' [1998] *Int. ALR* 68. These laws do not follow the Model Law in every respect.

that 'In matters governed by this Law, no court shall intervene except where so provided in this Law.' The Model Law requires that every national court should refuse to hear proceedings covered by a written arbitration agreement and should refer the parties to arbitration, unless it finds that the agreement is null and void, inoperative or incapable of being performed.[47] The arrangement of the arbitration itself is left almost entirely to the agreement of the parties or to the discretion of the tribunal. The Law stipulates certain rules which are to be applied in the absence of agreement on matters such as the presumed receipt of communications, [48] the number of arbitrators,[49] and the amendment of pleadings.[50] These rules correspond to the UNCITRAL Arbitration Rules.

Under the Model Law the national courts (or other authority designated by the State under the legislation)[51] may intervene to support and supervise the arbitral process in a limited range of circumstances. For example, the courts may act as appointing authorities where the parties are unable to agree upon the appointment of arbitrators, and may determine challenges to the arbitrators.[52] The courts may, on appeal from the arbitral tribunal, determine challenges to the tribunal's jurisdiction;[53] and the court may assist the arbitration by ordering interim measures of protection[54] or the taking of evidence.[55] The courts are also given a limited jurisdiction to set aside arbitral awards on the application of one of the parties, on specific grounds which are set out in the Model Law and which correspond to the grounds for non-recognition of foreign arbitral awards in article V of the 1958 New York Convention, which we are about to mention.[56] The courts may refuse to recognise or enforce foreign arbitral awards on the same grounds.[57]

4. International agreements on arbitration

Arbitration rules ensure the orderly conduct of arbitrations. National laws on arbitration offer the support of the courts to arbitrations within the State and give recognition to resulting arbitral awards. But in order that arbitration be an effective instrument for the settlement of international disputes it is necessary that agreements to arbitrate and arbitral awards are recognised internationally. This is

---

[47] UNCITRAL Model Law, arts. 7, 8.
[48] Ibid., art. 3.
[49] Ibid., art. 10.
[50] Ibid., art. 23.
[51] Ibid., art. 6.
[52] Ibid., arts. 10–15.
[53] Ibid., art. 16.
[54] Ibid., art. 9.
[55] Ibid., art. 27.
[56] Ibid., art. 34. See further chapter eight, p. 267.
[57] UNCITRAL Model Law, arts. 35, 36.

the essential task addressed by the conventions on international commercial arbitration.

The first significant international agreement was the 1923 Geneva Protocol.[58] The Protocol, which was ratified by around thirty States including the British Empire, most European States and the USA, established four main principles. First, the Parties agreed to recognise the validity of agreements to submit present or future disputes in commercial and other arbitrable matters[59] to arbitration, even if the arbitration were to be held in a third State. The reference to future disputes was significant: up to that time there was a view, adopted in some States, that while parties could agree to submit an existing dispute to arbitration they could not properly remove in advance the jurisdiction of the courts in respect of any and every dispute which might arise between them. The second principle was that the arbitral procedure should be governed by 'the will of the parties and by the law of the country in whose territory the arbitration takes place'. These two principles are the pillars on which arbitration still rests.[60] Third, the Parties agreed to ensure that arbitral awards rendered in their own territory would be enforceable abroad. And fourth, they agreed to ensure that their courts would decline to exercise jurisdiction in cases which the disputing parties had agreed to refer to arbitration.

The 1923 Protocol was an instrument of limited scope. More important in the context of international arbitration was the 1927 Geneva Convention on the Execution of Foreign Arbitral Awards.[61] The 1927 Convention provided for the recognition and enforcement of foreign arbitral awards in the courts of Contracting States, subject to five conditions: that the award was rendered under a valid arbitration agreement; that the subject matter was arbitrable; that the tribunal complied with the procedures prescribed by the agreement and the *lex arbitri*; that the award be final and not open to challenge; and that recognition and enforcement be not contrary to the public policy or to the principles of the law of the country in which the award is sought to be relied on.[62] In addition, recognition and enforcement had to be refused if the award had been annulled in the country where it was rendered, or if the party against which it was made was unable to present his case, or if the tribunal had acted in excess of its jurisdiction; and recognition and enforcement might be refused if it could be shown that there were other grounds on which the award could be challenged under the *lex arbitri*.[63] The Convention went on to lay down the procedures under which recognition and enforcement of foreign arbitral awards should be accorded.

---

[58] 27 *LNTS* 157.
[59] On arbitrability or justiciability see chapter one pp. 10–13, and chapter eight, p. 202.
[60] See further chapter eight, pp. 230–31.
[61] 92 *LNTS* 301.
[62] 1927 Geneva Convention, art. 1.
[63] Ibid., arts. 2, 3.

As international commerce resumed after World War II, attention was turned to the revision of the 1927 Geneva regime. In 1953 the ICC proposed consideration of a system of 'decollated' awards: that is, awards not underpinned or controlled by any national legal system but deriving their authority entirely from the consent of the parties, and entitled to recognition and enforcement in the courts of all States on that basis. Most States would not accept a duty to enforce awards which were not governed by any system of national law, and the ICC proposal was rejected in favour of the negotiation of a new international convention. The result was the 1958 New York Convention on the Recognition and Enforcement of Foreign Arbitral Awards.[64] This Convention, considered in more detail below,[65] offered a more streamlined system based on the same basic principles as the 1927 Geneva Convention. States Parties undertook to recognise agreements to arbitrate and to ensure that their courts would decline to exercise jurisdiction in cases covered by arbitration agreements.[66] They agreed to recognise and enforce awards rendered in other Contracting States, either generally or on the basis of reciprocity.[67] And they agreed to an exhaustive list of grounds on which recognition and enforcement of foreign awards could be refused. Those grounds, set out in article V, are, broadly speaking: the incapacity of a party; the absence of a fair hearing; a lack of jurisdiction on the part of the tribunal; an impropriety in the constitution of the tribunal or the conduct of its proceedings; that the award is not binding; that the dispute is not arbitrable; or that recognition or enforcement is contrary to the public policy of the State where it is sought.[68] The 1958 Convention provides a simplified procedure for recognition and enforcement. It is necessary only to produce to the court where recognition or enforcement is sought an authenticated copy of the award and of the arbitration agreement: recognition or enforcement is then automatic unless the other party persuades the court to exercise its right to refuse on one or more of the grounds set out in article V.

The New York Convention has proved a great success as its list of States Parties indicates;[69] and ratification of it is an almost essential for any State whose traders wish to participate in the more highly developed international markets. It remains the pre-eminent international convention on recognition and enforcement of

---

[64] 330 *UNTS* 3. See A. J. van den Berg, *The New York arbitration convention of 1958: towards a uniform judicial interpretation* (Deventer, 1981). For preparatory works, commentary, and national decisions on the Convention see G. Gaja, *International Commercial Arbitration: New York Convention* (Dobbs Ferry, NY, 1975, loose-leaf). The *Yearbook Commercial Arbitration* publishes national decisions, periodically consolidated in commentaries on the Convention: see, e.g., (1994) 19 *Yearbook Commercial Arbitration* 475.

[65] See chapter eight, p. 266, below.

[66] 1958 New York Convention, art. II.

[67] Ibid., art. III.

[68] The provisions of the 1958 New York Convention, art. V, are considered in more detail in chapter eight, below.

[69] It had been ratified by around 120 States, as at the end of 1998.

arbitral awards,[70] but it is not the only one. In 1961 a number of European States adopted the European (or Geneva) Convention on International Commercial Arbitration.[71] This Convention establishes the right to resort to *ad hoc* or institutional arbitration, and provides rules to be applied in default of agreement by the parties. It sets out the grounds on which challenges to the jurisdiction of a tribunal may be made, and regulates the jurisdiction of national courts in arbitration matters and the grounds upon which they may set aside awards; and it provides for the recognition and enforcement of foreign awards. It was designed to be a stricter alternative to the New York Convention, binding European States (and any others who chose to join the system) more closely than the New York Convention to respect the autonomy of arbitration as an institution and to recognise and enforce awards. It was also intended to provide a special framework for arbitration in East–West trade. However, in practice, its relatively limited application[72] means that it has limited importance, and it is largely overshadowed by the New York Convention.

The New York Convention spawned a number of other, primarily regional, arrangements, too. These include the 1972 Moscow Convention on the Settlement by Arbitration of Disputes Arising from Economic, Scientific and Technical Co-operation,[73] and the 1975 Inter-American (Panama) Convention on International Commercial Arbitration.[74] These, too, are not dissimilar from the New York Convention, but (though of some regional importance) are of much less international significance.

---

[70] Note that the Brussels and Lugano Conventions on Jurisdiction and Judgments in Civil and Commercial Matters do not apply to arbitral awards: see J. G. Collier, *The Conflict of Laws*, 2nd edn. (Cambridge, 1994), 138–9; D. T. Hascher, 'Recognition and enforcement of arbitration awards and the Brussels Convention' (1996) 12 *Arbitration International* 233, and 'Recognition and enforcement of judgments on the existence and validity of an arbitration clause under the Brussels Convention' (1997) 13 *Arbitration International* 33.

[71] 21 April 1961, 484 *UNTS* 364; and see the amendments made in the Agreement Relating to the Application of the European Convention on International Commercial Arbitration, 17 December 1962, 523 *UNTS* 94.

[72] It had only 27 parties at the end of 1998, although they did include the UK, France, Germany, Italy and the Russian Federation.

[73] (1974) 13 *ILM* 5. See H. Strohbach, 'General Introduction' (1976) 1 *Yearbook of Commercial Arbitration* 4. On current Russian practice see G. P. Hendrix, 'Business litigation and arbitration in Russia' (1997) 31 *International Lawyer* 1075.

[74] (1975) 14 *ILM* 336. See A. M. Garro, 'Enforcement of Arbitration Agreements and Jurisdiction of Arbitral Tribunals in Latin America' (1984) 1 *Journal of International Arbitration* 293; C. R. Norberg, 'General Introduction to Inter-American Commercial Arbitration' (1978) 3 *Yearbook Commercial Arbitration* 1 (with the text of the Convention at 15). At the end of 1998, the Panama Convention had 17 States Parties, including the USA. See further <http://www.sice. oas.org/ftaa/iacac2e.htm>.

5. Concluding remarks

It is worth emphasising again the crucial importance of international commercial arbitration in the settlement of international disputes, which is beyond question despite its astonishing neglect by many public international lawyers. The days when the claims of every expropriated company were presented on the inter-State plane by the company's national State are gone. It is now quite usual for foreign investors and host States, and for companies engaging in other transactions with foreign States, to agree to settle their disputes by international commercial arbitration, in tribunals where the company and the State litigate against each other on a footing of equality. Those tribunals apply the law chosen by the parties, and this commonly involves the application of public international law.[75] It is in these tribunals, rather than in the rare cases where diplomatic claims are presented to inter-State tribunals on behalf of companies by States, that international disputes are predominantly settled and that international law is increasingly applied and made.

---

[75] See chapter eight, p. 239.

4

MIXED ARBITRATIONS

1. The International Centre for the Settlement of Investment Disputes (ICSID)   59

   1.1 The ICSID framework   60
   1.2 ICSID procedure   68

2. The Iran-US Claims Tribunal   73

   2.1 The Hostages Crisis   74
   2.2 The Algiers Accords   75
   2.3 The Iran-US Claims Tribunal   76

One of the most remarkable developments in international dispute settlement procedures has been the rapid growth of the institution of mixed arbitrations: that is to say, arbitrations between States on the one hand and non-State entities, usually corporations or, less frequently, individuals, on the other. The two most striking examples of tribunals handling mixed arbitrations are the tribunals established under the auspices of the International Centre for the Settlement of Investment Disputes ('ICSID'), and the Iran–US Claims Tribunal. They are the subject of this chapter.

1. The International Centre for the Settlement of Investment Disputes (ICSID)

The ICSID scheme was devised by the World Bank (the International Bank for Reconstruction and Development). In 1964 the Executive Directors of the Bank were asked to draft a convention 'establishing facilities and procedures which would be available on a voluntary basis for the settlement of investment disputes between contracting States and nationals of other contracting States through conciliation and arbitration'.[1] The resulting draft, which became the Washington

---

[1] IBRD res. 214, 10 September 1964. For accounts of earlier attempts to establish schemes for the settlement of investment disputes see: G. Schwarzenberger, 'The Abs-Shawcross Draft Convention on Investments Abroad' (1961) 14 *Current Legal Problems* 213; id., *Foreign Investments and International Law* (London, 1969), 153–69.

Convention on the Settlement of Investment Disputes between States and Nationals of Other States (the 'ICSID Convention'),[2] was intended to strengthen the partnership between countries in the cause of economic development and to stimulate the flow of international private capital into those countries that wish to attract it, by overcoming the fear of arbitrary and uncompensated expropriation.

The Convention procedures were designed to provide a balance between the interests of investors and of host States. It was thought desirable to establish a dispute settlement mechanism to which both the investor and the State could become irrevocably committed and which either could invoke, and which was detached from the municipal laws of both the investor and the host State. There had been mixed (State/non-State) arbitrations over investment disputes in the past, organised on an *ad hoc* basis.[3] These had been organised on the basis of contractual agreements made between the State and the company, and followed the pattern of private international commercial arbitration.[4] What was needed now was a standing system which States and investors could incorporate in their agreements by reference, thus avoiding the need for the negotiation of a new settlement procedure in every case. The aim seems to have been achieved. The ICSID Convention has been a great success: it has been ratified by over 125 States, from all geographical and political blocs, and accession to the Convention appears to be a high priority for newly independent States keen to attract foreign investment.[5]

1.1 The ICSID framework

1.1.1 Organs

Somewhat like the Permanent Court of Arbitration,[6] ICSID is not itself a tribunal but rather a framework within which arbitration and conciliation can occur. ICSID, which has its seat at the World Bank headquarters in Washington, DC,

---

[2] 575 *UNTS* 159; (1965) 4 *ILM* 532.

[3] See, e.g.: *Petroleum Development (Trucial Coast) Ltd.* v. *Sheikh of Abu Dhabi* (1951) 18 *ILR* 122, (1952) 1 *ICLQ* 247; *Saudi Arabia* v. *Arabian American Oil Co. (Aramco)* (1958) 27 *ILR* 117; *Sapphire International Petroleum Ltd.* v. *National Iranian Oil Co.* (1963) 35 *ILR* 136, (1964) 13 *ICLQ* 1011. And, for a brilliant account of the shortcomings of mixed arbitrations, see V. V. Veeder, 'The *Lena Goldfields* arbitration: the historical roots of three ideas' (1998) 47 *ICLQ* 747.

[4] See, for examples of agreements containing such clauses, *Egypt-Egyptian Petroleum Corporation/ESSO*, Concession Agreement of 14 December 1974, (1975) 14 *ILM* 915, art. XXI; *Libyan National Oil Co./Occidental of Libya Inc.*, Agreement of 7 February 1974, (1975) 14 *ILM* 645, section XII; *Syria-Syrian Petroleum Co.-Pecten Ash Sham Co./Syria Shell Petroleum Development BV/Deminex Petroleum Syria GmbH*, Contract for the Exploration, Development and Production of Petroleum, 21 August 1985, (1987) 26 *ILM* 1186, art. XXIII.

[5] The 1998 ICSID Annual Report records 144 States as signatories of the Convention, of which 129 have deposited instruments of ratification. Parties include former COMECON States, and several Latin America States—both groups long averse to compulsory international dispute settlement procedures.

[6] See chapter two, pp. 35–8, above.

has an Administrative Council chaired by the President of the World Bank, in which each Member State has one vote, usually exercised by its World Bank representative.[7] The Administrative Council is responsible for the adoption of the rules of procedure for conciliation and arbitration proceedings, and generally for supervising the operation of ICSID. Its only other permanent organ is the Secretariat, whose Secretary-General and Deputy Secretary-General are precluded from exercising any political functions and are elected by the Administrative Council.[8] Again like the PCA, ICSID maintains lists ('Panels') of persons 'of high moral character and recognized competence in the fields of law, industry or finance, who may be relied upon to exercise independent judgment',[9] and who may serve as conciliators or arbitrators. Each State Party may designate four persons, who need not be its nationals, to the Panel of Conciliators and four to the Panel of Arbitrators: in addition, the Chairman of ICSID may designate a further ten to each Panel, paying due regard to the need to assure on the Panels the representation of the principal legal systems of the world and of the main forms of economic activity. Panel members serve for renewable six-year terms.[10] It is from the Panels that parties to investment disputes are expected to select arbitrators or conciliators.

1.1.2 Jurisdiction

The jurisdiction of ICSID is set out in article 25 of the ICSID Convention:

> The jurisdiction of the Centre shall extend to any legal dispute arising directly out of an investment, between a Contracting State (or any constituent subdivision or agency of a Contracting State designated to the Centre by that State) and a national of another Contracting State, which the parties to the dispute consent in writing to submit to the Centre. When the parties have given their consent, no party may withdraw its consent unilaterally.

The jurisdiction is tightly defined.[11] It extends only to disputes which are both legal and arise directly out of an investment, although the latter requirement is generous enough to embrace, for example, disputes arising from the taxation of investments.[12] Moreover, two levels of submission to ICSID must both exist: the references to Contracting States and nationals of other Contracting States require that the ICSID Convention should have been ratified by both of the States in question; and the reference to the written consent of the parties to the dispute requires that there should have been a further, explicit acceptance of ICSID

---

[7] ICSID Convention, arts. 2–8.

[8] ICSID Convention, arts. 9–11.

[9] ICSID Convention, art. 14(1).

[10] ICSID Convention, arts. 12–16.

[11] See G. Delaume, 'ICSID Arbitration: Practical Considerations' (1984) 1(2) *Journal of International Arbitration* 101.

[12] See *Kaiser Bauxite Company* v. *The Government of Jamaica* (1975) 1 *ICSID Reports* 296.

procedures by the disputing parties. These elements of the definition are considered further below; but it should be noted that they were all modified in 1978 by the ICSID Additional Facility,[13] which was intended to open up ICSID to a wider range of disputes.

The ICSID Additional Facility extends the jurisdiction of the Centre to include disputes between parties only one (rather than both) of which is a Contracting State or a national of a Contracting State, and to disputes which do not arise directly out of an investment. It also enables ICSID to engage in purely fact-finding procedures, and not only in conciliation or arbitration. Some States have made reference to the Additional Facility in investment protection treaties,[14] and it was first utilised in two disputes involving Mexico in 1997.[15] The following account is, however, focused on the main ICSID Convention procedures, which are much more commonly used.

1.1.3 Submission to ICSID jurisdiction

The first of the two levels of submission to ICSID required by Article 25 is the ratification of the Convention. A State may make its ratification subject to a notification that it wishes to include certain categories of dispute within, or exclude certain categories of dispute from, the jurisdiction of the Centre.[16] A few States have made such notifications: for instance, Saudi Arabia 'reserves the right of not submitting all questions relating to oil and pertaining to acts of sovereignty' to ICSID, and Turkey has excluded disputes relating to real property rights in Turkey.[17] But such notifications have no real purpose or effect other than as a declaration of the policy of the State concerning submission of disputes to ICSID: further consent by the State to submit particular disputes to the Centre is still required; and a notification that certain categories of dispute are excluded should not override any such further consent which does submit particular disputes to the Centre.[18]

---

[13] See the ICSID Arbitration (Additional Facility) Rules, 1 *ICSID Reports* 213, (1982) 21 *ILM* 1443; cf. A. Broches, 'The "Additional Facility" of the International Centre for the Settlement of Investment Disputes' (1979) 4 *Yearbook Commercial Arbitration* 373.

[14] See ICSID, *Bilateral Investment Treaties 1959–1996: Chronological Country Data and Bibliography* (Washington, DC, 1997); R. Dolzer and M. Stevens, *Bilateral Investment Treaties* (The Hague, 1995), 139–40; *News from ICSID*, Winter 1985, 6.

[15] *Metalclad Corporation* v. *United Mexican States* (Case ARB(AF)/97/1); *Robert Azinian and others* v. *United Mexican States* (Case ARB(AF)/97/2).

[16] ICSID Convention, art. 25(4).

[17] *Contracting States and measures taken by them for the purpose of the Convention*, ICSID Doc. ICSID/8 (September 1998), 3.

[18] See *Kaiser Bauxite Company* v. *The Government of Jamaica* (1975) 1 *ICSID Reports* 296; *Alcoa Minerals of Jamaica, Inc.* v. *The Government of Jamaica* (1975) 1 *ICSID Reports* 296n, 4 *Yearbook Commercial Arbitration* 206 (1979); J. T. Schmidt, 'Arbitration under the Auspices of the International Centre for the Settlement of Investment Disputes (ICSID): Implications of the decision in *Alcoa Minerals of Jamaica, Inc.* v. *Government of Jamaica*' (1976) 17 *Harvard International Law Journal* 90.

The second level of submission is the written consent of the parties to submit the particular dispute which has arisen to ICSID settlement procedures. No particular form is required for this consent.[19] It may be expressed in a concession agreement between the host State and the investor.[20] This is expressly contemplated by some national laws. For instance, the Former Yugoslavian Investment Law provided that disputes 'shall be settled by a competent Yugoslavian Court, unless provisions have been made in the concession agreement for such disputes to be settled by arbitration tribunals set up under the [ICSID Convention] or by other arbitration'. Alternatively, the municipal legislation of the host State may itself provide for ICSID settlement. For example, the Investment Code of Togo provides that: 'Any dispute which may arise between the Government of Togo and the investor concerning one or more clauses of the present Law shall be settled amicably. In the event that the dispute persists, it shall be submitted to ICSID.'[21] Here, the legislation is in effect an offer to submit disputes to ICSID, which may be accepted by the investor in several different ways: the investor may secure the inclusion of an ICSID submission clause in a concession agreement regulating its investment, or it may request ICSID settlement in an application for permission to make its investment;[22] or it may simply submit a written request to ICSID invoking the Law as the basis of ICSID jurisdiction.[23]

Submission to ICSID may also be effected in a bilateral investment protection treaty. In 1997 it was reported that there were around 1,100 such treaties, over 900 of which provided for ICSID arbitration.[24] The case of *Asian Agricultural Products Ltd.* v. *Democratic Socialist Republic of Sri Lanka*,[25] for example, was submitted to ICSID on the basis of a provision in the 1980 UK–Sri Lanka Agreement for the Promotion and Protection of Investments.[26] The ICSID Tribunal was content to base its jurisdiction upon this provision and a written application by Asian Agricultural Products to the Centre: no additional agreement between Sri Lanka and the company was required.

---

[19] *Amco Asia Corp. and others* v. *Indonesia*, award of 25 September 1983, 1 *ICSID Reports* 389 at 400, (1984) 23 *ILM* 351 at 369.

[20] See, e.g., *Amco Asia Corp. and others* v. *Indonesia*, award of 25 September 1983, 1 *ICSID Reports* 389 at 401, (1984) 23 *ILM* 351 at 370.

[21] Law 85–03, of 29 January 1985, art. 4: *News from ICSID*, Summer 1986, 8. See further A. Parra, 'Principles governing foreign investments, as reflected in national investment codes' (1992) 7 *ICSID Review—FILJ* 428.

[22] See, e.g., *Amco Asia Corp. and others* v. *Indonesia*, award of 25 September 1983, 1 *ICSID Reports* 389 at 392, (1984) 23 *ILM* 351 at 356.

[23] Cf. *SPP(ME)Ltd. and SPP Ltd.* v. *Egypt*, Decision of 14 April 1988, 3 *ICSID Reports* 131.

[24] A. A. Escobar, 'Three aspects of ICSID's administration of arbitration proceedings', *News from ICSID*, Summer 1997, 4. See further ICSID, *Bilateral Investment Treaties 1959–1996: Chronological Country Data and Bibliography* (Washington, DC, 1997); R. Dolzer and M. Stevens, *Bilateral Investment Treaties* (The Hague, 1995), ch. 5.

[25] Award of 27 June 1990, 4 *ICSID Reports* 245, (1991) 30 *ILM* 577.

[26] (1980) 19 *ILM* 886, art. 8.

The nature of the obligation varies from treaty to treaty.[27] Some contain immediately effective submissions of all future disputes to ICSID. For example, the 1980 treaty between the United Kingdom and Sri Lanka, invoked in the *Asian Agricultural Products* case, stipulated that:

> Each Contracting Party hereby submits to the International Centre for the Settlement of Investment Disputes . . . for settlement by conciliation or arbitration under [the ICSID Convention] any legal disputes arising between that Contracting Party and a national or company of the other Contracting Party concerning an investment of the latter in the territory of the former.

Other treaties require further negotiations. The 1979 Malaysia–Sweden treaty, for instance, states that '[i]n the event of a dispute arising . . . it shall upon the agreement of both the Parties to the dispute be submitted to arbitration' under ICSID; and the 1970 Kenya–Netherlands treaty simply binds each contracting State to 'give sympathetic consideration to a request' from a national of the other to submit an investment dispute to ICSID. Some treaties attach conditions to submission to ICSID: for example, the 1983 Senegal–US treaty excludes from the agreement to submit to ICSID all disputes arising from export guarantee, credit and insurance programmes; and some UK treaties provide for recourse to ICSID only when 'agreement cannot be reached within three months between the parties to the dispute through pursuit of local remedies or otherwise'.[28]

Submission to ICSID is also becoming a feature of multilateral treaty practice, and it may be expected that this development will lead to a considerable increase in the workload of ICSID tribunals. Both the NAFTA Agreement[29] and the European Energy Charter,[30] for example, contain submissions to ICSID by the States Parties, which may be activated simply by the initiation of proceedings by the investor. It is also possible to refer disputes to ICSID by agreement after the dispute has arisen, as happened in the *MINE* case.[31]

1.1.4 Parties to disputes

A particular problem arises from the requirement that the dispute arise between one State and the nationals of another. It is not uncommon for the investment

---

[27] For a sample of treaty clauses see *News from ICSID*, Summer 1984, 16, and Winter 1985, 12; and see ICSID, *Bilateral Investment Treaties 1959–1996: Chronological Country Data and Bibliography* (Washington, DC, 1997); R. Dolzer and M. Stevens, *Bilateral Investment Treaties* (The Hague, 1995), ch. 5; K. J. Vandevelde, *United States Investment Treaties. Policy and practice.* (Deventer, 1992), ch. 9.

[28] See further G. Delaume, 'ICSID and Bilateral Investment Protection Treaties', *News from ICSID*, Winter 1982, 13.

[29] Art. 1120, NAFTA Agreement, (1993) 32 *ILM* 289 and 605. See chapter six, pp. 111–15 below.

[30] Art. 26(4), European Energy Charter, (1995) 34 *ILM* 360. See T. A. Wälde, 'Investment arbitration under the Energy Charter Treaty', (1996) *Arbitration International* 429; G. Turner, 'Investment Protection through Arbitration' [1998] *Int. ALR* 166.

[31] Award of 6 January 1988, 4 *ICSID Reports* 54.

laws of States to require that foreign investment be directed into the State through a company incorporated in that State. This has the advantage for the State of avoiding complications which might otherwise arise in exercising its jurisdiction over the company for tax and other purposes. But it also has the effect of rendering the 'foreign' investment 'domestic': if the investment is expropriated, it is the property of a *domestic* company which is taken, and under the traditional rules of international law it might be argued that there is no breach of any duty owed by the State to aliens. The ICSID Convention recognises this difficulty and offers a means of overcoming it in the provisions which define the concept of 'National of another Contracting State' under the Convention.

Article 25(2) of the ICSID Convention deals first with individual nationals. They are persons who had the nationality of a Contracting State other than the State party to the dispute on the date at which the parties consented to submit to ICSID conciliation or arbitration and also at the date when the application invoking the ICSID procedures was registered by the applicant with the ICSID Secretariat—an application of the continuous nationality principle.[32] The definition, therefore, falls back on each State's own definition of its nationals. However, the article specifically excludes dual nationals: that is, persons who also had the nationality of the Contracting State party to the dispute at either of the relevant dates. This is in marked contrast with the practice of the Iran-US Claims Tribunal, which did much to develop the concept of dominant nationality in allowing claims by dual nationals and which asserted that its practice reflected the current state of customary international law.[33]

Article 25(2)(b) deals with the nationality of companies, and it is here that the problem of compulsory local incorporation of foreign investments is tackled, through what is known as the 'foreign control' clause. The first part of article 25(2)(b) includes within the definition of a 'national of another Contracting State', 'any juridical person which had the nationality of a Contracting State other than the State party to the dispute on the date on which the parties consented to submit such dispute to conciliation or arbitration'. The determination of nationality, as in the case of individual nationals, remains a matter for the law of the State concerned.[34] Article 25(2)(b) then continues, also including within the definition 'any juridical person which had the nationality of the Contracting State party to the dispute on that date and which, because of foreign control, the parties have

---

[32] See chapter eight, p. 192.

[33] See below, p. 80 and chapter eight, p. 192.

[34] See further below, p. 80 and chapter eight, p. 192. The ICSID Convention does not stipulate how States should determine the nationality of companies; but the 'foreign control' provision which follows in art. 25(2)(b) implies that the nationality of controlling shareholders is irrelevant and that nationality is to be determined on the basis of the place of incorporation and/or *siége social* of the company.

agreed should be treated as a national of another Contracting State for the purposes of this Convention'.

This 'foreign control' clause permits the parties to a dispute to agree to treat a company incorporated by the investor in the host State as a vehicle for its investment, and controlled by the investor, as a 'national of another Contracting State', even though the company will have the nationality of the host State. This agreement will often be expressed in a bilateral investment protection treaty. For example, the 1980 Sri Lanka–UK treaty contained an agreement to apply ICSID article 25(2)(b) to investment disputes arising between one State Party and nationals of the other, and to treat any company, incorporated in the host State, 'in which before such a dispute arises the majority of shares are owned by nationals or companies of the other Contracting Party' as a national of that other Contracting Party.[35] The company party to an investment dispute may rely upon the treaty to establish the agreement of the host State to apply the 'foreign control' clause.

It is not necessary that agreement be expressed in a treaty. There may be evidence of an implied agreement between the host State and the investor to activate the 'foreign control' clause. One early arbitration applied a strict test. In *Holiday Inns SA, Occidental Petroleum et al.* v. *Government of Morocco*,[36] the ICSID tribunal refused to infer an intention on the part of the Moroccan Government to treat four Moroccan subsidiaries of Holiday Inns as foreign corporations. It noted that the 'foreign control' clause was an exception to the general principles of the ICSID Convention and stated that an implied agreement to apply the clause would only be inferred 'in the event that specific circumstances would exclude any other interpretation of the intention of the parties'.

However, a more liberal approach, more conducive to the general aims of the ICSID system, was taken in a later case. The long-running case of *Amco Asia Corporation, Pan American Development Limited and P. T. Amco Indonesia* v. *Republic of Indonesia*[37] illustrates ICSID jurisdiction based on an implied agreement between the host State and the investor. It also shows a tribunal, with admirable pragmatism, seeking to reinforce the advances made by ICSID in investment protection by accepting that the right to ICSID arbitration is a corollary of the investment, which can be transferred along with that investment.

Amco, a US corporation, wished to build a hotel complex in Indonesia in collaboration with an Indonesian company. An Indonesian company, P. T. Amco, was established as a vehicle for the investment, as was required by Indonesian investment laws as a condition for obtaining tax concessions. Amco's letters of

---

[35] Art. 8: (1980) 19 *ILM* 886.

[36] Case No. ARB/72/1. See P. Lalive, 'The First World Bank Arbitration (*Holiday Inns* v. *Morocco*)—Some Legal Problems' (1980) 51 *BYIL* 123, reprinted in 1 *ICSID Reports* 645.

[37] See the summary in 1 *ICSID Reports* 377.

application for various tax concessions and permissions from the Indonesian Investment Board requested ICSID arbitration of disputes. The application was made in the name of, and approval was subsequently granted to, P. T. Amco, to whom all of Amco's interests in the project were transferred. With the approval of the Indonesian Government a portion of Amco's shares in the Indonesian company were subsequently transferred to Pan American, a Hong Kong corporation. Disputes arose concerning the operation of the project, and P. T. Amco's investment licence was cancelled and its property seized.

In January 1981 Amco, Pan American, and P. T. Amco filed a request for arbitration with ICSID. Indonesia argued that it had not consented to ICSID arbitration with Amco or Pan American, but only with P. T. Amco. The applicants argued that Indonesia had held out an 'offer' to submit to ICSID arbitration in its investment literature, which had been accepted by submitting the investment application and which became binding on approval of that application; and that the government-approved share transfer to Pan American carried with it a right to ICSID arbitration. The ICSID tribunal, stressing that submission to ICSID and agreement on the application of the 'foreign control' clause demanded no particular formalities, upheld the applicants' arguments. The nature of the dealings indicated that Indonesia had agreed to treat P. T. Amco as a foreign corporation controlled by Amco; and the right to ICSID arbitration attached to the investment, so that it was extended to Pan American by the approved share transfer to that company.[38]

Despite the wording of article 25(2)(b), it may be an unnecessary complication to seek evidence of an identifiable 'agreement' between the parties. *Amco Asia* may be better read as indicating that it is enough if each party to the dispute has at some point consented to the application of the 'foreign control' clause. Nonetheless, the requirement of foreign control is an 'objective Convention limit beyond which ICSID jurisdiction cannot exist', so that if there is in fact no such control the ICSID tribunal will lack jurisdiction even if the parties have agreed to treat the company as one falling within article 25(2)(b).[39]

The 'foreign control' clause is permissive, not obligatory. Unless States agree to invoke it, the ICSID Convention will not apply to disputes between a State and a company incorporated under its laws as a vehicle for foreign investment.[40] This contrasts with the position in the Iran-US Claims Tribunal, where companies incorporated in third States but controlled by Iranian or US nationals were

---

[38] Decision on jurisdiction, 25 September 1983, 1 *ICSID Reports* 389, (1984) 23 *ILM* 351.

[39] See *Vacuum Salt Products Limited* v. *Government of the Republic of Ghana*, Award of 16 February 1994, 4 *ICSID Reports* 320. The Tribunal in that case declined jurisdiction because of the lack of foreign control.

[40] Although such disputes would fall within the scope of the ICSID Additional Facility: above, p. 62.

automatically entitled to present claims. On the other hand, in the Iran-US Tribunal, Iranian and US-incorporated companies could not present claims unless they were also controlled by nationals of those countries, whereas in ICSID the absence of national control is not an obstacle to the presentation of a claim by a foreign corporation.[41]

1.2 ICSID procedure[42]

If a legal dispute subject to ICSID jurisdiction arises, either party to the dispute may request the ICSID Secretary-General to initiate ICSID conciliation[43] or arbitration.[44] In either case the Secretary-General is obliged to register the request unless he finds, on the basis of information contained in the request, that the dispute is manifestly outside the jurisdiction of ICSID.[45]

1.2.1 Conciliation

Requests for conciliation are rare. By mid-1998, only three requests for conciliation had been registered and only two of those proceeded to a Conciliation Commission.[46] Conciliation Commissions, consisting either of a sole conciliator or an odd number of conciliators, are established by the agreement of the parties, failing which the Chairman of the ICSID Administrative Council makes the appointments. The parties may choose any person to sit on the Commission; but the Secretary-General's choice is limited to persons on the Panel of Conciliators. The Commission, which is the judge of its own competence, is required to clarify the issues in dispute and endeavour to bring about agreement between the parties. It may recommend terms of settlement.[47]

---

[41] *Amco Asia Corporation, Pan American Development Limited and P. T. Amco Indonesia v. Republic of Indonesia,* Decision on jurisdiction, 25 September 1983, 1 *ICSID Reports* 389, (1984) 23 *ILM* 351. The position may be different in cases where the investor company, although incorporated in a third State, is controlled by a national of the host State. The provisions of ICSID art. 25(2)(a) on dual nationality suggest that claims by such corporations might be disallowed.

[42] The detailed Rules governing conciliation and those for arbitration proceedings are reprinted in 1 *ICSID Reports,* 51–194.

[43] ICSID Convention, art. 28.

[44] ICSID Convention, art. 36.

[45] As has been done: see *News from ICSID,* Summer 1985, 10.

[46] In *Tesoro Petroleum Corporation* v. *Government of Trinidad and Tobago,* the Report of the Conciliation Commission (Lord Wilberforce) was issued on 27 November 1985. Conciliation was requested in 1982 in *SEDITEX Engineering Beratungsgesellschaft für die Textilindustrie mbH* v. *Government of the Democratic Republic of Madagascar,* but the case was withdrawn before the Conciliation Commission was established. A new request for conciliation was received in 1994, and the Conciliation Commission drew up its report in 1996.

[47] ICSID Convention, arts. 28–35.

1.2.2 Arbitration

Requests for ICSID arbitration are more common, almost fifty having been made since the first request in 1972.[48] The ICSID arbitration system is intended to be self-contained. Consent to ICSID arbitration (but not consent to ICSID conciliation) is presumed to exclude all other remedies, although that presumption may be rebutted.[49] For instance, a Contracting State may stipulate that local remedies must be exhausted before it engages in ICSID arbitration.[50] Once the obligation to submit to ICSID arbitration is engaged, however, national courts must dismiss claims properly submitted to ICSID. So, for example, the Belgian and Swiss courts in the *MINE* litigation dismissed applications for the indication of provisional measures in a dispute of which ICSID was seised.[51] Similarly, Contracting States are bound not to give diplomatic protection nor bring international claims in respect of disputes involving their nationals, which the nationals have submitted or consented to submit to ICSID arbitration, unless the State party to the dispute has failed to comply with an ICSID award in the dispute.[52]

Either party to a dispute within the jurisdiction of ICSID may request the Secretary-General to establish an Arbitral Tribunal. The parties choose an uneven number of arbitrators, three in the absence of agreement, and the persons to act as arbitrators. If the parties are unable to agree, each nominates one arbitrator and those two agree upon a third person to act as president of the tribunal. The Chairman of the Administrative Council[53] is empowered to appoint any arbitrators not appointed by the parties, in such a way as to ensure that the majority of arbitrators are not nationals of either of the Contracting States (i.e., the host State

---

[48] See the ICSID *Annual Reports, and ICSID Cases,* Doc. ICSID/16/Rev. 3, 31 March 1994. Details of cases are reported in *News from ICSID* and the *ICSID Review—Foreign Investment Law Journal,* and the texts of many awards are reprinted in the *ICSID Reports* (Cambridge, 1993 onwards).

[49] ICSID Convention, art. 26.

[50] And presumably the parties to a dispute may always agree between themselves upon an alternative dispute settlement procedure.

[51] National decisions: 4 *ICSID Reports* 32, (1985) 24 *ILM* 1639 (Belgium); 4 *ICSID Reports* 35, (1987) 26 *ILM* 382 (Switzerland). And see the award of 6 January 1988, *Maritime International Nominees Establishment* v. *Government of the Republic of Guinea,* 4 *ICSID Reports* 54 at 69. Cf. G. Delaume, 'ICSID Arbitration and the Courts' (1983) 77 *AJIL* 785; Friedland, 'Provisional Measures in ICSID' (1986) *Arbitration International* 335. But see the award of 26 April 1986 of the ICSID tribunal in the *Atlantic Triton* case, in which it appears to be suggested that national courts might retain a concurrent jurisdiction to order interim conservatory measures: 3 *ICSID Reports* 3 at 35–7; and see also, to the same effect, the decisions of the French courts in *Atlantic Triton:* 3 *ICSID Reports* 4, 10. Cf. the decision of the New Zealand High Court in the dispute between Mobil and the Government of New Zealand, *Attorney-General* v. *Mobil Oil NZ Ltd.* (1987) 4 *ICSID Reports* 117. See also ICSID Convention, art. 47.

[52] ICSID Convention, art. 27. This does not preclude informal diplomatic exchanges to facilitate a settlement.

[53] The President of the World Bank is *ex officio* the Chairman: ICSID Convention, art. 5.

or the investor's national State) involved.[54] The Chairman may choose only from the Panel of Arbitrators, but the parties may choose anyone to act as an arbitrator.

The tribunal determines its own competence.[55] So, it may, for instance, decide whether a dispute exists in cases where the respondent alleges that there is none.[56] It is bound to decide cases 'in accordance with such rules of law as may be agreed by the parties', and in the absence of agreement 'shall apply the law of the Contracting State party to the dispute (including its rules on the conflict of laws) and such rules of international law as may be applicable'.[57] There is also a power to decide cases *ex aequo et bono*, if the parties so agree.[58]

Perhaps the most important provision is that embodying the principle of non-frustration: that is to say, the principle that the refusal of one of the parties to co-operate will not frustrate the arbitral process. Under article 45, while the non-appearance of either party is not to be deemed an admission of the other's assertions, neither will it prevent the tribunal from proceeding: the party which does appear may request the tribunal to render an award.[59] It seems that the remedies available to the tribunal are confined to awards of damages. Tribunals may not, for example, order the liquidation of enterprises.[60]

Awards are binding and are not subject to any appeal or other remedy other than those provided within the ICSID system itself—another aspect of the self-contained nature of the system.[61] The hope was that by barring recourse to municipal courts in appeals on points of law or actions to quash awards, and so on, ICSID arbitration would be a swift, predictable procedure. That hope has not been wholly realised.

The Convention offers four procedures for questioning awards. First, either party may, within 45 days of the date of the award, request the tribunal to decide any question which it had omitted to decide or to rectify minor errors in the text of the

---

[54] ICSID Convention, art. 38; *Kaiser Bauxite Company* v. *The Government of Jamaica* (1975) 1 *ICSID Reports* 296; *AGIP SPA* v. *The Government of the People's Republic of the Congo* (1979) 1 *ICSID Reports* 306.

[55] ICSID Convention, art. 41.

[56] *AGIP S.p.A.* v. *Government of the People's Republic of the Congo*, award of 30 November 1979, 1 *ICSID Reports* 306 at 317, (1982) 21 *ILM* 726 at 730.

[57] ICSID Convention, art. 42. O. Chukwumerije, 'International law and article 42 of the ICSID Convention' (1997) 14(3) *Journal of International Arbitration* 79. See further chapter eight, pp. 239–48.

[58] As was done during the proceedings in *S.A.R.L. Benvenuti & Bonfant* v. *Government of the People's Republic of the Congo*, award of 8 August 1980, 1 *ICSID Reports* 335 at 349 (where the date is given wrongly), (1982) 21 *ILM* 740 at 752.

[59] See *American Manufacturing & Trading, Inc.* v. *Republic of Zaire*, award of 21 February 1997, (1997) 36 *ILM* 1531.

[60] *Adriano Gardella* v. *Ivory Coast*, award of 29 August 1977, 1 *ICSID Reports* 283 at 294. Tribunals may recommend provisional measures, under art. 47 of the Convention.

[61] ICSID Convention, art. 53.

award.[62] Second, either party may request an interpretation of the award where the parties disagree as to its meaning.[63] Third, either party may, within 90 days, request the revision of the award where new facts come to light which could decisively affect the award and the applicant's ignorance of them was not due to negligence. But it is the fourth procedure, annulment, which has compromised the aims of swiftness and finality in ICSID procedures.

Article 52 lays down five grounds on which an award may be annulled on the application of either party within 120 days of the date of the award. The grounds are that: the tribunal was improperly constituted; the tribunal manifestly exceeded its powers; an arbitrator was corrupt; there were serious departures from fundamental rules of procedure; and there was a failure to state reasons. Challenges are determined by a three-person *ad hoc* Committee appointed by the Chairman of the Administrative Council from the Panel of Arbitrators. If the application is successful the award is annulled in whole or in part, but may be submitted to a new ICSID tribunal at the request of either party. In practice the grounds for annulment are broader than they might appear. For instance, in *Amco Asia* it was held that a tribunal had manifestly exceeded its powers by failing to apply fundamental provisions of Indonesian law to certain aspects of the case;[64] and in the *Klöckner* arbitration, between a European multinational corporation which built a fertilizer factory in Cameroon and the Government of that country, an award was annulled because of a failure to apply Cameroonian law.[65] These decisions are some way from the typical case of annulment for procedural irregularities, and come very close to being appeals on points of law.

The annulment of an award can prolong the litigation substantially. For instance, the initial request for arbitration in *Klöckner* was made in April 1981, the tribunal constituted in October 1981, and the award rendered October 1983. So far, so good. But an application for annulment was made in February 1984, and an *ad hoc* Committee was constituted in March 1984. The *ad hoc* Committee took a remarkably liberal view of its powers to annul awards, notably in two respects. First, it considered that the grounds for review set out in article 52 were not exhaustive, and that a failure to meet any of the standards set elsewhere in the ICSID Convention might justify annulment; and secondly, it decided that it need

---

[62] ICSID Convention, art. 49(2). Awards were rectified in *Adriano Gardella S.p.A. v. Government of Côte d'Ivoire*, Case No. ARB/74/1 (unpublished), and *Amco Asia Corporation, Pan American Development Limited and P. T. Amco Indonesia v. Republic of Indonesia*, awards of 5 June 1990 and 17 October 1990, 1 *ICSID Reports* 569, 638 (where the dates are given wrongly).

[63] ICSID Convention, art. 50.

[64] *Amco Asia Corporation, Pan American Development Limited and P. T. Amco Indonesia v. Republic of Indonesia*, ad hoc Committee Decision of 16 May 1986, 1 *ICSID Reports* 509, (1986) 25 *ILM* 1439.

[65] *Klöckner Industrie-Anlagen GmbH, Klöckner Belge SA and Klöckner Handelmaatshappij BV v. United Republic of Cameroon and Société Cameroonaise des Engrais*, ad hoc Committee Decision of 3 May 1985, (1986) 1 *ICSID Review—Foreign Investment Journal* 89, 2 *ICSID Reports* 95.

not consider the gravity of the defect in deciding whether or not to annul. It annulled the first award in May 1985. Resubmission to a new ICSID tribunal was requested in June 1985 and the second tribunal, constituted in March 1986, rendered its award in January 1988. Perhaps unsurprisingly, this second award was then the subject of an application for annulment. The saga was not brought to an end until May 1990, when the second *ad hoc* Committee dismissed the application.

A similar fate befell the *Amco* case. After awards upholding the jurisdiction of the tribunal and indicating provisional measures in 1983,[66] an award on the merits was rendered in 1984.[67] That award was challenged and annulled in 1986.[68] The case was resubmitted to a new ICSID tribunal and awards on jurisdiction and on the merits were rendered in 1988 and 1991.[69] The second award was challenged, and that application rejected in part in 1992. It is hard to resist the conclusion that the ICSID system was reaching the point where the initial arbitration was little more than a first instance hearing, with a near-certain possibility of review and retrial by another tribunal. Even if there are some merits in the free availability of review, they do not advance the goal of swift and final settlement of investment disputes which motivated the establishment of ICSID. (It should be noted, however, that around half of the cases sent to ICSID for arbitration are settled by the parties before a final award is rendered, and that in these cases the ICSID system does lead to swift and final settlements.)

The delays caused by repeated annulment requests were heavily criticised, and ICSID tribunals were accused of operating a 'hair-trigger' policy, under which relatively minor procedural defects were regarded as sufficient to warrant the annulment of an award.[70] Fortunately, in a subsequent case the opportunity was taken to pull back from the excessively liberal approach to annulment adopted by the *Klöckner* Committee.[71] In *MINE* v. *Guinea*, an application was made by Guinea for the partial annulment of a unanimous ICSID award in favour of MINE (Maritime International Nominees Establishment), which had entered into a joint venture with the Government of Guinea in the shipping field. The *ad hoc* Committee rejected the view that *any* breach of the ICSID Convention could justify annulment, and concentrated instead upon the defects listed in

---

[66] 1 *ICSID Reports* 377; 89 *ILR* 379; (1984) 23 *ILM* 351 (jurisdiction). 1 *ICSID Reports* 410; 89 *ILR* 402; (1985) 24 *ILM* 365 (provisional measures).

[67] 1 *ICSID Reports* 413; 89 *ILR* 405; (1985) 24 *ILM* 1022.

[68] 1 *ICSID Reports* 509; 89 *ILR* 514; (1986) 25 *ILM* 1439.

[69] 1 *ICSID Reports* 543; 89 *ILR* 552; (1988) 27 *ILM* 1281 (jurisdiction II, 1988). 1 *ICSID Reports* 569; (1991) 118 *Journal de droit international* 172; 89 *ILR* 580 (award II, 1990).

[70] See, e.g., M. Reisman, 'The breakdown of the control mechanism in ICSID arbitration' (1989) 4 *Duke Law Journal* 739.

[71] The *Amco Asia* case has a similar history, with applications for annulment of two successive awards: see 1 *ICSID Reports* 377.

article 52, rejecting at the same time the notion that it must annul the award if any defect were found, regardless of the gravity of the defect, even in respect of article 52 violations. The *ad hoc* Committee stated that it might 'refuse to exercise its authority to annul an award where annulment is clearly not required to remedy procedural injustice and annulment would unjustifiably erode the binding force and finality of ICSID awards'.[72] Confidence in the ability of ICSID to deliver swift solutions appears to have been restored;[73] and the Centre's caseload is increasing steadily—fourteen new cases were registered in the fiscal years 1997 and 1998 alone.

1.2.3 Enforcement of ICSID awards

The ICSID Convention obliges each Contracting State to recognise and enforce pecuniary obligations imposed by awards of ICSID tribunals as if they were final judgments of the State's own courts.[74] This obligation does not, however, require States to override their laws on sovereign immunity,[75] so it may still prove difficult to enforce an ICSID award against a State in a court where the law provides extensive immunity from enforcement for foreign sovereigns.[76] Were a State to refuse to satisfy an ICSID award against it, however, the refusal would amount to a breach of its treaty obligation, and the national State of the investor would be entitled to pursue the matter on the international plane.[77]

2. The Iran-US Claims Tribunal

The second mixed tribunal that we consider is the Iran-US Claims Tribunal, which is much the most experienced of the standing international tribunals. Around 4,000 cases have been finalised by the Tribunal by award, decision or order since it was brought into existence as part of the complex arrangements that followed on from the 'hostage' crisis of 1979. We explain the background to this tribunal at some length because of its value as an illustration of the way in which

---

[72] *Maritime International Nominees Establishment* v. *Government of the Republic of Guinea, ad hoc* Committee Decision of 22 December 1989, 4 *ICSID Reports* 79, at 86.

[73] See A. Broches, 'Observations on the Finality of ICSID Awards', *Selected Essays* (Dordrecht, 1995), ch. 14.

[74] Art. 54. For example, see the implementing legislation in the UK, the Arbitration (International Investment Disputes) Act 1966. Enforcement is by way of registration in the High Court.

[75] ICSID Convention, art. 55. See, e.g., *Maritime International Nominees Establishment* v. *Republic of Guinea* (US Court of Appeals, DC, 1982) 4 *ICSID Reports* 8.

[76] See further chapter eight, pp. 270–3.

[77] See ICSID Convention, art. 27; and A. Broches, 'The Convention on the Settlement of Investment Disputes' (1972) 136 *HR* 331, at 379.

the domestic and international context of disputes shapes the dispute settlement process.[78]

2.1 The Hostages Crisis

The crisis which developed between the United States and Iran following the detention of fifty-two US nationals by activists in the Iranian Islamic revolution on 4 November 1979 is an object lesson in dispute settlement. The immediate focus was on securing the release of the US hostages, held in the US embassy compound in Tehran. This was the subject of the US application to the ICJ in the *Hostages* case,[79] and of an unsuccessful attempt in April 1980 by the US to rescue the hostages by force. But the conflict rapidly expanded to include many other matters. The US complained of mistreatment of its nationals and expropriation of their property and of breaches of contracts by the Iranian authorities. Iran complained of persistent US intervention in its domestic affairs[80] and of breaches of contracts by US nationals, and threatened to withdraw all of its considerable assets from the USA—a move which would have removed the assets to which successful litigants against Iran and its State enterprises in US courts would have looked for the satisfaction of awards not paid voluntarily by Iran. That move was precluded by US President Carter's use in November 1979 of powers under the International Emergency Economic Powers Act 1979, to freeze all Iranian assets in the USA or under US jurisdiction or control.[81] During the following year a substantial proportion of the frozen assets were attached in judicial proceedings begun in US and foreign courts.[82] In addition, severe trade sanctions had been imposed on Iran.

The freezing of Iranian assets put a major constraint upon the US negotiating position. It could not negotiate the freedom of the hostages in return for the unblocking of the assets without securing adequate assured compensation for those claimants against Iran who had already instituted proceedings in the courts. Iran was unlikely to agree either to a settlement which left the assets frozen until the existing claims were settled, or to a lump sum settlement, which would in any event have taken too long to work out. Instead, a radical solution was sought and accepted by both sides.

---

[78] See further G. H. Aldrich, *The Jurisprudence of the Iran-United States Claims Tribunal* (Oxford, 1996), Introduction; W. Mapp, *The Iran-United States Claims Tribunal: the first ten years 1981–1991,* (Manchester, 1993); R. Khan, *The Iran-United States Claims Tribunal: controversies, cases and contribution* (Dordrecht, 1990); S. H. Amin, 'Iran-United States claims settlement' (1983) 32 *ICLQ* 750.

[79] *US Consular and Diplomatic Staff in Tehran,* ICJ Rep. 1980, 1.

[80] See above, chapter 1, p. 15.

[81] (1979) 18 *ILM* 1549. See further H. E. Moyer and L. A. Mabry, 'Export Controls as Instruments of Foreign Policy: The History, Legal Issues, and Policy Lessons of Three Recent Cases' (1983) 15 *Law and Policy of International Business* 1.

[82] See Note (1981) 69 *California Law Review* 837.

2.2 The Algiers Accords

The Algerian Government, acting at the request of the parties, had been an active and skilful mediator between the parties; and on 19 January 1981 the parties signed the Algiers Accords, which established the basis for the settlement of the crisis.[83] The Accords contained a number of elements, of which the General Declaration and the associated Undertakings of the US and Iran, and the Claims Settlement Declaration are the most important.

The General Declaration was in the form of a declaration by the Algerian Government, made on the basis of formal adherences received from Iran and the US of the interdependent commitments made by the two Governments. As a matter of international law it undoubtedly constitutes a treaty binding Iran and the US.[84] The Declaration was based on two 'general principles': first, the US was to restore, so far as possible, the financial position of Iran to that existing before 14 November 1979; and second, each State was to terminate all litigation between its Government and the nationals of the other State and settle those claims by binding arbitration. The latter principle required the US to terminate existing proceedings in US courts, to nullify judicial attachments of Iranian assets, and to prohibit further litigation against Iran other than through the agreed arbitration procedure.[85]

The General Declaration and associated Undertakings went on to amplify the two basic principles. The essence of the arrangement was that the frozen Iranian assets were to be paid into the Netherlands Central Bank and released to Iran when Algeria certified that the hostages had safely departed from Iran. However, $1 billion was to be retained in the Dutch bank for the satisfaction of awards made by the arbitral tribunal established under the Algiers Accords; and if the amount in the account fell below $500 million, it was to be made up to that amount promptly by Iran. The US agreed to revoke all trade sanctions imposed on Iran since 4 November 1979 and to withdraw all claims against Iran pending before the ICJ.[86] Further, the US agreed to bar the prosecution by the US and its nationals, and by anyone in US courts, of all pending or future claims against Iran arising prior to the date of the Declaration from the seizure and detention of US nationals and damage to their property in the Embassy compound, or from acts

---

[83] The documents making up the Algiers Accords are reprinted in 1 *Iran-US CTR* 3, and (1981) 20 *ILM* 224.

[84] Cf. *Textron Inc.* v. *Iran* (arbitral award, 1981) 6 *Iran-US CTR* 328 at 353.

[85] See the (unsuccessful) constitutional challenge to this aspect of the settlement, in *Dames and Moore* v. *Reagan*, 453 US 654 (1981). Cf. M. F. Hertz, 'The Hostages crisis and domestic litigation: an overview', in R. B. Lillich (ed.), *The Iran-United States Claims Tribunal 1981–1983* (Charlottesville, Va., 1984), 136.

[86] See G. Wegen, 'Discontinuance of International Proceedings: The Hostages Case' (1982) 76 *AJIL* 717.

in the course of the Islamic Revolution not attributable to the Iranian Government that injured US nationals or their property.[87] Acts which were attributable to the Government of Iran were to be submitted to the Iran-US Claims Tribunal, established by the Algiers Accords. The US also undertook not to interfere in Iran's internal affairs and to take certain steps related to the return to Iran of the assets of the family of the deposed Shah. The Declaration ended with a provision that any disputes arising from it would be submitted for binding settlement to the Iran-US Claims Tribunal, whose awards were to be enforceable in the courts of any country.

2.3 The Iran-US Claims Tribunal

The Claims Settlement Declaration[88] established the Iran-US Claims Tribunal, with its seat at The Hague, to decide certain claims by the nationals of the US against Iran and Iranian nationals against the US (and contractual claims between the two Governments) that had not been settled within six months by the parties directly concerned. Formally, at least, priority was given to negotiation as the procedure for settling the disputes.[89] But it was recognised from the outset that very large numbers of claims would end up before the Tribunal,[90] which would have to be constituted in a manner capable of handling such a volume of litigation.

The Tribunal has nine members, referred to as judges; three are chosen by Iran, three by the US, and three by the other six.[91] In its early years the Tribunal suffered a number of resignations and challenges to judges, and it was necessary to resort to the agreed procedure under which the Secretary-General of the Permanent Court of Arbitration nominated an Appointing Authority: in this case he appointed the Chief Justice of the Netherlands' Supreme Court.[92] The Appointing Authority nominated judges to the vacant positions.[93] The Tribunal sits either in three-person chambers or, rarely, for important cases in plenary session. It operates under a modified version of the UNCITRAL Arbitration

---

[87] General Declaration, para. 11.

[88] (1981) 20 *ILM* 230.

[89] Claims Settlement Declaration, arts. I, II.

[90] Up to 30 September 1998 the following had been filed: 309 awards, 27 partial awards, 235 awards on agreed terms, and 17 partial awards on agreed terms; 52 interlocutory awards, 27 interim awards, and 2 combined interim and interlocutory awards; 877 terminations by Order or Decision; and 129 Decisions in 136 cases. A total of 3,922 cases had been finalised by award, decision or order. 469 oral proceedings had been held. The total amounts awarded to the US and Iranian parties at that date were: US—US$2,158,055,473.43, plus the US$ equivalents of £303,196, DM 297,051 and Rls. 97,132,598; Iran—US$1,012,516,179.13, plus the US$ equivalent of Rls. 7,977,343. The awards are published in the *Iran-US Claims Tribunal Reports*.

[91] Claims Settlement Declaration, art. III.

[92] See further G. H. Aldrich, *The Jurisprudence of the Iran-United States Claims Tribunal* (Oxford, 1996), Introduction.

[93] See the account in S. A. Baker and M. D. Davis, *The UNCITRAL Arbitration Rules in Practice: The Experience of the Iran-United States Claims Tribunal* (Deventer, 1992), 18–36.

Rules.[94] The UNCITRAL Rules were designed for *ad hoc* arbitrations, and changes were needed in order to facilitate the handling of large numbers of cases by the Tribunal. The modifications deal for the most part with the formalities and time limits for the presentation of claims and of evidence. Further reference is made to these Rules below.[95] All awards of the Tribunal are final and binding, and enforceable in any foreign court in accordance with the local law.[96]

The most innovatory aspects of the Tribunal are evident in the provisions concerning the submission of cases to it and the law that it is directed to apply to them. It is these provisions which give the Tribunal its hybrid or 'mixed' character, combining some of the characteristics of inter-State arbitration with some of the characteristics of international commercial arbitration between private parties.[97] States, in the form of their governments, and private persons are given equal juridical status before the Tribunal.

Three categories of case may be submitted to the Tribunal:

(1) claims by US nationals against Iran, or by Iranian nationals against the US, and associated counter-claims;

(2) 'official' claims by the US and Iran against each other arising out of contractual arrangements between them for the purchase and sale of goods and services; and

(3) cases concerning the interpretation or performance of the obligations set out in the General Declaration in the Algiers Accords.[98]

Attempts to push the Tribunal beyond these limits on its jurisdiction were unsuccessful.[99]

2.3.1 Claims of nationals

It is convenient to take each category of claims in turn, beginning with the claims of nationals. Certain, but not all, claims by the nationals of one State against the other State may be taken to the Tribunal. It is necessary that the claims were outstanding (whether or not they had been filed with a court) at the date of the Claims Settlement Declaration, and that they should 'arise out of debts, contracts

---

[94] Claims Settlement Declaration, art. III(2).

[95] See S. A. Baker and M. D. Davis, *The UNCITRAL Arbitration Rules in Practice: The experience of the Iran-United States Claims Tribunal* (Kluwer, Deventer & Boston, 1992), 1–3 and *passim*; see further chapter eight.

[96] Claims Settlement Declaration, art. IV.

[97] See D. Lloyd-Jones, 'The Iran-US Claims Tribunal: Private Rights and State Responsibility' (1984) 24 *Virginia Journal of International Law* 259.

[98] Claims Settlement Declaration, art. II(1),(2),(3).

[99] See, e.g., Case *A/2* (1982) 1 *Iran-US CTR* 101, in which the Tribunal refused to hear claims brought by Iran against US nationals.

(including letters of credit or bank guarantees), expropriations or other measures affecting property rights'.[100]

To the extent that it arose after the date of the Declaration, a claim is outside the jurisdiction of the Tribunal. The point arose in *Kimberley-Clark Corp.* v. *Bank Markazi*.[101] Kimberley-Clark had made a licence agreement with Iran for making Kleenex tissues. It claimed royalties due under the agreement for the period from 1980 to the date of the award, which Bank Markazi refused to pay, and also damages in respect of the period from the date of the award up to the end of the licence. The Tribunal held that it had jurisdiction only in respect of royalties due before 19 January 1981 (unless the claimants could prove that there had been an anticipatory breach of the contract before that date, which they could not). It had no jurisdiction over royalties due later, and claims in respect of them could be brought before US courts, albeit without the advantages of the security fund established for the satisfaction of Tribunal awards against Iran.

Similarly, claims falling outside the categories of debts, contracts, expropriations and other measures affecting property rights are not within the jurisdiction of the Tribunal. For instance, it has dismissed claims for damages arising from the assassination of a US national,[102] and for damages for psychological damage caused to an Iranian at school in the USA,[103] as having no connection whatever with contract or property rights.[104] On the other hand, the Tribunal sometimes adopted a generous interpretation of the categories which are within its jurisdiction, extending the notion of debt or contract to include claims based upon unjust enrichment,[105] and the concept of expropriation to include deprivation of the power of control and management of enterprises.[106]

Some matters were specifically excluded from the jurisdiction of the Tribunal. First there are the matters, set out in the General Declaration (paragraph 11), in respect of which the US undertook to bar the prosecution of claims: i.e., claims related to ' (A) the seizure of the fifty-two United States nationals on November 4, 1979, (B) their subsequent detention, (C) injury to United States property or property of the United States nationals within the United States Embassy com-

---

[100] Claims Settlement Declaration, art. II(1).

[101] (1983) 2 *Iran-US CTR* 334.

[102] *Grimm* v. *Iran* (1983) 2 *Iran-US CTR* 78.

[103] *Haddadi* v. *US* (1985) 8 *Iran-US CTR* 20.

[104] And see the case of *Hoffland Honey Co.* v. *NIOC* (1983) 2 *Iran-US CTR* 41, where a Wisconsin bee-keeper unsuccessfully claimed $2,866,122 from the National Iranian Oil Co., for damage to his 36,140 colonies of bees, which allegedly resulted from chemicals manufactured in the USA by companies using Iranian oil, and used on the bees. He had no contractual or other link with NIOC.

[105] *Isaiah* v. *Bank Mellat* (1983) 2 *Iran-US CTR* 232. But the Tribunal did not accept that arbitral awards constituted contractual debts: *Bendore-Derozzi* v. *Iran* (1984) 6 *Iran-US CTR* 130.

[106] *Starrett Housing Corp.* v. *Iran* (1983) 4 *Iran-US CTR* 122, (1984) 23 *ILM* 1091.

pound in Tehran after November 3, 1979, and (D) injury to the United States nationals or their property as a result of popular movements in the course of the Islamic Revolution in Iran which were not an act of the Government of Iran'.[107] Also excluded were any possible Iranian claims arising from the abortive US attempt to rescue the hostages by force.[108]

The very acts which had precipitated the crisis, and which carried the highest political charge, were therefore put outside the jurisdiction of the Iran-US Claims Tribunal and, indeed, any other tribunal. No procedure was laid down for their settlement. The US had initially applied to the ICJ in the *Hostages* case only for a determination of Iranian liability to make reparation for the detention of the hostages; and that it obtained.[109] It reserved the determination of the amount of compensation payable to a later stage in the proceedings; and that stage the US discontinued, as required by the Algiers Accords. Although, in withdrawing the case from the ICJ, the US reserved the right to reinstate proceedings if Iran failed to live up to its commitments,[110] for practical purposes all claims arising from the seizure of the hostages were abandoned. Nonetheless, Iran suffered heavy penalties as a result of the crisis. Bilateral trade with the US fell from around $5.7 billion in 1977 to around $500 million in 1980; Iran was subjected to a wide range of trade sanctions; and not only did it lose US economic and military support itself, but it subsequently saw increased US support for Iraq during the Iran-Iraq War, which began in 1980. There are other forms of retribution than those which are to be found in the rules of the courts.

The second category of excluded claims were those 'arising under a binding contract between the parties specifically providing that any disputes thereunder shall be within the sole jurisdiction of the competent Iranian courts in response to the Majlis position'.[111] This so-called 'Iranian Forum clause' exception generated much jurisprudence in the early days of the Tribunal, which contrived to strike a judicious balance between upholding its own jurisdiction and upholding contractual agreements consigning disputes to the Iranian courts. Iran had argued that the Iranian Forum clause provision excluded from the Tribunal's jurisdiction all cases arising from contracts which contained a reference to Iran as a forum for dispute settlement. US claimants sought to argue that it applied only where a binding clause gave exclusive jurisdiction over all disputes arising from the contract to the Iranian courts, and that any such clause made before the Islamic Revolution would no longer bind the US parties anyway because the post-revolutionary courts were fundamentally different from the pre-revolutionary

---

[107] On (D), see *Ultra Systems Inc.* v. *Iran* (1983) 2 *Iran-US CTR* 100.
[108] *Haji-Bagherpour* v. *US* (1983) 2 *Iran-US CTR* 38.
[109] ICJ Rep. 1980, 3.
[110] See the US letter withdrawing the case, dated 6 April 1981: (1981) 20 *ILM* 889.
[111] Claims Settlement Declaration, art. II(1). The Majlis is the Iranian Parliament.

courts envisaged in such clauses.[112] The Tribunal took a group of nine cases concerning the main variants of dispute settlement clauses in contracts. It refused to enter into the question whether the clauses or contracts in which they appeared could be said to be 'binding', taking the surprisingly robust view that the word 'binding' was redundant.[113] To that extent, it met Iranian concerns that the US argument would have entirely undermined the exclusion of the 'Iranian Forum' cases. But it also held that only in cases where the contract expressly stipulated that Iranian courts had sole jurisdiction over each and every dispute arising from the contract did the Iranian Forum clause exception apply and take the case outside the Tribunal's jurisdiction.[114]

Perhaps the most significant aspect of these national claims is that most of the claimants were themselves entitled to present them, acting in their own names on a level of parity with the respondent Government, and conducting and compromising the litigation as they saw fit, before a tribunal where their cases ran alongside inter-State claims. It requires either considerable mental agility, or a lesser degree of intellectual ossification, to explain why these non-State litigants should not be considered to be full actors in the international legal system. Only where the claims amounted to less than $250,000 were the national claimants obliged to follow the traditional international law procedure, by having their claims presented on their behalf by their national government.[115]

The definition of 'nationals' for the purpose of these jurisdictional provisions is notable. Natural persons who are citizens of Iran or the US are, of course, included; and the Tribunal has rendered some important decisions in which it has upheld the application of the 'dominant nationality' test in cases of dual nationality.[116] So, too, are corporations and other legal entities organised under the laws of Iran or the US. But unlike the traditional position in international law, exemplified by the *Barcelona Traction* case,[117] in which the nationality of the shareholders is in general irrelevant, the Claims Settlement Declaration stipulated that claims of such legal persons are included only 'if, collectively, natural persons who are citizens of such country hold, directly or indirectly, an interest in such corporation or entity equivalent to fifty per cent or more of its capital stock'.[118] On the other

---

[112] Cf. the English case, *Carvalho* v. *Hull Blyth (Angola) Ltd.* [1979] 1 WLR 1278, where a similar argument succeeded.

[113] *Halliburton Co.* v. *Doreen/IMCO* (1982) 1 *Iran-US CTR* 242.

[114] See T. L. Stein, 'Jurisprudence and Jurists' Prudence: The Iranian-Forum Clause Decisions of the Iran-US Claims Tribunal' (1984) 78 *AJIL* 1.

[115] Claims Settlement Declaration, art. III(3).

[116] *Esphahanian* v. *Bank Tejarat* (1983) 2 *Iran-US CTR* 157; *Golpira* v. *Government of Iran* (1983) 2 *Iran-US CTR* 171; *Case A/18* (1984) 5 *Iran-US CTR* 251, 428. Note the powerful dissents by the Iranian judges, whose views led them to refuse to participate in some such cases: cf. *Saghi* v. *Iran* (1987) 14 *Iran-US CTR* 3. See further below, chapter eight, p. 192.

[117] ICJ Rep. 1970, 3. See further below, chapter eight, p. 193.

[118] Art. VII(1).

hand, and again departing from the *Barcelona Traction* principle, citizens of the US who owned claims against Iran through the medium of a *non*-US company which they controlled were entitled to bring claims (as, *mutatis mutandis*, are Iranian nationals).[119] These provisions are discussed further below.[120]

By contrast, the definitions of the respondent States for the purposes of the national claims were straightforward. They included the Governments of Iran and the United States, any political subdivisions of Iran or the United States, and any agency, instrumentality or entity controlled by the Government of Iran or the United States or any political subdivision thereof.[121] Claims could, therefore, be brought against State-controlled trading corporations; and the Tribunal interpreted these provisions as extending its jurisdiction to entities indirectly controlled by the relevant Government.[122]

2.3.2 Official claims

Article II(2) of the Claims Settlement Declaration gave the Tribunal jurisdiction over official claims of the US and Iran against each other arising out of contracts for the sale of goods and services. The US succeeded in having these direct claims between the two States held back until the closing stages of the Tribunal's activities. This strategy avoided any possible risk that Iran might withdraw its co-operation from the Tribunal once its own, very substantial, claims against the US had been adjudicated. Consequently there have been few awards under this head. One early award established that claims for customs duties are not within the Tribunal's jurisdiction.[123]

2.3.3 Interpretative cases

Article II(3) of the Claims Settlement Declaration empowered the Tribunal to rule upon the interpretation and performance of the General Declaration, and article VI(4) gave it a similar power in relation to the Claims Settlement Declaration itself. The Tribunal, which sits in plenary session in these 'interpretation' cases, exercised this power to rule upon various technical questions concerning the operation of the Tribunal and the security account from which awards against Iran are satisfied.[124] The important award on admissibility in dual nationality cases, *Case A/18*, was also rendered under this heading.[125]

---

[119] Claims Settlement Declaration, art. VII(2).

[120] See further below, chapter eight, p. 192.

[121] Claims Settlement Declaration, art. VII(3),(4).

[122] See, e.g., *Economy Forms Corp.* v. *Iran* (1983) 3 *Iran-US CTR* 42; *Rexnord Inc.* v. *Iran* (1983) 2 *Iran-US CTR* 6; *Raygo Wagner Equipment Co.* v. *Star Line Iran Co.* (1982) 1 *Iran-US CTR* 411.

[123] *Iranian Customs* v. *US, Case B/3* (1985) 8 *Iran-US CTR* 89.

[124] See, e.g., *Case A/1 (Security Account)* (1983) 1 *Iran-US CTR* 189, (1983) 22 *ILM* 591; *Case A/15 (Excess Iranian Funds)* (1986) 12 *Iran-US CTR* 40, (1987) 26 *ILM* 1562.

[125] (1984) 5 *Iran-US CTR* 251, 428.

2.3.4 Applicable law

The 'mixed' nature of the Tribunal is evident from the stipulations concerning the applicable law. Article V of the Claims Settlement Declaration states:

> The Tribunal shall decide all cases on the basis of respect for law, applying such choice of law rules and principles of commercial and international law as the Tribunal determines to be applicable, taking into account relevant usages of the trade, contract provisions and changed circumstances.

The Tribunal was therefore empowered to apply rules of public international law and of private law as the circumstances of the cases demand.

2.3.5 Enforcement of Iran-US Claims Tribunal Awards

Awards against Iran and its agencies are satisfied by payments from the security account established under the Algiers Accords and regularly topped up by Iran. US claimants are therefore secure. There is no comparable provision for securing awards in favour of Iranian claimants against the US. The Algiers Accords were framed to produce a pragmatic solution to an acute problem, and not to reinforce the doctrine of the sovereign equality of States or the courtesies of international diplomacy. The resulting imbalance has, however, revealed some of the difficulties of the international arrangements.[126]

One case, *A/21*,[127] arose from the failure of a US defendant to pay monies awarded to Iran on a counter-claim. The Iranian Government then initiated an interpretative case in the Tribunal. The Iranian Government argued that the US Government was obliged to satisfy all Tribunal awards against US nationals who refused to pay: i.e., it sought to establish in respect of US defendants a position comparable to that resulting from the establishment of the Security Fund in respect of Iranian defendants. The US argued that US courts were available for the enforcement of Tribunal awards. The Tribunal rejected the Iranian submission, but said that it would reconsider the position were Iran ultimately to be denied a remedy in US courts. The particular claim which sparked off *Case A/21* was then submitted to the US courts in the *Gould* case.[128] Gould, against whom the Tribunal had made the original award, argued that, as an unrecognised Government, the Government of Iran had no *locus standi* to bring the case, and that the award was not enforceable under the New York Convention.[129] The US Court, however, deferred to strong arguments from the US Government that the

---

[126] For a discussion of the constitutional problems in the US arising from the deduction of 2% of awards payable to US nationals by the US Government, for administrative costs, see *Sperry Corp.* v. *US* 853 F 2d. 904, (1989) 86 *AJIL* 86.

[127] (1987) 14 *Iran-US CTR* 324.

[128] *Ministry of Defence of Iran* v. *Gould Inc.* (1988) 82 *AJIL* 591; and see further 969 Fed.2d 764 (9th Cir., 1992).

[129] See chapter eight, p. 266, below.

claim should be allowed: it accepted that *locus standi* was a matter within the discretion of the Executive, whose lead the Court would follow, and that the judicial interest in securing effective arbitral proceedings overrode any technical obstacles to enforcement under the New York Convention.[130]

The latter point had been addressed, with the same result, by the English courts in *Dallal* v. *Bank Mellat*.[131] Dallal, a US national, had sued the Iranian Bank Mellat in the US courts. His action was terminated by the Algiers Accords and subsequent US Presidential Decree staying such actions and providing for their adjudication by the Iran-US Claims Tribunal. The Presidential Decree also provided that the Tribunal's awards should be final as a matter of US law. Dallal's claim was rejected on the merits by the Tribunal. Dallal then sought to bring an action in the English courts, where Bank Mellat argued that the claim should be struck out as an abuse of process because the claim had already been tried by a tribunal of competent jurisdiction. Both the New York Convention and English common law require, however, that arbitral awards be valid under the *lex arbitri* if they are to be recognised or enforced, and the Iran-US Claims Tribunal awards did not comply with certain technical requirements of the Dutch Code of Civil Procedure. Nonetheless, the English court held that because the Tribunal had been created by treaty between two Governments to adjudicate upon cases between parties within the jurisdiction of those Governments, and whose laws recognised the Tribunal's competence, and because the Tribunal had its seat in a third State which had consented to its operation, it was impossible for an English court to treat the Tribunal as incompetent. Dallal's application was dismissed.

Gould and *Dallal* demonstrate the readiness of municipal tribunals to accept the arrival of mixed tribunals as an integral part of the international dispute settlement procedure. The contrast with earlier cases such as the *Socobel* litigation[132] is marked: whether time has increased the willingness of municipal tribunals to regard the multiplicity of international tribunals as their equal partners in an international dispute settlement system, or whether the cases turn on their own peculiar features, remains to be seen.

The Iran-US Claims Tribunal and the ICSID system offer clear illustrations of the ability of the legal system to cater for litigation between States on the one hand and corporations and individuals on the other, whatever juridical apartheid may be demanded by traditional international legal doctrine. They are a hybrid, combining the characteristics of both inter-State arbitrations and international commercial arbitrations.

---

[130] Enforcement could, however, be refused on the grounds set out in article V of the New York Convention: see *Iran Aircraft Industries* v. *Avco Corp.* 980 F 2d 141 (2d Cir., 1992). See further, chapter eight, p. 267, below.

[131] [1986] QB 441.

[132] See chapter eight, p. 264, below.

5

DISPUTE SETTLEMENT IN THE LAW OF THE SEA

1. Introduction   84

2. The International Tribunal for the Law of the Sea   87

3. The International Court of Justice   90

4. Annex VII arbitral tribunals   90

5. Annex VIII special arbitral tribunals   91

6. General provisions   92

1. Introduction

The dispute settlement provisions in the 1982 United Nations Convention on the Law of the Sea[1] (the '1982 Convention') are remarkable for their detail and variety,[2] which surpass even that of the 1899/1907 Hague Convention. The range of potential disputes is such that no single procedure for dispute settlement is appropriate. For example, there may be inter-State disputes of the kind that have in the past been brought before the International Court of Justice. These may be essentially legal in nature, as are disputes concerning jurisdiction over fishing on the high seas;[3] or they may be inter-State disputes that involve the appreciation of a host of non-legal factors, such as disputes over maritime boundaries.[4] They may, on the other hand, not be inter-State disputes. For example, a case arising from the seizure of a foreign vessel and its crew for fishing in a State's exclusive fisheries zone

---

[1] (1982) 21 *ILM* 1245. See R. R. Churchill and A. V. Lowe, *The Law of the Sea*, 3rd edn. (Manchester, 1999).

[2] See further S. Oda, 'Dispute Settlement Prospects in the Law of the Sea' (1995) 44 *ICLQ* 863.

[3] See, e.g., the Application by Spain dated 28 March 1995 instituting proceedings against Canada with respect to a dispute relating to the Canadian Coastal Fisheries Protection Act: 1995 ICJ Rep. 87. The ICJ decided that it lacked jurisdiction over the case: 1998 ICJ Rep. 432.

[4] See, e.g., the *Gulf of Maine* case, ICJ Rep. 1984, 246.

would initially be brought before the arresting State's own domestic courts,[5] although it is possible that the case might subsequently, and after the exhaustion of local remedies, be taken up by the fishermen's national State and pursued as an inter-State claim in the International Court[6] or some other international tribunal.[7] This much is common to international disputes as they have arisen under classical international law. But the 1982 Law of the Sea Convention has pressed far beyond the bounds of the classical approach to the Law of the Sea and it has in consequence been necessary to provide for new kinds of dispute.

There are many instances of such innovations in the 1982 Convention, but two examples will serve to make the point. First, and most obviously, the 1982 Convention regulates the activities not only of States but also of corporations. Part XI of the Convention, as modified by the 1994 Agreement Relating to the Implementation of Part XI of the United Nations Convention on the Law of the Sea of 10 December 1982,[8] provides for the licensing of companies by the International Seabed Authority established by the 1982 Convention to mine the mineral resources lying on the seabed beyond the limits of national jurisdiction. Those companies may be privately owned or State owned; and they may be operating alongside the Enterprise, an international organisation established by the 1982 Convention to exploit the international seabed on behalf of mankind. Relations between these various entities are laid down partly in the Convention, and partly under licences and contracts to be concluded between them once exploitation begins. In addition, the activities on the international seabed of particular companies will naturally be regulated under their national laws. The international seabed provisions, therefore, may give rise both to classical disputes between States or between States and international organisations in relation to the exercise of rights and discharge of obligations under the Convention, and also to various kinds of 'mixed' disputes between States and international organisations and non-State entities—the corporations exploiting the international seabed. For instance, States are obliged by the 1982 Convention to ensure that mining companies that have their nationality and have concluded contracts with the International Seabed Authority co-operate fully with the Authority in seeking to agree fair and reasonable terms for the transfer of proprietary mining technology to the Enterprise and to developing States wishing to mine the deep seabed.[9] Failure to do so might give rise to a dispute between a company's national State on the one hand and the Enterprise or a developing State on the other, concerning the interpretation and application of those treaty obligations. Again, mining companies have to make royalty or profit-sharing payments to the Authority,

---

[5] See, e.g., *Mortensen* v. *Peters* (1906) SLT 227.

[6] See, e.g., the *Anglo-Norwegian Fisheries* case, ICJ Rep. 1951, 116.

[7] See, e.g., the *North Atlantic Coast Fisheries* arbitration (1910) 11 *UNRIAA* 167.

[8] (1994) 33 *ILM* 1309. Hereafter referred to in this chapter as 'the 1994 Agreement'.

[9] 1994 Agreement, Annex, section 5, Transfer of Technology.

calculated on the basis of their production, and disputes might arise between the Authority and a company over the amount due; or a company which has made technology available to the Enterprise or a developing State under a contract may be involved in a dispute arising from that contract.

A second category of potential disputes that fits uneasily into the more common international dispute settlement procedures is that which concerns provisions in the 1982 Convention that give States discretion in certain areas. For instance, in the 200-mile Exclusive Economic Zones which States are allowed to establish under the Convention, the coastal State is empowered to set limits on fish catches at levels that ensure that the fish stocks are not endangered by overfishing. The coastal State must also determine the harvesting capacity of its own fishing vessels, and is obliged to allow third States access to any surplus catch which the fishery might be able to sustain.[10] Complaints may arise from a failure to set realistic limits on fish catches or to allocate surpluses to other States. The essence of such disputes would not be legal: there is relatively little room for argument over what the treaty obligations are. Rather it would concern the propriety of the State's exercise of discretion in determining the total allowable catch, its own harvesting capacity, and hence the surplus available to third States. Those are, clearly, matters requiring the expert interpretation of scientific evidence.

In order to take account of the variety in the kinds of dispute that might arise, and also to accommodate the considerable differences of opinion between States as to the most suitable form of dispute settlement procedure, the 1982 Convention set out an elaborate scheme.[11] Unlike the 1958 Conventions on the Law of the Sea, whose dispute settlement provisions appeared in a short optional protocol[12] ratified by around thirty States, the dispute settlement provisions of the 1982 Convention are an integral part of the Convention itself, inseparable from the substantive provisions of the Convention. They are an essential part of the balance between the interests of the various States that gave the 1982 Convention the quality of a 'package deal', no part of which is separable from the others.

Lest the point be lost in the discussion of the detailed provisions, it should be emphasised that the dispute settlement scheme in the 1982 Convention has two parts. Section 1 (General Provisions) of Part XV of the Convention sets out the fundamental principles. Article 279 provides that States must settle disputes in accordance with articles 2(3) and 33 of the UN Charter. The clear implication of that is spelled out in article 280, which provides that States have the right to settle any dispute between them by peaceful means of their own choosing. The same

---

[10] 1982 Convention, arts. 61, 62.

[11] The best account is in the University of Virginia Center for Oceans Law and Policy, *United Nations Convention on the Law of the Sea 1982: A Commentary*, vol. V (eds. M. H. Nordquist, S. Rosenne and L. B. Sohn) (Dordrecht, 1989).

[12] 450 *UNTS* 169.

principles apply to disputes between States and non-State entities—including both international organisations such as the Authority and the Enterprise, and the seabed mining companies.[13] When a dispute arises the parties must 'proceed expeditiously to an exchange of views regarding its settlement by negotiation or other peaceful means' (as they must where they have sought unsuccessfully to settle it or where it is necessary to consult in order to agree on the manner of implementing a settlement which has been reached).[14] Those peaceful means might be established in advance by agreement between them: for example, most fisheries disputes between EU States would have to be submitted, under the EC Treaty, to the Court of Justice of the European Communities.[15] If the means of settling the dispute have not been established in advance, the parties are free to have recourse to any procedure, although (somewhat oddly) the Convention singles out the possibility of recourse to (voluntary) conciliation for explicit mention.[16] Only where settlement is not possible by means chosen by the parties to the dispute would the elaborate dispute settlement provisions of the 1982 Convention come into play.

Section 2 of Part XV of the 1982 Convention sets out the 'compulsory procedures entailing binding decisions', as it terms them, to which parties must have recourse if the means chosen by them fail to settle the dispute.[17] That obligation is subject to a number of exceptions, with which we deal below. The parties are in fact given considerable freedom in choosing the precise 'compulsory procedure' that must be pursued in such circumstances. There are four main choices: the International Tribunal for the Law of the Sea (the 'ITLOS'); the International Court of Justice; an 'Annex VII' arbitral tribunal; and an 'Annex VIII' special arbitral tribunal. We will deal with each in turn, although it is not possible in this work to do more than outline the most significant provisions.

2. The International Tribunal for the Law of the Sea[18]

The International Tribunal for the Law of the Sea is established by Annex VI of the 1982 Convention, and has its seat in Hamburg. It has twenty-one judges,

---

[13] 1982 Convention, art. 285.

[14] Ibid., art. 283.

[15] Ibid., art. 282. EC Treaty arts. 38–47, 170.

[16] The conciliation procedure, based on a five-person *ad hoc* conciliation commission to which each party appoints two members, is set out in Annex V of the Convention. Reports of a conciliation commission do not bind the parties.

[17] 1982 Convention, art. 286.

[18] The rules of procedure and other documents concerning the Tribunal, and reports of its cases, can be obtained at the UN Law of the Sea web site: <www.un.org/Depts/los/>. See further T. Treves, 'The Law of the Sea Tribunal: its status and scope of jurisdiction after November 16, 1994' (1995) 55 *ZAORV* 421–51; T. Eitel, 'A comment', ibid., 452–6.

elected by secret ballot for nine-year terms[19] by parties to the Convention from among those of recognised competence in the Law of the Sea. No two judges may be of the same nationality, and the composition of the Tribunal as a whole must be representative of the world's principal legal systems. As in the International Court of Justice, each State party to a dispute before the Tribunal may appoint a judge *ad hoc* if there is no judge of its nationality already on the Tribunal.[20] The provisions on activities incompatible with membership of the Tribunal, or with sitting in any particular case before it, are similar to those applicable to judges of the International Court of Justice.[21]

While all available members are to sit in any case before the ITLOS, some may not be so able. Accordingly, a quorum of eleven is set. The Tribunal is also empowered to sit in chambers for four categories of case. First, the Tribunal may itself establish chambers of three or more members to hear particular categories of case, which might include, for instance, disputes concerning environmental or fisheries matters.[22] Second, it may form a chamber for a particular dispute, if the parties so request.[23] Third, it is to form each year a five-member chamber to hear cases by the accelerated summary procedure and to prescribe provisional measures when the full Tribunal is not in session.[24] And fourth, it is to establish an eleven-member Sea-Bed Disputes Chamber, which may itself form three-member *ad hoc* chambers, to hear disputes arising from Part XI (the International Sea-Bed Area) of the Convention brought by States Parties to the Convention, the International Sea-Bed Authority, the Enterprise, or mining companies having contracts with the Authority.[25] These provisions allow a certain degree of selection among the judges, in order to ensure that those whose particular skills (and perhaps nationalities) are most appropriate for any given case may sit in that case. In addition, the Tribunal and its chambers have the power to appoint, in consultation with the parties, non-voting scientific or technical experts to assist it.[26]

The procedure of the Tribunal and its chambers, in relation to matters such as non-appearing respondents and so on, is very similar to that of the International Court of Justice. Decisions of the Tribunal and its chambers are, naturally, binding, but only on the parties to the case and only in respect of that dispute.[27] That principle is qualified by the provisions concerning intervention, which mirror

---

[19] Transitional provisions give some of the initial members shorter terms: 1982 Convention, Annex VI, art. 5.

[20] Ibid., Annex VI, art. 17.

[21] Ibid., Annex VI, arts. 7, 8, 9.

[22] Ibid., Annex VI, art. 15(1).

[23] Ibid., Annex VI, art. 15(2).

[24] Ibid., art. 290 and Annex VI, arts. 15(3), 25(2).

[25] Ibid., arts. 186–91 and Annex VI, arts. 35–40.

[26] Ibid., art. 289.

[27] Ibid., art. 296 and Annex VI, art. 33.

those in the Statute of the International Court. State Parties to the Convention having an interest of a legal nature which may be affected by a decision in any dispute may request from the Tribunal permission to intervene.[28] State Parties to the Convention also have a right to intervene in cases where the interpretation or application of the Convention is in question.[29] There is no provision entitling States not parties to the 1982 Convention to intervene. Where a State has intervened, it is bound by the decision in the same way as the parties to the dispute.

Decisions of the Sea-Bed Disputes Chamber (and any chambers established by it),[30] but not decisions of the Tribunal and its other chambers, are further stated to be 'enforceable in the territories of the States Parties in the same manner as judgments or orders of the highest court of the State Party in whose territory the enforcement is sought'.[31] This provision is similar to that in article 54 of the ICSID Convention, and the reason for its inclusion is also similar. The Sea-Bed Disputes Chamber may, as we have noted, adjudicate upon disputes between corporations and States or international organisations. Such cases would have the nature of commercial arbitrations, and it is thought appropriate that the decisions in them should be enforceable in broadly the same way as are international commercial arbitration or ICSID awards. Indeed, recourse to international commercial arbitration is specified as an alternative to use of the Sea-Bed Disputes Chamber, although in order to safeguard as far as possible the uniform interpretation of the Convention it is provided that commercial arbitration tribunals shall have no jurisdiction to decide any question of interpretation of the Convention but must instead refer such questions to the Sea-Bed Disputes Chamber for a ruling which must then be applied by the commercial arbitral tribunal.[32]

The ITLOS heard its first case in 1997. The case concerned provisions of the 1982 Convention that require the 'prompt release' of vessels arrested for certain fisheries or pollution offences on payment of a bond.[33] Under article 292, where it is alleged that the 'prompt release' obligation has not been complied with, the question of release can be submitted to the ITLOS by the flag State.[34] St Vincent and the Grenadines complained that the Republic of Guinea had wrongly detained the M/V *Saiga*, which was alleged to have been unlawfully supplying bunkering oil to fishing vessels in Guinean waters. Though charged with a customs offence,

---

[28] Ibid., Annex VI, art. 31.
[29] Ibid., Annex VI, art. 32.
[30] Ibid., Annex VI, art. 15(5).
[31] Ibid., Annex VI, art. 39.
[32] Ibid., arts. 187, 188. Cf. the operation of the 'preliminary ruling' provisions in art. 177 of the EC Treaty: see L. N. Brown and T. Kennedy, *The Court of Justice of the European Communities* (London, 1994), ch. 10.
[33] 1982 Convention, arts. 73(2), 220(6),(7), and 226(1)(c). See the *International Journal of Marine and Coastal Law*, Special Issue. The International Tribunal for the Law of the Sea: establishment and prompt release procedures (1996), vol. 11, Number 2 (137–232).
[34] Or another tribunal agreed by the States concerned.

in respect of which the 1982 Convention does not impose a 'prompt release' obligation, the majority of the judges in the ITLOS decided that the case should be treated as a fisheries offence, and ordered the release of the vessel.[35] The order was made with exemplary speed: the whole procedure took only three weeks, during which hearings were held, from the date that the initial application was faxed to the ITLOS.[36]

3. The International Court of Justice

The second of the possible fora listed in article 287 of the 1982 Convention is the International Court of Justice. The International Court is discussed below, in chapter seven.

4. Annex VII arbitral tribunals[37]

Arbitral tribunals established under Annex VII of the Law of the Sea Convention are available to hear disputes between States, and also for disputes involving international organisations, such as the European Community.[38] Cases arising from complaints made by individuals or corporations must, therefore, be espoused by their national State in accordance with the usual rules concerning the nationality of claims, the exhaustion of local remedies, and so on. Tribunals are to be composed of five members, one chosen by each of the parties and the other three members chosen jointly by the parties, from a panel to which each State Party to the Convention may nominate four people. If the disputants cannot agree upon the three jointly chosen arbitrators, these are to be appointed by the President of the Law of the Sea Tribunal. Arbitrators must have some experience in maritime affairs, but not, it seems, necessarily in the Law of the Sea: it is, therefore, possible

---

[35] 110 *ILR* 736, (1998) 37 *ILM* 360. The minority, which included the President and Vice-President of the Tribunal, would have declined jurisdiction. The analysis in the minority judgments is persuasive: see A. V. Lowe, '*The M/V Saiga*: the first case in the International Tribunal for the Law of the Sea' (1999) 48 *ICLQ* 187.

[36] The vessel was, however, not immediately released. St Vincent subsequently made another, and legally quite distinct, application to the ITLOS, alleging that Guinea had violated its obligations under the 1982 Convention by its treatment of the *Saiga*. Those proceedings continued despite the subsequent release of the *Saiga*.

[37] See K. Oellers-Frahm, 'Arbitration—a promising alternative of dispute settlement under the Law of the Sea Convention' (1995) 55 *ZAORV* 457.

[38] 1982 Convention, art. 305, Annex VII, art. 13, and Annex IX. Disputes involving deep seabed mining companies fall within the exclusive jurisdiction of the Sea-Bed Disputes Chamber. In the absence of any other provision of the Convention giving *locus standi* to companies, it seems that companies may not institute cases in Annex VII tribunals: see further the University of Virginia Center for Oceans Law and Policy, *United Nations Convention on the Law of the Sea 1982: A Commentary*, vol. V (eds. M. H. Nordquist, S. Rosenne and L. B. Sohn) (Dordrecht, 1989), 437.

to select arbitrators whose expertise lies in a technical field, such as fisheries management or environmental matters. This may, indeed, open the door for arbitral decisions based less upon the law than upon compromises based on an interpretation of a 'reasonable' response to the factual circumstances of the dispute.[39] Parties having the same interest are to appoint an arbitrator jointly by agreement between them.[40]

Annex VII arbitral tribunals are to decide upon their own rules of procedure,[41] but the basic framework that is envisaged appears to be broadly similar to that under the UNCITRAL Arbitration Rules. There is a provision for a majority vote, to be taken even if one or two of the arbitrators is absent or abstains, and for the President of the Tribunal to exercise a casting vote.[42] The absence of a party is no bar to the rendering of an award, although the Tribunal must satisfy itself that the applicant's case is well founded in fact and in law. Awards are final and without appeal.[43]

5. Annex VIII special arbitral tribunals

Many disputes turn essentially on disagreements over facts and their evaluation, rather than on questions of law. The 1982 Convention makes special provision for the handling of such disputes. Special arbitral tribunals may be established under Annex VIII of the Law of the Sea Convention to deal with four categories of specialised disputes: those concerning fisheries, environmental protection, marine scientific research, or navigation (including pollution and dumping).[44] Special arbitral tribunals are limited, like Annex VII tribunals, to disputes to which States and international organisations are parties. States Parties to the Convention may nominate experts in the relevant field (who may be technical, rather than legal, experts) to each of four lists, each dealing with one of these categories, maintained respectively by the FAO, UNEP, IOC and IMO.[45] Each party to the dispute may choose two arbitrators (of whom only one may be a national) for each case, preferably from the appropriate list, and a President, who is to be a national of a third State, is chosen by agreement of the parties, failing which the Secretary-General of the United Nations is to make the appointment unless the parties agree upon another appointing authority.[46] The rules governing the

---

[39] See the comments of Judge Oda, 'Dispute Settlement Prospects in the Law of the Sea' (1995) 44 *ICLQ* 863 at 867.
[40] 1982 Convention, Annex VII, art. 3(g).
[41] Ibid., Annex VII, art. 5.
[42] Ibid., Annex VII, art. 8.
[43] Ibid., Annex VII, art. 11.
[44] Ibid., Annex VIII, art. 1.
[45] Ibid., Annex VIII, art. 2.
[46] Ibid., Annex VIII, art. 3.

operation of special arbitral tribunals are in principle the same as those applicable to Annex VII tribunals.[47]

Special arbitral tribunals may also be used as fact-finding commissions to inquire into and establish the facts in relation to disputes within the four specialised categories. This must be done by agreement between the parties. In such cases the findings of fact are conclusive between the parties, who are then free to choose some other process, such as negotiation or arbitration, for the settlement of the dispute.[48]

6. General provisions

There are certain limitations upon the jurisdiction of all of these tribunals; or, to put it another way, the obligation to submit disputes to any of these procedures is not absolute, but is subject to exceptions *ratione materiae.* Some limitations are prescribed by the Convention itself. The first is general. No dispute concerning the exercise by a coastal State of its sovereign rights or jurisdiction is subject to the 'compulsory procedures entailing binding decisions' set out in Section 2 of Part XV of the 1982 Convention unless it is alleged (a) that the State has violated the freedoms set out in the Convention of navigation, overflight and pipe- and cable-laying, and other internationally lawful uses of the seas, or (b) that a State exercising any such freedom has violated the Convention or coastal laws adopted in conformity with the Convention, or (c) that the coastal State has acted in contravention of certain internationally adopted rules and standards on marine pollution.[49] Secondly, States are not obliged to submit to the compulsory procedures disputes arising from the refusal to give permission to conduct scientific research in their 200-mile Exclusive Economic Zones or continental shelves, although if they do not submit such disputes to these procedures they must be submitted to a compulsory conciliation procedure.[50] Similar provisions apply to certain disputes over Exclusive Economic Zone fisheries.[51] And, as was noted above, disputes concerning the exploitation of the international seabed area must be submitted to the Sea-Bed Disputes Chamber of the Law of the Sea Tribunal.

The Convention also gives States Parties the right to impose other limitations, thereby opting out of the compulsory dispute settlement procedures in respect of

---

[47] 1982 Convention, Annex VIII, art. 4.

[48] Ibid., Annex VIII, art. 5.

[49] Ibid., art. 297(1).

[50] Ibid., art. 297(2). Uruguay and Cape Verde, for example, have announced that they will not submit to the compulsory procedures in respect of such disputes: see United Nations (1994) 25 *Law of the Sea Bulletin*, 11, 38.

[51] 1982 Convention, art. 297(3). Again, Uruguay and Cape Verde have announced that they will not submit to the compulsory procedures in respect of such disputes.

certain defined categories of dispute. These optional exceptions, set out in article 298 of the Convention, cover disputes concerning military activities, disputes in respect of which the Security Council is exercising its functions, and delimitation disputes. In the case of the first two, if a State Party opts out of the compulsory settlement procedures it is subject only to the general international law duty to settle the dispute by agreed and peaceful means. In the case of the third category, delimitation disputes, a State that opts out is bound to accept compulsory conciliation;[52] and if conciliation is unsuccessful the parties must submit the dispute to one of the compulsory settlement procedures unless they agree on some other procedure.[53] Several States have invoked the optional exceptions under article 298. Most, such as Russia and other Eastern European States and Tunisia, have excepted all three categories of dispute. Others have excepted only some: Iceland, for instance, has excepted only questions of continental shelf delimitation.[54] Where a State exercises this right to exclude certain categories of dispute from the compulsory settlement procedures, the exclusion operates reciprocally, so that the State cannot institute compulsory settlement procedures in respect of such disputes.[55] States are, of course, free to agree upon reference of the dispute to any procedure they choose, even if they have excluded it from the compulsory dispute settlement provisions.[56]

States Parties to the Convention may indicate which of the four means for the settlement of disputes concerning the interpretation or application of the Convention they have chosen, at any time on or after signature of the Convention.[57] Any State Party to the Convention that has not selected one of the available fora under article 287 is deemed to have accepted 'Annex VII' arbitration. Any dispute that is not settled by means chosen by the parties or by the voluntary conciliation procedure under section 1 of this Part of the Convention must be submitted to one of these fora at the request of any party to the dispute.[58] If both parties have chosen the same forum under article 287, it goes to that body; otherwise, the dispute is to be referred to an 'Annex VII' arbitral tribunal unless the parties agree otherwise.[59]

---

[52] The provisions of Annex V of the 1982 Convention apply to compulsory conciliation.

[53] Delimitation disputes involving questions of title to territory may be excluded entirely from the compulsory settlement procedures: 1982 Convention, art. 298(1)(a).

[54] Relevant declarations are conveniently set out in United Nations, *The Law of the Sea. Declarations and statements with respect to the United Nations Convention on the Law of the Sea* (New York, 1977), 102–4, updated by the list at <www.un.org/Depts/los/los_decl.htm>.

[55] 1982 Convention, art. 298(3). Cf. the operation of the reciprocity principle in the ICJ: below, chapter seven, pp. 141–51.

[56] 1982 Convention, art. 299.

[57] Ibid., art. 287(1).

[58] Ibid., art. 286.

[59] Ibid., art. 287.

Practice in the choice of tribunal is varied. Many States have as yet made no choice, although they are free to do so at any time in the future. Among those who have chosen, the Law of the Sea Tribunal (chosen by Belgium, Germany, Greece, Oman, Tanzania, and Uruguay, among others) and the International Court (chosen by States including Belgium, Germany and Oman, among others, but explicitly rejected by Cuba and Guinea-Bissau[60]) are the most popular.[61] States need not choose the same forum for every purpose: for example, some Eastern European States have chosen 'Annex VII' arbitration as the 'basic' means for dispute settlement, but have chosen Annex VIII special arbitration for disputes concerning fisheries, environmental protection, scientific research and navigation, and the Law of the Sea Tribunal for disputes concerning the prompt release of detained vessels and their crews.[62]

Certain basic principles are laid down for the operation of all four of the 'article 287' tribunals when hearing and determining law of the sea cases. First, all are to apply the Convention 'and other rules of international law not incompatible with this Convention', unless the parties to the dispute agree to a determination *ex aequo et bono*.[63] The Sea-Bed Disputes Chamber will also have to apply the terms of contracts made between the mining companies and the International Sea-Bed Authority and regulations adopted by that Authority.[64] Whether this stipulation is sufficient to ensure that there is no fragmentation in the jurisprudence on the subject remains to be seen.[65] Certainly, there is a risk that the ITLOS in particular, whose bench is likely in its early years to include many with first-hand experience of the drafting of the Convention, may adopt approaches to treaty interpretation based less on the general canons of interpretation set out in the Vienna Convention on the Law of Treaties than on personal understanding of the nature of the compromises reached at UNCLOS III. Similarly, the special arbitral tribunals may decide cases as much on the basis of solutions which appear workable for the future as on analyses of pre-existent rights and duties of States. Neither development is undesirable in itself; but it would be unfortunate if a split appeared between the jurisprudence of these tribunals and that of the International Court.

---

[60] Ironically, given that Guinea-Bissau subsequently instituted proceedings in the International Court against Senegal in respect of a maritime boundary award: see *Arbitral Award of 31 July 1989*, ICJ Rep. 1990, 64, and ICJ Rep. 1991, 53.

[61] Information on the choices made is set out from time to time in the United Nations *Law of the Sea Bulletin* and on the UN Law of the Sea web site, <www.un.org/Depts/los/>.

[62] The provisions on prompt release appear in art. 292 of the 1982 Convention.

[63] 1982 Convention, art. 293.

[64] Ibid., Annex VI, art. 38.

[65] See A. E. Boyle, 'Dispute settlement and the Law of the Sea Convention: problems of fragmentation and jurisdiction' (1997) 46 *ICLQ* 37; J. A. Charney, 'The implications of expanding international dispute settlement systems: the 1982 Convention on the Law of the Sea' (1996) 90 *AJIL* 69.

All of the tribunals are to apply the exhaustion of local remedies rule as it exists in general international law.[66] All are empowered to appoint two or more non-voting scientific or technical experts in consultation with the parties and appoint them to assist with the decision of disputes involving scientific or technical matters.[67] All may prescribe provisional measures.[68] And all may make preliminary determinations, at the request of a party or on their own initiative, that the application is an abuse of legal process or prima facie unfounded.[69] This latter provision, designed to spare States the need to defend manifestly ill-founded and mischievous applications, is unusual. Whether it leads to a substantial saving of time, or to two consecutive trials of the merits of the case, remains to be seen. All decisions are to be taken by majority vote, all are to be reasoned, and all are final and binding on the parties.

---

[66] 1982 Convention, art. 295. See further chapter eight, pp. 195–8, below.
[67] Ibid., art. 289.
[68] Ibid., art. 290.
[69] Ibid., art. 294. Cf. art. 27(2) of the European Convention on Human Rights.

6

THE SETTLEMENT OF INTERNATIONAL ECONOMIC DISPUTES

1. The GATT and WTO systems	96
1.1 The GATT system	96
1.2 The WTO system	99
2. Regional trade dispute settlement systems	104
2.1 The EU system	105
2.2 COMESA—the Common Market for Eastern and Southern Africa	107
2.3 ECOWAS—the Economic Community of Western African States	109
2.4 Other African economic organisations	110
2.5 NAFTA—the North American Free Trade Agreement	111
2.6 Mercosur—Mercado Común del Sur/the Southern Common Market	116
3. International financial disputes	117
3.1 The IMF	117
3.2 The World Bank	119
3.3 The Multilateral Investment Guarantee Agency (MIGA)	121
4. Concluding remarks	123

1. The GATT and WTO systems

1.1 The GATT system

The procedures for the settlement of disputes arising under the General Agreement on Tariffs and Trade (GATT),[1] and now under the World Trade Organisation (WTO)[2] that has replaced it, are remarkable for their departure

---

[1] The GATT is reproduced in S. Zamora and R. A. Brand (eds.), *Basic Documents of International Economic Law* (Chicago, 1990) (hereafter, *Zamora & Brand*), vol. 1, 3. A useful overview of the development of the GATT and the WTO dispute settlement systems is to be found in J. H. Jackson, 'Dispute settlement and the WTO: emerging problems' (1998) 1 *Journal of International Economic Law* 329.

[2] See J. H. Jackson, *The World Trading System: Law and Policy of International Economic Relations*, 2nd edn. (Cambridge, Mass., 1997); J. H. Jackson, W. J. Davey and A. O. Sykes, *Legal Problems of International Economic Relations*, 3rd edn. (St Paul, Minn., 1995); A. Qureshi, *The World Trade Organisation* (Manchester, 1996); M. J. Trebilcock and R. Howse, *The Regulation of*

from the principle that disputes resolved by formal mechanisms should be settled on the basis of what is an essentially retrospective analysis of the rights and duties of the parties at the time that the dispute arose. Rather, the GATT/WTO system proceeds by an analysis of whether benefits (rather than rights) that the parties expected to derive from the substantive rules of the GATT/WTO have been nullified or impaired, or the achievement of any objective of the agreement is being impaired, and then to an essentially prospective analysis of what measures might produce a workable solution to the dispute for the future.

The GATT, originally adopted as part of the abortive International Trade Organisation in 1947 and applied on a 'provisional' basis from that date, sought to liberalise world trade by establishing the fundamental principles of non-discrimination and Most Favoured Nation treatment between the Contracting Parties as the bases of the international trade order. Those obligations were supplemented by provisions concerning matters such as subsidies and dumping and other non-tariff barriers to trade, and concerning the reductions of tariff barriers which were subsequently negotiated in a series of GATT negotiating rounds.[3]

The original GATT dispute settlement system has been described as 'the history of improvising on the extremely inadequate language of Article XXIII [of the GATT], which concerns remedies for "nullification and impairment" of negotiated liberalisation commitments'.[4] After a period in which the Contracting Parties dealt with complaints by one member against another on an *ad hoc* basis, by the establishment of working parties to which the States selected nominated representatives to serve, the practice arose of establishing panels of individuals, serving in their personal capacities and in a more nearly 'judicial' role, to report on complaints. That practice was the basis of the procedures set out in the 1979 Understanding Regarding Notification, Consultation, Dispute Settlement and Surveillance, to which was annexed the Agreed Description of the Customary Practice of the GATT in the Field of Dispute Settlement.[5]

The foundations of the GATT scheme lay in the provisions concerning notification and consultation. Several GATT provisions obliged Contracting Parties to notify the GATT of specific trade measures, and articles 2 and 3 of the 1979 Understanding obliged them 'to the maximum extent possible, to notify the Contracting Parties of their adoption of trade measures affecting the operation of

---

International Trade (London, 1995). See also the WTO web site, <http://www.wto.org/wto/index.htm>.

[3] Useful introductions to the GATT can be found in K. Dam, *The GATT: Law and International Economic Organisation* (Chicago, 1970), and R. Hudec, *The GATT Legal System and World Trade Diplomacy* (New York, 1975).

[4] J. H. Jackson, *GATT Machinery and the Tokyo Round Agreements* (1983), quoted in J. H. Jackson and W. J. Davey, *Legal Problems of International Economic Relations*, 2nd edn. (St Paul, Minn., 1986), 333.

the General Agreement'. Notification was the prelude to consultation. Under articles 4–6 of the Understanding, Contracting Parties were obliged to respond to requests for consultations promptly, and to conduct consultations expeditiously with a view to reaching mutually satisfactory conclusions. These provisions implemented articles XXII and XXIII(1) of the GATT. If consultation failed to resolve the dispute, the parties might invite the use of good offices.[6] If that failed, under article XXIII(2) a party could refer the matter to the GATT CONTRACTING PARTIES (the capitalised term signifies the Contracting Parties acting jointly) for consideration.[7] If a party so requested, the CONTRACTING PARTIES would establish a GATT dispute settlement panel.[8]

When panel proceedings were initiated, the GATT Director-General would nominate three or five members, normally governmental but serving in their individual capacities, of the panel, to whom the parties would raise objections only for compelling reasons.[9] The parties, and any Contracting Party having a substantial interest in the matter, had the right to be heard by the panel, which also had the right to call for information from any individual or government on its own motion.[10] The panel would review the facts and the applicability of GATT provisions, and try to assist the parties towards a mutually satisfactory resolution of the dispute.[11] The written reports of the panel, which would record either any agreed settlement which had developed between the parties or its own findings and recommendations, was transmitted to the Council of the GATT (a body open to all GATT Contracting Parties), which had the power formally to adopt the reports, thereby giving them binding force.[12] The CONTRACTING PARTIES could recommend steps such as the abandonment of the disputed trade measures, and could authorise a Contracting Party to suspend the application to any other contracting party of specified concessions or obligations under the Agreement—in essence, to take authorised retaliatory measures, such as the suspension of tariff concessions.[13]

One notable feature of the system was, as has been noted, its dependence not upon *breach* of the GATT but rather upon the 'nullification or impairment' of

---

⁵ GATT, 26th Supp. *BISD* 210 (1980); and see the 1982 modifications, 29th Supp. *BISD* 13 (1983) and (1983) 22 *ILM* 445; see GATT, *Guide to GATT Law and Practice*, 6th edn. (Geneva, 1994), 583 at 590. A valuable account of the old GATT dispute settlement procedures is to be found in O. Long, *Law and its Limitations in the GATT Multilateral Trade System* (Dordrecht, 1985).

⁶ 1979 Understanding, art. 8. On good offices, see above, chapter two, p. 27.

⁷ GATT, art. XXIII(2).

⁸ 1979 Understanding, art. 10.

⁹ Ibid., arts. 11–14, and Annex, art. 6.

¹⁰ Ibid., art. 15, and Annex, art. 6.

¹¹ Ibid., Annex, arts. 3, 6.

¹² Ibid., arts. 16–23.

¹³ This was done only once. See the 1952 Report on the Netherlands Measures of Suspension of Obligations to the United States, 1st Supp. *BISD* 32 (1953).

benefits accruing to the parties under the GATT. A breach of the GATT was treated as prima facie proof of such nullification or impairment, but no more than that.[14] A breach might, at least in theory, be found not to have led to nullification or impairment;[15] and nullification or impairment could be proved, on the basis of a detailed justification by the complainant, even in the absence of a breach.[16]

These GATT procedures were only one part of the system for the settlement of trade disputes. Many separate agreements prescribing their own dispute settlement procedures were concluded under the GATT umbrella: for example, the Code on Subsidies and Countervailing Duties,[17] and the Revised Anti-Dumping Code.[18] While these separate procedures were broadly comparable to that described above, no two were identical.[19] The untidiness of this lack of harmonisation of GATT dispute settlement procedures, and the danger of fragmentation within the system, was apparent from the outset; but constraints of time prevented the consolidation of the system during the Tokyo Round negotiations which produced the 1979 amendments to the GATT. This was remedied in the Uruguay Round negotiations which concluded in 1994 and established the World Trade Organisation as the successor to the GATT.[20]

1.2 The WTO system

The Dispute Settlement Understanding (DSU), annexed to the WTO Agreement, lays down a unified system of dispute settlement, based on that set out in articles XXII and XXIII of the GATT.[21] While WTO agreements on specific

---

[14] 1979 Understanding, Annex, art. 5. And see the 1962 Panel Report on Uruguayan Complaints, 11 *BISD* 95 (1963).

[15] The 1988 Panel Report on United States Taxes on Petroleum and Certain Imported Substances (the 'Superfund' report) suggested that a breach creates a practically irrefutable presumption of nullification or impairment, 34th Supp. *BISD* 136 at 156–8 (1988), (1988) 27 *ILM* 1596 at 1611–12. It is not clear how far this view will prevail in the WTO: see J. H. Jackson, 'Dispute settlement and the WTO: emerging problems' (1998) 1 *Journal of International Economic Law* 329 at 337–8; and see art. 3(8) of the 1994 WTO Understanding on Rules and Procedures Governing the Settlement of Disputes (1994) 33 *ILM* 1226. Cf. J. Pauwelyn, 'Evidence, proof and persuasion in WTO dispute settlement: who bears the burden?' (1998) 1 *Journal of International Economic Law* 222.

[16] See the 1950 Report on the Australian Subsidy on Ammonium Sulphate, 2 *BISD* 188 (1952).

[17] GATT Doc. MTN/NTM/W/236, 5 April 1979; reproduced in (1979) 18 *ILM* 579.

[18] See GATT Doc. MTN/NTM/W/232, 11 April 1979; reproduced in (1979) 18 *ILM* 621.

[19] See R. Hudec, 'GATT Dispute Settlement After the Tokyo Round, An Unfinished Business' (1980) 13 *Cornell International Law Journal* 145.

[20] An excellent concise account of the WTO is to be found in A. Qureshi, *The World Trade Organisation: Implementing International Trade Norms* (Manchester, 1996).

[21] The 1994 Understanding on Rules and Procedures Governing the Settlement of Disputes is reproduced in (1994) 33 *ILM* 1226. For general treatments of the system see P. Pescatore, W. J. Davey and A. F. Lowenfeld, *Handbook of WTO/GATT Dispute Settlement* (New York, 1991—loose-leaf); N. Komuro, 'The WTO dispute settlement mechanism—coverage and procedure' (1995) *Journal of World Trade* 5; E.-U. Petersmann (ed.), *International trade law and the GATT/WTO dispute settlement system* (London, 1997); id., *The GATT/WTO dispute settlement*

topics may modify or supplement the new procedure, the DSU is in principle applicable to all WTO disputes,[22] although the power to adopt interpretations of the WTO Agreement and the associated Multilateral Trade Agreements has been vested exclusively in the Ministerial Conference and General Council (on both of which all Contracting Parties are entitled to be represented).[23] It seems likely that 'interpretations', which must be adopted by a three-quarters majority of the Members, will be confined to formal interpretations which have something of the character of interpretative protocols, marking a clear policy choice: it can scarcely be possible for any dispute settlement procedure to operate without making routine interpretations of the agreements. The effect of this provision, therefore, is to reserve the competence to make a final and authoritative interpretation of the agreements to the political organs of the WTO.

The WTO Dispute Settlement Body (DSB) on which representatives of all Contracting Parties are entitled to sit[24] is set up to administer the system, with the power to establish panels, adopt reports from panels and the new Appellate Body also established in 1994, to survey the implementation of the rulings and recommendations of panels, and to authorise the suspension of concessions and other obligations.[25] Like the GATT, it is based upon the notion of the 'nullification or impairment' of benefits, rather than upon the notion of breach, of the WTO obligations. Under the various agreements which make up the WTO system it is the DSB which recommends steps to end the dispute or gives a ruling authorising the complainant to suspend WTO obligations in respect of the respondent Member.[26] It takes its decisions by consensus.[27]

Notification[28] and consultation[29] again form the basis of the system, with good offices, conciliation and mediation offered to assist the parties in developing a

---

system: International law, International organizations and dispute settlement (London, 1997); *International Journal of International Economic Law*, Special Issue: WTO Dispute Settlement System, vol. 1, no. 2 (June 1998); T. J. Schoenbaum, 'WTO dispute settlement: praise and suggestions for reform' (1998) 47 *ICLQ* 647; A. W. Sharpe, 'The first three years of WTO dispute settlement: observation and comment' (1998) 1 *Journal of International Economic Law* 277; 'Special Issue: WTO dispute settlement system' (1998) 1(2) *Journal of International Economic Law*.

[22] 1994 Understanding, arts. 1 and 23.

[23] 1994 Agreement Establishing the World Trade Organisation, art. IX(2), reproduced in (1994) 33 *ILM* 1144.

[24] Ibid., art. IV.

[25] 1994 Understanding, art. 2.

[26] See, e.g., the 1994 General Agreement on Trade in Services, art. XXIII, reproduced in (1994) 33 *ILM* 1168.

[27] 1994 Understanding, art. 2(4).

[28] Prescribed by the substantive agreements which form a part of the WTO system: see the Uruguay Round documents reproduced in (1994) 33 *ILM* 1125.

[29] Also prescribed by the substantive agreements which form a part of the WTO system: see the Uruguay Round documents reproduced in (1994) 33 *ILM* 1125; and art. 4 of the 1994 Understanding.

solution to their dispute.[30] Disputes not resolved by using those procedures must, if the complaining party so requests, be submitted to a panel to be established by the DSB, unless the DSB decides by consensus (which means the absence of formal objection by any Member) not to establish a panel.[31] There is, accordingly, a strong bias in favour of acceding to requests for the establishment of panels.

Panels are composed of three members (unless the parties agree on a panel of five), who are well qualified in international trade law or policy and serve in their individual capacities.[32] Panel members are nominated by the Secretariat, and the parties are not to oppose nominations except for good reasons. If there is no agreement on the panellists within twenty days of the establishment of the panel, its composition is determined by the Director-General of the WTO in consultation with the chairman of the DSB and the chairman of the Council or Committee established under the WTO agreement in question.

The terms of reference of panels may be drawn up by the Chairman of the DSB, in consultation with the parties. Unless the parties to the dispute agree otherwise, panels are required to examine the complaint in the light of the relevant provisions in the WTO agreement in question, and to make such findings as will assist the DSB in making the recommendations or rulings provided for in that agreement.[33] Panel reports form part of the WTO *acquis* and, while not legally binding precedents, exercise a considerable influence on later panels.[34]

There are notable provisions dealing with third party interests. If more than one Member State requests the establishment of a panel in relation to the same matter a single panel is, whenever feasible, established to consider the multiple complaints. Written submissions by each complainant are made available to all, and each has the right to be present when another presents its case. If a single panel is not established, 'to the greatest extent possible the same persons shall serve as panellists on each of the separate panels' and panel timetables shall be harmonised.[35] Third parties may be interested, but not be complainants. Their interests are safeguarded by article 10 of the 1994 Understanding, which gives them the opportunity to be heard by the panel, and the right to receive the submissions of the parties and to have their own submissions transmitted to the parties. They may, of course, themselves have recourse to the dispute settlement procedures if they consider that measures under consideration by a panel nullify or impair benefits accruing

---

[30] 1994 Understanding, art. 5.

[31] Ibid., art. 6.

[32] See further on their duties of impartiality, confidentiality, etc., the WTO Rules of Conduct for the Understanding on Rules and Procedures Governing the Settlement of Disputes, 3 December 1997 (1997) 36 *ILM* 477.

[33] 1994 Undertaking, art. 7.

[34] See the discussion in D. Palmeter and P. C. Mavroidis, 'The WTO legal system: sources of law' (1998) 92 *AJIL* 398.

[35] 1994 Understanding, art. 9.

to them under one of the WTO agreements covered by the procedures; and if they do so the dispute would if possible be submitted to the original panel.

The normal working procedures of the panels are set out in an appendix to the 1994 Understanding.[36] Panels meet in closed session, to which the parties and any third parties which have notified their interest in the case present their views. The panel may request information from any body or individual. Parties are not present during the deliberations of the panel, which remain confidential. The drafting of the panel report proceeds in two stages. The first is the Interim Review Stage.[37] After hearing the parties' statements the panel drafts the descriptive (factual and argument) sections of its report and sends the draft to the parties, who have a fixed time to comment upon it. The panel then issues an interim report, including both the descriptive sections and the panel's findings and conclusions. Again, the parties have a set time within which to comment upon it and to request a further meeting of the panel and the parties to discuss matters raised in the comments. The panel then drafts its final report, which must include a discussion of the arguments raised at the interim review stage, as well as 'the findings of fact, the applicability of relevant provisions and the basic rationale behind any findings and recommendations that it makes'.[38]

Panels should report within six months from the date that their composition and terms of reference are agreed, although extensions taking the overall time limit up to nine months, or even more in cases of complaints against developing countries, are permitted. If an agreement has been reached by the parties, the procedure is much simpler: the report simply records the settlement and gives a brief description of it. Panel reports are automatically adopted by the DSB unless either (i) a party to the dispute appeals against the report, or (ii) the DSB decides by consensus not to adopt the report.[39]

The 1994 Understanding provided, in article 17, for the establishment of a standing seven-member Appellate Body by the DSB.[40] The first members, who are broadly representative of WTO membership but unaffiliated with any government, were appointed in 1995. The Appellate Body sits in divisions of three persons, selected on the basis of rotation.[41] Appeals may be made to the Appellate Body by the parties only, although third parties which have notified the DSB of a substantial interest in the matter may make submissions to and be heard by the Appellate Body. Appeals are limited to questions of law and legal interpretations in the panel report, and the Appellate Body may uphold, modify or reverse the

---

[36] 1994 Understanding, art. 12 and Appendix 3.
[37] Ibid., art. 15.
[38] Ibid., art. 12.
[39] Ibid., art. 16.
[40] Ibid., art. 17.
[41] Appellate Body, Working Procedures for Appellate Review, Rule 6.

panel's legal findings; but it seems that the Appellate Body cannot remit the matter to a panel for reconsideration. [42]

Appellate Body reports, like unappealed panel reports, are automatically adopted by the DSB unless there is a consensus against adoption.[43] This is a reversal of the previous GATT procedure, according to which a consensus was required for the adoption of a panel report, without which the report did not have legal force. One consequence is that the parties to a dispute cannot now block the adoption of a report if they have reached an accommodation between themselves in the light of that report,[44] although they could have done so in the past by preventing the consensus in favour of adoption that was then needed. Whether this facilitates the development of a satisfactory regime for international trade or impedes it by limiting the scope for flexible responses to disputes remains to be seen. If it were desired to preserve that flexibility, utilisation of arbitration as a means of settling WTO disputes, as is permissible under the 1994 Understanding,[45] could be a more desirable procedure.

Strict time limits are laid down. Unless otherwise agreed by the parties, unappealed panel reports should be considered by the DSB within nine months, and Appellate Body reports should be considered within twelve months.[46] At the DSB meeting, the Member States concerned explain their intentions regarding compliance with recommendations in the panel or Appellate Body report, for which they may be allowed a reasonable period of time (up to fifteen months from the date of the establishment of the panel). The DSB keeps compliance under surveillance.[47] If the Member State concerned persists in its failure to comply with the recommendations, the complainant State may seek the authority of the DSB to suspend the application to the Member concerned of concessions or other obligations under the agreement that has been violated.[48] Such concessions or obligations should relate to the same sector; but if that is not practicable or effective, concessions or obligations relating to another sector, or even arising under another WTO agreement, may be suspended. If the Member State concerned objects to the level of suspension authorised, which should be equivalent to the level of the violation, the matter is to be referred to arbitration, which is final.[49]

The WTO is an inter-State organisation. Implementation of WTO obligations is effected through municipal laws and tribunals, such as the International Trade

---

[42] 1994 Understanding, art. 17(6), (13).

[43] Ibid., art. 17(14).

[44] See, e.g., the handling of the *Tuna* dispute: 'Agora: Trade and Environment' (1992) 86 *AJIL* 700 at 702, n. 13.

[45] Art. 25.

[46] 1994 Understanding, art. 20.

[47] Ibid., art. 21.

[48] Ibid., art. 22.

[49] Ibid., art. 22.

Commission and the Court of International Trade in the United States.[50] Accordingly, it might have been thought that complaints that States had failed to comply with GATT/WTO obligations might be subject to the rule of exhaustion of local remedies. In fact, it appears that no government has ever tried to argue this point. The rights and duties under the GATT/WTO are inter-State matters, and the admissibility of complaints by States has never been conditional on the prior exhaustion of local remedies.[51]

The WTO dispute settlement provisions have been remarkably successful. By the end of 1998 more than 150 cases had been initiated, which represents something like a fourfold increase on the rate at which GATT procedures were invoked.[52] As the WTO has now cleared the way for the appearance of private counsel, rather than only government lawyers, in WTO dispute proceedings, and thus made it more practicable for corporations to press their national governments to activate WTO procedures, this pace may be expected to continue.[53] Furthermore, given that there were 133 States Parties to the WTO by mid-1998, and that all are bound by the dispute settlement system, the DSU represents the most extensive network of compulsory dispute settlement obligations in contemporary international law. It is almost inevitable that the WTO procedures will exert a gravitational pull, drawing into the WTO system disputes that could not easily find a forum elsewhere, and recasting them as 'trade' disputes.[54]

2. Regional trade dispute settlement systems

While the WTO system is set to become the most important of international trade dispute settlement systems, it is by no means the only one. Some regional economic organisations have well-developed dispute settlement systems. There is not space in this book to examine the practice of every regional system, but we set out a number of examples to illustrate this body of practice.

---

[50] E. McGovern, *International trade regulation* (Exeter, 1995—loose-leaf).

[51] See Ernst-Ulrich Petersmann, 'The Dispute Settlement System of the World Trade Organisation and the Evolution of the GATT Dispute Settlement System since 1948' (1994) 31 *Common Market Law Review* 1157 at 1240. This article offers an incisive analysis of all aspects of the WTO Dispute Settlement System.

[52] Panel reports and related documents and information may be found at <http://www.wto.org/wto/dispute/dispute.htm>.

[53] See the Appellate Body Report on the Regime for the Importation, Sale and Distribution of Bananas, WT/DS27/AB/R, 9 September 1997, <http://www.wto.org/wto/dispute/bananas.htm>, (1998) 37 *ILM* 243. See also the panel discussion, 'Is the WTO dispute settlement mechanism responsive to the needs of traders? Would a system of direct access by private parties yield better results?' (1998) 32(2) *Journal of World Trade* 147–65.

[54] Cf. the handling of the EU-US 'Helms-Burton' dispute: A. V. Lowe, 'US Extraterritorial Jurisdiction: The Helms-Burton and D'Amato Acts' (1997) 46 *ICLQ* 378; (1997) 36 *ILM* 529. See also T. L. Brewer and S. Young, 'Investment issues at the WTO: the architecture of rules and the settlement of disputes' (1998) 1 *Journal of International Economic Law* 457.

2.1 The EU system

Pre-eminent among the regional economic organisations is the European Community. The disputes settlement provisions of the European Community treaties are well covered in many basic texts,[55] and that treatment will not be duplicated in this chapter. No more than a brief outline of the major provisions will be given here.

The European Court—or, to give it its proper name (which avoids the common confusion of the EC Court with the quite separate Court established under the European Convention on Human Rights), the Court of Justice of the European Communities—is the judicial body which serves all three European Communities, that is, the European Economic Community, the European Coal and Steel Community, and EURATOM.[56] In practice, its role in relation to the Economic Community is of overwhelmingly greater significance than its role in relation to the other two Communities, and it is that which will be treated here. The Court has fifteen judges, who must be independent and be qualified for high judicial office or jurists of recognised competence. One is nominated by each Member State, appointed by the common accord of the Member States. The judges elect one of their number to act as President. While all fifteen judges may sit in a case, and will do so whenever a Member State or Community institution is a party to the case and so requests, it may also sit in chambers of three or five judges.

The Court is assisted by nine Advocates-General who act rather like *amici curiae*. After the parties have presented their arguments to the Court, but before the Court decides the case, the Advocate General to whom the case is allocated gives an independent and impartial opinion to the Court proposing the terms of a decision which would accord with the 'Community interest'. Opinions are highly influential and often followed by the Court, but they are not binding upon it. The Court, which deliberates in private but renders its judgments in public, has decided over 4,000 cases since it was established.

The European Court has jurisdiction over a wide range of disputes. First, there are direct actions brought by the Commission[57] or by a Member State[58] against a

---

[55] Perhaps the most accessible is L. N. Brown and T. Kennedy, *The Court of Justice of the European Communities*, 4th edn. (London, 1994).

[56] The Member States are Austria, Belgium, Denmark, Finland, France, Germany, Greece, Ireland, Italy, Luxembourg, Netherlands, Portugal, Spain, Sweden and the UK. A separate Court, the EFTA Court, has jurisdiction with regard to EFTA States Parties to the European Economic Area Agreement (Iceland, Liechtenstein and Norway), which in effect expands the scope of the Common Market to certain non-EU States. See the EFTA Court web site: <http://www.efta.int/structure/court/efta-crt.cfm>.

[57] EC Treaty, art. 169.

[58] Ibid., art. 170.

Member State that is alleged to be in breach of its obligations under the treaty. In these cases, the Court gives a declaratory judgment, with which the State must comply.[59] In this capacity its role is analogous to that of the International Court of Justice, as it is when it exercises its competence to give, at the request of the Council, the Commission, or a Member State, an advisory opinion on the compatibility of a proposed international agreement between the Community and other international organisations or States.[60] However, the European Court has competences which extend well beyond that of the more usual type of international tribunal.

A second kind of jurisdiction derives from article 177 of the EC Treaty. National courts in Member States may request the European Court to give preliminary rulings on questions of Community Law necessary for decisions in cases before them; and courts of last resort must make such a reference to the European Court. This, in effect, gives individuals the power to raise matters before the European Court, via a reference from the national Court. In such cases the Court renders its judgment interpreting Community Law, but the application of the law is a matter for the national court that referred the question.

Under a third set of powers, the Court may rule upon challenges to the legality of acts of the Community,[61] and to refusals of Community institutions to act in circumstances where they are obliged to act.[62] Cases may be brought before the Court by Community institutions and by Member States, and, subject to very restrictive rules on the *locus standi* of applicants, by individuals and legal persons directly and individually affected by those measures.[63]

The Court also has the power to determine claims for damages made against the Community arising from its non-contractual liability,[64] and over staff cases.

Cases brought by individuals or legal persons challenging the legality of a Community act, or a failure to act, or concerning the Community's non-contractual liability, and staff cases, are heard by the Court of First Instance (CFI). Such actions include the challenges by such applicants to fines and other orders imposed on them by the Commission acting in its role as enforcer of the Community's competition policy. The CFI was established in 1989 to relieve the Court of some of its growing workload, freeing it to concentrate upon the cases between the Member States and the Community institutions, and on the preliminary references under article 177 that are the crucial means by which the uniform application of EC law in Member States' courts is secured. The CFI, like the

---

[59] EC Treaty, art. 171.
[60] Ibid., art. 228(6).
[61] Ibid., arts. 173, 174.
[62] Ibid., art. 175.
[63] Ibid., art. 173.
[64] Ibid., arts. 178, 215.

European Court, has one judge nominated by each Member State; but the CFI has no advocates-general attached to it. The CFI often sits in three- or five-judge chambers, but may sit in plenary session for important cases. There is a right of appeal from the CFI to the European Court on points of law.

The most striking characteristic of European Community law is its complete integration into the municipal legal orders of its Member States. Community law, promulgated by the Council and Commission of the Community, is directly effective in the Member States, and prevails over Member States' laws in case of inconsistency. Member States' courts are obliged to give effect to it and to respect these principles of direct effect and supremacy. Accordingly, the Community legal order is (to borrow a term from the discussion of arbitration) 'mixed', in the sense that it is an order in which both States (and international organisations) and individuals and legal persons are full actors. To that extent it is utterly different from the WTO legal system. The inter-State obligations and the private rights and duties under EC Law form a seamless whole, integrated into a system in which both national and Community courts play distinct and complementary roles.

The European Community is by far the most sophisticated and complex of regional international organisations. That reflects its ambition to advance further into the area of political integration of the Member States, the early stages of which were secured by the establishment of the European Union by the Maastricht Treaty. That Treaty, the Treaty on European Union concluded in 1992, established the European Union by adding to the European Community proper (i.e., the integrated version of the European Economic Community, the European Coal and Steel Community, and EURATOM) two further pillars in which the Member States co-operate over, respectively, a Common Foreign and Security Policy, and Justice and Home Affairs. No other regional organisation has yet reached, or even adopted the explicit aim of reaching, such a degree of integration. There are, nonetheless, several other regional economic organisations with their own dispute settlement systems, which deserve brief mention.

2.2 COMESA—the Common Market for Eastern and Southern Africa

The most nearly comparable system is that created by the 1993 Treaty Establishing the Common Market for Eastern and Southern Africa (COMESA).[65] The COMESA States intend to secure the establishment of a customs union, removing (as does the European Community) obstacles to the free movement of goods, persons, services and capital, and to move towards eventual

---

[65] (1994) 33 *ILM* 1067. For an account of the development of COMESA and its relationship to the Southern African Customs Union (SACU), the Southern African Development Community (SADC), and the pan-continental African Economic Community (AEC), see M. R. A. Heiman, 'The drive towards regionalisation in Southern Africa: fictional reality' (1997) 9 *AJICL* 639.

monetary union. In addition, the treaty provides for co-operation and harmonisation of national policies and measures in a wide range of fields, including transport, industry, agriculture, and economic and social development. But the most striking aspect of the COMESA regime is that, again like the European Community, it provides for the direct effect within the legal systems of Member States of measures adopted by COMESA institutions.[66]

The jurisdiction of the Court of Justice established by the COMESA Treaty[67] is correspondingly broad. It has jurisdiction over inter-State disputes and disputes between the Member States and the COMESA Council (the body that adopts COMESA laws).[68] COMESA itself may take action against defaulting Member States: the Council is to decide, after an initial report on the situation by the Secretary-General, whether to handle the dispute itself or to refer it to the Court.[69] Any person resident in the Community may refer to the Court questions of the compatibility with the Treaty of measures taken by COMESA or its Member States.[70] There is in the Treaty no equivalent of the restrictive European Community law provisions on *locus standi,* requiring that the applicant show that he is directly and individually concerned by the measure impugned (although the COMESA Court may, of course, develop such restrictions in its case law); but there is a requirement that applicants must first exhaust local remedies in the national courts and tribunals of the Member State.[71] Courts and tribunals in Member States have a right, similar to that in article 177 of the European Community Treaty, to request preliminary rulings on the interpretation of the Treaty by the COMESA Court when necessary to enable them to give judgment in a case before them. The clear implication is that national courts will, like their European counterparts, apply COMESA law directly, as part of their national law.[72] The Court also has jurisdiction over staff cases and claims based on the non-contractual liability of COMESA,[73] and the power to give advisory opinions to COMESA and its Member States regarding questions of law arising from the provisions of the Treaty.[74]

The COMESA Court has on it only seven judges, of which only one may be a national of any one Member State, appointed for a five-year term with the possibility of one renewal for a further five years. The judges, and the President of the

---

[66] COMESA Treaty, (1994) 33 *ILM* 1067, art. 10.

[67] Ibid., arts. 19–44.

[68] Ibid., art. 24.

[69] Ibid., art. 25.

[70] Ibid., art. 26.

[71] Ibid.

[72] The COMESA Treaty, art. 29(2), gives decisions of the COMESA Court on the interpretation of the Treaty precedence over decisions of national courts.

[73] Ibid., art. 27.

[74] Ibid., art. 32.

Court, are appointed by the Authority, which consists of the Heads of State or Government of the Member States. Additional judges may be appointed at the request of the Court.[75]

2.3 ECOWAS—the Economic Community of West African States

A second notable regional economic system in Africa is ECOWAS, the Economic Community of West African States. The treaty establishing ECOWAS was concluded in 1975,[76] and amended in 1993.[77] ECOWAS has sixteen Member States.[78] The aims of ECOWAS are broad, including co-operation and harmonisation of national policies in economic fields such as agriculture, industry, natural resources and tourism, and the staged establishment of a customs union and of an economic and monetary union (in which respects it resembles the European Community) leading to co-operation in political, judicial, security and cultural matters (in which respects it resembles the expanded European Union).[79] Unlike the European Community and COMESA, ECOWAS does not prescribe measures that have direct effect in the legal orders of its Member States. Accordingly, disputes arising under the ECOWAS treaty are inter-State disputes, and do not have the mixed character of some European Community disputes resulting from the direct application of EC law to individuals and legal persons.

A Protocol to the ECOWAS Treaty on the Community Court of Justice was adopted in 1991.[80] Again unlike the position in the European Community, not all Member States are represented on the ECOWAS Court. It has seven judges, no two of whom may be of the same nationality, appointed by the ECOWAS Authority of Heads of State and Government from a list of nominees (who, in an unusual example of ageism in international tribunals, must be between the ages of 40 and 60 on appointment) submitted by Member States.[81] The judges, who serve for a term of five years, renewable once only, are independent of Member States and must be qualified for the highest judicial office or be jurists of recognised competence in international law.[82] The Court has jurisdiction over contentious cases between Member States or between Member States and ECOWAS institutions regarding the interpretation or application of the Treaty which are not

---

[75] Ibid., arts. 8, 20, 21.
[76] (1975) 14 *ILM* 1200.
[77] (1996) 8 *AJICL* 187; (1996) 35 *ILM* 660.
[78] Benin, Burkina Faso, Cape Verde, Côte d'Ivoire, The Gambia, Ghana, Guinea, Guinea Bissau, Liberia, Mali, Mauritania, Niger, Nigeria, Senegal, Sierra Leone and Togo.
[79] See the 1993 ECOWAS Treaty, arts. 25–68.
[80] (1996) 8 *AJICL* 228. See K. O. Kufuor, 'Securing Compliance with the Judgments of the ECOWAS Court of Justice' (1996) 8 *AJICL* 1.
[81] ECOWAS Treaty, 1993, arts. 1, 3.
[82] 1991 ECOWAS Court Protocol, arts. 3, 4.

settled amicably by direct agreement,[83] and cases instituted by the Authority of Heads of State and Government against a Member State or an ECOWAS institution in cases of failure to discharge treaty obligations, actions beyond the limits of authority, or abuse of powers conferred by the Treaty.[84] In 1991 this provision was amended slightly so as to give the Court express jurisdiction in respect of such cases brought by Member States on behalf of nationals, after attempts to reach an amicable settlement have failed—a competence that was doubtless implicit in the original, 1975, formula.[85] Also in the 1991 Protocol, the Court was given the power to render advisory opinions on 'questions of the Treaty'—presumably, questions of the interpretation and application of the provisions of the Treaty. [86]

2.4 Other African economic organisations

Provisions on dispute settlement, either similar to those in the ECOWAS Treaty or much less refined, can also be found in the 1992 Treaty of the Southern African Development Community,[87] the 1991 Treaty Establishing the African Economic Community (AEC),[88] the 1989 Treaty Establishing the Arab Mahgreb Union (UMA),[89] and the 1983 Treaty for the Establishment of the Economic Community of Central African States (CEEAC).[90]

The African regional economic organisations (and the pan-continental AEC) all adopt the same broad approach to dispute settlement: a court is established to decide upon questions of treaty interpretation and application in the context of inter-State disputes. They have plainly been inspired, to a greater or lesser degree, by the European Community dispute settlement system. The approach adopted in the 1992 Treaty establishing the North American Free Trade Area (NAFTA),[91]

---

[83] ECOWAS Treaty 1975, art. 56; ECOWAS Treaty 1993, art. 76; 1991 ECOWAS Court Protocol, art. 9.

[84] ECOWAS Treaty, 1993, art. 7(3)(g).

[85] ECOWAS Treaty 1993, art. 76; 1991 ECOWAS Court Protocol, art. 9.

[86] ECOWAS Treaty 1993, art. 76; 1991 ECOWAS Court Protocol, art. 10.

[87] (1993) 5 *AJICL* 418 (art. 32).

[88] (1991) 3 *AJICL* 792 (arts. 18, 87). See also the 1998 Protocol on the Relationship between the African Economic Community and the Regional Economic Communities (1998) 10 *AJICL* 157. The Protocol was signed on behalf of ECOWAS, SADC, COMESA, UMA, CEEAC (the Economic Community of Central African States), and IGAD (the Intergovernmental Authority for Development). See B. Thompson, 'Economic integration efforts in Africa: a milestone—the Abuja Treaty' (1993) 5 *AJICL* 743 (1993).

[89] The skeletal treaty can be found at (1989) 1 *Proceedings of the African Society of International & Comparative Law* 288 (art. 13).

[90] (1984) 23 *ILM* 945, arts. 16–18, 83.

[91] For the NAFTA Treaty, signed on 11 and 17 December 1992, see (1993) 32 *ILM* 289 and 605. See F. M. Abbott, *Law and policy of regional integration: the NAFTA and western hemispheric integration in the World Trade Organization system* (Dordrecht, 1995); L. A. Glick, *Understanding the North American Free Trade Agreement: legal and business consequences of NAFTA*, 2nd edn. (Deventer, 1994); J. J. Norton and T. L. Bloodworth (eds.), *NAFTA and beyond: a new framework for doing business in the Americas* (Dordrecht, 1995).

to which we turn next, is very different, and much more like the WTO than it is like the European Community system.[92]

2.5 NAFTA—the North American Free Trade Agreement

NAFTA, which established the free trade area between the USA, Canada and Mexico, entered into force in 1994. Its objects include the elimination of barriers to trade in goods and services, and the promotion of fair competition, investment, and the protection of intellectual property rights in the Member States.[93] It contains a number of distinct procedures for dispute settlement, which are intimately linked with the provisions for consultation and co-operation in the harmonisation and development of national economic policies and regulations. Here it is possible only to outline the most significant aspects of the NAFTA dispute settlement system.[94]

The main inter-State dispute settlement provisions appear in Chapter 20 of the 1992 NAFTA Treaty. That Chapter establishes a Free Trade Commission, on which each Member State has a cabinet-level representative, to oversee the implementation of the Agreement and resolve disputes concerning its interpretation or application.[95] Member States are obliged to overcome difficulties wherever possible through co-operation and consultation,[96] but a comprehensive dispute settlement procedure is provided in case they should not succeed in doing so. To the extent that the subject matter of the dispute falls both within the NAFTA and GATT (now the WTO) treaties, the dispute may be settled in either forum at the discretion of the complaining Party.[97]

First, consultation,[98] and good offices, mediation and conciliation by the Free Trade Commission[99] are available to the States Parties. Should those steps fail, the Parties may request the establishment by the Commission of a five-person Arbitral Panel.[100] If a third Party (in practice, the third Party, as there are only three Parties to NAFTA) has a substantial interest in the matter it is entitled to join the

---

[92] For a discussion of some of the differences between the WTO and NAFTA approaches see R. H. Steinberg, 'Trade-environment negotiations in the EU, NAFTA, and WTO: regional trajectories of rule development' (1997) 91 *AJIL* 231 at 245–8.

[93] 1992 NAFTA Treaty, art. 102.

[94] See further J. R. Holbein and D. J. Musch, *North American Free Trade Agreements: Dispute Settlement* (Dobbs Ferry, NY, 1992—loose-leaf); D. S. Huntington, 'Settling disputes under the North American Free Trade Agreement' (1993) 34 *Harvard International Law Journal* 407; J. I. Garvey, 'Trade law and quality of life—dispute resolution under the NAFTA Side Accords on Labor and the Environment' (1995) 89 *AJIL* 439.

[95] 1992 NAFTA Treaty, art. 2001.

[96] Ibid., art. 2003.

[97] Ibid., art. 2005.

[98] Ibid., art. 2006.

[99] Ibid., art. 2007.

[100] Ibid., art. 2008.

proceedings as a complaining party.[101] If the third Party does not intervene, it may not thereafter initiate or continue with a dispute settlement procedure under NAFTA or the WTO in respect of the same matter in the absence of a significant change in economic or commercial circumstances;[102] but the third Party is entitled to attend all hearings and to make written and oral submissions to a panel even if it is not a 'disputing party'.[103]

States Parties agree upon a roster of up to thirty panellists with expertise in law, international trade or other relevant fields.[104] The complaining Party or Parties choose two panellists who are nationals of the Party complained against, and the Party complained against chooses two panellists who are nationals of the complaining Party or Parties; and the disputing Parties agree upon the fifth panellist, who chairs the panel, failing which the State(s) on one side of the dispute is chosen by lot, and the State(s) so chosen chooses a chairperson who is not one of its (or their) nationals.[105]

The panel may seek technical information and advice from experts, and may establish a Scientific Review Board to give a written report on any factual issue concerning environmental, health, safety or other scientific matters raised by a disputing party in the proceedings.[106] The panel proceeds in a judicial fashion, and first renders an Initial Report setting out its findings of fact, its determination as to whether the measure at issue is inconsistent with the NAFTA Treaty or nullifies or impairs benefits which the complaining Party or Parties could reasonably have expected to accrue under the Treaty, and the panel's recommendations for the resolution of the dispute.[107] It then receives the comments of the Parties, in the light of which it may hold further hearings and reconsider its report.[108] It then presents its Final Report to the Free Trade Commission.[109] Unless the Parties agree otherwise, the Initial Report is to be presented within ninety days of the appointment of the last panellist, and the Final Report within a further thirty days.

On receipt of the Final Report the Parties must agree upon the resolution of the dispute, in conformity with the determinations and recommendations of the panel.[110] As in the WTO system, the suspension of benefits of equivalent effect to the impugned measure may operate as a sanction.[111]

---

[101] 1992 NAFTA Treaty, art. 2008(3).
[102] Ibid., art. 2008(4).
[103] Ibid., art. 2013.
[104] Ibid., art. 2009.
[105] Ibid., art. 2011.
[106] Ibid., arts. 2014, 2015.
[107] Ibid., art. 2016 and Annex 2004.
[108] Ibid., art. 2016.
[109] Ibid., art. 2017.
[110] Ibid., art. 2018.
[111] Ibid., art. 2019.

Special provision is made for the settlement of disputes concerning antidumping and countervailing duty obligations under the NAFTA Treaty. Such disputes are referred to a bi-national panel, drawn from a roster of retired judges who are citizens of the States Parties. Unlike the Chapter 20 Arbitral Panels, States may nominate whomsoever they choose to the bi-national panel, but the other States involved have a right of peremptory challenge; and if this results in vacancies on the panel, the remaining members are chosen by lot from among the persons nominated to the roster by the State which has failed to secure the appointment of its complement of panellists.[112] Determinations that antidumping or countervailing duties are to be imposed are made initially by bodies within each of the States Parties; but an 'involved (State) Party' may request that a final determination of such a domestic body, or an amendment to the State's legislation, be reviewed for its compatibility with the NAFTA Treaty or the GATT (now WTO Treaty) by a bi-national panel.[113] States may make such a request on their own initiative and (in an interesting reversal of the local remedies rule) must make a request if asked to do so by a person who would otherwise have the right to such a judicial review under the domestic law of the State: such domestic review is replaced by the bi-national panel procedure.[114]

Bi-national panel procedures are subject to strict time limits, which should result in the declaratory ruling being given by the panel in about ten months[115]—considerably shorter than the time taken for domestic review in the United States; and there are special provisions to prevent the subversion of the process by unnecessary delay.[116] Decisions of the bi-national panels are binding on the States, although the Treaty provides an extraordinary challenge procedure where it is alleged that the bi-national panel acted improperly.[117]

The NAFTA Treaty also provides for 'mixed arbitrations' of the kind that we discussed in previous chapters. Chapter 11 sets out basic safeguards for investments in NAFTA States, including entitlements to national and Most Favoured Nation treatment and safeguards against unlawful expropriation.[118] In addition to the inter-State procedures under Chapter 20 of the Treaty, Chapter 11 provides for investors of one State Party themselves to initiate proceedings in respect of disputes concerning the treatment of their investments by another State Party under the Treaty. Any dispute not resolved by negotiation may be submitted to arbitration.[119] The investor may choose between arbitration under ICSID or the ICSID

---

[112] Ibid., Annex 1901.2.
[113] Ibid., arts. 1903, 1904.
[114] Ibid., art. 1904(1), (5), (11).
[115] Ibid., art. 1904.
[116] Ibid., art. 1905.
[117] Ibid., art. 1904(9), (13), and Annex 1904.13.
[118] Ibid., arts. 1101–14.
[119] Ibid., arts. 1116–19.

Additional Facility or UNCITRAL Rules.[120] The States Parties have in NAFTA article 1122 given their consent to each of these alternative forms of arbitration: investors may give their consent to the arbitration when they initiate proceedings.[121] If the investor does opt for arbitration under the NAFTA treaty, it may not resort to other dispute settlement procedures: in other words, recourse to local remedies is precluded. Investors may present claims on their own behalf or on behalf of enterprises that are established in another State Party and which they own or control, provided that the enterprise concerned consents.[122] A Canadian company, for example, might bring a claim against the United States in respect of an alleged violation of the investment rights secured by the NAFTA Treaty of a US corporation controlled by the Canadian company: the provision thus has an effect similar to that of the ICSID 'foreign control' clause.[123]

The NAFTA Treaty regulates these mixed arbitral procedures in considerable detail, to ensure that the scheme integrates satisfactorily with the ICSID and UNCITRAL rules. For instance, the Secretary-General of ICSID is made the appointing authority, acting in circumstances where the parties fail to appoint or agree upon the appointment of an arbitrator;[124] other States Parties are entitled to notice of the proceedings;[125] and, in what is the most striking innovation, provision is made for the compulsory consolidation of arbitral proceedings that have a question of law or of fact in common, in the interests of the fair and efficient resolution of the claims.[126] Tribunals established under the NAFTA Treaty are to apply the Treaty 'and applicable rules of international law',[127] and if certain questions of interpretation of the Treaty arise they must be remitted by the arbitral tribunal to the Free Trade Commission, whose interpretations of the NAFTA treaty are binding.[128] Awards, which may order only monetary damages or restitution,[129] are enforceable under the procedures in the ICSID Convention, the 1958 New York Convention, or the 1975 Inter-American (Panama) Convention on International Commercial Arbitration.[130] If a State Party does not comply with an award, an inter-State arbitral panel may be established at the instance of the

---

[120] 1992 NAFTA Treaty, art. 1120. The option of ICSID Additional Facility arbitration is necessary because, as of June 1998, neither Canada nor Mexico was a party to the ICSID Convention. The first Additional Facility cases were initiated in 1997: see chapter four, p. 62, above.

[121] 1992 NAFTA Treaty, art. 1121. A similar provision appears in the European Energy Charter, art. 26: see (1995) 34 *ILM* 360 and G. Turner, 'Investment Protection through Arbitration' [1998] *Int. ALR* 166.

[122] 1992 NAFTA Treaty, arts. 1112, 1121.

[123] See above, chapter four, p. 65.

[124] 1992 NAFTA Treaty, art. 1124.

[125] Ibid., arts. 1127, 1129.

[126] Ibid., art. 1126. See further chapter eight, p. 209 below.

[127] 1992 NAFTA Treaty, art. 1131.

[128] Ibid., arts. 1131, 1132.

[129] Ibid., art. 1135.

[130] Ibid., art. 1136. See further chapters four, p. 73 above, and eight, p. 266 below.

investor's State to rule on the matter.[131] A broadly comparable, and in some respects more complex, dispute settlement scheme was proposed for the OECD's Multilateral Agreement on Investment, before negotiations on the draft were abandoned at the end of 1998.[132]

Two other provisions of the NAFTA Treaty merit mention here. First, the Free Trade Commission is empowered to deliver interpretations of the Treaty to any domestic tribunal in a Member State that has to decide upon a question of the interpretation or application of the Treaty.[133] This process is similar to that under article 177 of the EC Treaty; but it seems that the Commission's interpretation does not (as a matter of treaty obligation, at least) bind the domestic tribunal. It is clearly envisaged that such questions will regularly arise incidentally in domestic proceedings,[134] although States Parties are forbidden to provide any (direct) rights of action under their domestic laws for breaches of the Treaty resulting from measures adopted by another State Party.[135]

Secondly, there are noteworthy provisions relating to the procedures for dealing with certain categories of dispute, such as complaints concerning surges in imports of goods that cause serious injury to domestic producers.[136] Entities, including affected companies and representatives of domestic industries, may initiate 'Emergency Action Proceedings', which may lead to the adoption of temporary emergency measures to reduce the import surge. Such proceedings may also be initiated by the States themselves. Rather than laying down the detailed rules for such proceedings, the NAFTA Treaty simply requires Member States to establish their own domestic procedures and prescribes certain basic rules and principles that must feature in the domestic system.[137] This approach is akin to the harmonisation of legal procedures in Member States, and is an elegant solution to the problems which can arise when it is sought to integrate international judicial procedures into a range of widely differing national legal systems. A similar approach is adopted in relation to disputes that might arise concerning matters such as intellectual property rights,[138] and publishing of and appeals within the State concerned against decisions of its own governmental bodies applying NAFTA trade measures.[139]

---

[131] 1992 NAFTA Treaty, arts. 1136, 2008.

[132] See the OECD web site, <http://www.oecd.org/daf/cmis/mai/negtext.htm>.

[133] 1992 NAFTA Treaty, art. 2020.

[134] See ibid., art. 2022, which encourages the use of arbitration and acceptance of the 1958 New York Convention or the 1975 Inter-American Convention on International Commercial Arbitration in order to render arbitration effective.

[135] 1992 NAFTA Treaty, art. 2021.

[136] Ibid., Chapter 8.

[137] Ibid., art. 803 and Annex 803.3.

[138] Ibid., arts. 1714–18.

[139] Ibid., arts. 1801–6.

2.6 Mercosur—Mercado Común del Sur/the Southern Common Market

The NAFTA Treaty is much the most sophisticated of the American regional trade agreements. The 1991 Mercosur Agreement,[140] in contrast, provided simply that disputes are to be settled by direct negotiations, failing which the Council of the Common Market (the 'Common Market Group') is to make recommendations.[141] That provision was amplified in the Protocol of Brasilia signed on 17 December 1991,[142] itself subsequently developed by the Protocol of Ouro Preto of 17 December 1994. The most notable provision of the revised system is that complaints of breaches of the Treaty, made either by States or individuals within the Mercosur States, are to be submitted first to the National Sections of the inter-State Mercosur Trade Commission, and then, if the matter is not resolved, to the Trade Commission itself, which rules on the matter if it can reach a consensus on the matter. If the Trade Commission cannot reach a consensus the matter is referred to the intergovernmental Common Market Group for a decision or, ultimately, to the *ad hoc* Arbitration Panel established under the Protocol of Brasilia and based in Asunción, Paraguay.[143] Mercosur also has a dispute system, established by the Protocol of Colonia, for mixed arbitrations concerning investment disputes.[144]

There are many other regional trade organisations, of varying degrees of vitality, whose constitutions provide for the settlement of disputes between their members.[145] In addition, there are dispute settlement systems in other economic

---

[140] Argentina–Brazil–Paraguay–Uruguay, Treaty establishing a Common Market, 26 March 1991 (the Treaty of Asunción), (1991) 30 *ILM* 1041. Bolivia and Chile are associate members. See M. Haines-Ferrari, 'Mercosur: a new model of Latin American economic integration' 25 *Case Western Journal of International Law* 413.

[141] Mercosur Treaty, 1991, Annex III, (1991) 30 *ILM* 1041.

[142] Text at < http://www.sice.oas.org/root/trade/mrcsrs/decisions/AN0191.STM>.

[143] Protocol of Ouro Preto, Annex, (1995) 34 *ILM* 1244. See C. A. Bizai and R. B. Mattarollo, 'Dispute resolution in Mercosur' [1996] *International Trade Law and Regulation* 150; and see G. Mancero-Bucheli, 'Anti-competitive practices by private undertakings in ANCOM and MERCO-SUR: an analysis from the perspective of EC Law' (1998) 47 *ICLQ* 149 for a discussion of the procedure in a specific context.

[144] Text at <http://www.sice.oas.org/root/trade/mrcsrs/decisions/AN1193.STM>: see art. 9. The scheme is similar to that in the NAFTA treaty.

[145] See, for example, the 1973 Treaty Establishing the Caribbean Community and Common Market (CARICOM), Annex, Chapter Two, arts. 11, 12, which provide for the arbitration of disputes; (1973) 12 *ILM* 1033; reproduced in *Zamora & Brand*, vol. 2, 643 at 664. Cf. the 1976 Treaty of Amity and Co-operation in Southeast Asia, of the Association of Southeast Asian Nations (ASEAN), arts. 13–18, which provides for the use of good offices, mediation, inquiry and conciliation, with the consent of all Parties concerned; (1988) 27 *ILM* 160, reproduced in *Zamora & Brand*, vol. 2, 699.

treaties, although these commonly utilise existing institutions, such as negotiation and mediation,[146] arbitration,[147] or the International Court of Justice.[148]

3. International financial disputes

It is a curiosity of the international system that disputes arising from international monetary relations are handled in a fundamentally different way from those concerning international trade relations.

3.1 The IMF

The Articles of the International Monetary Fund[149] contain only the most attenuated of dispute settlement provisions. The IMF is charged with the promotion of currency exchange stability and multilateral payments systems, in order to facilitate the expansion and balanced growth of trade and to minimise disequilibrium in the international balances of payments of its members.[150] It does so by allocating to Member States quotas, measured in units of account calculated in relation to a basket of currencies and known as Special Drawing Rights (SDRs). Members pay their quotas to the Fund, mostly (as to 75 per cent) in their own currency,[151] and in addition the IMF itself may borrow money on world markets.[152] In essence, a Member State needing foreign currency to pay for imports buys the foreign currency using its own currency or the SDRs allocated to it, and is obliged to repay the 'loan' by repurchasing its own currency at a future date and at an exchange rate based on the SDR.[153] Members undertake a number of general obligations, such as the duties not to impose foreign exchange restrictions without the approval of the IMF, to make unenforceable under their domestic law exchange contracts contrary to the exchange control regulations of the State whose currency is the subject of the contract, and to avoid discriminatory currency practices.[154] These duties are reinforced by obligations to supply information to the IMF and to

---

[146] See, e.g., the 1995 Agreement on Co-operation for the Sustainable Development of the Mekong River Basin, arts. 34 and 35, (1995) 34 *ILM* 864.

[147] See, e.g., the 1989 Basel Convention on the Control of Transboundary Movements of Hazardous Wastes and their Disposal, art. 20 and Annex VI, (1989) 28 *ILM* 649.

[148] See, e.g., the 1970 European Patent Co-operation Treaty, art. 59; (1970) 9 *ILM* 978, reproduced in *Zamora & Brand*, vol. 2, 833; the 1971 Universal Copyright Convention, art. XV; 25 *United States Treaties* 1341, reproduced in *Zamora & Brand*, vol. 2, 813.

[149] Reproduced in *Zamora & Brand*, vol. 1, 321.

[150] Art. I.

[151] Art. III.

[152] See the General Arrangements to Borrow, in *Zamora & Brand*, vol. 1, 401. Note para. 20, requiring that questions of interpretation under the arrangements 'shall be settled to the mutual satisfaction of the Fund, the participant raising the question, and all other participants'.

[153] Art. V.

[154] Art. VIII.

consult with the Fund and other members concerning any difficulties that might arise.[155]

Disputes are handled by an internal, non-judicial procedure. Article XXIX provides that any question of the interpretation of the articles is to be submitted (the procedure is compulsory) for decision to the Executive Board, on which sit the five Executive Directors appointed by the Member States with the largest quotas and fifteen others elected by the other Member States.[156] Any member particularly affected by the question has a right to be represented if it is not entitled to appoint an Executive Director. There is a rarely used right of appeal for any member against a ruling of the Executive Board, to the Board of Governors, on which sit representatives of every Member State. The Board refers the question to the Committee on Interpretation.[157] The decision of the Committee stands unless it is overturned by a decision carried by 85 per cent of the votes of the Board of Governors (votes of members are weighted according to the size of their IMF quotas[158]). The Board's decision is final. This procedure is supplemented by article VIII of the 1947 Agreement between the United Nations and the International Monetary Fund, which authorises the IMF to seek an advisory opinion from the International Court of Justice under article 65 of the ICJ Statute on 'any legal questions arising within the scope of the Fund's activities other than questions relating to the relationship between the Fund and the United Nations or any specialised agency'.[159] That power has never been used. Disputes between the Fund and a member that has withdrawn from it, or between the Fund and any member should the Fund ever be liquidated, may, again under article XXIX of the IMF Articles, be submitted to arbitration. This power has never been used.

Failures by Member States to comply with Fund obligations are also dealt with internally. For example, the Fund has the power under articles V(5), VI(1), XIV(3) and XXIII(2) to suspend the rights of a member to use Fund facilities, including the use of SDRs for currency swaps. The defaulting party is given the right to present its case, but does not have the right to use the Fund facilities until the matter is resolved. The Fund has the power under article XXVI (as amended in 1992)[160] to declare a defaulting member ineligible to use Fund facilities. A member persisting, after a declaration of ineligibility to use Fund resources, in its failure to comply with its IMF obligations may have its voting rights and certain other rights of participation suspended, by a decision of 70 per cent of the Fund's voting power. After a

---

[155] e.g., Arts. VIII (5)–(7), XI(2), XIV, XVI(3), XXII.

[156] For the composition of the Executive Board, see art. XII.

[157] See J. Gold, *The Rule of Law in the International Monetary Fund* (IMF Pamphlet No. 32, 1980), 43–51.

[158] Art. XII(5).

[159] For the settlement of intra-UN disputes, see art. 58 of the UN Charter; and see B. Simma (ed.), *The Charter of the United Nations: A Commentary* (Oxford, 1995), 816–19.

[160] For the text of the 1992 amendments see (1992) 31 *ILM* 1307.

reasonable period following suspension, the defaulting State may be required to withdraw from membership of the Fund, by a decision of the Board of Governors carried by a majority holding 85 per cent of the total votes in the IMF.

The IMF system, then, is based upon notification and consultation and the consideration by the expert policy-making organs of complaints made either by Member States or by the IMF itself. While differences concerning Fund policies are common, recognisable complaints are rare, and there is a strong preference for dealing with them informally. The emphasis is heavily upon the resolution of difficulties as a part of the continuing development of strategies and policies for advancing the Fund's goals.

3.2 The World Bank

The World Bank—the International Bank for Reconstruction and Development (IBRD)—has a system rather different from that of the IMF, as a result of its different role. The World Bank provides loans in the true sense—loans of money that the borrower does not otherwise have, rather than conversions of money it does have into a foreign currency. Questions of interpretation of the Bank's Articles of Agreement[161] are, as in the case of the IMF, referred to the Bank's Executive Directors with a right of appeal to the Board of Governors. There is provision, again similar to that in the IMF, for the arbitration of disputes arising between the Bank and withdrawing members, and between the Bank and any members on the winding up of the Bank.[162] There are also similar provisions on the suspension of rights of membership.[163]

The Bank operates by concluding loan agreements with Member States, and the dispute settlement provisions relating to specific agreements are of more practical significance than those relating to the Articles of Agreement. In the past the general approach has been confined to providing for the submission of such disputes to arbitration.[164] Concerned at criticisms of the lack of accountability and transparency in World Bank projects that had a significant impact on the lives of communities in the project area, in 1993 the World Bank established a novel and remarkable procedure—the Inspection Panel.[165]

---

[161] Reproduced in *Zamora & Brand*, vol. 1, 427.

[162] Art. IX.

[163] Art. VI.

[164] See *International Disputes: The Legal Aspects. Report of a Study Group of the David Davies Memorial Institute of International Studies* (London, 1972), 228.

[165] Technically, the initiative took the form of parallel identical resolutions of the IBRD and the International Development Association (IDA), one of the World Bank affiliates which, together with the International Financial Corporation and the Multilateral Investment Guarantee Agency make up the World Bank Group. IBRD Resolution No. 93–10 and IDA Resolution No. IDA 93–6, both of 22 September 1993 (hereafter in this section, 1993 Resolution), reproduced in (1995) 34 *ILM* 520. See K. V. S. K. Nathan, 'The World Bank Inspection Panel: court or quango?' (1995) 12(2) *Journal of International Arbitration* 135.

The Inspection Panel consists of three Inspectors, nominated by the President of the World Bank and appointed by the Executive Directors. Its role is described in the Operating Procedures adopted by the Inspection Panel in 1994:

> The Panel has authority to receive Requests which complain of a violation of the Bank's policies and procedures[166] from the following people or entities:
>
> (a) any group of two or more people in the country where the bank-financed project is located who believe that as a result of the Bank's violation their rights or interests have been, or are likely to be adversely affected in a direct and material way. They may be an organisation, association, society or other grouping of individuals; or
> (b) a duly appointed local representative acting on explicit instructions as the agent of adversely affected people; or
> (c) in the exceptional case [where there is no adequate or appropriate representation in the country where the project is located] a foreign representative acting as agent of adversely affected people; or
> (d) an Executive Director of the Bank in special cases of serious alleged violations of the bank's policies and procedures.[167]

The violation may take the form of a failure by the Bank to check on the borrower's fulfilment of its obligations under the loan agreement, as well as failures committed directly by the Bank.[168]

The chairperson of the Inspection Panel, to whom the Request must be addressed, may refuse to register Requests that are clearly outside the panel's mandate, or are filed after 95 per cent of the loan has been disbursed, or are manifestly absurd or anonymous, or that emanate from an unqualified requester, or (in an interesting analogue to the local remedies rule) where no effort has first been made to resolve the matter with the Bank's Management.[169] Requests that are registered are notified promptly to the Bank's Management, which has twenty-one days within which to respond.[170] Within a further twenty-one days the Inspection Panel, which is an investigative and not a judicial body, must conduct a preliminary review of the case, without investigating Management actions in depth, and recommend to the Executive Directors whether a full investigation should take place.[171] The materiality of the (threatened) damage, the seriousness of the alleged breach, and the adequacy of the Management's proposed remedial actions are to

---

[166] The Bank's Operational Policies, Bank Procedures and Operational Directives are published.

[167] The Inspection Panel for the International Bank for Reconstruction and Development, International Development Association: Operating Procedures (hereafter in this section, Operating Procedures) para. 4, (1995) 34 *ILM* 510. The 'two or more people' mentioned in (a) must represent some commonality of interests, and not simply their own interests: see the Memorandum by the IBRD Senior Vice-President and General Counsel, (1995) 34 *ILM* 525, at 527.

[168] See the 1993 Resolution, para. 12.

[169] Operating Procedures, (1995) 34 *ILM* 510, paras. 2, 16–22.

[170] Ibid., paras. 17, 18, 27–9.

[171] Ibid., paras. 30–7. The role of the Inspection Panel and the interpretation of its Operating Procedures were discussed in the Memorandum by the IBRD Senior Vice-President and General Counsel: (1995) 34 *ILM* 525.

be taken into account in framing the recommendation.[172] The Inspection Panel may recommend that no further action be taken if the Management has dealt appropriately with the subject matter of the Request and has either demonstrated clearly that it followed Bank policies and procedures or admitted its failure to do so but proposed remedial action which the panel judges will adequately correct the failure and any adverse effects that the failure has already caused.[173]

The Board of Executive Directors appears to have an unconstrained discretion in deciding whether or not to accept the Inspection Panel's recommendation: thus, it may decide to establish an investigation even where the panel has not recommended it, and vice versa.[174] Where it decides upon an investigation, the matter is remitted to the Inspection Panel. The Inspection Panel has wide-ranging powers to obtain information in various ways, including the holding of public meetings in the project area; and any member of the public may supply the Inspection Panel with information that they believe relevant to the investigation.[175] After the Inspection Panel's report is submitted to the Board, the Bank Management has six weeks in which to send its response to the Board. The Board then decides upon what action, if any, is necessary. The Inspection Panel's Report, the Management's recommendations, and the Board's decision are all published.[176]

The first case before the Inspection Panel, in 1994, concerned the Arun III hydroelectric project in Nepal, and subsequent Requests have concerned projects such as the Power VI project in Tanzania, the Rondonia Natural Resources Management project in Brazil, and the Hydroelectric Dams in the Biobio River project in Chile.[177] These procedures, although they may appear formal, are in essence no more than an institutionalised consultation process. The Bank decides how it is to respond to the complaint, and the role of the Inspection Panel is to put the case clearly before the Bank's Executive Directors. That is not to say that the new system is insignificant: on the contrary, it is an important step towards securing transparency and fairness in the operations of international organisations, bold in its involvement of 'communities' in the process. It may prove to be a powerful influence on developments in other organisations.

3.3 The Multilateral Investment Guarantee Agency (MIGA)

The Multilateral Investment Guarantee Agency (MIGA), a member of the World Bank Group of organisations, was established by Convention in 1985[178] to pro-

---

[172] Operating Procedures, para. 35.
[173] Ibid., para. 33.
[174] Ibid., para. 39.
[175] Ibid., paras. 42–51.
[176] Ibid., paras. 52–7.
[177] Current information can be found on the internet at www.worldbank.org.
[178] For the text of the MIGA Convention see (1985) 24 *ILM* 1598; also reproduced in *Zamora & Brand*, vol. 1, 497.

vide foreign investors with financial guarantees against non-commercial risks. These include, for instance, currency transfer risks arising from restrictions and delays in conversion and transfer of local currency; expropriation; war risks; and breaches or repudiation of contracts where the investor has no access to a competent court or arbitral forum or is unable to enforce the forum's decision.[179] Investors pay a premium to secure insurance cover under a contract of guarantee made with MIGA.[180] If MIGA compensates the investor under the contract, it becomes subrogated to the rights of the investor against the host State.[181]

Disputes concerning the interpretation of the MIGA Convention follow the IMF pattern of reference to the MIGA Board.[182] Disputes between MIGA and the investor arising from a contract of guarantee are to be settled by arbitration in accordance with the rules set out in the contract.[183] Disputes between MIGA and its Member States are more complex. If the dispute arises between a Member State and MIGA in its capacity as subrogee the procedures in Annex II to the MIGA Convention are to be followed, unless some other method is agreed.[184] Annex II prescribes, first, negotiation. If the dispute is not resolved within 120 days by negotiation, either party may submit it to conciliation (to which the parties may also agree to have recourse in place of negotiation). If the parties cannot agree upon a conciliator, they may jointly request the Secretary-General of ICSID or the President of the ICJ to make the appointment; and unless otherwise agreed the conciliator is to determine the rules of procedure, being guided by the ICSID Conciliation Rules.[185] If the parties do refer the dispute to conciliation, they may not have recourse to arbitration, which is the third possible stage in the process, unless the conciliator fails to report within 180 days of appointment or the parties fail within 60 days after receipt of the conciliator's report to settle the dispute. If they do not choose to resort to conciliation, they may proceed straight to arbitration. Arbitration may be initiated by notice by either party. Each party nominates an arbitrator, agreeing on a third to act as President of the tribunal. In default of such appointments or agreement, the arbitrators are appointed by the Secretary-General of ICSID. The arbitration follows the broad lines of the ICSID procedures. Thus, the tribunal is to apply 'the provisions of [the MIGA] Convention, any relevant agreement between the parties to the dispute, the Agency's by-laws and regulations, the applicable rules of international law, the domestic law of the member concerned as well as the applicable provisions of the investment contract, if any'. The reference to the contract allows the parties the freedom to choose

---

[179] MIGA Convention, arts. 2, 11.
[180] Ibid., art. 16.
[181] Ibid., art. 18.
[182] Ibid., art. 56.
[183] Ibid., art. 58.
[184] Ibid., art. 57(2).
[185] On ICSID, see chapter four, pp. 59–73 above.

some other law to govern the contract. Awards are final, binding and enforceable as if they were final court judgments, in all Member States.[186] Any other disputes between Member States and MIGA, not covered by the procedure for interpretation of the Convention, are also to be resolved by the Annex II procedures.

4. Concluding remarks

The foregoing account by no means exhausts the range of dispute settlement procedures in international economic agreements. There are procedures of considerable interest in institutions such as the International Labour Organisation (ILO), whose Governing Body (composed of representatives of government, of employers and of workers from each Member State) appoints Commissions of Inquiry to investigate complaints of non-compliance by Member States with ILO obligations.[187] There are other institutions that simply apply or adapt more traditional dispute settlement procedures to their own particular situation, in the way that the Common Fund for Commodities Agreement provides for questions of the interpretation or application of the Agreement to be decided by the Executive Board, coupled with a right for any Member to have the matter referred for a final decision to the Governing Council (or, if the Council is unable to reach a decision by a three-quarters majority, by arbitration).[188] And there are institutions that are, in effect, concretised conflicts: the various international commodity agreements, for instance, institutionalise the conflict between producers and consumers, so that the working of the institution is a continuing exercise in conflict management. Space precludes the further consideration of these important and fascinating bodies here; but the examples given in this chapter will serve as an introduction to the main procedures for the settlement of disputes in the economic sphere.

---

[186] MIGA Convention, Annex II.
[187] Constitution of the ILO, arts. 26–34; and see the ILO web site for details of the work of Commissions of Inquiry: <http://www.ilo.org>.
[188] UN Doc. TD/IPC/CF/CONF.24, arts. 52, 53.

7

THE INTERNATIONAL COURT
OF JUSTICE

1. Participation	124
2. Composition of the Court and election of judges: Dismissal	126
3. Sittings: Chambers	127
4. Disqualification of judges	129
5. *Ad hoc* judges	130
6. President; Vice-President; Registrar; Seat	131
7. Competence and jurisdiction in contentious cases	132
7.1 All cases which the parties refer to the Court	133
7.2 Matters specially provided for in the UN Charter	135
7.3 *Forum prorogatum*	136
7.4 Treaties or conventions in force	137
7.5 'Transferred' jurisdiction	139
7.6 The Optional Clause	140
8. Admissibility	155
8.1 Hypothetical nature of the case	156
8.2 The case has become 'moot'	157
8.3 Lack of interest in the subject matter	157
8.4 Legal interest of a third State	158
8.5 Other examples	161
9. Intervention	162
9.1 Construction of a convention	163
9.2 An interest of a legal nature	164
10. Interim (provisional) measures of protection	168
10.1 Jurisdiction	169
10.2 The exercise of discretion	171
10.3 The scope of interim measures	173
10.4 Relationship to the claim on the merits	174
10.5 Enforcement of interim measures	174
11. Procedure of the Court	175
12. Effect of judgments	177
13. Enforcement of judgments	178

14. Interpretation and revision of judgments   179

15. Non-appearance   180

16. Advisory Opinions   182

The International Court of Justice was created in 1945 by its Statute, which forms part of the Charter of the United Nations.[1] Unlike its predecessor, the Permanent Court of International Justice, which existed from 1923 to 1945 during the life of the League of Nations, but which was not an organ of the League, the International Court is the principal judicial organ of the United Nations (Charter, article 92). The Court has its own Rules of Procedure, which it establishes within the framework of the Statute and which it can alter. The Rules presently in force are those of 1978.[2]

1. Participation

The UN Charter, article 93, provides that two classes of State may become parties to the Statute of the Court. These are (a) all members of the United Nations, which are *ipso facto* parties to the Statute, and (b) non-members, which may become parties on conditions to be determined in the case of each State by the General Assembly on the recommendation of the Security Council. San Marino and Switzerland became parties by the latter route. (Liechtenstein, which was such a party, is now a member of the United Nations.)

By the Statute, article 35, the Court is open (a) to all parties to the Statute, and (b) to other States, subject to conditions laid down by the Security Council, which

---

[1] The Statute is almost identical with that of its predecessor, the PCIJ, which was drafted in 1920 by a Committee of Jurists. The rules governing amendment of the Statute are those which govern amendment of the UN Charter itself (Charter, arts. 108–9), so making the Statute virtually unalterable. The Charter's provisions concerned with the Court are contained in Ch. XIV, arts. 92–6. A prime source of information about the Court is the annual *Yearbook of the International Court of Justice*, published by the United Nations. For general discussions of the role of the Court see L. Gross, *The Future of the International Court of Justice* (Dobbs Ferry, NY, 1976); V. Lowe and M. Fitzmaurice (eds.), *Fifty Years of the International Court of Justice* (Cambridge, 1996) (hereafter, *Fifty Years of the ICJ*); A. S. Muller, D. Rais, and J. M. Thuranszky (eds.), *The International Court of Justice. Its Future Role after Fifty Years* (The Hague, 1997); Sir R. Jennings, 'The Role of the International Court of Justice' (1997) 68 *BYIL* 1. See also G. Z. Capaldo (ed.), *Repertory of Decisions of the International Court of Justice (1947–1992)*, 2 vols. (Dordrecht, 1995).

[2] See ICJ Acts and Documents No. 5 (1989), 93, to be found also in S. Rosenne, *Documents on the International Court of Justice*, 3rd edn. (1st bilingual edition) (Dordrecht, 1994) 205. See also S. Rosenne, *Law and Practice of the International Court of Justice*, 3rd edn. (The Hague, 1997), vol. 4, 1821; G. Guyomar, *Commentaire du Règlement de la Cour Internationale de Justice* (Paris, 1983); S. Rosenne, *Procedure in the International Court: a commentary on the 1978 Rules of the International Court of Justice* (The Hague, 1983).

must not place them in a position of inequality before the Court. Examples of States which were allowed to participate in proceedings before they became members of the UN are: Albania, in the *Corfu Channel* case (1949), Italy, in the *Monetary Gold* case (1954), and the Federal Republic of Germany, in the *North Sea Continental Shelf* cases (1969).

By becoming a party to the Statute, a State accepts the jurisdiction of the court over, and the exercise of its powers in, certain matters. These are: first, the jurisdiction of the Court to determine its own jurisdiction (*compétence de la compétence*) (article 36(b)),[3] secondly, its jurisdiction to indicate interim (or provisional) measures of protection (article 41),[4] and thirdly, its power to allow intervention in proceedings by a third State which has an interest of a legal nature which may be affected by the decision in the case (article 62).[5] However, as will be seen, the mere fact that a State has become a party to the Statute does not give the Court jurisdiction to adjudicate on a particular dispute to which that State is a party. It is necessary that the parties to the dispute have agreed to the Court exercising its jurisdiction in respect of that dispute.[6]

2. Composition of the Court and election of judges: Dismissal

Article 2 of the Statute states that the Court shall consist of a body of independent judges, i.e. independent of their national States, who are (a) elected regardless of nationality, and (b) of high moral character, and who (c) either (i) 'possess the qualifications required in their respective countries for appointment to the highest judicial offices', such as English barristers of sufficient seniority, or (ii) are 'jurisconsults of recognised competence in international law', such as professors of the subject. It will be seen from article 2(c)(i) that knowledge of international law is not required, although it is usual for judges of the Court to have a specialist knowledge of the subject. Of the six British nationals who have been judges of the Court, five were professors (three at Cambridge, one at Oxford and one at London) and the fifth had been legal adviser to the Foreign Office.

Article 3 states that there shall be fifteen judges and that no two may be nationals of the same State. In fact, election is usually dependent on regional arrangement and a desire to secure the representation of the main legal systems of the world. At the present time (1998), this distribution is five Western (USA, France, Germany, Netherlands, United Kingdom), three African (one representing the Francophone civil law systems, one the Anglophone common law systems and one

---

[3] See p. 144, and chapter eight, p. 227, below.
[4] See p. 168, and chapter eight, p. 248, below.
[5] See p. 164, below.
[6] See p. 132, below.

representative of Islamic law systems), three Asian, two Eastern European and two Latin American judges. Among the judges there is almost always one judge of the nationality of each of the permanent members of the UN Security Council, USA, Russia, UK, France and China, though China had no representation from 1967–85.

The election of judges is governed by articles 4–15 of the Statute. It is effected by the General Assembly and the Security Council acting and voting separately. The main provision is that candidates who secure an absolute majority of votes in both organs are elected.[7] Judges are elected for nine years; one-third of the Court retires by rotation every three years. Casual vacancies are filled in the same way and a judge who is elected to fill a casual vacancy serves until the date at which his predecessor would have retired. Candidates are nominated not, as are members of governing bodies of other international organisations, by States but by the national groups of the Permanent Court of Arbitration, these being the panels of individuals nominated by States party to the Hague Convention on the Pacific Settlement of Disputes 1907.[8] This is intended to insulate the election from direct interference by States, but it is a highly theoretical form of insulation since States usually get who they want as nominees.

By article 18 of the Statute a member of the Court may be dismissed by the other members, but only if, in the opinion of the other members, he has ceased to fulfil the required conditions.

3. Sittings: Chambers

Normally, the full court sits to hear cases, although the quorum consists of only nine members (Statute, article 25). Article 26 enables the Court to form Chambers of two kinds. First, article 26(1) states that the Court 'may from time to time form one or more Chambers, composed of three or more judges as the Court may determine, for dealing with particular categories of cases'. The first such Chamber was created in July 1993 to deal with environmental cases.[9] Article 26(2) states that the Court 'may at any time' form an *ad hoc* Chamber for dealing with a particular case, in which event the number of judges is determined by the Court with the approval of the parties.[10] This facility was not used until the 1980s,

---

[7] Art. 10(1). If more than one national of the same State obtains an absolute majority the eldest of them only is considered as elected. A special procedure is laid down for selection of judges where insufficient candidates have obtained an absolute majority (arts. 11–12). This procedure has never been resorted to.

[8] Under art. 44 of the 1907 Convention. See chapter two, p. 37, above.

[9] ICJ Communiqué No. 93/20, 19 July 1993.

[10] A judgment of a Chamber is regarded as a judgment of the Court: Statute, art. 27.

but in the *Gulf of Maine* case (1984)[11] and the Burkina Faso/Mali *Frontier Dispute* case (1986)[12] Chambers of five judges decided the case.[13] The first of these cases raised a problem which was settled therein, though not, perhaps, very satisfactorily. Article 26(2) of the Statute provides that the *number* of judges to constitute a Chamber is to be determined by the Court with the approval of the parties. In that case the contending States (USA and Canada) agreed between themselves not only on the number of judges but also on the individual judges who would compose the Chamber. They also agreed that if the Court did not appoint their selected judges, they would withdraw the case from the Court and instead submit it to an arbitral tribunal composed of those five members.[14] The Court itself 'balloted' to select those five judges. But two of the judges of the Court (Judges Morozov and El Khani) disagreed with this way of proceeding on the ground that, in violation of the Statute, the Court had allowed itself to be dictated to and in effect had not done the selecting itself.[15] Article 17(2) of the Rules of Court requires the President to ascertain the views of the parties regarding the *composition* of the Chamber. One judge has argued that if this authorises consultation regarding anything other than the number of judges, the provision may be *pro tanto* ultra vires.[16]

What is the relationship between the Court and a Chamber? Is the Chamber simply a delegate of the Court so that the Court continues to control it after it is constituted? This question was raised by the application by Nicaragua to be allowed to intervene in the *Land, Island and Maritime Frontier* case between El Salvador and Honduras (1990).[17] The application was made to the Court itself and not to the Chamber which had already been constituted. The Court held that the application must be made to the Chamber and not to itself.[18] A Chamber is subject to the Court only with regard to its composition. Once the Chamber is constituted

---

[11] ICJ Rep. 1984, 246.

[12] ICJ Rep. 1986, 554.

[13] See also the *Elettronica Sicula (ELSI)* case, ICJ Rep. 1987, 3 and *Land, Island and Maritime Frontier* case (*El Salvador/Honduras*), ICJ Rep. 1987, 10. No cases have been decided by Chambers since those four cases, the procedure having apparently fallen out of favour during the 1990s. For discussion of *ad hoc* Chambers, see S. M. Schwebel, 'Ad hoc chambers of the International Court of Justice' (1987) 81 *AJIL* 831; S. Oda, 'Further thoughts on the chambers procedure of the International Court of Justice', (1988) 82 *AJIL* 556; E. Valencia-Ospina, 'The use of chambers in the International Court of Justice', in *Fifty Years of the ICJ*, 487.

[14] In the *Beagle Channel* Arbitration (1978), (1978) 17 *ILM* 634, Chile and Argentina had agreed on one ex-member and four sitting members of the Court to compose the Arbitration Tribunal.

[15] ICJ Rep. 1982, 9.

[16] See the dissenting judgment of Judge Shahabuddeen in the *Land, Island and Maritime Frontier* case, ICJ Rep. 1990, 3 at 18. See also J. G. Collier, 'The International Court of Justice and the peaceful settlement of disputes', in *Fifty Years of the ICJ*, 364.

[17] ICJ Rep. 1990, 3.

[18] Nicaragua later made an application to the Chamber, which acceded to it in part: ICJ Rep. 1990, 92.

it *is* the Court; it is not an agent of or subject to control by the full Court and there is no appeal to the latter. It is 'for the tribunal seised of a principal issue to deal also with any issue subsidiary thereto'; 'a chamber formed to deal with a particular case therefore deals not only with the merits of the case, but also with incidental proceedings arising in that case'.[19]

Is the Court obliged to create a Chamber at the request of the parties? Article 26(1) and (2) of the Statute appear to be permissive: the Court '*may* at any time form a chamber', but article 26(3) uses obligatory language: cases '*shall* be heard and determined by the chamber . . . if the parties so request'. There is no problem with a Chamber created under article 26(1). It already exists and article 26(3) requires the Court to refer the case to the Chamber. But a problem arises with an *ad hoc* Chamber since none exists unless the parties ask for one to be created. Therefore it may be asked whether the Court could refuse on policy grounds to form an *ad hoc* Chamber where the point of law involved in the case is so important or fundamental that it requires consideration by the full Court. We believe that the Court could refuse, relying on the wording of article 26(2).[20]

It should be added that article 29 of the Statute provides for the creation of a third kind of Chamber to hear cases by way of summary procedure. Although such a Chamber has been created every year, none has ever met.

4. Disqualification of judges

Article 17(2) of the Statute provides that a judge cannot participate in deciding a case if he has acted as agent, counsel or advocate, or as a member of a national or international court, or of a commission of inquiry, in the case.[21]

Article 24 deals with two situations. First, if for some special reason a member of the Court considers that he should not take part in the decision of a case, he must inform the President.[22] Secondly, if the President considers that for some special reason a judge should not sit in a case, he must give him notice accordingly; and any dispute over this between the member and the President shall be settled by the

---

[19] ICJ Rep. 1990, 3 at 4. See also *Frontier Dispute* case (*Burkina Faso/Mali*), ICJ Rep. 1986, 3; *Elettronica Sicula* case, ICJ Rep.1989, 15.

[20] The parties would probably settle the matter, for they might well decide to discontinue the proceedings before the Court and refer their dispute to arbitration instead.

[21] Art. 17 of the Statute contains the obvious rule that no member of the Court may act as agent, counsel, or advocate in any case.

[22] In the *Anglo-Iranian Oil Co.* case, ICJ Rep. 1952, 89, Sir Benegal Rao of India did not sit. He had been on the Security Council when it considered an earlier UK complaint that Iran had not complied with the Court's order of interim measures in the case. The French judge Basdevant did not take part in the Advisory Opinion in the *Effect of Awards of Compensation Made by the United Nations Administrative Tribunal* case, ICJ Rep. 1954, 7, since his daughter was the President of that Tribunal.

Court. This happened in the *South West Africa* cases (1965),[23] where the Australian President, Sir Percy Spender, instructed the Pakistan national, Sir Mohammed Zafrullah Khan, not to sit. No reason was given, but he had been a member of the Pakistan delegation to the UN General Assembly when it considered South West Africa and had taken a strong position against South Africa. He had also been nominated as an *ad hoc* judge by the applicant States before his election to the Court.

A State may itself object to a judge or judges. In the *Namibia* case (1971),[24] in which the General Assembly sought an advisory opinion, South Africa objected to Sir Mohammed (who was by then the President of the Court), Judge Padilla Nervo, a Mexican, and Judge Morozov of the Soviet Union, all of whom had participated in General Assembly criticism of South Africa's presence in South West Africa. The President did not instruct them not to sit and the Court overruled the objection, saying that the fact that the three judges had been in the delegations of their States was not material and that their having been government spokesmen did not prevent them from being judicially impartial. But four judges voted against Judge Morozov's participation, since he had, according to Judge Petrén, 'taken a spectacular role' in the preparation of one of the Security Council resolutions which endorsed and took as its point of departure a General Assembly resolution which had to be assessed by the Court in the present advisory opinion.[25]

5. *Ad hoc* judges

Article 31 of the Statute provides that the fact that a judge is a national of one of the parties does not debar him from continuing to sit in a case. But it continues by providing that in cases where a party has a judge of its nationality on the Court, the other party may choose another person to sit as a judge in the case. If neither has a judge of its nationality each party may choose a person to sit as a judge.[26] An *ad hoc* judge need not be, and often is not, a national of the State which appoints him. If several parties have the same interest in the case, as for example being joint applicants, they are reckoned as one party only.[27]

---

[23] ICJ Rep. 1965, 9. It has been cynically suggested that Sir Mohammed was 'persuaded' not to sit by Sir Percy in order to secure a tied vote, so enabling Sir Percy to use his casting vote.

[24] ICJ Rep. 1971, 16.

[25] For a fuller account of these cases see S. Rosenne in L. Gross (ed.), *The Future of the International Court of Justice* (Dobbs Ferry, NY, 1976), vol. 1, 377, at 388–90, reproduced in D. J. Harris, *Cases and Materials on International Law*, 5th edn. (London, 1998), 990–2. The cases are possibly distinguishable in that the first involved contentious proceedings, the second advisory only.

[26] This also applies to the formation of a Chamber of the Court (see p. 127, above).

[27] ICJ Statute, art. 31(5). In the *South West Africa* cases, ICJ Rep. 1966, 6, the two applicant States, Ethiopia and Liberia, were allowed to appoint one judge jointly.

This institution of *ad hoc* judges is open to forceful criticisms. Amongst these are that it is contrary to the basic principle of judicial impartiality; that in the cases in which they have been appointed, *ad hoc* judges have in their judgments usually espoused the view of the States which appointed them (the occasions upon which national judges have voted against their own State are also comparatively rare, however); that an *ad hoc* judge could make the difference to a decision (though this has not yet happened); and that in cases where each side appoints an *ad hoc* judge, they cancel each other out, so that in such cases they are unnecessary. But arguments in favour of the institution have been put forward, the most persuasive being that it increases the confidence of States in the Court, particularly when the other party has a judge of its nationality on the Court, in that the presence of an *ad hoc* judge may reassure the party which has appointed him that the nuances of its pleadings have been understood by at least one member of the Court. Moreover, even though the *ad hoc* judge does not (or is not supposed to) represent the State which appointed him, he may fulfil a useful function in supplying a national point of view in the deliberations of the Court. The right to appoint *ad hoc* judges may be regarded as a concession to diplomatic susceptibilities. It has, in fact, done no particular harm.

Difficulties have arisen in the case of Advisory Opinions, where there are actually no parties to the case but a State may think it has a legal interest which may be affected. Article 68 of the Statute states that 'in exercising its advisory functions the Court shall be guided by the provisions of the present Statute which apply in contentious cases to the extent to which it recognises them to be applicable'. The Permanent Court of International Justice frequently granted applications to nominate an *ad hoc* judge, but although the International Court of Justice did so in the *Western Sahara* case (1975),[28] in the *Namibia* case (1971)[29] it had refused to do so, perhaps misconstruing its own rules of procedure.[30]

6. President; Vice-President; Registrar; Seat

By the Statute, article 21(1), the Court is to elect its President and Vice-President for terms of three years; they may be re-elected.[31] By article 21(2) the Court is to appoint its Registrar and may provide for the appointment of other officers. The

---

[28] ICJ Rep. 1975, 6.

[29] ICJ Rep. 1971, 16.

[30] The Rules of Court (art. 102 (3)) provide that when an advisory opinion is requested upon a legal question actually pending between two or more States, art. 31 of the Statute shall apply, as do the provisions of the Rules (arts. 36–7) concerning the application of that article. See further M. Pomerance, 'The admission of judges *ad hoc* in advisory proceedings: some reflections in the light of the *Namibia* case' (1973) 67 *AJIL* 446.

[31] See the excellent discussion of the role of the President in S. Rosenne, 'The President of the International Court of Justice', in *Fifty Years of the ICJ*, 406.

President and Registrar must reside at the seat of the Court, which is The Hague. The Court may, however, sit and exercise its functions elsewhere whenever it considers this desirable (article 22). It did so for the first time in April 1997, when it visited the site of the Gabcíkovo-Nagymaros project at the invitation of the parties.[32]

7. Competence and jurisdiction in contentious cases

Only States may be parties in cases before the Court (Statute, article 34(1)).[33] This precludes individuals and corporations from bringing an action before the Court. Moreover, although certain international organisations may request advisory opinions of the Court (article 65),[34] they may not be parties to contentious cases (States, on the other hand, may not request advisory opinions). As of April 1998, the Court had dealt with seventy-six inter-State contentious disputes and twenty-two requests for advisory opinions.

The position of public international organisations in respect of contentious cases is stated in article 34(2) and (3) of the Court's Statute. The Court may request them to provide information relevant to cases before it and must receive any such information presented by such organisations on their own initiative. When the constituent instrument of such an organisation or a convention adopted thereunder is in question in a case before the Court, the Registrar must notify the organisation concerned and communicate to it copies of all the written proceedings.

The fundamental rule respecting the jurisdiction of the Court is that it depends on consent: the parties must have voluntarily conferred jurisdiction on the Court. The claimant State has consented by bringing the case before the Court,[35] but unless the defendant State has given its consent, the Court will still lack jurisdiction to hear the case.

The methods of conferring jurisdiction are for the most part set out in article 36 of the Statute. Article 36(1) provides that:

> The jurisdiction of the Court comprises all cases which the parties refer to it and all matters specially provided for in the Charter of the United Nations or in treaties and conventions in force.

---

[32] See ICJ Rep. 1997, 3.

[33] Though the Court regularly receives applications from individuals—approximately 1,200 in the year from August 1996: see ICJ, *Yearbook 1996–1997*, 204.

[34] See p. 182, below.

[35] However, in the *Monetary Gold* case, ICJ Rep. 1954, 19 (which is discussed at pp. 158–60 and 165 below), Italy, which had agreed to the Court's jurisdiction over the dispute, successfully argued that it should not exercise its jurisdiction.

And article 36(2), which will be dealt with later, provides for States to make unilateral declarations accepting the compulsory jurisdiction of the court over future disputes. It is known as the 'Optional Clause'.

There are, in fact, four ways (a fifth will also be discussed) in which jurisdiction can be conferred. Two of these confer jurisdiction before any dispute has arisen, that is (i) where a treaty or convention in force between the States in question provides for it, and (ii) where there are declarations under article 36(2); and two do so after a dispute has arisen, that is (iii) where the States in question specially agree to refer their dispute to the Court, and (iv) where the doctrine of *forum prorogatum* (a kind of implied submission) applies.

However, we will take the methods in the order in which they appear in article 36.

7.1 All cases which the parties refer to the Court

The Court plainly has jurisdiction over cases which the parties refer to it: that is to say, cases referred by a special agreement which defines the exact nature of the dispute, made between the parties to the dispute after it has arisen. Most cases which the Court has decided on the merits have come to it this way, even if, as in the *Minquiers and Ecrehos* case (1953),[36] both States (there, the United Kingdom and France) have made 'Optional Clause' declarations under article 36(2), for it enables the parties to agree on the wording of the precise point on which they want the Court's judgment.

---

[36] ICJ Rep. 1953, 47. All but two of the cases decided in the 1980s on their merits came to the Court on this basis: cf. *Tunisia/Libya Continental Shelf* case, ICJ Rep. 1982, 18; *Gulf of Maine* case, ICJ Rep. 1984, 246; *Libya/Malta Continental Shelf* case, ICJ Rep. 1985, 13; *Burkina Faso/Mali Frontier Dispute* case, ICJ Rep. 1986, 554. Only two cases were decided on their merits which were referred to the Court some other way and in one, the *Case concerning US Diplomatic and Consular Staff in Tehran*, ICJ Rep. 1980, 3, Iran refused to appear at all on the ground that the Court had no jurisdiction. In the second, the United States refused to argue the merits of the case after the Court had held that it had jurisdiction: *Case concerning US Military and Paramilitary Activities in and against Nicaragua* (*Nicaragua* v. *US*), ICJ Rep. 1986, 3. In the 1990s rather more cases were initiated by unilateral applications made by States invoking compromissory clauses in bilateral or multilateral treaties: see, e.g., *Case concerning Questions of Interpretation and Application of the 1971 Montreal Convention arising from the Aerial Incident at Lockerbie* (*Libya* v. *United Kingdom; Libya* v. *USA*), ICJ Rep. 1992, 3 and 114; *Case concerning Application of the Convention on the Prevention and Punishment of the Crime of Genocide* (*Bosnia and Herzegovina* v. *Yugoslavia*), ICJ Rep. 1993, 3, 325; *Case concerning Oil Platforms* (*Iran* v. *USA*), ICJ Rep. 1996, 803; *Land and Maritime Boundary between Cameroon and Nigeria* (*Cameroon* v. *Nigeria*), ICJ Rep. 1996, 13; *Request for an examination of the situation in accordance with paragraph 63 of the Court's Judgment of 20 December 1974 in the Nuclear Tests* (*New Zealand* v. *France*) case, ICJ Rep. 1995, 288; *Fisheries Jurisdiction* (*Spain* v. *Canada*), ICJ Rep. 1995, 87 and 1998, 432; *Case concerning the Vienna Convention on Consular Relations* (*Paraguay* v. *United States of America*), ICJ Rep. 1998, 248. Nonetheless, cases continue to be brought by special agreement: see, e.g., *Territorial Dispute* (*Libyan Arab Jamahiriya/Chad*), ICJ Rep. 1994, 6; *Case concerning Gabcíkovo-Nagymaros project* (*Hungary/Slovakia*), ICJ Rep. 1997, 3; *Case concerning Kasikili/Sedudu Island* (*Botswana/Namibia*), ICJ Rep. 1998, 6.

Simple though this seems, three problems have arisen. First, there can be a dispute over whether the parties have indeed agreed to refer the case. In the *Aegean Sea Continental Shelf* case (1975)[37] between Greece and Turkey, Greece argued that a joint communiqué, issued after negotiations, which said that the two States would consider referring the dispute to the Court, amounted to an agreement so to refer it. The Court held that it did not, and that the communiqué dealt only with the possibility of the two States making such an agreement.

Secondly, there can be a dispute as to how, under an agreement, the Court can be seised of a case. Extremely complicated questions of interpretation of agreements for the reference of a dispute to the Court arose in two cases concerned with *Maritime Delimitation and Territorial Questions between Qatar and Bahrain: Jurisdiction and Admissibility.*[38] The main question which arose for decision was whether, in agreeing to submit their dispute to the ICJ, the two States had concluded any legally binding commitment which entitled either State to submit it unilaterally. Qatar argued that they had; Bahrain denied this. The two States had for some time been in dispute over certain territories. In 1987 the King of Saudi Arabia, with the agreement of Qatar and Bahrain, established a Tripartite Committee charged with preparing the submission of the dispute to the ICJ. At the Committee's fourth meeting Bahrain proposed what came to be called the 'Bahraini Formula' by which 'The Parties request the Court to decide any matter of territorial right or other title or interest which may be a matter of difference between them; and to draw a single maritime boundary between their respective maritime areas of seabed, subsoil and superadjacent waters.' This was rejected by Qatar which, at the sixth and final meeting in December 1988, put forward an alternative form of words, which Bahrain rejected. However, the parties did agree in principle what was the subject matter of their dispute, but disagreed on how it was to be submitted to the Court. In December 1990, at a meeting at Doha, Qatar accepted the Bahraini Formula. The parties agreed to a further period for the exercise by the Saudi King of his good offices, and that if this did not produce a settlement by the end of May 1991, the matter could be placed before the ICJ. The minutes of the agreement ('the Doha Minutes') were signed by Qatar and Bahrain. No settlement ensued and in July 1991 Qatar submitted a unilateral application to the Court which, however, referred to only part of the areas in dispute. In its judgment of July 1994 the Court held that the Doha Minutes amounted to an international agreement giving rise to mutual rights and obligations but that the application did not comply with the agreement, which required the submission of the whole of the dispute. The Court then proceeded to 'afford the parties the opportunity to submit the whole of the dispute' and to fix 30

---

[37] ICJ Rep. 1976, 3.
[38] ICJ Rep. 1994, 112; ICJ Rep. 1995, 6.

November 1994 as the date by which the parties were jointly or separately to take action to this end.

These decisions are very curious. As Judge Schwebel pointed out, in a separate opinion, by its judgment the Court had not decided any dispute, either the substantive territorial dispute or that over jurisdiction or admissibility.[39] Moreover, the Court, realising that it was incompetent at the stage to make any such decision, in effect offered itself as a conciliator.[40]

This attempt at conciliation failed and on 30 November 1994 Qatar unilaterally submitted what the Court accepted was the whole of the dispute. However, Bahrain wrote to the Court stating that, in its view, the Doha Minutes permitted only a joint application to the Court, and did not give Qatar the right to seise the Court of the dispute unilaterally (a right which the Court itself had failed to assert in its previous judgment). By a somewhat unusual process of interpretation[41] the Court decided that the parties had agreed to the possibility of a unilateral application and held that Qatar had submitted the dispute to the Court.

The third problem arose in the *Monetary Gold Removed from Rome in 1943* case (1954),[42] where it was held that where a State which is not a party to the case (in that case Albania) has a legal interest which forms the very subject matter of the case, the Court will decline to exercise jurisdiction.[43] This was so, even though in that case a party to a multilateral convention providing for settlement by the ICJ had referred the case to the Court, and then objected to it exercising its jurisdiction.

7.2 Matters specially provided for in the UN Charter

Article 36(1) of the Statute refers to '*matters specially provided for in the Charter of the United Nations*'. It was originally intended to provide in the UN Charter that certain types of dispute would be compulsorily determined by the International

---

[39] ICJ Rep. 1994, 112 at 130 and see the dissenting opinion of Judge Oda, ICJ Rep. 1995, 6 at 39.

[40] See J. G. Collier, 'The International Court of Justice and the peaceful settlement of disputes', in *Fifty Years of the ICJ*, 364, at 371–2; and for a fuller discussion of these cases see E. Lauterpacht, '"Partial judgments" and the inherent jurisdiction of the International Court of Justice', ibid., 465–86.

[41] The Court found the text of the Minutes clear when interpreted 'in accordance with the ordinary meaning to be given to its [*sic*] terms in their context and the light of [their] object and purpose . . .'. It did not find it necessary to resort to supplementary means of interpretation. However it did look at the *travaux préparatoires* in order to see if they provided confirmation of the Court's interpretation. They did not; as Judge Schwebel (dissenting) said (at 35) '[w]hat the text and context . . . leave so unclear, is, however, crystal clear when those Minutes are analysed with the assistance of the *travaux préparatoires* . . . a reasonable evaluation of [which] sustains only the position of Bahrain'. See, for cogent criticism, the note by M. Evans (1995) 44 *ICLQ* 691.

[42] ICJ Rep. 1954, 19. See for a similar problem with a different solution: *Libya/Malta Continental Shelf (Application by Italy for Permission to Intervene)* case, ICJ Rep. 1984, 3, (pp. 164–8 below). See also the *East Timor* case, ICJ Rep. 1995, 90.

[43] See p. 165, below for further discussion of the *Monetary Gold* principle.

Court.[44] However, the only relevant provision of the Charter as it was finally adopted is article 36, which says merely that where, in pursuance of the pacific settlement of disputes, it is making recommendations as to the method of their adjustment, the Security Council 'should . . . take into consideration that legal disputes should as a general rule be referred by the parties to the [ICJ]'. In the *Corfu Channel* case (1948)[45] the United Kingdom argued that such a recommendation to the parties by the Security Council conferred jurisdiction on the Court. The Court did not find it necessary to deal with this argument, but seven judges disagreed with it, pointing to the word 'recommendation', which is not mandatory. If this is so, the Charter contains no provision as envisaged by the Statute article 36(1) and the words above are redundant.

7.3 *Forum prorogatum*[46]

Forum prorogatum is the name given to the situation where one State refers the case to the Court and the other does some act which can be regarded as submission to the jurisdiction, such as appearing and arguing the case on its merits. In the *Anglo-Iranian Oil Co.* case (1952)[47] the Court held that an appearance by Iran to argue that the Court lacked jurisdiction could not constitute a submission to it. Though the United Kingdom argued in the *Corfu Channel* case[48] that the Court had jurisdiction on this basis, and it is sometimes said[49] that in that case the Court relied on *forum prorogatum* to found its jurisdiction, this is not altogether clear since Albania expressly accepted both the admissibility of the case and the Court's jurisdiction in a letter addressed to the Court which, the Court said, removed all difficulties over jurisdiction.[50]

A case heard by the PCIJ may provide a clearer example. In the *Rights of Minorities in Polish Upper Silesia* case (1928)[51] Poland first objected to the jurisdiction in its second written pleadings (the rejoinder), having argued the merits of the case in its first written pleadings (counter-memorial), and the Court held it had jurisdiction, since submission of arguments on the merits without objecting to the jurisdiction must be taken to indicate a desire for a judgment on the merits.[52]

---

[44] I. Brownlie, *Principles of Public International Law*, 5th edn. (Oxford, 1998), 716.

[45] ICJ Rep. 1948, 18. See generally C. H. M. Waldock, '*Forum prorogatum* or acceptance of a unilateral summons to appear before the International Court' (1948) 2 *ILQ* 377.

[46] See the 1996 address by the President of the Court to the General Assembly, 'The *forum prorogatum* before the International Court of Justice: the resources of an institution or the hidden face of consensualism', ICJ, *Yearbook 1996–1997*, 216.

[47] ICJ Rep. 1952, 93.

[48] ICJ Rep. 1948, 5.

[49] See, e.g., *Merrills*, 123–4; D. J. Harris, *Cases and Materials in International Law*, 5th edn. (London, 1998), 999.

[50] However, just before the Court made this ruling the United Kingdom and Albania announced that they had agreed to submit the case to the Court by special agreement; it seems clear, therefore, that *forum prorogatum* was not the only foundation of the Court's jurisdiction.

[51] PCIJ, Ser. A, No. 15 (1928). See also the *Mavrommatis Jerusalem Concessions (Merits)* case, ibid., No. 5 (1925), 27.

7.4 Treaties or conventions in force

The parties to a treaty may include in it a provision for reference to the ICJ of any dispute arising out of the treaty. Such a provision is known as a 'compromissory clause'.[53] It is useful to distinguish between (i) treaties specifically for the settlement of disputes, and (ii) treaties on any matter which include a dispute settlement clause. Many such treaties, of both kinds, exist. As to (i), dispute settlement treaties, these may be multilateral or bilateral. A prime example of a multilateral treaty is the General Act for the Pacific Settlement of Disputes 1928 (which was revised in 1949).[54] It includes provisions concerning conciliation, arbitration and judicial settlement. The provisions regarding judicial settlement permit one party to take another before the Court, which bear a close similarity to the Optional Clause of the Statute of the ICJ.

Two questions have arisen concerning the General Act. First, is it still in force? Australia relied on it against France in the *Nuclear Tests* cases (1974).[55] France argued that the Act was no longer in force since it had never been invoked, had been forgotten and had been overtaken by the Statute of the ICJ (though this argument was hardly tenable since the General Act was revised in 1949 when the Statute was already in force). While the Court held on quite different grounds that the case had become inadmissible, four judges in a joint dissenting judgment stated that nothing had happened to make the General Act obsolete. In the *Aegean Sea Continental Shelf* case (1975)[56] Greece relied on the General Act against Turkey. The Court held that the principle of reciprocity entitled Turkey to rely on a reservation made by Greece to the General Act, and so seems impliedly to have affirmed the continuing validity of the General Act at that time.[57]

Secondly, if a State has made a reservation to its Optional Clause declaration[58] but not to the General Act, can its Optional Clause reservation be read into its ratification of the General Act?[59] The dissenting judges in the *Nuclear Tests* case[60] held that it could not.

---

[52] For an outline of the Court's procedure, including the order of pleadings, see pp. 175–6, below.

[53] See generally J. Charney, 'Compromissory Clauses and the Jurisdiction of the International Court of Justice' (1989) 83 *AJIL* 85.

[54] 93 *LNTS* 543 (General Act); 71 *UNTS* 101 (Revised General Act).

[55] ICJ Rep. 1974, 327.

[56] ICJ Rep. 1978, 3.

[57] As to the doctrine of reciprocity in relation to optional clause reservations see pp. 150–1, below.

[58] As to reservations to optional clause reservations see pp. 141–50, below.

[59] The converse situation, of a limitation on the Court's jurisdiction existing under compromissory clauses in a treaty but not under optional clause declarations, was raised in the *Case concerning Land and Maritime Boundary between Cameroon and Nigeria*, where the Court held that the limitation could not affect the declarations: ICJ Rep. 1998, 275, judgment of 11 June 1998, paras. 61–73.

[60] ICJ Rep. 1974, 327.

Since 1974 several States including France, the United Kingdom and India have either denounced the General Act or have said it no longer exists and its present status is unclear.

With respect to (ii), treaties which contain clauses referring disputes arising under them to the Court, again these may be multilateral, like the Optional Protocols to the Vienna Convention on Diplomatic Relations 1961, and that on Consular Relations 1963 which conferred jurisdiction on the Court in the *Hostages* case (1980),[61] or they may be bilateral. Examples of bilateral treaties are the Spanish–Belgian Commercial Treaty 1927, which gave jurisdiction in the *Barcelona Traction* case (1964),[62] the Exchanges of Notes concerning fisheries between the United Kingdom and Germany on the one hand and Iceland on the other hand, of 1960, which gave jurisdiction in the (Icelandic) *Fisheries Jurisdiction* case (1973),[63] the Treaty of Friendship, Navigation and Commerce concluded between the USA and Nicaragua at Managua 1956, article XXIV(2) of which gave jurisdiction in the *Nicaragua* v. *US* case (1984),[64] and the Treaty of Amity, Economic Relations and Consular Rights 1955, between the United States and Iran, article XXI(2) of which gave jurisdiction in the *Oil Platforms* (*Iran* v. *USA*) case.[65] As the last of those cases clearly demonstrated, the Court's jurisdiction will extend only to disputes falling within the scope of the compromissory clause.

A problem concerning such clauses has arisen in two cases in which a State argued that the treaty was no longer in force. In the *Appeal Relating to the Jurisdiction of the Council of the International Civil Aviation Organisation* case (1972),[66] Pakistan complained to the ICAO of breaches of the Chicago Convention on Civil Aviation 1944 and a bilateral Air Transit Agreement with India. India objected to the ICAO Council hearing the complaint but the Council rejected India's objection. India then asked the Court to declare that this rejection was wrong, relying on the jurisdictional clauses in the same treaties to establish the Court's jurisdiction. But its objection to the Council's action was that those treaties were no longer in force. So Pakistan argued that in relying before the Court on the clauses, India must be admitting that the treaties remained in existence. The Court held, not altogether logically,[67] that Pakistan's argument was 'unacceptable'; a party must be free to invoke the jurisdictional clauses in a treaty without prejudicing its arguments on the merits. Note that the difficulty in this case was that the claimant State sought to rely on the jurisdictional provision of a

---

[61] ICJ Rep. 1980, 3.
[62] ICJ Rep. 1964, 6.
[63] ICJ Rep. 1973, 3.
[64] ICJ Rep. 1984, 392. See further p. 148, below.
[65] ICJ Rep. 1996, 803.
[66] ICJ Rep. 1972, 46.
[67] See D. W. Greig, *International Law*, 2nd edn. (London, 1976), 636.

treaty which that State itself claimed was no longer in force. There is no difficulty in the converse case where the claimant State relies on that provision but the defendant claims that the treaty is not in force. In the (Icelandic) Fisheries Jurisdiction case (1973),[68] the United Kingdom and Germany relied on jurisdictional provisions in their Exchanges of Notes of 1960 with Iceland, which terminated the 'Cod War'. Iceland seemed to take the position (it refused to appear before the Court, but published various statements of its views) that the Exchanges of Notes had been terminated by fundamental change of circumstances. The Court held that there had been no such change. But even if it were ultimately to turn out that there had been, whether or not this was so was the very point at issue and the jurisdiction clause continued to exist to enable the court to decide it.[69]

7.5 'Transferred' jurisdiction

A further basis of the Court's jurisdiction is to be found in the notion of 'transferred' jurisdiction. When, in 1945, the Permanent Court of International Justice was replaced by the International Court of Justice, it was thought necessary to preserve provisions in treaties which conferred jurisdiction on the former court. Article 37 of the Statute of the International Court of Justice therefore provides that whenever

> a treaty or convention in force provides for reference of a matter to . . . the Permanent Court of International Justice, the matter shall, as between the parties to the present Statute, be referred to the International Court of Justice.

There are two essential requirements. First, the treaty must still be in force. There is usually no difficulty in this, since either it is or it is not still in force.[70] Secondly, the parties to the treaty must also be parties to the Statute. This also seems free of difficulty, since either they are or they are not. But matters were complicated by the decision of the Court in the *Aerial Incident* case (1959),[71] which concerned 'Optional Clause' declarations. It was held that for such declarations to be 'transferred' from the PCIJ to the ICJ, under Article 36(5) of the Statute (which provides that 'they shall be deemed, as between the parties to the present Statute to be acceptances of the compulsory jurisdiction of the ICJ'), the States must not only be parties to the Statute at the time the case is referred to the Court but also must

---

[68] ICJ Rep. 1973, 3.

[69] This conclusion is similar to that of the House of Lords in *Heyman* v. *Darwins Ltd.* [1942] AC 356 regarding the effect of frustration of a contract which contains an arbitration clause. For a further discussion of this problem in connection with the arbitral process, see chapter eight, p. 215, below.

[70] In the series of cases concerned with South West Africa (Namibia) the Court held that the Mandate between the League of Nations and South Africa concerning the territory was still in force despite the demise of the League. See, e.g., *South West Africa* cases, ICJ Rep. 1962, 319; *ibid.*, 1966, 6.

[71] ICJ Rep. 1959, 127. See further pp. 153–4, below, where art. 36(5) is set out in full.

have been so at the inception of the Court in 1945, which the respondent State, Bulgaria, was not. In the *Barcelona Traction* (*Belgium* v. *Spain*) case (1964),[72] however, Article 37 was interpreted differently; the Court held that its words must be given their plain meaning and all that was needed was that the treaty was still in force. The fact that Spain was not a party to the Statute in 1945 was immaterial. The distinction drawn by the Court between article 36(5) and article 37 seems tenuous and highly artificial. The Court's reasoning in the *Barcelona Traction* case seems preferable to its reasoning in the *Aerial Incident* case.

7.6 The Optional Clause[73]

The term 'Optional Clause' refers to article 36(2) of the Statute, and confers what is sometimes called 'compulsory' jurisdiction. But the word 'compulsory' is misleading. It is optional for States to make jurisdiction compulsory; they are not compelled to make it so. Article 36(2) provides that by communicating with the UN Secretary-General:

> The States parties to the present Statute may at any time declare that they recognise as compulsory *ipso facto* and without special agreement, in relation to any other State accepting the same obligation, the jurisdiction of the Court in all legal disputes concerning:
> a. The interpretation of a treaty;
> b. Any question of international law;
> c. The existence of any fact which, if established, would constitute a breach of an international obligation;
> d. The nature or extent of the reparation to be made for the breach of an international obligation.

This is too verbose; (a), (c) and (d) are really redundant. Since they are all questions of international law they are covered by (b).

Several problems arise out of Article 36(2).

7.6.1 The character of the relationships created by a declaration

It is obvious that a declaration under article 36(2) is a unilateral act of the State making it, but it seems that it creates a bilateral relationship, or a series of bilateral relationships between the States which make declarations. The article refers to the making of declarations 'in relation to any other State accepting the same obligation' and the mutual obligations arise at the time the second declaration is made

---

[72] ICJ Rep. 1964, 6.

[73] For full accounts of the then current position regarding the Optional Clause and learned analysis of the various types of reservations see articles by C. H. M. Waldock, 'Decline of the Optional Clause' (1955–6) 32 *BYIL* 244 and by J. G. Merrills, 'The Optional Clause today' (1979) 50 *BYIL* 87 and 'The Optional Clause revisited' (1993) 64 *BYIL* 17. See also R. Szafarz, *The Compulsory Jurisdiction of the International Court of Justice* (Dordrecht, 1993).

even though the declaration has not been communicated to the other contending State. So, once State *A* has filed a declaration, State *B* cannot, unless it has reserved the right to do so, withdraw its declaration so as to deprive the Court of jurisdiction over a case between *A* and *B*, as the Court held in the *Right of Passage* case (1957),[74] the *Nuclear Tests* cases (1974)[75] and the *Nicaragua* v. *US* case (1984).[76]

7.6.2 Reservations[77]

Article 36(3) provides that declarations may be made unconditionally or on condition of 'reciprocity on the part of several or certain States'. Thus, for example, if Egypt were to accept the compulsory jurisdiction if the United States and Bolivia have done so or do so, and if these States have not, then, even if Portugal has accepted it, the Court would not have jurisdiction over a dispute between Portugal and Egypt. Article 36(3) also permits declarations to be made for a certain time, for example, ten years. However, only one State seems to have made a declaration containing precisely the first,[78] and none exactly the second, of these conditions of acceptance.[79] But many States have made conditions or reservations of other kinds.

For example, States have frequently made reservations excluding disputes arising before a certain date or, even if the dispute arises after such a date, if it arises out of facts or situations existing before that date (see the Belgian reservation in the *Electricity Company of Sofia and Bulgaria* case (1939)).[80] Another example is the condition of reciprocity *simpliciter* as in the *Norwegian Loans* case (1957)[81] where the Norwegian condition of reciprocity was in issue.

The United Kingdom's declaration of 1969[82] contains both these reservations. It also contains reservations excluding from the jurisdiction of the Court disputes which the United Kingdom has agreed with the other party or parties to settle by some other means of peaceful settlement, or has already submitted to arbitration by agreement with any States which had not at the time of submission accepted the Court's compulsory jurisdiction; disputes with a Commonwealth country

---

[74] ICJ Rep. 1957, 125.

[75] ICJ Rep. 1974, 253 and 457.

[76] ICJ Rep. 1984, 392.

[77] See S. A. Alexandrov, *Reservations and Unilateral Declarations Accepting the Compulsory Jurisdiction of the International Court of Justice* (Dordrecht, 1995).

[78] Brazil, in its declaration of 1921, which is no longer in force. The reference to reciprocity in art. 36(3) was inserted by the Committee of Jurists who drafted the Statute of the PCIJ in 1920. This was done to meet the wish of the Brazilian member of the Committee to enable a State to make its acceptance of the Court's jurisdiction conditional on a similar acceptance by one or more of the then Great Powers.

[79] Conditions which have limited acceptance of jurisdiction to a fixed period have provided for their continuance in force until notice is given to terminate them.

[80] PCIJ, Ser. A/B, No. 77 (1939), discussed at p. 147, below.

[81] ICJ Rep. 1957, 9, discussed at p. 151, below.

[82] Misc. No. 4 (1969), Cmnd. 3872.

with regard to situations or facts existing before 1 January 1969; and disputes where the other Party has accepted compulsory jurisdiction only in relation to or for the purposes of the dispute, or where the other party accepted it less than twelve months prior to the filing of the application bringing the dispute before the Court. The United Kingdom also reserves the right to add to, amend or withdraw any of its reservations or any it may add, with effect from the moment of giving notice to the Secretary-General. In the light of the decision of the Court in the *Nicaragua* v. *US* case,[83] which will shortly be discussed, this last reservation is of greater importance than may have been supposed in 1969.

The Assembly of the League of Nations gave its approval, by resolutions of 1924 and 1928, to the making of such conditions or reservations even though these are not expressly authorised by article 36 itself.[84] The ICJ referred to States' freedom in this respect in the *Nicaragua* v *US* case.[85] To what extent, if at all, are States limited in their freedom to make any reservation they think fit? It is submitted that such as are clearly incompatible with the Statute of the ICJ would be impermissible; indeed, States have never really tried to make such reservations. In the *Norwegian Loans* case (1957) Judge Lauterpacht gave examples of such reservations, such as those which say that oral proceedings of the Court should be secret, that a judgment should not be binding unless it is unanimous, or that it should contain no reasons, or that judges of a certain nationality or nationalities should be excluded. These would all conflict with the Statute, of which the Court is the 'guardian'.[86] It may also be observed that the Vienna Convention on the Law of Treaties 1969, article 19(c), permits States to make reservations to treaties unless a reservation is, *inter alia* 'incompatible with the object and purpose of the treaty'.[87]

The Court has never squarely faced the problem. At any rate, it has never decided whether a particular condition or reservation was 'illegal' and impermissible in this respect or what the consequences would be if it were. The matter has, however, been addressed by individual judges in their separate or dissenting judgments in two cases, *Norwegian Loans* (1957) and *Interhandel* (1959), which we discuss below.[88]

We now turn to a discussion of several kinds of reservation which States have made.

---

[83] ICJ Rep. 1984, 392.

[84] The wording of art. 36 of the Statute of the PCIJ was, in this respect, identical to that of art. 36 of the Statute of the ICJ.

[85] ICJ Rep. 1984, 392 at 418.

[86] ICJ Rep. 1957, 9 at 45–67.

[87] For a discussion of the problems raised by the concept of incompatible reservations, see C. Redgwell (1993) 64 *BYIL* 245.

[88] ICJ Rep. 1957, 9; 1959, 6. See further p. 151, below.

7.6.2.1 *Domestic jurisdiction*[89]

Frequently, States have included in their declarations a reservation from the Court's jurisdiction of disputes which are 'within the domestic jurisdiction' of those States. Theoretically, this reservation is unnecessary since, if a matter is, by international law, within the domestic jurisdiction of States, then international law has no application to it. Moreover, it adds little or no protection to the State which makes it since it does not even purport to prevent the Court determining, objectively, whether a particular dispute does or does not fall within domestic jurisdiction.

7.6.2.2 *'Automatic' reservations*[90]

The term 'automatic' or 'self-judging' reservation refers to a particular reservation that was contained in the US declaration of 1946, or variants upon it. In that declaration the US did not simply reserve from the jurisdiction of the Court disputes which were within the domestic jurisdiction of the USA: to make certain that it would achieve its aim it excepted 'disputes with regard to matters which are essentially within the domestic jurisdiction of the United States of America *as determined by the United States of America'*. This is sometimes known as the 'Connolly Amendment', because it was introduced by the US Senator Connolly into the US declaration which President Truman proposed to make, as a condition of giving the Senate's advice and consent to the declaration (as is required by the Constitution of the USA). A similar device was employed by France; and in the UK declaration of 1957 a similar reservation was made with respect to national security. The latter was partially removed in 1963 and disappeared altogether in 1969.[91]

The first time that such a reservation was pleaded was in the *Norwegian Loans* case,[92] in which France, which had made such a reservation, brought an action against Norway, which had not. The Norwegians prayed in aid the condition of reciprocity[93] which was contained in their own declaration so as to use the French reservation in their own favour, and declared that the matter fell within Norwegian domestic jurisdiction. This was accepted by the ICJ. Since neither State challenged the validity of the reservation and the Court declined jurisdiction anyway, it was not, in the Court's view, necessary to decide whether the reservation was valid. Soon afterwards, in the *Interhandel* case,[94] Switzerland brought a

---

[89] See G. Arangio-Ruiz, 'The plea of domestic jurisdiction before the International Court of Justice: substance or procedure?', in *Fifty Years of the ICJ*, 440.

[90] See J. Crawford, 'The legal effect of automatic reservations to the jurisdiction of the International Court' (1979) 50 *BYIL* 63.

[91] Ten States have made such reservations, of which five remained in force in 1996.

[92] ICJ Rep. 1957, 9.

[93] See p. 151, below.

[94] ICJ Rep. 1959, 6.

claim against the USA, which pleaded this reservation as one of five objections to the jurisdiction of the Court. But it later claimed not to be seriously relying on it, and the Court again did not rule upon the point since it dismissed the case on one of the other preliminary objections to its jurisdiction (failure to exhaust of local remedies).

However, several judges in these two cases considered the matter and concluded that this type of reservation was contrary to the Statute and so invalid in so far as the reservation gave the declaring State the sole right, to the exclusion of the Court, to judge the question of the Court's jurisdiction. The leading proponents of this view were judges Lauterpacht and Klaestad. The former said[95] that it followed from the existence of the 'automatic' reservations that there existed no valid declaration of acceptance of the jurisdiction of the Court by France or the USA respectively and so, whatever the States thought, the Court must decline jurisdiction. Judge Klaestad, on the other hand, regarded the invalid reservation as severable from the rest of the United States' declaration, which was to that extent a valid declaration.[96]

These judges in *Interhandel* faced two questions. The first question was whether such a 'self-judging' reservation was valid at all. They concluded that it was not valid and gave two reasons for this: first, that it rendered the declaration devoid of any real legal obligation; secondly, that it conflicted with the Statute itself. Since article 36(6) gives the Court the sole right to be the judge of whether it has jurisdiction, it is illegal and impermissible to allow a State which is a party to the dispute to be the judge of this. But these reasons are not entirely convincing, for the first might not be true; a State may not determine that the matter is within its domestic jurisdiction in the particular case and may accept that the Court has jurisdiction over it. In the *Nicaragua* v. *US* case[97] the Court's jurisdiction was challenged by the USA, not on the basis of the automatic reservation, but upon different reservations. It would have hardly been credible for the USA to say that carrying out hostile activities in and around Nicaragua was a matter within the domestic jurisdiction of the USA.

Nor is the second reason entirely sound. Article 36(6) only gives the Court the sole power to judge its own jurisdiction where there exists a dispute between the contending States as to whether jurisdiction does or does not exist. There are two possibilities: (a) if we assume for the sake of argument that the reservation is *possibly invalid* then such a dispute can arise, one State saying it *is* valid and invoking it, the other saying it is invalid. The Court can settle the consequent dispute as to its

---

[95] ICJ Rep. 1957, 9 at 43–66 (*Norwegian Loans*); ICJ Rep. 1959, 6 at 116–19 (*Interhandel*).

[96] ICJ Rep. 1959, 6 at 77–8. And cf. the decision of the European Court of Human Rights in the *Belilos* case (1988) ECHR Ser. A, No. 132.

[97] ICJ Rep. 1984, 392. On this case see generally D. W. Greig (1991) 62 *BYIL* 119–281, where this, and almost all other, aspects of the case are exhaustively discussed.

jurisdiction (there is no jurisdiction if the reservation is valid, jurisdiction exists if it is not). But to say that the automatic reservation is ineffective to bestow jurisdiction assumes the potential correctness of what it is sought to prove. On the other hand, (b), if we assume that the reservation is *valid* then there can hardly be a dispute as to whether the court has jurisdiction, since if, say, the USA has decided that the matter is within its domestic jurisdiction, then the Court has no jurisdiction at all. If, on the other hand, the USA has decided that the matter is *not* within its domestic jurisdiction the court *has* jurisdiction.

The second question facing the judges in *Norwegian Loans* and *Interhandel* was, supposing the reservation to be invalid, what is the consequence of this? Here, there are three possibilities: (i) the words 'in the opinion of' or 'as determined by' the USA or whatever country, should be deleted; or (ii) the reservation in its entirety should be struck out, leaving the rest of the acceptance operative; or (iii) the whole declaration is vitiated and a nullity, so the court has no jurisdiction. None of the judges opted for (i) but they differed as between (ii) and (iii). Judge Lauterpacht, for example, thought that to cut words out of the declaration and leave the rest there, as entailed by alternatives (i) or (ii), would foist on the USA or France an international obligation other than it intended to be bound by, because without the reservation the USA (or France) would never have become a party to the optional clause at all. Therefore, (iii) was the only real possibility and the invalidity of the reservation infected the declaration altogether. Other judges thought that the invalid reservation could be severed from the rest, and the declaration as a whole left standing. The USA *had* intended to make a declaration accepting the Court's jurisdiction, and the Senate debates on the Connolly amendment showed that the Senate was concerned to make it clear that matters which were within the United States domestic jurisdiction by international law should clearly be excluded from the Court's 'compulsory' jurisdiction. Of these two views, that of Judge Lauterpacht is possibly the more convincing.[98]

However, it is possible to advance other alternatives. For example, the Court might accept both the declaration and the reservation as valid in so far as they relate to matters which could conceivably fall within a State's domestic jurisdiction, but also consider that there are some matters, such as boundary disputes or allegations of the unlawful use of force, which could not conceivably do so. In such a case the Court might well assert the right to review or reject an attempt by a State to invoke its automatic domestic jurisdiction reservation.

---

[98] Similar reasoning appears in the Separate Opinion of President Schwebel in the *Spain/Canada Fisheries Jurisdiction* case, judgment of 4 December 1998, ICJ Rep. 1998, 432. But, for arguments to the contrary, see the powerful dissenting opinion of Judge Bedjaoui in that case. See also I. F. I. Shihata, *The Power of the International Court to Determine its Own Jurisdiction* (The Hague, 1965), 271–304.

The question has not been definitively answered. The Court itself did not raise the point in either the *Hostages* case (1980),[99] where the USA was the claimant State, or in the *Nicaragua v. US* case (1984),[100] where it was the respondent.

It is to be noted that at the present time only five States (Liberia, Malawi, Mexico, the Philippines and Sudan) have such a reservation in their acceptance.[101] (The United States withdrew its entire acceptance in 1985.)

7.6.2.3 *Limitation of jurisdiction to certain categories of case*

Reservations may limit the jurisdiction of the Court to certain categories of case. For instance, in 1931 Persia (Iran) accepted the compulsory jurisdiction of the Court, but only in respect of disputes arising out of treaties concluded by it after that date. So, in the *Anglo-Iranian Oil Company* case (1952),[102] the United Kingdom claimed that a concession granted to the Company by Persia in 1933, replacing earlier concessions, was a treaty. (The UK Government was the major shareholder in the Company.) The Court held, however, that since the concession was not an agreement between the two States, it was not a treaty, and declined jurisdiction. More recently, Canada has excluded from the jurisdiction of the Court disputes arising from certain of its enactments concerning the seas adjacent to its coasts. The effect of this reservation was questioned in the *Spain/Canada Fisheries Jurisdiction* case.[103] Though a minority of the judges expressed considerable unease at this manipulation of the 'reservations' system, the majority adhered to the Court's previous case law, and to the implications of the principle of consensual jurisdiction in the Court, and held that the Court lacked jurisdiction over a dispute involving such an enactment.

7.6.2.4 *Time limitations*

Frequently, acceptance of compulsory jurisdiction is only granted in respect of disputes arising after a particular date. In the *Interhandel* case (1959)[104] the Court was faced with a clause in the United States reservation which took this form. According to that clause, the United States accepted jurisdiction with respect to disputes 'hereafter [i.e., after 26 August 1946] arising'. The United States and Switzerland had been at odds about the dispute in the *Interhandel* case before 1946; but with respect to the claim in issue, that is, the claim for restitution to Interhandel of its assets, this had only been requested in 1948 and rejected then by the United States. The dispute therefore arose only in May of that year, and the

---

[99] ICJ Rep. 1980, 3.
[100] ICJ Rep. 1984, 392.
[101] See ICJ, *Yearbook 1996–1997*, 84–125.
[102] ICJ Rep. 1952, 93.
[103] Judgment of 4 December 1998, ICJ Rep. 1998, 432.
[104] ICJ Rep. 1959, 6.

United States' objection to jurisdiction on this ground was dismissed.[105] A variant on this kind of reservation, such as is to be found in the current United Kingdom declaration, is to accept jurisdiction only over disputes which arise after a certain date with regard to situations or facts subsequent to that date. This is sometimes called the 'Belgian' formula, and is a more draconian limitation than that contained in the previous formula, since a dispute may arise after a certain date, but the situation or facts out of which it arises may exist before that date.[106] No doubt if the United States had used the 'Belgian' formula it would have succeeded in the *Interhandel* case.

The 'Belgian' formula can give rise to two difficulties: (a) it is not always easy to determine when a dispute arose, and (b) it is often very difficult to decide when the situation or facts out of which it arose first existed. The Court has been faced with the matter several times. The first was in the *Phosphates in Morocco* case (1938).[107] In 1906 the General Act of Algeçiras, dealing with Morocco, then under French control, was concluded. In 1911 France and Germany concluded a Convention which laid down an 'open-door' policy for Morocco and regulated mining concessions, to which Italy acceded. In 1918–19 phosphate mining licences were issued to French nationals who assigned them to an Italian. But in 1920 the French created a State phosphate monopoly and in 1925 the Italian's rights were refused recognition and Italy complained. The refusal was finally confirmed by France. In 1931 France had accepted compulsory jurisdiction 'over any dispute which may arise after the ratification of the present declaration with regard to situations or facts subsequent to such ratification'. The Court held that it had no jurisdiction in a case brought by Italy against France; the dispute, and the facts out of which it arose, clearly existed before 1931.

On the other hand, in the *Electricity Company of Sofia and Bulgaria* case (1939) the Court held that it had jurisdiction.[108] In 1898 an electricity concession was granted by Bulgaria to a French company which in 1908 transferred it to a Belgian company. The concession was nationalised by Bulgaria during the First World War, but restored by the Treaty of Neuilly in 1920. In 1925 an arbitrator laid down electricity prices. In 1926 Belgium accepted compulsory jurisdiction 'in any dispute arising after the ratification of the present declaration with regard to situations or facts subsequent to this ratification'. In 1934, the Bulgarian State mines administration imposed a coal tariff against which the company protested,

---

[105] We discuss this case, and the effect given in it to the United States reservation, further below, p. 151.

[106] The current Indian declaration of 1974 goes even further, since it excludes 'disputes prior to the date of this declaration, including any dispute the foundations, reasons, facts, causes, origins, definitions, allegations or bases of which existed prior to this date, even if they are submitted or brought to the knowledge of the Court hereafter'. See ICJ *Yearbook 1996–1997*, 100.

[107] (1938) PCIJ, Ser. A/B, No. 74 (1938).

[108] (1939) PCIJ, Ser. A/B, No. 77 (1939).

but proceedings in the local courts went against the company. In 1936 Bulgaria imposed a discriminatory income tax. Belgium protested at these actions and took the case to the Court. The Court held that the dispute clearly arose after 1926. Further, the situation or facts came into existence after that year. The 1925 arbitral award was the source of the company's rights, but gave rise to no dispute. The facts out of which the dispute arose were those which came about in 1934–6: 'The only situations or facts which must be taken into account from the standpoint of the compulsory jurisdiction . . . are those which must be considered as being the source of the dispute.' In effect, the Permanent Court substituted the words 'caused by' for 'with regard to' in the reservation, since one fact, the Award, had existed in 1925.

This formula was also considered in the *Right of Passage* case (1960).[109] India's declaration of 1940 limited the Court's jurisdiction to disputes arising after 5 February 1930 with respect to situations or facts which existed only after that date. The Court alluded to the *Electricity Company of Sofia and Bulgaria* case and found that there had been no controversy at all over Portugal's right of passage over Indian territory, which had existed for several centuries, until 1954. India's argument that the dispute arose out of a situation or facts existing before 1930 was, therefore, rejected.

7.6.2.5 'Multilateral treaty' reservations

In the United States declaration of 1946 there was included a reservation regarding disputes arising under a multilateral treaty. This is known as the Vandenberg amendment, after the US Senator who introduced it. The Court would not have compulsory jurisdiction 'unless all parties to the treaty affected by the decision are parties to the case or unless the United States specially agrees'.

In the *Nicaragua* v. *US* case (1984; 1986),[110] the United States explained that the reason for this reservation was to prevent the Court deciding in a case between two parties to the treaty what the treaty means. This decision would only be binding between those two parties and not between them and the other parties or between the other parties *inter se*. This the USA considered undesirable.

On one interpretation of the Vandenberg amendment, advanced by the USA, the word 'affected' would entail that *all* the parties would have to be before the Court. So, as Nicaragua was alleging that the United States had indulged in the wrongful use of force contrary to, in particular, the Charter of the United Nations (and that of the Organisation of American States of 1948) all members of the UN would have to be parties to the case to satisfy the Vandenberg amendment. Another interpretation of 'affected', and that which was eventually adopted by the

---

[109] ICJ Rep. 1960, 6.
[110] ICJ Rep. 1984, 392; ICJ Rep. 1986, 14.

Court,[111] was that it entailed only that those States whose rights and obligations would be affected by the decision should be parties. Since the Court so held, and because El Salvador would be affected by the decision,[112] it followed that the Court could not entertain the case in so far as Nicaragua relied on those multilateral conventions.[113]

7.6.2.6 *Resort to other means of peaceful settlement*

Some States (such as the United Kingdom in its current declaration) have excluded from the Court's jurisdiction 'disputes in regard to which the parties have agreed [and some declarations add "or shall agree"] to have recourse to some other method of settlement'. The ICJ has twice recently had to deal with objections to the jurisdiction based on such reservations.

In the *Certain Phosphate Lands in Nauru* case (1992),[114] Nauru alleged that Australia had breached provisions of the trusteeship agreement under which Australia was responsible for Nauru before the latter's independence in 1968. Australia attempted to challenge the Court's jurisdiction by relying on such a reservation concerning other methods of settlement that was included in its declaration. It argued that any dispute over the conduct of the trusteeship fell within the jurisdiction of the UN General Assembly and Trusteeship Council and should be regarded as having been settled by the unconditional termination of the trusteeship over Nauru. Thus Australia and Nauru had agreed to have 'recourse to some other method of peaceful settlement'. The Court rejected this argument. The arrangements during the trusteeship period were irrelevant. The terms of both article 36(2) of the Statute and the Australian declaration only cover disputes between States. Until independence, Nauru was not a State; and after independence no relevant agreement had been concluded between Australia and the Republic of Nauru.[115]

In the *Arbitral Award* case (*Guinea-Bissau v. Senegal*),[116] the Court was asked to determine the validity of an arbitral award concerning the maritime boundary of the two States. In their acceptances of the Court's jurisdiction both States had

---

[111] The Court did not decide this point at the jurisdictional stage in 1984, but joined the US objection to the merits.

[112] This was because the United States claimed to justify its actions in part upon the basis of its exercising a right of self-defence collectively with El Salvador against unlawful force directed by Nicaragua against that State.

[113] The Court decided the case on the basis of customary international law. Judges Schwebel (USA) and Sir Robert Jennings (UK) strongly dissented from the Court's decision to do this. The Court had decided in 1984 by 14–1 that it possessed jurisdiction by virtue of the bilateral Treaty of Managua 1956.

[114] ICJ Rep. 1992, 240.

[115] Australia could presumably have avoided the Court's jurisdiction had it excluded from its declaration disputes arising out of facts or situations existing during the trusteeship.

[116] ICJ Rep. 1991, 53. See the note by F. Beveridge (1992) 41 *ICLQ* 891.

made reservations of the kind under discussion, and also reservations regarding earlier disputes. The Court held, correctly, that neither kind of reservation precluded its taking jurisdiction. The dispute arose out of the award and concerned its application. It did not arise from the dispute which had given rise to the award, and which had been subject to the obligation to resort to arbitration.

7.6.3 Condition of reciprocity

Article 36(2) provides that a State may make a declaration which is effective to confer jurisdiction on the Court in respect of another State which accepts '*the same obligation*'. Thus a declaration operates reciprocally. But this principle of reciprocity contained in article 36(2) entails also that both of the parties must have accepted the obligation to subject the particular dispute to the Court. In other words, if it falls within a reservation contained in a declaration of *either* party it is excluded from the Court's jurisdiction should either party rely on the reservation and whether or not it is also excluded from the Court's jurisdiction by a reservation of the other party.[117]

As the Court put it in the *Interhandel* case, 'Reciprocity in the case of Declarations accepting the compulsory jurisdiction of the Court enables a party to invoke a reservation to that acceptance which it has not expressed in its own Declaration but which the other Party has expressed in its Declaration.'[118]

This is exemplified by the *Electricity Company of Sofia and Bulgaria* case.[119] Belgium instituted proceedings against Bulgaria. Belgium's declaration contained a reservation excluding disputes arising out of situations or facts existing before 1926; but Bulgaria's did not. The parties agreed that Bulgaria had the right to rely on Belgium's reservation on the basis of reciprocity and to argue that the Court had no jurisdiction, and the PCIJ also agreed that Bulgaria could do this.[120]

However many States, such as the United Kingdom, have accepted the Court's jurisdiction 'on *condition* of reciprocity'. Does this have any significance, or does it add nothing to the *principle* of reciprocity contained in article 36(2)? Often, as in the last-mentioned case, this is immaterial, since the operation of the principle and of such a condition will lead to the same result. The ICJ has usually treated the principle and the condition as identical, as it did in the *Right of Passage* case.[121] But this is not always strictly correct.

---

[117] Should neither party rely on it, the jurisdiction of the Court might be regarded as founded upon *forum prorogatum*, as to which see p. 136 above.

[118] ICJ Rep. 1959, 6 at 23.

[119] (1939) PCIJ, Ser. A/B, No. 77.

[120] Although the Court ultimately held, as we have seen (pp. 147–8, above), that the dispute was not excluded by the reservation and that it had jurisdiction.

[121] ICJ Rep. 1957, 125 at 145.

In one case, the distinction between them was crucial. In the *Norwegian Loans* case[122] France instituted proceedings against Norway. France's declaration reserved from the Court's jurisdiction all 'matters which are essentially within the *national jurisdiction as understood by the Government of the French Republic*'. Norway's declaration had no kindred reservation. Norway claimed to rely on the French reservation and to deny the court had jurisdiction since the matter was within the *national jurisdiction of Norway as understood by the Government of Norway*. The Court allowed Norway to do this and held that it had no jurisdiction. But this is not the same situation as that in the *Electricity Company of Sofia and Bulgaria* case. The French declaration did not exclude matters within Norway's national jurisdiction as understood by Norway. Therefore the dispute did not fall within the 'reserved' area in the French declaration. The Court observed that[123] '[i]n accordance with the condition of reciprocity to which the acceptance of the compulsory jurisdiction is made subject in both Declarations . . . Norway, equally with France, is entitled to except from the compulsory jurisdiction of the Court disputes understood by Norway to be essentially within its national jurisdiction'. That is to say, the dispute was excluded by the *condition* of reciprocity contained in the Norwegian declaration and not by the operation of the *principle* stated in article 36(2).

This being so, the condition made in a State's declaration has some purpose and is not redundant.

One last point. In the *Interhandel* case[124] the USA tried to effect the converse: i.e. when Switzerland brought an action against it the United States sought to put into Switzerland's declaration a reservation that was not contained therein, but was contained in the declaration made by the USA. The United States' declaration of 1946 excluded from the Court's jurisdiction disputes arising before 26 August 1946. On 26 July 1948, the United States finally rejected the Swiss Government's diplomatic representations on behalf of the Swiss company, Interhandel. On 28 July 1948 the Swiss Government made a declaration accepting the Court's jurisdiction, but with no reservation as to time. The United States argued that it could apply the 'past disputes' reservations in its own declaration to the Swiss acceptance date. The court rejected this possibility. Reciprocity enables one party to rely on a reservation contained in the declaration of the other party; it does not permit a State to rely on a reservation which is not included in the declaration of the other party.

---

[122] ICJ Rep. 1957, 9.
[123] Ibid., at 24.
[124] ICJ Rep. 1959, 6. See also *Nicaragua* v. *US*, ICJ Rep. 1984, 392 at 419.

7.6.4 *Withdrawal or termination of declaration*

A State may withdraw or terminate its declaration, at any rate if it has reserved the right to do so (as has the United Kingdom). If a period of notice is specified in the declaration, the termination will be valid if notice is given within that period.[125] If it has not done so and the declaration has an indefinite duration, the matter is not entirely clear. In the *Nicaragua* v. *US* case (1984) the Court said[126] that if the United States had not limited its right to do so by stating (in its declaration) that such change was to take place only on six months' notice it could have modified or terminated its declaration, 'a power which is inherent in any unilateral act of a State'. But the Court later said that 'the right of immediate termination of declarations with indefinite duration is far from established', and added that it appeared that declarations should be treated by analogy with the law of treaties 'which requires a reasonable time [of notice] for withdrawal or termination'.[127]

However, it is clear that a State cannot withdraw a declaration after the Court has been seised of a case so as to deprive it of jurisdiction. Nor can the Court, once seised of a case, be deprived of jurisdiction by expiration of a declaration by lapse of time. This is the so-called rule in the *Nottebohm* case.[128] Liechtenstein became a party to the Statute, made a declaration and referred the case against Guatemala to the Court just before Guatemala's declaration expired. Guatemala argued that the Court had thereby subsequently lost jurisdiction over the case. The Court held that this was not so: it said that 'an extrinsic fact such as the subsequent lapse of the Declaration, by reason of expiry of the period or by denunciation, cannot deprive the Court of the jurisdiction already established'.[129]

It is convenient to mention here that when a declaration is made it takes effect as soon as it is deposited with the UN Secretary-General. It is not necessary that other States be informed, or even aware, of the deposit: the declarant State may proceed immediately to initiate proceedings against another State that has accepted the jurisdiction of the Court, because the jurisdictional nexus is immediately established.[130]

---

[125] *Nicaragua* v. *US*, ICJ Rep. 1984, 392 at 418.

[126] Ibid., at 419. And see S. Oda, 'Reservations in the Declarations of acceptance of the Optional Clause and the period of validity of those Declarations: the effect of the Shultz letter' (1988) 59 *BYIL* 1.

[127] *Nicaragua* v. *US*, ICJ Rep. 1984, 392 at 420. The Vienna Convention on the Law of Treaties 1969, art. 46, requires twelve months' notice of termination. But note the limitations on the treaty analogy, discussed by the Court in the *Spain/Canada Fisheries Jurisdiction* case, judgment of 4 December 1998, ICJ Rep. 1998, 432.

[128] ICJ Rep. 1953, 121.

[129] Ibid., at 123.

[130] *Case concerning Land and Maritime Boundary between Cameroon and Nigeria*, judgment of 11 June 1998, paras. 21–47, ICJ Rep. 1998, 275.

7.6.5 Variation of the terms of a declaration

A State may, in its declaration, reserve the right to vary it by adding new or cancelling existing reservations; the United Kingdom, for instance, has done this. The Court upheld the validity of such a reservation, by which the variation would be effective as from the moment of its notification to the UN Secretary-General, in the *Right of Passage* case (1957).[131] India had objected to a reservation in the Portuguese declaration which was in such terms, mainly on the ground of its uncertainty and on its alleged offensiveness to the principle of reciprocity.[132] The Court also held, however, that such a reservation could not be used so as to deprive the Court of jurisdiction over a case which had already been submitted to it.

The State must have made such a reservation in order to be able to vary an existing declaration. The United States' declaration of 1946 contained no right to amend or vary it, but was expressly to remain in force for five years and thereafter until six months after notice might be given to terminate it. On 6 May 1984, the United States gave notice that the 1946 declaration was not to apply to 'disputes with any Central American States or arising out of or related to events in Central America' and that 'notwithstanding the terms of the [1946] declaration, this proviso shall take effect immediately and shall remain in force for two years'. In the *Nicaragua* v. *US* case (1984),[133] the Court held that this purported change was ineffective. The United States could only withdraw its declaration in accordance with the terms thereof (i.e. on six months' notice): it could not keep the declaration in force and vary it. The United States had reserved the right to do the former, but not the latter.

One last point regarding reservations. It is important to emphasise that the fact that a case comes within a reservation to an optional clause declaration does not affect the possibility that the Court has jurisdiction on another basis, as was held in the *Nicaragua* v. *US* case.[134]

7.6.6 'Transferred' declarations

This matter has already been mentioned in connection with article 37.[135] Article 36(5) of the Statute provides that:

> Declarations made under article 36 of the Statute of the Permanent Court of International Justice and which are still in force shall be deemed, *as between the parties to the present Statute*, to be acceptances of the compulsory jurisdiction of the

---

[131] ICJ Rep. 1957, 125.
[132] For the principle of reciprocity, see p. 150, above.
[133] ICJ Rep. 1984, 392 at 421.
[134] See p. 138 above and see the *Appeal Relating to the Jurisdiction of the Council of the International Civil Aviation Organisation* case, ICJ Rep. 1972, 46 at 53.
[135] p. 139, above.

International Court of Justice for the period which they still have to run and in accordance with their terms.

In the *Aerial Incident* case (1959)[136] the Court said that this meant that such declarations ceased to be in force in 1945 when the PCIJ was dissolved unless the State in question at once became a party to the Statute of the ICJ. Since Bulgaria was not a party at that time, Israel could not rely on Bulgaria's PCIJ declaration to found jurisdiction. This decision seems very technical and involves reading the words underlined thus: 'as between the [present] parties to the present Statute' which is not what article 36(5) says. It was, as we have seen, distinguished in a highly artificial manner in the *Barcelona Traction* case (1964).[137]

In the *Nicaragua* v. *US* case (1984),[138] Nicaragua had made an unconditional declaration under the Statute of the PCIJ in 1929 and relied on this to institute proceedings against the United States. The declaration was ineffective unless Nicaragua was a party to the Statute of the PCIJ, which it had signed but did not appear to have ratified. The League of Nations had no official record of any instrument of ratification, and Nicaragua itself was unclear about the matter. The United States argued that Nicaragua's declaration was never 'in force', and so was not 'transferred' by article 36(5). The Court held that the declaration did not, under the wording of that provision, have to have had 'binding force', but merely that it must have been 'made under' the Statute of the PCIJ. Nicaragua did become a party to the Statute of the ICJ in 1945, and so the declaration of 1929 could be transferred.[139] It also held that by reason of the acceptance by Nicaragua and other States without demur of the listing in UN and ICJ publications of Nicaragua as a declarant under the Optional Clause, those States (including the United States and Nicaragua, if an action had been brought against it) would be estopped from denying that this was the case. It is submitted that none of this strange reasoning is very satisfactory; the Court rejected certain cogent arguments of the United States on this point.[140]

7.6.7 The Optional Clause: Summary

It has to be said that the Optional Clause system, as a method of endowing the Court with compulsory jurisdiction, has not been a great success. In 1925,

---

[136] ICJ Rep. 1959, 127.

[137] ICJ Rep. 1964, 6.

[138] ICJ Rep. 1984, 392.

[139] Unless the *Aerial Incident* case is correct, the same would be true if Nicaragua had not become a party to the Statute until after 1945.

[140] These were based on the fact that a note of caution about Nicaragua's declaration was sounded in the publications referred to and that in 1943 and 1955 Nicaragua had told the United States that it was not necessarily in force. See the dissenting judgments of Judges Schwebel and Sir Robert Jennings. See also G. L. Scott and C. L. Carr, 'The ICJ and compulsory jurisdiction: the case for closing the clause' (1987) 81 *AJIL* 57.

twenty-three of the thirty-six States party to the Court's Statute had made optional clause declarations. In 1945, twenty-three of the fifty-one States Parties had done so. Twenty years later, in 1965, forty of the 118 States Parties had made optional clause declarations. And the position in 1996 was summarised thus:

> In July 1996 there were only 59, from the following regional groups: Africa 17 (11 of them since 1966); Latin America 9; Asia 5; Europe and other States 28. It must be added that 12 other States that had at one time recognized the compulsory jurisdiction of the ICJ have withdrawn their acceptance of such jurisdiction, 7 of them after they had been made respondents in proceedings before the Court.[141]

Of the five permanent members of the Security Council, Russia and China have never made such declarations, France withdrew its declaration in 1974 after the *Nuclear Tests* case and the United States did likewise in 1985 after the *Nicaragua* v. *US (Jurisdiction)* case. Only the United Kingdom has a declaration in force at the present time. Furthermore, as we have seen, most of the declarations (around two-thirds of them) that are in force are subject to different forms of, and quite often numerous, reservations. Some of these are very far-reaching. The result of all this is that the Court's compulsory jurisdiction is extremely limited and in only half a dozen cases decided since the Second World War has jurisdiction been based upon optional clause declarations.

Among the reasons for this are that States do not want to be involved in international litigation (or arbitration) unless they think they have a good chance of winning. Moreover, they do not like to be made defendants. It does not do much for their international standing. Also, a defendant State is not in a position to take part in defining the questions to be put to the Court. In these respects, submission of the dispute by special agreement is much more congenial. When the United States withdrew its declaration it emphasised that it had no objection to conferring jurisdiction in this way, and it has indeed since done so.[142]

8. Admissibility

A distinction must be made between objections by the respondent State to the jurisdiction of the Court and objections on the ground that the case is not admissible. Both objections prevent the Court hearing and determining the merits of the case, but lack of jurisdiction may prevent the Court from hearing any cases against the defendant State, whereas non-admissibility does not. Or, put differently, lack of jurisdiction means that the Court cannot hear a particular case at all, whereas non-admissibility means sometimes that the Court could have heard the

---

[141] On the ICJ web site, from which the most recent statistics, and other details and documents concerning the Court's activity, can be obtained: <http://www.icj-cij.org/>.

[142] In the *Elettronica Sicula* case, ICJ Rep. 1989, 15.

case at one time, but cannot do so now, or that it cannot hear it now, but might do so in the future (as with non-exhaustion of local remedies). In the *Interhandel* case (1959),[143] the Court treated non-exhaustion of local remedies as a matter of admissibility rather than of jurisdiction, though the respondent State had pleaded it as an objection to the Court's jurisdiction.

Some objections to admissibility are common to both arbitral and judicial methods of settlement and are discussed elsewhere in this book. These include non-compliance with the nationality of claims and exhaustion of local remedies rules.[144] We discuss here some objections which have either been dealt with only by the ICJ or which have produced particular problems in cases heard by it.

8.1 Hypothetical nature of the case

As we noted above,[145] in the *Northern Cameroons* case (1963)[146] the Court rejected a case brought by Cameroon against the United Kingdom in which it had claimed maladministration by the United Kingdom as Trustee of the former Trust Territory of Northern Cameroons (which had by a United Nations plebiscite decided to join Nigeria rather than Cameroon, after which the General Assembly terminated the trusteeship). The Court regarded the case as hypothetical and lacking in any real purpose, since nothing would come of any possible decision by the Court.

This decision was not applied in the *Certain Phosphate Lands in Nauru* case[147] where the Court was faced with a dispute between Nauru and Australia, a member together with the United Kingdom and New Zealand of the Administering Authority of Nauru while it was under Trusteeship. Australia argued that the termination of the Trusteeship Agreement in 1967 precluded subsequent allegations of breaches of the Agreement being examined by the Court. The Court held that the dispute already existed before termination of the Agreement and that everyone then knew that the differences continued. So the termination had done nothing to settle these differences. Even though the General Assembly Resolution 2347 (XXII), which terminated the Trusteeship, did not expressly reserve Nauru's possible rights, it did not give a discharge to the Administering Authority from possible responsibility. The Australian objection was dismissed.[148]

---

[143] ICJ Rep. 1959, 6, 26.
[144] Chapter eight, 191–8.
[145] Chapter one, p. 13.
[146] ICJ Rep. 1963, 15.
[147] ICJ Rep. 1992, 240.
[148] The Court also dismissed Australia's objections based on (i) a condition in its own acceptance of compulsory jurisdiction that there was an agreement with Nauru to settle the dispute by other methods, (ii) Nauru's alleged waiver, (iii) passage of time. It upheld Australia's objection to Nauru's claim to the assets of the British Phosphates Commissioners as a new claim additional to the dispute originally submitted to the Court. Australia's objection, also unsuccessful, based on the fact that the

8.2 The case has become 'moot'

We also noted above[149] the decision in the *Nuclear Tests* cases (1974),[150] in which the Court dismissed cases brought by Australia and New Zealand against France to test the legality of French nuclear tests in the Pacific. It held that a French Government statement that it would undertake no more such testings was intended by France to be binding and consequently was binding on France in international law, so that Australia had achieved its objective. This extraordinary decision[151] provoked a joint dissent from four judges, but it enabled the Court to avoid determining the legality of the testing of nuclear weapons.[152]

On the other hand, in the (Icelandic) *Fisheries Jurisdiction* case,[153] the Court decided that the conclusion of an interim agreement between the United Kingdom and Iceland, which established a *modus vivendi* while the Court was hearing the case, did not prevent the Court continuing to hear it. An actual controversy between the States still existed.

8.3 Lack of interest in the subject matter

The Court will declare the case inadmissible if the claimant State has no interest in the case. This may be because of a general principle concerning the degree of interest which must exist. Thus in the *South West Africa* cases (1966),[154] after the Court had heard the merits of the case, it held that Ethiopia and Liberia did not have 'sufficient interest' of their own to bring a case against South Africa alleging breaches of the League of Nations Mandate over South West Africa (Namibia) merely because they had been members of the League. Members of the League had no direct recourse against mandatories but could only use the machinery of the League, which had ceased to exist with the demise of the League.

United Kingdom and New Zealand were not parties to the case, will be discussed later. See p. 159, below.

[149] Chapter one, p. 13.

[150] ICJ Rep. 1974, 327.

[151] Extraordinary, since it is inconceivable that France, which had refused to become a party to the Nuclear Test Ban Treaty 1963, intended any such thing: see A. Rubin, 'The international effects of unilateral declarations' (1977) 71 *AJIL* 1, esp. at 24–8.

[152] The Court was diplomatic about this. It was only with the change of Government in Australia in 1973 that that country alleged that nuclear testing was illegal. Before that, nuclear tests had, indeed, taken place in Australia itself. An attempt to persuade the Court to examine the situation was made by New Zealand in response to France's announcement in June 1995 that it proposed to conduct nuclear weapons tests. This attempt was rebuffed by an Order of the Court of 22 September 1995: ICJ Rep. 1995, 288: see the note by R. Volterra [1996] 55 *CLJ* 3.

[153] ICJ Rep. 1974, 3. See also p. 139 above.

[154] ICJ Rep. 1966, 6. See I. Brownlie, *Principles of Public International Law*, 5th edn. (Oxford, 1998), 469–76.

Or a State may have no legal interest, in the sense of *locus standi*. In the *Barcelona Traction* case (1970),[155] the Court dismissed Belgium's action against Spain because the alleged injury was to the company, which was Canadian. The alleged preponderant Belgian shareholding did not give Belgium a legal interest in the case, since the alleged injury did not affect the shareholders' legal rights but only the legal rights of the company itself.[156]

8.4 Legal interest of a third State

We have seen that, in the *Monetary Gold Removed from Rome in 1943* case,[157] the Court declined to exercise its jurisdiction in a case referred to it under a special agreement. In that case a State (Albania) which was not a party to the proceedings had a legal interest which would fall to be determined in the Court's decision. This rule seems to be concerned with admissibility.

The facts of the case were as follows. Gold, which originally belonged to Albania and was removed by the Italians to Rome during World War II, was then removed thence to Germany by the Germans. Italy had a claim to the gold by way of reparation for a previous international wrong allegedly done to it by Albania arising from the nationalisation of a bank. An arbitrator held that the gold belonged to the Albanian National Bank. France, the United Kingdom and the USA formed a Tripartite Commission under a Treaty of 1946 to deal with restitution, to the countries from which it had been looted, of monetary gold found in the possession of Germany. The United Kingdom had a claim on the gold by way of satisfaction of the judgment debt owed to it by Albania arising out of the *Corfu Channel* case. The ICJ had jurisdiction over the *Monetary Gold* case by a special agreement (the Washington Agreement 1951) between the members of the Tripartite Commission and Italy. Italy instituted proceedings against the three States under this agreement. Then, surprisingly, Italy objected to the Court exercising its jurisdiction.[158]

The Court upheld Italy's principal objection, which was that since the Italian claim was based on its right of redress for the wrong committed by Albania, the determination of the case would depend on a decision upon the international responsibility of Albania. The latter issue would be, said the Court, 'the very

---

[155] ICJ Rep. 1970, 3.

[156] See further, chapter eight, pp. 193–5.

[157] ICJ Rep. 1954, 19, see p. 135, above.

[158] The reason for Italy's objection is unclear. H. Lauterpacht observed that 'although in the *Monetary Gold* case the Court declined jurisdiction at the instance of one of the parties—the applicant party—it is possible that it would have done so *proprio motu* on the ground that the application asked it to determine the legality of the conduct of a State which was not a party to the dispute. This being so, it is not apparent why the applicant State itself felt called upon to question the jurisdiction which it had invoked': *Development of International Law by the International Court* (London, 1958), 102–3; and see also *ibid.*, 342–3.

subject-matter' of its decision. Albania had not given its consent to the Court deciding this issue, so the Court could not exercise its jurisdiction over the Italian claim.

The *Monetary Gold* case was distinguished in the *Nicaragua* v. *US* case (1984).[159] There, the Court rejected the United States' argument that it should rule Nicaragua's application inadmissible because the case also concerned the legal interests of three States which were not parties to the case, El Salvador, Costa Rica and Honduras. Whereas, in the *Monetary Gold* case, Albania's responsibility was the 'very subject-matter' of the decision, in the *Nicaragua* case, the third States' interests might, at most, only be affected by it.

Again, the *Monetary Gold* principle was regarded by a Chamber of the Court as inapplicable to the rights of Nicaragua in the Gulf of Fonseca in the *Land, Island and Maritime Frontier* case (1990)[160] between El Salvador and Honduras. This was a case in which Nicaragua sought to intervene under article 62 of the Court's Statute and will be discussed in that context, where we submit that the disregard of the *Monetary Gold* principle is open to criticism.[161]

The decision in the *Monetary Gold* case was again distinguished in the *Certain Phosphate Lands in Nauru* case (1992),[162] between Nauru and Australia. Nauru brought an action concerning the rehabilitation of phosphate lands in Nauru which had been worked out before Nauruan independence in 1968. Nauru had, after World War I, been placed under the mandate of His Britannic Majesty as sovereign of the United Kingdom, Australia and New Zealand; and the Trusteeship Agreement of 1947 continued the same arrangements. The three States were to be the 'Administering Authority', though Australia was to undertake the actual administration, until the three States should conclude any agreement to vary these arrangements. No such agreement was ever made. Australia, relying on the *Monetary Gold* case, argued that Nauru's claim was really against the Administering Authority, so that the UK and New Zealand were indispensable parties to the dispute and their responsibility was involved; the case was therefore inadmissible. The Court held, however, that the cases were not *in pari materia*, and that the interests of the United Kingdom and New Zealand did not form the 'very subject-matter'[163] of any judgment the Court might give; the determination of their responsibility was not a prerequisite to determination of Australia's. A finding against Australia, though it 'might well have legal implications' for the UK and New Zealand, might only 'affect these'. The Court also

---

[159] ICJ Rep. 1984, 392.
[160] ICJ Rep. 1990, 92.
[161] p. 168, below.
[162] ICJ Rep. 1992, 240. See the note by I. Scobbie (1993) 42 *ICLQ* 710.
[163] This has become the standard test. Cf. *Case concerning Land and Maritime Boundary between Cameroon and Nigeria*, judgment of 11 June 1998, para. 79, ICJ Rep. 1998, 275.

suggested that the interests of the 'third States' would be protected by article 59 of the Statute. But the same could have been said of Albania in the *Monetary Gold* case.

Four judges (President Sir Robert Jennings and Judges Oda, Ago and Schwebel) dissented on this part of the judgment (Judge Oda dissented on almost every part of it), believing that there was no way the Court could decide whether Australia was liable for all or only part of the claim of Nauru without adjudicating upon the obligations and responsibility of the UK and New Zealand. The President thought that it was 'manifest' that the interests of those two States would constitute the 'very subject-matter' of a judgment by the Court.

Australia had better luck with this argument in the *East Timor* case (1995).[164] East Timor was a Portuguese colony from the sixteenth century, but Portugal left in 1975. Indonesia then occupied the territory, and its incorporation into Indonesia was recognised *de jure* by Australia in 1978. Thereafter, Australia and Indonesia negotiated to delimit their continental shelves in the 'Timor Gap', between the south coast of East Timor and the north coast of Australia. A treaty creating a 'Zone of Co-operation' in the area was concluded in 1989 and Australia implemented this by legislation. The Court had compulsory jurisdiction over Australia but not over Indonesia, so Portugal instituted proceedings against Australia. Portugal claimed that by its dealings Australia had acted unlawfully, by infringing the rights of the East Timorese people to self-determination and of Portugal as administering authority. Australia's principal objection to the ICJ hearing the case was that the Court could not act if to do so would involve it ruling on the lawfulness of Indonesia's entry into and presence in East Timor, on the validity of the 1989 treaty, or on Indonesia's rights thereunder, Indonesia not being a party to the proceedings. That is, Australia's behaviour could not be separated from Indonesia's.

The Court applied the *Monetary Gold* principle, saying that it could not assess Australia's behaviour without considering why Indonesia could not lawfully have concluded the 1989 Treaty. It added that 'the very subject matter of the Court's decision would necessarily be a determination whether, having regard to the circumstances in which Indonesia entered and remained in East Timor, it could or could not have acquired the power to enter into treaties on behalf of East Timor relating to the resources of the latter's continental shelf. The Court could not make such a determination in the absence of the consent of Indonesia'.

It is not easy to identify precisely the factors which led the Court to apply the *Monetary Gold* principle so differently in each of these cases.

---

[164] ICJ Rep. 1995, 90. See the note by V. Lowe [1995] 54 *CLJ* 484.

Adoption of the *Monetary Gold* principle is as far as the Court has gone in the direction of requiring that 'essential' or 'indispensable' parties must be before it in order for it to have or exercise jurisdiction to decide the case before it. That is to say, unless the third party's rights or obligations form the very subject matter of the decision, the Court will proceed even though a third party's interests *might* be affected by it. The Court has pointed out that a third party's interests are protected by article 59 of the Statute, which provides that the 'decision of the Court has no binding force except between the parties and in respect of that particular case'. Moreover, the third State may, if it wishes, apply to intervene in the case under articles 62 or 63 of the Statute, or may institute proceedings itself.[165] If it does not do so, the Court has no power to compel a third State to appear before it.

Thus, in the *Nicaragua* v. *US* case (1984),[166] the United States objected that the application of Nicaragua was inadmissible because Nicaragua had failed to bring before the Court other parties (El Salvador, Costa Rica and Honduras), whose presence and participation was necessary for the protection of their rights and for the determination of the issues raised by the application. The Court rejected the objection, giving the above reasons. As indicated it repeated these in dismissing a similar objection by Australia in the *Certain Phosphate Lands in Nauru* case.[167]

The relationship between the *Monetary Gold* principle and the right of third States to intervene will be discussed later.[168]

8.5 Other examples

In the *Nicaragua* v. *US* case (1984),[169] the Court rejected several United States' objections to admissibility in addition to the objection based on the *Monetary Gold* case principle.[170] These included:

1. Nicaragua's allegations of United States' unlawful use of force were, under the Charter of the United Nations, exclusively a matter for the Security Council and not for the Court to deal with. This was rejected on the obvious ground that article 24 of the Charter only gives the Security Council 'primary' responsibility for

---

[165] In the *Monetary Gold* case itself, Albania had not instituted any proceedings and it had refused to apply to be allowed to intervene in the case.

[166] ICJ Rep. 1984, 392 especially at 431. For the fate of El Salvador's request to intervene under art. 63 of the Statute see p. 163, below.

[167] ICJ Rep. 1992, 240. See also the *Frontier Dispute* case (*Burkina Faso/Mali*), ICJ Rep. 1986, 14 for the position of Niger, the third State; and the *Land, Island and Maritime Frontier* case (*El Salvador/Honduras*), ICJ Rep. 1990, 92 in which Nicaragua sought to intervene. This case is discussed at p. 166, below. In the *Certain Phosphate Lands in Nauru* case, Judge Schwebel, dissenting, trenchantly criticised both this reasoning and the Court's judgment in the *Nicaragua* v. *US* case: ICJ Rep. 1992, 240 at 332–5.

[168] See p. 167, below.

[169] ICJ Rep. 1984, 392. And see T. D. Gill, *Litigation Strategy in the International Court: a case study of the* Nicaragua *v.* United States *dispute* (Dordrecht, 1989).

[170] See p. 158, above.

such matters. Moreover, Nicaragua's application to the Court was not, it held, an unauthorised appeal from decisions of the Security Council, as the United States had argued.[171]

2. The Court could not properly deal with the matter since, if Nicaragua was correct, the use of force was still going on. The Court could not make a judicial assessment of an unstable situation. But the Court held that this (and the difficulty of ascertaining the facts) merely put an extra burden on the parties of producing sufficient evidence of their allegations.

3. Just as failure to exhaust domestic remedies leads to inadmissibility, so does failure to exhaust international remedies. Nicaragua had not exhausted these, since regional negotiations (the Contadora process) were still continuing. The Court rejected this argument, pointing out that if it were correct in law, the respondent State could render the claim endlessly inadmissible by dragging out the negotiations.[172]

In the subsequent *Nicaragua* v. *Honduras* case (1988)[173] the Court rejected Honduras's objections to the admissibility of Nicaragua's complaints. These were, in brief: (a) that Nicaragua's application was politically motivated; (b) that Nicaragua had 'artificially extracted' one issue out of the context of general conflict existing in Central America; (c) that the dispute was *res judicata* in that the case in a broader context had been considered by the Court in other cases (i.e. the *Nicaragua* v. *US* case);[174] (d) that Nicaragua had not complied with a treaty provision (Pact of Bogotá 1948) requiring that settlement should have been effected by 'direct negotiations through the usual diplomatic channels'; and (e) that the claim was barred by another requirement of the Pact (article 32) that when any 'pacific procedure' has been started, no other procedure can be commenced until the former procedure has been concluded.

9. Intervention[175]

Articles 62 and 63 of the Statute deal with two situations in which a third State may intervene in a case brought between two other States. These are methods by which the Court acquires jurisdiction without the specific consent of the parties

---

[171] See K. Skubiszewski, 'The International Court of Justice and the Security Council', in *Fifty Years of the ICJ*, 606.

[172] The Court had earlier held that the fact that negotiations are being actively pursued is not a bar to recourse to judicial settlement or arbitration: *Aegean Sea Continental Shelf* case, ICJ Rep. 1978, 3 at 13.

[173] *Border and Transborder Armed Actions* case, ICJ Rep. 1988, 69.

[174] See further, chapter one, p. 15.

[175] See J. M. Ruda, 'Intervention before the International Court of Justice', in *Fifty Years of the ICJ*, 487.

to the case being necessary.[176] Article 62 deals with cases in which the State seeking to intervene considers that it has an interest of a legal nature; article 63 with cases which involve the construction of a treaty to which the putative intervenor is a party. The latter provision is the more straightforward and we deal with it first.

9.1 Construction of a convention

Article 63 provides that:

> 1. Whenever the construction of a Convention to which States other than those concerned in the case are parties is in question, the Registrar shall notify all such States forthwith.[177]
> 2. Every State so notified has the right to intervene in the proceedings; but if it uses this right, the construction given by the judgment will be equally binding upon it.

The requirements for intervention are, therefore: first, there must be a multilateral convention and secondly, that the interpretation of its provisions must be an element in the case.

Article 63(2) provides that the judgment on the construction of the convention given by the Court binds the intervening State. It is important to note that that State does not have to show that the Court otherwise has jurisdiction over disputes between it and the States involved in the case.[178]

The Court may refuse to allow the State to intervene if the conditions specified are not complied with; if they are complied with, then the State has a *right* to do so (unlike the type of intervention under article 62). The Court allowed Cuba to intervene within narrow limits in the *Haya de la Torre* case (1951)[179] (a sequel to the *Asylum* case[180]) between Colombia and Peru when it argued that the interpretation of the Havana Convention on Asylum 1928 was involved.

But in the *Nicaragua* v. *US* case (1984)[181] the Court decided by a 9–6 majority not to hold a hearing on El Salvador's application to intervene. No reason was given.[182] The Court then decided by a majority of 14–1 that El Salvador's application was inadmissible at that stage of the proceedings since it was addressed to matters which presupposed both that the Court had jurisdiction and that Nicaragua's

---

[176] See generally, S. Rosenne, *Intervention in the International Court of Justice* (Dordrecht, 1993); C. Chinkin, *Third parties in International Law* (Oxford, 1993).

[177] This type of intervention has its origins in the 1907 Hague Convention for the Peaceful Settlement of Disputes, art. 84(2).

[178] Compare art. 62 (below), where this requirement has, in the past, been suggested to exist.

[179] ICJ Rep. 1951, 71.

[180] ICJ Rep. 1950, 266.

[181] ICJ Rep. 1984, 215.

[182] Five judges voted with the majority on this only because they thought that El Salvador had insufficiently specified the treaty provisions to which its application referred and the construction for which El Salvador contended. That State had not complied with the Rules of Court, nor, probably, with art. 63 of the Statute.

complaints were admissible. The US judge, Judge Schwebel, strongly dissented from both decisions, from the first by arguing that the denial of a hearing to El Salvador was tantamount to a breach of natural justice and from the second decision on the ground that El Salvador was seeking a construction of provisions of the UN Charter and other conventions which related to the questions of admissibility already raised by Nicaragua and the US.[183]

9.2 An interest of a legal nature

Article 62 deals with a different and more general situation:

> 1. Should a State consider that it has an interest of a legal nature which may be affected by the decision in the case it may submit a request to the Court to be permitted to intervene.
> 2. It shall be for the Court to decide upon this request.

It is important to note that the requesting State has no right, as it has under article 63, to intervene; it is for the Court itself to allow or to refuse it to do so.

The Rules of Court require the State seeking to intervene to set out (a) that it has an interest of a legal nature and that this interest could be affected by the decision in the case, (b) the precise object of its intervention, and (c) any basis of jurisdiction as between it and the parties.[184] By (c), added in 1978, the Court seemingly imposed the requirement that the intervening State has to show that there is some pre-existing jurisdictional link between it and one or both of the parties to the case which would have entitled it to bring an independent action against them.[185]

Requirements (a) and (c) need further discussion. The latter will be discussed first. It was first mentioned by Judge Ignacio-Pinto in the *Nuclear Tests* cases (1973),[186] in which Fiji sought to intervene in the cases brought by Australia and New Zealand against France. Since there was no jurisdictional link *aliunde* between Fiji and France this was the only way Fiji could 'sue' France. When the Court held that the case had become 'moot', there was, of course, no case for Fiji to intervene in.[187] But some members of the Court said that the State seeking to intervene 'must be in a position in which it could itself bring the respondent before the Court'. Judge Aréchaga based this on his reading and interpretation of article 62 of the Court's Statute and its *travaux préparatoires*. He said that the assumption when it was originally drafted in 1921 had been that the Court would have automatic compulsory

---

[183] ICJ Rep. 1984, 215 at 223.

[184] Rules of Court, art. 81.

[185] See the comment by P. C. Jessup (1981) 75 *AJIL* 903; C. Chinkin, 'Third-party intervention before the International Court of Justice' (1986) 80 *AJIL* 495.

[186] ICJ Rep. 1973, 320 at 322. In the *S.S. 'Wimbledon'* case, PCIJ, Ser. A, No. 1 (1923) the Permanent Court allowed Poland to intervene, but said nothing of importance about the principles governing intervention.

[187] ICJ Rep. 1974, 530.

jurisdiction. But when the Statute was finally adopted this had been replaced by 'optional' compulsory jurisdiction and the assumption had gone. Hence the jurisdictional import of article 62 remained as it originally was, and required such a link.[188] It could, of course, be argued to the contrary that the fact that article 62 was not altered expressly to require a jurisdictional link when the original assumption disappeared, means that such a link is not required.[189]

In the *Tunisia/Libya Continental Shelf* case (1981),[190] those two States specially agreed to ask the Court to lay down the principles and rules applicable to the determination of their continental shelf boundary, though the Court was not itself to determine the actual boundary. Malta was concerned about the likely effect on its own continental shelf claims. It had no jurisdictional basis on which it could have instituted proceedings against Tunisia and Libya. The Court rejected Malta's application to intervene. It thought that Malta did not wish to be bound by the result of the case (indeed, Malta had expressly said this). Moreover, it held that Malta had not explained what was its legal interest and how it might be affected by a decision.[191] The Court therefore did not have to give a decision about the jurisdictional link. (In fact all this did not really matter to Malta, since it had, in effect, argued its case before the Court when applying to intervene.)

In the *Libya/Malta Continental Shelf* case (1984),[192] Malta adopted the reverse stance and opposed an Italian request to intervene in the case concerning the delimitation of the continental shelf, which Libya and Malta had submitted to the Court by special agreement. Malta argued that in a sense this was a 'private' case between these two States and that this 'privacy' would be lost by Italian intervention.[193] The Court held that Italy could not intervene because it had not demonstrated an interest of a legal nature which might be affected by its decision. However, the Court expressly took note of Italy's continental shelf claims and said that it would in its judgment take account of the existence of other States having claims in the region and that its decision would expressly state that it did not prejudice Italy's declared interest.[194] (Again, Italy in fact obtained by this what it really wanted.)

Thus, in these two cases, it was not decided whether a jurisdictional link was required. (In the *Libya/Malta* case, the Court declined to decide the matter; but

---

[188] ICJ Rep. 1974, 530 at 538.

[189] Moreover, the Statute was revised in 1945, but no amendment was made to art. 62.

[190] ICJ Rep. 1981, 3.

[191] Malta would not be bound by the decision in the case: Statute, art. 59.

[192] ICJ Rep. 1984, 3.

[193] This is a dubious argument. If States want privacy they should go to arbitration, where there is no right of intervention.

[194] If the Court believes that a third State's legal interests would be the very subject matter of the decision in the case, it should decline to exercise its jurisdiction under the principle enunciated in the *Monetary Gold* case, ICJ Rep. 1954, 19, see p. 158, above.

several judges expressed their views.) In a case such as *Nuclear Tests* where a third State seeks to intervene on one side and there are a recognisable plaintiff and defendant in the case, it can plausibly be argued that there is a need for the intervening State to have a jurisdictional link with the defendant. Further, in 1978, after the *Nuclear Tests* case, a change was made in the Rules of Court, article 81(2) of which now requires that the applicant has to set out in its application, *inter alia*, *any basis of jurisdiction* as between the State applying to intervene and the parties. This did not appear in the previous version of the Rules, and this change may support the view that the Court adopted the opinion of Judge Aréchaga. If this is so, it could be ultra vires, since if he was wrong in his interpretation of article 62 of the Statute, the Court attempted to add to the only two requirements expressly stated in its Statute.

In any case, it is unclear how this jurisdictional link could apply in cases such as the two *Continental Shelf* cases (in which it was not mentioned), where there is no recognisable defendant, the case having been brought by agreement—or, indeed, how article 81(2)(c) of the Rules of Court could be complied with. In any event, a Chamber of the Court has, as will be seen, subsequently rejected the necessity of showing the existence of such a link.

With respect to the legal interest which might be affected by the Court's decision, the two *Continental Shelf* cases demonstrate, first, that it is the operative sentence (the *dispositif*), and not the whole reasoning of the Court (as Malta had argued in the first case) which constitutes the decision of the Court; and secondly, that, as the Court held in that case, the 'interest' is not merely a general interest in the outcome of the case, but a specific legal interest of the intervenor.

After 1984, it very much appeared that the possibility of intervention under article 62 was a dead letter, since the Court seemed to have set its face against it. However, several important problems were dealt with, including some of those mentioned, when, for the first time, a third State was allowed (by a Chamber of the Court) to intervene in respect of part of a case between two others. In the *Land, Island and Maritime Frontier* case (1990) between El Salvador and Honduras,[195] Nicaragua requested the Chamber to be permitted to intervene. As the Chamber said, it might have to decide five issues concerning the frontier between two parties. As regards the land frontier, Nicaragua did not seek to intervene as this could not possibly affect it. The four other issues concerned the islands in the Gulf of Fonseca, the delimitation of the maritime frontier therein, the juridical status of the waters of the Gulf,[196] and the status of and delimitation

---

[195] ICJ Rep. 1990, 92; and see [1991] *CLJ* 216.

[196] El Salvador claimed that the Central American Court of Justice had decided in 1917, in a case between itself and Nicaragua, that the Gulf of Fonseca was an undivided condominium of the three coastal States. Honduras, not a party to that decision, was claiming that the Gulf, as between itself, El Salvador and Honduras, was held in divided shares and proposed a dividing line between these.

of the frontier in the waters beyond the Gulf. The Chamber permitted Nicaragua to intervene, but only as regards the question of the juridical status of the Gulf, for it was only in respect of that issue that it had shown a legal interest which might be affected by the decision.[197] Several important problems were dealt with by the Chamber, including two previously mentioned.

First, the quandary into which the intervenor had seemed to be put by the Court's holdings, on the one hand, in the *Tunisia/Libya* and *Libya/Malta* cases that a mere general interest in the principles the Court might apply in determining the case was insufficiently specific and, on the other hand, in the *Monetary Gold* case[198] that if a third party's rights are the very subject matter in issue, the Court must decline to hear the case because the third party is not an actual party to the case, was to some extent avoided. Nicaragua clearly had a legal interest in the status of the Gulf of Fonseca in consequence of the judgment of 1917;[199] but the Court held that its rights were not the issue to be decided in the present case, since Honduras had only proposed dividing lines between itself and El Salvador. This seems to overlook the fact that Nicaragua's rights would have been directly affected by a decision denying that a condominium existed in the Gulf.

Secondly, though the intervenor bears the burden of demonstrating convincingly what it asserts, according to the Chamber it need not show that its claimed interest *would* or *must*, but only that it *might* be affected by the decision.

Thirdly, contrary to what had previously been suggested,[200] the Chamber denied that the intervenor must show that there is a jurisdictional link between itself and the parties. In the Court's Statute, intervention appears not in Chapter II (Competence), but in Chapter III (Procedure) and in the Rules of Court in Section D (Incidental Proceedings).[201] The Court's power to permit intervention is not acquired from consent to its jurisdiction. Rather, it derives from that consent which States give, by becoming parties to its Statute, to the Court's exercising such a power. Intervention exists, indeed, for the very purpose of permitting a State, which, because of the absence of a jurisdictional link, cannot be a party to the case, to put its point of view. This follows from the fact that the intervenor does not become a party so as to allow it to have its own claims adjudicated (and to appoint an *ad hoc* judge). Intervention is not a substitute for contentious proceedings. The intervenor only acquires the right to be heard, not the other rights nor the obligations of a party to the case. In its judgment on the merits, the Court

---

[197] The case is distinguishable from the *Libya/Malta* case in this respect. The dispute here concerned separable questions; this was not so in the *Libya/Malta* case.

[198] ICJ Rep. 1954, 19; see p. 158, above.

[199] See n. 196 above.

[200] See pp. 164–5, above

[201] The wording of art. 81(2)(c) of the Rules (p. 164, above) was said by the Chamber (at 135), surprisingly perhaps, to show that a jurisdictional link is *not* a condition of intervention.

emphasised that its finding that there was a condominium over the waters of the Gulf of Fonseca was not binding on Nicaragua, the intervenor.[202]

It should not be thought, however, that the Court has now become very liberal with respect to intervention. Nicaragua was only allowed to intervene with respect to the one issue on which one party, Honduras, argued that it should be permitted to do so. It remains to be seen whether intervention will ever be allowed if both parties object to it.

10. Interim (provisional) measures of protection[203]

After a State has referred a dispute to the Court, it may wish, as may a litigant in a domestic court, to prevent the defendant from taking steps or doing something which would change the factual situation and render the court's future judgment nugatory, to some extent at least.[204] In English law, this is done by asking for an interim or interlocutory injunction.[205] The Statute of the ICJ calls such proceedings 'provisional measures', but these are more usually referred to as 'interim measures of protection'.

Article 41 provides that:

1. The Court shall have the power to indicate, if it considers that circumstances so require, any provisional measures which ought to be taken to preserve the respective rights of either party.[206]
2. Pending the final decision, notice of the measures suggested shall forthwith be given to the parties and to the Security Council.

Five points require discussion: (1) the jurisdiction of the Court in a contentious case and its ability to indicate interim measures; (2) the identification of circumstances that would warrant an indication; (3) the right which it is sought to

---

[202] ICJ Rep. 1992, 351.

[203] J. Sztucki, *Interim Measures in the Hague Court* (Deventer, 1983); J. Elkind, *Interim Protection, a Functional Approach* (The Hague, 1981); M. H. Mendelson, 'Interim measures of protection in cases of contested jurisdiction' (1972–3) 46 *BYIL* 259; P. J. G. Goldsworthy, 'Interim measures of protection in the International Court of Justice' (1974) 68 *AJIL* 258. And see J. G. Merrills, 'Interim measures of protection and the substantive jurisdiction of the International Court' [1977] 36 *CLJ* 86 and 'Interim measures of protection in the recent jurisprudence of the International Court of Justice' (1995) 44 *ICLQ* 90, where he analyses the cases since 1980.

[204] From this it follows that the power to indicate such provisional measures does not permit the Court to grant, on an application to indicate them, an interim judgment on the merits of the case: *Factory at Chorzów*, Jurisdiction, PCIJ, Ser. A, No. 9, 4 at 21 (1927).

[205] For the basic principles concerning the grant of an interim injunction see *American Cyanamid Ltd.* v. *Ethicon* [1975] 1 All ER 504, HL.

[206] The power of a tribunal to order interim measures was described in the *Electricity Company of Sofia and Bulgaria* case, PCIJ, Ser. A/B, No. 77 (1939), 194 at 199 as 'a general principle of law' and by Judge Fitzmaurice in the *Northern Cameroons* case, ICJ Rep. 1963, 15 at 103, as an 'inherent' power.

protect; (4) the relationship to the merits of the claim; and (5) the effect and enforcement of an order indicating such measures.

10.1 Jurisdiction

The problem of jurisdiction only arises, obviously, if the respondent State contests the jurisdiction of the Court to hear the case brought against it. Interim measures may be sought as a matter of urgency at the start of the proceedings by the party which initiates them and may be 'pre-preliminary' to the stage of 'preliminary' objections at which objections to the jurisdiction are heard and decided upon. That is to say, the Court may have to decide whether to order interim measures before it decides whether it has jurisdiction. It may transpire that it has no jurisdiction. If it is clear at the pre-preliminary stage that it has no jurisdiction, then it cannot make an order. If it is unclear at that time, then what test as regards its jurisdiction should the Court adopt?

At least five different tests have been suggested; one of them seems to have found favour with the Court. They are:

1. The Court must have a clearly established jurisdiction. This was proposed by dissenting judges (though not the Court itself) in the *Anglo-Iranian Oil Co.* case (1951),[207] by Judge Forster (dissenting) in the *Nuclear Tests* (1973),[208] and in the separate opinion of Judge Morozov in the *Aegean Sea Continental Shelf* case (1976).[209] But this is inconsistent with the practice of the Court. Moreover, the question at issue arises before the question of jurisdiction is considered; its consideration may take a great deal of time. By the time jurisdiction is clearly established the claimant State's case may have been rendered pointless by the respondent's conduct. The risks were graphically illustrated in the *Breard* case (*Paraguay* v. *USA*), in which Paraguay sought an order of interim measures indicating that the United States should not execute M. Breard pending the hearing of Paraguay's claim that his death sentence was the result of proceedings in which Paraguay's right under the 1964 Vienna Convention on Consular Relations to assist its nationals had been violated. Paraguay made its application on 3 April 1998, and the execution was scheduled for 14 April. On 9 April 1998 the Court issued an Order calling on the United States to take all measures at its disposal to prevent the execution of M. Breard. M. Breard was executed on 14 April 1998.[210]
2. At the opposite extreme is the view that the question of jurisdiction is irrelevant to the ordering of interim measures. This cannot be accepted. It is not consistent with the Court's practice and conflicts with the voluntary principle of submission to the Court.

---

[207] ICJ Rep. 1951, 89.
[208] ICJ Rep. 1973, 99.
[209] ICJ Rep. 1976, 3.
[210] Order of 9 April 1998, ICJ Rep. 1998, 248. See 'Agora: *Breard*' (1998) 92 *AJIL* 666–712.

3. A third test is that it must be 'reasonably probable' that the Court has jurisdiction. In theory this is a good test, but in practice it would involve the Court too much in investigating the question of jurisdiction at the pre-preliminary stage. Though it has been suggested in separate opinions in several cases, such as the *Anglo-Iranian Oil Co.* case,[211] the (Icelandic) *Fisheries Jurisdiction* case,[212] the *Nuclear Tests* cases,[213] and the *Aegean Sea Continental Shelf* case,[214] it has not been adopted by the Court.

4. A fourth approach stipulates that the question of jurisdiction is only one of the circumstances which are to be taken into account. Judge Aréchaga suggested this in the *Nuclear Tests* case[215] and the *Aegean Sea* case,[216] basing his view on the fact that the Court's power is based on article 41 of the Statute, and not on the jurisdictional instruments made by the parties. But this cannot be correct; the Court could not possibly balance the other circumstances against the question of its jurisdiction.

5. Finally, there is the 'possibility' or 'prima facie' test. Judge Lauterpacht suggested in the *Interhandel* case (1957)[217] that there must be an instrument which *prima facie* confers jurisdiction on the Court and which contains no reservation which obviously excludes the dispute from that jurisdiction.

This test was adopted by the Court in the (Icelandic) *Fisheries Jurisdiction*[218] and *Nuclear Tests* cases.[219] In the *Nicaragua* v. *US* case (1984),[220] Nicaragua attempted to found jurisdiction on the two States' optional clause declarations. Though the Court later held that it had no jurisdiction on this basis,[221] it made an order indicating interim measures; it said that it need not satisfy itself as to its jurisdiction before so doing, but it must find, as it had done in this case, that there was a prima facie basis for it. In the *Case concerning the Land and Maritime Boundary between Cameroon and Nigeria* (1996),[222] the Court said that it 'may not indicate provi-

---

[211] ICJ Rep. 1951, 89.

[212] ICJ Rep. 1972, 12.

[213] ICJ Rep. 1973, 99.

[214] ICJ Rep. 1976, 3.

[215] ICJ Rep. 1973, 99 at 143.

[216] ICJ Rep. 1976, 3 at 16.

[217] ICJ Rep. 1957, 105 at 118–19.

[218] ICJ Rep. 1972, 12.

[219] ICJ Rep. 1973, 99. See also *Case concerning the Arbitral Award of 31 July 1989 (Guinea-Bissau* v. *Senegal)*, ICJ Rep. 1990, 64, and *Case concerning Passage through the Great Belt (Finland* v. *Denmark)*, ICJ Rep. 1991, 12 (this case was settled). The Court had effectively avoided the issue in the *Aegean Sea Continental Shelf* case, ICJ 1976, 3, saying merely that it was not called upon to pre-judge jurisdiction over the merits. It declined to make an order for other reasons (see p. 172, below).

[220] ICJ Rep. 1984, 169.

[221] ICJ Rep. 1984, 392. The Court held that it had jurisdiction under the bilateral Treaty of Managua 1956.

[222] ICJ Rep. 1996, 13 at 21. The provisions upon which the Court based its competence were optional clause declarations made by each of the States.

sional measures unless the provisions invoked by the Applicant appear, *prima facie*, to afford a basis on which the jurisdiction of the Court might be founded'.[223] A similar approach was taken in the *Breard* case.[224]

A slight variation in approach occurred in the 1995 case concerning New Zealand's *Request for an Examination of the Situation in accordance with Paragraph 63 of the Court's 1974 Judgment in the Nuclear Tests Case* (*New Zealand v. France*). New Zealand sought the indication of interim measures in the context of its claim that proposed French underground nuclear tests fell within the terms of paragraph 63 of the 1974 judgment, which stated that 'if the basis of this judgment were to be affected, the Applicant could request an examination of the situation in accordance with the provisions of the Statute'. Part of the basis of the judgment was the obligation which the Court had found that France unilaterally made not to engage in atmospheric testing. The Court held that because it concerned underground testing it had no bearing on the 1974 judgment, which was confined to atmospheric testing. The Court dismissed the New Zealand request *in limine*; it did not even proceed to discuss the possibility of the existence of jurisdiction.[225] This approach is, of course, compatible with the Court's earlier jurisprudence; it illustrates the possibility that the absence of prima facie admissibility will be as fatal to a claim for interim measures as the absence of prima facie jurisdiction.

10.2 The exercise of discretion

If the first question is solved, then in what circumstances should interim measures be indicated? Article 41 of the Statute says that the purpose of such measures is 'to preserve the rights of the parties'. In the *Anglo-Iranian Oil Co.* case[226] the Court took a fairly generous attitude, saying that it must be concerned to preserve the rights which it might subsequently adjudge to belong to the parties and whose breach would not be reparable by payment of compensation ordered in any later judgment on the merits. In the *Nuclear Tests* case[227] the Court was satisfied that it should order interim measures to restrain French nuclear testing in order to preserve the rights of Australia.

In the *Aegean Sea Continental Shelf* case[228] the Court took a more restrictive line. Greece sought an order to prevent any further Turkish activities in the disputed

---

[223] The Court has adhered to the prima facie test in subsequent cases, e.g. the *Bosnian Genocide* case brought by Bosnia-Herzegovina against Yugoslavia (Serbia and Montenegro), p. 172 below.

[224] *Case concerning the Vienna Convention on Consular Relations* (*Paraguay* v. *USA*), Order of 9 April 1998, ICJ Rep. 1998, 248.

[225] ICJ Rep. 1995, 288.

[226] ICJ Rep. 1951, 89.

[227] ICJ Rep. 1973, 99.

[228] ICJ Rep. 1976, 3. In the *Great Belt* case (n. 219 above) the Court refused to make an order on the ground that, in the existing circumstances, to do so was not urgent. This is to say, in effect, that there was no prospect of immediate irreparable damage to Finland.

areas on two grounds: (i) to preserve Greece's rights and prevent irreparable prejudice to them; (ii) to prevent Turkey aggravating the dispute and prejudicing friendly relations. But as to (i), the Court could not identify what irreparable prejudice Greece might suffer. Turkish exploration did not affect Greece's legal rights since a violation of its rights over the shelf could be satisfied by a judicial declaration to that effect. As to (ii), on the same day that Greece applied to the Court it put its case to the Security Council, which urged the two Governments to do all in their power to sort out the situation: this covered the ground that Greece was asking the Court to cover and it was not clear that either State would fail to comply with the Security Council resolution. The Court accordingly refused to order interim measures.

In the *Nicaragua* v. *US* case[229] Nicaragua asked the Court to order the United States to cease and desist from helping the Contras and to stop its own military action and use of force against Nicaragua. The Court unanimously ordered the United States to stop laying mines and blocking access to Nicaraguan ports and (with the dissent only of the United States' judge) fully to respect Nicaragua's sovereignty and not to jeopardise it by military action or the use of force prohibited by the UN Charter.[230] Further, unanimously, the Court ordered that no action must be taken by either State which might extend or prolong the dispute or which would have an effect on such of the rights of the two States as might be determined by the Court's future judgment on the merits.

The Court indicated provisional measures in the case concerning *Application of the Convention on the Prevention and Punishment of the Crime of Genocide* (1993)[231] brought by Bosnia-Herzegovina against Yugoslavia (Serbia and Montenegro), where the Court found that it prima facie possessed jurisdiction under the compromissory clause in the Genocide Convention.[232] It told the respondent to take all measures within its power to prevent the commission of genocide and to ensure that military, paramilitary or irregular armed units and other organisations or persons which might be subject to its direction or control, did not indulge in genocidal conduct. It also stated, in what has become a common provision, that neither State should take action which might aggravate or

---

[229] ICJ Rep. 1984, 169.

[230] This seems a rather theoretical thing to order by way of interim measures. The Court made this order, although it had refused to do so in the *Aegean Sea Continental Shelf* case, because there was no overlap between the reference to the Court and a Security Council resolution as there had been in the *Aegean Sea* case.

[231] ICJ Rep. 1993, 3. On this, and the second application (ibid., 325), see the note by C. Gray (1994) 43 *ICLQ* 704.

[232] The Court was, for the first time in an application for interim measures, faced with a question of jurisdiction *ratione personae* over the merits. The question was whether Serbia-Montenegro was a successor to the Federal Republic of Yugoslavia and thus a party to the Statute of the Court. On this, the Court only committed itself to the extent of finding that it prima facie had jurisdiction under art. 35(2) thereof.

extend the dispute or make it more difficult of solution. The Court rejected an argument that it should not indicate interim measures while the Security Council was seised of the dispute.[233] In dealing with a further application by Bosnia-Herzegovina, and a new application from Yugoslavia (Serbia and Montenegro), for orders for provisional measures the Court could find no new prima facie jurisdictional bases to support such orders and simply reaffirmed its earlier interim measures and required them to be implemented.[234]

On the other hand, in the case concerning *Questions of Interpretation and application of the 1971 Convention arising from the Aerial Incident at Lockerbie* (1992),[235] the Court declined to indicate interim measures against the United Kingdom and United States at the request of Libya, over strong dissenting judgments and with several separate declarations or opinions, on the ground that certain Security Council Resolutions (whose passing had been procured by those States) prevailed over the rights claimed by Libya under the 1971 Convention. Also, the Court considered that an indication of such measures would be likely to impair the rights of the United Kingdom and the United States under those resolutions.

10.3 The scope of interim measures

Though the remedy which is sought in the application for provisional measures need not be the same as the one sought in the principal claim, the rights which it is sought to protect by provisional measures must be those which are the subject matter of the proceedings before the Court and not merely those which would be affected by the possible outcome of those proceedings.

In the *Arbitral Award* case (*Guinea-Bissau* v. *Senegal*) (1990),[236] Guinea-Bissau instituted proceedings concerning a dispute with Senegal over the existence and validity of an award made on 3 January 1989 by an Arbitral Tribunal for the Determination of the Maritime Boundary between the two States. It complained of actions which it alleged had been taken by the Senegalese navy against fishing vessels in the maritime area which Guinea-Bissau regarded as being in dispute and requested the Court to indicate provisional measures to safeguard the rights of the parties, in terms that 'they shall abstain in the disputed area from any act or action of any kind whatever, during the whole duration of the proceedings until the decision is given by the Court'. Senegal admitted its naval actions but argued that they

---

[233] The Court applied the principle of its decision in the *Nicaragua* v. *US* case, ICJ Rep. 1984, 392. On the question of admissibility, see p. 155, above.

[234] ICJ Rep. 1993, 325.

[235] ICJ Rep. 1992, 3 and 113. For a highly critical comment see Lowe [1992] 51 *CLJ* 408.

[236] *Case concerning the Arbitral Award of 31 July 1989*, ICJ Rep. 1990, 64. (For the judgment of the Court on the validity of the award, see ICJ Rep. 1991, 53.) In the *Bosnian Genocide* case, ICJ Rep. 1993, 3 and 325, the Court refused to indicate those interim measures which were requested but were not connected with the alleged breaches of the Genocide Convention, which, the Court had decided, alone prima facie gave it jurisdiction over the merits.

were taken within the maritime area granted to it by a Franco–Portuguese agreement of 1960 which the Arbitral Tribunal had held was binding on Guinea-Bissau and itself. The Court declined to accede to this request for provisional measures. The dispute before it was not the one over maritime delimitation which had been dealt with by the Arbitral Tribunal, but rather one as to the existence and validity of the Tribunal's award. Accordingly, the rights sought to be made the subject of provisional measures were not the subject of the proceedings before the Court on the merits and they could not be subsumed by its judgment thereon. Further, even if the Court were ultimately to decide that the Tribunal's award was inexistent or null and void, such decision would not entail that Guinea-Bissau's maritime arc claims were well founded, nor would it resolve the dispute over the maritime claims.

10.4 Relationship to the claim on the merits

With respect to the relationship between a request for interim measures and the merits of the principal claim, although in domestic law systems the court will usually inquire whether the case presents a serious issue to be tried (as in England) or (as in the civil law) whether there is a probable or prima facie prospect of success on the merits, the International Court seems to have treated the merits as irrelevant, although in fact it often seems to discuss them—and indeed the applicant (and the respondent) States often argue the case pretty fully on the merits so as to assist them in persuading the Court to indicate the requested measures.[237]

10.5 Enforcement of interim measures

As regards the effect and enforcement of interim measures orders, left to oneself one would suppose that an order of interim measures would be binding and so place the party against which it is made under an obligation to comply with it, as with such orders made in other jurisdictions. But it has been pointed out that article 41 of the Statute contains very restrained language (the Court may *indicate* provisional measures which *ought to be* taken, and 'notice of the measures *suggested* shall be given'); and it has been argued that the order setting out interim measures is not a judgment or a decision of the Court (see articles 59 and 94 of the Statute). So, it is said, the parties are not bound by the measures indicated.

Against this is the fact that Rules 73–8 of the Rules of Procedure use the term 'decision' in the context of interim measures; indeed, though not a 'judgment', why should an 'order' not be a 'decision'? Moreover, as a general principle of law the parties to a dispute which is *sub judice* are obliged to abstain from an act which

---

[237] This matter is fully discussed by L. Collins, 'Provisional and protective measures in international litigation' (1992) 234 *HR* 9, at 224. See also the separate opinion of Judge Shahabuddeen in the *Great Belt* case, ICJ Rep. 1991, 12 at 34.

would nullify a subsequent judgment. Though the Court has never expressed a view on the matter,[238] the preponderant view is said to be that an indication of interim measures is not binding.[239] It is our opinion that it is, for if it is not, it seems pointless for the Court to make an indication. Whether or not this is so,[240] it is unfortunately clear that States have in practice taken little notice of such orders, since virtually none has been complied with.[241]

It is thought that enforcement of an order of interim measures could not be sought through the Security Council (see Charter, article 94(2)) since that only refers to a 'judgment'.[242]

11. Procedure of the Court

The rules governing procedure are governed by the Rules of Court 1978, articles 39–64.[243] Only a brief outline of the usual procedure will be given here. The Court has said from time to time that it does not wish to be bound by excessive formality, and the procedure described below has been modified in some cases.[244]

Proceedings are started by the *application*. This sets out the claimant State's cause of action, the facts respecting the leading issues and the basis of jurisdiction on which the applicant relies. It is deposited with the Registrar and sent to all members of the Court and to the respondent State. In its written pleadings—the *memorial*—the claimant elaborates on its application; it sets out fully the facts and

---

[238] In the *Nuclear Tests* cases, where France refused to comply with the Court's order, the Court could have decided this question but did not advert to it.

[239] L. Collins, 'Provisional and protective measures in international litigation' (1992) 234 *HR* 9, at 216–20. However, Fitzmaurice regarded it as binding, see 'The law and practice of the International Court of Justice, 1951–4: questions of jurisdiction, competence and procedure' (1958) 34 *BYIL* 1. H. Lauterpacht in *Development of International Law by the International Court of Justice* (London, 1958), 253–4 uses more guarded language. In the *Bosnian Genocide* case, ICJ Rep. 1993, 325, in separate opinions, Judges Weeramantry, at great length (373–87), and Ajibola (at 397) discussed the question and concluded, persuasively, that it is binding, the latter judge saying that this is 'quite clear'.

[240] For a slightly different view see S. Oda, 'Provisional Measures', in *Fifty Years of the ICJ*, 541 at 554–6.

[241] For example, they were ignored in the *Anglo-Iranian Oil Co.*, *Fisheries Jurisdiction*, *Nuclear Tests*, *Hostages* and *Nicaragua* v. *US* cases, and had little discernible impact in the *Bosnian Genocide* case. In some of these and in the Trial of *Pakistani Prisoners of War* and *Aegean Sea* cases, the respondent State did not appear.

[242] H. Mosler, in B. Simma (ed.), *The Charter of the United Nations* (Oxford, 1995), 103–4, agrees with this conclusion.

[243] For a full analysis see S. Rosenne, *The Law and Practice of the International Court of Justice*, 3rd edn. (The Hague, 1997), vol. 3. See also the accounts in the *Yearbooks* of the Court: e.g., ICJ, *Yearbook 1996–1997*, 144–63.

[244] The Court also adopts, and periodically revises, rules governing its working methods, which may modify the effect of the Rules of the Court. See, e.g., ICJ Communiqué 98/14, 6 April 1998, for an account of the changes adopted in order to cope with the Court's congested list and budgetary crisis.

argues the necessary points of law. Any evidence is usually in writing and will be accepted by the Court unless the respondent disputes it.

The respondent State files its *counter-memorial*, which argues the case on its merits and deals with the facts and the law. The claimant may then *reply* to the counter-memorial and the respondent put in a *rejoinder* to the reply.[245] The written pleadings are followed by the oral pleadings, and then by the deliberation and judgment of the Court.

But very few cases run so smoothly, and they are those where the case reaches the Court by agreement between the States in which the Court is seised of the case by a joint application to it. In other cases the respondent State may and usually does raise objections to the jurisdiction of the Court or as to admissibility. The objections to the jurisdiction may be raised at any time before the date for filing the counter-memorial.

If this occurs the Court holds a preliminary hearing and if it finds it has no jurisdiction that is an end of the case, otherwise the case then continues normally.

At the oral hearing usually the claimant State begins; the respondent State replies; then the claimant, then the respondent. The parties may present witnesses, but oral evidence is very rare.

At the conclusion of the hearing the judges deliberate in private (Statute, article 54(3)). Usually one judge or two draft the judgment which is then modified and approved by all the judges who agree with it.[246] The judgment is given in open court (article 58). The judges individually have the right to append declarations to the Court's judgment, or give separate concurring judgments, or they may give judgments dissenting from that of the Court (article 57). This could have the strange consequence that a decision of the Court is arrived at by an eight to seven majority, six judges giving separate concurring opinions. The judgment of the Court would then be that of two judges.

---

[245] The Court may permit the simultaneous, rather than consecutive, submission of written pleadings: see ICJ Communiqué 98/14, 6 April 1998.

[246] The internal practice of the Court is governed by a Resolution of 12 April 1976 concerning the Internal Practice of the Court, ICJ Acts and Documents No. 5 (1989), 165, contained also in 30 *Yearbook of the International Court of Justice*, 119. See, for an account by a former President of the Court, Sir Robert Jennings, 'The internal judicial practice of the International Court of Justice' (1988) 59 *BYIL* 31. The efficiency of the Court's procedures and working methods was the subject of a recent report by a Study Group of the British Institute of International and Comparative Law: see (1996) 45 *ICLQ* (Supplement). See also ICJ Communiqué 98/14, 6 April 1998.

12. Effect of judgments

According to the Statute, article 59, 'The decision of the Court has no binding force except between the parties in respect of that particular case.' By article 60 a judgment is final and without appeal.

The purpose of article 59 is to prevent the application of the common law doctrine of *stare decisis* from applying to judgments of the court; that is, to exclude the attribution to them of the binding force of precedent. This has not prevented the Court relying on its own judgments and, indeed, from distinguishing them. But article 59 has also been relied on by the Court and individual judges and by jurists as being the juridical basis on which the obligation of the parties to a particular case to give effect to its decision rests. It is curious that such negative language should create a positive obligation; the obligation of the parties seems to be taken for granted by article 59. The obligation is, it may be suggested, a general principle of law.

Article 59 is also sometimes regarded as being the juridical foundation of the application of the principle of *res judicata* to decisions of the Court. This also seem to be an unwarranted and unnecessary derivation from the wording of article 59. *Res judicata* is clearly a general principle of law. As Judge Anzilotti put it in his dissenting opinion in the *Chorzów Factory (Interpretation)* case (1927):[247]

> It appears to me that if there be a case in which it is legitimate to have recourse, in the absence of conventions and custom, to 'the general principles of law recognised by civilised nations', mentioned in [article 38(1)(c)] of the Statute, that case is assuredly the present one. Not without reason was the binding effect of *res judicata* expressly mentioned by the Committee of Jurists entrusted with the preparation of a plan for the establishment of a Permanent Court of International Justice, amongst the principles mentioned in 'the above-mentioned article'.

Res judicata means that the cause of action is merged in the decision of a court of competent jurisdiction and that the parties and those who claim through them and the Court and other tribunals cannot reopen the case on its merits in subsequent proceedings. This form of *res judicata* is known in English law as 'cause of action estoppel'. The word 'decision' refers only to the operative part of the judgment and not to the reasoning by which it was arrived at.

It has not been decided whether 'issue estoppel' also applies to judgments of the Court. According to that doctrine (by English law) any issue of fact which the court has to determine in order to decide the case cannot be reopened, provided that the issue in the second case and the parties to it are identical with those in the

---

[247] PCIJ, Ser. A, No. 13, 27. See also *Certain German Interests in Polish Upper Silesia* case, ibid. No. 7 (1926) and the *Factory at Chorzów (Merits)* case, ibid. No. 17 (1928). See also chapter eight, pp. 261–3, below, for a further discussion of *res judicata*.

first case and that the decision in the latter is final on the merits.[248] There seems no reason why it should not apply.

13. Enforcement of judgments

With respect to enforcement, article 94(1) of the UN Charter obliges Member States to comply with decisions of the Court. Article 94(2) provides that if a party to a case fails to carry out a judgment, the other may have recourse to the Security Council 'which may, if it deems it necessary, make *recommendations* or *decide upon measures* to give effect to the judgment'. The question which arises from this is whether the Security Council must follow the Court's decision or whether it can vary it. Although, on the face of it, it could do the latter, this would be most unsatisfactory, and the Council has not done this. In fact, until recently, all decisions were, sooner or later,[249] complied with. Moreover many cases are not concerned with reparation; only declarations of status, or other declaratory judgments, are sought and these do not require enforcement.

Enforcement through the Security Council is fraught with difficulties. In the *Nicaragua* v. *US* case, for instance, because of the use by the United States of its veto, the Security Council was unable to demand that the United States should comply with the duties cast upon it by the Court's judgment.[250]

If the Security Council lacks the political will (and the General Assembly lacks the legal power) to deal with a disobedient party, what can the other State do to try to enforce the Court's judgment? It could take non-forcible measures such as reprisals, for example by seizing the assets of the defaulting State within its jurisdiction. It could try to gain the co-operation of a third State by asking it to use its own power to deprive the defaulting State of certain rights. But this is not very plausible, since the third State would have little interest or, indeed, obligation in the matter when the Security Council has made no recommendation or decision under article 94(2).[251]

---

[248] For the requirements of English law, see *Carl Zeiss Stiftung* v. *Rayner & Keeler (no. 2)* [1967] 1 AC 853; *The Sennar (no. 2)* [1986] 1 WLR 490.

[249] The decision in the *Corfu Channel* case, ICJ Rep. 1949, 4, that Albania should pay damages to the United Kingdom, was unsatisfied until the dispute over this was settled by a Memorandum of Understanding on 8 May 1992: see (1992) 63 *BYIL* 781.

[250] The United Kingdom, France and Thailand abstained. Nicaragua took its case to the General Assembly, which by 94 votes to 3 (United States, El Salvador, Israel) and 47 abstentions, called for full and immediate compliance.

[251] This is not to say, however, that while third States have never adopted measures specifically with a view to the enforcement of a judgment of the Court, they have never resorted to measures to bring pressure to bear on the respondent State in the context of the dispute underlying the case, as happened in the Hostages crisis or after the Lockerbie incident, when sanctions were imposed on Iran and Libya respectively.

It is, lastly, possible that the claimant State could bring an action in the municipal courts of its own State or a third State to obtain the seizure of the debtor State's property situated in that State. There is no specific case on this point, but there are obvious difficulties in the way of such actions, as was shown in the *Socobel* case.[252] The case arose from a judgment of the Permanent Court of International Justice obtained by Belgium which determined that Greece was obliged by an arbitral award to pay compensation to the Belgian company Socobel. The Belgian courts held that Socobel could not enforce the judgment because, *inter alia*, it was not a party to the case in the Permanent Court. Municipal laws on State immunity and non-justiciability present further obstacles.

14. Interpretation and revision of judgments

The Statute, article 60, provides that 'In the event of a dispute as to the meaning or scope of the judgment, the Court shall construe it upon the request of any party.' It does not mention 'revision' or 'correction'.

The conditions upon which the Court will act were stated in the *Asylum* case (1950).[253] Colombia requested an interpretation of the Court's judgment.[254] It claimed to have discovered 'gaps' therein. The Court laid down two conditions for the admissibility of a request for interpretation. First, the real purpose of the request must be to obtain an interpretation: '[t]his signifies that its object must be solely to obtain clarification of the meaning and scope of what the Court has decided with binding force and not to obtain an answer to questions not so decided. Any other construction of article 60 . . . would nullify the provision of the article that the judgment is final and without appeal.' Secondly, there must in addition exist a *dispute* as to the meaning or scope of the judgment. Colombia's 'gaps' were in fact questions which the Court had not been called on to answer. Moreover, there was no dispute; the mere fact that one party finds the judgment 'obscure' and the other 'perfectly clear' (as did Peru), does not constitute a dispute. There must be a difference as to the meaning of a particular point.

In the *Tunisia/Libya Continental Shelf* case,[255] Tunisia requested the *revision, interpretation* and *correction* of the Court's judgment of 1982.[256] The Court stated as to *revision*, that there must be a new fact of such a nature as to be a decisive factor which would mean revision of at least the part of the judgment which would have been different in the light thereof. The fact must not have been discoverable at the

---

[252] (1951) 18 *ILR* 3. See further chapter eight, p. 263.
[253] ICJ Rep. 1950, 395. In the *Anglo-French Continental Shelf Arbitration*, the Court of Arbitration did give an interpretation of its award: see 54 *ILR* 139.
[254] ICJ Rep. 1950, 266.
[255] ICJ Rep. 1985, 192.
[256] ICJ Rep. 1982, 18.

time of the case by the State now putting it forward. Tunisia alleged that the real boundary point of a petroleum concession was different from what the Court had earlier been led to believe. This the Court rejected, saying that the fact could have been discovered at the time of the case and in any event the Court's reasoning had been wholly unaffected by the allegedly wrong boundary point. As to *interpretation*, the Court held that the request was partly admissible but that, as to one matter, the Court had clarified the point in its discussion of the request for revision. The Court did interpret its judgment on a second matter. On *correction*, Tunisia argued that there was an error in the judgment. The Court said that Tunisia had misunderstood an earlier part of the judgment so that this part of the request was without object and the Court need not deal with it.

15. Non-appearance

The deliberate refusal of a respondent State to appear before the Court, even in order to object to the Court's jurisdiction when a claim is brought against it, is a relatively recent phenomenon, but in the (Icelandic) *Fisheries Jurisdiction* (1972),[257] *Nuclear Tests* (1974),[258] *Trial of Pakistani Prisoners of War* (1973),[259] *Aegean Sea* (1976)[260] and the *Hostages* (1980)[261] cases, Iceland, France, India, Turkey and Iran respectively failed to appear and contented themselves with either ignoring the proceedings or writing letters to the Court simply asserting that it had no jurisdiction. In the *Nicaragua* v. *US* case (1986),[262] for the first time, a State (the USA) took part in the jurisdictional stage of the proceedings and, when it lost, refused to participate in the Court's hearing on the merits.[263]

Non-appearance places the Court and the claimant State in a difficult situation. In all the cases there existed an instrument which prima facie showed that the respondent State had accepted the jurisdiction. There was either a bilateral agreement, an optional clause declaration or a general convention such as the General Act of Geneva 1928. Article 53 of the Statute is relevant to this situation. It provides that:

(1) Whenever one of the parties does not appear before the Court, or fails to defend its case, the other party may call upon the Court to decide in favour of its claim.

---

[257] ICJ Rep. 1974, 3.
[258] ICJ Rep. 1974, 253.
[259] ICJ Rep. 1973, 328.
[260] ICJ Rep. 1978, 3.
[261] ICJ Rep.1980, 3.
[262] ICJ Rep. 1986, 14.
[263] The leading writers on the matter are J. Elkind, *Non-appearance before the International Court of Justice* (Dordrecht, 1984), and H. W. A. Thirlway, *Non-appearance before the International Court of Justice* (Cambridge, 1985).

That is to say the Court may give what is known as a default judgment. Article 53(2) continues:

> The Court must, before doing so, satisfy itself, not only that it has jurisdiction in accordance with Articles 36 and 37, but also that the claim is well founded in fact and in law.

In such cases, the Court, it seems, has insisted on establishing, not just that it prima facie has jurisdiction but that it really has jurisdiction.[264] It appears to have bent over to be fair to the absent respondent State; but, in doing so, it may well have been unfair to the claimant State. Professor O'Connell, arguing for Greece in the *Aegean Sea* case,[265] pointed out the problems. The Court has to avoid seeming to take sides with the claimant, and has to be satisfied by the claimant that the claim is well founded in fact and law without hearing the respondent's arguments. Yet the claimant does not know what arguments it has to meet—does it have to deal only with such points as the respondent puts to the Court in any communication it addresses to the Court? Or does it have to think up other arguments in order to knock them down? Or does it have to imagine what might be in the minds of members of the Court? As, in such cases, the respondent has failed to comply with article 62 of the Rules of Court regarding the making of preliminary objections, the question arises whether it should then be treated leniently. And the entire aim of a non-appearing State differs from that of a true litigant: it is not concerned to win the case but rather not to appear to lose it, in that if it does not appear it can say the Court has given a judgment which is academic and so not really binding on it. The late Sir Gerald Fitzmaurice, a former judge of the Court, insisted that the Court has not really condemned strongly enough the non-appearing States' behaviour and attitude and has effectively penalised the claimant State.[266]

In the *Nicaragua v. US* case[267] the withdrawal of the USA after the Court had held it had jurisdiction left the Court in a very awkward position. The points of law involved were both difficult and important and the Court did not hear the United States' arguments about them. With respect to the facts, these were not at all clear; Nicaragua put forward evidence and witnesses whom the Court had to believe, since there was no effective challenge to the evidence or cross-examination of the witnesses. In the circumstances, criticisms of the Court and its judgment in the case, especially from American commentators, are difficult to accept, to put it mildly.

---

[264] Compare the jurisdiction to indicate provisional (interim) measures of protection, p. 168 above.

[265] ICJ Rep. 1976, 3.

[266] (1980) 51 *BYIL* 89.

[267] ICJ Rep. 1986, 14. See the numerous articles by American lawyers in (1987) 81 *AJIL* 1–183.

16. Advisory Opinions

The International Court of Justice may be asked to give an advisory opinion.[268] Such an opinion, which is not binding, may be given on *any legal question* at the request of whatever body may be authorised in accordance with the UN Charter to make such a request (Statute article 65(1)). Article 96(1) of the UN Charter empowers the General Assembly or the Security Council to do so. Article 96(2) allows other organs of the United Nations and specialised agencies to request an opinion, but only if they are authorised by the General Assembly to do so and *the legal question arises within the scope of their activities.*

This limitation on the authority of such other organs or specialised agencies, as compared with the authority of the General Assembly or Security Council, was emphasised by the Court when, in 1996, it declined to give an opinion to the World Health Organisation. The Assembly of the WHO had asked the Court for an advisory opinion as to the legality of the use by a State of nuclear weapons in armed conflict in view of their possible effects on the environment and on health. The Court observed that the WHO was only authorised to deal with, *inter alia,* the effects on health of the use of nuclear weapons and to take preventive measures for the protection of the health of populations in the event of such weapons being used. It was not authorised to deal with the legality of their use in view of their health and environmental effects; and these effects would be the same whether or not the use which caused them was illegal.[269] On the same day, the Court gave an opinion to the General Assembly (though a somewhat unsatisfactory opinion) on the legality of the threat or use of nuclear weapons.[270]

Organs of the United Nations which have been authorised to request opinions are the Economic and Social Council (ECOSOC) and the Trusteeship Council, the Interim Committee of the General Assembly and the Committee for Applications for Review of Judgments of the UN Administrative Tribunals. There have in recent years been moves to have the Secretary-General authorised to do so, but this has not yet been done. Fifteen of the sixteen specialised agencies have been given such authority (the odd one out being the Universal Postal Union). These include, for example, the World Bank, the International Monetary Fund, the World Health Organisation, the International Maritime Organisation and the

---

[268] A tribunal can give an advisory opinion only if it is empowered to do so by its constituent instrument. Several tribunals are so authorised. Cf. e.g., the European Court of Human Rights (Second Protocol to the European Convention on Human Rights); the Inter-American Court of Human Rights (American Convention on Human Rights, 1969, art. 64); and the European Court of Justice (see arts. 177 and 228(b) of the EC Treaty) which also have such a power, as does the International Tribunal on the Law of the Sea.

[269] ICJ Rep. 1996, 66.

[270] *Legality of the Threat or Use of Nuclear Weapons,* ICJ 1996, 66, 226; and see V. Lowe [1996] 55 *CLJ* 45.

International Labour Organisation.[271] The International Atomic Energy Authority also has such authority, though it is not, strictly speaking, a specialised agency. It is to be noted that States are not permitted to ask for advisory opinions, though all States entitled to appear before the Court must be given notice of the request and they and international organisations may make written or oral statements relating to the question at issue (Statute, article 66).[272]

Not all requests for advisory opinions concern disputes between States, but they may do so; and the request may concern the legal question which lies at the heart of the dispute of which the international organisation or organ thereof is seised. Examples of such disputes are the *Nationality Decrees Issued in Tunis and Morocco* case (1923),[273] the *Interpretation of Peace Treaties* case (1950)[274] and the *Western Sahara* case (1975).[275] Or the dispute may be between an international organisation and its members and a State, as with the *Namibia* case (1971)[276] and the ECOSOC request in the case concerning the *Difference Relating to Immunity from Legal Process of a Special Rapporteur of the Commission on Human Rights.*[277] In such cases, the provision of article 68 of the Statute is of significance. This says that '[i]n the exercise of its advisory functions the Court shall further be guided by the provisions of the present Statute which apply in contentious cases to the extent to which it recognises them to be applicable'. Article 102(2) of the Rules of Court 1978 repeats this and says that: 'For this purpose, it shall above all consider whether the request for the advisory opinion relates to a legal question actually pending between two or more States.'

The relevance of this to the appointment of *ad hoc* judges has already been discussed. But its chief application may be in cases in which a State or States parties to the dispute to which the request is closely related do not consent to the Court examining the question at issue. In the *Status of Eastern Carelia* case (1923),[278] the PCIJ refused a request for an opinion from the League of Nations which concerned a dispute between Finland and the Soviet Union, because the latter State

---

[271] For examples, see the *Constitution of IMCO*, Advisory Opinion, ICJ Rep. 1960, 150; *Judgments of the Administrative Tribunal of the ILO upon Complaints Made against UNESCO*, Advisory Opinion, ICJ Rep. 1956, 77; *Interpretation of the Agreement of 25 March 1951 between the WHO and Egypt* (WHO Regional Headquarters), Advisory Opinion, ICJ Rep. 1980, 73; and see D. Pratap, *The Advisory Jurisdiction of the International Court* (Oxford, 1972). For a recent discussion, see R. Higgins, 'A comment on the current health of Advisory Opinions', in *Fifty Years of the ICJ*, 567.

[272] As many did in the proceedings in the case concerning *Legality of the Threat or Use of Nuclear Weapons*, ICJ Rep. 1996, 1.

[273] PCIJ, Ser. B, No. 4 (1923).

[274] ICJ Rep. 1950, 65.

[275] ICJ Rep. 1975, 12.

[276] ICJ Rep. 1971, 16.

[277] ICJ Rep. 1998, 423.

[278] PCIJ, Ser. B, No.5 (1923). Compare the *Interpretation of Article 3, Paragraph 2, of the Treaty of Lausanne* (Frontier Between Turkey and Iraq), 1925, Advisory Opinion, PCIJ, Ser. B, No. 12.

was not a member of the League at that time and had not given its consent to the examination of the question by the Court.[279] But two points serve to differentiate the position under the UN Charter and the Statute of the ICJ. The first is that the ICJ is the principal judicial organ of the UN, whereas the PCIJ was not an organ of the League; the other is that the Statute of the PCIJ gave power to that Court to give opinions on 'disputes', whereas that of the ICJ gives power to the ICJ to give them on 'any legal question'. It was in the light of these considerations that the ICJ distinguished *Eastern Carelia* in the *Peace Treaties* case.[280] The real distinction is that the question in the latter case, unlike that in the former case, did not relate to the merits of the dispute but to the creation of the machinery for its settlement. Furthermore, the lack of consent of an interested party was treated as no obstacle to giving an opinion in the later *Namibia* case[281] although South Africa's rights and obligations seem clearly to have been in issue.

In the *Western Sahara* case (1975),[282] the UN General Assembly was engaged in the process of decolonisation of what was Spanish Sahara (or Spanish West Africa). The General Assembly requested an advisory opinion on (i) the legal status of the territory, and (ii) its legal ties with Morocco and with Mauritania at the time Spain colonised the territory. One of Spain's objections to the Court giving an opinion was that the questions were closely linked to Spain's dispute with Morocco as to how decolonisation should be carried out, and that Spain had not consented to this dispute being decided in contentious proceedings. The Court distinguished the *Eastern Carelia* case. In that case, it said, the Soviet Union had in no way consented to the PCIJ exercising its advisory jurisdiction; that State was not at the relevant time a member of the League of Nations, nor was it a party to the Statute of the PCIJ. Spain, on the other hand, had given its general consent to the ICJ exercising its advisory jurisdiction since it was a member of the UN and a party to the Statute of the ICJ. The Court also pointed out that a dispute had arisen between Morocco and Mauritania over the status of the territory of Western Sahara after Spain had left the territory. The matter was within the framework of the General Assembly's decolonisation proceedings, and the purpose of seeking the advisory opinion was to obtain assistance in decolonising the territory, not to bring a dispute or legal controversy before the Court. Moreover, the issue between Morocco and Spain was not one as to the legal right to the territory in 1975 but as to the rights of Morocco at the time of colonisation. An opinion on the latter could not affect the rights of Spain in 1975. That is to say, it did not affect the merits of the dispute between the States. The Court said merely that 'the consent of an interested State continues to be relevant, not for the Court's com-

---

[279] The Court also said that the case involved an enquiry into the facts and this made the participation of both Finland and the Soviet Union essential.
[280] ICJ Rep. 1950, 65.
[281] ICJ Rep. 1971, 16.
[282] ICJ Rep. 1975, 12.

petence, but for the appreciation of the propriety of giving an opinion'. In other words, it is relevant not to whether the Court can give an opinion, but to whether it should do so.

The Court clearly thought that its function was to give guidance as to their functions to international organisations and not to decide questions pending between States, and that only compelling reasons should lead it to decline to render an opinion. But this may be true in theory and not necessarily in practice. It can hardly be doubted that the Court's opinion in the *Namibia* case [283] had an effect on South Africa's legal position with respect to that territory.

The request must be for an opinion on a *legal* question. This seems to preclude a request concerning a political question. However, although the Court has been at times urged to decline a request for this reason,[284] it has never done so; indeed it is difficult, if not impossible, to do so if the question is put in a legal form.

We have dealt with advisory opinions because they have their uses in assisting in the settlement of disputes, as the *Western Sahara* case shows. The Permanent Court was quite frequently asked to give advisory opinions for this purpose. The International Court of Justice has not found this to be a very large part of its curriculum. It has been asked for around three times as many judgments in inter-State cases as for advisory opinions; and more of the advisory opinions have been concerned with constitutional questions affecting international organisations than with legal disputes between particular States.

---

[283] ICJ Rep. 1971, 16.
[284] See, e.g., *Certain Expenses of the United Nations*, ICJ Rep. 1962, 151.

PART TWO:

PROCEDURE

8

THE ARBITRAL PROCESS

1. Introduction	190
2. Admissibility	191
2.1 Nationality of claims	191
2.2 Exhaustion of local remedies	195
3. Submission to jurisdiction	198
3.1 Written agreement	200
3.2 Existing or future differences	201
3.3 Defined legal relationship	202
3.4 Arbitrability	202
3.5 Capacity	204
3.6 Validity	206
4. Who is covered by the arbitration agreement?	207
5. Third parties: Intervention and joinder	208
6. Contents of the arbitration agreement	210
7. Arbitration clauses and submission agreements	212
8. The autonomy of the arbitration clause	212
9. Refusal to arbitrate and the denial of justice	216
10. Establishment and procedure of arbitral tribunals	218
10.1 Time limits	218
10.2 Appointment of arbitrators	219
10.3 Challenge to and disqualification of arbitrators	222
11. Powers and duties of arbitrators	223
12. The authority of truncated tribunals	225
13. Challenges to the tribunal's jurisdiction	227
14. *Lex arbitri*	229
15. Delocalisation	232
16. Procedure	235
17. Applicable law	239
18. Remedies	248

18.1 Interim measures	248
18.2 Final remedies	250
19. The award	**253**
20. Challenges to awards	**257**
21. Effects of the award	**261**
22. Enforcement of judgments and awards	**263**
22.1 The New York Convention	266
22.2 State immunity	270

1. Introduction

There are certain stages and problems common to all judicial procedures for the settlement of international disputes. The identity of the problems, and of the solutions, is evident when tribunals operate under the same rules—as, for example, international commercial arbitration tribunals and the Iran-US Claims Tribunal operate under the UNCITRAL Arbitration Rules. In fact, the similarities are more pervasive, as the frequency with which international courts and arbitral tribunals of all kinds refer to each other's jurisprudence indicates.[1] There are clear signs of a body of international procedural law emerging. The following account of the law is in principle applicable to all international tribunals subject, of course, to express stipulations to the contrary in the rules under which they operate. For convenience, however, reference will ordinarily be made to the law as it operates in the context of arbitrations.

The question of submission to the jurisdiction of the tribunal may appear to be the obvious starting point. It is, however, common to raise objections to the continuation of proceedings by a tribunal that appears to have jurisdiction. Many such preliminary objections are concerned with the question whether there exists a dispute of a nature that can properly be put to the dispute settlement procedure. This question ought, logically, to be determined before the procedure is initiated; and so we consider it first. This discussion is followed by a consideration of the question of submission to the jurisdiction of the tribunal, and of the rules concerning the establishment and operation of the tribunal, and then of the question of the law applicable to the proceedings, the *lex arbitri*. The determination of the law applicable to the substance of the dispute and the particular problems of 'internationalised' contracts are discussed in the following pages. The final sec-

---

[1] See, e.g., the decision of the Iran-US Claims Tribunal on questions of dual nationality, *Case A/18*(1984) 5 *Iran-US CTR*251, 428. The practice is noticeably more common in individual opinions in the International Court of Justice than in the judgments of the Court itself.

tions deal with challenges to and revision of awards, and the recognition and enforcement of awards.

2. Admissibility

Preliminary objections to the jurisdiction of the tribunal seek to have the proceedings terminated prior to the consideration of the merits of the claim, on the ground that the proceedings have not properly been instituted. They may address various issues. It may be said that the dispute is non-justiciable, or (in the case of inter-State disputes) that the claimant State has no right to present the case, or that a requirement that local remedies be exhausted before the claim is pursued on the plane of international law has not been fulfilled.

The justiciability of disputes, which distinguishes between those disputes that are and those that are not suitable for settlement by tribunals according to the law, was discussed in chapter one.[2] While objections to the justiciability of disputes are often raised as preliminary objections, the objection is rarely upheld. As we noted above, as long as a dispute remains in existence, tribunals are usually able to isolate a specifically legal issue upon which it is proper for them to rule.

In the case of international disputes arising—as most do—from injuries to the nationals (individual or corporate) of a State, rather than from injuries caused directly to the State itself, there are two further preliminary points which should be noted. The first is the principle of general international law that claims for such injuries can be brought only by the national State of the injured person, and the second is the related principle that the international claim can be brought only after local remedies available in the wrongdoing State have been exhausted. These principles are well canvassed in general texts on international law, and we make no attempt here to give a comprehensive exposition of them. However, both principles have been substantially modified in the operations of certain international tribunals. Indeed, the modifications lie at the very heart of the quiet revolution that has taken place in international dispute settlement over the past half-century. It is right that these modifications should be noted here.

2.1 Nationality of claims[3]

The requirement that claims in respect of injuries sustained by individuals or corporations be pursued on the international plane only by the State of which those injured are nationals is a consequence of the classical view that in doing so 'a State is in reality asserting its own right, the right to ensure in the person of its

---

[2] See pp. 10–16, above; and see further, on the question of arbitrability, pp. 202–3 below.
[3] See Sir A. Watts, 'Nationality of claims: some relevant concepts', in *Fifty Years of the ICJ*, 424.

nationals respect for the rules of international law'.[4] It is further required, in principle, that there should have been continuous nationality:[5] that is, the person injured must have been a national of the claimant State at the time that the injury was sustained and have remained a national up to the date of the presentation of the claim. It is left to each State to determine under its own laws which individuals and corporations are its nationals.[6] Other States are bound to accept such determinations, in so far as they are consistent with international law. The major exception, established in the *Nottebohm* case,[7] is that a State with which an individual has a long-standing and close connection is not obliged to recognise, for the purposes of diplomatic protection, a grant of nationality by a State with which the individual has no real connection.[8]

In the case of persons having dual nationality, the general rule is said to be that either national State may bring a claim against a third State.[9] Further, it is sometimes said, in apparently general terms, that the State of dominant nationality, with which the individual has demonstrably stronger links, may bring a claim against the other State, the State of 'subordinate' nationality.[10] The jurisprudence of the Iran-US Claims Tribunal is consistent with such a rule:[11] but the better view is that the reasoning behind the Iran-US Claims Tribunal decisions is more narrowly confined. The tribunal considered that there is a difference between cases where a claim is presented by a national State and cases (such as those before it) where the claim is presented by the nationals themselves. In the latter case, the tribunal's position might be said to be analogous to that of a third State in an inter-State claim. There is general agreement that third States must at least accept claims made by the State of dominant nationality[12] (whether or not it is accepted that they must also accept claims from the State of subordinate nationality). Accordingly, the tribunal should accept claims where the claimant is asserting the

---

⁴ *Panevezys-Saldutiskis Railway* case (1939) PCIJ Ser. A/B, No. 76, at 16.

⁵ This rule has sometimes been modified by treaty. See M. M. Whiteman, *Digest of International Law* (Washington, DC, 1963–73), vol. 8, 1233 (1967). See further R. B. Lillich and G. A. Christenson, *International Claims: Their Preparation and Presentation* (Syracuse, 1962), 9–12; *Oppenheim*, 511–15.

⁶ Art. 1, Hague Convention on Certain Questions Relating to the Conflict of Nationality Laws, 1930, 179 *LNTS* 89. *Oppenheim*, 853–7.

⁷ ICJ Rep. 1955, 4.

⁸ Note that *Nottebohm* did not establish any *positive* requirement that there be a genuine link between an individual and the national State (see *Flegenheimer* (1958) 25 *ILR* 91), and that it was not a case concerning dual nationality—Nottebohm lost his original, German, nationality on taking Liechtenstinian citizenship.

⁹ But see *Oppenheim* 516–17, where a different view is taken, obliging the third State to accept claims only from the State of dominant nationality.

¹⁰ See, e.g., *Mergé* (1955) 22 *ILR* 443.

¹¹ The leading cases are *Esphahanian* v. *Bank Tejarat* (1983) 2 *Iran-US CTR* 157, and Case *A/18* (1984) 5 *Iran-US CTR* 251.

¹² See art. 5 of the Hague Convention on Certain Questions Relating to the Conflict of Nationality Laws, 1930, 179 *LNTS* 89.

dominant nationality against the State of subordinate nationality; but it does not necessarily follow that in an *inter*-State claim the State of subordinate nationality must accept a claim brought by the State of dominant nationality.[13] That question appears to be open, as a matter of international law: but the trend is towards acceptance of the principle of dominant nationality in most contexts.

These rules concerning the nationality of claims arising from injuries to individuals are followed in almost all tribunals, but some exceptions run contrary to the trend. The main exception is ICSID, which operates under what is, in effect, a restrictive interpretation of the usual dual nationality rules. The ICSID Convention does not extend to claims brought by an individual national of one State against another State whose nationality he or she also has: the 'dominant nationality' approach has no application here.[14]

The rules concerning the nationality of corporations for the purposes of diplomatic protection are well known, and many were discussed in the voluminous pleadings in the *Barcelona Traction* case.[15] The clearest rule is that a corporation does not necessarily have the nationality of the majority of its shareholders. It will ordinarily have the nationality of the State in which it is incorporated and has its seat of management.[16] According to the *Barcelona Traction* judgment, in certain circumstances the nationality of its shareholders may be relevant and the shareholders' national State might be permitted to bring a claim. The most notable instances are, first, cases where the corporation has ceased to exist as a legal person, as where it has been wound up and/or struck from the register of corporations; and secondly, where the corporation's national State lacks the capacity to act on its behalf;[17] thirdly, the International Court noted that there was a theory according to which the shareholders' national State might be permitted to bring a claim where the wrongdoing State is itself the State of incorporation.[18] The Court did not, however, decide whether the theory was correct. Of these the third is the most significant. Many States require foreign investments to be made in the State through the vehicle of a locally incorporated company. Were it not for the third

---

[13] Indeed, art. 4 of the 1930 Hague Convention on Certain Questions Relating to the Conflict of Nationality Laws, 1930, 179 *LNTS* 89 unequivocally asserts that 'a State may not afford diplomatic protection to one of its nationals against a State whose nationality such person also possesses'.

[14] Art. 25(2)(a). Any such claims could, of course, be pursued using non-ICSID procedures.

[15] ICJ Rep. 1970, 3.

[16] The necessity for the coincidence of the State of incorporation and the seat of corporate management was not settled by the *Barcelona Traction* judgment. The Court did not have to decide the issue because Canada was both the State of incorporation and the seat of corporate management: see ICJ Rep. 1970, 3 at 43.

[17] A situation where the national State has no effective government (see *Republic of Somalia* v. *Woodhouse*, Drake [1993] Q.B. 54) might be an example of the second situation.

[18] Cf. the *Mexican Eagle Company* case (1938) Cmd. 5758; cf. B. A. Wortley, 'The Mexican Oil Dispute 1938–1946' (1957) 43 *Transactions of the Grotius Society* 15. See also the United Kingdom Rules regarding the Taking Up of International Claims by Her Majesty's Government, July 1983 (1983) 54 *BYIL* 520, Rule VI.

exception, diplomatic protection of such foreign-controlled companies, and hence of much foreign investment, would be practically impossible, except perhaps in circumstances where the investment is protected by an international agreement between the host State and the national State of the foreign investor.[19]

International tribunals ordinarily apply the rules as they are described above. The main modification effected by the constitutive documents of certain tribunals is the consolidation of the 'foreign control' exception to the basic *Barcelona Traction* rule. Perhaps the most important example is the provision in article 25(2)(b) of the ICSID Convention. That permits (but does not require) each Contracting State to treat a corporation which has its nationality as a national of another Contracting State if that corporation is foreign controlled. For instance, in *AMCO Asia* v. *Indonesia* it was held that Indonesia had by its conduct consented to treat a foreign controlled company as a foreign national, thus allowing it to bring a claim against Indonesia under the ICSID procedures.[20] As we noted above, it must be proved that the company was in reality 'foreign controlled': an agreement to treat a company not so controlled as if it were foreign controlled will not be effective to confer jurisdiction on an ICSID tribunal.[21]

A broadly similar provision, which has generated rather more jurisprudence, was included in the Iran-US Claims Settlement Declaration. The Iran-US Claims Tribunal was required to treat as claims of Iranian or United States' nationals claims which formally belonged to corporations controlled by Iranian or United States' nationals.[22]

The Iran-US Claims Tribunal was also bound by a rule which was the mirror image of the foreign control rule. Instead of following the normal rule of allowing all corporations incorporated in Iran or the United States to be treated as Iranian or United States nationals, the Claims Settlement Declaration imposed a further 'genuine link' condition. It required not only that the corporation be incorporated under Iranian or United States law, but also that 50 per cent or more of the stock be held by Iranian or United States nationals, as the case might be. No such condition of the validity of grants of nationality to corporations has yet been established in customary international law, and it was included in the Iran-US Declaration in order to preserve the essentially bilateral character of the settlement rather than as the seed of a new legal doctrine. The provision clearly gives

---

[19] See the *ELSI* case, ICJ Rep. 1989, 15; and see further pp. 196–7 below. If the USA could take action against Italy in that case to enforce a *treaty* obligation, is there any reason why it could not have taken action to enforce any comparable *customary* law rights protecting US shareholders? If so, what would be left of the *Barcelona Traction* rule?

[20] (1984) 23 *ILM* 351; 89 *ILR* 368, 379.

[21] See chapter four, p. 67, above (*Vacuum Salt Products Limited* v. *Government of the Republic of Ghana*, Award of 16 February 1994, 4 *ICSID Reports* 320).

[22] Claims Settlement Declaration, art. VII(2). See *Pomeroy* v. *Iran* (1983) 2 *Iran-US CTR* 372.

rise to difficulties, because in the case of corporations with many shareholders and widely traded stock it is not easy to determine the nationality of the stockholders.

The details of this problem have been addressed by the Iran-US Claims Tribunal in a series of cases. The approach that has been taken, following the jurisprudence of earlier tribunals,[23] is to operate on the basis of presumptions. If the claimant can establish a prima facie case that 50 per cent of its stock is held by nationals, and the respondent offers no evidence in rebuttal, the claim to nationality is regarded as made out. The Tribunal was assisted by the existence of requirements under US law that the names and addresses of holders of all holdings of more than 5 per cent of the shares in a US corporation be notified to US authorities, and by statistical data showing that only 4.3 per cent of portfolio investments by small shareholders in US corporations are owned by foreigners and only 0.2 per cent had more than 50 per cent of their shares owned by foreigners. The Tribunal has, accordingly, been satisfied that US 'nationality' in this narrow sense is established where the claimant has produced a certificate that the corporation in question is incorporated in the USA and where the total number of shares owned by holders of blocks of 5 per cent or more of the shares is less than 40 per cent of the shares in the corporation. In such cases, because of the likelihood that only around 4.3 per cent of shares will be held by foreign shareholders (giving 40 per cent plus around 4.3 per cent as possibly foreign-owned), it 'will draw the reasonable inference that more than 50 per cent of such stockholders are US citizens'.[24] If the holders of such blocks together own more than 40 per cent of the shares in the corporation, the claimants must produce additional evidence to satisfy the Tribunal that the necessary number of holders are US nationals.[25]

These provisions apart, international tribunals follow the usual rules concerning the nationality of claims. There are, however, many difficulties that arise where the losses which form the subject of the claims have been insured. The question of the subrogation of the insurer to the rights of the insured is a matter of considerable complexity, in which much turns upon the details of insurance policies and insurance practice. We do not treat this issue further in the present text.[26]

2.2 Exhaustion of local remedies

The final preliminary issue to be treated before examining the arbitration process proper is the exhaustion of local remedies. Under general international law where a wrong is done to an alien which is imputable to a State, the alien must give the

---

[23] *Parker,* 4 *RIAA* 39 (1926); *Certain Norwegian Loans,* ICJ Rep. 1957, 39–40.

[24] *Flexi-Van Leasing, Inc.* v. *Iran* (1982) 70 *ILR* 496, at 504–5.

[25] *Management of Alcan* v. *Ircable Corp.* (1983) 2 *I-USCTR* 294. Cf. *General Motors Corp.* v. *Iran* (1983) 3 *I-USCTR* 1.

[26] See further D. J. Bederman, 'Beneficial Ownership of International Claims' (1989) 38 *ICLQ* 924, and references therein; *Oppenheim,* 514.

State the opportunity of redressing that wrong by seeking a remedy from the State's own legal system. Until all such local remedies have been exhausted by the injured alien, the alien's national State may not pursue a claim in respect of the injury on the international plane. The failure to exhaust local remedies thus operates as a procedural bar[27] to the pursuit of an international claim.

The failure to exhaust local remedies has been raised frequently by respondent States as a preliminary objection to judicial or arbitral proceedings.[28] As it was put in the *Interhandel* case, 'A State may not even exercise its diplomatic protection, and much less resort to any kind of international procedure of redress, unless its subject has previously exhausted the legal remedies offered him by the State of whose action he complains.'[29] The doctrine extends to cases where the injured person has failed to make full use of the available remedies. So, in the *Ambatielos* arbitration, the failure of Ambatielos (who claimed that the United Kingdom had violated contractual obligations towards him) to call a material witness at the appropriate stage in the English court proceedings was held to constitute a failure to exhaust local remedies.[30]

It is necessary for the State invoking the failure to exhaust local remedies to prove both that there was a real remedy available and that recourse to it would not have been futile.[31] The approach to this burden of proof is, however, pragmatic. In the *ELSI* case, the International Court held that 'for an international claim to be admissible, it is sufficient if the essence of the claim has been brought before the competent tribunals and pursued as far as permitted by local laws and procedures, and without success'.[32] The doctrine does not require that every conceivable argument, however improbable the chances of its success, be raised in the local courts.

---

[27] Some have suggested that the local remedies rule is substantive, and that no international wrong arises until local remedies have been exhausted without success: see, e.g., the 1998 ILC Draft Articles on State Responsibility, arts. 21, 22, and Commentary thereon. The Draft Articles appear in UN Doc. A/51/10 and Corr. 1, 125; the ILC Commentaries on the Draft Articles, drawn from the ILC annual reports, were consolidated by the Secretariat in Doc. 97–02583 (January 1997). The position stated in the text is, in our view, correct. See C. F. Amerasinghe, *Local Remedies in International Law* (Cambridge, 1990), 319–58.

[28] See, e.g., *Losinger* (1936) PCIJ, Ser. A/B, No. 67, at 129–35, and the pleadings of the United Kingdom in *Anglo-Iranian Oil Co.*, ICJ Rep. 1952, 93, and of France in *Compagnie du Port, des Quais et des Entrepôts de Beyrouth and Société Radio-Orient (France v. Lebanon)*, ICJ Rep. 1960, 186. See also T. Meron, 'The Incidence of the Rule of Exhaustion of Local Remedies' (1959) 35 *BYIL* 93; S. M. Schwebel and J. G. Wetter, 'Arbitration and the Exhaustion of Local Remedies' (1966) 60 *AJIL* 484; J. L. Simpson & H. Fox, *International Arbitration* (London, 1959), ch. VI; A. A. C. Trindade, *The Application of the Rule of Exhaustion of Local Remedies in International Law* (Cambridge, 1983).

[29] ICJ Rep. 1959, 6 at 46.

[30] (1956) 23 *ILR* 306. For a criticism of the finding see D. W. Greig, *International Law*, 2nd edn. (London, 1976), 590–2. For the associated proceedings in the International Court see ICJ Rep. 1953, 10.

[31] *Finnish Shipowners* (1934) 3 *UNRIAA* 1479.

[32] ICJ Rep. 1989, 15 at 46; 84 *ILR* 311 at 352.

As is well known, attempts have been made in the form of the 'Calvo Clause' to strengthen the duty to pursue local remedies to the point where all other remedies are excluded.[33] Such clauses in contracts made by States purport to bind the parties to submit all disputes to the local courts, and to express the renunciation by the private party to the contract of all its rights under international law, including the right to diplomatic protection.[34] The significance of these clauses has declined substantially as States have sought to attract foreign investors, and they are not now common.[35] Nor have they, as a matter of international law, ever been capable of entirely achieving the ends which they sought. Calvo Clauses could not bind the foreign investor's national State not to exercise diplomatic protection on behalf of the investor.[36] They could, however, reinforce the local remedies doctrine; and in the *North American Dredging Company* case a Calvo Clause was held effective to create an obligation to exhaust local remedies before a claim was submitted to the US-Mexican General Claims Commission, even though the treaty establishing that Commission stipulated that no claim was to be disallowed or rejected by the application of the doctrine of the exhaustion of local remedies. [37] The Commission held that if the treaty had intended to override the reintroduction of the local remedies doctrine by means of Calvo Clauses, it ought to have done so expressly.

The exhaustion of local remedies doctrine is applied by most international tribunals,[38] but is subject to important modifications in respect of some tribunals. In the case of ICSID, for example, the duty to exhaust local remedies is made optional: it may, but need not, be required by the respondent State.[39] Indeed, under customary law, too, States are free to waive the duty.[40] For instance, no exhaustion of local remedies was required prior to recourse to the Iran-US Claims Tribunal.

---

[33] A. H. Feller, 'Some Observations on the Calvo Clause' (1933) 27 *AJIL* 461; A. V. Freeman, 'Recent Aspects of the Calvo Doctrine' (1946) 40 *AJIL* 121; K. Lipstein, 'The Place of the Calvo Clause in International Law' (1945) 22 *BYIL* 130; D. R. Shea, *The Calvo Clause* (Minneapolis, 1955); D. P. O'Connell, *International Law*, 2nd edn. (London, 1970), 1059–66; D.W. Greig, *International Law*, 2nd edn. (London, 1976); M. Sornarajah, *The Pursuit of Nationalized Property* (Dordrecht, 1986), 135–8.

[34] For an example see the clause discussed in the *North American Dredging Company* case (1926) 4 *UNRIAA* 26.

[35] Nor yet unknown. See, e.g., arts. 50, 51 of the Andean Investment Code 1970, (1971) 10 *ILM* 152.

[36] *North American Dredging Company* (1926) 4 *UNRIAA* 26. See M. Sornarajah, *The Pursuit of Nationalised Property* (Dordrecht, 1986), 135–7 for a suggestion that Calvo Clauses could have a wider effect, precluding the pursuit of international law remedies and even precluding international law liability.

[37] *North American Dredging Company* (1926) 4 *UNRIAA* 26 at 33.

[38] See, e.g., J. E. S. Fawcett, *The Application of the European Convention on Human Rights* (Oxford, 1987), 356 ff.

[39] ICSID Convention, art. 26. See above, chapter four, p. 69.

[40] *ELSI*, ICJ Rep. 1989, 15 at 42.

One particular context where the duty to exhaust local remedies is regarded as having been waived is the case of contractual agreements made by States to submit disputes with foreign nationals to arbitration. The rationale for this is that the arbitration *is* the 'local remedy', freely substituted by the State for the local courts.[41] Indeed, under the New York Convention the local courts would be bound to refuse to accept claims covered by an obligation to arbitrate. As arbitrator Mahmassani said in the *LIAMCO* arbitration, 'the Arbitral Tribunal constituted in accordance with such [sc., an arbitration] clause and procedure should have exclusive competence. No other tribunal or authority, local or otherwise, has competence in this matter.'[42]

The principles stated above relate to the exhaustion of 'local' remedies. There is no duty to exhaust international procedures, such as bilateral negotiations, before taking an international dispute before a judicial tribunal.[43]

With these preliminary matters discussed, we turn to a consideration of the arbitration process proper.

3. Submission to jurisdiction

All international litigation, in the sense in which the term is used in this book, is consensual. There has to be at some stage a voluntary submission to the jurisdiction of the tribunal, whether it be the ICJ, an ICSID arbitration panel, or any other tribunal. Indeed, the very possibility of submission is the first issue to be faced. There is no difficulty in the concept of submission by States to the jurisdiction of the ICJ, and the various modes of submission have already been discussed. But submission of private (i.e., non-State) parties to arbitration is more problematic.

Arbitrations are, from one perspective, systems of privatised justice adopted by parties who have opted out of national legal systems. They challenge the State's monopoly of justice. It is no surprise that States have sometimes sought to limit the right to opt for arbitration. On the other hand, since parties are generally free to compromise litigation before national courts, from another perspective arbi-

---

[41] By parity of reasoning, if the local law invests a foreign (or international) tribunal with jurisdiction, and the injured individual has a right of access to that tribunal, it, too, should be treated as 'local'. In European States this position might arise by virtue of the provisions of instruments such as the Brussels Convention on Civil Jurisdiction and Judgments and the European Convention on Human Rights.

[42] 62 *ILR* 140, 179–80; (1981) 20 *ILM* 1, 42. Cf. S. M. Schwebel, *International Arbitration: Three Salient Problems* (Cambridge, 1987), 119 ff.; and see the case of *Elf Aquitaine Iran* (1986) 11 *Yearbook Commercial Arbitration* 104–5.

[43] *Case concerning Land and Maritime Boundary between Cameroon and Nigeria*, ICJ Reports 1998, 275, judgment of 11 June 1998, para. 56.

tration is simply a particular application of the parties' freedom to settle disputes on the terms that they choose. These approaches can be seen to underlie the distinction between two different categories of arbitration agreement. One, often referred to as submission agreements, is the category of agreements to submit *existing* disputes to arbitration; the other, often referred to as arbitration clauses, is that of agreements in contracts to refer any *future* disputes to arbitration.[44]

Many States in the early part of the twentieth century accepted the validity of submission agreements but not of arbitration clauses.[45] The 1923 Geneva Protocol on Arbitration Clauses marked a major step forward by securing the recognition of the validity of agreements 'whether relating to existing or future differences between parties'.[46] States Parties agreed to oblige their courts to refuse to assert jurisdiction over disputes covered by valid arbitration clauses.[47] Similar obligations are now imposed by the 1958 New York Convention.[48]

The central role of the New York Convention in international arbitration gives a particular importance to the requirements relating to arbitration agreements that it prescribes for the recognition and enforcement of arbitral awards. Article II of the Convention requires that States Parties recognise arbitration agreements which:

a) are in writing;
b) cover differences which have arisen or may arise between the parties . . .
c) . . . which differences arise from a defined legal relationship, whether contractual or not, and
d) which concern a subject matter capable of settlement by arbitration.

In addition, article V.1(a) of the New York Convention permits the refusal of recognition and enforcement of arbitral awards in cases where:

e) the parties lacked capacity under the law applicable to them; or
f) the arbitration agreement is not valid under the law to which the parties have subjected it or, failing any indication thereon, under the law of the country where the award was made.

---

[44] On the distinction between submission agreements and arbitration clauses, see *Redfern & Hunter*, 130.

[45] This attitude persisted among certain Latin American States, at least until the conclusion of the 1975 Panama Convention: see C. R. Norberg, 'General Introduction to Inter-American Commercial Arbitration' (1978) 3 *Yearbook Commercial Arbitration* 1; A. M. Garro, 'Enforcement of Arbitration Agreements and Jurisdiction of Arbitral Tribunals in Latin America' (1984) 1 *Journal of International Arbitration* 293.

[46] Art. 1. 24 September 1923, 27 *LNTS* 157; M. O. Hudson, *International Legislation* (New York, 1931–50), vol. 2, 1062.

[47] Art. 4.

[48] Art. II(3). 10 June 1958, 330 *UNTS* 3.

Since the possibility of having the resulting award recognised and enforced is usually a basic aim of the parties,[49] article V in effect lays down two further requirements for arbitration agreements.

We will consider these requirements in turn.

3.1 Written agreement

While the New York Convention and many other conventions and national laws require agreements to arbitrate to be in writing,[50] this is essentially a matter of evidence. Under some laws it is sufficient if the underlying agreement is evidenced by an instrument in writing which the parties have expressly or impliedly accepted and which refers to standard conditions for arbitration.[51] There is no a priori necessity for a written agreement.[52] The doctrine of *forum prorogatum*, developed in the International Court, demonstrates the possibility of inferring an agreement to submit to the jurisdiction of a tribunal in the absence of a formal agreement in writing.[53] If the proceedings can be instituted and the resulting award enforced without recourse to the New York Convention, or to any other convention or system of national law which requires a written arbitration agreement, then an arbitration could be based upon an oral agreement, were it possible to prove the existence of such an agreement.

There are, of course, compelling policy reasons for requiring written agreements. The duty to submit to a tribunal, the ousting of the jurisdiction of national courts, the delimitation of the jurisdiction of the tribunal and the ordering of its proceedings, are all important matters upon which anything less than explicit and recorded agreement is unsatisfactory.

The requirement of a written agreement in the New York Convention was intended to preclude reliance on oral agreements, rather than to prescribe any particular form of record of the arbitration agreement. Thus, the Convention and

---

[49] The parties are not always concerned with recognition or enforcement. Each may be satisfied that the other will comply voluntarily with the award, or they may seek an award only on the question of liability.

[50] Geneva Convention (1927), art. 1(a); Geneva Convention (1961), art. II(2); ICSID Convention 1965, art. 25(1); UNCITRAL Model Law, art. 7(2). France, Code of Civil Procedure, art. 1443, *Redfern & Hunter*, 750; Switzerland, Private International Law Act 1987, art. 178, *Redfern & Hunter*, 785; USA, Federal Arbitration Act 1925, s. 2, *Redfern & Hunter*, 792; UK, Arbitration Act 1996, s. 5. Again, note that the 'UK' Act affects only English law: see s. 2. Scots law is somewhat different. We refer to it as a 'UK' Act only for convenience, and because our primary focus is on the international, inter-State aspect of dispute settlement.

[51] e.g., Netherlands, Code of Civil Procedure, art. 1021; UK Arbitration Act 1996, s. 6.

[52] Note the 1961 European Convention on International Commercial Arbitration, 484 *UNTS* 364, art. I.2.a of which makes provision for unwritten arbitration agreements.

[53] *Corfu Channel (Preliminary Objection)*, ICJ Rep. 1948, 15. See also C. M. H. Waldock, '*Forum prorogatum* or acceptance of a unilateral summons to appear before the International Court' (1948) 2 *ILQ* 377, and, on *forum prorogatum* in the ICJ, chapter seven, p. 136, above.

many national arbitration laws include within the category of written acceptances other methods of communication, such as exchanges of letters, telegrams and faxes.[54] No particular form of words is required, but many institutions have published model arbitration clauses. For instance, the LCIA suggests the following clause for inclusion in contracts:

> Any dispute arising out of or in connection with this contract, including any question regarding its existence, validity or termination, shall be referred to and finally resolved by arbitration under the UNCITRAL Arbitration Rules, which Rules are deemed to be incorporated by reference into this clause.
> Any arbitration commenced pursuant to this clause shall be administered by the LCIA.
> The appointing authority shall be the LCIA.
> The standard LCIA administrative procedures and schedule of costs shall apply.
> The number of arbitrators shall be [one/three].
> The place of arbitration shall be [city and/or country].
> The language to be used in the arbitral proceedings shall be [ ].
> The governing law of the contract shall be the substantive law of [ ].[55]

The agreement to arbitrate must, however, be precise. For example, the following clause was held to be ineffective as a submission to arbitration:

> In case of dispute, the parties undertake to submit to arbitration, but in case of litigation the Tribunal de la Seine shall have exclusive jurisdiction.[56]

3.2 Existing or future differences

The provision in the New York Convention (article II.1) that the Contracting States must recognise arbitration agreements which apply to 'all or any differences which have arisen or which may arise' between the parties is more an assertion of the ambit of the Convention than a statement of a condition of its applicability. As has been noted, many States did, and a few still do, refuse to recognise the validity of agreements to refer future disputes to arbitration.[57] In proceedings based on the New York Convention, States Parties must give effect to agreements to settle both existing and future disputes, and recognise and enforce arbitral awards based on such agreements; and a failure to do so would constitute a breach of the treaty obligation and a denial of justice which could itself be the subject of international proceedings.

---

[54] New York Convention, art. II(2); UNCITRAL Model Law, art. 7(2); Switzerland, Private International Law Act 1987, art. 178(1).

[55] See <http://www.lcia-arbitration.com/lcia/rulecost/rulecost.htm#recom>. For other Model Clauses see *Redfern & Hunter*, 535–40.

[56] Tribunal de grande instance de Paris (1 Feb. 1979, 16 Oct. 1979), (1980) *Revue de l'arbitrage* 97, at 101.

[57] See above, p. 199; cf. *Redfern & Hunter*, 135–6.

3.3 Defined legal relationship

Subject to their duties to submit to procedures under the UN Charter, States may in principle agree to give any tribunal jurisdiction over as broad a range of disputes as they choose. There is no a priori limitation upon the nature of the relationship from which a dispute must emerge if it is to be arbitrable. To this bald statement two qualifications must be made. First, certain disputes are not capable of settlement by the application of legal rules and principles: non-justiciablity will therefore operate as a limitation upon the category of disputes which are arbitrable.[58] Secondly, the constitutions of permanent international tribunals commonly limit their jurisdiction to certain kinds of dispute, and it may be impossible for them to be seised of other kinds of dispute.[59]

The position of private and mixed arbitrations is different. Resort to arbitration as an alternative to national courts is a privilege, not a right. As the next section explains, there are limitations upon the kinds of dispute that may be submitted to mixed or private arbitration. Moreover, submission to arbitration must be founded on an agreement, and since that agreement will necessarily establish a specific relationship between the parties it follows naturally that the agreement to arbitrate should be limited to disputes arising out of that relationship. For these reasons the New York Convention requires that all agreements to submit to arbitration be limited to disputes arising out of a defined relationship, which is usually established by the contract containing an arbitration clause.[60]

3.4 Arbitrability

States are, in principle, free to submit disputes of any kind to arbitration. Only the possibility of a tribunal giving a ruling of *non liquet*[61] or non-justiciability[62] operates to circumscribe the concept of an arbitrable dispute. In the case of disputes involving private parties, however, States may insist upon certain categories of dispute remaining within the jurisdiction of national courts. No municipal law permits private parties completely to exclude the jurisdiction of national legal

---

[58] See chapter one, p. 10, above.

[59] See, for instance, the ICSID Convention, art. 25.

[60] Though in such cases the cause of action need not be contractual, as long as the dispute is connected with the contract: see, e.g., *Lonrho Ltd. v. Shell Petroleum Company and British Petroleum Ltd.* (1979) 4 *Yearbook Commercial Arbitration* 320; *Rubino-Sammartano*, 105–6.

[61] In essence, *non liquet* is an acknowledgement that the matter is in principle one regulated by the law, but that the tribunal cannot determine the rule that can be applied. Non-justiciability is a term used in two senses: (i) the matter is not susceptible of legal decision at all, or (ii) the matter is regulated by law but it is inappropriate for the tribunal to apply the relevant rule. Meaning (ii) is sometimes found in decisions of municipal tribunals in which they refuse to rule upon questions of international law, regarding them as the proper preserve of international tribunals: see, e.g., *Buttes Gas and Oil Co. v. Hammer* [1982] AC 888, noted by J. G. Collier in [1982] 41 *CLJ* 18.

[62] See above, chapter one, p. 10.

systems. Unspeakable commercial skulduggery may be litigated through arbitration in private *Genevois* hotel suites; but if the parties resort to murder they will inevitably end up in public State courts.

One way of describing such limitations on the freedom to arbitrate is to say that certain disputes are non-arbitrable. Under the New York Convention States are not bound either to recognise arbitration agreements (article II.1), or to recognise and enforce awards resulting from arbitration agreements (article V.2), in cases where the subject matter of the dispute is not considered by the State to be capable of settlement by arbitration. Neither the New York Convention, nor any other convention, stipulates that certain disputes are inherently non-arbitrable. Conventions merely limit their own fields of application. This may be done by stipulating in the convention a particular limitation, such as the provision which limits ICSID arbitrations to disputes arising out of investments. But it is more generally done by reference to the provisions of national laws concerning arbitrability. It is national law which determines what disputes are or are not arbitrable.

This question would typically arise before the courts of the State where the arbitration is to take place, or where enforcement of the award is sought, in which case the court would determine the question of arbitrability under its own law. However, if the parties had chosen as the law governing the arbitration (the *lex arbitri*) the law of a third State, the court could also rest a refusal of recognition or enforcement upon the non-arbitrability of the dispute under the *lex arbitri*.[63]

There is a considerable variety among national laws in the categories of disputes that are stipulated to be not arbitrable. Among those most frequently encountered are disputes falling within the realms of family law, criminal law, insolvency, and certain aspects of intellectual property law. The common principle that unites those categories is the prominence of the public interest in seeing the uniform and public application of the law with due regard for the interests of persons other than the litigants themselves. To put it another way, only those disputes which can be compromised by the parties can be arbitrated. The trend in State practice is towards widening the category of arbitrable disputes. One notable development was the decision of the US Supreme Court in the *Mitsubishi* case,[64] in which the Court, reversing the effect of earlier decisions, upheld the arbitrability of issues of

---

[63] *Redfern & Hunter*, 138.

[64] *Mitsubishi Motors Corp.* v. *Soler Chrysler-Plymouth Inc.*, 473 US 614 (1985), (1985) 24 *ILM* 1064. Cf. W. F. Fox, '*Mitsubishi v Soler* and its Impact on International Commercial Arbitration' (1985) 19 *Journal of World Trade Law* 579; T. E. Carbonneau, '*Mitsubishi*: The Folly of Quixotic Internationalism' (1986) 2 *Arbitration International* 116; A. Lowenfeld, 'The *Mitsubishi* case: Another View' (1986) 2 *Arbitration International* 178; W. Park, 'National Law and Commercial Justice: Safeguarding Procedural Integrity in International Arbitration' (1989) 63 *Tulane Law Review* 647; J. H. Dalhuisen, 'The arbitrability of competition issues' (1995) 11 *Arbitration International* 151. Volume 12(2) of *Arbitration International* (1996) is a special issue on arbitrability in international commercial arbitration.

US antitrust law arising out of international commercial disputes. Similar developments are evident elsewhere. For instance, decisions in the 1990s in several European civil law jurisdictions held competition law and consumer law disputes to be arbitrable: the trend is clearly away from the approach represented by article 2061 of the French Civil Code, which states that 'an arbitration clause shall be void unless the law provides otherwise' and towards that represented by article 177 of the 1987 Swiss law on private international law, which states that 'any claim of a patrimonial nature may be the subject of arbitration'.[65]

Even if a dispute is arbitrable under the relevant national law, it may be excluded from conventional procedures. About one-third of the States Parties to the New York Convention have exercised their right under article I.3 to confine the application of the Convention to disputes arising from relationships which are, under their own laws, considered to be 'commercial'. This commonly excludes disputes relating to matters such as employment and bankruptcy.

3.5 Capacity

If the arbitration agreement is to be valid, it is in principle necessary that the parties be competent to conclude it. Even if the subject matter of the dispute is arbitrable, the parties may as a matter of law not be competent to agree to arbitrate it. For instance, the laws of some States prohibit the making of arbitration agreements by the State itself or by governmental agencies; and other laws make the conclusion of such agreements by public bodies conditional upon specific authorisation. It is convenient to mention here laws that stand on the borderline between the regulation of contractual capacity and the regulation of contractual terms. For example, under a 1988 decree of the Ruler of Dubai, contracts between public authorities in Dubai and foreign companies must not include clauses providing for arbitration by tribunals based outside Dubai.[66]

The New York Convention (article V.1(a)) refers to the capacity of the parties 'under the law applicable to them', but stipulates neither what that law might be nor how or by whom that question is to be determined. Article V of the New York Convention is concerned with the recognition and enforcement of arbitral awards, and the question may arise before a court where such recognition or enforcement is sought. The question may also arise if an action is brought to stay court proceedings and enforce an arbitration agreement. In this context the New York Convention (article II.3) would treat the question of capacity as one going to the validity of the arbitration agreement, and as such the question would also

---

[65] A. Kirry, 'Arbitrability: current trends in Europe' (1996) *Arbitration International* 373; M. de Boissesson and T. Clay, 'Recent developments in arbitration in civil law countries' [1998] *Int. ALR* 150.

[66] See (February 1989) 4(2) *International Arbitration Report*, 16–17.

concern the arbitral tribunal, whose jurisdiction depends upon the validity of the agreement. In each of these cases the prevailing view is that the court should apply the conflict of laws rules of the forum to determine what is the applicable law.

There is considerable support for the application of the law of the country with which the contract is most closely connected, or the law of his domicile and residence, to determine a natural person's capacity to contract. In the case of corporations, their capacity to do so is governed by their constitution and law of the place of incorporation and by the law which governs the contract in question.[67] The law of the place of incorporation has been employed for this purpose by international arbitral tribunals. For instance, in the *Liamco* case, arbitrator Mahmassani decided the capacity of Liamco by reference to Delaware corporation law. He determined the capacity of Libya by reference to the Libyan Arbitration Act of 1955.[68]

A particular problem arises in relation to the capacity of a State. Can a State invoke the provisions of its own law governing its capacity so as to invalidate an arbitration agreement to which it is a party? It was said in the *Benteler* case that: 'the present state of international arbitration law is that a State may not use its national law to contest its own consent to arbitrate'.[69] This certainly accords with the jurisprudence on the denial of justice,[70] and with the approach in recent legislation.[71] However, the point should not be pressed too far. In the context of inter-State arbitration agreements the law of treaties would be applicable. The Vienna Convention on the Law of Treaties, while adopting the general rule that States may not invoke provisions of their internal law regarding their competence in order to invalidate consent to be bound by a treaty, does permit States to rely upon manifest violations of rules of internal law of fundamental importance.[72] A failure to fulfil a requirement set out in the constitution to obtain parliamentary consent to accede to a treaty would be an example of a manifest and fundamental

---

[67] Dicey and Morris, *Conflict of Laws*, 12th edn. (London, 1993), Rule 181, p. 1271 and Rule 156, p. 1111; *Janred Properties Ltd.* v. *ENIT* [1989] 2 All ER 444 (CA); J. G. Collier, *Conflict of Laws*, 2nd edn. (Cambridge, 1994), 202–3. And see ICC Case 5832 (1988), in S. Jarvin, Y. Derains and J. J. Arnaldez, *ICC Arbitral Awards 1986–1990* (Paris, 1994), 352.

[68] *Libyan American Oil Co. (Liamco)* v. *Government of the Libyan Arab Republic* (1981) 62 *ILR* 140, 177–8; (1981) 20 *ILM* 1, 39–40.

[69] *Benteler* v. *Belgium* (1983), (1984) 1 *Journal of International Arbitration* 184, (1985) *European Commercial Cases* 101. Cf. *Elf Aquitaine Iran* v. *National Iranian Oil Co.*, (1982), (1986) 11 *Yearbook Commercial Arbitration* 97, 103. And see J. Paulsson, 'May a State invoke its internal law to repudiate consent to international commercial arbitration?' (1986) 2 *Arbitration International* 90.

[70] See below, p. 217.

[71] The 1987 Swiss Arbitration Act (art. 177(2)) provides that 'a state or an enterprise held, or an organisation controlled by it . . . cannot rely on its own law in order to contest its capacity to be a party to an arbitration': (1989) 6 *International Business Law Journal* 805, also in (1988) 27 *ILM* 37. Cf. *ICC Case No. 6162* (1992) 17 *Yearbook Commercial Arbitration* 153.

[72] Art. 46.

violation. There seems no good reason why the same principle should not apply to 'contractual' arbitration agreements made by States with non-State entities.[73]

3.6 Validity

The jurisdiction of an arbitral tribunal, the duty to recognise the arbitration agreement, and the duty to recognise and enforce the resulting award, all depend upon the validity of the arbitration agreement. The question of its validity may, therefore, be raised at the beginning of the process, as a challenge to the tribunal's jurisdiction, or to an attempt to litigate the dispute before the courts in violation of the agreement; or it may be raised as a defence to the recognition or enforcement of the award, or in proceedings for the annulment of the award.

The invalidity of the arbitration agreement can arise from defects of form or substance. Defects of form are unusual, since most legal systems require no more than that the agreement be written. However, some States may impose further rules, such as a requirement that the agreement be signed both by the parties and by their lawyers. A failure to comply with these rules would result in the formal invalidity of the agreement. The substantive invalidity of the agreement would result from a failure to comply with rules concerning the content, rather than the form, of the agreement. For example, substantive invalidity would result from an attempt to include non-arbitrable disputes within the agreement.

If the parties stipulate the law that they have agreed should govern the arbitration agreement, the formal and substantive validity of the agreement would be determined by that law. If the parties have not stipulated the law that is to govern the agreement, the tribunal or court before which the issue is raised must decide which law is to be applied. The New York Convention,[74] and the UNCITRAL Model Law,[75] support the view that the *lex loci arbitri*—the law of the place where the arbitration takes place—should be applied. There is, however, a strong tendency for tribunals to seek out and apply a law under which the arbitration agreement will be valid. Thus, the 1987 Swiss law provides:

> As regards to its substance, the arbitration agreement shall be valid if it conforms either to the law chosen by the parties, or to the law governing the subject-matter of the dispute, in particular the law governing the main contract, or if it conforms to Swiss law.[76]

There is a similar tendency to uphold the formal validity of the agreement wherever possible.

---

[73] For a case where international public policy was invoked to prevent a State relying on such constitutional limitations, see ICC proceedings No. 4381 (1986), *Clunet* 1986, 1106, quoted in *Rubino-Sammartano*, 153–4.

[74] Art. V.1(a).

[75] Art. 36(1)(a)(i).

[76] Art. 178(2): 6 *International Business Law Journal* 805 (1989); (1988) 27 *ILM* 37.

4. Who is covered by the arbitration agreement?

Once a valid arbitration agreement has been concluded, it may be necessary to determine precisely who are the parties to it. This problem usually arises where one corporate affiliate has signed on behalf of others. For instance, in *ICC Case No. 4402*, the Court of Arbitration held that signature of an arbitration agreement by a subsidiary was to be regarded prima facie as sufficient to bind its parent company, although the tribunal to which the case was consigned subsequently found on the facts that there was insufficient evidence of express or implied agreement on the part of the parent to bind the parent to arbitrate.[77]

The question may also arise in circumstances where the significance of signature by a government agency is in doubt. In the *Pyramids* arbitration the question arose whether the initialling of an arbitration agreement by an Egyptian Government Minister rendered the Egyptian Government a party to that agreement or was no more than an administrative formality. The arbitral tribunal held that it made the Government a party; but the French courts, to which an application for the annulment of the award was made, disagreed, and set aside the award.[78]

A related issue, which arose in the *Holiday Inns* arbitration, concerns succession to rights and duties under arbitration agreements. In that case the Moroccan Government had made an agreement containing an ICSID arbitration clause with two companies, subsidiaries respectively of Holiday Inns Inc., and Occidental Petroleum; and on the same day the two parent companies had agreed to guarantee all obligations under the basic agreement made by their subsidiaries. In response to a Moroccan argument that the parent companies were not entitled to be parties to the ICSID arbitration, the tribunal held that 'any party on whom rights and obligations under the Agreement have devolved is entitled to the benefits and subject to the burdens of the arbitration clause'.[79] The assumption of guarantors' obligations was sufficient to entitle the parent companies to be parties to the arbitration. Similarly, an ICSID tribunal has treated the transfer of 90 per cent of the shares in a company covered by an ICSID arbitration clause as transferring all rights attached to the shares, including the right to arbitrate.[80]

The principle that the right and duty to have recourse to arbitration for the settlement of contractual disputes flows with obligations arising under the contract was

---

[77] *ICC Case No. 4402* (1983) 8 *Yearbook Commercial Arbitration* 204, (1984) 9 *Yearbook Commercial Arbitration* 138. Cf. *ICC Case No. 4131, Dow Chemical et al.* v. *Isover Saint Gobain* (1984) 9 *Yearbook Commercial Arbitration* 131.

[78] 3 *ICSID Reports* 45, 79, 96; (1983) 22 *ILM* 752. The case was later taken up within the ICSID mechanism: see 3 *ICSID Reports* 101; (1993) 32 *ILM* 933.

[79] Unpublished; but see the account by Lalive, 'The First "World Bank" Arbitration (*Holiday Inns* v. *Morocco*)—Some Legal Problems' (1980) 51 *BYIL* 123; 1 *ICSID Reports* 645.

[80] *Amco Asia* v. *Indonesia*, 1 *ICSID Reports* 389, 402–3; (1984) 23 *ILM* 351, 371–4.

upheld in the idiosyncratic award in the *Westland Helicopters* case.[81] Proceeding from the premise that four States which had jointly established a commercial corporation having a distinct legal personality were, as a matter of law, presumed to remain liable for the obligations of that corporation, the tribunal held that:

> If it is true that the four States are bound by the obligations entered into by the Arab Organisation for Industrialisation, these four States are equally bound by the arbitration clause concluded by the Arab Organisation for Industry.

While the award was subsequently annulled by a Swiss court which rejected the (rather dubious) premise,[82] the reasoning that links substantive obligations and the obligation to arbitrate stands and is sound.[83]

5. Third parties: Intervention and joinder

Few topics so clearly illustrate the distinction between judicial and arbitral proceedings as the right of third parties to intervene, and it is convenient to deal with that topic in the context of submission. Under the Statute of the International Court, as we have seen,[84] States have a right to intervene in proceedings concerning the construction of a treaty to which they are parties.[85] Further, the Court may, but is not obliged to, permit them to intervene in other proceedings in which they have a legal interest which may be affected by the decision in the case.[86] As a matter of principle, no such right exists in relation to arbitrations. The arbitral process is ultimately founded upon the consent of the arbitrating parties; and no one may intervene in the proceedings without their consent.[87] Exceptionally, however, a right of intervention may be given by treaty. For instance, the 1899 Hague Convention (article 56) and its 1907 revision (article 84) gave a right of intervention to treaty parties when the construction of a treaty was at issue in arbitration. Such provisions are unusual; and the general right of intervention under the Hague Conventions appears not to have been invoked. Those provisions, allow-

---

[81] *Westland Helicopters Ltd.* v. *Arab Organization for Industrialisation, United Arab Emirates, Saudi Arabia, Qatar, Egypt and the Arab-British Helicopter Co.* (1984) 23 *ILM* 1071.

[82] *Westland Helicopters Ltd.* v. *AOI* (Annulment Proceedings, 1988), (1989) 28 *ILM* 687. For subsequent proceedings in the English courts see *Westland Helicopters Ltd* v. *Arab Organization for Industrialisation* [1995] Q.B. 282.

[83] Cf. *ICC Case No. 2626, Clunet* 1978, 981; *ICC Case No. 1704, Clunet* 1978, 977. See also the *SGTM/EPIDC* case, below, p. 215. But note the complications that may arise: D. Girsberger and C. Hausmaninger, 'Assignment of rights and agreement to arbitrate' (1992) *Arbitration International* 121.

[84] Chapter seven, pp. 163–8.

[85] Art. 63.

[86] Art. 62.

[87] The principle is regarded as an axiomatic inference from the consensual nature of arbitration: see the 1875 rules on arbitration drafted by the Institut de droit international, reproduced in W. Evans Darby, *International Tribunals,* 4th edn. (London, 1904), 488.

ing a right of intervention where the interpretation of a treaty is in issue, have, however, been echoed in some modern treaty regimes. Similar provisions may be found in the rules governing proceedings before certain standing tribunals in specialised dispute settlement regimes, such as the European Court of Justice,[88] the International Tribunal for the Law of the Sea,[89] and the WTO dispute settlement bodies.[90] There is still, however, no general right of intervention without the consent of the parties in *ad hoc* arbitrations or arbitrations conducted under international commercial arbitration rules.[91]

Just as there is no right of intervention so there is, as it were, no duty of intervention—or to put it another way, no third party can be compelled to join international proceedings without its consent and the consent of the original parties to the proceedings. The inability of third parties to insist upon a right of intervention, and of the parties to insist upon third parties joining the arbitration, can give rise to serious difficulties.[92] For instance, there may be an arbitration initiated by a State against a contractor, claiming damages arising from delay in the completion of a construction project. The contractor may assert in its defence that the delay was caused by the State, and that defence may be rejected. But the contractor may have subcontracted the works; and when the contractor in turn brings proceedings against the subcontractor the second arbitral tribunal may uphold the subcontractor's defence that the delay was the fault of the State, leaving the contractor with two inconsistent awards and the liability to pay the compensation awarded by the first tribunal.[93] Had the dispute been heard in a court, the subcontractor could simply have been joined to the main action regardless of the consent of the parties; but this is in principle not possible in an arbitration.

Several approaches to the improvement of this situation have been pursued. As was noted above, the NAFTA provisions on the arbitration of investment disputes provide for the compulsory consolidation of arbitral proceedings having questions of fact or law in common.[94] Recourse to these NAFTA arbitration provisions is a matter of choice, and therefore the parties must be taken to have agreed to any consolidation of proceedings that might occur. The provisions accordingly leave the principle of consent intact. Indeed, as is recognised in several arbitration laws, the parties are free to agree upon consolidation in any case.[95]

---

[88] See, e.g., art. 37 of the Statute of the Court of Justice of the European Communities.

[89] See the 1982 Law of the Sea Convention, Annex VI, art. 32.

[90] See art. 10 of the 1994 WTO Understanding on Rules and Procedures Governing the Settlement of Disputes, (1994) 33 *ILM* 1226.

[91] See, e. g., art. 41 of the Netherlands Arbitration Institute Arbitration Rules, reproduced in *Redfern & Hunter*, 645 at 669.

[92] See also the discussion of the *Monetary Gold* principle, above, chapter seven, pp. 158–61.

[93] For the fabled paradigmatic case, see Kerr LJ, 'Arbitration v. Litigation: the Macao Sardine case' (1987) 3 *Arbitration International* 79. For the *res judicata* aspect of this issue, see p. 262, below.

[94] NAFTA, art. 1126. See chapter four, p. 114, above.

[95] See, e.g., the UK Arbitration Act 1996, s. 35.

Some national laws have gone further, and provided for the mandatory consolidation of arbitrations, on application of one or more parties to the national courts.[96]

National courts have also sought to do what they can to ameliorate the inconvenience caused by the difficulties impeding third party intervention. One example is the *ADGAS* arbitration.[97] ADGAS initiated arbitration in London against a US company, the main contractor on a project. The US company denied liability and claimed that the fault was that of a Japanese subcontractor. The US company initiated arbitration against the Japanese subcontractor in London. Neither ADGAS nor the Japanese company would agree to the Japanese company joining the first arbitration; and the US and Japanese company could not agree upon the single arbitrator to be appointed for the second arbitration. The Court of Appeal, stressing the undesirability of separate arbitrations which might result in inconsistent decisions, exercised its powers under section 10 of the Arbitration Act 1950[98] and appointed the same arbitrator to each of the two arbitrations.

Where 'third parties' do join in proceedings, different problems may arise. For example, the representation of co-applicants or co-respondents having different interests in the litigation may cause difficulties. We deal with this aspect of multi-party arbitrations below.[99]

6. Contents of the arbitration agreement

There are certain matters which are, or at least should be, settled in every arbitration agreement, either explicitly in the agreement itself or by reference to a set of arbitration rules in which the matter is dealt with. These matters are discussed in greater detail below; but it is convenient to summarise them here.[100]

The agreement should deal with the constitution of the tribunal, prescribing the number of arbitrators and manner of their appointment. In cases where the arbitration is to be held in a State whose law does not give the local courts the power

---

[96] See, e.g., art. 1046 of the Netherlands Arbitration Act 1986; and cf. T. Hascher, 'Consolidation or arbitration by American courts' (1984) 1 *Journal of International Arbitration* 131; H. S. Miller, 'Consolidation in Hong Kong: the *Shui On* case' (1987) 3 *Arbitration International* 87.

[97] See *Abu Dhabi Gas Liquefaction Co. Ltd.* v. *Eastern Bechtel Corp.* [1982] 2 Lloyd's Rep. 425; (1982) 21 *ILM* 1057.

[98] See now the Arbitration Act 1996, s. 18.

[99] See pp. 221 (*Dutco*); 262 (binding force). See also the Annual Reports of the International Law Association, (1994) *Sixty Sixth Report*, 689, (1996) *Sixty Seventh Report*, 603.

[100] See further the UNCITRAL Notes on Organizing Arbitral Proceedings: UN Doc., GAOR A/51/71; *UNCITRAL Yearbook 1996, part one*, paras. 11–54; also available on the UNCITRAL web site <http://www.un.or.at/uncitral>. R. Ceccon, 'UNCITRAL Notes on Organizing Arbitral Proceedings and the Conduct of Evidence—a new approach to international arbitration' (1997) 14/2 *Journal of International Arbitration* 67.

to appoint arbitrators if one of the parties refuses to do so, it is also important to specify an appointing authority who can make the appointment in such circumstances. The agreement should also provide a mechanism for the filling of vacancies caused by the death or incapacity of arbitrators.

It is important that the agreement specifies the country where the arbitration is to take place since the law of the country where the arbitration has its seat will, as the *lex loci arbitri*, ordinarily apply to determine the extent to which the local courts may assist and intervene in the arbitration. That law may also impose certain mandatory requirements in relation to the conduct of the proceedings; and a failure to comply with any such requirements may render the award unenforceable. Indeed, unless the country is a party to the New York Convention or some other multilateral or bilateral agreement on the recognition and enforcement of awards, there may be considerable difficulty in enforcing an award even if it does comply with the requirements of the *lex loci arbitri*. Such legal considerations are of the greatest importance;[101] only when they have been dealt with should considerations of convenience, such as the location of the place in relation to the home bases of the parties, and the availability of accommodation, and secretarial and translation and other facilities, be allowed to determine the final choice. Even then, it should be recalled that the arbitration rules may empower a tribunal to meet at places other than its seat,[102] and so offer a way in which administrative convenience can be reconciled with the need to have regard to the *lex arbitri*.

The arbitration agreement should also specify the law to which it is subject. That law will, in the case of an arbitration clause included in a contract, be presumed to be the applicable law of the contract as a whole. But the parties may choose a different law. Since invalidity under the applicable law of the arbitration agreement may nullify that agreement, the choice of the applicable law is important.

In order to ensure the efficacy of the arbitration, it is usual to include default procedures, authorising the tribunal to proceed to render a full and final award even if one of the parties refuses to co-operate in the arbitration proceedings. Other provisions, such as clauses dealing with the language of proceedings, costs, time limits, the manner of dealing with documentary evidence and witnesses, and so on, may, of course, be included; but in reality these matters are commonly left to be decided by the tribunal itself.

In practice, the normal way of dealing with these issues is to set down the main elements—the appointment of arbitrators and place of arbitration—and then to

---

[101] See generally A. Samuel, 'The effect of the place of arbitration on the enforcement of the agreement to arbitrate' (1992) 8 *Arbitration International* 257; W. W. Park, *International Forum Selection* (The Hague, 1995).

[102] See, e.g., art. 20(2) of the UNCITRAL Arbitration Rules.

incorporate by reference one of the standard sets of arbitration rules such as the UNCITRAL or ICC rules.

7. Arbitration clauses and submission agreements

Arbitration clauses in contracts are drafted before the disputes arise, and before the balance of power and interests between the parties in any particular dispute which might arise can be known. This, and the unwillingness while concluding a contract to dwell on the possibility of a breakdown in the relationship, explains the brevity of arbitration clauses and the policy of relying on standard arbitration rules which have proved their practical utility and impartiality.

The situation is different where an arbitration agreement is negotiated in order to settle a dispute which has already arisen. Here the balance of power and interests, and any peculiarities of the dispute which may fit awkwardly within the standard rules, are already known. Submission agreements (as arbitration agreements drafted to cover existing disputes are generally known) tend to be drafted in much greater detail than arbitration clauses in contracts. A definition of the dispute, which marks out the limits of the tribunal's jurisdiction, will be included; and it is usual to make express provision for matters such as costs and time limits which might be left to be settled by the tribunal under an arbitration clause. The parties may set out a complete set of procedural rules for the tribunal; and even in cases where they adopt a standard set they are likely to supplement or modify its provisions, in the way that, for instance, the UNCITRAL Rules were modified for use by the Iran-US Claims Tribunal.[103]

8. The autonomy of the arbitration clause

At first sight the inclusion of an arbitration clause in a contract appears to give rise to a paradox. One of the parties may claim that the contract has been terminated. The contract may stipulate arbitration as the sole procedure for settling disputes. The tribunal's jurisdiction depends upon the contract. Therefore (so the paradox runs) the tribunal cannot be established without presupposing the continuing validity of the contract, which is the very point in issue. On the other hand, if this presupposition is not made, a party could avoid the obligation to arbitrate by the simple expedient of claiming that the contract is terminated. This paradox is troubling enough in the context of mixed arbitrations, where there is at least a possibility that a municipal court might hold that it has jurisdiction so as to afford the parties an alternative forum in which to have the dispute tried. The problem is

---

[103] See above, chapter three, p. 50, chapter four, p. 73.

more acute in the context of inter-State proceedings, where there may be no alternative tribunal with jurisdiction over the dispute.

All lawyers will know that the solution to this problem must be to give the tribunal jurisdiction; and the only doubt is how this conclusion is to be justified. The device which permits this conclusion is the principle of the 'autonomy of the arbitration clause'—the principle that the arbitration clause (or 'compromissory clause' or *compromis*, as it is termed in the context of the ICJ) is independent of the agreement (contract or treaty) in which it is included, and survives the termination of that agreement. Various arguments have been put forward to justify this principle.[104]

It is sometimes said to be an application of the more fundamental principle that each tribunal is the judge of its own competence. But that principle only requires that a duly established tribunal should have such competence, and does not address the problem of the tribunal the validity of whose establishment is the very question in dispute. Then there is the argument that the parties must be presumed to have intended that all disputes, including those relating to the validity of the agreement, be settled by the tribunal for which the arbitration clause provides. This argument is more attractive than it is compelling. If the parties did in fact intend that result, the conclusion can be justified as an application of normal principles governing the interpretation of agreements. If they did not in fact intend that result, there has to be some other justification for imposing that 'intention' upon them.[105]

Perhaps the only satisfactory explanation of the principle of the autonomy of the arbitration clause is that tribunals seek to uphold the efficacy of agreements providing for the reference of disputes to tribunals. Jurists have agonised over the logic of the principle; but the views which count are those of the tribunals which rule on the validity of arbitration clauses, and they have consistently upheld the autonomy of the *compromis*.[106] To adopt any other view would be to allow one of the parties to frustrate the arbitration process.

This reasoning has been adopted by the ICJ, notably in the *ICAO Council*[107] and *Fisheries Jurisdiction*[108] cases. In the former case the Court said:

> If a mere allegation, as yet unestablished, that a treaty was no longer operative could be used to defeat its jurisdictional clauses, all such clauses would become potentially

---

[104] See generally on this topic S. M. Schwebel, *International Arbitration: Three Salient Problems* (Cambridge, 1987), ch. I.

[105] Cf. P. Lalive, 'Problèmes relatifs à l'arbitrage international commercial' (1967) 120 *HR* 569.

[106] As does the UK Arbitration Act 1996, s. 7. See further A. Rogers and R. Launders, 'Separability—the indestructible arbitration clause' (1994) 10 *Arbitration International* 77.

[107] ICJ Rep. 1972, 46.

[108] ICJ Rep. 1973, 3; and see Judge Fitzmaurice SO, at 31. See also Judge Carneiro's dissenting opinion in the *Anglo-Iranian Oil Company* case, ICJ Rep. 1952, 93 at 164.

a dead letter, even in cases like the present, where one of the very questions at issue on the merits, and as yet undecided, is whether or not the treaty is operative—i.e., whether it has been validly terminated or suspended.[109]

International arbitral tribunals have taken the same view. For example, in the *Losinger* case,[110] it was said that:

> the unilateral annulment of a contract has no effect on the arbitration clause, which remains in force, at least until the legal position has been established regarding the grounds of annulment and the consequences of annulment.

The principle operated to give the tribunal jurisdiction in cases such as *Lena Goldfields*,[111] where one of the parties purported to annul the agreement in which the arbitration clause appeared, and in the arbitrations arising out of the Libyan oil nationalisations.[112]

It will be noted that the formulation of the principle of the autonomy of the arbitration clause set out above itself presupposes that the agreement in which the clause appears was at least initially valid and in force. This point was taken in the *Elf Aquitaine* arbitration,[113] where it was noted that:

> An arbitration clause may not always be operative in cases where it is clearly indicated by the facts and circumstances that there never existed a valid contract between the parties.

The logic of this is irresistible. If the purported agreement was void *ab initio*, for example because it was procured by coercion, there is no argument for holding the parties to a compromissory clause included in it. On the other hand a mere allegation that the agreement was void *ab initio* should not have this effect. The most practical solution is to allow the establishment of the tribunal if there is an arguable or a prima facie case[114] made out for the validity of the agreement, and to accept that the tribunal might, after hearing a full argument, hold that the agreement was void and that it had consequently lacked jurisdiction all along.

---

[109] ICJ Rep. 1972, 46 at 53–4.

[110] PCIJ, Ser. C, No. 78 (1936), at 105.

[111] (1930), reprinted in (1950) 36 *Cornell Law Quarterly* 44. See further A. Nussbaum, 'The arbitration between Lena Goldfields Ltd and the Soviet Government' (1950) 36 *Cornell Law Quarterly* 31; V. V. Veeder, 'The *Lena Goldfields* Arbitration: the historical roots of three ideas' (1998) 47 *ICLQ* 747.

[112] See, e.g., *Texaco Overseas Petroleum Co. (TOPCO) and California Asiatic Oil Co. v. Libya*, 53 *ILR* 389 at 402–13; *LIAMCO v. Libya*, 62 *ILR* 140 at 178, (1981) 20 *ILM* 1 at 40.

[113] *Elf Aquitaine Iran v. National Iranian Oil Co.* (1986) 11 *Yearbook Commercial Arbitration* 97.

[114] In *Benincasa v. Dentalkit Srl.*, Case C–269/95, [1998] All ER (EC) 135, the European Court of Justice held that a jurisdiction clause, which was formally valid under art. 17 of the Brussels Convention 1968, was effective to confer jurisdiction, though the plaintiff argued that the contract in which the clause was contained was void. What the precise burden of proof should be is unclear. It is also unclear whether giving the burden of proof a qualifying label would have any practical significance.

This is the approach adopted in the ICC Rules, whose organisational framework makes the process clear. Like other sets of arbitration rules, the ICC Rules treat arbitration clauses as independent of the agreements in which they are included.[115] Under the ICC system, requests for arbitration are made in the first instance to the Secretariat of the ICC Court of Arbitration.[116] If one of the parties challenges the existence or validity of the arbitration agreement, the Court of Arbitration will direct that the arbitration should proceed if a prima facie case for the existence of the agreement is made out: the arbitrator then takes the definitive decision upon the existence of the arbitration agreement, and may find that the tribunal lacks jurisdiction to proceed further.[117]

Technically, the most satisfactory description of the position is that the *compromis*, even if embedded in another agreement, is treated as an independent agreement, rather than as merely a severable provision of the main agreement. In this way its validity is not automatically terminated if the main agreement falls. Although it has sometimes been suggested that the arbitration agreement should be treated as a collateral contract, this is undesirable because, if the consideration for the arbitration agreement is the conclusion of the main contract, the collateral contract may fail for want of consideration if the main contract is found to be void *ab initio*, entailing the logical difficulties noted above. A better view is that the arbitration agreement is an entirely independent agreement consisting of reciprocal promises to submit disputes arising from the main transaction to arbitration. This may be a characterisation imposed on the situation, rather than a reflection of the parties' actual intentions; but it does have the merit of providing the soundest basis upon which to found arbitral proceedings.[118]

Before leaving the question of the effect of the annulment of an agreement upon arbitration clauses contained therein, a word should be said about the related (if somewhat unusual) question of the effect of the annulment of one of the parties. This issue arose in the *SGTM/EPIDC* arbitration.[119] In 1972 SGTM, a private corporation, instituted under a contractual arbitration clause arbitral proceedings in Geneva against EPIDC, which had been established as an agency of the East

---

[115] ICC 1998 Rules, art. 6(4). Cf., e.g., UNCITRAL Rules, art. 21(2); UNCITRAL Model Law art. 16(1); Netherlands Arbitration Institute Arbitration Rules, art. 9(5).

[116] ICC 1998 Rules, art. 6, See further, chapter three, p. 47.

[117] ICC 1998 Rules, art. 6. See *ICC Case No. 4402* (1983) 8 *Yearbook Commercial Arbitration* 204, and (1984) 9 *Yearbook Commercial Arbitration* 138. See also the Stockholm Chamber of Commerce Arbitration Rules, ss. 11, 14, *Redfern & Hunter*, 678.

[118] Cf. the discussions in the English courts: *Heyman* v. *Darwins Ltd.* [1942] AC 356 (HL). And see *Bremer Vulkan Schiffbau und Maschinenfabrik* v. *South India Shipping Corp. Ltd.* [1981] AC 909, at 980 (HL), per Lord Diplock: 'The Arbitration Clause contains a self-contained contract collateral or ancillary to the shipbuilding contract itself.'

[119] *Société des Grands Travaux de Marseille* v. *East Pakistan Industrial Development Corporation* (1980) 5 *Yearbook Commercial Arbitration* 177. Cf. G. R. Delaume, 'State contracts and transnational arbitration' (1981) 75 *AJIL* 784 at 789–90.

Pakistan Government. The Government of Bangladesh, which had supplanted the former government of East Pakistan when Bangladesh gained independence in 1971, subsequently transferred all EPIDC assets to the newly-formed Bangladesh Industrial Development Corporation (BIDC) and declared all arbitration proceedings to which EPIDC had been party to have abated. Then, shortly before the arbitration began, the Government dissolved BIDC and vested all its assets in the Government of Bangladesh, and announced that the Government would consider making *ex gratia* payments to creditors of BIDC. The arbitration clause survived, but the respondent did not. What effect should this have on the arbitration? The arbitrator, drawing on rules of Swiss and Bangladeshi law, held that the Government of Bangladesh had succeeded to EPIDC's liabilities. This decision was annulled in a controversial decision by the Swiss courts, on the ground that the arbitrator had misapplied Swiss law and was not entitled to extend his jurisdiction to BIDC and the Government of Bangladesh, which were not parties to the arbitration agreement.[120] The result of the Swiss court decision—that a State can evade an obligation to arbitrate by dissolving the nominal respondent—is too unattractive to be likely to survive unmodified, and runs counter to the principle that rights and duties arising from arbitration agreements are deemed to be transferred together with the control of the company.[121]

9. Refusal to arbitrate and the denial of justice

It is commonly considered that a denial of justice occurs where a government, in the face of a valid arbitration agreement made with an alien, prevents an arbitration from proceeding, whether by a simple refusal to participate in the arbitration, by the dissolution of the respondent party, or in any other manner. In Judge Schwebel's words:

> If the alien's right to arbitration is negated by the contracting State, a wrong ensues, whatever the law governing the contract, the arbitration agreement, or the arbitral process, no less than a wrong under international law ensues if a State takes the property of an alien without just compensation whether or not the right to that property derives from its municipal law.[122]

This view derives considerable support from international practice. The claim of denial of justice was raised by Switzerland in the *Losinger* case against a refusal by

---

[120] Swiss Federal Tribunal, 5 May 1976, (1980) 5 *Yearbook Commercial Arbitration* 217; cf. P. Lalive, 'Jurisprudence suisse de droit international privé' (1978) 34 *Annuaire Suisse de Droit International* 392.

[121] See above, pp. 207–8.

[122] S. M. Schwebel, *International Arbitration: Three Salient Problems* (Cambridge, 1987), 66. Cf. F. A. Mann, 'State Contracts and International Arbitration' (1967) 42 *BYIL* 1.

Yugoslavia to arbitrate,[123] and by the UK against a similar refusal by Iran in the *Anglo-Iranian Oil Company* case,[124] although both cases foundered at the stage of preliminary objections. Similarly, many arbitral awards support the view that unilateral action by a State which deprives a respondent company of a previously agreed right of access to arbitration is unlawful and constitutes a denial of justice.[125] It should be noted that in this context there is no duty to exhaust local remedies: the provision for arbitration is regarded as having been substituted, by or with the agreement of the State, for the State's own courts.[126]

It is also a settled rule that States, having agreed to arbitration, cannot invoke State immunity as a bar to the arbitral proceedings.[127] A plea of State immunity was rejected by the arbitrator in the *Solel Boneh* case[128] on the elegant, if antiquated,[129] ground that State immunity derived from the principle *par in parem non habet imperium*. He said:

> As arbitrator, I am myself no representative or organ of any State. My authority as arbitrator rests upon an agreement between the parties to the dispute . . . I do not consider that the doctrine of sovereign immunity has any application whatsoever in arbitration proceedings which are, as in Sweden, conducted independently of the local courts.

That reasoning gives rise to difficulties in circumstances where the local courts are competent to intervene in arbitral proceedings. The conclusion is better justified on the ground that the arbitration agreement constitutes a waiver of immunity for the purposes of the arbitral proceedings themselves and any court proceedings concerning the conduct of the arbitration, although not necessarily a waiver in respect of any temporary or permanent enforcement measures.[130]

---

[123] PCIJ, Ser. C., No. 78, at 313, 317, 365, 367.

[124] See the United Kingdom pleadings in that case, and cf. the dissenting opinion of Judge Carneiro, ICJ Rep. 1952, 164 ff. See also the cases of *Electricité de Beyrouth Company (France v. Lebanon)*, ICJ Rep. 1954, 107, and *Compagnie du Port, des Quais et des Entrepôts de Beyrouth and Société Radio-Orient (France v. Lebanon)*, ICJ Rep. 1960, 186. And see the US protests over the refusal of Libya to arbitrate the expropriation of US oil interests: *Digest of United States Practice in International Law, 1975*, 490, and (1981) 75 *AJIL* 487–8.

[125] S. M. Schwebel, *International Arbitration: Three Salient Problems* (Cambridge, 1987), ch. II, cites many such awards.

[126] See above, p. 198.

[127] J. G. Wetter, 'Pleas of Sovereign Immunity and Act of State Sovereignty before International Arbitral Tribunals' (1985) 2 *Journal of International Arbitration* 7.

[128] *Solel Boneh International v. Uganda* (1975) *Journal de droit international* 938.

[129] See, e.g., *Oppenheim*, 341 ff.

[130] See, e.g., the UK State Immunity Act 1978, ss. 2, 9; C. Schreuer, *State Immunity: Some Recent Developments* (Cambridge, 1989), chapter six.

10. Establishment and procedure of arbitral tribunals

10.1 Time limits

Once a dispute subject to an obligation to arbitrate has arisen, the arbitration procedure must be initiated and the arbitral tribunal established. In commercial contracts and concessions containing arbitration clauses, and in sets of arbitration rules, there is often prescribed a limited time after the dispute has arisen, within which the claimant is entitled to initiate arbitration and after which the claim becomes time barred. The laws of some countries, which may operate as the *lex arbitri*, may empower the local courts to extend time limits prescribed by such arbitration agreements.[131] Even where no such time limit is set out in the arbitration agreement itself, the law applicable to the contractual obligations may, as a matter of substantive law, set a limitation period for the pursuit of the claim.[132] In such a case the plea that the claim is time barred is likely to be considered by the arbitral tribunal after arbitration has been initiated: if upheld, the claim would be dismissed. Furthermore, quite apart from the existence of prescribed time limits, arbitrators may also be given the power to dismiss claims in the event of inordinate and inexcusable delay in the pursuit of the claim.[133]

Prescribed maximum time limits, within which a claim may be initiated and after which a claim is barred, are unlikely to be found in inter-State arbitration agreements,[134] because States allow themselves greater latitude and greater choice of means in the settlement of disputes. There are, however, occasional treaty provisions to similar effect. For instance, the Optional Protocol to the 1961 Vienna Convention on Diplomatic Relations, concerning the Compulsory Settlement of Disputes, provides that within two months of one party notifying another that a dispute exists the parties may agree to go to arbitration, and after the expiry of that period either party may bring the matter to the ICJ.[135] But it will be noted that the two-month limit here does not operate to bar later proceedings, but only to limit the time within which the parties may opt for arbitration rather than recourse to

---

[131] See, e.g., the UK Arbitration Act 1996, ss. 12, 50, 79.

[132] Some systems of law (e.g., English common law) have treated this question as a matter of procedure, governed by the law of the place of the arbitration, rather than a matter of substance, governed by the proper law of the contract. The current trend in municipal law, however, is to treat it as a question of substance. See, e.g., the European Convention on the Law Applicable to Contractual Obligations 1980 (the Rome Convention), art. 10(1)(d), enacted into UK law by the Contracts (Applicable Law) Act 1990, and the Foreign Limitation Periods Act 1984; J. G. Collier, *Conflict of Laws*, 2nd edn. (Cambridge, 1994), 67–8.

[133] See, e.g., the UK Arbitration Act 1996, s. 41 (reversing the effect of the decision in *Bremer Vulkan Schiffbau und Maschinenfabrik* v. *South Indian Shipping Corporation Ltd.* [1981] AC 909).

[134] Apart from cases involving the presentation of claims by a State on behalf of its nationals. See, e.g., the instances quoted in the UN Secretariat, *Commentary on the Draft Convention on Arbitral Procedure*, UN Doc. A/CN.4/92 (1955), 147–8.

[135] 500 *UNTS* 95.

the International Court. It is more common to find provisions envisaging *minimum* time limits, before the expiry of which the parties may not have recourse to arbitration. For example, the 1963 US–Trinidad and Tobago Agreement Relating to Investment Guarantees provides that any dispute unresolved at the end of three months from a request for negotiation shall be referred by either government to arbitration.[136]

In addition to such explicit provisions, there is a general rule of international law applicable in the context of inter-State arbitrations, barring claims where there has been excessive delay in their presentation. The rule, generally based upon the doctrine of extinctive prescription and the notion that States are deemed to have waived claims not pursued,[137] is unclear in its content. In particular, there is no clear time limit prescribed; and it seems that the time will vary according to the nature of the claim and the circumstances of the case.

Time limits may apply not merely to the first presentation of the claim, but also to the various stages of the establishment and operation of the arbitral tribunal.

10.2 Appointment of arbitrators

The first stage in the establishment of the arbitral tribunal is the designation of its members. Arbitration clauses will not specify the arbitrators, but only the procedure by which they are to be chosen and appointed. Submission agreements relating to disputes which have already arisen, however, may name the arbitrators,[138] although they do not always do so.[139]

Where the arbitrators are not named, the arbitration agreement will indicate the procedure for their appointment. It will normally call for the appointment of an odd number of arbitrators, usually one or three. Alternatively it may stipulate that the arbitration is to be conducted in accordance with one of the sets of arbitration rules, which rules will determine this issue. For instance, article 8 of the 1998 ICC Rules states that if the parties have not decided upon the number of arbitrators there is to be a sole arbitrator unless the dispute is such as to warrant the appointment of three arbitrators.[140]

---

[136] 471 *UNTS* 141. Cf. the Sri Lanka–UK Agreement for the Protection and Promotion of Investments 1980, (1980) 19 *ILM* 886.

[137] See, e.g., the *Ambatielos* claim (1956) 23 *ILR* 306 at 314; *Tagliaferro* (1903) 10 *UNRIAA* 592 at 593; D. P. O'Connell, *International Law* (London, 1970), 1066–7.

[138] See, e.g., the France–UK Arbitration Agreement of 10 July 1975 concerning the delimitation of the continental shelf, *UKTS* No. 137 (1975), Cmnd. 6280.

[139] See, e.g., the Canada–USA Convention for the Settlement of Difficulties (arising from the operation of the Trail smelter) of 15 April 1935, 162 *LNTS* 73.

[140] See also the UNCITRAL Arbitration Rules, art. 5, and the UNCITRAL Model Law, art. 10(2).

Most arbitral tribunals in disputes involving States have three members. The usual pattern is that each party nominates one arbitrator, the third being chosen by agreement between the parties[141] or between the two nominated arbitrators.[142] Such a constitution offers an assurance to each party that its views can be interpreted and represented to the tribunal, even though the arbitrators are required to be impartial.

It is common to make provision for the appointment of arbitrators in the event of the parties failing to appoint. For instance, the 1998 ICC Rules provide that if a party fails to nominate 'its' arbitrator within thirty days, or to agree upon a third arbitrator, the ICC Court of Arbitration is to make the appointment.[143] The ICSID Convention contains a similar provision.[144] In other cases, the parties might specifically agree upon a named person or institution to act as the appointing authority where there is a failure to nominate or agree upon an arbitrator. The President of the International Court of Justice was named as an appointing authority in an agreement made between Egypt, the Egyptian General Petroleum Company and Esso, for example.[145] There may occasionally be a double default, with the appointing authority failing to make an appointment. The UNCITRAL Arbitration Rules, used as the basis of the Iran-US Claims Tribunal, provide for this eventuality by specifying that the Secretary-General of the Permanent Court of Arbitration is to act if the appointing authority designated by the parties does not do so within sixty days;[146] and the ICC has asserted the right of its Court of Arbitration to act in default of a designated appointing authority.[147]

If the parties make no appointment, and if they designate no appointing authority (or the authority fails to act), the *lex arbitri* may itself stipulate a default procedure. For example, section 17 of the United Kingdom (English) Arbitration Act states that where each party is to appoint an arbitrator and one fails to do so, or to do so within the set time, the other may appoint a sole arbitrator, whose decision shall bind the parties. Such provisions are not common. It is more usual for the *lex arbitri* to empower the courts to act. Many States have laws giving their courts the power to appoint arbitrators in such circumstances.[148] If there is no such power

---

[141] e.g., art. 37, ICSID Convention.

[142] e.g., UNCITRAL Arbitration Rules, art. 7(1).

[143] Art. 8.

[144] Art. 38.

[145] Text reproduced in (1975) 14 *ILM* 933 (art. xxi).

[146] Arts. 6(2),(3) and 7(2),(3).

[147] Preliminary award in *Case No. 2321* (1974), in S. Jarvin and Y. Derains, *ICC Arbitral Awards 1974–1985* (Deventer, 1990), 8.

[148] See, e.g., the UK Arbitration Act 1996, ss. 18, 19 (and see the earlier provisions in the Arbitration Act 1950, s. 10 and Arbitration Act 1979, s. 6(4), used in *Abu Dhabi Gas Liquefaction Co. Ltd.* v. *Eastern Bechtel Corp.* [1982] 2 Lloyd's Rep. 425), (1982) 21 *ILM* 1057. Cf. the French Code of Civil Procedure, art. 1444; the Netherlands Arbitration Act 1986, art. 1027, in *Redfern & Hunter*, Appendices.

vested in a court having jurisdiction over the arbitration, or the courts decline to exercise the power, the process grinds to a halt. The existence of an arbitration agreement will, under article II(3) of the New York Convention, operate to bar trial of the dispute in the courts of a State Party. But there is in general no further means of compelling the establishment of the tribunal and the conduct of the arbitration. In this respect arbitration is less advantageous to an applicant than is the International Court of Justice, under article 53 of whose Statute cases may be tried notwithstanding the non-appearance of one of the parties.[149]

A particular problem arises in the case of multi-party arbitrations. One major reason for the practice of allowing each party to nominate an arbitrator in bilateral disputes is to secure the confidence of the parties. Each of them will know that there is someone on the tribunal who will understand, and if necessary explain to the other arbitrators, the nuances of the party's case. The need for this becomes apparent when it is recalled that the parties in the dispute may come from very different legal traditions, each of which has complex and subtle concepts not easily grasped on first acquaintance, and that those concepts may lie at the heart of the pleadings, if not of the case itself. Similarly, each party is given the reassurance that flows from the ability to appoint an arbitrator likely to understand and be broadly sympathetic to the manner of argument on the (often highly technical) merits of the case. This reasoning applies with equal force no matter how many parties there might be. But what about where three or more parties have bound themselves to take disputes arising between them to a single tribunal composed of, say, three judges?

This problem arose in the *Dutco* litigation.[150] A dispute arose between Dutco and two of its German contracting partners, BKMI and Siemens, who were all involved in a project in Oman. Dutco sought arbitration against the two German companies under the ICC Rules, as had been agreed. The ICC established a three-person tribunal. Dutco was asked to nominate one arbitrator, and BKMI and Siemens were asked jointly to nominate another arbitrator. BKMI and Siemens considered themselves to have different interests, and did not wish to nominate an arbitrator jointly, although they did so (under protest) in order to avoid the possibility of the ICC exercising its default powers to make the appointment itself.[151] After unsuccessfully challenging the tribunal's jurisdiction, Siemens applied to the French courts, as the courts of the *lex arbitri*. In 1992 the Cour de cassation,

---

[149] See chapter seven, p. 189, above. Cf. H. W. A. Thirlway, *Non-appearance before the International Court of Justice* (Cambridge, 1985).

[150] *Dutco* (*Siemens AG and BKMI Industrienlagen GmbH* v. *Dutco Consortium Construction Co.*) (French Cour de Cassation, 1992): see C. Seppala (April 1993) 8(4) *International Arbitration Report* 25; J-L Délvolvé, 'Multipartism: The *Dutco* Decision of the French Cour de cassation' (1993) 9 *Arbitration International* 197; A. S. Rau and E. F. Sherman, 'Tradition and innovation in international arbitral procedure' (1995) 30 *Texas International Law Journal* 89 at 108–18.

[151] See the power in art. 2(4) of the 1988 ICC Rules, reproduced in (1989) 28 *ILM* 231, and *Redfern & Hunter*, 577.

overturning a lower court judgment, held that the tribunal was improperly constituted. In cases where two parties have different interests,[152] a principle of (French) public order demands that the parties in an arbitration be treated on a footing of equality as far as rights to appoint arbitrators are concerned; and the parties cannot contract out of that right in advance of the dispute arising, although they may do so once the dispute has arisen and they can know what their precise interests are. This decision makes it difficult to accommodate multi-party disputes in arbitral proceedings, although arbitration institutions are developing a variety of ways of circumventing the problem. For example, the ICC and LCIA Rules now provide that the administering authority (the ICC or LCIA Court) will appoint *all* members of the tribunal in multi-party disputes, unless the parties agree upon joint nominations.[153]

10.3 Challenge to and disqualification of arbitrators[154]

It is possible that one of the parties may object to an arbitrator nominated by another party; and, regrettably, challenges to arbitrators are apparently becoming more common.[155] Arbitration rules provide for such challenges to be made, upon defined grounds. The UNCITRAL Rules, for instance, provide that arbitrators may be challenged if circumstances exist which give rise to justifiable doubts as to their impartiality or independence, and oblige them to disclose any circumstances which might lead to such doubts.[156] Tribunals tend to adopt a robust approach, accepting that in the relatively small world of international litigation it is very likely that individuals (whether parties, counsel or arbitrators) will know each other—indeed, regarding such knowledge as lying at the root of the confidence that the parties have in arbitral process—and that that is not incompatible with the need for impartiality.[157] On the other hand, an arbitrator who is a director of a

---

[152] The ICC and the French Cour d'appel considered that the German parties shared a common interest. The companies persuaded the Cour de cassation that they did not. Acceptance of the divergence of interests appears to have been crucial to the decision of the Cour de cassation.

[153] ICC 1998 Rules, art. 10; LCIA 1998 Rules, art. 8; and see the similar provision in art. 1046 of the Netherlands Arbitration Act 1986. See further I. Dore, *Theory and Practice of Multiparty Commercial Arbitration* (London, 1990).

[154] W. M. Tupman, 'Challenge and Disqualification of Arbitrators in International Commercial Arbitration' (1989) 38 *ICLQ* 26; G. A. Alvarez, 'The challenge of arbitrators' (1990) 6 *Arbitration International* 203; M. Bedjaoui, 'Challenge of arbitrators', in A. J. van den Berg (ed.), *International Arbitration in a Changing World: International Council for Commercial Arbitration Congress series no. 6* (Deventer, 1994), 85.

[155] See, e.g., the challenges in the ICSID arbitrations noted by W. M. Tupman, ibid., at 44, and the extensive practice of the Iran-US Claims Tribunal described in S. A. Baker and M. D. Davis, *The UNCITRAL Arbitration Rules in Practice* (Deventer, 1992), 37–71.

[156] Arts. 9, 10.

[157] See, e.g., the challenge in the *Amco Asia* v. *Indonesia* case in ICSID, noted at 1 *ICSID Reports* 376, 380, 389.

corporation that has appointed him probably cannot meet the required standard of impartiality.[158]

The arbitration rules may themselves lay down a procedure for dealing with such challenges. Normally, the challenge is communicated initially to the other party. Unless the other party accepts the challenge and replaces the arbitrator, or the arbitrator concerned withdraws, the challenge is put to the appointing authority, who decides upon it.[159] Alternatively, the tribunal itself may deal with the issue. Under the ICC 1998 Rules the decision on a challenge is made by the ICC Court of Arbitration;[160] and under the ICSID Rules challenges to one arbitrator are decided by the other members of a three-person tribunal.[161]

Challenges may also be raised before the courts of the seat of the arbitration, invoking the provisions of the local law as the *lex arbitri*. Most national laws empower the courts to remove arbitrators on certain specified grounds, such as partiality.[162] The precise grounds vary from jurisdiction to jurisdiction.

11. Powers and duties of arbitrators

The powers of arbitrators derive from two sources: the arbitration agreement (which may include a reference to a set of arbitration rules which confer powers on the arbitrators), and the law of the place where the tribunal has its seat—the *lex arbitri*. In addition the *lex arbitri* may give local courts certain powers to assist the arbitrators.[163]

Arbitration rules typically give arbitrators the powers necessary to control the proceedings satisfactorily and to render the award. For instance, under the UNCI-TRAL Rules arbitrators are given powers to determine the language of proceedings and time limits, to appoint experts, and, unless agreed by the parties, to determine the law applicable to the dispute. Local laws typically give certain procedural powers to arbitrators acting within the country, such as the power to take

---

[158] See, e.g., the discussion in the *Holiday Inns* v. *Morocco* case in ICSID: 1 *ICSID Reports* 645. For an inter-State (Saudi Arabia–United Kingdom) example see the *Buraimi Oasis* arbitration (1955), J. G. Wetter, *The International Arbitral Process*, Vol. 3 (New York, 1979), 357.

[159] e.g., UNCITRAL Arbitration Rules, arts. 11, 12.

[160] Art. 11.

[161] ICSID Arbitration Rules, Rule 9. If the two arbitrators cannot agree, or in the case of a challenge to a sole arbitrator or to the majority of arbitrators in a tribunal, the decision is taken by the Chairman of the Administrative Council of ICSID.

[162] See, e.g., the UK Arbitration Act 1996, s. 24 (which requires that the parties first exhaust removal procedures specified in the arbitration agreement); Netherlands Arbitration Act 1986, arts. 1033–5; Swiss Private International Law Act 1987, art. 180.

[163] S. Jarvin, 'The sources and limits of the arbitrator's powers', in J. D. M. Lew (ed.), *Contemporary Problems in International Arbitration* (London, 1986), 50.

evidence under oath and to call for evidence in the parties' control.[164] Local courts may also, under the local law, be given the power to do such things as compel witnesses to give evidence, either to the court or directly to the arbitral tribunal.[165]

The arbitration rules under which the tribunal is constituted may themselves lay down express organisational guidelines on matters such as the location and duration of sittings, the language of the proceedings, the form in which claims and counter-claims and evidence are to be submitted, the keeping of records of hearings, and so on. The UNCITRAL, ICC and most other sets of arbitration rules contain provisions on some or all of these matters. If there are no relevant provisions, and the parties do not settle the rules by agreement, the tribunal itself settles such organisational matters, whether or not specific powers are given in respect of them.[166] However, two points must be emphasised. First, the tribunal does not have absolute freedom to organise its proceedings: it must comply with any mandatory provisions of the local law. That law may, for instance, either require or forbid arbitrators to take evidence under oath.[167] Secondly, the choice of the country—or more strictly, the legal jurisdiction—in which the tribunal will have its seat is of major importance, because that decision usually determines the *lex arbitri* and, consequently, the extent to which local courts will be able to assist or otherwise intervene in the arbitral process. For this reason some, but not all,[168] arbitration rules remove from the tribunal the decision on the location of the seat: thus, for instance, article 14 of the ICC 1998 Arbitration Rules stipulates that the ICC Court of Arbitration is to fix the place of arbitration unless it is agreed upon by the parties.

Specific mention must be made of the power of arbitrators to order interim measures of protection. The rules under which the tribunal operates may confer a power to order such measures.[169] There is some support for the view that this is an inherent power of a tribunal: the interim award of the Iran-US Claims Tribunal in *E-Systems, Inc.* v. *Iran* referred to 'an inherent power to issue such orders as may be necessary to conserve the respective rights of the parties and to ensure that this Tribunal's jurisdiction and authority are made fully effective'.[170] But since the

---

[164] See, e.g., UK Arbitration Act 1996, ss. 34, 38.

[165] See, e.g., UK Arbitration Act 1996, ss. 43, 44; Netherlands Arbitration Act 1986, art. 1042. Note that the 1970 Hague Convention on the Taking of Evidence Abroad in Civil or Commercial Matters does not apply to arbitrations. See further D. S. Underhill and B. Valentin, 'Securing evidence for foreign arbitrations' [1998] *Int. ALR* 205.

[166] See UNCITRAL Arbitration Rules, art. 15; ICC 1988 Arbitration Rules, art. 15; ICSID Rules of Procedure, Rules 19, 20.

[167] See further *Rubino-Sammartano*, chs. 16, 19.

[168] e.g., art. 16 of the UNCITRAL Arbitration Rules leaves the decision to the tribunal.

[169] See, e.g., the UNCITRAL Arbitration Rules, art. 26; ICC 1998 Rules, art. 23; ICSID Rules, art. 39.

[170] (1983) 2 *Iran-US CTR* 57.

basis of such powers is the contractual agreement between the parties establishing the tribunal, those powers can in principle only extend to the parties themselves. If the tribunal wishes to enforce against a third party an order to take or comply with protective measures—for example, ordering a bank to freeze an account in which one of the parties holds funds—the tribunal must seek the assistance of the local courts. Provisions empowering courts to assist tribunals in this way are common.[171] We return to this point below, when we consider the remedies available in international dispute settlement.[172]

The duties of arbitrators derive from the arbitration agreement.[173] Clearly, the duty of conducting fair proceedings and rendering an impartial and reasoned award within a reasonable time is the primary duty, implicit in any reference of a dispute to arbitrators and sometimes explicitly imposed upon the arbitrators by the *lex arbitri*.[174] More precise duties may be spelled out in the rules governing the arbitration. These may include a requirement that the arbitrator(s) draw up a statement of the tribunal's terms of reference and a summary of the case,[175] and that certain stages of the procedure be completed within specified time limits.[176] Further duties to act with due diligence and in a judicial manner may be imposed on arbitrators by the local law and enforceable against them through the local courts.[177]

12. The authority of truncated tribunals

It is convenient to deal at this point with what is known as the problem of the authority of truncated tribunals, that is to say, the question whether a tribunal can proceed to render a valid award if one or more of the arbitrators refuse to co-operate in the arbitral process or to sign the final award. Such refusal has been a

---

[171] See, e.g., UK Arbitration Act 1996, s. 44; Swiss Private International Law Act 1987, art. 183. See further *Rubino-Sammartano*, ch. 17. The local courts may also be empowered to support the tribunal in enforcing the tribunal's orders directed to the parties: see the UK Arbitration Act 1996, s. 42.

[172] See p. 248, below.

[173] And also from professional ethics. See, for instance, the International Bar Association, 'Ethics for International Arbitrators', reprinted in *Redfern & Hunter*, 708; J. Paulsson, 'Ethics, elitism, eligibility' (1997) 14/4 *Journal of International Arbitration* 13. Cf. the WTO Rules of Conduct for the Understanding on Rules and Procedures Governing the Settlement of Disputes, 3 December 1997, (1997) 36 *ILM* 477.

[174] See, e.g., the UK Arbitration Act 1996, ss. 1, 33.

[175] See, e.g., ICC 1998 Rules, art. 18.

[176] See, e.g., ICC 1998 Rules, art. 24; the ICSID Rules of Procedure, Rules 13, 46.

[177] *Redfern & Hunter*, 262–71. It is interesting to speculate whether an action for breach of statutory duty might lie against miscreant arbitrators under ss. 1 and 33 of the UK Arbitration Act 1996, for example. But note that arbitrators are commonly given wide immunity from suit in respect of the discharge of their functions: see, e.g., ibid., s. 74.

persistent phenomenon in international arbitration from the time of the Jay Treaty arbitrations[178] up to the present day.[179]

Were a tribunal faced with such non-co-operation to take the view that it could no longer function and give a valid award, the only obstacle to either party stopping the proceedings at any stage would be the independence of the arbitrators; and at least where the parties each appoint one or more arbitrators, this protection may prove insufficient. Given the fact that, *ex hypothesi*, the parties have already agreed to arbitrate and have established the tribunal and seised it of the dispute, there is little to be said in favour of giving them this power to impede the proceedings. Accordingly, tribunals have repeatedly asserted that they may continue to hear a case and to render an award in the absence of one of the party-appointed arbitrators.

For example, in the *Lena Goldfields* arbitration between a British company and the Soviet Government,[180] the Soviet arbitrator was instructed to withdraw when the Soviet Government purported to dissolve the concession which was the subject of the dispute; but he withdrew only after the three-man tribunal for which the concession provided had been established. The remaining two members met and decided that they were competent to render an award, and they subsequently did so.[181] That case, often cited as authority for the proposition that a truncated tribunal has the authority to render a final award, is less clear than might appear, because the arbitration agreement itself provided that two arbitrators could render an award where the third defaulted. However, as Judge Schwebel has pointed out, the case must at least support the proposition that a truncated tribunal is *capable* of having the authority to render an award in circumstances where the parties intend that it should have that authority and have manifested that intent (as the parties here had done in the arbitration agreement).[182]

From the point of view of effectiveness, the solution adopted in *Lena Goldfields* was and is obvious. But it was not always so. In the early days of arbitration, when arbitrators were regarded as exercising an essentially diplomatic function, exploring the possibilities of a settlement on behalf of those who appointed them, the consent of each party to every stage of the arbitral process was a natural corollary of the perceived nature of the process. Only when arbitrators came to be seen as

---

[178] G. Schwarzenberger, *International Law as applied by International Courts and Tribunals*, vol. 4 (London, 1986), chs. 1–2.

[179] See the extraordinary events in the Iran-US Claims Tribunal: S. A. Baker and M. D. Davis, *The UNCITRAL Arbitration Rules in Practice: The Experience of the Iran-United States Claims Tribunal* (Deventer, 1992), 37–9, 172–3.

[180] See (1950) 36 *Cornell Law Review* 31, and V. V. Veeder, 'The *Lena Goldfields* Arbitration: the historical roots of three ideas' (1998) 47 *ICLQ* 747.

[181] The dispute was eventually settled by diplomatic negotiations, which resulted in the award being partly implemented.

[182] Comparable provisions giving authority to truncated tribunals can be found in, e.g., the UNCITRAL Rules (art. 31) and the 1998 ICC Rules (art. 25).

exercising an essentially judicial function could the non-frustration of the work of a truncated tribunal become the guiding principle.

This shift began to occur around the end of the last century, and was regarded as well established by the time that the International Court decided the *Peace Treaties* case in 1950.[183] There the Court observed that, unlike the position where no tribunal had ever been validly constituted, the withdrawal of an arbitrator from a validly constituted tribunal did not deprive the remaining arbitrators of the right to proceed to render an award.[184] This view is now supported by a considerable body of practice.[185]

13. Challenges to the tribunal's jurisdiction

The jurisdiction of the tribunal flows from the agreement of the parties. It follows that the tribunal has no competence in matters outside the remit given to it by the parties, although jurisdictional deficiencies can be cured at any stage by the agreement of the parties. This limitation upon the tribunal's jurisdiction is fundamental to the validity of its proceedings. In consequence, for instance, the New York Convention permits the refusal of recognition and enforcement of an award which deals with 'a difference not contemplated by or not falling within the terms of the submission to arbitration' or which 'contains decisions on matters beyond the scope of the submission to arbitration'.[186] Challenges to the jurisdiction of tribunals are increasingly common.

It is generally accepted that the tribunal may determine its own competence, subject to possible review of its decision by a competent court (which may be the court administering the *lex arbitri* or a court in which recognition or enforcement is sought). The mechanisms of challenge vary under different sets of arbitration rules. Article 21(1) of the UNCITRAL Rules stipulates that:

> The arbitral tribunal shall have the power to rule on objections that it has no jurisdiction, including any objections with respect to the existence or validity of the arbitration clause or of the separate arbitration agreement.[187]

In accordance with the principle of the autonomy of the arbitration agreement[188] it is, however, noted that where the tribunal is concerned with an arbitration

---

[183] Though there were survivals of the earlier, 'diplomatic', view of arbitration: see the *Buraimi Oasis* arbitration (1955), in J. G. Wetter, *The International Arbitral Process*, Vol. III (New York, 1979), 357.

[184] ICJ Rep. 1950, 221 at 229.

[185] See the cases discussed in S. M. Schwebel, *International Arbitration: Three Salient Problems* (Cambridge, 1987), ch. III.

[186] Art. V(1)(c).

[187] Cf. art. 16 of the UNCITRAL Model Law.

[188] See above, p. 212.

clause in a contract, 'a decision by the arbitral tribunal that the contract is null and void shall not entail *ipso jure* the invalidity of the arbitration clause'.[189] Jurisdictional challenges are generally taken as preliminary questions,[190] which are resolved by an interlocutory award. The ICC system is somewhat different. Instead of the tribunal itself deciding on a jurisdictional challenge, the decision is taken initially by the ICC Court of Arbitration. If that Court is satisfied of the prima facie existence of a valid arbitration agreement, the matter is remitted to the arbitral tribunal, which takes the final decision.[191] Some arbitration agreements may provide for an appeal from a ruling by the arbitral tribunal on its jurisdiction to a second arbitral tribunal;[192] others may achieve the same result by requiring— as does the ICSID system—that rulings on jurisdictional challenges take the form of awards (either preliminary, or joined with awards on the merits), which accordingly become open to challenge by proceedings for the annulment of that award.[193]

The courts administering the *lex arbitri* commonly provide a further forum in which jurisdictional challenges may be raised. If the tribunal rules that it has jurisdiction, a dissatisfied party may challenge the ruling in those courts,[194] although that right may be restricted in various ways. For instance, the law may require that the application to the court be made by agreement between the parties or with the permission of the arbitral tribunal;[195] or it may be stipulated that a jurisdictional challenge may be made only in conjunction with an application for the annulment of the final award.[196] A similar result could be achieved even in the absence of an express right to challenge the tribunal's jurisdiction by the expedient of initiating litigation over the dispute in the State's courts. If the claimant wished to proceed with the arbitration, it would have to persuade the court that the dispute was covered by a valid agreement to arbitrate,[197] and the jurisdiction of the arbitral tribunal would thus be put directly in issue. In all cases, a party that continues to participate in proceedings without raising a formal objection to the tribunal's jurisdiction at an early stage risks by virtue of its acquiescence losing entirely the right to object.[198]

---

[189] UNCITRAL Rules, art. 21(2).

[190] UNCITRAL Rules, art. 21(3),(4).

[191] ICC 1998 Rules, art. 6: cf. *ICC Case No. 4402* (1984) 9 *Yearbook Commercial Arbitration* 138. The principle of the autonomy of the arbitration clause is given effect in the ICC Rules in art. 6(4).

[192] This is envisaged by art. 1052(6) of the Netherlands Arbitration Act 1986.

[193] See the ICSID Rules, arts. 41, 50, 52.

[194] See, e.g., the UNCITRAL Model Law, art. 16(3).

[195] e.g., UK Arbitration Act 1996, ss. 31, 32.

[196] See, e.g., art. 1052(4) of the Netherlands Arbitration Act 1986.

[197] New York Convention, art. II.

[198] See the UK Arbitration Act 1996, ss. 32, 73; cf. art. 16 of the UNCITRAL Model Law, which prescribes a 30-day time limit for challenges.

Jurisdictional challenges are of three main kinds. First, there are allegations that there has been no agreement whatever to arbitrate or that a putative agreement was void *ab initio*. In such cases, if the challenge is well founded, the tribunal clearly has no jurisdiction to entertain the dispute, and if it does proceed to render an award that award is not entitled to recognition or enforcement.[199] Secondly, there are cases where an agreement to arbitrate did exist initially, but it is alleged that the agreement has subsequently been terminated by the invalidity of the contract in which it is contained. As we have seen, the principle of the autonomy of the arbitration clause provides for the continued validity of the agreement in such cases, so that the tribunal may properly proceed to render an award. Thirdly, there are cases where the continuing validity of the arbitration agreement is not disputed but it is alleged that some aspects of the applicant's claim (or of a counterclaim) fall outside the ambit of the agreement.[200] Again, if that allegation is well founded, the tribunal clearly lacks jurisdiction over such aspects.

14. *Lex arbitri*

We have dealt above with the question of the validity of the agreement to arbitrate. That question may involve the reference of questions to more than one legal system. The capacities of the parties may fall for determination under legal systems different from that which governs the arbitration agreement and the performance of obligations arising under it. Once the tribunal is established the possibility of references to yet other legal systems arises in connection with the conduct of the arbitration.

A clear distinction must be drawn between the law which is applied to determine the merits of a case (here called the 'applicable law') and the law which underpins and governs the arbitral process. The latter, the *lex arbitri*, is the subject of this section.

The *lex arbitri* is of great importance. Its scope was well described by Steyn J (as he then was) in *Paul Smith* v. *H & S Holdings Inc.*:

> The law governing the arbitration comprises the rules governing interim measures (e.g., court orders for the preservation or storage of goods), the rules empowering the exercise by the court of supportive measures to assist an arbitration which has run into difficulties (e.g., filling a vacancy in the composition of the tribunal, if there is no other mechanism) and rules providing for the exercise by the court of its supervisory jurisdiction over arbitrations (e.g., removing an arbitrator for misconduct).[201]

---

[199] New York Convention, art. V(1)(a).
[200] We return to this aspect below, at p. 260, in the context of challenges to arbitral awards.
[201] [1992] 2 Lloyd's Rep. 127 at 130. Cf., G. Zekos, 'Court's intervention in commercial and maritime arbitration under US law' (1997) 14 *Journal of International Arbitration* 99.

The *lex arbitri* will often be different from the applicable law.[202] The parties may, for instance, have subjected the contract (and hence, in principle, the merits of the case) to, say, English law, but have opted for arbitration in Paris, in which case French law is likely to be the *lex arbitri*.

The distinction is illustrated neatly by the English case of *Whitworth Street Estates Manchester) Ltd.* v. *James Miller & Partners Ltd.*[203] An English company contracted with a Scottish company to work on a building in Scotland. The parties had chosen to arbitrate in Scotland. After the arbitration the English company requested the arbitrator to state a case to the English High Court, seeking a review of the arbitral award on a point of law. This was possible under English law, but not under Scots law, which regarded the arbitrator as the final adjudicator on questions of law as well as fact. The House of Lords upheld the arbitrator's refusal to state a case, because, although English law, it held, governed the contract, Scots law was the *lex arbitri* and governed the arbitration.

The *Whitworth Street Estates* case also illustrates the common presumption that the *lex arbitri* is the law of the seat of the arbitration. That principle has been asserted with great vigour by some of the most distinguished lawyers in this field. For example, Lord Mustill said 'the inference that the parties when contracting to arbitrate in a particular place consented to having the arbitral process governed by the law of that place is irresistible'.[204] Nonetheless, the position has not gone entirely unquestioned, and the approach to the determination of the *lex arbitri* is much influenced by fundamental conceptions of the nature of arbitration.

There are three major theories about the nature of arbitration.[205] One, the 'jurisdictional theory', maintains that arbitration is rooted in the sovereignty of States and their authority to prescribe methods for dispute resolution which may, or must, be adopted within their borders. On this view, the freedom to arbitrate disputes is granted by the law of the State, and consequently subject to any constraints imposed by that law. The theory therefore points to the law of the State where the arbitration takes place—the *lex loci arbitri*—as the law which governs the conduct of the arbitration and the status of the award.

A second, 'contractual', theory asserts that the validity of arbitration proceedings and awards springs from the freedom of the parties to make contractual arrangements for the ordering of their affairs. This might be thought to imply that the

---

[202] See D. R. Thomas, 'The Proper Law of Arbitration Agreements' [1984] *LMCLQ* 304, and 'The Curial Law of Arbitration Proceedings' [1984] *LMCLQ* 491.

[203] [1970] AC 583 (HL).

[204] *Channel Tunnel Group Ltd.* v. *Balfour Beatty Construction Ltd.* [1993] AC 334 at 357–8 (HL).

[205] For a concise account see J. D. M. Lew, *The Applicable Law in International Commercial Arbitration* (Dobbs Ferry, NY, 1976), 51–61; A. Kassis, *Problèmes de base de l'arbitrage: arbitrage juridictionnel et arbitrage contractuel* (Paris, 1987).

parties are also free to choose the *lex arbitri*.[206] As has been pointed out,[207] however, the argument presupposes that there exists a legal system which confers this freedom of contract upon the parties; and accordingly this approach is not as independent of the State and the *lex loci arbitri* as might at first appear.

A third theory acknowledges this last point, but has it that arbitration has become so firmly established that it should be treated as an autonomous legal institution and not forced into inappropriate legal categories. This 'autonomy' theory supports the freedom of the parties to choose the *lex arbitri*, this being consonant with the general principle of party autonomy which is said to underlie arbitration.

These theories are of little importance in themselves, and in the crude form in which they have been presented above they are of little interest. But they do have a significant influence upon the attitude taken to the role of local courts in exercising control over arbitral proceedings.

The orthodox position has long been that known as the 'seat' theory, which broadly corresponds to the 'jurisdictional' approach to arbitration. The 'seat' theory asserts that arbitral proceedings are governed by the law of the place in which the arbitration is held and has its 'seat': the *lex arbitri* is the *lex loci arbitri*. The arbitral tribunal, like the courts and other tribunals in the country in which it has its seat, is governed by the law of that country.

This position is supported by a number of international conventions and decisions. For instance, article V(1)(e) of the New York Convention permits a foreign court to refuse to recognise or enforce an arbitral award which has been set aside or suspended by a competent authority of the country in which the award was made. Similarly, the tribunals in the *Sapphire*[208] and *BP*[209] arbitrations applied the law of the seat of the arbitration as the *lex arbitri*. There are powerful policy arguments in favour of this approach. As the reference to the New York Convention implies, a failure to comply with the law of the seat may render the award unenforceable in foreign courts: an arbitrator seeking to give an effective award cannot ignore the mandatory provisions of the *lex loci arbitri*. Again, the State in which the arbitration takes place has an interest in the maintenance of basic principles of fairness and justice in the arbitral proceedings.[210] But it has been argued by

---

[206] Cf. *SEEE* v. *World Bank, Yugoslavia and France* (1985) 82 *ILR* 59 at 69 (Court of Appeal, Rouen, France, 1984); *Texaco/Calasiatic* v. *Libya* (1977), (1978) 17 *ILM* 1 at 7.

[207] See F. A. Mann, 'Lex Facit Arbitrum', in P. Sanders (ed.), *International Arbitration: Liber Amicorum for Martin Domke* (The Hague, 1967), 'State Contracts and International Arbitration' (1967) 42 *BYIL* 1, and 'England Rejects "Delocalised" Contracts and Arbitration' (1984) 33 *ICLQ* 193.

[208] *Sapphire International Petroleum Co.* v. *NIOC* (1963) 35 *ILR* 136 at 138.

[209] *BP* v. *Libya* (1973) 53 *ILR* 297 at 308–11.

[210] See W. Park, 'The *Lex Loci Arbitri* and International Commercial Arbitration' (1983) 32 *ICLQ* 21; and 'National Law and Commercial Justice: Safeguarding Procedural Integrity in International Arbitration' (1989) 63 *Tulane Law Review* 647.

proponents of the 'delocalisation' approach that these considerations should not be decisive.

15. Delocalisation

Automatic application of the law of the seat as the *lex arbitri* may, it is said, produce results which appear arbitrary and undesirable. One distinguished commentator gives this example: the parties have decided on ICC arbitration, and the ICC has stipulated that the arbitration will be held in State A, with which neither the parties nor the dispute nor any of the arbitrators has any connection. A majority award is rendered, but the arbitrator appointed by the loser refuses to sign. Under the ICC Rules such an award is valid; but under the law of State A all arbitrators are required to sign the award, and this award is consequently invalid.[211] The choice of State A was fortuitous, and unconnected with the subject matter of the dispute. Why should such invalidity prevent the recognition and enforcement of the award in State B, whose laws (like the ICC Rules, upon which the parties had agreed) accept the validity of majority awards?

Such consequences have led some, mainly continental, jurists to propose the delocalisation of international commercial arbitration, i.e., the releasing of arbitrations from the legal requirements of the State in which the arbitration happened to be conducted, including its mandatory procedural rules governing arbitration. In other words, they advocate the freedom of the parties to choose something other than the *lex loci arbitri* as the *lex arbitri*. They also advocate the freedom of the parties to select, to govern their contract, some law other than the municipal law of any country.

There is some support for the delocalisation theory. Article 15 of the 1998 ICC Rules provides that the arbitration is to be governed by those Rules and, where the Rules are silent, by any rules the parties or the tribunal may settle on, 'whether or not reference is thereby made to the rules of procedure of a national law to be applied to the arbitration'.[212] The implication is that the parties may choose *not* to have any municipal procedural law applied to the arbitration. And in the *Gotaverken* case the Paris Court of Appeal, which had been asked to set aside an award rendered in France, interpreted article 11 as enabling the parties to detach an award from any municipal law;[213] and in the meantime a Swedish court had

---

[211] J. Paulsson, 'Delocalisation of International Commercial Arbitration: When and Why It Matters' (1983) 32 *ICLQ* 53 at 58–9; T. Rensmann, 'Anational arbitral awards—legal phenomenon or academic phantom?' (1998) 15/2 *Journal of International Arbitration* 37.

[212] Art. 11 of the 1988 ICC Rules used the formula 'whether or not reference is thereby made to a municipal procedural law to be applied to the arbitration'.

[213] Art. V(1)(d) of the New York Convention appears to adopt a similar stance; but it is not interpreted in this way: see *Redfern & Hunter*, 84, and A. J. van den Berg, *The New York Arbitration Convention of 1958* (The Hague, 1981), 34–9.

treated that award as enforceable without asking whether the award was binding under French law, basing its finding of the binding force of the award solely on the parties' contractual agreement to arbitrate.[214] The acceptance by the French and Swedish courts that the award was effectively delocalised meant that no court, applying the *lex arbitri,* was able to annul the award; however, the award could be challenged, on the grounds set out in the New York Convention,[215] in a court where its recognition or enforcement was sought.

There are some other precedents. The mixed arbitral tribunals established under the Peace Treaties after World War I were apparently not subject to any *lex loci arbitri.*[216] The *Aramco* tribunal refused to apply the law of its seat as the *lex arbitri,* on the ground that the law on sovereign immunity precluded the subjection of a State in a mixed arbitration to the law of another State;[217] and this, along with the intention of the parties to remove the dispute from the jurisdiction of the local courts, was given as a reason for applying international law as the *lex arbitri* in the *Texaco* case.[218] But the sovereign immunity argument, whatever validity it might have had in days when the doctrine of absolute immunity prevailed, cannot be persuasive now that the doctrine of restricted immunity holds sway.[219] Indeed, despite the persuasiveness of the argument of the proponents of delocalisation, that approach to the *lex arbitri* has as yet failed to take root.

Powerful arguments of principle and policy may be made against delocalisation. The freedom to settle disputes by arbitration is a concession, a derogation from the monopoly claimed by the State in the administration of justice; and the concession is made subject to such conditions, including the supervision and regulation of arbitral proceedings by the local law, as the State may choose. The parties, or the arbitrators, may wish to have the assistance of the local courts during the proceedings, and the courts may refuse to give it if the arbitration is in some sense insulated from the local law. The residual ability to challenge the award at the stage of recognition or enforcement is less than satisfactory, because it obliges the party making the challenge to do so by way of a defence to proceedings in a jurisdiction chosen by the other party. And courts may be reluctant to recognise or enforce awards which are not grounded in some system of national law.[220] The more widely adopted view was expressed by an English Court in *Bank Mellat* v. *Helliniki Techniki SA*:

---

[214] See J. Paulsson, 'Arbitration Unbound: Award Detached from the Law of its Country of Origin' (1981) 30 *ICLQ* 358.

[215] Art. V.

[216] R. David, *Arbitration in International Trade* (Deventer, 1985), 305, quoting a decision of the German-Roumanian Tribunal of 16 June 1925.

[217] *Saudi Arabia* v. *Aramco* (1958) 27 *ILR* 117.

[218] *Texaco/Calasiatic* v. *Libya* (1977), (1978) 17 *ILM* 1 at 7–9.

[219] Cf., *BP* v. *Libya* (1974) 53 *ILR* 297 at 309.

[220] Ibid.

Despite suggestions to the contrary by some learned writers under other systems, our jurisprudence does not recognise the concept of arbitral procedures floating in the transnational firmament, unconnected with any municipal system of law.[221]

There is no general acceptance of the claim that parties have the right to choose to detach themselves from systems of national law. Nonetheless, the underlying policy arguments in favour of delocalisation have found some favour with national legislatures; and if courts are reluctant to accept that the parties can by simple agreement free themselves from the shackles of the local law, legislatures have in recent years done much to loosen those shackles. For example, the 1981 French Decree on International Arbitration[222] severely limited the extent to which French law impinges upon international arbitrations and the grounds on which the French courts may interfere with them. This approach is also evident in instruments such as the Belgian legislation of 1985,[223] and the Swiss law of 1987;[224] and the UK Arbitration Act 1996 allows the parties to an international arbitration having its seat in England to agree, for example, to exclude the jurisdiction of English courts in appeals on points of law.[225] Paradoxically, the delocalisationists had to await the intervention of the very laws which they sought to escape in order to achieve their aims.

The position generally adopted is, in short, that the parties may not simply by their own agreement free themselves of the mandatory provisions of the *lex loci arbitri*, but that those provisions are steadily diminishing in their scope. As long as the parties comply with those mandatory rules, they may structure the arbitration as they wish. They may 'delocalise' to the extent of choosing another law to govern the procedure, but they may not escape the supervisory jurisdiction of the courts of the seat or any mandatory provisions of the law of the seat. The point is illustrated by the curious case of *Union of India* v. *McDonnell Douglas Corp.*,[226] which concerned a contract that provided for arbitration in accordance with the procedure set out in the Indian Arbitration Act 1940, with the seat of the arbitration in London. In an English court Saville J, as he then was, held that the law governing the arbitration was Indian law, but that the parties had submitted to the supervisory jurisdiction of the English courts and that English law was in that sense the procedural law, which would prevail where it was inconsistent with Indian arbitration law. The choice of Indian law as the law stipulating the arbitral procedure was, in essence, treated in the same way as it would have been had the

---

[221] [1984] QB 291 at 301 (per Kerr LJ); see also *Naviera Amazonica Peruana SA* v. *Campania Internacional de Seguros de Peru* [1988] 1 Lloyd's Rep. 116 at 119.

[222] (1981) 20 *ILM* 917.

[223] 1985 Revision of the Belgian Judicial Code, (1986) 25 *ILM* 725.

[224] Statute on International Arbitration, (1988) 27 *ILM* 37.

[225] Ss. 2, 69; cf., ss. 42–5.

[226] [1993] Lloyd's Rep. 48.

parties chosen arbitration in England with, say, the UNCITRAL Rules stipulating the arbitral procedure.

These considerations do not apply to inter-State arbitrations. A sense of the propriety of abstention by the local courts in the business of inter-State tribunals, coupled with the limitations imposed by the international law principle of the sovereign equality of States and domestic law rules on State immunity, effectively secures the right of the disputing States to control proceedings in such tribunals as they wish. Thus, as we noted above,[227] the validity of awards of the Iran-US Claims Tribunal, whose seat is at The Hague, were upheld by the English courts, even though they did not entirely comply with the requirements of Netherlands law.[228]

16. Procedure

The procedure governing an arbitration is almost always determined, in greater or lesser detail, in advance.[229] The first task is the settling of the terms of the arbitration—the *compromis*. The *compromis* will generally specify the identity of the parties, the scope and nature of the dispute (and consequently the limits of the tribunal's jurisdiction), the manner in which the tribunal is to be formed and the place where it is to sit, the procedure to be followed by the tribunal, the law applicable to the merits, the form of the award, and certain provisions on costs and fees.[230] It is usual for the parties to settle these questions themselves. If they do not do so, the matter is left for the tribunal, which may proceed on the application of one of the parties as long as there is enough agreement evident to enable the tribunal to proceed with its work.[231] Indeed, this principle has sometimes been stated in the arbitration agreement itself.[232]

Occasionally, provision has been made for the *compromis* to be settled by a third party. The 1907 Hague Convention for the Pacific Settlement of Disputes provided, in article 53, that the Permanent Court of Arbitration could settle the *compromis* if the parties agreed to have recourse to it for the purpose. Not surprisingly,

---

[227] Chapter four, p. 83, above.

[228] *Dallal* v. *Bank Mellat* [1986] QB 441.

[229] Occasionally agreement is reached on the arbitration of a dispute without agreement on even basic elements of procedure. See, e.g., the confusion surrounding the *Wal Wal* arbitration: (1935) 29 *AJIL* 690; 3 *UNRIAA* 1657; P. B. Potter, 'The *Wal Wal* Arbitration' (1936) 30 *AJIL* 27.

[230] See UN Secretariat, *Commentary on the Draft Convention on Arbitral Procedure*, UN Doc. A/CN.4/92 (1955), 34–44.

[231] Cf. art. 8 of the ILC's 1958 Model Rules on Arbitral Procedure, and the Commentary thereon: *Yearbook of the ILC*, 1958(ii) 78, 87.

[232] See, e.g., the 1898 Arbitration Treaty between Italy and Argentina, art. 2: W. Evans Darby, *International Tribunals*, 4th edn. (London, 1904), 400.

given the degree of co-operation between States which any arbitration presupposes, the provision remained a dead letter.

We have dealt above with the formation of the tribunal, and will consider the questions of the applicable law and of final and interim awards below. Here we deal with the procedure of the tribunal itself. The rules of procedure derive from three sources. First, there are the provisions contained in the various sets of arbitration rules, such as the UNCITRAL and ICC Rules, one of which may have been selected by the parties in the arbitration agreement. Secondly, there may be additional rules prescribed by the *lex arbitri*. Thirdly, there is a growing, if elusive, body of practice from which there is evolving a kind of common law governing the conduct of arbitrations.[233]

Representation of parties It is clear that, whether or not express provision is made, the parties have the right to be represented before the tribunal. The roles of counsel and agents for the parties are distinct.[234] Counsel present the case to the tribunal under the direction of the party whom they act. The agent is the representative of the party, and is responsible for the overall management of that party's case. A strict distinction between these functions has been observed in some cases. Thus, when in the *Behring Sea Fur Seal Arbitration* the US agent announced that he would present a motion to the tribunal and that counsel would argue it, the President of the Tribunal stated: 'We will not recognise the agents as arguing the matter. We recognise them as representing the government. Counsel will argue the matters, and we will dispose of them.'[235] These days, however, the distinction is not always strictly observed, and agents may argue all or part of the case before the tribunal.

The acts of the agents bind the States that they represent.[236] Accordingly, an agreement between the agents for each of the parties has the same effect as an agreement between the parties themselves. It may, for instance, operate to bind the tribunal to take a particular view of the ambit of its jurisdiction;[237] similarly, undertakings

---

[233] The work by V. S. Mani, *International Adjudication: Procedural Aspects* (The Hague, 1980) is one of the few studies of this topic. See also K. S. Carlston, *The Process of International Arbitration* (New York, 1946); J. G. Wetter, 'The conduct of arbitration' (1985) 2/2 *Journal of International Arbitration* 7. A valuable and detailed analysis of procedural issues in the form of hypothetical problems is to be found in P. Sanders, *Comparative Arbitration Practice and Public Policy in Arbitration: International Council for Commercial Arbitration Congress series no. 3* (Deventer, 1987), 19–174.

[234] See, e.g., Hague Convention 1899, art. 37; Hague Convention 1907, art. 62; ICJ Statute, art. 42.

[235] Moore, *Int. Arb.*, vol. 1, 910.

[236] See the comments of Verzijl in *Georges Pinson* (French-Mexican Mixed Commission, 1924) 5 *UNRIAA* 325 at 355–6.

[237] *Franco-US Air Transport Services Agreement* arbitration (1963) 38 *ILR* 182 at 188–9.

given to the tribunal by agents concerning the future conduct of their States are binding upon those States.[238]

Procedural fairness There are certain fundamental principles, all deriving from the notion of a fair trial, which must be observed in the proceedings. Most basic is the principle *audi alteram partem*, which is enshrined in all the sets of arbitration rules and would in any event operate as a general principle of law. The principle implies not only a right to be heard, but a right to have the arguments which each party wishes to advance heard.[239] The point arose in the *Wal Wal* arbitration, in which the attempt by the Italian agent to deny the Ethiopian agent the right to raise questions concerning sovereignty over the place where the military clash which was the subject of the arbitration occurred was roundly condemned.[240] And in the *Hostages* case the International Court was clearly willing to consider broad accusations made in the Iranian media concerning the propriety of the reception of the Shah of Iran by the United States, even though they could not affect the legal claim in issue in that case.[241] That principle would have very limited value if the tribunal were entitled to disregard the manner in which a party has chosen to defend its actions, and to substitute its own conception of that case.[242] The apparent willingness of the International Tribunal for the Law of the Sea to override the respondent State's choice in this respect in the case of the M/V *Saiga* is difficult to reconcile with this principle.[243]

Secondly, there is an entitlement to proper deliberation by a duly constituted tribunal. It goes without saying that the tribunal should function collectively, with all members able to participate in the hearings and subsequent deliberations. It was for this reason that the Court of Arbitration in the *Beagle Channel* case was at pains to make clear that Judge Petrén, who died four months before the award was rendered, had taken part in all of the deliberations up to the date of his death, had put his views on record, and had participated in the first reading of the draft of the award.[244]

---

[238] *Certain German Interests in Polish Upper Silesia*, Merits, 1926, PCIJ, Ser. A, No. 7, 13 (1926); *Mavrommatis Jerusalem Concessions (Merits)*, PCIJ, Ser. A, No. 5, 37 (1925); *Free Zones of Upper Savoy and the District of Gex*, PCIJ, Ser. A/B, No. 46 (1932).

[239] And cf. art. 70 of the Hague Convention of 1907.

[240] See V. S. Mani, *International Adjudication: Procedural Aspects* (The Hague, 1980), 21–3, citing the criticisms by Lapradelle, one of the Ethiopian-appointed arbitrators and quoting a work by the other Ethiopian-appointed arbitrator, P. B. Potter, *The Wal Wal Arbitration* (Washington, DC, 1938), 60ff.

[241] ICJ Rep. 1980, 3 at 41.

[242] Although, as the International Court of Justice observed in the *Spain/Canada Fisheries Jurisdiction* case, ICJ Rep. 1998, 432, judgment of 4 December 1998 para. 30, where the parties disagree on the nature of the dispute between them, the court must determine on an objective basis, in the light of the parties' submissions and other evidence, what the dispute dividing the parties is.

[243] (1998) 110 *ILR* 736; (1998) 37 *ILM* 360. See above, chapter five, p. 89.

[244] (1978) 17 *ILM* 632 at 643. Argentina did not list Judge Petrén's death among the reasons for its rejection of the award.

Thirdly, the parties are entitled to have a reasoned award. This is implicit in the judicial nature of arbitration. Despite an attempt by the Russian delegation at the 1899 Conference to remove the requirement, the Hague Conventions of 1899 and 1907 stipulate that the award must give the reasons on which it is based.[245] The requirement serves to ensure that the tribunal has understood and given due consideration to the arguments advanced by the parties, and to facilitate acceptance of the award by them. The parties may, of course, agree to have the dispute settled by an unreasoned award.

Other principles, such as the right to an impartial tribunal free from corruption and to proceedings free from fraud, might be added to the list.[246] However, there is little point in attempting to draw up an exhaustive catalogue of procedural rights, because there is no reason why any conduct that is considered to violate fundamental norms of natural justice should not suffice as a ground for challenging an award.

The remedy for any such violation is, in principle, the nullification of the award. One of the most famous instances is the set of *Umpire* cases in 1857, where several awards rendered by an umpire, who did not give the respondent, New Grenada, the opportunity to be heard on the merits of claims made against it by the United States, were nullified and the claims retried *de novo*.[247] The principle is, however, well established in contemporary practice.

There may be several different tribunals competent to rule on an application for the nullification of an award. The award may have been rendered under a system, such as the ICSID system, which itself provides for annulment proceedings.[248] The International Court of Justice has ruled on the validity of awards rendered in inter-State arbitrations,[249] although its jurisdiction to do so depends (as it does in all cases) upon the consent of the parties. National courts may be given the competence to annul awards, in their roles as tribunals applying the *lex arbitri*.[250] And a national court asked to recognise or enforce an award may refuse to do so on the ground of a procedural irregularity.[251] We return to this point below, when we consider challenges to arbitral awards.

---

[245] Art. 79, in the 1907 text.

[246] See generally V. S. Mani, *International Adjudication: Procedural Aspects* (The Hague, 1980); the papers in Part I of A. J. van den Berg (ed.), *I. Preventing Delay and Disruption of Arbitration. II. Effective Proceedings in Construction Cases: International Council for Commercial Arbitration Congress series no. 5* (Deventer, 1991), 15–345; A. J. Okekeifere, 'The UNCITRAL Model Law and the problem of delay in commercial arbitration' (1997) 14/1 *Journal of International Arbitration* 125; J. Trappe, 'The arbitration proceedings—fundamental principles and the rights of the parties' (1998) 15/3 *Journal of International Arbitration* 93.

[247] Moore, *Int. Arb.*, vol. 2, 1396–409.

[248] ICSID Convention, art. 52.

[249] See the *Arbitral Award Made by the King of Spain on 23 December 1906*, ICJ Rep. 1960, 192, and the Guinea Bissau/Senegal *Arbitral Award of 31 July 1989*, ICJ Rep. 1991, 53.

[250] See, e.g., the UNCITRAL Model Law, art. 34; the UK Arbitration Act 1996, ss. 67–71.

[251] New York Convention, art. V. And see, e.g., *Parsons & Whittemore Overseas Co., Inc. v. Société Générale de l'Industrie du Papier* 508 F 2d 969 (2d Cir. 1974), (1975) 14 *ILM* 504.

17. Applicable law

Most disputes arise from disagreements over facts, rather than law; and most disputes which are legal disputes arise from the interpretation of agreements whose validity is not in question. Nonetheless, the choice of the law applicable to determine the merits of a dispute is an important matter, because it determines the rules which are applicable to, for example, the interpretation of an agreement, the permissible means of performance, and the consequences of breach. The law applicable to the merits ('the applicable law') is, as we have seen, quite distinct from the *lex arbitri*. The governing principle is that the parties are free to choose the applicable law.

In some circumstances the choice of the tribunal dictates the applicable law. Thus, States which agree to litigate disputes before the International Court of Justice have *ipso facto* agreed to the choice of applicable law stipulated in the Court's Statute. Article 38(1) of the Statute requires the Court to apply treaties, customary international law and general principles of law in order to decide cases before it, unless the parties have specifically agreed to a determination of the dispute *ex aequo et bono* in accordance with article 38(2). But that simple and uncontroversial proposition conceals a more complex practical position.

First, since in general[252] treaties prevail over custom the parties are free to modify their rights and duties *inter se* by the conclusion of a treaty. Similarly, the institutions of local custom and persistent objection can modify the application to the parties of general rules of customary international law. The *compromis* submitting a dispute to the International Court can, in principle, constitute a modification by treaty of the rules applicable between the parties. Accordingly, the parties can in effect direct the Court to decide the case on the basis of some law other than general international law. The possibility of something of this kind occurring was admitted in the *Tunisia/Libya Continental Shelf* case.[253] The Special Agreement under which the dispute was submitted to the Court contained a provision stipulating that 'the Court shall take its decision according to equitable principles, and the relevant circumstances which characterise the area, as well as the new accepted trends in the Third Conference on the Law of the Sea'. The Court accepted that it would have been possible for the parties to have identified in the Special Agreement certain specific developments in the Law of the Sea which were to be applied in their bilateral relations, which would have been binding as a *lex specialis*. But it held that the parties had not been so specific, and that in this case the Court could not go further than it would go in any case, applying new trends to the extent that they had become part of customary international law. Such a *lex*

---

[252] The rules on *jus cogens* constitute the exception.
[253] ICJ Rep. 1982, 18 at 21, 38.

specialis would operate, not in derogation from the sources of law stipulated in article 38(1) of the Statute, but rather as an application of them, because treaty law and customary international law admit the possibility of the creation of such special rules.

Secondly, public international law permits States to choose the law to which they will submit their contractual undertakings. For instance, the 1966 Denmark–Malawi Loans Agreement was expressly subjected to Danish law,[254] and there can be no doubt that a tribunal would have upheld the validity of this choice of law.

As far as mixed arbitrations are concerned, the general principle that the parties are free to choose the applicable law—the principle of party autonomy—prevails.[255] Tribunals have found various routes to this conclusion, including findings that international law itself allows such party autonomy,[256] and that the conflict of laws rules applicable in the arbitration themselves allowed the parties to choose the applicable law.[257] In the case of arbitrations conducted under established procedures, the instrument governing the arbitration commonly prescribes the principle of party autonomy.[258] Although the principle is generally accepted, its operation is tempered by the common practice of subjecting contracts made with States to the law of the State party.[259] Given that most such contracts envisage performance in the territory of the State, such a choice of law is obvious and convenient.

The basic principle, then, is clear. A tribunal will, at least as a general rule, uphold an express choice of law by the parties, no matter what that law might be and regardless of whether the parties, or the transaction, have any real connection with the chosen legal system. Indeed, one commentator has remarked that there is no known case in which an arbitrator has set aside the parties' express choice of law on the ground of lack of connection with the intended legal system.[260]

---

[254] 586 *UNTS* 3. See F. A. Mann, 'About the Proper Law of Contracts between States', reprinted in Mann, *Studies in International Law* (Oxford, 1973), 241.

[255] See J. D. M. Lew, *Applicable Law in International Commercial Arbitration* (Dobbs Ferry, NY, 1978). Cf. P. Lalive in ICC award No. 1512, 24 February 1971 (1975) 1 *Yearbook Commercial Arbitration* 128 at 130.

[256] e.g., Dupuy, Sole Arbitrator, in *Texaco* v. *Libya* (1977) 53 *ILR* 389 at 422, (1978) 17 *ILM* 1 at 11.

[257] This was one ground canvassed by Cavin, Sole Arbitrator, in *Sapphire International Petroleum Ltd.* v. *National Iranian Oil Company* (1963) 35 *ILR* 136 at 170–1. Another option is simply to assert that the parties enjoy such autonomy: see Mahmassani in *LIAMCO* v. *Libya* (1977) 62 *ILR* 140 at 171, citing in support Dicey and Morris's *Conflict of Laws* and McNair, 'The General Principles of International Law Recognised by Civilised Nations' (1957) 33 *BYIL* 1.

[258] See, e.g., the European Convention 1961, art. VII(1); UNCITRAL Arbitration Rules, art. 33.1; ICC 1998 Rules, art. 17; ICSID Convention, art. 42. Cf. the Rome Convention on the Law Applicable to Contractual Obligations, art. 3.1.

[259] See E. Paasivirta, *Participation of States in International Contracts* (Helsinki, 1990), 57 *et seq.*

[260] O. Lando, 'The law applicable to the merits of the dispute', in J. D. M. Lew, *Contemporary Problems in International Arbitration* (London, 1986), 101 at 104. Cf. Dupuy in the *Texaco* arbitration (1978) 17 *ILM* 11, at para. 25.

The parties' choice of law may, however, be limited by the application of the rules of some other system. For instance, the Rome Convention on the Law Applicable to Contractual Obligations,[261] to which EU countries are, or may become, parties provides in article 3(1) that a contract 'shall be governed by the law chosen by the parties'. However, article 3(3) limits the application of the chosen law by providing that this 'shall not, where all the other elements relevant to the situation are connected with one country, prejudice the application of the rules of law of that country which cannot be derogated from by contract', which rules are called mandatory rules. Moreover, articles 7(1)[262] and 7(2) of the Convention provide for the application of mandatory rules of third countries and of the forum country respectively where these are mandatory irrespective of the law otherwise applicable to the contract. An example of the former would be a contract the performance of which was illegal according to the law of the place where it was intended to perform it—say, a contract to build a brewery in a strict Islamic State, or to supply technology to a State to which such exports are forbidden under the law of the State where the technology originates.[263]

In the nature of things, choices of law that seek to evade mandatory rules in State/non-State contracts are unlikely to arise, if only because the parties will not risk making a contract which cannot lawfully be performed. There is one context, however, in which the issue might give rise to real problems in practice. The arbitral tribunal might sit in a State whose courts would refuse to enforce certain contracts on the ground that to do so would conflict with local public policy. What if the brewery were contracted to be built in a State permitting the consumption of alcohol, but the arbitration was conducted in a strict prohibitionist State? It has been said that a tribunal which 'applies a foreign law as the law chosen by the parties is not obliged to apply provisions of that law which are incompatible with its own mandatory rules or with those of another country with which the contract has a close connection'.[264] Of course, this is a problem which could and should be avoided by choosing a more appropriate forum for the arbitration. But the principle remains: even in arbitration, tribunals will not allow themselves to be used for the circumvention of mandatory laws which apply to transactions properly

---

[261] Convention on the Law Applicable to Contractual Relations, (1980) OJ L266. The provisions of the Convention are enacted, with two exceptions (arts. 7(1) and 10(1)(e)), into UK law by the Contracts (Applicable Law) Act 1990.

[262] The UK, Germany, Ireland and Luxembourg entered reservations to art. 7(1) of the Rome Convention. Art. 7(1) has not been enacted into English law: Contracts (Applicable Law) Act 1990, s. 2(2). Art. 7(1) seems to be exemplified by such English cases as *Foster* v. *Driscoll* [1921] 1 KB 470 (CA) and *Regazzoni* v. *K. C. Sethia (1944) Ltd.* [1958] AC 301. These cases must now be regarded therefore as being examples of the refusal to enforce a contract that is contrary to English public policy, as provided for by art. 16 of the Convention. See J. G. Collier, *Conflict of Laws*, 2nd edn. (Cambridge, 1994), 210–12.

[263] *Redfern & Hunter*, 100–1; Rome Convention, art. 7(1).

[264] *Redfern & Hunter*, 100–1.

within their reach. To this extent, the autonomy of the parties does not give them a wholly unrestricted freedom to choose the applicable law.[265]

An express choice of the applicable law may be made at any time. Normally, it will be made in the agreement to which it relates (and one wonders how any competent lawyer can permit the signature of an international agreement which does not stipulate an applicable law). But the choice may be made by the parties in the arbitration agreement, or even in an agreement made during the course of the arbitration.[266] It is even conceivable that the parties might agree during the arbitration upon an applicable law different from that which was originally stipulated to govern their agreement, although there is a presumption that this will not be so.[267]

It is usual to choose a system of national law as the applicable law. This has the benefit of ensuring, so far as is possible, that there will be rules applicable to any unforeseen aspect of the relations between the parties. However, there are significant disadvantages with this approach. The law chosen may well be amended after the conclusion of the agreement, and any amendments may significantly modify the rights of the parties.

It has been said that 'any contract which is not a contract between states acting in their capacity as subjects of international law, is based on the municipal law of some country'.[268] Two implications may be read into this. The first is that the *choice* of an applicable law must be rooted in some system of municipal law permitting such a choice. The second is that a chosen law must be a system of municipal law. Neither is now regarded as correct. As these matters are of great importance in many mixed arbitrations, it is worthwhile to spend some time considering them.

As to the first of the implications, it is itself rooted in an increasingly dated view of arbitration as an extension of the freedom to contract and to compromise claims that is maintained in all major legal systems. That view is in the process of replacement by a conception of arbitration as an institution independent of national legal systems, which does not need to be explained in terms of contractual free-

---

[265] The point was established in cases such as *Vita Food Products Inc.* v. *Unus Shipping Co. Ltd.* [1939] AC 277. Cf. the papers in P. Sanders (ed.), *Comparative Arbitration Practice and Public Policy in Arbitration: International Council for Commercial Arbitration Congress series no. 3* (Deventer, 1987), 177–362; O. Chukwumerije, 'Mandatory rules of law in international commercial arbitration' (1993) 5 *AJICL* 561; H. W. Baade, 'The operation of foreign public law' (1995) 30 *Texas International Law Journal* 429; A. N. Zhilsov, 'Mandatory and public policy rules in international commercial arbitration' (1995) 42 *Netherlands International Law Review* 81; M. Blessing, 'Mandatory rules of law *versus* party autonomy in international arbitration' (1997) 14/4 *Journal of International Arbitration* 24.

[266] See, e.g., the ICC case cited by *Redfern & Hunter*, 99.

[267] See *Aminoil/Kuwait* (1982) 21 *ILM* 976 at 1000.

[268] *Serbian Loans*, PCIJ, Ser. A, No. 20, 41 (1920).

doms under the law or whatever. While the older view preserves a certain doctrinal purity it appears to have no significant practical consequences. As to the second implication, it is simply false. It has always been a more complicated matter than the quotation suggests, because a tribunal deciding on the applicable law may decide either to refer to the internal provisions of a municipal law *tout court* or to refer to a municipal law including its private international law provisions, which may require a reference to some other law for the determination of particular aspects of a dispute. That point should not be overstated: any such reference is usually made to some other municipal law, and it is highly unusual for *renvoi* to apply in the law of contract.[269] But the more significant point is that it is permissible—indeed, common—for the parties to choose as the applicable law a set of rules other than a municipal legal system.

The primary reason for choosing a law other than that of the State party to the contract is the desire to insulate the rights and duties negotiated by the parties and secured in the contract from the risk of changes resulting from the amendment of municipal laws. There is a significant risk that the State party might amend its rights and obligations, to the detriment of the non-State party, by the enactment of legislation.[270] The point was well put in the *Sapphire* case:

> the foreign company was bringing financial and technical assistance to Iran, which involved it in investments, responsibilities and considerable risks. It therefore seems natural that they should be protected against any legislative changes which might alter the character of the contract, and that they should be assured of some legal security. This could not be guaranteed to them by the outright application of Iranian law, which it is within the power of the Iranian State to change.[271]

Attempts have been made to alleviate the problem by including clauses providing for the revision of the agreement in case of hardship or changed circumstances; but they do not seek to guarantee rights that have been agreed and fixed in the contract.[272] Indeed, they do quite the opposite, offering a route out of difficulties in which one or other party may find itself under the contract. The 'guarantee' which the investor might seek takes the form, in international contracts, of a stabilisation clause: i.e., a clause that designates as the applicable law a law which it is not within the power of the State party to change unilaterally.

---

[269] See *Amin Rasheed Shipping Corporation* v. *Kuwait Insurance Co.*, [1984] AC 50. The Rome Convention on the Law Applicable to Contractual Relations (enacted into UK law by the Contracts (Applicable Law) Act 1990), art. 15, excludes the application of *renvoi*. Cf. UK Arbitration Act 1996, s. 46(2).

[270] See, e.g., the manner in which Jamaica purported to revise the terms of a 1968 bauxite concession by increasing taxes in its Bauxite Production Levy legislation in 1974: J. T. Schmidt, 'Arbitration under the Auspices of the International Centre for the Settlement of Investment Disputes (ICSID): Implications of the decision in *Alcoa Minerals of Jamaica, Inc.* v. *Government of Jamaica*' (1976) 17 *Harvard International Law Journal* 90.

[271] (1963) 35 *ILR* 136 at 171.

[272] See W. Peter, *Arbitration and Renegotiation of International Investment Agreements*, 2nd edn. (The Hague, 1995).

In the earlier part of the twentieth century this 'insulating' of the contract from variation by the legislation of the State party was sometimes attempted by subjecting the contract to the law of the State as it stood at a designated date.[273] This scarcely answers the problem, because the law so incorporated may be viewed simply as a shorthand definition of a body of specific rules which the parties have adopted by reference as terms of the contract, which remain just as subject as are expressly adopted clauses to legislative change. A second device is the subjection of the contract to 'general principles of law' or 'general principles of international law',[274] which by definition cannot be varied by unilateral action on the part of a single State. Something of this kind was done by the tribunals in the *Abu Dhabi*[275] and *Sapphire*[276] arbitrations, and, more clearly in accordance with the parties' wishes, in the *Aramco* arbitration.[277]

A variation of the use of general principles is the choice of the so-called *lex mercatoria* as the applicable law. The *lex mercatoria* is the term used to describe an ill-defined body of general principles of international trade law, which is capable of interpretation so as to eliminate from its scope idiosyncratic rules which may apply within particular systems of national law.[278] One might be forgiven for suspecting that the *lex mercatoria* is in essence an attempt to cloak with the semblance of legal certainty what is no more than a decision that the agreement be subjected to the rule of common sense (or the particular variant of common sense which prevails in the business community). National courts have shown great caution in accepting it as a legitimate choice of law, although its acceptance is not unknown.[279] For present purposes, however, the choice of the *lex mercatoria* may be regarded as equivalent to the choice of general principles of law.

---

[273] See, e.g., *Lena Goldfields* (1930), (1950) 36 *Cornell Law Quarterly* 44; *Redfern & Hunter*, 104, and references therein, and C. Greenwood, 'State contracts in international law—the Libyan oil arbitrations' (1982) 53 *BYIL* 27.

[274] Or even something as vague as a stipulation that the case be decided 'according to an equitable rather than a strictly legal interpretation': see, e.g., the *Orion Compania Espanola de Seguros* v. *Belfort Maatschappij* [1962] 2 Lloyd's Rep. 257.

[275] *Petroleum Development Ltd.* v. *Sheikh of Abu Dhabi* (1951) 18 *ILR* 144 at 149.

[276] *Sapphire International Petroleum Ltd.* v. *National Iranian Oil Company* (1963) 35 *ILR* 136 at 172–3.

[277] *Saudi Arabia* v. *Arabian American Oil Company (Aramco)* (1958) 27 *ILR* 117 at 167–9.

[278] See T. E. Carbonneau (ed.), *Lex Mercatoria and Arbitration: A Discussion of the New Law Merchant* (Dobbs Ferry, NY, 1990).

[279] See, e.g., *Deutsche Schachtbau- und Tiefbohrgesellschaft mbH* v. *R'As al-Khaimah National Oil Co. (RAKOIL)* [1990] 1 AC 295; *Société Pabalk Ticaret Sirketi* v. *Société anon. Norsolor* (Vienna Supreme Court, 1982) (1984) 9 *Yearbook Commercial Arbitration* 159. Cf. O. Lando, 'The *Lex Mercatoria* in International Commercial Law' (1985) 34 *ICLQ* 747; G. Delaume, 'Comparative Analysis as a Basis of Law in State Contracts: the Myth of the *Lex Mercatoria*' (1989) 63 *Tulane Law Review* 613; D. W. Rivkin, 'Enforceability of Arbitral Awards based on *Lex Mercatoria*' (1993) 9 *Arbitration International* 67. And see the *Norsolor* saga, in J. D. M. Lew (ed.), *Contemporary Problems in International Arbitration* (London, 1986), 120.

The choice of general principles of law as the applicable law offers effective insulation from unilateral changes in municipal law, but at the price of certainty. General principles are necessarily vague; they do not provide the kind of detailed code appropriate to complex commercial transactions; and the manner of their application is not always a predictable matter. In an attempt to overcome these drawbacks, the more recent practice has been to subject contracts to 'hybrid' clauses, in which the applicable law is a combination of national law (which provides the detail and predictability) and international law (which provides a safeguard against unilateral change). One such clause was in issue in the *Texaco* arbitration. It read:

> This concession shall be governed by and interpreted in accordance with the principles of the law of Libya common to the principles of international law and in the absence of such common principles then by and in accordance with the general principles of law, including such of those principles as may have been applied by international tribunals.[280]

Similar clauses were contained in the concession agreements underlying the *BP* and *Liamco* arbitrations; and although there were significant differences in the interpretations attached to them by the different tribunals, they were all regarded as proper choices of law by the parties and as affording a measure of insulation from unilateral changes of the municipal (Libyan) law, and—although this point is less clearly established—as converting a cancellation of the contract in breach of its terms which was merely wrongful in terms of municipal law into a wrongful taking in international law, thus attracting a higher award of damages than would have been made for a lawful expropriation.[281]

Thus far we have been concerned with the express choice by the parties of the law applicable to the contract by means of a clause in the contract itself. Similar principles would apply to an express choice of applicable law made not in the contract but afterwards, in the arbitration agreement. For instance, the parties may agree to ICSID arbitration, in which case they would be bound by article 42(1) of the ICSID Convention, which provides that:

> The Tribunal shall decide the dispute in accordance with such rules of law as may be agreed by the parties. In the absence of such agreement, the Tribunal shall apply the

---

[280] *Texaco Overseas Petroleum Company and California Asiatic Oil Company* v. *The Government of the Libyan Arab Republic* (1975, 1977) 53 *ILR* 389 at 442.

[281] On the differences in interpretation and the effect of the clauses on damages, see C. Greenwood, 'State contracts in international law—the Libyan oil arbitrations' (1982) 53 *BYIL* 27 at 46–8. Note also the limitations upon the permissible scope and interpretations of such contractual bindings of the State, which flow from the principle of the State's permanent sovereignty over natural resources: *Government of Kuwait* v. *American Independent Oil Company (AMINOIL)* (1982) 66 *ILR* 519 at 589. Cf. M. Sornarajah, 'Power and justice in foreign investment arbitration' (1997) 14/3 *Journal of International Arbitration* 103; N. Nassar, 'Internationalization of State contracts: ICSID, the lost citadel' (1997) 14/3 *Journal of International Arbitration* 184.

law of the Contracting State party to the dispute (including its rules on the conflict of laws) and such rules of international law as may be applicable.

But what if neither the contract nor the arbitration agreement contains any express provision on the applicable law?

It may be possible to imply a choice of law. Strictly, such an inference should only be made where (to use the terms of article 3 of the Rome Convention on the Law Applicable to Contractual Obligations) it can be 'demonstrated with reasonable certainty by the terms of the contract or the circumstances of the case' that the parties had intended a particular law to be applied. Sometimes it is said that the choice of the forum, or the nature of the contract, implies a choice of law;[282] but in practice this approach leaves considerable freedom to the tribunal and fades almost imperceptibly into the next category, that of cases where the parties have made no choice of law at all, either express or implied.

Here, two possibilities present themselves. First, the parties may have expressly authorised the tribunal to determine what is the applicable law. For instance, in the *AMINOIL* case the arbitration agreement provided that:

> The law governing the substantive issues between the Parties shall be determined by the Tribunal, having regard to the quality of the Parties, the transnational character of their relations and the principles of law and practice prevailing in the modern world.[283]

That clause alludes to a view adopted in the *Texaco* arbitration, to the effect that contracts which, because of their subject matter, duration and conclusion between States and corporations, may be placed in the category of economic development agreements should be regarded as having been internationalised, in the sense of the submission of the rights and duties arising under them to international law.[284] The *AMINOIL* clause allowed the Tribunal almost complete liberty in determining the applicable law. So, too, do the more recent rules governing international commercial arbitration. For example, article 17(1) of the 1998 ICC Rules stipulates that:

> The parties shall be free to agree upon the rules of law to be applied by the Arbitral Tribunal to the merits of the dispute. In the absence of any such agreement, the Arbitral Tribunal shall apply the rules of law which it determines to be appropriate.

Here it is made quite clear that the tribunal is empowered to determine not the *law* (which might have been thought to imply a choice of a legal system) but the *rules* of law, which would enable the tribunal to choose some rules from one legal system and others from another.

---

[282] *Revere Copper* v. *OPIC* (1978) 56 *ILR* 258, (1978) 17 *ILM* 1321.

[283] *Government of Kuwait* v. *AMINOIL* (1982) 66 *ILR* 519 at 533 (art. III.2).

[284] *Texaco Overseas Petroleum Company and California Asiatic Oil Company* v. *The Government of the Libyan Arab Republic* (1975, 1977) 53 *ILR* 389 at 452–7. Cf. *Revere Copper* v. *OPIC* (1978) 56 *ILR* 258, (1978) 17 *ILM* 1321.

Other clauses may be more constraining. Sometimes a less direct approach is taken, directing the tribunal not to apply the *law* it considers appropriate, but to apply the choice of law rule under the system of conflict of laws that it considers most appropriate and thence to apply the rules of the chosen law. For example, article VII(1) of the European Convention provides that:

> failing any indication by the parties as to the applicable law, the arbitrators shall apply the proper law under the rule of conflict that the arbitrators deem applicable . . . the arbitrators shall take account of the terms of the contract and trade usages.

This may be thought unnecessarily pedantic; and it is hard to see that it leads to conclusions any different from those which would apply were the tribunal directed simply to apply the most appropriate law.[285]

In the foregoing cases, even though the tribunal has considerable freedom to choose the law, that freedom derives from a specific authorisation by the parties in the arbitration agreement. It might be regarded as a delegation by the parties of the choice of the applicable law. But what of cases where the parties have made absolutely no provision on the matter, whether by expressly or impliedly choosing the applicable law themselves or by authorising the tribunal to choose it?

In such cases it is clearly necessary that the tribunal apply some law, and equally clear that it is within the inherent powers of the tribunal to make such a choice. The question remains, however, whether in doing so the tribunal is constrained by the conflict of laws rules of the *lex arbitri*. International practice on this matter is not settled. Older cases suggest that the arbitrator is indeed bound by the conflicts rules of the forum.[286] More recently the practice has been for the arbitrator to be empowered by the *lex arbitri* to choose the conflicts rules that he deems applicable,[287] or for the tribunal to do so on its own initiative.[288] And most recently the tendency has been for the *lex arbitri* to dispense with this formality altogether, and to allow the arbitrator to proceed straight to the choice of the substantive law that he deems applicable. In line with the general trend towards increasing autonomy for international arbitration tribunals, the laws of many States now allow a tribunal a practically unfettered freedom to choose the applicable law. For instance, the French Code of Civil Procedure, as amended in 1981, provides that:

---

[285] The 1988 ICC Arbitration Rules directed the arbitrator to apply 'the law designated as the proper law by the rule of conflict which he deems appropriate' (art. 13(3)); but that provision was replaced by art. 17(1) of the 1998 Rules, quoted above.

[286] See, e.g., *Czarnikow* v. *Roth, Schmidt & Co.* [1922] 2 KB 478.

[287] UNCITRAL Model Law, art. 28(2); UK Arbitration Act 1996, s. 46(3), and see S. R. Shackleton, 'The applicable law in international arbitration under the new English Arbitration Act 1996' (1997) 13 *Arbitration International* 375; cf. UNCITRAL Arbitration Rules, art. 33.

[288] e.g., *Sapphire International Petroleum Ltd.* v. *National Iranian Oil Co.* (1963) 35 *ILR* 136; *ICC Case 6719* (1991), in J. J. Arnaldez, Y. Derains and D. Hascher, *ICC Arbitral Awards 1991–1995* (Paris, 1997), 567.

The arbitrator shall settle the dispute in accordance with the rules which the parties have chosen, and in the absence of such a choice, in accordance with those rules which he considers to be appropriate.[289]

Once the applicable law is chosen, the tribunal applies it as would a municipal court. Arbitral procedure may be more flexible than that of courts; but the tribunal cannot ignore or modify rules of law that it has held to be applicable to the dispute before it. Indeed, to do so would expose the award to challenge, as an award rendered in excess of the tribunal's jurisdiction.[290]

18. Remedies

The question of the available remedies will have surfaced at an early stage in the proceedings. Indeed, the initial application to the tribunal will have specified the kind of relief that is sought from the tribunal. The remedies which a tribunal may order are, broadly speaking, of two kinds: interim (or provisional) measures, and final measures. Interim measures are indicated by the tribunal prior to the conclusion of the case. Their primary purpose is to safeguard the position of the parties and to prevent them from taking any action which might frustrate the final measures indicated by the tribunal.

18.1 Interim measures[291]

The power of a tribunal to order interim measures is commonly set out in the instrument establishing the tribunal. For instance, article 47 of the ICSID Convention empowers ICSID tribunals to recommend such measures,[292] and article 47 of the ICJ Statute authorises the Court to indicate provisional measures.[293] Similar provisions are set out in the statutes of other permanent tribunals,[294] and in many institutional rules.[295] Tribunals commonly make orders for such measures in the form of interim awards.

---

[289] Cf. the Netherlands: Art. 1054(2), Code of Civil Procedure; Switzerland, Private International Law Act, Ch. 12, art. 187; and see the Rome Convention on the Law Applicable to Contractual Obligations, art. 4(1).

[290] See p. 257, below.

[291] See L. Collins, 'Provisional and Protective Measures in International Litigation' (1992) 111 *HR* 9; S. Oda, 'Provisional measures: the practice of the International Court of Justice', in *Fifty Years of the International Court of Justice*, 541; Z. Stalev, 'Interim measures of protection in the context of arbitration', in A. J. van den Berg (ed.), *International Arbitration in a Changing World: International Council for Commercial Arbitration Congress series no. 6* (Deventer, 1994), 103; D. A. Redfern, 'Arbitration and the courts: interim measures—is the tide about to turn?' (1995) 30 *Texas International Law Journal* 71.

[292] See above, chapter four, p. 69.

[293] See chapter seven, pp. 168–75, above.

[294] See, e.g., the tribunals operating under the Law of the Sea dispute settlement system: 1982 Law of the Sea Convention, art. 290 and Annex VI, art. 25.

[295] See, e.g., UNCITRAL Arbitration Rules, art. 26; UNCITRAL Model Law, art. 17; ICC 1998 Rules, art. 23; London Court of International Arbitration 1998 Rules, art. 25.

One shortcoming of these provisions is that while they may bind the parties, who have in effect agreed to be bound by the interim measures by virtue of their acceptance of the jurisdiction of the tribunal, they cannot bind third parties. This may be crucial. For instance, property owned by one party to the dispute might be held by a third party (as a bank might hold a bank account), and the other party to the dispute may wish to ensure that the property is not dissipated or moved out of a State where it can easily be attached. The third party is, of course, subject to the law of the place in which it is located; but it is not subject to the authority of the tribunal, which flows from the agreement between the parties. This statement of elementary principle points to the solution to the problem. It is necessary to seek the assistance of the local courts, applying the *lex arbitri,* in such cases.[296] The need for the assistance of the local courts is explicitly recognised in a number of sets of arbitration rules.[297]

We have seen that national legislation on arbitration commonly empowers national courts to assist in arbitrations by, for example, appointing arbitrators where the parties have failed to do so.[298] Such powers may extend to the making of orders to assist the tribunal in other ways, including the making of interim orders on matters such as security for costs and the protection of property in issue in the case.[299] Whether or not the local courts will exercise any powers they might have to assist the parties in this way is a matter for the local law; and in some circumstances the courts will refuse to intervene. Thus, in *Bank Mellat v. Helliniki Techniki SA*[300] the English Court of Appeal was asked to make an order for security for costs, under section 12(6) of the Arbitration Act 1950, which empowered the Court to make orders to assist arbitrations.[301] It refused to do so on the ground that the arbitration, which was between a Greek claimant and an Iranian respondent and concerned a contract for the development of land in Iran, had no connection with England. Neither party carried on business in England; no aspect of the contract touched England. The only connection with England was the stipulation for ICC arbitration in London, and that was considered insufficient connection to warrant the Court exercising its discretion to make the order sought.

---

[296] See K. Groves, 'Virtual reality: effective injunctive relief in relation to international arbitrations' [1998] *Int. ALR* 188.

[297] See, e.g., ICC 1998 Rules, art. 23(2); Netherlands Arbitration Institute Rules, art. 37; UNCITRAL Arbitration Rules, art. 26(3).

[298] See p. 220, above.

[299] See, e.g., the UK Arbitration Act 1996, s. 44; Swiss Private International Law Act 1987, art. 183; UNCITRAL Model Law, art. 9.

[300] [1983] 3 All ER 428. Cf. *Channel Tunnel Group Ltd. v. Balfour Beatty Construction Ltd.* [1992] QB 656, in which it was decided that the powers would not be exercised in relation to an arbitration held abroad, even if English law was designated as the *lex arbitri.*

[301] See now ss. 38, 41(5) and 42 of the 1996 Arbitration Act.

One thread in the reasoning in *Bank Mellat* was the inappropriateness, as a general principle, of intervention by the local courts in international arbitrations.[302] That argument is most clearly demonstrated in the context of ICSID arbitrations, as we noted above.[303] Indeed, it is a clear aim of the ICSID system to remove ICSID arbitrations from the reach of intervention by national courts as far as is possible. ICSID is, however, unusual in the fullness of its commitment to independence from national legal systems. The more general practice is for local courts to be allowed by arbitration rules to intervene in appropriate circumstances to order interim measures of protection, and to regard themselves as at least having a discretion to do so.

18.2 Final remedies

The extraordinary neglect of the question of final remedies in international law is a reflection of the paucity of general principle and the—perhaps consequential—profusion of intricately argued decisions on the topic which give the impression of a case by case approach to the problem. Nonetheless, some general points can be briefly made.

First, it is plain that the normal remedies in international tribunals of all kinds are the award of monetary compensation and the rendering of declaratory judgments.[304] Logically, the declaratory judgment, in the sense of a judgment determining the rights and duties of the parties, must be the starting point, because such a determination is the implicit foundation of every award of monetary damages.[305] Moreover, many cases, particularly in inter-State disputes, contain no request for monetary reparation at all: they are confined to requests for the interpretation of agreements or the determination of the rights and duties of the parties.

The power to make declaratory awards is, of course, necessarily inherent in the tribunal. Indeed, it is the *raison d'être* of all tribunals. As was made clear in the *Aramco* award, there is no objection whatever to parties limiting themselves to claims for declaratory relief.[306] Declaratory awards have as their function, as it was put in the classic statement in the *Chorzów Factory* case, 'to ensure recognition of a situation at law, once and for all, and with binding force as between the Parties; so that the legal position thus established cannot again be called in question in so far as the legal effects ensuing therefrom are concerned'.[307] The declaration

---

[302] See the remarks of Robert Goff LJ, as he then was, [1983] 3 All ER 428 at 441–2.

[303] See the references to the *Atlantic Triton* case, p. 69, above.

[304] See the UK Arbitration Act 1996, s. 48.

[305] See I. Brownlie, 'Remedies in the International Court of Justice', in *Fifty Years of the International Court of Justice*, 557.

[306] 27 *ILR* 117 (1963).

[307] PCIJ, Ser. A, No. 13, 20 (1927).

implies an obligation to adjust the position of the parties as necessary to bring that position into line with their legal obligations. This may follow practically automatically from the judgment, as in cases of the determination of title to disputed territory; or it may imply an obligation to alter domestic legislation, as where such legislation is found to violate international law. In the latter case, the tribunal may order injunctive relief. And in some cases, the declaration may itself constitute sufficient reparation: that was, for example, the position in relation to the International Court's ruling on the violation of Albanian sovereignty by one of the British naval operations in issue in the *Corfu Channel* case.[308]

In other cases the determination of the rights and duties of the parties may be the prelude to an assessment of damages, either by the tribunal itself or by direct negotiation between the parties. In many instances in international relations the issue of legal principle is more important than the question of material compensation for any injury suffered. For instance, in the *Hostages* case, the United States did not pursue the claim for monetary reparation against Iran, contenting itself with a declaration of its rights and, as has been noted above, proceeding to negotiate a resolution to the crisis in the Algiers Accords.[309] Similarly, in the *BP* case, BP requested merely declaratory relief, leaving the assessment of damages to a later stage.[310]

As far as monetary compensation is concerned, it has sometimes been suggested that its proper role is as an alternative to restitution in kind, which is the primary remedy in international law.[311] In practice, however, in international and mixed arbitrations restitution, in the sense of the restoration of the position of the parties to the *status quo ante* by the return of property and amendment of legislation which may have affected that property, is ordered very rarely indeed, and certainly cannot be regarded as the primary remedy. There is, indeed, some remaining doubt as to the very right of a tribunal, in the absence of an express power in the *compromis*, to order *restitutio in integrum*.[312] But the main reasons for the rarity of orders for restitution, and cognate remedies such as specific performance, are pragmatic. Where property has been confiscated, the loss of confidence between the parties may preclude the resumption of the prior relationship; property destroyed may be incapable of satisfactory repair; and restitution alone would not effect reparation for consequential economic loss or for moral or personal injury. Where tribunals do refer to restitution it is almost always merely as the first step towards the calculation of monetary damages.

---

[308] ICJ Rep. 1949, 4.

[309] ICJ Rep. 1980, 4, at para. 90. See further chapter four, pp. 73–83, above.

[310] (1973) 53 *ILR* 297.

[311] See, e.g., *Chorzów Factory (Merits)*, PCIJ, Ser. A, No. 17, 1 at 47 (1928). Cf. the remarks of arbitrator Dupuy in *Texaco* (1978) 17 *ILM* 3.

[312] See C. Gray, *Judicial Remedies in International Law* (Oxford, 1987), ch. 1, and 193–200. And see the discussion by Judge Lagergren in *BP* v. *Libyan Arab Republic* (1973) 53 *ILR* 297 at 334–48.

The inherent power of a tribunal to award monetary compensation is beyond doubt, and the great majority of claims involve claims for such compensation.[313] Questions of great complexity arise in the calculation of the quantum of damages and interest. As to quantum, that is a matter which depends in large measure upon the substantive obligation which has been breached, rather than an abstract matter detached from the substance of the claim. For example, it is widely accepted that the measure of damages in cases of lawful takings of alien property differs from that in unlawful takings, as a result of differences in the heads under which damages can be recovered.[314] The question of the recoverability of interest is also complex and controversial. There is general agreement that tribunals have the power to award interest on damages, but controversy persists in relation to questions such as whether interest dating back to the time of the injury is recoverable for unliquidated or only for liquidated claims.[315]

Space precludes further examination of this topic,[316] but attention must be drawn to the question of the variety of possible sources of the tribunal's power to order the various remedies. The matter is clearly illustrated in the context of the award of interest. The power to make such awards may be given to the tribunal by the parties, either explicitly or by virtue of its inclusion in a set of institutional rules that they have adopted, or by agreement at some later stage.[317] But it may also arise under the *lex arbitri*. For instance, the English Arbitration Act 1996 provides that, unless the parties stipulate otherwise, arbitral tribunals are empowered to award simple or compound interest on sums awarded, up to the date of the award, or the date of payment.[318] This is, however, a matter on which national laws vary widely. The general prohibition in Islamic law on the levying of interest, for instance, constrains the ability of the laws of Islamic States to make provisions similar to those in the English Act. A third possible source of the power to award interest is the substantive law applicable to the dispute. A contract may itself stipulate the payment of interest in the event of breach, although strictly such a stipulation should be distinguished from interest payable by way of damages. But the applicable law of the contract may also permit or require the payment of interest: this is,

---

[313] The power to award punitive damages is much more controversial, although the US Supreme Court has upheld the arbitrator's power to do so where expressly or impliedly authorised to do so by a domestic arbitration clause: see *Mastrobuono* v. *Shearson Lehman Hutton, Inc.* 115 S Ct. 1212 (1995); and see the analysis and summary of practice in other States in J. Y. Gotanda, 'Awarding punitive damages in international commercial arbitrations in the wake of *Mastrobuono* v. *Shearson Lehman*' (1997) 38 *Harvard International Law Journal* 59.

[314] See, e.g., *Amoco International Finance Corp.* v. *Iran* (1987) 83 *ILR* 501 at 563–71. Cf. I. Brownlie, *Principles of Public International Law*, 5th edn. (Oxford, 1998), 540–2.

[315] See C. Gray, *Judicial Remedies in International Law* (Oxford, 1987), 29–33.

[316] See further T. E. Elder, 'The case against arbitral awards of specific performance in transnational commercial disputes' (1997) 13 *Arbitration International* 1.

[317] See. e.g., the London Court of International Arbitration 1998 Rules, art. 26.6.

[318] S. 49.

for example, the position under German law.[319] There is a possible conflict between the applicable law and the *lex arbitri* in these cases: the applicable law may stipulate, and the *lex arbitri* forbid, the award of interest, for instance. Any such conflict is likely to be determined by deciding whether the question of interest is procedural, in which case it is probable that the *lex arbitri* would prevail, or substantive, in which case the applicable law would probably prevail.

In principle, a similar reference to the *lex arbitri* and the applicable law is permissible in the case of other remedies, although it is unlikely to arise in practice except in relation to awards of monetary compensation.

Before leaving this heading it is convenient to say a little about costs. In inter-State proceedings it is usual for each State to bear its own costs, and for the costs of the tribunal to be divided equally between the parties. In mixed arbitrations practice is more varied. Sometimes in *ad hoc* arbitrations each side bears its own costs and the loser bears the costs of the tribunal. In arbitrations before permanent tribunals, or conducted under one or other set of institutional rules, the general practice is for the tribunal to decide upon costs.[320] Again, the *lex arbitri* may bestow the power to make such a decision upon the tribunal.[321]

19. The award

The procedure for rendering an award is the subject of detailed provision under many sets of rules. The Statute of the International Court, for instance, provides for private deliberation by the judges to be followed by a reasoned majority decision, which may be accompanied by separate opinions from judges whose opinions are not represented in the majority decision.[322] In the context of the ICJ such rules are important because they dictate the manner in which the Court will deliver its judgment; and the provision for separate opinions clearly encourages—or at least permits—the judges on the Court to contribute to the reappraisal and development of international law in a way that would be made much more difficult were the Court obliged to deliver a single judgment.

In the case of arbitrations the procedure for the rendering of awards has an additional importance, because a failure to observe the prescribed procedures may render the award unenforceable. There is little difficulty in the case of arbitrations before a sole arbitrator. The arbitrator makes his or her decision, and beyond ensuring that it is properly reasoned and complies with requirements for signature

---

[319] *Redfern & Hunter*, 404–5.
[320] See, e.g., ICC 1998 Rules, arts. 30, 31; UNCITRAL Arbitration Rules, arts. 38–40.
[321] See, e.g., the UK Arbitration Act 1996, ss. 59–65.
[322] ICJ Statute, arts. 54–8. See chapter seven, pp. 175–6, above.

and other formalities[323] that is the end of the matter. The position of tribunals with more than one member is more difficult. In some cases the arbitration rules provide for decisions to be taken by a simple majority. This is the case in arbitrations under the UNCITRAL and ICSID rules, for example.[324] But sometimes the principle of majority decision is varied. For example, under the ICC Rules if there is no majority for any award—as where each of three arbitrators takes a different view of the matter—the award is to be made by the Chairman of the tribunal alone.[325] Another variation appears in the 1966 Strasbourg Uniform Law prepared by the Council of Europe,[326] article 22.3 of which provides that in determining the amount of compensation payable if a majority cannot be obtained for any particular sum the votes for the highest sum are to be counted as votes for the next highest sum until a majority is obtained. And in some arbitration rules, the Chairman is given the power to make procedural rulings.[327]

It cannot be said that separate or dissenting opinions are encouraged in international arbitration. ICSID is unusual among the permanent institutions in expressly permitting them,[328] although some sets of rules for administered arbitration expressly permit such opinions.[329] The general position appears to be that such opinions are permissible as long as they are not forbidden by the tribunal's rules or by the *lex arbitri*.[330]

It has already been noted that tribunals commonly issue not merely final awards but also interim awards dealing with matters such as jurisdiction, admissibility, applicable law, procedure, liability and interim measures of protection. Such awards can do much to structure and expedite the proceedings and save much time in unnecessary or misdirected pleading. Tribunals are often expressly empowered to make interim awards, either in relation to specified matters or generally.[331] If there is no express power, one may be implied under the *lex arbitri*.[332] In the absence of an express power or one implied by law, it is arguable that the tribunal's inherent right to order its own procedure (subject to the terms of the

---

[323] See, e.g., art. 32 of the UNCITRAL Arbitration Rules.

[324] UNCITRAL Arbitration Rules, art. 31; ICSID Rules of Procedure, Rule 16.

[325] ICC 1998 Rules, art. 25. Cf. Euro-Arab Chambers of Commerce Rules, art. 24-2.

[326] Annexed to the European Convention Providing a Uniform Law on Arbitration 1966, *European Treaty Series* No. 56; and see R. David, *Arbitration in International Trade* (Deventer, 1985), 164.

[327] e.g., London Court of International Arbitration 1985 Rules, art. 5.3, reprinted in *Redfern & Hunter*, 619. In the 1998 Rules the Chairman's power to make procedural rulings depends upon the prior consent of the other arbitrators: see art. 14(3).

[328] ICSID Rules, art. 47(3).

[329] e.g., Stockholm Chamber of Commerce Arbitration Rules, art. 28; and cf. the old USSR Chamber of Commerce and Industry Arbitration Rules, para. 35.

[330] On the role of the *lex arbitri* see *Redfern & Hunter*, 399.

[331] See, e.g., the UNCITRAL Arbitration Rules, art. 24(4); ICSID Rules, Rule 41(4).

[332] e.g., the UK Arbitration Act 1996, s. 47.

instrument under which it is established and of the *lex arbitri*) entails a right to make interim awards when it sees fit.

If the respondent fails to participate in the proceedings, the power of the tribunal to render a default award will arise. This power is usually provided in the instrument establishing the tribunal. Thus, the Statute of the International Court provides that where one of the parties does not appear before the Court, or fails to defend its case, the Court must, if the other party calls upon it to do so, decide in favour of the claim, on condition that the Court has satisfied itself that it has jurisdiction and that the claim is well founded in fact and law.[333] The ICSID Rules contain a similar provision;[334] and comparable provisions can be found in other sets of arbitration rules.[335] These powers to render default awards, which of course depend upon the prior acceptance by the parties of the rules in question, represent a major step in the direction of the compulsory settlement of international disputes by judicial processes.

It sometimes happens that the parties will agree the terms of settlement of a dispute during the proceedings before the tribunal. In such circumstances they might choose simply to withdraw the case and revoke the mandate of the tribunal. In inter-State cases this is an appropriate action: the *Great Belt* case, for example, was withdrawn from the International Court immediately before pleadings on the merits were due to begin, following an agreement upon the terms of a settlement between Finland and Denmark.[336] This course of action may be less appropriate in mixed arbitrations, where the parties may be unwilling to lose the advantage of having the terms of the settlement put in a form which would permit the enforcement of those terms through national courts were one party to fail to comply with them voluntarily. This advantage can be secured by having the terms of settlement adopted by the tribunal and embodied in a consent award, which is then enforceable in the same way as any other award. The UNCITRAL Rules and the 1998 ICC Rules give the tribunal the power to embody the agreed terms in a consent award in this way.[337] And even the Rules of the International

---

[333] Art. 53. See chapter seven, p. 180, above.

[334] Rule 42.

[335] e.g., ICC 1998 Rules, art. 6(2), (3); Netherlands Arbitration Institute Arbitration Rules, art. 36; Stockholm Chamber of Commerce Arbitration Rules, Rule 21; UNCITRAL Arbitration Rules, art. 28.

[336] See the note by M. Koskenniemi, 'Note' (1993) 32 *ILM* 101, and 'L'affaire du passage par le Grand-Belt' (1992) 38 *AFDI* 905.

[337] UNCITRAL Arbitration Rules, art. 34; ICC 1998 Rules, art. 26 (replacing art. 17 of the 1988 ICC Rules, which *obliged* the tribunal to record an agreed settlement as an award). Cf. ICSID Rules, Rule 43; the London Court of International Arbitration 1998 Rules, art. 26.8, and the Netherlands Arbitration Institute Rules, art. 54, all of which empower but do not oblige the tribunal to furnish a consent award. The Netherlands Rules are unusual in expressly giving the tribunal the right to refuse, without giving reasons, a request for a consent award.

Court provide for the recording of the terms of the settlement in the order for the removal of the case from the list, if the parties so desire.[338]

After the award has been made it may be necessary to correct minor errors in it, or to seek an interpretation of it. The International Court Rules permit applications for the revision and interpretation of judgment to be made,[339] as do many sets of arbitration rules.[340] So, too, do national arbitration laws.[341] One well-known instance of rectification occurred in the *Anglo-French Continental Shelf* arbitration, in which the United Kingdom sought, with partial success, the revision of the award in order to correct technical errors in the drawing of the delimitation line.[342]

Finally in this context, it should be noted that in the case of mixed arbitrations, it is important that the award should be enforceable. This is less of a problem in the case of inter-State awards, because a State willing to settle a dispute by arbitration is unlikely to renege upon the decision and, as will be seen, if pressure for execution of the settlement is necessary it is likely to operate in the political arena rather than through national courts, where problems of sovereign immunity—particularly in relation to non-commercial transactions—present themselves.

In order to ensure that an award is enforceable through national courts it is essential that care be taken to comply with any formal requirements which might apply to it. This need is reflected in article 35 of the ICC 1998 Rules, which requires the tribunal to 'make every effort to make sure that the Award is enforceable at law'.[343] Formal requirements may be laid down in the *lex arbitri*, or in the arbitration rules themselves, which often set out requirements with a view to ensuring that all of the most common requirements to be found in various national laws are covered. These formal requirements may concern matters such as the signing and dating of the award and the inclusion of recitals specifying the identities of the arbitrators and the parties, the seat of the arbitration, the relief sought, and the decision on the substance of the claim and on costs. It is, in addition, necessary to ensure that the award is properly reasoned, which implies the need both to set out the

---

[338] ICJ 1978 Rules, art. 88.

[339] ICJ 1978 Rules, arts. 98–101. See chapter seven, p. 179, above.

[340] e.g., the UNCITRAL Arbitration Rules, arts. 35, 36; ICSID Rules, Rules 50–1; London Court of International Arbitration 1998 Rules, art. 27; Netherlands Arbitration Institute Rules, art. 52. See D. D. Caron and L. F. Reed, 'Post award proceedings under the UNCITRAL Arbitration Rules' (1995) 11 *Arbitration International* 429; A. N. Vollmer and A. J. Bedford, 'Post-award arbitral proceedings' (1995) 15/1 *Journal of International Arbitration* 37.

[341] See, e.g., the UK Arbitration Act 1996, s. 57; French Code of Civil Procedure, art. 1475; Netherlands Arbitration Act 1986, art. 1060.

[342] (1979) 18 *ILM* 397, 462. And see art. 10(2) of the *compromis*. Max-Planck-Institut, *Dispute Settlement in Public International Law* (Berlin, 1984), 863 at 865.

[343] Other rules oblige the tribunal to deal with formalities that are commonly required in national laws as conditions of the validity of awards: see, e.g., UNCITRAL Arbitration Rules, art. 32; ICSID Rules, art. 47.

facts and to explain fully the chain of argument which connects them to the decision.

20. Challenges to awards

Not all awards are perfect, and some may be so flawed in their logic or in the process by which factual and legal determinations were made that they ought not to stand. Where a party takes this view of an award it may seek its annulment. The process is often called recourse against an award.

There is weighty authority for the view that arbitral awards are inherently liable to annulment, if they are sufficiently flawed, and that the only problem is finding a tribunal with the jurisdiction to entertain the challenge. The parties may have consented to the jurisdiction of some tribunal in such matters, in which case that tribunal will have the competence to annul the award. Thus, when the International Court was asked by Nicaragua to annul an arbitral award rendered many years previously by the King of Spain, the Court did not doubt that it was competent to do so.[344] The same position was taken by the Court in a dispute between Guinea Bissau and Senegal concerning a maritime boundary award;[345] and a similar view prevails in arbitral practice.[346]

Clearly, the prospect of annulment materially weakens the utility of an award as a final disposition of the dispute. If judicial settlement is to serve its proper function, annulment proceedings must be closely controlled.[347] Some form of controlled annulment is available for all international judgments. The system is at its weakest in the case of the International Court, whose judgments are said to be final and without appeal;[348] but even here a kind of controlled annulment can be achieved through the mechanism for the enforcement of International Court judgments. The UN Charter provides that States Parties to International Court cases undertake to comply with its judgments; but if a discontented party refuses to do so there is no automatic enforcement. Rather, it is provided that the Security Council 'may, if it deems necessary, make recommendations or decide upon measures to be taken to give effect to the judgment'.[349] Were the Security Council to

---

[344] *Arbitral Award Made by the King of Spain on 23 December 1906*, ICJ Rep 1960, 192. The Court did not in fact annul the award.

[345] *Arbitral Award of 31 July 1989*, ICJ Rep. 1991, 53. The original award appears at 83 *ILR* 1. See H. W. A. Thirlway, 'Procedural law and the International Court of Justice', in *Fifty Years of the ICJ*, 389; S. M. Schwebel, 'May the majority vote of an international arbitral tribunal be impeached?' (1997) 13 *Arbitration International* 145.

[346] See, e.g., the *North Eastern Boundary* case, *Lapradelle–Politis*, vol. 1, 355.

[347] For a searching analysis of this matter see W. M. Reisman, *Systems of Control in International Adjudication and Arbitration* (Durham, North Carolina, 1992).

[348] ICJ Statute, art. 60.

[349] UN Charter, art. 94. See chapter seven, p. 178, above.

be persuaded that the Court had erred in some respect in its judgment, that fact would doubtless influence any measures which it might recommend.

In the case of arbitrations the position is more tightly regulated. The review of *ad hoc* inter-State awards by the International Court is, of course, controllable by the parties through their control over the acceptance of the Court's jurisdiction. Mixed arbitrations operate under a rather different system. The outstanding example is ICSID, whose elaborate provisions starkly demonstrate the dangers of too readily allowing claims for annulment to be brought. ICSID is a self-contained system. Its awards cannot be challenged before national courts. But, as we noted above,[350] applications for annulment may be made by either party to the Secretary-General of ICSID under article 52 of the ICSID Convention. The application is remitted to a new, three-person *ad hoc* ICSID Committee, which has the power to annul the award in whole or in part. This scheme, which has its intellectual roots in proposals made in the 1920s to give the Permanent Court of International Justice a supervisory competence in respect of arbitral awards,[351] has proved a mixed blessing. ICSID dealt with fourteen arbitrations in its first seventeen years of existence, with considerable expedition; but the remarkable readiness of *ad hoc* Committees to annul awards for relatively minor defects, signalled in the *Klöckner* and *AMCO* cases, undermined confidence in the regime. That confidence was not restored until the decision in the *MINE* proceedings, which indicated that only a substantial defect, falling clearly within the grounds listed in article 52 of the ICSID Convention, would justify annulment.[352]

Other mixed arbitrations have rather different systems for the review of awards. The ICC system, it will be recalled, involves the submission of the draft award to the ICC Court of Arbitration, which may lay down modifications as to the form of the award, paying particular attention to any mandatory requirements of the law of the place of arbitration.[353] This procedure, which sometimes gives rise to fears that the ICC Court may stray beyond questions of form and into the merits of the award, is helpful in avoiding any formal defects which might preclude the subsequent enforceability of the award in national courts. This is unusual.[354] In other systems of administered arbitration, the award is the responsibility of the tribunal alone. When an award has been rendered, it is liable to challenge in two

---

[350] See chapter four, pp. 71–3, above.

[351] See on this, and on review procedures generally, W. M. Reisman, *Systems of Control in International Adjudication and Arbitration* (Durham, North Carolina, 1992), ch. 3 and *passim.*

[352] See chapter four, p. 72, above.

[353] ICC 1998 Rules, art. 27 and Internal Rules of the (ICC) International Court of Arbitration, art. 7. The equivalent provisions in the 1988 ICC texts (arts. 21 and 17 respectively) directed the ICC Court to pay attention to both the 'law applicable to the proceedings' and the mandatory rules of the place of arbitration. It seems that it is now assumed that the *lex loci arbitri* and the *lex arbitri* will always be the same.

[354] But not unique. See, e.g., the Rules of the Euro-Arab Chambers of Commerce, reprinted in *Redfern & Hunter*, 554, art. 24.

main fora: the courts of the country of the *lex arbitri* (or of the seat of the arbitration, if that be different),[355] and the courts in which the recognition or enforcement of the award is sought. We will deal with the latter when we discuss recognition and enforcement. Here we consider challenges under the *lex arbitri*.

The availability of recourse against an award in municipal courts is a matter for the local law, and there are substantial variations between different States. In the past it has been more common than it is now for national laws to permit appeals against arbitral awards. For example, the English Arbitration Act 1950 permitted appeals to the courts on points of law by way of case stated. In line with developments in other countries, that possibility was severely curtailed by the Arbitration Act 1979, which permitted parties to international arbitrations to contract out, by means of an 'exclusion agreement', of the right of appeal to the courts in such cases, as does the 1996 Act which replaced the 1979 Act.[356] Exclusion of this right of appeal promotes the speedy delivery of a final award by the tribunal chosen by the parties and eliminates the risk of a reluctant litigant being dragged from the privacy of an arbitration into the public gaze of a municipal court. At the same time it is desirable to have some possibility of recourse to local courts in order to control the more egregious cases of deficient awards, notably those involving serious procedural irregularities. This is the route taken by many of the reforms of national legislation on arbitration during the past two decades.[357]

The present pattern is well represented by the UNCITRAL Model Law, which has been widely used as a model for the reform of national law. It provides, in article 34, for recourse against awards rendered in international arbitrations[358] which have taken place in the State[359] only on certain specified grounds, which mirror

---

[355] *Redfern & Hunter*, 431–2. And see above, pp. 231–5. See also the note by Z. Mody and T. T. Arvind on a 1998 Indian Supreme Court Decision, '*Bombay Gas Company Ltd* v. *Mark Victor Mascarenhas—challenge to a foreign award*' [1998] *Int. ALR* 178. It has been suggested that an International Court of Arbitral Awards be established to exercise the review function: see, in M. Hunter, A. Marriott and V. V. Veeder (eds.), *The Internationalisation of International Arbitration: the LCIA centenary conference* (London, 1995), the papers by H. M. Holtzmann, 'A task for the 21st century: creating a new international court for resolving disputes on the enforceability of arbitral awards' (109), and S. M. Schwebel, 'The creation and operation of an International Court of Arbitral Awards' (115).

[356] Arbitration Act 1979, ss. 1, 3, 4; Arbitration Act 1996, s. 69. See *Arab African Energy Corporation Ltd.* v. *Olieproduktion Nederland BV* [1983] 2 Lloyd's Rep. 419; *Marine Contractors Inc.* v. *Shell Petroleum Development Co. of Nigeria Ltd.* [1984] 2 Lloyd's Rep. 77. Cf. D. R. Thomas, *The Law and Practice relating to Appeals from Arbitration Awards* (London, 1994).

[357] See, e.g., the French Code of Civil Procedure, arts. 1442–507; Netherlands Arbitration Act 1986. The Belgian law of 1985 and the Swiss Private International Law Act of 1987 have been criticised as virtual abdications of the responsibility to exercise control over the propriety of awards rendered within the State: see W. M. Reisman, *Systems of Control in International Adjudication and Arbitration* (Durham, North Carolina, 1992), 127–34.

[358] For the definition of 'international', which focuses on the parties coming from different States, see art. 1(3),(4).

[359] Art. 1(2).

the grounds on which recognition or enforcement of arbitral awards may be refused under the New York Convention. Those grounds are that:

(a) the party making the application furnishes proof that:

(i) a party to the arbitration agreement was . . . under some incapacity; or the said agreement is not valid under the law to which the parties have subjected it or, failing any indication thereon, under the law of this State; or

(ii) the party making the application was not given proper notice of the appointment of an arbitrator or of the arbitral proceedings or was otherwise unable to present his case; or

(iii) the award deals with a dispute not contemplated by or not falling within the terms of the submission to arbitration, or contains decisions on matters beyond the scope of the submission to arbitration, provided that, if the decisions on matters submitted to arbitration can be separated from those not so submitted, only that part of the award which contains decisions on matters not submitted to arbitration may be set aside; or

(iv) the composition of the arbitral tribunal or the arbitral procedure was not in accordance with the agreement of the parties, unless such agreement was in conflict with a provision of this Law from which the parties cannot derogate,[360] or, failing such agreement, was not in accordance with this Law; or

(b) the court finds that:

(i) the subject-matter of the dispute is not capable of settlement by agreement by arbitration under the Law of this State; or

(ii) the award is in conflict with the public policy of this State.

These grounds have been discussed above, in the context of the requirements for a valid arbitration; but there is one further important point to be made in relation to them. The grounds for review are set in the particular context of international arbitration, in which parties from different States will already have proceeded to a 'settlement' of the award in accordance with a procedure, less formal than litigation in court, agreed between them. Accordingly, it is not intended that the same standards of review should be applied to international arbitrations as might be applied to purely domestic proceedings involving no foreign element. This is particularly evident in relation to the public policy ground. In French law, for instance, a clear notion of 'international public policy', more restricted than domestic public policy, has been developed.[361]

---

[360] The Law contains provisions on matters such as proof of delivery of communications (art. 3), the appointment of arbitrators (art. 11), challenges to arbitrators (art. 13), interim measures (art. 17) and so on, from which the parties may derogate by agreement. If a party proceeds with the arbitration with knowledge of a breach of a non-derogable requirement of the Law or any requirement of the arbitration agreement, and without prompt objection, the right to object is deemed to have been waived: art. 4.

[361] French Code of Civil Procedure, art. 1502.

National laws prescribe time limits within which applications for the review of awards must be lodged. In the UNCITRAL Model Law the time limit is three months.[362]

The consequences of a challenge to an award depend upon how the court has dealt with the challenge, and in turn upon the powers and provisions of the national law which the court applies. The award may, of course, be confirmed. The court may remit the award to the tribunal: this would be appropriate, for example, in cases where the challenge is based upon the fact that the tribunal did not discharge its mandate because it failed to address certain aspects of the dispute, but failed in a manner which does not impugn the validity of the decisions which it did reach.[363] Or the court may decide to annul and set aside the award.

The consequences of nullity themselves vary from State to State. In some, it is the award alone which is annulled, the arbitration agreement remaining in force so that the parties must return their dispute to arbitration. That may in practice involve no more than the remission of the matter by the parties to the tribunal, which may correct the errors and reissue the award in proper form. In other States, and particularly in cases where the ground of invalidity is the corruption of an arbitrator or a defect in the jurisdiction of the tribunal, annulment results, or may be decided by the court to result, in the annulment of the arbitration agreement, too.[364] In such a case, unless the parties make a new arbitration agreement, they may seek a judicial settlement only through the courts.

21. Effects of the award

Once a valid award has been rendered it has the status of *res judicata* between the parties. In the case of International Court judgments this principle is generally regarded as implicit in articles 59 and 60 of its Statute;[365] and a similar position obtains in respect of other standing tribunals.[366] But the principle does not depend upon the inclusion of a specific provision in the tribunal's constitutive instrument. *Res judicata* is a general principle of international law, albeit one which has attracted relatively little attention. The principle was stated in the *Amco v. Indonesia (Resubmission: Jurisdiction)* award, rendered under the auspices of ICSID, as follows: 'The general principle announced in numerous cases is that a

---

[362] Art. 34(3). Some time limits are much shorter. English law sets a limit of 28 days: UK Arbitration Act 1996, s. 70(3).

[363] See, e.g., ibid., ss. 68(3), 69(7).

[364] See A. Samuel, *Jurisdictional Problems in International Commercial Arbitration: A Study of Belgian, Dutch, English, French, Swedish, Swiss, U.S. and West German Law* (Zurich, 1989), 255–9. Cf. the UK Arbitration Act 1996, s. 71(4).

[365] Though it is not explicitly stated. See above, chapter seven, p. 177.

[366] See, e.g., art. 53 of the ICSID Convention.

right, question or fact *distinctly put in issue and distinctly determined* by a court of competent jurisdiction as a ground of recovery, cannot be disputed.'[367] A valid award from a properly constituted arbitral tribunal undoubtedly counts as a determination by a court of competent jurisdiction.

According to one much-quoted authority, there are three conditions for the application of the principle of *res judicata*. They are: identity of parties; identity of cause; and identity of object (or subject matter) in the subsequent proceedings.[368] Their application is not without difficulty in the context of international arbitration. For example, the requirement of identity of parties precludes the easy application of the principle in the context of multi-party disputes, where parallel arbitrations between on the one hand a government and a main contractor, and on the other hand the main contractor and a subcontractor, may lead to incompatible determinations of facts and liability—a difficulty compounded by the lack of a general right of intervention or joinder in arbitral proceedings.[369] Furthermore, the confidentiality of arbitral proceedings[370] means that the award in one tribunal may not be available to the tribunal in another; and even if the earlier award is available, the pleadings may not be, so that the tribunal cannot easily decide what matters were 'distinctly put in issue and distinctly determined' by the earlier tribunal.

International law has no doctrine of *stare decisis*. Neither arbitral awards nor even International Court judgments have, strictly speaking, any legal authority beyond their status as *res judicata*. They bind only the parties, and only in respect of the case in which they are delivered. Nonetheless it is natural that in practice awards and judgments will exercise a very powerful influence upon other tribunals in relation to determinations of fact and responsibility, and in relation to their appraisal

---

[367] 1 *ICSID Reports* 543 at 550, 89 *ILR* 552 at 560, citing the *Orinoco Steamship Company* case (1910) 10 *UNRIAA* 184 at 276. See also the *Pious Fund of the Californias* arbitration (1902), J. B. Scott, *Hague Court Reports* (1916), 1 at 5. Cf. the Dissenting Opinion of Judge Koretsky in *South West Africa (Second Phase)*, ICJ Rep. 1966, 6 at 332, citing, *inter alia, Corfu Channel*, ICJ Rep. 1949, 4 at 35, and *Rights of Nationals of the United States of America in Morocco*, ICJ Rep. 1952, 176 at 213. The general principle is subject to a number of qualifications, of which the most important is that a decision may be revised if it was based upon a manifest error of law, such as the overlooking of a relevant treaty: *Trail Smelter* arbitration (*USA* v. *Canada*, 1941) 3 *UNRIAA* 1938 at 1957.

[368] Judge Anzilotti, *Chorzów Factory*, PCIJ, Ser. A, No. 13, at 23–7. Cf. S. Rosenne, *The Law and Practice of the International Court*, 3rd edn. (The Hague, 1997), vol. 3, 1655–68; *Trail Smelter* arbitration (1941) 3 *UNRIAA* 1938 at 1952. See also D. W. Bowett, '*Res judicata* and the limits of rectification of decisions of international tribunals' (1996) 8 *AJICL* 577; V. Lowe, '*Res judicata* and the Rule of Law in international arbitration' (1996) 8 *AJICL* 38.

[369] See above, p. 208. Cf. Mahir Jalili, 'French Setback to Multiparty Arbitration' (February 1992) 7(2) *International Arbitration Report* 20, for an example of the difficulties.

[370] See the symposium on the Australian High Court decision in *Esso/BHP* v. *Plowman* (1995) 183 *CLR* 10: (1995) 11 *Arbitration International* 231–340 (including the text of the decision). Cf. P. Neill, 'Confidentiality in arbitration' (1996) 12 *Arbitration International* 287; A. Rogers and D. Miller, 'Non-confidential arbitration proceedings' (1996) 12 *Arbitration International* 319.

of the law.[371] And the more distinguished the members of the tribunal, and the more painstaking its examination of the facts and the law, the greater that influence will be.

22. Enforcement of judgments and awards

The final stage in our examination of the process of the 'judicial' settlement of international disputes concerns the enforcement of the judgment or award. Mention has already been made of the power of the UN Security Council to decide upon any necessary measures to be taken in the event of a State failing to comply with a judgment of the International Court of Justice.[372] That power is subject to important limitations. First, failures to comply with judgments are not necessarily threats to international peace and security, so that the powers under Chapter VII of the UN Charter may not be available to the Security Council. Secondly, the powers are in any event subject to the right of veto by the Permanent Members of the Security Council. The United States, for example, vetoed a resolution drafted after Nicaragua had asked the Council to take action against it after the judgment in the *Nicaragua* case in 1986.

It is true that the record of compliance with International Court judgments is far from perfect: the *Corfu Channel*, *Fisheries Jurisdiction*, *Hostages*, *Nicaragua*, and *Bosnian Genocide* cases, for example, all yielded judgments long unsatisfied by the respondents; and the record of compliance with interim measures is even worse. Nonetheless, the measure of the International Court's success must be its contribution to the confinement and resolution of disputes, rather than the degree of compliance with its orders. Seen in that light, and against the background of the fact that most of the judgments which have not been complied with have been overtaken, often very quickly, by political developments, the record of the Court appears more impressive. The judgment is in truth often no more than one element in a much broader strategy seeking the resolution of the dispute through essentially political channels.

International Court judgments are necessarily inter-State judgments, and it is therefore extremely unlikely that their enforcement through national courts would be sought. Were such enforcement ever to be sought, a practically insuperable obstacle would arise, as became apparent in the *Socobel* saga. Socobel, a Belgian company, obtained an arbitral award in its favour against the Greek State. Greece did not pay; and, for a number of technical reasons concerning the law of the time on the enforcement of foreign arbitral awards, Socobel could not enforce

---

[371] See R. Y. Jennings, 'The Judiciary, International and National, and the Development of International Law' (1996) 45 *ICLQ* 1.

[372] UN Charter, art. 94. See above, chapter seven, p. 178.

the award. Belgium took up the matter, and in 1939 obtained a ruling from the Permanent Court of International Justice that Greece was obliged to pay.[373] After World War II, funds allocated to Greece under the Marshall Aid programme were paid into a Belgian bank; and Socobel, armed with the Permanent Court judgment, sought to attach them. While a Greek plea of sovereign immunity was rejected, the Belgian court held that Socobel could not enforce the Permanent Court judgment, *inter alia* because Socobel was not a party to it.[374] That logic is likely to defeat all similar attempts by non-State entities to enforce International Court judgments through national courts. This objection would disappear if the State, rather than its national, were to seek enforcement; but there would remain formidable obstacles arising from rules of national law on State immunity and on non-justiciability.

Awards against States resulting from mixed arbitrations are different. There is no doubt that such awards bind the State, which must carry them out in good faith. Indeed, this principle was upheld by the Permanent Court in the *Socobel* case itself. In most cases, awards are voluntarily complied with: around 95 per cent of ICC awards, for example, are said to be voluntarily satisfied. But where they are not, procedures for their enforcement exist. The Iran-US Claims Tribunal, noted above, was exceptional in having a security account specially established to guarantee payment of awards by Iran.[375] The usual position is that enforcement has to be sought through the mechanisms made generally available to disputing parties within national legal systems.

Negotiations are the obvious way to obtain satisfaction from a reluctant loser; and as we have remarked above, it is not uncommon for an arbitration to be envisaged from the outset as no more than a means of obtaining an award which will form the basis for negotiating a final settlement. The national State of the non-State party may involve itself. The *Lena Goldfields* award, for instance, was not immediately executed by the Soviet Government; but when it was linked by the British Government to negotiations on a trade agreement, a settlement quickly followed. The powers of the Security Council under article 94 of the UN Charter are not available in the case of failures to comply with arbitral awards;[376] but States have a wide range of measures which they can adopt unilaterally in order to bring pressure upon a State to comply with an award, or with an International Court judgment. For example, diplomatic links may be reduced or severed, visa and trade restrictions may be tightened, loans and investments may be suspended, and assets of the defaulting State may be frozen. But in practice even the few awards

---

[373] *Société Commercial de Belgique* case, PCIJ Ser. A/B, No. 78; 9 *ILR* 521. See chapter seven above, p. 179.

[374] *Socobel* v. *The Greek State* (1951) 18 *ILR* 3.

[375] See chapter four, p. 79, above.

[376] Although such powers had existed in the League of Nations Covenant: see art. 13(4).

from mixed arbitrations with which there is no voluntary compliance very rarely need any such action, because there is a system of routine enforcement readily available to the parties.

We should more properly refer to the recognition and enforcement of arbitral awards. Recognition occurs when a court regards the award as a definitive determination of the dispute so that, for example, the parties may not relitigate the matter. Enforcement occurs when a court takes the award and, at the request of the successful party, orders measures for its execution, such as the seizure of the respondent's property, in the same way as it would in respect of a court judgment. Enforcement presupposes recognition, but moves beyond it; and where we refer to enforcement, we use the term to include recognition.

Enforcement under the law of the country in which the arbitration has its seat is straightforward. If the State permits arbitration of disputes, permitting the enforcement of the resulting awards through the courts is a natural consequence.[377] Foreign arbitral awards are a little more problematic. The State has an interest in ensuring that only just decisions are enforced, or to put it another way, in not lending the support of its coercive powers to unjust proceedings. It also has an interest in maintaining certain substantive standards; it may, for instance, refuse to enforce awards which appear to promote an activity incompatible with fundamental moral principles in the State, such as awards arising out of contracts illegal in that State. For these reasons national laws vary in the conditions which they attach to the enforcement of awards from tribunals located in other States, over whose proceedings they have had no control. There are, moreover, variations in national laws on sovereign immunity which will make it easier to proceed to enforce an award against a State in some States than in others. These variations will, of course, be exploited by the parties. While a successful litigant will always choose to enforce the award in one of the States where the respondent has assets, the terms of the local law on enforcement will be a powerful influence in the choice from among those States.[378]

It is possible that a State may have municipal legislation on the recognition and enforcement of foreign arbitral awards which is a purely national matter, standing independently of any international regime. But it is desirable to secure a degree of predictability and reciprocity in the enforcement of arbitral awards, and a number

---

[377] The link was established clearly by the Geneva Protocol on Arbitration Clauses 1923.

[378] See the papers in A. J. van den Berg (ed.), *International Arbitration in a Changing World: International Council for Commercial Arbitration Congress series no. 6* (Deventer, 1994): M. Lalonde, 'The post-arbitral phase in North America and Western Europe' (127); A. H. El-Ahdab, 'The post-arbitral phase' (165); M. Gaudet, 'The enforcement of awards relating to international trade' (203); C. N. Brower, 'Correction and completion of awards; enforcement of partial and final awards; collaboration by courts for an award to be effective; impact of "international public policy" on arbitration' (213).

of international agreements have been concluded for this purpose. Among them are the Geneva Convention on the Execution of Foreign Arbitral Awards 1927;[379] the Amman Arab Convention on Commercial Arbitration;[380] the European Convention on International Commercial Arbitration 1961;[381] and the Inter-American Convention on International Commercial Arbitration 1975.[382] In practice, much the most important in the present context is the 1958 New York Convention on the Recognition and Enforcement of Foreign Arbitral Awards.[383] Its pre-eminence is underlined by the fact that the UNCITRAL Model Law, intended as a pattern for national arbitration laws regardless of whether or not the States concerned are parties to the New York or any other arbitration convention, is designed around the terms of the New York Convention.

22.1 The New York Convention

The New York Convention, in essence, seeks to ensure that in the States Parties to it: (i) arbitration agreements are recognised as valid, and as precluding litigation of the dispute in the State's courts; (ii) foreign arbitral awards are recognised and enforced, except in certain exceptional circumstances; and (iii) the grounds on which recognition or enforcement might be refused are strictly limited. The Convention does not regulate 'domestic' awards. It applies only to arbitral awards rendered in any State (or, if a State invokes the 'reciprocity' provision in article I(3), any other State Party[384]) other than that in which recognition or enforcement is sought, and to arbitral awards rendered in the State in which recognition or enforcement is sought but which are not considered by that State to be 'domestic' awards.[385] The provisions concerning the validity and effectiveness of agreements to arbitrate have been considered above:[386] here we are concerned with the provisions on recognition and enforcement.

---

[379] 92 *LNTS* 302.

[380] *Bergsten*, Document II.14; and cf. on the 1952 Arab League Convention on the Enforcement of Foreign Judgments and Awards, S. Saleh, *Commercial Arbitration in the Middle East* (London, 1984), ch. 25, and A. H. El-Ahdab, 'Enforcement of arbitral awards in Arab countries' (1995) 11 *Arbitration International* 169.

[381] 484 *UNTS* 364.

[382] (1975) 14 *ILM* 336; and see A. J. van den Berg, 'The New York Convention 1958 and the Panama Convention 1975: redundancy or compatibility?' (1989) 5 *Arbitration International* 214.

[383] 330 *UNTS* 38.

[384] More than half of the Contracting States to the New York Convention (numbering 113, as of November 1997) have invoked this provision. Note also the further provision in art. I(3) permitting a Contracting State to limit its obligations under the Convention to differences arising out of legal relationships which are considered 'commercial' under its law: more than one-third of the Contracting States have invoked this provision.

[385] Art. I. A State might treat awards in inter-State arbitrations, or of bodies such as the Iran-US Claims Tribunal, as non-domestic, even though the arbitrations happen to be held on its territory; and it may similarly treat awards involving at least one foreign party, or concerning foreign property, as non-domestic. See further, *Rubino-Sammartano*, 15–24.

[386] See p. 206, above.

States may act unilaterally, by the enactment of suitable legislation, so as to ensure that foreign arbitral awards are enforced within their territories. This is, however, less than satisfactory in practice, because actual and potential parties to arbitrations will need to understand the law of each of the different States in which proceedings might be brought, and those laws may impose onerous burdens upon parties seeking enforcement.[387] International Conventions simplify the matter by securing the application of uniform rules in the States Parties to them. The rules themselves may, of course, be more or less helpful to litigants. The 1927 Geneva Convention, for example, while helpful in establishing uniform conditions for the recognition or enforcement of foreign arbitral awards, imposed upon the party seeking the recognition or enforcement the burden of proving that the award met certain conditions, including its finality under the law of the seat of the arbitration and its compatibility with the public policy of the forum where enforcement is sought. That procedure was irksome to successful parties seeking enforcement, and even to the losing party, on whom the costs of fulfilling the conditions were likely to fall. The New York Convention[388] is more helpful to litigants. The party seeking enforcement need only produce certified copies (or translations if necessary) of the award and of the agreement under which it was made: recognition and enforcement is then automatic,[389] unless the party against which it is sought proves the existence of one or more of the grounds upon which the New York Convention permits the refusal of recognition and enforcement.[390]

The grounds for the refusal of recognition and enforcement are exhaustively set out in article V of the New York Convention. The first (article V(1)(a)) is that:

> The parties [sc., or a party] to the [sc., arbitration] agreement . . . were, under the law applicable to them, under some incapacity, or the said agreement is not valid under the law to which the parties have subjected it or, failing any indication thereon, under the law of the country where the award was made.

This ground goes to the very validity of the award: in the absence of a valid agreement to arbitrate, the tribunal could have no authority to render the award. The court may refuse recognition and enforcement in these circumstances, even if one of the parties had raised the question during the arbitration and the arbitral tribunal had decided that the agreement to arbitrate was valid. This point was considered above, in the context of the validity of arbitration agreements.[391]

---

[387] See *Rubino-Sammartano*, 485–9.

[388] Which was enacted into English law by the UK Arbitration Act 1975. See now the Arbitration Act 1996, Part III.

[389] Assuming that the Contracting State has fulfilled its obligations to implement the Convention in its national law: see *Navigation Maritime Bulgare (Bulgaria)* v. *P. T. Nizwar (Indonesia)*, Supreme Court of Indonesia, 1984, (1986) 11 *Yearbook Commercial Arbitration* 508.

[390] Arts. III, IV and V.

[391] See pp. 214–15, above.

The next three grounds concern procedural defects in the arbitration. They are (article V(1)) that:

(b) The party against whom the award is invoked was not given proper notice of the appointment of the arbitrator or of the arbitration proceedings or was otherwise unable to present his case; or

(c) The award deals with a difference not contemplated by or not falling within the terms of the submission to arbitration, or it contains decisions on matters beyond the scope of the submission to arbitration, provided that, if the decisions on matters submitted to arbitration can be separated from those not so submitted, that part of the award which contains decisions on matters submitted to arbitration may be recognised and enforced; or

(d) The composition of the arbitral authority or the arbitral procedure was not in accordance with the agreement of the parties, or, failing such agreement, was not in accordance with the law of the country where the arbitration took place.

Although the Convention does not expressly say so, these grounds are generally interpreted as authorising the refusal of recognition and enforcement only in the case of serious procedural irregularities.[392] Again, these matters have been considered above, in the context of arbitral procedure.[393]

The fifth ground on which recognition and enforcement of the award may be refused at the request of the party against whom it is invoked is (article V(1)(e)) that:

The award has not yet become binding on the parties,[394] or has been set aside or suspended by a competent authority of the country in which, or under the law of which, that award was made.[395]

This provision is supplemented by article VI, which permits the court in which recognition and enforcement is sought to adjourn its proceedings in order to await the outcome of an application to a competent authority referred to in article V(1)(e) to have the award set aside or suspended. Article VI also permits the court to order the party against whom enforcement is sought to give a suitable security in such cases.[396]

---

[392] For an instance of refusal under art. V(1)(b) ('unable to present his case') see *Iran Aircraft Industries* v. *Avco Corp.*, 980 F 2d 141 (2d Cir. 1992).

[393] See pp. 218–25; 227–9, above.

[394] The award is, in principle, binding upon publication to the parties. As to the question of binding character, see *Rossell NV* v. *Oriental Shipping (UK) Ltd.* [1991] 2 Lloyd's Rep. 625, where it was held that an agreement that any proceedings to confirm or vacate a New York award would be brought in the USA did not prevent enforcement in England, as it did not deprive the award of its binding character and it did not amount to an agreement not to enforce the award.

[395] i.e., the *lex loci arbitri* or *lex arbitri* (which will normally be the same). The effect of the rather odd decision of the English House of Lords in *Hiscox* v. *Outhwaite* [1992] 1 AC 56, holding that the award is made where it is signed not where the arbitration has its seat, was reversed by s. 53 of the Arbitration Act 1996.

[396] Cf. UNCITRAL Model Law, art. 36.

In addition to these five grounds on which the losing party may request the court to refuse recognition and enforcement to the award, there are two further grounds in the New York Convention on which the court itself may decide, whether or not the losing party raises the matter, to refuse recognition and enforcement. These, set out in article V(2), are that:

(a) The subject-matter of the difference is not capable of settlement by arbitration under the law of that country; or
(b) The recognition of the award would be contrary to the public policy of that country.

These grounds preserve the integrity of the court, freeing it from any obligation to enforce awards which would be regarded under the *lex fori* as improper even if they were untainted by procedural defects. We have already discussed the requirements of arbitrability[397] and compatibility with public policy;[398] but the general pro-enforcement tendency of States' courts, evident in the more restricted concepts of non-arbitrability and public policy which are applied in the context of international (as opposed to purely domestic) arbitrations, deserves to be emphasised.

Under the New York Convention recognition or enforcement of the award may be refused only on one or more of the grounds set out in article V; no other ground suffices to justify a refusal. Courts occasionally refuse on other grounds and, one suspects, chiefly for domestic political or economic reasons such as the fear of upsetting a foreign State against which enforcement is sought: but such actions are not compatible with the Convention and undermine its value as an impartial system for international co-operation in the administration of justice.[399]

If recognition or enforcement is refused by a court, whether in accordance with the New York Convention or otherwise, that refusal does not invalidate the initial award. A court in another State may take a different view, and permit enforcement. Naturally, if the ground for refusing enforcement is the invalidity of the agreement or a gross procedural irregularity, it is probable that all courts will take

---

[397] See p. 202, above. Cf. the *Liamco* award in the US courts, where enforcement was initially refused on this ground: below, n. 416.

[398] See p. 234, above. Cf. *Parsons & Whittemore Overseas Co. Inc.* v. *Société Générale de l'Industrie du Papier*, 508 F 2d 969 (1974), (1975) 14 *ILM* 504; *Westacre Investments Inc.* v. *Jugoimport-SPDR Holding Co. Ltd.* [1998] 3 WLR 770, [1998] 4 All ER 570. See further the papers in P. Sanders (ed.), *Comparative Arbitration Practice and Public Policy in Arbitration: International Council for Commercial Arbitration Congress series no. 3* (Deventer, 1987), 177–362; D. Miller, 'Public policy in international commercial arbitration in Australia' (1993) 9 *Arbitration International* 167; E. H. Bouzari, 'The public policy exception to the enforcement of international arbitral awards: implications for NAFTA jurisprudence' (1995) 30 *Texas International Law Journal* 205; G. Born, *International Civil Litigation in the United States* (The Hague, 1996), 1040–52; and R. B. von Mehren, 'Enforcement of Foreign Arbitral Awards in the United States' [1998] *Int. ALR* 198.

[399] *Libya* v. *Libyan American Oil Co. (LIAMCO)* (Switzerland, 1981) 62 *ILR* 228, (1981) 20 *ILM* 151.

the same view; but where a refusal is based on, say, public policy, significant differences may exist from court to court. This point underlines the main distinction between the effects of a successful challenge to an award under the *lex arbitri*, which nullifies the award and renders it unenforceable in all States,[400] and a successful application for the refusal of recognition and enforcement, whose legal effects are confined to the legal system of the refusing court.

For this system to operate properly it is necessary that courts *should* refuse to recognise and enforce awards set aside under the *lex arbitri*, in accordance with article V(1)(e) of the New York Convention. And the same is true of awards tainted by the other defects set out in article V(1). The maintenance of the propriety of arbitral procedures by controls exercised by courts at the point of enforcement is an essential element of the New York scheme. Accordingly, while the English language text of the New York Convention stipulates that recognition and enforcement 'may' be refused in the stated circumstances, there are powerful arguments, based both on the rules of treaty interpretation and on policy grounds, that courts *must* refuse recognition and enforcement in the case of a material violation of the standards set out in article V(1)(a)–(e) of the Convention.[401] On the other hand, that is not what the text says;[402] and there are some decisions to the contrary, which assert that awards may be recognised and enforced under the provisions of the court's national law even if they would not be enforceable under the New York Convention.[403] Indeed, there may be provisions in bilateral or regional conventions, such as the 1961 European Convention, which permit or require recognition and enforcement in circumstances falling within the grounds for refusal listed in article V of the New York Convention;[404] and the ICSID Convention imposes a seemingly absolute obligation on States Parties to recognise and enforce ICSID awards.[405]

22.2 State immunity

The obligation to recognise and enforce an award, as discussed above, requires that the award be given a status similar to that of a domestic court judgment. But

---

[400] See above, p. 227.

[401] See W. M. Reisman, *Systems of Control in International Adjudication and Arbitration* (Durham, North Carolina, 1992), 115–20. The argument does not apply to the grounds in art. V(2), which entitle the court to protect its *own* interests.

[402] See J. Paulsson, '*May* or *Must* under the New York Convention: an exercise in syntax and linguistics' (1998) 14 *Arbitration International* 227.

[403] See, e.g., the *Norsolor* case in the French Cour de cassation, 9 October 1984, *Clunet*, 1985, 680, and (1986) 11 *Yearbook Commercial Arbitration* 484; and the *Chromalloy* case, 939 F Supp. 907 (DDC, 1996), G. H. Sampliner, 'Enforcement of nullified foreign arbitral awards: *Chromalloy* revisited' (1997) 14/3 *Journal of International Arbitration* 141.

[404] See *Rubino-Sammartano*, 491–4; European Convention 1961, art. IX.

[405] Art. 54. The control function exercised by courts under art. V of the New York Convention is arguably supplanted by the procedures for the review of awards provided in the ICSID Convention itself.

even court judgments may not be enforceable: the respondent may be a State, and enjoy immunity from the jurisdiction of the local courts. The court from which recognition and enforcement is sought is bound by its national law on State immunity.

It has been noted already that State immunity is not regarded as an obstacle to the arbitration itself. The agreement to arbitrate is taken as a valid waiver of immunity; and this principle may properly be regarded as entailing the agreement by the State that the resultant award be recognised and the concomitant duty to fulfil the terms of the award.[406] Difficulties arise, however, in the context of the enforcement of arbitral awards, because of the extensive immunity enjoyed by States from measures of execution. Detailed studies of State immunity in the context of international arbitration are available elsewhere;[407] this, the concluding section on the arbitral process, is confined to brief remarks on the key points.

There is a considerable degree of convergence in national laws on the immunity of States from suit. The principle of restrictive immunity, according to which States are immune from suits in respect of matters which are exercises of its public authority (*acta jure imperii*) but not in respect of commercial transactions into which it has entered (*acta jure gestionis*), is generally accepted.[408] Moreover, there is no doubt that an agreement to arbitrate amounts to a waiver of immunity in respect of the arbitration.[409] But national laws on the immunity of a State from measures of execution are more diverse. For example, under English law, any property of a foreign State 'for the time being in use or intended for use for commercial purposes' may be attached;[410] but property declared by the relevant ambassador to be used for non-commercial purposes may not be attached unless the applicant proves that it is not so used, and bank accounts of a diplomatic mission may not be attached unless the applicant shows that the account was

---

[406] See above, p. 217.

[407] C. Schreuer, *State Immunity: Recent Developments* (Cambridge, 1987); J. R. Crawford, 'Execution of Judgments and Foreign Sovereign Immunity' (1981) 75 *AJIL* 820; G. B. Sullivan, 'Implicit Waiver of Sovereign Immunity by Consent to Arbitration: Territorial Scope and Procedural Limits' (1983) 18 *Texas International Law Journal* 329; H. Fox, 'Sovereign Immunity and Arbitration' in J. D. M. Lew (ed.), *Contemporary Problems in International Arbitration* (London, 1986), 323, and in the same volume papers by G. Delaume (313) and G. Bernini and A. J. van den Berg (359); G. Delaume, 'State contracts and transnational arbitration' (1981) 75 *AJIL* 784; P. Trooboff, 'Foreign State immunity: emerging consensus on principles' (1986) 200 *HR* 235; A. van Blankenstein, 'Enforcement of an arbitral award against a State: with whom are you dealing?', in S. Muller and W. Mijs (eds.), *The Flame Rekindled: New Hope for International Arbitration* (Dordrecht, 1994), 159.

[408] See I. Brownlie, *Principles of Public International Law*, 5th edn. (Oxford, 1998), ch. XVI; *Oppenheim*, 339–76; and the symposium in (1981) 10 *Netherlands Yearbook of International Law*, for useful accounts and analyses of this topic.

[409] See above, p. 217; and further: J. G. Wetter, 'Pleas of Sovereign Immunity and Act of Sovereignty before International Arbitral Tribunals' (1985) 2 *Journal of International Arbitration* 7; M. Sornarajah, *International Commercial Arbitration* (Singapore, 1990), ch. 7.

[410] State Immunity Act 1978, s. 13(4).

earmarked by the foreign State solely for the settlement of commercial liabilities.[411] On the other hand, courts in France have held that commercial property of a State may be attached only if it is used for the commercial activity upon which the claim was based;[412] and US courts have held that bank accounts are liable to attachment unless earmarked for non-commercial purposes.[413]

There is a trend towards the limitation of State immunity from execution in actions for the enforcement of arbitral awards, perhaps most clearly illustrated by 1988 amendments to the US Foreign Sovereign Immunities Act;[414] but the existence and variety of national laws on immunity from execution present a significant obstacle to the enforcement of arbitral awards, often entangled with other obstacles to enforcement. Certainly, international law does not at present support the principle sometimes advanced, that the agreement of a State to submit to arbitration entails a waiver of its immunity in respect of all subsequent proceedings arising out of the arbitration, including proceedings for the enforcement of the award.[415]

The attempts to enforce the *Liamco* award illustrate the point. In the French courts, the order which Liamco initially obtained for the attachment of Libyan assets was annulled by the Tribunal de Grande Instance of Paris after Libya invoked sovereign immunity and Liamco was unable to show immediately which assets were used for commercial and which for non-commercial purposes. In the United States, Liamco was refused recognition and enforcement of the award on the ground that the dispute put in issue the validity of Libya's nationalisation decrees and was therefore not arbitrable (under article V(2)(a) of the New York Convention) because of the act of State doctrine—a decision later vacated by the Court of Appeals. In Switzerland, the Federal Supreme Court annulled an order for the attachment of Libyan assets which Liamco had obtained from the Zurich District Court: the Supreme Court held that there was an insufficient relationship between the dispute and Swiss law to warrant the enforcement of the award (which had been rendered in Geneva) against Libya, but gave no ruling on Libya's claim to immunity. And in Sweden, Liamco obtained a court ruling that Libya had waived its immunity by consenting to arbitration. That ruling, which did not specify which Libyan assets were liable to seizure, was the subject of an appeal to

---

[411] *Alcom Ltd.* v. *Republic of Colombia* [1984] AC 580, 74 *ILR* 170. Cf. *Oppenheim,* 350.

[412] *Société Eurodif* v. *Iran,* 111 *Clunet* 598 (1984). Cf. J. Paulsson, 'Sovereign Immunity from Jurisdiction: French Case Law Revisited' (1985) 19 *International Lawyer* 277.

[413] *Birch Shipping Corp.* v. *Embassy of the United Republic of Tanzania,* 507 F Supp. 311 (1980), 63 *ILR* 524.

[414] Public Law 100–669, (1989) 28 *ILM* 396. And see E. Paasivirta, *Participation of States in International Contracts and Arbitral Settlement of Disputes* (Helsinki, 1990), 318–22.

[415] See, e.g., Sucharitkul, Sixth Report on the Jurisdictional Immunities of States and Their Property, *Yearbook of the International Law Commission, 1984,* vol. II, Part 1, para. 255; *Ipitrade International SA* v. *Federal Republic of Nigeria,* 465 F Supp. 824 (1978); and for comment see M. Sornarajah, *International Commercial Arbitration* (Singapore, 1990), ch. 7, especially at 207–13.

the Supreme Court; but that, and all other actions, were overtaken by a compensation agreement negotiated between Libya and Liamco in 1981.[416] The anticipation of such idiosyncratic variations between national laws is the key to the successful selection of a forum in which enforcement is to be sought—as, indeed, it is to all aspects of international litigation.

---

[416] See R. B. von Mehren and P. N. Kourides, 'International Arbitrations Between States and Foreign Private Parties: the Libyan Nationalisation Cases' (1981) 75 *AJIL* 476 at 545–9. For the court decisions see: 106 *Journal de droit international* 859 (1979) (France); *Libyan American Oil Co. (Liamco)* v. *Socialist People's Libyan Arab Jamahiriya*, 482 F Supp. 1175 (1980), 62 *ILR* 220, (1981) 20 *ILM* 161 (USA); *Socialist People's Libyan Arab Jamahiriya* v. *Libyan American Oil Co. (Liamco)*, (1981) 20 *ILM* 151, 62 *ILR* 228 (Switzerland); *Libyan American Oil Co. (Liamco)* v. *Socialist People's Libyan Arab Jamahiriya*, 62 *ILR* 225, (1981) 20 *ILM* 893 (Sweden).

APPENDICES

APPENDICES—CONTENTS

Appendix 1. The Manila Declaration on the Peaceful Settlement of
International Disputes   279

Appendix 2. Hague Convention on the Pacific Settlement of
Disputes, 1907   285

Appendix 3. ICSID Convention   302

Appendix 4. UNCITRAL Arbitration Rules   319

Appendix 5. UNCITRAL Model Law   334

Appendix 6. Statute of the International Court of Justice   346

Appendix 7. Rules of the International Court of Justice   359

APPENDIX 1. THE MANILA DECLARATION ON THE PEACEFUL SETTLEMENT OF INTERNATIONAL DISPUTES

UN General Assembly Resolution 37/10, 15 November 1982

The General Assembly,

Having examined the item entitled 'Peaceful settlement of disputes between States',

Recalling its resolutions 34/102 of 14 December 1979, 35/160 of 15 December 1980 and 36/110 of 10 December 1981,

Reaffirming the need to exert utmost efforts in order to settle any conflicts and disputes between States exclusively by peaceful means and to avoid any military action and hostilities, which can only make more difficult the solution of those conflicts and disputes,

Considering that the question of the peaceful settlement of disputes should represent one of the central concerns for States and for the United Nations and that the efforts to strengthen the process of the peaceful settlement of disputes should be continued,

Convinced that the adoption of the Manila Declaration on the Peaceful Settlement of International Disputes should enhance the observance of the principle of peaceful settlement of disputes in the relations between States and contribute to the elimination of the danger of recourse to force or to the threat of force, to the relaxation of international tensions, to the promotion of a policy of co-operation and peace and of respect for the independence and sovereignty of all States, to the enhancing of the role of the United Nations in preventing conflicts and settling them peacefully and, consequently, to the strengthening of international peace and security,

Considering the need to ensure a wide dissemination of the text of the Declaration,

1. *Approves* the Manila Declaration on the Peaceful Settlement of International Disputes, the text of which is annexed to the present resolution;

2. *Expresses* its appreciation to the Special Committee on the Charter of the United Nations and on the Strengthening of the Role of the Organization for its important contribution to the elaboration of the text of the Declaration;

3. *Requests* the Secretary-General to inform the Governments of the States Members of the United Nations or members of specialized agencies, the Security Council and the International Court of Justice of the adoption of the Declaration;

4. *Urges* that all efforts be made so that the Declaration becomes generally known and fully observed and implemented.

ANNEX

Manila Declaration on the Peaceful Settlement of International Disputes

The General Assembly,

Reaffirming the principle of the Charter of the United Nations that all States shall settle their international disputes by peaceful means in such a manner that international peace and security, and justice, are not endangered,

Conscious that the Charter of the United Nations embodies the means and an essential framework for the peaceful settlement of international disputes, the continuance of which is likely to endanger the maintenance of international peace and security,

Recognizing the important role of the United Nations and the need to enhance its effectiveness in the peaceful settlement of international disputes and the maintenance of international peace and security, in accordance with the principles of justice and international law, in conformity with the Charter of the United Nations,

Reaffirming the principle of the Charter of the United Nations that all States shall refrain in their international relations from the threat or use of force against the territorial integrity or political independence of any State, or in any other manner inconsistent with the purposes of the United Nations,

Reiterating that no State or group of States has the right to intervene, directly or indirectly, for any reason whatsoever, in the internal or external affairs of any other State,

Reaffirming the Declaration on Principles of International Law concerning Friendly Relations and Co-operation among States in accordance with the Charter of the United Nations,

Bearing in mind the importance of maintaining and strengthening international peace and security and the development of friendly relations among States, irrespective of their political, economic and social systems or levels of economic development,

Reaffirming the principle of equal rights and self-determination of peoples as enshrined in the Charter of the United Nations and referred to in the Declaration on Principles of International Law concerning Friendly Relations and Co-operation among States in accordance with the Charter of the United Nations and in other relevant resolutions of the General Assembly,

Stressing the need for all States to desist from any forcible action which deprives peoples, particularly peoples under colonial and racist regimes or other forms of alien domination, of their inalienable right to self-determination, freedom and independence, as referred to in the Declaration on Principles of International Law concerning Friendly Relations and Co-operation among States in accordance with the Charter of the United Nations,

Mindful of existing international instruments as well as respective principles and rules concerning the peaceful settlement of international disputes, including the exhaustion of local remedies whenever applicable,

Determined to promote international co-operation in the political field and to encourage the progressive development of international law and its codification, particularly in relation to the peaceful settlement of international disputes,

Solemnly declares that:

I

1. All States shall act in good faith and in conformity with the purposes and principles enshrined in the Charter of the United Nations with a view to avoiding disputes among themselves likely to affect friendly relations among States, thus contributing to the maintenance of international peace and security. They shall live together in peace with one another as good neighbours and strive for the adoption of meaningful measures for strengthening international peace and security.

2. Every State shall settle its international disputes exclusively by peaceful means in such a manner that international peace and security, and justice, are not endangered.

3. International disputes shall be settled on the basis of the sovereign equality of States and in accordance with the principle of free choice of means in conformity with obligations under the Charter of the United Nations and with the principles of justice and international law. Recourse to, or acceptance of, a settlement procedure freely agreed to by States with regard to existing or future disputes to which they are parties shall not be regarded as incompatible with the sovereign equality of States.

4. States parties to a dispute shall continue to observe in their mutual relations their obligations under the fundamental principles of international law concerning the sovereignty, independence and territorial integrity of States, as well as other generally recognized principles and rules of contemporary international law.

5. States shall seek in good faith and in a spirit of co-operation an early and equitable settlement of their international disputes by any of the following means: negotiation, inquiry, mediation, conciliation, arbitration, judicial settlement, resort to regional arrangements or agencies or other peaceful means of their own choice, including good offices. In seeking such a settlement, the parties shall agree on such peaceful means as may be appropriate to the circumstances and the nature of their dispute.

6. States parties to regional arrangements or agencies shall make every effort to achieve pacific settlement of their local disputes through such regional arrangements or agencies before referring them to the Security Council. This does not preclude States from bringing any dispute to the attention of the Security Council or of the General Assembly in accordance with the Charter of the United Nations.

7. In the event of failure of the parties to a dispute to reach an early solution by any of the above means of settlement, they shall continue to seek a peaceful solution and shall consult forthwith on mutually agreed means to settle the dispute peacefully. Should the parties fail to settle by any of the above means a dispute the continuance of which is likely to endanger the maintenance of international peace and security, they shall refer it to the Security Council in accordance with the Charter of the United Nations and without prejudice to the functions and powers of the Council set forth in the relevant provisions of Chapter VI of the Charter.

8. States parties to an international dispute, as well as other States, shall refrain from any action whatsoever which may aggravate the situation so as to endanger the maintenance of international peace and security and make more difficult or impede the peaceful settlement of the dispute, and shall act in this respect in accordance with the purposes and principles of the United Nations.

9. States should consider concluding agreements for the peaceful settlement of disputes among them. They should also include in bilateral agreements and multilateral conventions to be concluded, as appropriate, effective provisions for the peaceful settlement of disputes arising from the interpretation or application thereof.

10. States should, without prejudice to the right of free choice of means, bear in mind that direct negotiations are a flexible and effective means of peaceful settlement of their disputes. When they choose to resort to direct negotiations, States should negotiate meaningfully, in order to arrive at an early settlement acceptable to the parties. States should be equally prepared to seek the settlement of their disputes by the other means mentioned in the present Declaration.

11. States shall in accordance with international law implement in good faith all the provisions of agreements concluded by them for the settlement of their disputes.

12. In order to facilitate the exercise by the peoples concerned of the right to self-determination as referred to in the Declaration on Principles of International Law concerning Friendly Relations and Co-operation among States in accordance with the Charter of the United Nations, the parties to a dispute may have the possibility, if they agree to do so and as appropriate, to have recourse to the relevant procedures mentioned in the present Declaration, for the peaceful settlement of the dispute.

13. Neither the existence of a dispute nor the failure of a procedure of peaceful settlement of disputes shall permit the use of force or threat of force by any of the States parties to the dispute.

II

1. Member States should make full use of the provisions of the Charter of the United Nations, including the procedures and means provided for therein, particularly Chapter VI, concerning the peaceful settlement of disputes.

2. Member States shall fulfil in good faith the obligations assumed by them in accordance with the Charter of the United Nations. They should, in accordance with the Charter, as appropriate, duly take into account the recommendations of the Security Council relating to the peaceful settlement of disputes. They should also, in accordance with the Charter, as appropriate, duly take into account the recommendations adopted by the General Assembly, subject to Articles 11 and 12 of the Charter, in the field of peaceful settlement of disputes.

3. Member States reaffirm the important role conferred on the General Assembly by the Charter of the United Nations in the field of peaceful settlement of disputes and stress the need for it to discharge effectively its responsibilities. Accordingly, they should:

(a) Bear in mind that the General Assembly may discuss any situation, regardless of origin, which it deems likely to impair the general welfare or friendly relations among nations and, subject to Article 12 of the Charter, recommend measures for its peaceful adjustment;

(b) Consider making use, when they deem it appropriate, of the possibility of bringing to the attention of the General Assembly any dispute or any situation which might lead to international friction or give rise to a dispute;

(c) Consider utilizing, for the peaceful settlement of their disputes, the subsidiary

organs established by the General Assembly in the performance of its functions under the Charter;

(d) Consider, when they are parties to a dispute brought to the attention of the General Assembly, making use of consultations within the framework of the Assembly, with a view to facilitating an early settlement of their dispute.

4. Member States should strengthen the primary role of the Security Council so that it may fully and effectively discharge its responsibilities, in accordance with the Charter of the United Nations, in the area of the settlement of disputes or of any situation the continuance of which is likely to endanger the maintenance of international peace and security. To this end they should:

(a) Be fully aware of their obligation to refer to the Security Council such a dispute to which they are parties if they fail to settle it by the means indicated in Article 33 of the Charter;

(b) Make greater use of the possibility of bringing to the attention of the Security Council any dispute or any situation which might lead to international friction or give rise to a dispute;

(c) Encourage the Security Council to make wider use of the opportunities provided for by the Charter in order to review disputes or situations the continuance of which is likely to endanger the maintenance of international peace and security;

(d) Consider making greater use of the fact-finding capacity of the Security Council in accordance with the Charter;

(e) Encourage the Security Council to make wider use, as a means to promote peaceful settlement of disputes, of the subsidiary organs established by it in the performance of its functions under the Charter;

(f) Bear in mind that the Security Council may, at any stage of a dispute of the nature referred to in Article 33 of the Charter or of a situation of like nature, recommend appropriate procedures or methods of adjustment;

(g) Encourage the Security Council to act without delay, in accordance with its functions and powers, particularly in cases where international disputes develop into armed conflicts.

5. States should be fully aware of the role of the International Court of Justice, which is the principal judicial organ of the United Nations. Their attention is drawn to the facilities offered by the International Court of Justice for the settlement of legal disputes, especially since the revision of the Rules of the Court.

States may entrust the solution of their differences to other tribunals by virtue of agreements already in existence or which may be concluded in the future.

States should bear in mind:

(a) That legal disputes should as a general rule be referred by the parties to the International Court of Justice, in accordance with the provisions of the Statute of the Court;

(b) That it is desirable that they:

    (i) Consider the possibility of inserting in treaties, whenever appropriate, clauses providing for the submission to the International Court of Justice of disputes which may arise from the interpretation or application of such treaties;

(ii) Study the possibility of choosing, in the free exercise of their sovereignty, to recognize as compulsory the jurisdiction of the International Court of Justice in accordance with Article 36 of its Statute;

(iii) Review the possibility of identifying cases in which use may be made of the International Court of Justice.

The organs of the United Nations and the specialized agencies should study the advisability of making use of the possibility of requesting advisory opinions of the International Court of Justice on legal questions arising within the scope of their activities, provided that they are duly authorized to do so.

Recourse to judicial settlement of legal disputes, particularly referral to the International Court of Justice, should not be considered an unfriendly act between States.

6. The Secretary-General should make full use of the provisions of the Charter of the United Nations concerning the responsibilities entrusted to him. The Secretary-General may bring to the attention of the Security Council any matter which in his opinion may threaten the maintenance of international peace and security. He shall perform such other functions as are entrusted to him by the Security Council or by the General Assembly. Reports in this connection shall be made whenever requested to the Security Council or the General Assembly.

Urges all States to observe and promote in good faith the provisions of the present Declaration in the peaceful settlement of their international disputes;

Declares that nothing in the present Declaration shall be construed as prejudicing in any manner the relevant provisions of the Charter or the rights and duties of States, or the scope of the functions and powers of the United Nations organs under the Charter, in particular those relating to the peaceful settlement of disputes;

Declares that nothing in the present Declaration could in any way prejudice the right to self-determination, freedom and independence, as derived from the Charter, of peoples forcibly deprived of that right and referred to in the Declaration on Principles of International Law concerning Friendly Relations and Co-operation among States in accordance with the Charter of the United Nations, particularly peoples under colonial and racist regimes or other forms of alien domination; nor the right of these peoples to struggle to that end and to seek and receive support, in accordance with the principles of the Charter and in conformity with the above-mentioned Declaration;

Stresses the need, in accordance with the Charter, to continue efforts to strengthen the process of the peaceful settlement of disputes through progressive development and codification of international law, as appropriate, and through enhancing the effectiveness of the United Nations in this field.

APPENDIX 2. HAGUE CONVENTION ON THE PACIFIC SETTLEMENT OF DISPUTES, 1907

Convention for the Pacific Settlement of International Disputes

His Majesty the German Emperor, King of Prussia; the President of the United States of America; the President of the Argentine Republic; His Majesty the Emperor of Austria, King of Bohemia, etc., and Apostolic King of Hungary; His Majesty the King of the Belgians; the President of the Republic of Bolivia; the President of the Republic of the United States of Brazil; His Royal Highness the Prince of Bulgaria; the President of the Republic of Chile; His Majesty the Emperor of China; the President of the Republic of Colombia; the Provisional Governor of the Republic of Cuba; His Majesty the King of Denmark; the President of the Dominican Republic; the President of the Republic of Ecuador; His Majesty the King of Spain; the President of the French Republic; His Majesty the King of the United Kingdom of Great Britain and Ireland and of the British Dominions beyond the Seas, Emperor of India; His Majesty the King of the Hellenes; the President of the Republic of Guatemala; the President of the Republic of Haiti; His Majesty the King of Italy; His Majesty the Emperor of Japan; His Royal Highness the Grand Duke of Luxembourg, Duke of Nassau; the President of the United States of Mexico; His Royal Highness the Prince of Montenegro; the President of the Republic of Nicaragua; His Majesty the King of Norway; the President of the Republic of Panama; the President of the Republic of Paraguay; Her Majesty the Queen of the Netherlands; the President of the Republic of Peru; His Imperial Majesty the Shah of Persia; His Majesty the King of Roumania; His Majesty the Emperor of All the Russias; the President of the Republic of Salvador; His Majesty the King of Servia; His Majesty the King of Siam; His Majesty the King of Sweden; the Swiss Federal Council; His Majesty the Emperor of the Ottomans; the President of the Oriental Republic of Uruguay; the President of the United States of Venezuela;

Animated by the sincere desire to work for the maintenance of general peace;

Resolved to promote by all the efforts in their power the friendly settlement of international disputes;

Recognizing the solidarity uniting the members of the society of civilized nations;

Desirous of extending the empire of law and of strengthening the appreciation of international justice;

Convinced that the permanent institution of a Tribunal of Arbitration accessible to all, in the midst of independent Powers, will contribute effectively to this result;

Having regard to the advantages attending the general and regular organization of the procedure of arbitration;

Sharing the opinion of the august initiator of the International Peace Conference that it is expedient to record in an International Agreement the principles of equity and right on which are based the security of States and the welfare of peoples;

Being desirous, with this object, of insuring the better working in practice of Commissions of Inquiry and Tribunals of Arbitration, and of facilitating recourse to arbitration in cases which allow of a summary procedure;

Have deemed it necessary to revise in certain particulars and to complete the work of the First Peace Conference for the pacific settlement of international disputes;

The High Contracting Parties have resolved to conclude a new Convention for this purpose, and have appointed the following as their Plenipotentiaries:

(Here follow the names of Plenipotentiaries.)

Who, after having deposited their full powers, found in good and due form, have agreed upon the following:

PART I. *The Maintenance of General Peace*

ARTICLE 1

With a view to obviating as far as possible recourse to force in the relations between States, the Contracting Powers agree to use their best efforts to ensure the pacific settlement of international differences.

PART II. *Good Offices and Mediation*

ARTICLE 2

In case of serious disagreement or dispute, before an appeal to arms, the Contracting Powers agree to have recourse, as far as circumstances allow, to the good offices or mediation of one or more friendly Powers.

ARTICLE 3

Independently of this recourse, the Contracting Powers deem it expedient and desirable that one or more Powers, strangers to the dispute, should, on their own initiative and as far as circumstances may allow, offer their good offices or mediation to the States at variance.

Powers strangers to the dispute have the right to offer good offices or mediation even during the course of hostilities.

The exercise of this right can never be regarded by either of the parties in dispute as an unfriendly act.

ARTICLE 4

The part of the mediator consists in reconciling the opposing claims and appeasing the feelings of resentment which may have arisen between the States at variance.

ARTICLE 5

The functions of the mediator are at an end when once it is declared, either by one of the parties to the dispute or by the mediator himself, that the means of reconciliation proposed by him are not accepted.

ARTICLE 6

Good offices and mediation undertaken either at the request of the parties in dispute or on the initiative of Powers strangers to the dispute have exclusively the character of advice, and never have binding force.

ARTICLE 7

The acceptance of mediation cannot, unless there be an agreement to the contrary, have the effect of interrupting, delaying, or hindering mobilization or other measures of preparation for war.

If it takes place after the commencement of hostilities, the military operations in progress are not interrupted in the absence of an agreement to the contrary.

ARTICLE 8

The Contracting Powers are agreed in recommending the application, when circumstances allow, of special mediation in the following form:

In case of a serious difference endangering peace, the States at variance choose respectively a Power, to which they intrust the mission of entering into direct communication with the Power chosen on the other side, with the object of preventing the rupture of pacific relations.

For the period of this mandate, the term of which, unless otherwise stipulated, cannot exceed thirty days, the States in dispute cease from all direct communication on the subject of the dispute, which is regarded as referred exclusively to the mediating Powers, which must use their best efforts to settle it.

In case of a definite rupture of pacific relations, these Powers are charged with the joint task of taking advantage of any opportunity to restore peace.

PART III. *International Commissions of Inquiry*

ARTICLE 9

In disputes of an international nature involving neither honour nor vital interests, and arising from a difference of opinion on points of facts, the Contracting Powers deem it expedient and desirable that the parties who have not been able to come to an agreement by means of diplomacy, should, as far as circumstances allow, institute an International Commission of Inquiry, to facilitate a solution of these disputes by elucidating the facts by means of an impartial and conscientious investigation.

ARTICLE 10

International Commissions of Inquiry are constituted by special agreement between the parties in dispute.

The Inquiry Convention defines the facts to be examined; it determines the mode and time in which the Commission is to be formed and the extent of the powers of the Commissioners.

It also determines, if there is need, where the Commission is to sit, and whether it may remove to another place, the language the Commission shall use and the languages the use of which shall be authorized before it, as well as the date on which each party must deposit its statement of facts, and, generally speaking, all the conditions upon which the parties have agreed.

If the parties consider it necessary to appoint Assessors, the Convention of Inquiry shall determine the mode of their selection and the extent of their powers.

ARTICLE 11

If the Inquiry Convention has not determined where the Commission is to sit, it will sit at The Hague.

The place of meeting, once fixed, cannot be altered by the Commission except with the assent of the parties.

If the Inquiry Convention has not determined what languages are to be employed, the question shall be decided by the Commission.

ARTICLE 12

Unless an undertaking is made to the contrary, Commissions of Inquiry shall be formed in the manner determined by Articles 45 and 57 of the present Convention.

ARTICLE 13

Should one of the Commissioners or one of the Assessors, should there be any, either die, or resign, or be unable for any reason whatever to discharge his functions, the same procedure is followed for filling the vacancy as was followed for appointing him.

ARTICLE 14

The parties are entitled to appoint special agents to attend the Commission of Inquiry, whose duty it is to represent them and to act as intermediaries between them and the Commission.

They are further authorized to engage counsel or advocates, appointed by themselves, to state their case and uphold their interests before the Commission.

ARTICLE 15

The International Bureau of the Permanent Court of Arbitration acts as registry for the Commissions which sit at The Hague, and shall place its offices and staff at the disposal of the Contracting Powers for the use of the Commission of Inquiry.

ARTICLE 16

If the Commission meets elsewhere than at The Hague, it appoints a Secretary-General, whose office serves as registry.

It is the function of the registry, under the control of the President, to make the necessary arrangements for the sittings of the Commission, the preparation of the Minutes, and, while the inquiry lasts, for the charge of the archives, which shall subsequently be transferred to the International Bureau at The Hague.

ARTICLE 17

In order to facilitate the constitution and working of Commissions of Inquiry, the Contracting Powers recommend the following rules, which shall be applicable to the inquiry procedure in so far as the parties do not adopt other rules.

ARTICLE 18

The Commission shall settle the details of the procedure not covered by the special Inquiry Convention or the present Convention, and shall arrange all the formalities required for dealing with the evidence.

ARTICLE 19

On the inquiry both sides must be heard.

At the dates fixed, each party communicates to the Commission and to the other party the statements of facts, if any, and, in all cases, the instruments, papers, and documents which it considers useful for ascertaining the truth, as well as the list of witnesses and experts whose evidence it wishes to be heard.

ARTICLE 20

The Commission is entitled, with the assent of the Powers, to move temporarily to any place where it considers it may be useful to have recourse to this means of inquiry or to send one or more of its members. Permission must be obtained from the State on whose territory it is proposed to hold the inquiry.

ARTICLE 21

Every investigation, and every examination of a locality, must be made in the presence of the agents and counsel of the parties or after they have been duly summoned.

ARTICLE 22

The Commission is entitled to ask from either party for such explanations and information as it considers necessary.

ARTICLE 23

The parties undertake to supply the Commission of Inquiry, as fully as they may think possible, with all means and facilities necessary to enable it to become completely acquainted with, and to accurately understand, the facts in question.

They undertake to make use of the means at their disposal, under their municipal law, to insure the appearance of the witnesses or experts who are in their territory and have been summoned before the Commission.

If the witnesses or experts are unable to appear before the Commission, the parties will arrange for their evidence to be taken before the qualified officials of their own country.

ARTICLE 24

For all notices to be served by the Commission in the territory of a third Contracting Power, the Commission shall apply direct to the Government of the said Power. The same rule applies in the case of steps being taken on the spot to procure evidence.

The requests for this purpose are to be executed so far as the means at the disposal of the Power applied to under its municipal law allow. They cannot be rejected unless the Power in question considers they are calculated to impair its sovereign rights or its safety.

The Commission will equally be always entitled to act through the Power on whose territory it sits.

ARTICLE 25

The witnesses and experts are summoned on the request of the parties or by the Commission of its own motion, and, in every case, through the Government of the State in whose territory they are.

The witnesses are heard in succession and separately in the presence of the agents and counsel, and in the order fixed by the Commission.

ARTICLE 26

The examination of witnesses is conducted by the President.

The members of the Commission may however put to each witness questions which they consider likely to throw light on and complete his evidence, or get information on any point concerning the witness within the limits of what is necessary in order to get at the truth.

The agents and counsel of the parties may not interrupt the witness when he is making his statement, nor put any direct question to him, but they may ask the President to put such additional questions to the witness as they think expedient.

ARTICLE 27

The witness must give his evidence without being allowed to read any written draft. He may, however, be permitted by the President to consult notes or documents if the nature of the facts referred to necessitates their employment.

ARTICLE 28

A Minute of the evidence of the witness is drawn up forthwith and read to the witness. The latter may make such alterations and additions as he thinks necessary, which will be recorded at the end of his statement.

When the whole of his statement has been read to the witness, he is asked to sign it.

ARTICLE 29

The agents are authorized, in the course of or at the close of the inquiry, to present in writing to the Commission and to the other party such statements, requisitions, or summaries of the facts as they consider useful for ascertaining the truth.

ARTICLE 30

The Commission considers its decisions in private and the proceedings are secret.

All questions are decided by a majority of the members of the Commission.

If a member declines to vote, the fact must be recorded in the Minutes.

ARTICLE 31

The sittings of the Commission are not public, nor the Minutes and documents connected with the inquiry published except in virtue of a decision of the Commission taken with the consent of the parties.

ARTICLE 32

After the parties have presented all the explanations and evidence, and the witnesses have all been heard, the President declares the inquiry terminated, and the Commission adjourns to deliberate and to draw up its Report.

ARTICLE 33

The Report is signed by all the members of the Commission.

If one of the members refuses to sign, the fact is mentioned; but the validity of the Report is not affected.

ARTICLE 34

The Report of the Commission is read at a public sitting, the agents and counsel of the parties being present or duly summoned.

A copy of the Report is given to each party.

ARTICLE 35

The Report of the Commission is limited to a statement of facts, and has in no way the character of an Award. It leaves to the parties entire freedom as to the effect to be given to the statement.

ARTICLE 36

Each party pays its own expenses and an equal share of the expenses incurred by the Commission.

PART IV. *International Arbitration*

CHAPTER I. *The System of Arbitration*

ARTICLE 37

International arbitration has for its object the settlement of disputes between States by Judges of their own choice and on the basis of respect for law.

Recourse to arbitration implies an engagement to submit in good faith to the Award.

ARTICLE 38

In questions of a legal nature, and especially in the interpretation or application of International Conventions, arbitration is recognized by the Contracting Powers as the most effective, and, at the same time, the most equitable means of settling disputes which diplomacy has failed to settle.

Consequently, it would be desirable that, in disputes about the above-mentioned questions, the Contracting Powers should, if the case arose, have recourse to arbitration, in so far as circumstances permit.

ARTICLE 39

The Arbitration Convention is concluded for questions already existing or for questions which may arise eventually.

It may embrace any dispute or only disputes of a certain category.

ARTICLE 40

Independently of general or private Treaties expressly stipulating recourse to arbitration as obligatory on the Contracting Powers, the said Powers reserve to themselves the right of concluding new Agreements, general or particular, with a view to extending compulsory arbitration to all cases which they may consider it possible to submit to it.

CHAPTER II. *The Permanent Court of Arbitration*

ARTICLE 41

With the object of facilitating an immediate recourse to arbitration for international differences, which it has not been possible to settle by diplomacy, the Contracting Powers undertake to maintain the Permanent Court of Arbitration, as established by the First Peace Conference, accessible at all times, and operating, unless otherwise stipulated by the parties, in accordance with the rules of procedure inserted in the present Convention.

ARTICLE 42

The Permanent Court is competent for all arbitration cases, unless the parties agree to institute a special Tribunal.

ARTICLE 43

The Permanent Court sits at The Hague.

An International Bureau serves as registry for the Court. It is the channel for communications relative to the meetings of the Court; it has charge of the archives and conducts all the administrative business.

The Contracting Powers undertake to communicate to the Bureau, as soon as possible, a certified copy of any conditions of arbitration arrived at between them and of any Award concerning them delivered by a special Tribunal.

They likewise undertake to communicate to the Bureau the laws, regulations, and documents eventually showing the execution of the Awards given by the Court.

ARTICLE 44

Each Contracting Power selects four persons at the most, of known competency in questions of international law, of the highest moral reputation, and disposed to accept the duties of Arbitrator.

The persons thus elected are inscribed, as Members of the Court, in a list which shall be notified to all the Contracting Powers by the Bureau.

Any alteration in the list of Arbitrators is brought by the Bureau to the knowledge of the Contracting Powers.

Two or more Powers may agree on the selection in common of one or more Members.

The same person can be selected by different Powers. The Members of the Court are appointed for a term of six years. These appointments are renewable.

Should a Member of the Court die or resign, the same procedure is followed for filling the vacancy as was followed for appointing him. In this case the appointment is made for a fresh period of six years.

ARTICLE 45

When the Contracting Powers wish to have recourse to the Permanent Court for the settlement of a difference which has arisen between them, the Arbitrators called upon to form the Tribunal with jurisdiction to decide this difference must be chosen from the general list of Members of the Court.

Failing the direct agreement of the parties on the composition of the Arbitration Tribunal, the following course shall be pursued:

Each party appoints two Arbitrators, of whom one only can be its national or chosen from among the persons selected by it as Members of the Permanent Court. These Arbitrators together choose an Umpire.

If the votes are equally divided, the choice of the Umpire is intrusted to a third Power, selected by the parties by common accord.

If an agreement is not arrived at on this subject each party selects a different Power, and the choice of the Umpire is made in concert by the Powers thus selected.

If, within two months' time, these two Powers cannot come to an agreement, each of them presents two candidates taken from the list of Members of the Permanent Court, exclusive of the members selected by the parties and not being nationals of either of them. Drawing lots determines which of the candidates thus presented shall be Umpire.

ARTICLE 46

The Tribunal being thus composed, the parties notify to the Bureau their determination to have recourse to the Court, the text of their 'Compromis', and the names of the Arbitrators.

The Bureau communicates without delay to each Arbitrator the 'Compromis', and the names of the other members of the Tribunal.

The Tribunal assembles at the date fixed by the parties. The Bureau makes the necessary arrangements for the meeting.

The members of the Tribunal, in the exercise of their duties and out of their own country, enjoy diplomatic privileges and immunities.

ARTICLE 47

The Bureau is authorized to place its offices and staff at the disposal of the Contracting Powers for the use of any special Board of Arbitration.

The jurisdiction of the Permanent Court may, within the conditions laid down in the regulations, be extended to disputes between non-Contracting Powers or between Contracting Powers and non-Contracting Powers, if the parties are agreed on recourse to this Tribunal.

ARTICLE 48

The Contracting Powers consider it their duty, if a serious dispute threatens to break out between two or more of them, to remind these latter that the Permanent Court is open to them.

Consequently, they declare that the fact of reminding the parties at variance of the provisions of the present Convention, and the advice given to them, in the highest interests of peace, to have recourse to the Permanent Court, can only be regarded as friendly actions.

In case of dispute between two Powers, one of them can always address to the International Bureau a note containing a declaration that it would be ready to submit the dispute to arbitration.

The Bureau must at once inform the other Power of the declaration.

ARTICLE 49

The Permanent Administrative Council, composed of the Diplomatic Representatives of the Contracting Powers accredited to The Hague and of the Netherland Minister for Foreign Affairs, who will act as President, is charged with the direction and control of the International Bureau.

The Council settles its rules of procedure and all other necessary regulations.

It decides all questions of administration which may arise with regard to the operations of the Court.

It has entire control over the appointment, suspension, or dismissal of the officials and employees of the Bureau.

It fixes the payments and salaries, and controls the general expenditure.

At meetings duly summoned the presence of nine members is sufficient to render valid the discussions of the Council. The decisions are taken by a majority of votes.

The Council communicates to the Contracting Powers without delay the regulations adopted by it. It furnishes them with an annual Report on the labours of the Court, the working of the administration, and the expenditure. The Report likewise contains a résumé of what is important in the documents communicated to the Bureau by the Powers in virtue of Article 43, paragraphs 3 and 4.

ARTICLE 50

The expenses of the Bureau shall be borne by the Contracting Powers in the proportion fixed for the International Bureau of the Universal Postal Union.

The expenses to be charged to the adhering Powers shall be reckoned from the date on which their adhesion comes into force.

CHAPTER III. *Arbitration Procedure*

ARTICLE 51

With a view to encouraging the development of arbitration, the Contracting Powers have agreed on the following rules, which are applicable to arbitration procedure, unless other rules have been agreed on by the parties.

ARTICLE 52

The Powers which have recourse to arbitration sign a 'Compromis', in which the subject of the dispute is clearly defined, the time allowed for appointing Arbitrators, the form, order, and time in which the communication referred to in Article 63 must be made, and the amount of the sum which each party must deposit in advance to defray the expenses.

The 'Compromis' likewise defines, if there is occasion, the manner of appointing Arbitrators, any special powers which may eventually belong to the Tribunal, where it shall meet, the language it shall use, and the languages the employment of which shall be authorized before it, and, generally speaking, all the conditions on which the parties are agreed.

ARTICLE 53

The Permanent Court is competent to settle the 'Compromis', if the parties are agreed to have recourse to it for the purpose.

It is similarly competent, even if the request is only made by one of the parties, when all attempts to reach an understanding through the diplomatic channel have failed, in the case of:

1. A dispute covered by a general Treaty of Arbitration concluded or renewed after the present Convention has come into force, and providing for a 'Compromis' in all disputes and not either explicitly or implicitly excluding the settlement of the 'Compromis' from the competence of the Court. Recourse cannot, however, be had to the Court if the other party declares that in its opinion the dispute does not belong to the category of disputes which can be submitted to compulsory arbitration, unless the Treaty of Arbitration confers upon the Arbitration Tribunal the power of deciding this preliminary question.

2. A dispute arising from contract debts claimed from one Power by another Power as due to its nationals, and for the settlement of which the offer of arbitration has been accepted. This arrangement is not applicable if acceptance is subject to the condition that the 'Compromis' should be settled in some other way.

ARTICLE 54

In the cases contemplated in the preceding Article, the 'Compromis' shall be settled by a Commission consisting of five members selected in the manner arranged for in Article 45, paragraphs 3 to 6.

The fifth member is President of the Commission *ex officio*.

ARTICLE 55

The duties of Arbitrator may be conferred on one Arbitrator alone or on several Arbitrators selected by the parties as they please, or chosen by them from the Members of the Permanent Court of Arbitration established by the present Convention.

Failing the constitution of the Tribunal by direct agreement between the parties, the course referred to in Article 45, paragraphs 3 to 6, is followed.

ARTICLE 56

When a Sovereign or the Chief of a State is chosen as Arbitrator, the arbitration procedure is settled by him.

ARTICLE 57

The Umpire is President of the Tribunal *ex officio*.

When the Tribunal does not include an Umpire, it appoints its own President.

ARTICLE 58

When the 'Compromis' is settled by a Commission, as contemplated in Article 54, and in the absence of an agreement to the contrary, the Commission itself shall form the Arbitration Tribunal.

ARTICLE 59

Should one of the Arbitrators either die, retire, or be unable for any reason whatever to discharge his functions, the same procedure is followed for filling the vacancy as was followed for appointing him.

ARTICLE 60

The Tribunal sits at The Hague, unless some other place is selected by the parties.

The Tribunal can only sit in the territory of a third Power with the latter's consent.

The place of meeting once fixed cannot be altered by the Tribunal, except with the consent of the parties.

ARTICLE 61

If the question as to what languages are to be used has not been settled by the 'Compromis', it shall be decided by the Tribunal.

ARTICLE 62

The parties are entitled to appoint special agents to attend the Tribunal to act as intermediaries between themselves and the Tribunal.

They are further authorized to retain for the defence of their rights and interests before the Tribunal counsel or advocates appointed by themselves for this purpose.

The Members of the Permanent Court may not act as agents, counsel, or advocates except on behalf of the Power which appointed them Members of the Court.

ARTICLE 63

As a general rule, arbitration procedure comprises two distinct phases: pleadings and oral discussions.

The pleadings consist in the communication by the respective agents to the members of the Tribunal and the opposite party of cases, counter-cases, and, if necessary, of replies; the parties annex thereto all papers and documents called for in the case. This communication shall be made either directly or through the intermediary of the International Bureau, in the order and within the time fixed by the 'Compromis'.

The time fixed by the 'Compromis' may be extended by mutual agreement by the parties, or by the Tribunal when the latter considers it necessary for the purpose of reaching a just decision.

The discussions consist in the oral development before the Tribunal of the arguments of the parties.

ARTICLE 64

A certified copy of every document produced by one party must be communicated to the other party.

ARTICLE 65

Unless special circumstances arise, the Tribunal does not meet until the pleadings are closed.

ARTICLE 66

The discussions are under the control of the President. They are only public if it be so decided by the Tribunal, with the assent of the parties.

They are recorded in minutes drawn up by the Secretaries appointed by the President. These minutes are signed by the President and by one of the Secretaries and alone have an authentic character.

ARTICLE 67

After the close of the pleadings, the Tribunal is entitled to refuse discussion of all new papers or documents which one of the parties may wish to submit to it without the consent of the other party.

ARTICLE 68

The Tribunal is free to take into consideration new papers or documents to which its attention may be drawn by the agents or counsel of the parties.

In this case, the Tribunal has the right to require the production of these papers or documents, but is obliged to make them known to the opposite party.

ARTICLE 69

The Tribunal can, besides, require from the agents of the parties the production of all papers, and can demand all necessary explanations. In case of refusal the Tribunal takes note of it.

ARTICLE 70

The agents and the counsel of the parties are authorized to present orally to the Tribunal all the arguments they may consider expedient in defence of their case.

ARTICLE 71

They are entitled to raise objections and points. The decisions of the Tribunal on these points are final and cannot form the subject of any subsequent discussion.

ARTICLE 72

The members of the Tribunal are entitled to put questions to the agents and counsel of the parties, and to ask them for explanations on doubtful points.

Neither the questions put, nor the remarks made by members of the Tribunal in the course of the discussions, can be regarded as an expression of opinion by the Tribunal in general or by its members in particular.

ARTICLE 73

The Tribunal is authorized to declare its competence in interpreting the 'Compromis', as well as the other Treaties which may be invoked, and in applying the principles of law.

297

ARTICLE 74

The Tribunal is entitled to issue rules of procedure for the conduct of the case, to decide the forms, order, and time in which each party must conclude its arguments, and to arrange all the formalities required for dealing with the evidence.

ARTICLE 75

The parties undertake to supply the Tribunal, as fully as they consider possible, with all the information required for deciding the case.

ARTICLE 76

For all notices which the Tribunal has to serve in the territory of a third Contracting Power, the Tribunal shall apply direct to the Government of that Power. The same rule applies in the case of steps being taken to procure evidence on the spot.

The requests for this purpose are to be executed as far as the means at the disposal of the Power applied to under its municipal law allow. They cannot be rejected unless the Power in question considers them calculated to impair its own sovereign rights or its safety.

The Court will equally be always entitled to act through the Power on whose territory it sits.

ARTICLE 77

When the agents and counsel of the parties have submitted all the explanations and evidence in support of their case the President shall declare the discussion closed.

ARTICLE 78

The Tribunal considers its decisions in private and the proceedings remain secret.
All questions are decided by a majority of the members of the Tribunal.

ARTICLE 79

The Award must give the reasons on which it is based. It contains the names of the Arbitrators; it is signed by the President and Registrar or by the Secretary acting as Registrar.

ARTICLE 80

The Award is read out in public sitting, the agents and counsel of the parties being present or duly summoned to attend.

ARTICLE 81

The Award, duly pronounced and notified to the agents of the parties, settles the dispute definitively and without appeal.

ARTICLE 82

Any dispute arising between the parties as to the interpretation and execution of the Award shall, in the absence of an Agreement to the contrary, be submitted to the Tribunal which pronounced it.

ARTICLE 83

The parties can reserve in the 'Compromis' the right to demand the revision of the Award.

In this case and unless there be an Agreement to the contrary, the demand must be addressed to the Tribunal which pronounced the Award. It can only be made on the ground of the discovery of some new fact calculated to exercise a decisive influence upon the Award and which was unknown to the Tribunal and to the party which demanded the revision at the time the discussion was closed.

Proceedings for revision can only be instituted by a decision of the Tribunal expressly recording the existence of the new fact, recognizing in it the character described in the preceding paragraph, and declaring the demand admissible on this ground.

The 'Compromis' fixes the period within which the demand for revision must be made.

ARTICLE 84

The Award is not binding except on the parties in dispute.

When it concerns the interpretation of a Convention to which Powers other than those in dispute are parties, they shall inform all the Signatory Powers in good time. Each of these Powers is entitled to intervene in the case. If one or more avail themselves of this right, the interpretation contained in the Award is equally binding on them.

ARTICLE 85

Each party pays its own expenses and an equal share of the expenses of the Tribunal.

CHAPTER IV. *Arbitration by Summary Procedure*

ARTICLE 86

With a view to facilitating the working of the system of arbitration in disputes admitting of a summary procedure, the Contracting Powers adopt the following rules, which shall be observed in the absence of other arrangements and subject to the reservation that the provisions of Chapter III apply so far as may be.

ARTICLE 87

Each of the parties in dispute appoints an Arbitrator. The two Arbitrators thus selected choose an Umpire. If they do not agree on this point, each of them proposes two candidates taken from the general list of the Members of the Permanent Court exclusive of the members appointed by either of the parties and not being nationals of either of them; which of the candidates thus proposed shall be the Umpire is determined by lot.

The Umpire presides over the Tribunal, which gives its decisions by a majority of votes.

ARTICLE 88

In the absence of any previous agreement the Tribunal, as soon as it is formed, settles the time within which the two parties must submit their respective cases to it.

ARTICLE 89

Each party is represented before the Tribunal by an agent, who serves as intermediary between the Tribunal and the Government who appointed him.

ARTICLE 90

The proceedings are conducted exclusively in writing. Each party, however, is entitled to ask that witnesses and experts should be called. The Tribunal has, for its part, the right to demand oral explanations from the agents of the two parties, as well as from the experts and witnesses whose appearance in Court it may consider useful.

PART V. *Final Provisions*

ARTICLE 91

The present Convention, duly ratified, shall replace, as between the Contracting Powers, the Convention for the Pacific Settlement of International Disputes of the 29th July, 1899.

ARTICLE 92

The present Convention shall be ratified as soon as possible.

The ratifications shall be deposited at The Hague.

The first deposit of ratifications shall be recorded in a *procès-verbal* signed by the Representatives of the Powers which take part therein and by the Netherland Minister for Foreign Affairs.

The subsequent deposits of ratifications shall be made by means of a written notification, addressed to the Netherland Government and accompanied by the instrument of ratification.

A duly certified copy of the *procès-verbal* relative to the first deposit of ratifications, of the notifications mentioned in the preceding paragraph, and of the instruments of ratification, shall be immediately sent by the Netherland Government, through the diplomatic channel, to the Powers invited to the Second Peace Conference, as well as to those Powers which have adhered to the Convention. In the cases contemplated in the preceding paragraph, the said Government shall at the same time inform the Powers of the date on which it received the notification.

ARTICLE 93

Non-Signatory Powers which have been invited to the Second Peace Conference may adhere to the present Convention.

The Power which desires to adhere notifies its intention in writing to the Netherland Government, forwarding to it the act of adhesion, which shall be deposited in the archives of the said Government.

This Government shall immediately forward to all the other Powers invited to the Second Peace Conference a duly certified copy of the notification as well as of the act of adhesion, mentioning the date on which it received the notification.

ARTICLE 94

The conditions on which the Powers which have not been invited to the Second Peace Conference may adhere to the present Convention shall form the subject of a subsequent Agreement between the Contracting Powers.

ARTICLE 95

The present Convention shall take effect, in the case of the Powers which were not a party to the first deposit of ratifications, sixty days after the date of the *procès-verbal* of this deposit, and, in the case of the Powers which ratify subsequently or which adhere, sixty days after the notification of their ratification or of their adhesion has been received by the Netherland Government.

ARTICLE 96

In the event of one of the Contracting Parties wishing to denounce the present Convention, the denunciation shall be notified in writing to the Netherland Government, which shall immediately communicate a duly certified copy of the notification to all the other Powers informing them of the date on which it was received.

The denunciation shall only have effect in regard to the notifying Power, and one year after the notification has reached the Netherland Government.

ARTICLE 97

A register kept by the Netherlands Minister for Foreign Affairs shall give the date of the deposit of ratifications effected in virtue of Article 92, paragraphs 3 and 4, as well as the date on which the notifications of adhesion (Article 93, paragraph 2) or of denunciation (Article 96, paragraph 1) have been received.

Each Contracting Power is entitled to have access to this register and to be supplied with duly certified extracts from it.

In faith whereof the Plenipotentiaries have appended their signatures to the present Convention.

Done at The Hague, the 18th October 1907, in a single copy, which shall remain deposited in the archives of the Netherlands Government, and duly certified copies of which shall be sent, through the diplomatic channel, to the Contracting Powers.

APPENDIX 3. ICSID CONVENTION

CONVENTION ON THE SETTLEMENT OF INVESTMENT DISPUTES BETWEEN STATES AND NATIONALS OF OTHER STATES

PREAMBLE

The Contracting States

Considering the need for international cooperation for economic development, and the role of private international investment therein;

Bearing in mind the possibility that from time to time disputes may arise in connection with such investment between Contracting States and nationals of other Contracting States;

Recognizing that while such disputes would usually be subject to national legal processes, international methods of settlement may be appropriate in certain cases;

Attaching particular importance to the availability of facilities for international conciliation or arbitration to which Contracting States and nationals of other Contracting States may submit such disputes if they so desire;

Desiring to establish such facilities under the auspices of the International Bank for Reconstruction and Development;

Recognizing that mutual consent by the parties to submit such disputes to conciliation or to arbitration through such facilities constitutes a binding agreement which requires in particular that due consideration be given to any recommendation of conciliators, and that any arbitral award be complied with; and

Declaring that no Contracting State shall by the mere fact of its ratification, acceptance or approval of this Convention and without its consent be deemed to be under any obligation to submit any particular dispute to conciliation or arbitration,

Have agreed as follows:

CHAPTER I
International Centre for Settlement of Investment Disputes

Section 1
Establishment and Organization

Article 1

(1) There is hereby established the International Centre for Settlement of Investment Disputes (hereinafter called the Centre).

(2) The purpose of the Centre shall be to provide facilities for conciliation and arbitration of investment disputes between Contracting States and nationals of other Contracting States in accordance with the provisions of this Convention.

Article 2

The seat of the Centre shall be at the principal office of the International Bank for Reconstruction and Development (hereinafter called the Bank). The seat may be moved to another place by decision of the Administrative Council adopted by a majority of two-thirds of its members.

Article 3

The Centre shall have an Administrative Council and a Secretariat and shall maintain a Panel of Conciliators and a Panel of Arbitrators.

Section 2
The Administrative Council

Article 4

(1) The Administrative Council shall be composed of one representative of each Contracting State. An alternate may act as representative in case of his principal's absence from a meeting or inability to act.
(2) In the absence of a contrary designation, each governor and alternate governor of the Bank appointed by a Contracting State shall be *ex officio* its representative and its alternate respectively.

Article 5

The President of the Bank shall be *ex officio* Chairman of the Administrative Council (hereinafter called the Chairman) but shall have no vote. During his absence or inability to act and during any vacancy in the office of President of the Bank, the person for the time being acting as President shall act as Chairman of the Administrative Council.

Article 6

(1) Without prejudice to the powers and functions vested in it by other provisions of this Convention, the Administrative Council shall:

(a) adopt the administrative and financial regulations of the Centre;
(b) adopt the rules of procedure for the institution of conciliation and arbitration proceedings;
(c) adopt the rules of procedure for conciliation and arbitration proceedings (hereinafter called the Conciliation Rules and the Arbitration Rules);
(d) approve arrangements with the Bank for the use of the Bank's administrative facilities and services;
(e) determine the conditions of service of the Secretary-General and of any Deputy Secretary-General;
(f) adopt the annual budget of revenues and expenditures of the Centre;
(g) approve the annual report on the operation of the Centre.

The decisions referred to in sub-paragraphs (a), (b), (c) and (f) above shall be adopted by a majority of two-thirds of the members of the Administrative Council.
(2) The Administrative Council may appoint such committees as it considers necessary.

(3) The Administrative Council shall also exercise such other powers and perform such other functions as it shall determine to be necessary for the implementation of the provisions of this Convention.

Article 7

(1) The Administrative Council shall hold an annual meeting and such other meetings as may be determined by the Council, or convened by the Chairman, or convened by the Secretary-General at the request of not less than five members of the Council.
(2) Each member of the Administrative Council shall have one vote and, except as otherwise herein provided, all matters before the Council shall be decided by a majority of the votes cast.
(3) A quorum for any meeting of the Administrative Council shall be a majority of its members.
(4) The Administrative Council may establish, by a majority of two-thirds of its members, a procedure whereby the Chairman may seek a vote of the Council without convening a meeting of the Council. The vote shall be considered valid only if the majority of the members of the Council cast their votes within the time limit fixed by the said procedure.

Article 8

Members of the Administrative Council and the Chairman shall serve without remuneration from the Centre.

Section 3
The Secretariat

Article 9

The Secretariat shall consist of a Secretary-General, one or more Deputy Secretaries-General and staff.

Article 10

(1) The Secretary-General and any Deputy Secretary-General shall be elected by the Administrative Council by a majority of two-thirds of its members upon the nomination of the Chairman for a term of service not exceeding six years and shall be eligible for re-election. After consulting the members of the Administrative Council, the Chairman shall propose one or more candidates for each such office.
(2) The offices of Secretary-General and Deputy Secretary-General shall be incompatible with the exercise of any political function. Neither the Secretary-General nor any Deputy Secretary-General may hold any other employment or engage in any other occupation except with the approval of the Administrative Council.
(3) During the Secretary-General's absence or inability to act, and during any vacancy of the office of Secretary-General, the Deputy Secretary-General shall act as Secretary-General. If there shall be more than one Deputy Secretary-General, the Administrative Council shall determine in advance the order in which they shall act as Secretary-General.

Article 11

The Secretary-General shall be the legal representative and the principal officer of the Centre and shall be responsible for its administration, including the appointment of staff, in accordance with the provisions of this Convention and the rules adopted by the Administrative Council. He shall perform the function of registrar and shall have the power to authenticate arbitral awards rendered pursuant to this Convention, and to certify copies thereof.

Section 4
The Panels

Article 12

The Panel of Conciliators and the Panel of Arbitrators shall each consist of qualified persons, designated as hereinafter provided, who are willing to serve thereon.

Article 13

(1) Each Contracting State may designate to each Panel four persons who may but need not be its nationals.
(2) The Chairman may designate ten persons to each Panel. The persons so designated to a Panel shall each have a different nationality.

Article 14

(1) Persons designated to serve on the Panels shall be persons of high moral character and recognized competence in the fields of law, commerce, industry or finance, who may be relied upon to exercise independent judgment. Competence in the field of law shall be of particular importance in the case of persons on the Panel of Arbitrators.
(2) The Chairman, in designating persons to serve on the Panels, shall in addition pay due regard to the importance of assuring representation on the Panels of the principal legal systems of the world and of the main forms of economic activity.

Article 15

(1) Panel members shall serve for renewable periods of six years.
(2) In case of death or resignation of a member of a Panel, the authority which designated the member shall have the right to designate another person to serve for the remainder of that member's term.
(3) Panel members shall continue in office until their successors have been designated.

Article 16

(1) A person may serve on both Panels.
(2) If a person shall have been designated to serve on the same Panel by more than one Contracting State, or by one or more Contracting States and the Chairman, he shall be deemed to have been designated by the authority which first designated him or, if one such authority is the State of which he is a national, by that State.
(3) All designations shall be notified to the Secretary-General and shall take effect from the date on which the notification is received.

Section 5
Financing the Centre

Article 17

If the expenditure of the Centre cannot be met out of charges for the use of its facilities, or out of other receipts, the excess shall be borne by Contracting States which are members of the Bank in proportion to their respective subscriptions to the capital stock of the Bank, and by Contracting States which are not members of the Bank in accordance with rules adopted by the Administrative Council.

Section 6
Status, Immunities and Privileges

Article 18

The Centre shall have full international legal personality. The legal capacity of the Centre shall include the capacity:

(a) to contract;
(b) to acquire and dispose of movable and immovable property;
(c) to institute legal proceedings.

Article 19

To enable the Centre to fulfil its functions, it shall enjoy in the territories of each Contracting State the immunities and privileges set forth in this Section.

Article 20

The Centre, its property and assets shall enjoy immunity from all legal process, except when the Centre waives this immunity.

Article 21

The Chairman, the members of the Administrative Council, persons acting as conciliators or arbitrators or members of a Committee appointed pursuant to paragraph (3) of Article 52, and the officers and employees of the Secretariat

(a) shall enjoy immunity from legal process with respect to acts performed by them in the exercise of their functions, except when the Centre waives this immunity;
(b) not being local nationals, shall enjoy the same immunities from immigration restrictions, alien registration requirements and national service obligations, the same facilities as regards exchange restrictions and the same treatment in respect of travelling facilities as are accorded by Contracting States to the representatives, officials and employees of comparable rank of other Contracting States.

Article 22

The provisions of Article 21 shall apply to persons appearing in proceedings under this Convention as parties, agents, counsel, advocates, witnesses or experts; provided, however, that sub-paragraph (b) thereof shall apply only in connection with their travel to and from, and their stay at, the place where the proceedings are held.

Article 23

(1) The archives of the Centre shall be inviolable, wherever they may be.
(2) With regard to its official communications, the Centre shall be accorded by each Contracting State treatment not less favourable than that accorded to other international organizations.

Article 24

(1) The Centre, its assets, property and income, and its operations and transactions authorized by this Convention shall be exempt from all taxation and customs duties. The Centre shall also be exempt from liability for the collection or payment of any taxes or customs duties.
(2) Except in the case of local nationals, no tax shall be levied on or in respect of expense allowances paid by the Centre to the Chairman or members of the Administrative Council, or on or in respect of salaries, expense allowances or other emoluments paid by the Centre to officials or employees of the Secretariat.
(3) No tax shall be levied on or in respect of fees or expense allowances received by persons acting as conciliators, or arbitrators, or members of a Committee appointed pursuant to paragraph (3) of Article 52, in proceedings under this Convention, if the sole jurisdictional basis for such tax is the location of the Centre or the place where such proceedings are conducted or the place where such fees or allowances are paid.

CHAPTER II
Jurisdiction of the Centre

Article 25

(1) The jurisdiction of the Centre shall extend to any legal dispute arising directly out of an investment, between a Contracting State (or any constituent subdivision or agency of a Contracting State designated to the Centre by that State) and a national of another Contracting State, which the parties to the dispute consent in writing to submit to the Centre. When the parties have given their consent, no party may withdraw its consent unilaterally.
(2) 'National of another Contracting State' means:

(a) any natural person who had the nationality of a Contracting State other than the State party to the dispute on the date on which the parties consented to submit such dispute to conciliation or arbitration as well as on the date on which the request was registered pursuant to paragraph (3) of Article 28 or paragraph (3) of Article 36, but does not include any person who on either date also had the nationality of the Contracting State party to the dispute; and
(b) any juridical person which had the nationality of a Contracting State other than the State party to the dispute on the date on which the parties consented to submit such dispute to conciliation or arbitration and any juridical person which had the nationality of the Contracting State party to the dispute on that date and which, because of foreign control, the parties have agreed should be treated as a national of another Contracting State for the purposes of this Convention.

(3) Consent by a constituent subdivision or agency of a Contracting State shall require the approval of that State unless that State notifies the Centre that no such approval is required.

(4) Any Contracting State may, at the time of ratification, acceptance or approval of this Convention or at any time thereafter, notify the Centre of the class or classes of disputes which it would or would not consider submitting to the jurisdiction of the Centre. The Secretary-General shall forthwith transmit such notification to all Contracting States. Such notification shall not constitute the consent required by paragraph (1).

Article 26

Consent of the parties to arbitration under this Convention shall, unless otherwise stated, be deemed consent to such arbitration to the exclusion of any other remedy. A Contracting State may require the exhaustion of local administrative or judicial remedies as a condition of its consent to arbitration under this Convention.

Article 27

(1) No Contracting State shall give diplomatic protection, or bring an international claim, in respect of a dispute which one of its nationals and another Contracting State shall have consented to submit or shall have submitted to arbitration under this Convention, unless such other Contracting State shall have failed to abide by and comply with the award rendered in such dispute.

(2) Diplomatic protection, for the purposes of paragraph (1), shall not include informal diplomatic exchanges for the sole purpose of facilitating a settlement of the dispute.

CHAPTER III
Conciliation

Section 1
Request for Conciliation

Article 28

(1) Any Contracting State or any national of a Contracting State wishing to institute conciliation proceedings shall address a request to that effect in writing to the Secretary-General who shall send a copy of the request to the other party.

(2) The request shall contain information concerning the issues in dispute, the identity of the parties and their consent to conciliation in accordance with the rules of procedure for the institution of conciliation and arbitration proceedings.

(3) The Secretary-General shall register the request unless he finds, on the basis of the information contained in the request, that the dispute is manifestly outside the jurisdiction of the Centre. He shall forthwith notify the parties of registration or refusal to register.

Section 2
Constitution of the Conciliation Commission

Article 29

(1) The Conciliation Commission (hereinafter called the Commission) shall be constituted as soon as possible after registration of a request pursuant to Article 28.

(2) (a) The Commission shall consist of a sole conciliator or any uneven number of conciliators appointed as the parties shall agree.

(b) Where the parties do not agree upon the number of conciliators and the method of their appointment, the Commission shall consist of three conciliators, one conciliator appointed by each party and the third, who shall be the president of the Commission, appointed by agreement of the parties.

Article 30

If the Commission shall not have been constituted within 90 days after notice of registration of the request has been dispatched by the Secretary-General in accordance with paragraph (3) of Article 28, or such other period as the parties may agree, the Chairman shall, at the request of either party and after consulting both parties as far as possible, appoint the conciliator or conciliators not yet appointed.

Article 31

(1) Conciliators may be appointed from outside the Panel of Conciliators, except in the case of appointments by the Chairman pursuant to Article 30.

(2) Conciliators appointed from outside the Panel of Conciliators shall possess the qualities stated in paragraph (1) of Article 14.

Section 3

Conciliation Proceedings

Article 32

(1) The Commission shall be the judge of its own competence.

(2) Any objection by a party to the dispute that that dispute is not within the jurisdiction of the Centre, or for other reasons is not within the competence of the Commission, shall be considered by the Commission which shall determine whether to deal with it as a preliminary question or to join it to the merits of the dispute.

Article 33

Any conciliation proceeding shall be conducted in accordance with the provisions of this Section and, except as the parties otherwise agree, in accordance with the Conciliation Rules in effect on the date on which the parties consented to conciliation. If any question of procedure arises which is not covered by this Section or the Conciliation Rules or any rules agreed by the parties, the Commission shall decide the question.

Article 34

(1) It shall be the duty of the Commission to clarify the issues in dispute between the parties and to endeavour to bring about agreement between them upon mutually acceptable terms. To that end, the Commission may at any stage of the proceedings and from time to time recommend terms of settlement to the parties. The parties shall cooperate in good faith with the Commission in order to enable the Commission to carry out its functions, and shall give their most serious consideration to its recommendations.

(2) If the parties reach agreement, the Commission shall draw up a report noting the issues in dispute and recording that the parties have reached agreement. If, at any stage of

the proceedings, it appears to the Commission that there is no likelihood of agreement between the parties, it shall close the proceedings and shall draw up a report noting the submission of the dispute and recording the failure of the parties to reach agreement. If one party fails to appear or participate in the proceedings, the Commission shall close the proceedings and shall draw up a report noting that party's failure to appear or participate.

Article 35

Except as the parties to the dispute shall otherwise agree, neither party to a conciliation proceeding shall be entitled in any other proceeding, whether before arbitrators or in a court of law or otherwise, to invoke or rely on any views expressed or statements or admissions or offers of settlement made by the other party in the conciliation proceedings, or the report or any recommendations made by the Commission.

CHAPTER IV
Arbitration

Section 1
Request for Arbitration

Article 36

(1) Any Contracting State or any national of a Contracting State wishing to institute arbitration proceedings shall address a request to that effect in writing to the Secretary-General who shall send a copy of the request to the other party.

(2) The request shall contain information concerning the issues in dispute, the identity of the parties and their consent to arbitration in accordance with the rules of procedure for the institution of conciliation and arbitration proceedings.

(3) The Secretary-General shall register the request unless he finds, on the basis of the information contained in the request, that the dispute is manifestly outside the jurisdiction of the Centre. He shall forthwith notify the parties of registration or refusal to register.

Section 2
Constitution of the Tribunal

Article 37

(1) The Arbitral Tribunal (hereinafter called the Tribunal) shall be constituted as soon as possible after registration of a request pursuant to Article 36.

(2) (a) The Tribunal shall consist of a sole arbitrator or any uneven number of arbitrators appointed as the parties shall agree.

(b) Where the parties do not agree upon the number of arbitrators and the method of their appointment, the Tribunal shall consist of three arbitrators, one arbitrator appointed by each party and the third, who shall be the president of the Tribunal, appointed by agreement of the parties.

Article 38

If the Tribunal shall not have been constituted within 90 days after notice of registration of the request has been dispatched by the Secretary-General in accordance with paragraph

(3) of Article 36, or such other period as the parties may agree, the Chairman shall, at the request of either party and after consulting both parties as far as possible, appoint the arbitrator or arbitrators not yet appointed. Arbitrators appointed by the Chairman pursuant to this Article shall not be nationals of the Contracting State party to the dispute or of the Contracting State whose national is a party to the dispute.

Article 39

The majority of the arbitrators shall be nationals of States other than the Contracting State party to the dispute and the Contracting State whose national is a party to the dispute; provided, however, that the foregoing provisions of this Article shall not apply if the sole arbitrator or each individual member of the Tribunal has been appointed by agreement of the parties.

Article 40

(1) Arbitrators may be appointed from outside the Panel of Arbitrators, except in the case of appointments by the Chairman pursuant to Article 38.
(2) Arbitrators appointed from outside the Panel of Arbitrators shall possess the qualities stated in paragraph (1) of Article 14.

Section 3
Powers and Functions of the Tribunal

Article 41

(1) The Tribunal shall be the judge of its own competence.
(2) Any objection by a party to the dispute that that dispute is not within the jurisdiction of the Centre, or for other reasons is not within the competence of the Tribunal, shall be considered by the Tribunal which shall determine whether to deal with it as a preliminary question or to join it to the merits of the dispute.

Article 42

(1) The Tribunal shall decide a dispute in accordance with such rules of law as may be agreed by the parties. In the absence of such agreement, the Tribunal shall apply the law of the Contracting State party to the dispute (including its rules on the conflict of laws) and such rules of international law as may be applicable.
(2) The Tribunal may not bring in a finding of *non liquet* on the ground of silence or obscurity of the law.
(3) The provisions of paragraphs (1) and (2) shall not prejudice the power of the Tribunal to decide a dispute *ex aequo et bono* if the parties so agree.

Article 43

Except as the parties otherwise agree, the Tribunal may, if it deems it necessary at any stage of the proceedings,

(a) call upon the parties to produce documents or other evidence, and
(b) visit the scene connected with the dispute, and conduct such inquiries there as it may deem appropriate.

Article 44

Any arbitration proceeding shall be conducted in accordance with the provisions of this Section and, except as the parties otherwise agree, in accordance with the Arbitration Rules in effect on the date on which the parties consented to arbitration. If any question of procedure arises which is not covered by this Section or the Arbitration Rules or any rules agreed by the parties, the Tribunal shall decide the question.

Article 45

(1) Failure of a party to appear or to present his case shall not be deemed an admission of the other party's assertions.

(2) If a party fails to appear or to present his case at any stage of the proceedings the other party may request the Tribunal to deal with the questions submitted to it and to render an award. Before rendering an award, the Tribunal shall notify, and grant a period of grace to, the party failing to appear or to present its case, unless it is satisfied that that party does not intend to do so.

Article 46

Except as the parties otherwise agree, the Tribunal shall, if requested by a party, determine any incidental or additional claims or counterclaims arising directly out of the subject-matter of the dispute provided that they are within the scope of the consent of the parties and are otherwise within the jurisdiction of the Centre.

Article 47

Except as the parties otherwise agree, the Tribunal may, if it considers that the circumstances so require, recommend any provisional measures which should be taken to preserve the respective rights of either party.

Section 4
The Award

Article 48

(1) The Tribunal shall decide questions by a majority of the votes of all its members.

(2) The award of the Tribunal shall be in writing and shall be signed by the members of the Tribunal who voted for it.

(3) The award shall deal with every question submitted to the Tribunal, and shall state the reasons upon which it is based.

(4) Any member of the Tribunal may attach his individual opinion to the award, whether he dissents from the majority or not, or a statement of his dissent.

(5) The Centre shall not publish the award without the consent of the parties.

Article 49

(1) The Secretary-General shall promptly dispatch certified copies of the award to the parties. The award shall be deemed to have been rendered on the date on which the certified copies were dispatched.

(2) The Tribunal upon the request of a party made within 45 days after the date on which

the award was rendered may after notice to the other party decide any question which it had omitted to decide in the award, and shall rectify any clerical, arithmetical or similar error in the award. Its decision shall become part of the award and shall be notified to the parties in the same manner as the award. The periods of time provided for under paragraph (2) of Article 51 and paragraph (2) of Article 52 shall run from the date on which the decision was rendered.

Section 5
Interpretation, Revision and Annulment of the Award

Article 50

(1) If any dispute shall arise between the parties as to the meaning or scope of an award, either party may request interpretation of the award by an application in writing addressed to the Secretary-General.

(2) The request shall, if possible, be submitted to the Tribunal which rendered the award. If this shall not be possible, a new Tribunal shall be constituted in accordance with Section 2 of this Chapter. The Tribunal may, if it considers that the circumstances so require, stay enforcement of the award pending its decision.

Article 51

(1) Either party may request revision of the award by an application in writing addressed to the Secretary-General on the ground of discovery of some fact of such a nature as decisively to affect the award, provided that when the award was rendered that fact was unknown to the Tribunal and to the applicant and that the applicant's ignorance of that fact was not due to negligence.

(2) The application shall be made within 90 days after the discovery of such fact and in any event within three years after the date on which the award was rendered.

(3) The request shall, if possible, be submitted to the Tribunal which rendered the award. If this shall not be possible, a new Tribunal shall be constituted in accordance with Section 2 of this Chapter.

(4) The Tribunal may, if it considers that the circumstances so require, stay enforcement of the award pending its decision. If the applicant requests a stay of enforcement of the award in his application, enforcement shall be stayed provisionally until the Tribunal rules on such request.

Article 52

(1) Either party may request annulment of the award by an application in writing addressed to the Secretary-General on one or more of the following grounds:

  (a) that the Tribunal was not properly constituted;
  (b) that the Tribunal has manifestly exceeded its powers;
  (c) that there was corruption on the part of a member of the Tribunal;
  (d) that there has been a serious departure from a fundamental rule of procedure; or
  (e) that the award has failed to state the reasons on which it is based.

(2) The application shall be made within 120 days after the date on which the award was rendered except that when annulment is requested on the ground of corruption such

application shall be made within 120 days after discovery of the corruption and in any event within three years after the date on which the award was rendered.

(3) On receipt of the request the Chairman shall forthwith appoint from the Panel of Arbitrators an *ad hoc* Committee of three persons. None of the members of the Committee shall have been a member of the Tribunal which rendered the award, shall be of the same nationality as any such member, shall be a national of the State party to the dispute or of the State whose national is a party to the dispute, shall have been designated to the Panel of Arbitrators by either of those States, or shall have acted as a conciliator in the same dispute. The Committee shall have the authority to annul the award or any part thereof on any of the grounds set forth in paragraph (1).

(4) The provisions of Articles 41–45, 48, 49, 53 and 54, and of Chapters VI and VII shall apply *mutatis mutandis* to proceedings before the Committee.

(5) The Committee may, if it considers that the circumstances so require, stay enforcement of the award pending its decision. If the applicant requests a stay of enforcement of the award in his application, enforcement shall be stayed provisionally until the Committee rules on such request.

(6) If the award is annulled the dispute shall, at the request of either party, be submitted to a new Tribunal constituted in accordance with Section 2 of this Chapter.

Section 6
Recognition and Enforcement of the Award

Article 53

(1) The award shall be binding on the parties and shall not be subject to any appeal or to any other remedy except those provided for in this Convention. Each party shall abide by and comply with the terms of the award except to the extent that enforcement shall have been stayed pursuant to the relevant provisions of this Convention.

(2) For the purposes of this Section, 'award' shall include any decision interpreting, revising or annulling such award pursuant to Articles 50, 51 or 52.

Article 54

(1) Each Contracting State shall recognize an award rendered pursuant to this Convention as binding and enforce the pecuniary obligations imposed by that award within its territories as if it were a final judgment of a court in that State. A Contracting State with a federal constitution may enforce such an award in or through its federal courts and may provide that such courts shall treat the award as if it were a final judgment of the courts of a constituent state.

(2) A party seeking recognition or enforcement in the territories of a Contracting State shall furnish to a competent court or other authority which such State shall have designated for this purpose a copy of the award certified by the Secretary-General. Each Contracting State shall notify the Secretary-General of the designation of the competent court or other authority for this purpose and of any subsequent change in such designation.

(3) Execution of the award shall be governed by the laws concerning the execution of judgments in force in the State in whose territories such execution is sought.

Article 55

Nothing in Article 54 shall be construed as derogating from the law in force in any Contracting State relating to immunity of that State or of any foreign State from execution.

CHAPTER V
Replacement and Disqualification of Conciliators and Arbitrators

Article 56

(1) After a Commission or a Tribunal has been constituted and proceedings have begun, its composition shall remain unchanged; provided, however, that if a conciliator or an arbitrator should die, become incapacitated, or resign, the resulting vacancy shall be filled in accordance with the provisions of Section 2 of Chapter III or Section 2 of Chapter IV.
(2) A member of a Commission or Tribunal shall continue to serve in that capacity notwithstanding that he shall have ceased to be a member of the Panel.
(3) If a conciliator or arbitrator appointed by a party shall have resigned without the consent of the Commission or Tribunal of which he was a member, the Chairman shall appoint a person from the appropriate Panel to fill the resulting vacancy.

Article 57

A party may propose to a Commission or Tribunal the disqualification of any of its members on account of any fact indicating a manifest lack of the qualities required by paragraph (1) of Article 14. A party to arbitration proceedings may, in addition, propose the disqualification of an arbitrator on the ground that he was ineligible for appointment to the Tribunal under Section 2 of Chapter IV.

Article 58

The decision on any proposal to disqualify a conciliator or arbitrator shall be taken by the other members of the Commission or Tribunal as the case may be, provided that where those members are equally divided, or in the case of a proposal to disqualify a sole conciliator or arbitrator, or a majority of the conciliators or arbitrators, the Chairman shall take that decision. If it is decided that the proposal is well-founded the conciliator or arbitrator to whom the decision relates shall be replaced in accordance with the provisions of Section 2 of Chapter III or Section 2 of Chapter IV.

CHAPTER VI
Cost of Proceedings

Article 59

The charges payable by the parties for the use of the facilities of the Centre shall be determined by the Secretary-General in accordance with the regulations adopted by the Administrative Council.

Article 60

(1) Each Commission and each Tribunal shall determine the fees and expenses of its members within limits established from time to time by the Administrative Council and after consultation with the Secretary-General.

(2) Nothing in paragraph (1) of this Article shall preclude the parties from agreeing in advance with the Commission or Tribunal concerned upon the fees and expenses of its members.

Article 61

(1) In the case of conciliation proceedings the fees and expenses of members of the Commission as well as the charges for the use of the facilities of the Centre, shall be borne equally by the parties. Each party shall bear any other expenses it incurs in connection with the proceedings.

(2) In the case of arbitration proceedings the Tribunal shall, except as the parties otherwise agree, assess the expenses incurred by the parties in connection with the proceedings, and shall decide how and by whom those expenses, the fees and expenses of the members of the Tribunal and the charges for the use of the facilities of the Centre shall be paid. Such decision shall form part of the award.

CHAPTER VII
Place of Proceedings

Article 62

Conciliation and arbitration proceedings shall be held at the seat of the Centre except as hereinafter provided.

Article 63

Conciliation and arbitration proceedings may be held, if the parties so agree,

(a) at the seat of the Permanent Court of Arbitration or of any other appropriate institution, whether private or public, with which the Centre may make arrangements for that purpose; or

(b) at any other place approved by the Commission or Tribunal after consultation with the Secretary-General.

CHAPTER VIII
Disputes Between Contracting States

Article 64

Any dispute arising between Contracting States concerning the interpretation or application of this Convention which is not settled by negotiation shall be referred to the International Court of Justice by the application of any party to such dispute, unless the States concerned agree to another method of settlement.

CHAPTER IX
Amendment

Article 65

Any Contracting State may propose amendment of this Convention. The text of a proposed amendment shall be communicated to the Secretary-General not less than 90 days prior to the meeting of the Administrative Council at which such amendment is to be considered and shall forthwith be transmitted by him to all the members of the Administrative Council.

Article 66

(1) If the Administrative Council shall so decide by a majority of two-thirds of its members, the proposed amendment shall be circulated to all Contracting States for ratification, acceptance or approval. Each amendment shall enter into force 30 days after dispatch by the depositary of this Convention of a notification to Contracting States that all Contracting States have ratified, accepted or approved the amendment.

(2) No amendment shall affect the rights and obligations under this Convention of any Contracting State or of any of its constituent subdivisions or agencies, or of any national of such State arising out of consent to the jurisdiction of the Centre given before the date of entry into force of the amendment.

CHAPTER X
Final Provisions

Article 67

This Convention shall be open for signature on behalf of States members of the Bank. It shall also be open for signature on behalf of any other State which is a party to the Statute of the International Court of Justice and which the Administrative Council, by a vote of two-thirds of its members, shall have invited to sign the Convention.

Article 68

(1) This Convention shall be subject to ratification, acceptance or approval by the signatory States in accordance with their respective constitutional procedures.

(2) This Convention shall enter into force 30 days after the date of deposit of the twentieth instrument of ratification, acceptance or approval. It shall enter into force for each State which subsequently deposits its instrument of ratification, acceptance or approval 30 days after the date of such deposit.

Article 69

Each Contracting State shall take such legislative or other measures as may be necessary for making the provisions of this Convention effective in its territories.

Article 70

This Convention shall apply to all territories for whose international relations a Contracting State is responsible, except those which are excluded by such State by written notice to the depositary of this Convention either at the time of ratification, acceptance or approval or subsequently.

Article 71

Any Contracting State may denounce this Convention by written notice to the depositary of this Convention. The denunciation shall take effect six months after receipt of such notice.

Article 72

Notice by a Contracting State pursuant to Articles 70 or 71 shall not affect the rights or obligations under this Convention of that State or of any of its constituent subdivisions or agencies or of any national of that State arising out of consent to the jurisdiction of the Centre given by one of them before such notice was received by the depositary.

Article 73

Instruments of ratification, acceptance or approval of this Convention and of amendments thereto shall be deposited with the Bank which shall act as the depositary of this Convention. The depositary shall transmit certified copies of this Convention to States members of the Bank and to any other State invited to sign the Convention.

Article 74

The depositary shall register this Convention with the Secretariat of the United Nations in accordance with Article 102 of the Charter of the United Nations and the Regulations thereunder adopted by the General Assembly.

Article 75

The depositary shall notify all signatory States of the following:

(a) signatures in accordance with Article 67;
(b) deposits of instruments of ratification, acceptance and approval in accordance with Article 73;
(c) the date on which this Convention enters into force in accordance with Article 68;
(d) exclusions from territorial application pursuant to Article 70;
(e) the date on which any amendment of this Convention enters into force in accordance with Article 66; and
(f) denunciations in accordance with Article 71.

DONE at Washington, in the English, French and Spanish languages, all three texts being equally authentic, in a single copy which shall remain deposited in the archives of the International Bank for Reconstruction and Development, which has indicated by its signature below its agreement to fulfil the functions with which it is charged under this Convention.

APPENDIX 4. UNCITRAL ARBITRATION RULES

GENERAL ASSEMBLY RESOLUTION 31/98

UNCITRAL ARBITRATION RULES

Section I. Introductory Rules

Scope of application (article 1) and model Arbitration clause
Notice, calculation of periods of time (article 2)
Notice of arbitration (article 3)
Representation and assistance (article 4)

Section II. Composition of the Arbitral Tribunal

Number of arbitrators (article 5)
Appointment of arbitrators (articles 6 to 8)
Challenge of arbitrators (articles 9 to 12)
Replacement of an arbitrator (article 13)
Repetition of hearings in the event of the replacement of an arbitrator (article 14)

Section III. Arbitral Proceedings

General provisions (article 15)
Place of arbitration (article 16)
Language (article 17)
Statement of claim (article 18)
Statement of defence (article 19)
Amendments to the claim or defence (article 20)
Pleas as to the jurisdiction of the arbitral tribunal (article 21)
Further written statements (article 22)
Periods of time (article 23)
Evidence and hearings (articles 24 and 25)
Interim measures of protection (article 26)
Experts (article 27)
Default (article 28)
Closure of hearings (article 29)
Waiver of rules (article 30)

Section IV. The Award

Decisions (article 31)
Form and effect of the award (article 32)
Applicable law, *amiable compositeur* (article 33)
Settlement or other grounds for termination (article 34)

319

Interpretation of the award (article 35)
Correction of the award (article 36)
Additional award (article 37)
Costs (articles 38 to 40)
Deposit of costs (article 41)

RESOLUTION 31/98 ADOPTED BY THE GENERAL ASSEMBLY ON 15 DECEMBER 1976

31/98. Arbitration Rules of the United Nations Commission on International Trade Law

The General Assembly,

Recognizing the value of arbitration as a method of settling disputes arising in the context of international commercial relations,

Being convinced that the establishment of rules for *ad hoc* arbitration that are acceptable in countries with different legal, social and economic systems would significantly contribute to the development of harmonious international economic relations,

Bearing in mind that the Arbitration Rules of the United Nations Commission on International Trade Law have been prepared after extensive consultation with arbitral institutions and centres of international commercial arbitration,

Noting that the Arbitration Rules were adopted by the United Nations Commission on International Trade Law at its ninth session after due deliberation,

1. *Recommends* the use of the Arbitration Rules of the United Nations Commission on International Trade Law in the settlement of disputes arising in the context of international commercial relations, particularly by reference to the Arbitration Rules in commercial contracts;

2. *Requests* the Secretary-General to arrange for the widest possible distribution of the Arbitration Rules.

UNCITRAL ARBITRATION RULES

Section I. Introductory Rules

SCOPE OF APPLICATION

Article 1

1. Where the parties to a contract have agreed in writing* that disputes in relation to that contract shall be referred to arbitration under the UNCITRAL Arbitration Rules, then such disputes shall be settled in accordance with these Rules subject to such modification as the parties may agree in writing.

---

* MODEL ARBITRATION CLAUSE.
Any dispute, controversy or claim arising out of or relating to this contract, or the breach, termination or invalidity thereof, shall be settled by arbitration in accordance with the UNCITRAL Arbitration Rules as at present in force.
Note—Parties may wish to consider adding:

(a) The appointing authority shall be . . . (name of institution or person);
(b) The number of arbitrators shall be . . . (one or three);
(c) The place of arbitration shall be . . . (town or country);
(d) The language(s) to be used in the arbitral proceedings shall be . . .

2. These Rules shall govern the arbitration except that where any of these Rules is in conflict with a provision of the law applicable to the arbitration from which the parties cannot derogate, that provision shall prevail.

NOTICE, CALCULATION OF PERIODS OF TIME

Article 2

1. For the purposes of these Rules, any notice, including a notification, communication or proposal, is deemed to have been received if it is physically delivered to the addressee or if it is delivered at his habitual residence, place of business or mailing address, or, if none of these can be found after making reasonable inquiry, then at the addressee's last known residence or place of business. Notice shall be deemed to have been received on the day it is so delivered.

2. For the purposes of calculating a period of time under these Rules, such period shall begin to run on the day following the day when a notice, notification, communication or proposal is received. If the last day of such period is an official holiday or a non-business day at the residence or place of business of the addressee, the period is extended until the first business day which follows. Official holidays or non-business days occurring during the running of the period of time are included in calculating the period.

NOTICE OF ARBITRATION

Article 3

1. The party initiating recourse to arbitration (hereinafter called the 'claimant') shall give to the other party (hereinafter called the 'respondent') a notice of arbitration.

2. Arbitral proceedings shall be deemed to commence on the date on which the notice of arbitration is received by the respondent.

3. The notice of arbitration shall include the following:
   (a) A demand that the dispute be referred to arbitration;
   (b) The names and addresses of the parties;
   (c) A reference to the arbitration clause or the separate arbitration agreement that is invoked;
   (d) A reference to the contract out of or in relation to which the dispute arises;
   (e) The general nature of the claim and an indication of the amount involved, if any;
   (f) The relief or remedy sought;
   (g) A proposal as to the number of arbitrators (i.e. one or three), if the parties have not previously agreed thereon.

4. The notice of arbitration may also include:

   (a) The proposals for the appointments of a sole arbitrator and an appointing authority referred to in article 6, paragraph 1;
   (b) The notification of the appointment of an arbitrator referred to in article 7;
   (c) The statement of claim referred to in article 18.

REPRESENTATION AND ASSISTANCE

Article 4

The parties may be represented or assisted by persons of their choice. The names and addresses of such persons must be communicated in writing to the other party; such communication must specify whether the appointment is being made for purposes of representation or assistance.

Section II. Composition of the Arbitral Tribunal

NUMBER OF ARBITRATORS

Article 5

If the parties have not previously agreed on the number of arbitrators (i.e. one or three), and if within 15 days after the receipt by the respondent of the notice of arbitration the parties have not agreed that there shall be only one arbitrator, three arbitrators shall be appointed.

APPOINTMENT OF ARBITRATORS (ARTICLES 6 TO 8)

Article 6

1. If a sole arbitrator is to be appointed, either party may propose to the other:

(a) The names of one or more persons, one of whom would serve as the sole arbitrator; and

(b) If no appointing authority has been agreed upon by the parties, the name or names of one or more institutions or persons, one of whom would serve as appointing authority.

2. If within 30 days after receipt by a party of a proposal made in accordance with paragraph 1 the parties have not reached agreement on the choice of a sole arbitrator, the sole arbitrator shall be appointed by the appointing authority agreed upon by the parties. If no appointing authority has been agreed upon by the parties, or if the appointing authority agreed upon refuses to act or fails to appoint the arbitrator within 60 days of the receipt of a party's request therefor, either party may request the Secretary-General of the Permanent Court of Arbitration at The Hague to designate an appointing authority.

3. The appointing authority shall, at the request of one of the parties, appoint the sole arbitrator as promptly as possible. In making the appointment the appointing authority shall use the following list-procedure, unless both parties agree that the list-procedure should not be used or unless the appointing authority determines in its discretion that the use of the list-procedure is not appropriate for the case:

(a) At the request of one of the parties the appointing authority shall communicate to both parties an identical list containing at least three names;

(b) Within 15 days after the receipt of his list, each party may return the list to the appointing authority after having deleted the name or names to which he objects and numbered the remaining names on the list in the order of his preference;

(c) After the expiration of the above period of time the appointing authority shall appoint the sole arbitrator from among the names approved on the lists returned to it and in accordance with the order of preference indicated by the parties;

(d) If for any reason the appointment cannot be made according to this procedure, the appointing authority may exercise its discretion in appointing the sole arbitrator.

4. In making the appointment, the appointing authority shall have regard to such considerations as are likely to secure the appointment of an independent and impartial arbi-

trator and shall take into account as well the advisability of appointing an arbitrator of a nationality other than the nationalities of the parties.

Article 7

1. If three arbitrators are to be appointed, each party shall appoint one arbitrator. The two arbitrators thus appointed shall choose the third arbitrator who will act as the presiding arbitrator of the tribunal.

2. If within 30 days after the receipt of a party's notification of the appointment of an arbitrator the other party has not notified the first party of the arbitrator he has appointed:

(a) The first party may request the appointing authority previously designated by the parties to appoint the second arbitrator; or

(b) If no such authority has been previously designated by the parties, or if the appointing authority previously designated refuses to act or fails to appoint the arbitrator within 30 days after receipt of a party's request therefor, the first party may request the Secretary-General of the Permanent Court of Arbitration at The Hague to designate the appointing authority. The first party may then request the appointing authority so designated to appoint the second arbitrator. In either case, the appointing authority may exercise its discretion in appointing the arbitrator.

3. If within 30 days after the appointment of the second arbitrator the two arbitrators have not agreed on the choice of the presiding arbitrator, the presiding arbitrator shall be appointed by an appointing authority in the same way as a sole arbitrator would be appointed under article 6.

Article 8

1. When an appointing authority is requested to appoint an arbitrator pursuant to article 6 or article 7, the party which makes the request shall send to the appointing authority a copy of the notice of arbitration, a copy of the contract out of or in relation to which the dispute has arisen and a copy of the arbitration agreement if it is not contained in the contract. The appointing authority may require from either party such information as it deems necessary to fulfil its function.

2. Where the names of one or more persons are proposed for appointment as arbitrators, their full names, addresses and nationalities shall be indicated, together with a description of their qualifications.

CHALLENGE OF ARBITRATORS (ARTICLES 9 TO 12)

Article 9

A prospective arbitrator shall disclose to those who approach him in connexion with his possible appointment any circumstances likely to give rise to justifiable doubts as to his impartiality or independence. An arbitrator, once appointed or chosen, shall disclose such circumstances to the parties unless they have already been informed by him of these circumstances.

Article 10

1. Any arbitrator may be challenged if circumstances exist that give rise to justifiable doubts as to the arbitrator's impartiality or independence.

2. A party may challenge the arbitrator appointed by him only for reasons of which he becomes aware after the appointment has been made.

Article 11
1. A party who intends to challenge an arbitrator shall send notice of his challenge within 15 days after the appointment of the challenged arbitrator has been notified to the challenging party or within 15 days after the circumstances mentioned in articles 9 and 10 became known to that party.
2. The challenge shall be notified to the other party, to the arbitrator who is challenged and to the other members of the arbitral tribunal. The notification shall be in writing and shall state the reasons for the challenge.
3. When an arbitrator has been challenged by one party, the other party may agree to the challenge. The arbitrator may also, after the challenge, withdraw from his office. In neither case does this imply acceptance of the validity of the grounds for the challenge. In both cases the procedure provided in article 6 or 7 shall be used in full for the appointment of the substitute arbitrator, even if during the process of appointing the challenged arbitrator a party had failed to exercise his right to appoint or to participate in the appointment.

Article 12
1. If the other party does not agree to the challenge and the challenged arbitrator does not withdraw, the decision on the challenge will be made:

(a) When the initial appointment was made by an appointing authority, by that authority;
(b) When the initial appointment was not made by an appointing authority, but an appointing authority has been previously designated, by that authority;
(c) In all other cases, by the appointing authority to be designated in accordance with the procedure for designating an appointing authority as provided for in article 6.

2. If the appointing authority sustains the challenge, a substitute arbitrator shall be appointed or chosen pursuant to the procedure applicable to the appointment or choice of an arbitrator as provided in articles 6 to 9 except that, when this procedure would call for the designation of an appointing authority, the appointment of the arbitrator shall be made by the appointing authority which decided on the challenge.

REPLACEMENT OF AN ARBITRATOR

Article 13
1. In the event of the death or resignation of an arbitrator during the course of the arbitral proceedings, a substitute arbitrator shall be appointed or chosen pursuant to the procedure provided for in articles 6 to 9 that was applicable to the appointment or choice of the arbitrator being replaced.
2. In the event that an arbitrator fails to act or in the event of the *de jure* or *de facto* impossibility of his performing his functions, the procedure in respect of the challenge and replacement of an arbitrator as provided in the preceding articles shall apply.

REPETITION OF HEARINGS IN THE EVENT OF THE REPLACEMENT OF AN ARBITRATOR

Article 14

If under articles 11 to 13 the sole or presiding arbitrator is replaced, any hearings held previously shall be repeated; if any other arbitrator is replaced, such prior hearings may be repeated at the discretion of the arbitral tribunal.

Section III. Arbitral Proceedings

GENERAL PROVISIONS

Article 15

1. Subject to these Rules, the arbitral tribunal may conduct the arbitration in such manner as it considers appropriate, provided that the parties are treated with equality and that at any stage of the proceedings each party is given a full opportunity of presenting his case.

2. If either party so requests at any stage of the proceedings, the arbitral tribunal shall hold hearings for the presentation of evidence by witnesses, including expert witnesses, or for oral argument. In the absence of such a request, the arbitral tribunal shall decide whether to hold such hearings or whether the proceedings shall be conducted on the basis of documents and other materials.

3. All documents or information supplied to the arbitral tribunal by one party shall at the same time be communicated by that party to the other party.

PLACE OF ARBITRATION

Article 16

1. Unless the parties have agreed upon the place where the arbitration is to be held, such place shall be determined by the arbitral tribunal, having regard to the circumstances of the arbitration.

2. The arbitral tribunal may determine the locale of the arbitration within the country agreed upon by the parties. It may hear witnesses and hold meetings for consultation among its members at any place it deems appropriate, having regard to the circumstances of the arbitration.

3. The arbitral tribunal may meet at any place it deems appropriate for the inspection of goods, other property or documents. The parties shall be given sufficient notice to enable them to be present at such inspection.

4. The award shall be made at the place of arbitration.

LANGUAGE

Article 17

1. Subject to an agreement by the parties, the arbitral tribunal shall, promptly after its appointment, determine the language or languages to be used in the proceedings. This determination shall apply to the statement of claim, the statement of defence, and any further written statements and, if oral hearings take place, to the language or languages to be used in such hearings.

2. The arbitral tribunal may order that any documents annexed to the statement of claim or statement of defence, and any supplementary documents or exhibits submitted in the

course of the proceedings, delivered in their original language, shall be accompanied by a translation into the language or languages agreed upon by the parties or determined by the arbitral tribunal.

STATEMENT OF CLAIM

Article 18

1. Unless the statement of claim was contained in the notice of arbitration, within a period of time to be determined by the arbitral tribunal, the claimant shall communicate his statement of claim in writing to the respondent and to each of the arbitrators. A copy of the contract, and of the arbitration agreement if not contained in the contract, shall be annexed thereto.

2. The statement of claim shall include the following particulars

    (a) The names and addresses of the parties;
    (b) A statement of the facts supporting the claim;
    (c) The points at issue;
    (d) The relief or remedy sought.

The claimant may annex to his statement of claim all documents he deems relevant or may add a reference to the documents or other evidence he will submit.

STATEMENT OF DEFENCE

Article 19

1. Within a period of time to be determined by the arbitral tribunal, the respondent shall communicate his statement of defence in writing to the claimant and to each of the arbitrators.

2. The statement of defence shall reply to the particulars (b), (c) and (d) of the statement of claim (article 18, para. 2). The respondent may annex to his statement the documents on which he relies for his defence or may add a reference to the documents or other evidence he will submit.

3. In his statement of defence, or at a later stage in the arbitral proceedings if the arbitral tribunal decides that the delay was justified under the circumstances the respondent may make a counter-claim arising out of the same contract or rely on a claim arising out of the same contract for the purpose of a set-off.

4. The provisions of article 18, paragraph 2, shall apply to a counter-claim and a claim relied on for the purpose of a set-off.

AMENDMENTS TO THE CLAIM OR DEFENCE

Article 20

During the course of the arbitral proceedings either party may amend or supplement his claim or defence unless the arbitral tribunal considers it inappropriate to allow such amendment having regard to the delay in making it or prejudice to the other party or any other circumstances. However, a claim may not be amended in such a manner that the amended claim falls outside the scope of the arbitration clause or separate arbitration agreement.

PLEAS AS TO THE JURISDICTION OF THE ARBITRAL TRIBUNAL

Article 21

1. The arbitral tribunal shall have the power to rule on objections that it has no jurisdiction, including any objections with respect to the existence or validity of the arbitration clause or of the separate arbitration agreement.

2. The arbitral tribunal shall have the power to determine the existence or the validity of the contract of which an arbitration clause forms a part. For the purposes of article 21, an arbitration clause which forms part of a contract and which provides for arbitration under these Rules shall be treated as an agreement independent of the other terms of the contract. A decision by the arbitral tribunal that the contract is null and void shall not entail *ipso jure* the invalidity of the arbitration clause.

3. A plea that the arbitral tribunal does not have jurisdiction shall be raised not later than in the statement of defence or, with respect to a counter-claim, in the reply to the counter-claim.

4. In general, the arbitral tribunal should rule on a plea concerning its jurisdiction as a preliminary question. However, the arbitral tribunal may proceed with the arbitration and rule on such a plea in their final award.

FURTHER WRITTEN STATEMENTS

Article 22

The arbitral tribunal shall decide which further written statements, in addition to the statement of claim and the statement of defence, shall be required from the parties or may be presented by them and shall fix the periods of time for communicating such statements.

PERIODS OF TIME

Article 23

The periods of time fixed by the arbitral tribunal for the communication of written statements (including the statement of claim and statement of defence) should not exceed 45 days. However, the arbitral tribunal may extend the time-limits if it concludes that an extension is justified.

EVIDENCE AND HEARINGS (ARTICLES 24 AND 25)

Article 24

1. Each party shall have the burden of proving the facts relied on to support his claim or defence.

2. The arbitral tribunal may, if it considers it appropriate, require a party to deliver to the tribunal and to the other party, within such a period of time as the arbitral tribunal shall decide, a summary of the documents and other evidence which that party intends to present in support of the facts in issue set out in his statement of claim or statement of defence.

3. At any time during the arbitral proceedings the arbitral tribunal may require the parties to produce documents, exhibits or other evidence within such a period of time as the tribunal shall determine.

Article 25

1. In the event of an oral hearing, the arbitral tribunal shall give the parties adequate advance notice of the date, time and place thereof.

2. If witnesses are to be heard, at least 15 days before the hearing each party shall communicate to the arbitral tribunal and to the other party the names and addresses of the witnesses he intends to present, the subject upon and the languages in which such witnesses will give their testimony.

3. The arbitral tribunal shall make arrangements for the translation of oral statements made at a hearing and for a record of the hearing if either is deemed necessary by the tribunal under the circumstances of the case, or if the parties have agreed thereto and have communicated such agreement to the tribunal at least 15 days before the hearing.

4. Hearings shall be held in camera unless the parties agree otherwise. The arbitral tribunal may require the retirement of any witness or witnesses during the testimony of other witnesses. The arbitral tribunal is free to determine the manner in which witnesses are examined.

5. Evidence of witnesses may also be presented in the form of written statements signed by them.

6. The arbitral tribunal shall determine the admissibility, relevance, materiality and weight of the evidence offered.

INTERIM MEASURES OF PROTECTION

Article 26

1. At the request of either party, the arbitral tribunal may take any interim measures it deems necessary in respect of the subject-matter of the dispute, including measures for the conservation of the goods forming the subject-matter in dispute, such as ordering their deposit with a third person or the sale of perishable goods.

2. Such interim measures may be established in the form of an interim award. The arbitral tribunal shall be entitled to require security for the costs of such measures.

3. A request for interim measures addressed by any party to a judicial authority shall not be deemed incompatible with the agreement to arbitrate, or as a waiver of that agreement.

EXPERTS

Article 27

1. The arbitral tribunal may appoint one or more experts to report to it, in writing, on specific issues to be determined by the tribunal. A copy of the expert's terms of reference, established by the arbitral tribunal, shall be communicated to the parties.

2. The parties shall give the expert any relevant information or produce for his inspection any relevant documents or goods that he may require of them. Any dispute between a party and such expert as to the relevance of the required information or production shall be referred to the arbitral tribunal for decision.

3. Upon receipt of the expert's report, the arbitral tribunal shall communicate a copy of the report to the parties who shall be given the opportunity to express, in writing, their opinion on the report. A party shall be entitled to examine any document on which the expert has relied in his report.

4. At the request of either party the expert, after delivery of the report, may be heard at a

hearing where the parties shall have the opportunity to be present and to interrogate the expert. At this hearing either party may present expert witnesses in order to testify on the points at issue. The provisions of article 25 shall be applicable to such proceedings.

DEFAULT

Article 28

1. If, within the period of time fixed by the arbitral tribunal, the claimant has failed to communicate his claim without showing sufficient cause for such failure, the arbitral tribunal shall issue an order for the termination of the arbitral proceedings. If, within the period of time fixed by the arbitral tribunal, the respondent has failed to communicate his statement of defence without showing sufficient cause for such failure, the arbitral tribunal shall order that the proceedings continue.

2. If one of the parties, duly notified under these Rules, fails to appear at a hearing, without showing sufficient cause for such failure, the arbitral tribunal may proceed with the arbitration.

3. If one of the parties, duly invited to produce documentary evidence, fails to do so within the established period of time, without showing sufficient cause for such failure, the arbitral tribunal may make the award on the evidence before it.

CLOSURE OF HEARINGS

Article 29

1. The arbitral tribunal may inquire of the parties if they have any further proof to offer or witnesses to be heard or submissions to make and, if there are none, it may declare the hearings closed.

2. The arbitral tribunal may, if it considers it necessary owing to exceptional circumstances, decide, on its own motion or upon application of a party, to reopen the hearings at any time before the award is made.

WAIVER OF RULES

Article 30

A party who knows that any provision of, or requirement under, these Rules has not been complied with and yet proceeds with the arbitration without promptly stating his objection to such non-compliance, shall be deemed to have waived his right to object.

Section IV. The Award

DECISIONS

Article 31

1. When there are three arbitrators, any award or other decision of the arbitral tribunal shall be made by a majority of the arbitrators.

2. In the case of questions of procedure, when there is no majority or when the arbitral tribunal so authorizes, the presiding arbitrator may decide on his own, subject to revision, if any, by the arbitral tribunal.

FORM AND EFFECT OF THE AWARD

Article 32

1. In addition to making a final award, the arbitral tribunal shall be entitled to make interim, interlocutory, or partial awards.

2. The award shall be made in writing and shall be final and binding on the parties. The parties undertake to carry out the award without delay.

3. The arbitral tribunal shall state the reasons upon which the award is based, unless the parties have agreed that no reasons are to be given.

4. An award shall be signed by the arbitrators and it shall contain the date on which and the place where the award was made. Where there are three arbitrators and one of them fails to sign, the award shall state the reason for the absence of the signature.

5. The award may be made public only with the consent of both parties.

6. Copies of the award signed by the arbitrators shall be communicated to the parties by the arbitral tribunal.

7. If the arbitration law of the country where the award is made requires that the award be filed or registered by the arbitral tribunal, the tribunal shall comply with this requirement within the period of time required by law.

APPLICABLE LAW, *AMIABLE COMPOSITEUR*

Article 33

1. The arbitral tribunal shall apply the law designated by the parties as applicable to the substance of the dispute. Failing such designation by the parties, the arbitral tribunal shall apply the law determined by the conflict of laws rules which it considers applicable.

2. The arbitral tribunal shall decide as *amiable compositeur* or *ex aequo et bono* only if the parties have expressly authorized the arbitral tribunal to do so and if the law applicable to the arbitral procedure permits such arbitration.

3. In all cases, the arbitral tribunal shall decide in accordance with the terms of the contract and shall take into account the usages of the trade applicable to the transaction.

SETTLEMENT OR OTHER GROUNDS FOR TERMINATION

Article 34

1. If, before the award is made, the parties agree on a settlement of the dispute, the arbitral tribunal shall either issue an order for the termination of the arbitral proceedings or, if requested by both parties and accepted by the tribunal, record the settlement in the form of an arbitral award on agreed terms. The arbitral tribunal is not obliged to give reasons for such an award.

2. If, before the award is made, the continuation of the arbitral proceedings becomes unnecessary or impossible for any reason not mentioned in paragraph 1, the arbitral tribunal shall inform the parties of its intention to issue an order for the termination of the proceedings. The arbitral tribunal shall have the power to issue such an order unless a party raises justifiable grounds for objection.

3. Copies of the order for termination of the arbitral proceedings or of the arbitral award on agreed terms, signed by the arbitrators, shall be communicated by the arbitral tribunal to the parties. Where an arbitral award on agreed terms is made, the provisions of article 32, paragraphs 2 and 4 to 7, shall apply.

INTERPRETATION OF THE AWARD

Article 35

1. Within 30 days after the receipt of the award, either party, with notice to the other party, may request that the arbitral tribunal give an interpretation of the award.

2. The interpretation shall be given in writing within 45 days after the receipt of the request. The interpretation shall form part of the award and the provisions of article 32, paragraphs 2 to 7, shall apply.

CORRECTION OF THE AWARD

Article 36

1. Within 30 days after the receipt of the award, either party, with notice to the other party, may request the arbitral tribunal to correct in the award any errors in computation, any clerical or typographical errors, or any errors of similar nature. The arbitral tribunal may within 30 days after the communication of the award make such corrections on its own initiative.

2. Such corrections shall be in writing, and the provisions of article 32, paragraphs 2 to 7, shall apply.

ADDITIONAL AWARD

Article 37

1. Within 30 days after the receipt of the award, either party, with notice to the other party, may request the arbitral tribunal to make an additional award as to claims presented in the arbitral proceedings but omitted from the award.

2. If the arbitral tribunal considers the request for an additional award to be justified and considers that the omission can be rectified without any further hearings or evidence, it shall complete its award within 60 days after the receipt of the request.

3. When an additional award is made, the provisions of article 32, paragraphs 2 to 7, shall apply.

COSTS (ARTICLES 38 TO 40)

Article 38

The arbitral tribunal shall fix the costs of arbitration in its award. The term 'costs' includes only:

(a) The fees of the arbitral tribunal to be stated separately as to each arbitrator and to be fixed by the tribunal itself in accordance with article 39;

(b) The travel and other expenses incurred by the arbitrators;

(c) The costs of expert advice and of other assistance required by the arbitral tribunal;

(d) The travel and other expenses of witnesses to the extent such expenses are approved by the arbitral tribunal;

(e) The costs for legal representation and assistance of the successful party if such costs were claimed during the arbitral proceedings, and only to the extent that the arbitral tribunal determines that the amount of such costs is reasonable;

(f) Any fees and expenses of the appointing authority as well as the expenses of the Secretary-General of the Permanent Court of Arbitration at The Hague.

Article 39

1. The fees of the arbitral tribunal shall be reasonable in amount, taking into account the amount in dispute, the complexity of the subject-matter, the time spent by the arbitrators and any other relevant circumstances of the case.

2. If an appointing authority has been agreed upon by the parties or designated by the Secretary-General of the Permanent Court of Arbitration at The Hague, and if that authority has issued a schedule of fees for arbitrators in international cases which it administers, the arbitral tribunal in fixing its fees shall take that schedule of fees into account to the extent that it considers appropriate in the circumstances of the case.

3. If such appointing authority has not issued a schedule of fees for arbitrators in international cases, any party may at any time request the appointing authority to furnish a statement setting forth the basis for establishing fees which is customarily followed in international cases in which the authority appoints arbitrators. If the appointing authority consents to provide such a statement, the arbitral tribunal in fixing its fees shall take such information into account to the extent that it considers appropriate in the circumstances of the case.

4. In cases referred to in paragraphs 2 and 3, when a party so requests and the appointing authority consents to perform the function, the arbitral tribunal shall fix its fees only after consultation with the appointing authority which may make any comment it deems appropriate to the arbitral tribunal concerning the fees.

Article 40

1. Except as provided in paragraph 2, the costs of arbitration shall in principle be borne by the unsuccessful party. However, the arbitral tribunal may apportion each of such costs between the parties if it determines that apportionment is reasonable, taking into account the circumstances of the case.

2. With respect to the costs of legal representation and assistance referred to in article 38, paragraph (e), the arbitral tribunal, taking into account the circumstances of the case, shall be free to determine which party shall bear such costs or may apportion such costs between the parties if it determines that apportionment is reasonable.

3. When the arbitral tribunal issues an order for the termination of the arbitral proceedings or makes an award on agreed terms, it shall fix the costs of arbitration referred to in article 38 and article 39, paragraph 1, in the text of that order or award.

4. No additional fees may be charged by an arbitral tribunal for interpretation or correction or completion of its award under articles 35 to 37.

DEPOSIT OF COSTS

Article 41

1. The arbitral tribunal, on its establishment, may request each party to deposit an equal amount as an advance for the costs referred to in article 38, paragraphs (a), (b) and (c).

2. During the course of the arbitral proceedings the arbitral tribunal may request supplementary deposits from the parties.

3. If an appointing authority has been agreed upon by the parties or designated by the Secretary-General of the Permanent Court of Arbitration at The Hague, and when a party so requests and the appointing authority consents to perform the function, the arbitral tribunal shall fix the amounts of any deposits or supplementary deposits only after

consultation with the appointing authority which may make any comments to the arbitral tribunal which it deems appropriate concerning the amount of such deposits and supplementary deposits.

4. If the required deposits are not paid in full within 30 days after the receipt of the request, the arbitral tribunal shall so inform the parties in order that one or another of them may make the required payment. If such payment is not made, the arbitral tribunal may order the suspension or termination of the arbitral proceedings.

5. After the award has been made, the arbitral tribunal shall render an accounting to the parties of the deposits received and return any unexpended balance to the parties.

APPENDIX 5. UNCITRAL MODEL LAW

UNITED NATIONS COMMISSION ON INTERNATIONAL TRADE LAW

UNCITRAL MODEL LAW ON INTERNATIONAL COMMERCIAL ARBITRATION

(United Nations document A/40/17, Annex I)(As adopted by the United Nations Commission on International Trade Law on 21 June 1985)

CHAPTER I. GENERAL PROVISIONS

Article 1. **Scope of Application**[*]

(1) This Law applies to international commercial[**] arbitration, subject to any agreement in force between this State and any other State or States.

(2) The provisions of this Law, except articles 8, 9, 35 and 36, apply only if the place of arbitration is in the territory of this State.

(3) An arbitration is international if:

(a) the parties to an arbitration agreement have, at the time of the conclusion of that agreement, their places of business in different States; or
(b) one of the following places is situated outside the State in which the parties have their places of business:

(i) the place of arbitration if determined in, or pursuant to, the arbitration agreement;
(ii) any place where a substantial part of the obligations of the commercial relationship is to be performed or the place with which the subject-matter of the dispute is most closely connected; or

(c) the parties have expressly agreed that the subject-matter of the \arbitration agreement relates to more than one country.

(4) For the purposes of paragraph (3) of this article:

(a) if a party has more than one place of business, the place of business is that which has the closest relationship to the arbitration agreement;

---

* Article headings are for reference purposes only and are not to be used for purposes of interpretation.

** The term 'commercial' should be given a wide interpretation so as to cover matters arising from all relationships of a commercial nature, whether contractual or not. Relationships of a commercial nature include, but are not limited to, the following transactions: any trade transaction for the supply or exchange of goods or services; distribution agreement; commercial representation or agency; factoring; leasing; construction of works; consulting; engineering; licensing; investment; financing; banking; insurance; exploitation agreement or concession; joint venture and other forms of industrial or business co-operation; carriage of goods or passengers by air, sea, rail or road.

(b) if a party does not have a place of business, reference is to be made to his habitual residence.

(5) This Law shall not affect any other law of this State by virtue of which certain disputes may not be submitted to arbitration or may be submitted to arbitration only according to provisions other than those of this Law.

Article 2. **Definitions and Rules of Interpretation**

For the purposes of this Law:

(a) 'arbitration' means any arbitration whether or not administered by a permanent arbitral institution;
(b) 'arbitral tribunal' means a sole arbitrator or a panel of arbitrators;
(c) 'court' means a body or organ of the judicial system of a State;
(d) where a provision of this Law, except article 28, leaves the parties free to determine a certain issue, such freedom includes the right of the parties to authorize a third party, including an institution, to make that determination;
(e) where a provision of this Law refers to the fact that the parties have agreed or that they may agree or in any other way refers to an agreement of the parties, such agreement includes any arbitration rules referred to in that agreement;
(f) where a provision of this Law, other than in articles 25(a) and 32(2)(a), refers to a claim, it also applies to a counter-claim, and where it refers to a defence, it also applies to a defence to such counter-claim.

Article 3. **Receipt of Written Communications**

(1) Unless otherwise agreed by the parties:

(a) any written communication is deemed to have been received if it is delivered to the addressee personally or if it is delivered at his place of business, habitual residence or mailing address; if none of these can be found after making a reasonable inquiry, a written communication is deemed to have been received if it is sent to the addressee's last-known place of business, habitual residence or mailing address by registered letter or any other means which provides a record of the attempt to deliver it;
(b) the communication is deemed to have been received on the day it is so delivered.

(2) The provisions of this article do not apply to communications in court proceedings.

Article 4. **Waiver of Right to Object**

A party who knows that any provision of this Law from which the parties may derogate or any requirement under the arbitration agreement has not been complied with and yet proceeds with the arbitration without stating his objection to such non-compliance without undue delay or, if a time-limit is provided therefor, within such period of time, shall be deemed to have waived his right to object.

Article 5. **Extent of Court Intervention**

In matters governed by this Law, no court shall intervene except where so provided in this Law.

Article 6. **Court or other Authority for Certain Functions of Arbitration Assistance and Supervision**

The functions referred to in articles 11(3), 11(4), 13(3), 14, 16(3) and 34(2) shall be performed by . . . [Each State enacting this model law specifies the court, courts or, where referred to therein, other authority competent to perform these functions.]

CHAPTER II. ARBITRATION AGREEMENT

Article 7. **Definition and Form of Arbitration Agreement**

(1) 'Arbitration agreement' is an agreement by the parties to submit to arbitration all or certain disputes which have arisen or which may arise between them in respect of a defined legal relationship, whether contractual or not. An arbitration agreement may be in the form of an arbitration clause in a contract or in the form of a separate agreement.

(2) The arbitration agreement shall be in writing. An agreement is in writing if it is contained in a document signed by the parties or in an exchange of letters, telex, telegrams or other means of telecommunication which provide a record of the agreement, or in an exchange of statements of claim and defence in which the existence of an agreement is alleged by one party and not denied by another. The reference in a contract to a document containing an arbitration clause constitutes an arbitration agreement provided that the contract is in writing and the reference is such as to make that clause part of the contract.

Article 8. **Arbitration Agreement and Substantive Claim before Court**

(1) A court before which an action is brought in a matter which is the subject of an arbitration agreement shall, if a party so requests not later than when submitting his first statement on the substance of the dispute, refer the parties to arbitration unless it finds that the agreement is null and void, inoperative or incapable of being performed.

(2) Where an action referred to in paragraph (1) of this article has been brought, arbitral proceedings may nevertheless be commenced or continued, and an award may be made, while the issue is pending before the court.

Article 9. **Arbitration Agreement and Interim Measures by Court**

It is not incompatible with an arbitration agreement for a party to request, before or during arbitral proceedings, from a court an interim measure of protection and for a court to grant such measure.

CHAPTER III. COMPOSITION OF ARBITRAL TRIBUNAL

Article 10. **Number of Arbitrators**

(1) The parties are free to determine the number of arbitrators.
(2) Failing such determination, the number of arbitrators shall be three.

Article 11. **Appointment of Arbitrators**

(1) No person shall be precluded by reason of his nationality from acting as an arbitrator, unless otherwise agreed by the parties.
(2) The parties are free to agree on a procedure of appointing the arbitrator or arbitrators, subject to the provisions of paragraphs (4) and (5) of this article.

(3) Failing such agreement,

(a) in an arbitration with three arbitrators, each party shall appoint one arbitrator, and the two arbitrators thus appointed shall appoint the third arbitrator; if a party fails to appoint the arbitrator within thirty days of receipt of a request to do so from the other party, or if the two arbitrators fail to agree on the third arbitrator within thirty days of their appointment, the appointment shall be made, upon request of a party, by the court or other authority specified in article 6;

(b) in an arbitration with a sole arbitrator, if the parties are unable to agree on the arbitrator, he shall be appointed, upon request of a party, by the court or other authority specified in article 6.

(4) Where, under an appointment procedure agreed upon by the parties,

(a) a party fails to act as required under such procedure, or

(b) the parties, or two arbitrators, are unable to reach an agreement expected of them under such procedure, or

(c) a third party, including an institution, fails to perform any function entrusted to it under such procedure, any party may request the court or other authority specified in article 6 to take the necessary measure, unless the agreement on the appointment procedure provides other means for securing the appointment.

(5) A decision on a matter entrusted by paragraph (3) or (4) of this article to the court or other authority specified in article 6 shall be subject to no appeal. The court or other authority, in appointing an arbitrator, shall have due regard to any qualifications required of the arbitrator by the agreement of the parties and to such considerations as are likely to secure the appointment of an independent and impartial arbitrator and, in the case of a sole or third arbitrator, shall take into account as well the advisability of appointing an arbitrator of a nationality other than those of the parties.

Article 12. Grounds for Challenge

(1) When a person is approached in connection with his possible appointment as an arbitrator, he shall disclose any circumstances likely to give rise to justifiable doubts as to his impartiality or independence. An arbitrator, from the time of his appointment and throughout the arbitral proceedings, shall without delay disclose any such circumstances to the parties unless they have already been informed of them by him.

(2) An arbitrator may be challenged only if circumstances exist that give rise to justifiable doubts as to his impartiality or independence, or if he does not possess qualifications agreed to by the parties. A party may challenge an arbitrator appointed by him, or in whose appointment he has participated, only for reasons of which he becomes aware after the appointment has been made.

Article 13. Challenge Procedure

(1) The parties are free to agree on a procedure for challenging an arbitrator, subject to the provisions of paragraph (3) of this article.

(2) Failing such agreement, a party who intends to challenge an arbitrator shall, within fifteen days after becoming aware of the constitution of the arbitral tribunal or after

becoming aware of any circumstance referred to in article 12(2), send a written statement of the reasons for the challenge to the arbitral tribunal. Unless the challenged arbitrator withdraws from his office or the other party agrees to the challenge, the arbitral tribunal shall decide on the challenge.

(3) If a challenge under any procedure agreed upon by the parties or under the procedure of paragraph (2) of this article is not successful, the challenging party may request, within thirty days after having received notice of the decision rejecting the challenge, the court or other authority specified in article 6 to decide on the challenge, which decision shall be subject to no appeal; while such a request is pending, the arbitral tribunal, including the challenged arbitrator, may continue the arbitral proceedings and make an award.

Article 14. **Failure or Impossibility to Act**

(1) If an arbitrator becomes *de jure* or *de facto* unable to perform his functions or for other reasons fails to act without undue delay, his mandate terminates if he withdraws from his office or if the parties agree on the termination. Otherwise, if a controversy remains concerning any of these grounds, any party may request the court or other authority specified in article 6 to decide on the termination of the mandate, which decision shall be subject to no appeal.

(2) If, under this article or article 13(2), an arbitrator withdraws from his office or a party agrees to the termination of the mandate of an arbitrator, this does not imply acceptance of the validity of any ground referred to in this article or article 12(2).

Article 15. **Appointment of Substitute Arbitrator**

Where the mandate of an arbitrator terminates under article 13 or 14 or because of his withdrawal from office for any other reason or because of the revocation of his mandate by agreement of the parties or in any other case of termination of his mandate, a substitute arbitrator shall be appointed according to the rules that were applicable to the appointment of the arbitrator being replaced.

CHAPTER IV. JURISDICTION OF ARBITRAL TRIBUNAL

Article 16. **Competence of Arbitral Tribunal to Rule on its Jurisdiction**

(1) The arbitral tribunal may rule on its own jurisdiction, including any objections with respect to the existence or validity of the arbitration agreement. For that purpose, an arbitration clause which forms part of a contract shall be treated as an agreement independent of the other terms of the contract. A decision by the arbitral tribunal that the contract is null and void shall not entail *ipso jure* the invalidity of the arbitration clause.

(2) A plea that the arbitral tribunal does not have jurisdiction shall be raised not later than the submission of the statement of defence. A party is not precluded from raising such a plea by the fact that he has appointed, or participated in the appointment of, an arbitrator. A plea that the arbitral tribunal is exceeding the scope of its authority shall be raised as soon as the matter alleged to be beyond the scope of its authority is raised during the arbitral proceedings. The arbitral tribunal may, in either case, admit a later plea if it considers the delay justified.

(3) The arbitral tribunal may rule on a plea referred to in paragraph (2) of this article either as a preliminary question or in an award on the merits. If the arbitral tribunal rules

as a preliminary question that it has jurisdiction, any party may request, within thirty days after having received notice of that ruling, the court specified in article 6 to decide the matter, which decision shall be subject to no appeal; while such a request is pending, the arbitral tribunal may continue the arbitral proceedings and make an award.

Article 17. **Power of Arbitral Tribunal to Order Interim Measures**

Unless otherwise agreed by the parties, the arbitral tribunal may, at the request of a party, order any party to take such interim measure of protection as the arbitral tribunal may consider necessary in respect of the subject-matter of the dispute. The arbitral tribunal may require any party to provide appropriate security in connection with such measure.

CHAPTER V. CONDUCT OF ARBITRAL PROCEEDINGS

Article 18. **Equal Treatment of Parties**

The parties shall be treated with equality and each party shall be given a full opportunity of presenting his case.

Article 19. **Determination of Rules of Procedure**

(1) Subject to the provisions of this Law, the parties are free to agree on the procedure to be followed by the arbitral tribunal in conducting the proceedings.

(2) Failing such agreement, the arbitral tribunal may, subject to the provisions of this Law, conduct the arbitration in such manner as it considers appropriate. The power conferred upon the arbitral tribunal includes the power to determine the admissibility, relevance, materiality and weight of any evidence.

Article 20. **Place of Arbitration**

(1) The parties are free to agree on the place of arbitration. Failing such agreement, the place of arbitration shall be determined by the arbitral tribunal having regard to the circumstances of the case, including the convenience of the parties.

(2) Notwithstanding the provisions of paragraph (1) of this article, the arbitral tribunal may, unless otherwise agreed by the parties, meet at any place it considers appropriate for consultation among its members, for hearing witnesses, experts or the parties, or for inspection of goods, other property or documents.

Article 21. **Commencement of Arbitral Proceedings**

Unless otherwise agreed by the parties, the arbitral proceedings in respect of a particular dispute commence on the date on which a request for that dispute to be referred to arbitration is received by the respondent.

Article 22. **Language**

(1) The parties are free to agree on the language or languages to be used in the arbitral proceedings. Failing such agreement, the arbitral tribunal shall determine the language or languages to be used in the proceedings. This agreement or determination, unless otherwise specified therein, shall apply to any written statement by a party, any hearing and any award, decision or other communication by the arbitral tribunal.

(2) The arbitral tribunal may order that any documentary evidence shall be accompanied by a translation into the language or languages agreed upon by the parties or determined by the arbitral tribunal.

Article 23. Statements of Claim and Defence

(1) Within the period of time agreed by the parties or determined by the arbitral tribunal, the claimant shall state the facts supporting his claim, the points at issue and the relief or remedy sought, and the respondent shall state his defence in respect of these particulars, unless the parties have otherwise agreed as to the required elements of such statements. The parties may submit with their statements all documents they consider to be relevant or may add a reference to the documents or other evidence they will submit.

(2) Unless otherwise agreed by the parties, either party may amend or supplement his claim or defence during the course of the arbitral proceedings, unless the arbitral tribunal considers it inappropriate to allow such amendment having regard to the delay in making it.

Article 24. Hearings and Written Proceedings

(1) Subject to any contrary agreement by the parties, the arbitral tribunal shall decide whether to hold oral hearings for the presentation of evidence or for oral argument, or whether the proceedings shall be conducted on the basis of documents and other materials. However, unless the parties have agreed that no hearings shall be held, the arbitral tribunal shall hold such hearings at an appropriate stage of the proceedings, if so requested by a party.

(2) The parties shall be given sufficient advance notice of any hearing and of any meeting of the arbitral tribunal for the purposes of inspection of goods, other property or documents.

(3) All statements, documents or other information supplied to the arbitral tribunal by one party shall be communicated to the other party. Also any expert report or evidentiary document on which the arbitral tribunal may rely in making its decision shall be communicated to the parties.

Article 25. Default of a Party

Unless otherwise agreed by the parties, if, without showing sufficient cause,

(a) the claimant fails to communicate his statement of claim in accordance with article 23(1), the arbitral tribunal shall terminate the proceedings;

(b) the respondent fails to communicate his statement of defence in accordance with article 23(1), the arbitral tribunal shall continue the proceedings without treating such failure in itself as an admission of the claimant's allegations;

(c) any party fails to appear at a hearing or to produce documentary evidence, the arbitral tribunal may continue the proceedings and make the award on the evidence before it.

Article 26. Expert Appointed by Arbitral Tribunal

(1) Unless otherwise agreed by the parties, the arbitral tribunal

(a) may appoint one or more experts to report to it on specific issues to be determined by the arbitral tribunal;

(b) may require a party to give the expert any relevant information or to produce, or to provide access to, any relevant documents, goods or other property for his inspection.

(2) Unless otherwise agreed by the parties, if a party so requests or if the arbitral tribunal considers it necessary, the expert shall, after delivery of his written or oral report, participate in a hearing where the parties have the opportunity to put questions to him and to present expert witnesses in order to testify on the points at issue.

Article 27. Court Assistance in Taking Evidence

The arbitral tribunal or a party with the approval of the arbitral tribunal may request from a competent court of this State assistance in taking evidence. The court may execute the request within its competence and according to its rules on taking evidence.

CHAPTER VI. MAKING OF AWARD AND TERMINATION OF PROCEEDINGS

Article 28. Rules Applicable to Substance of Dispute

(1) The arbitral tribunal shall decide the dispute in accordance with such rules of law as are chosen by the parties as applicable to the substance of the dispute. Any designation of the law or legal system of a given State shall be construed, unless otherwise expressed, as directly referring to the substantive law of that State and not to its conflict of laws rules.

(2) Failing any designation by the parties, the arbitral tribunal shall apply the law determined by the conflict of laws rules which it considers applicable.

(3) The arbitral tribunal shall decide *ex aequo et bono* or as *amiable compositeur* only if the parties have expressly authorized it to do so.

(4) In all cases, the arbitral tribunal shall decide in accordance with the terms of the contract and shall take into account the usages of the trade applicable to the transaction.

Article 29. Decision Making by Panel of Arbitrators

In arbitral proceedings with more than one arbitrator, any decision of the arbitral tribunal shall be made, unless otherwise agreed by the parties, by a majority of all its members. However, questions of procedure may be decided by a presiding arbitrator, if so authorized by the parties or all members of the arbitral tribunal.

Article 30. Settlement

(1) If, during arbitral proceedings, the parties settle the dispute, the arbitral tribunal shall terminate the proceedings and, if requested by the parties and not objected to by the arbitral tribunal, record the settlement in the form of an arbitral award on agreed terms.

(2) An award on agreed terms shall be made in accordance with the provisions of article 31 and shall state that it is an award. Such an award has the same status and effect as any other award on the merits of the case.

Article 31. Form and Contents of Award

(1) The award shall be made in writing and shall be signed by the arbitrator or arbitrators. In arbitral proceedings with more than one arbitrator, the signatures of the majority

of all members of the arbitral tribunal shall suffice, provided that the reason for any omitted signature is stated.

(2) The award shall state the reasons upon which it is based, unless the parties have agreed that no reasons are to be given or the award is an award on agreed terms under article 30.

(3) The award shall state its date and the place of arbitration as determined in accordance with article 20(1). The award shall be deemed to have been made at that place.

(4) After the award is made, a copy signed by the arbitrators in accordance with paragraph (1) of this article shall be delivered to each party.

Article 32. **Termination of Proceedings**

(1) The arbitral proceedings are terminated by the final award or by an order of the arbitral tribunal in accordance with paragraph (2) of this article.

(2) The arbitral tribunal shall issue an order for the termination of the arbitral proceedings when:

(a) the claimant withdraws his claim, unless the respondent objects thereto and the arbitral tribunal recognizes a legitimate interest on his part in obtaining a final settlement of the dispute;

(b) the parties agree on the termination of the proceedings;

(c) the arbitral tribunal finds that the continuation of the proceedings has for any other reason become unnecessary or impossible.

(3) The mandate of the arbitral tribunal terminates with the termination of the arbitral proceedings, subject to the provisions of articles 33 and 34(4).

Article 33. **Correction and Interpretation of Award; Additional Award**

(1) Within thirty days of receipt of the award, unless another period of time has been agreed upon by the parties:

(a) a party, with notice to the other party, may request the arbitral tribunal to correct in the award any errors in computation, any clerical or typographical errors or any errors of similar nature;

(b) if so agreed by the parties, a party, with notice to the other party, may request the arbitral tribunal to give an interpretation of a specific point or part of the award.

If the arbitral tribunal considers the request to be justified, it shall make the correction or give the interpretation within thirty days of receipt of the request. The interpretation shall form part of the award.

(2) The arbitral tribunal may correct any error of the type referred to in paragraph (1)(a) of this article on its own initiative within thirty days of the date of the award.

(3) Unless otherwise agreed by the parties, a party, with notice to the other party, may request, within thirty days of receipt of the award, the arbitral tribunal to make an additional award as to claims presented in the arbitral proceedings but omitted from the award. If the arbitral tribunal considers the request to be justified, it shall make the additional award within sixty days.

(4) The arbitral tribunal may extend, if necessary, the period of time within which it

shall make a correction, interpretation or an additional award under paragraph (1) or (3) of this article.

(5) The provisions of article 31 shall apply to a correction or interpretation of the award or to an additional award.

CHAPTER VII. RECOURSE AGAINST AWARD

Article 34. **Application for Setting Aside as Exclusive Recourse Against Arbitral Award**

(1) Recourse to a court against an arbitral award may be made only by an application for setting aside in accordance with paragraphs (2) and (3) of this article.

(2) An arbitral award may be set aside by the court specified in article 6 only if:

(a) the party making the application furnishes proof that:

(i) a party to the arbitration agreement referred to in article 7 was under some incapacity; or the said agreement is not valid under the law to which the parties have subjected it or, failing any indication thereon, under the law of this State; or

(ii) the party making the application was not given proper notice of the appointment of an arbitrator or of the arbitral proceedings or was otherwise unable to present his case; or

(iii) the award deals with a dispute not contemplated by or not falling within the terms of the submission to arbitration, or contains decisions on matters beyond the scope of the submission to arbitration, provided that, if the decisions on matters submitted to arbitration can be separated from those not so submitted, only that part of the award which contains decisions on matters not submitted to arbitration may be set aside; or

(iv) the composition of the arbitral tribunal or the arbitral procedure was not in accordance with the agreement of the parties, unless such agreement was in conflict with a provision of this Law from which the parties cannot derogate, or, failing such agreement, was not in accordance with this Law; or

(b) the court finds that:

(i) the subject-matter of the dispute is not capable of settlement by arbitration under the law of this State; or

(ii) the award is in conflict with the public policy of this State.

(3) An application for setting aside may not be made after three months have elapsed from the date on which the party making that application had received the award or, if a request had been made under article 33, from the date on which that request had been disposed of by the arbitral tribunal.

(4) The court, when asked to set aside an award, may, where appropriate and so requested by a party, suspend the setting aside proceedings for a period of time determined by it in order to give the arbitral tribunal an opportunity to resume the arbitral proceedings or to take such other action as in the arbitral tribunal's opinion will eliminate the grounds for setting aside.

CHAPTER VIII. RECOGNITION AND ENFORCEMENT OF AWARDS

Article 35. **Recognition and Enforcement**

(1) An arbitral award, irrespective of the country in which it was made, shall be recognized as binding and, upon application in writing to the competent court, shall be enforced subject to the provisions of this article and of article 36.

(2) The party relying on an award or applying for its enforcement shall supply the duly authenticated original award or a duly certified copy thereof, and the original arbitration agreement referred to in article 7 or a duly certified copy thereof. If the award or agreement is not made in an official language of this State, the party shall supply a duly certified translation thereof into such language.[***]

Article 36. **Grounds for Refusing Recognition or Enforcement**

(1) Recognition or enforcement of an arbitral award, irrespective of the country in which it was made, may be refused only:

(a) at the request of the party against whom it is invoked, if that party furnishes to the competent court where recognition or enforcement is sought proof that:

(i) a party to the arbitration agreement referred to in article 7 was under some incapacity; or the said agreement is not valid under the law to which the parties have subjected it or, failing any indication thereon, under the law of the country where the award was made; or

(ii) the party against whom the award is invoked was not given proper notice of the appointment of an arbitrator or of the arbitral proceedings or was otherwise unable to present his case; or

(iii) the award deals with a dispute not contemplated by or not falling within the terms of the submission to arbitration, or it contains decisions on matters beyond the scope of the submission to arbitration, provided that, if the decisions on matters submitted to arbitration can be separated from those not so submitted, that part of the award which contains decisions on matters submitted to arbitration may be recognized and enforced; or

(iv) the composition of the arbitral tribunal or the arbitral procedure was not in accordance with the agreement of the parties or, failing such agreement, was not in accordance with the law of the country where the arbitration took place; or

(v) the award has not yet become binding on the parties or has been set aside or suspended by a court of the country in which, or under the law of which, that award was made; or

(b) if the court finds that:

(i) the subject-matter of the dispute is not capable of settlement by arbitration under the law of this State; or

---

*** The conditions set forth in this paragraph are intended to set maximum standards. It would, thus, not be contrary to the harmonization to be achieved by the model law if a State retained even less onerous conditions.

(ii) the recognition or enforcement of the award would be contrary to the public policy of this State.

(2) If an application for setting aside or suspension of an award has been made to a court referred to in paragraph (1)(a)(v) of this article, the court where recognition or enforcement is sought may, if it considers it proper, adjourn its decision and may also, on the application of the party claiming recognition or enforcement of the award, order the other party to provide appropriate security.

APPENDIX 6. STATUTE OF THE INTERNATIONAL COURT OF JUSTICE

STATUTE OF THE INTERNATIONAL COURT OF JUSTICE

Article 1

The International Court of Justice established by the Charter of the United Nations as the principal judicial organ of the United Nations shall be constituted and shall function in accordance with the provisions of the present Statute.

CHAPTER I
ORGANIZATION OF THE COURT

Article 2

The Court shall be composed of a body of independent judges, elected regardless of their nationality from among persons of high moral character, who possess the qualifications required in their respective countries for appointment to the highest judicial offices, or are jurisconsults of recognized competence in international law.

Article 3

1. The Court shall consist of fifteen members, no two of whom may be nationals of the same state.
2. A person who for the purposes of membership in the Court could be regarded as a national of more than one state shall be deemed to be a national of the one in which he ordinarily exercises civil and political rights.

Article 4

1. The members of the Court shall be elected by the General Assembly and by the Security Council from a list of persons nominated by the national groups in the Permanent Court of Arbitration, in accordance with the following provisions.
2. In the case of Members of the United Nations not represented in the Permanent Court of Arbitration, candidates shall be nominated by national groups appointed for this purpose by their governments under the same conditions as those prescribed for members of the Permanent Court of Arbitration by Article 44 of the Convention of The Hague of 1907 for the Pacific Settlement of International Disputes.
3. The conditions under which a state which is a party to the present Statute but is not a Member of the United Nations may participate in electing the members of the Court shall, in the absence of a special agreement, be laid down by the General Assembly upon recommendation of the Security Council.

Article 5

1. At least three months before the date of the election, the Secretary-General of the United Nations shall address a written request to the members of the Permanent Court of Arbitration belonging to the states which are parties to the present Statute, and to the members of the national groups appointed under Article 4, paragraph 2, inviting them to undertake, within a given time, by national groups, the nomination of persons in a position to accept the duties of a member of the Court.

2. No group may nominate more than four persons, not more than two of whom shall be of their own nationality. In no case may the number of candidates nominated by a group be more than double the number of seats to be filled.

Article 6

Before making these nominations, each national group is recommended to consult its highest court of justice, its legal faculties and schools of law, and its national academies and national sections of international academies devoted to the study of law.

Article 7

1. The Secretary-General shall prepare a list in alphabetical order of all the persons thus nominated. Save as provided in Article 12, paragraph 2, these shall be the only persons eligible.

2. The Secretary-General shall submit this list to the General Assembly and to the Security Council.

Article 8

The General Assembly and the Security Council shall proceed independently of one another to elect the members of the Court.

Article 9

At every election, the electors shall bear in mind not only that the persons to be elected should individually possess the qualifications required, but also that in the body as a whole the representation of the main forms of civilization and of the principal legal systems of the world should be assured.

Article 10

1. Those candidates who obtain an absolute majority of votes in the General Assembly and in the Security Council shall be considered as elected.

2. Any vote of the Security Council, whether for the election of judges or for the appointment of members of the conference envisaged in Article 12, shall be taken without any distinction between permanent and non-permanent members of the Security Council.

3. In the event of more than one national of the same state obtaining an absolute majority of the votes both of the General Assembly and of the Security Council, the eldest of these only shall be considered as elected.

Article 11

If, after the first meeting held for the purpose of the election, one or more seats remain to be filled, a second and, if necessary, a third meeting shall take place.

Article 12

1. If, after the third meeting, one or more seats still remain unfilled, a joint conference consisting of six members, three appointed by the General Assembly and three by the Security Council, may be formed at any time at the request of either the General Assembly or the Security Council, for the purpose of choosing by the vote of an absolute majority one name for each seat still vacant, to submit to the General Assembly and the Security Council for their respective acceptance.

2. If the joint conference is unanimously agreed upon any person who fulfils the required conditions, he may be included in its list, even though he was not included in the list of nominations referred to in Article 7.

3. If the joint conference is satisfied that it will not be successful in procuring an election, those members of the Court who have already been elected shall, within a period to be fixed by the Security Council, proceed to fill the vacant seats by selection from among those candidates who have obtained votes either in the General Assembly or in the Security Council.

4. In the event of an equality of votes among the judges, the eldest judge shall have a casting vote.

Article 13

1. The members of the Court shall be elected for nine years and may be re-elected; provided, however, that of the judges elected at the first election, the terms of five judges shall expire at the end of three years and the terms of five more judges shall expire at the end of six years.

2. The judges whose terms are to expire at the end of the above-mentioned initial periods of three and six years shall be chosen by lot to be drawn by the Secretary-General immediately after the first election has been completed.

3. The members of the Court shall continue to discharge their duties until their places have been filled. Though replaced, they shall finish any cases which they may have begun.

4. In the case of the resignation of a member of the Court, the resignation shall be addressed to the President of the Court for transmission to the Secretary-General. This last notification makes the place vacant.

Article 14

Vacancies shall be filled by the same method as that laid down for the first election subject to the following provision: the Secretary-General shall, within one month of the occurrence of the vacancy, proceed to issue the invitations provided for in Article 5, and the date of the election shall be fixed by the Security Council.

Article 15

A member of the Court elected to replace a member whose term of office has not expired shall hold office for the remainder of his predecessor's term.

Article 16

1. No member of the Court may exercise any political or administrative function, or engage in any other occupation of a professional nature.
2. Any doubt on this point shall be settled by the decision of the Court.

Article 17

1. No member of the Court may act as agent, counsel, or advocate in any case.
2. No member may participate in the decision of any case in which he has previously taken part as agent, counsel, or advocate for one of the parties, or as a member of a national or international court, or of a commission of enquiry, or in any other capacity.
3. Any doubt on this point shall be settled by the decision of the Court.

Article 18

1. No member of the Court can be dismissed unless, in the unanimous opinion of the other members, he has ceased to fulfil the required conditions.
2. Formal notification thereof shall be made to the Secretary-General by the Registrar.
3. This notification makes the place vacant.

Article 19

The members of the Court, when engaged on the business of the Court, shall enjoy diplomatic privileges and immunities.

Article 20

Every member of the Court shall, before taking up his duties, make a solemn declaration in open court that he will exercise his powers impartially and conscientiously.

Article 21

1. The Court shall elect its President and Vice-President for three years; they may be re-elected.
2. The Court shall appoint its Registrar and may provide for the appointment of such other officers as may be necessary.

Article 22

1. The seat of the Court shall be established at The Hague. This, however, shall not prevent the Court from sitting and exercising its functions elsewhere whenever the Court considers it desirable.
2. The President and the Registrar shall reside at the seat of the Court.

Article 23

1. The Court shall remain permanently in session, except during the judicial vacations, the dates and duration of which shall be fixed by the Court.
2. Members of the Court are entitled to periodic leave, the dates and duration of which shall be fixed by the Court, having in mind the distance between The Hague and the home of each judge.
3. Members of the Court shall be bound, unless they are on leave or prevented from

attending by illness or other serious reasons duly explained to the President, to hold themselves permanently at the disposal of the Court.

Article 24

1. If, for some special reason, a member of the Court considers that he should not take part in the decision of a particular case, he shall so inform the President.
2. If the President considers that for some special reason one of the members of the Court should not sit in a particular case, he shall give him notice accordingly.
3. If in any such case the member of the Court and the President disagree, the matter shall be settled by the decision of the Court.

Article 25

1. The full Court shall sit except when it is expressly provided otherwise in the present Statute.
2. Subject to the condition that the number of judges available to constitute the Court is not thereby reduced below eleven, the Rules of the Court may provide for allowing one or more judges, according to circumstances and in rotation, to be dispensed from sitting.
3. A quorum of nine judges shall suffice to constitute the Court.

Article 26

1. The Court may from time to time form one or more chambers, composed of three or more judges as the Court may determine, for dealing with particular categories of cases; for example, labour cases and cases relating to transit and communications.
2. The Court may at any time form a chamber for dealing with a particular case. The number of judges to constitute such a chamber shall be determined by the Court with the approval of the parties.
3. Cases shall be heard and determined by the chambers provided for in this Article if the parties so request.

Article 27

A judgment given by any of the chambers provided for in Articles 26 and 29 shall be considered as rendered by the Court.

Article 28

The chambers provided for in Articles 26 and 29 may, with the consent of the parties, sit and exercise their functions elsewhere than at The Hague.

Article 29

With a view to the speedy dispatch of business, the Court shall form annually a chamber composed of five judges which, at the request of the parties, may hear and determine cases by summary procedure. In addition, two judges shall be selected for the purpose of replacing judges who find it impossible to sit.

Article 30

1. The Court shall frame rules for carrying out its functions. In particular, it shall lay down rules of procedure.

2. The Rules of the Court may provide for assessors to sit with the Court or with any of its chambers, without the right to vote.

Article 31

1. Judges of the nationality of each of the parties shall retain their right to sit in the case before the Court.

2. If the Court includes upon the Bench a judge of the nationality of one of the parties, any other party may choose a person to sit as judge. Such person shall be chosen preferably from among those persons who have been nominated as candidates as provided in Articles 4 and 5.

3. If the Court includes upon the Bench no judge of the nationality of the parties, each of these parties may proceed to choose a judge as provided in paragraph 2 of this Article.

4. The provisions of this Article shall apply to the case of Articles 26 and 29. In such cases, the President shall request one or, if necessary, two of the members of the Court forming the chamber to give place to the members of the Court of the nationality of the parties concerned, and, failing such, or if they are unable to be present, to the judges specially chosen by the parties.

5. Should there be several parties in the same interest, they shall, for the purpose of the preceding provisions, be reckoned as one party only. Any doubt upon this point shall be settled by the decision of the Court.

6. Judges chosen as laid down in paragraphs 2, 3, and 4 of this Article shall fulfil the conditions required by Articles 2, 17 (paragraph 2), 20, and 24 of the present Statute. They shall take part in the decision on terms of complete equality with their colleagues.

Article 32

1. Each member of the Court shall receive an annual salary.

2. The President shall receive a special annual allowance.

3. The Vice-President shall receive a special allowance for every day on which he acts as President.

4. The judges chosen under Article 31, other than members of the Court, shall receive compensation for each day on which they exercise their functions.

5. These salaries, allowances, and compensation shall be fixed by the General Assembly. They may not be decreased during the term of office.

6. The salary of the Registrar shall be fixed by the General Assembly on the proposal of the Court.

7. Regulations made by the General Assembly shall fix the conditions under which retirement pensions may be given to members of the Court and to the Registrar, and the conditions under which members of the Court and the Registrar shall have their travelling expenses refunded.

8. The above salaries, allowances, and compensation shall be free of all taxation.

Article 33

The expenses of the Court shall be borne by the United Nations in such a manner as shall be decided by the General Assembly.

CHAPTER II
COMPETENCE OF THE COURT

Article 34

1. Only states may be parties in cases before the Court.
2. The Court, subject to and in conformity with its Rules, may request of public international organizations information relevant to cases before it, and shall receive such information presented by such organizations on their own initiative.
3. Whenever the construction of the constituent instrument of a public international organization or of an international convention adopted thereunder is in question in a case before the Court, the Registrar shall so notify the public international organization concerned and shall communicate to it copies of all the written proceedings.

Article 35

1. The Court shall be open to the states parties to the present Statute.
2. The conditions under which the Court shall be open to other states shall, subject to the special provisions contained in treaties in force, be laid down by the Security Council, but in no case shall such conditions place the parties in a position of inequality before the Court.
3. When a state which is not a Member of the United Nations is a party to a case, the Court shall fix the amount which that party is to contribute towards the expenses of the Court. This provision shall not apply if such state is bearing a share of the expenses of the Court.

Article 36

1. The jurisdiction of the Court comprises all cases which the parties refer to it and all matters specially provided for in the Charter of the United Nations or in treaties and conventions in force.
2. The states parties to the present Statute may at any time declare that they recognize as compulsory *ipso facto* and without special agreement, in relation to any other state accepting the same obligation, the jurisdiction of the Court in all legal disputes concerning:

a. the interpretation of a treaty;
b. any question of international law;
c. the existence of any fact which, if established, would constitute a breach of an international obligation;
d. the nature or extent of the reparation to be made for the breach of an international obligation.

3. The declarations referred to above may be made unconditionally or on condition of reciprocity on the part of several or certain states, or for a certain time.
4. Such declarations shall be deposited with the Secretary-General of the United Nations, who shall transmit copies thereof to the parties to the Statute and to the Registrar of the Court.
5. Declarations made under Article 36 of the Statute of the Permanent Court of International Justice and which are still in force shall be deemed, as between the parties to

the present Statute, to be acceptances of the compulsory jurisdiction of the International Court of Justice for the period which they still have to run and in accordance with their terms.

6. In the event of a dispute as to whether the Court has jurisdiction, the matter shall be settled by the decision of the Court.

Article 37

Whenever a treaty or convention in force provides for reference of a matter to a tribunal to have been instituted by the League of Nations, or to the Permanent Court of International Justice, the matter shall, as between the parties to the present Statute, be referred to the International Court of Justice.

Article 38

1. The Court, whose function is to decide in accordance with international law such disputes as are submitted to it, shall apply:

a. international conventions, whether general or particular, establishing rules expressly recognized by the contesting states;

b. international custom, as evidence of a general practice accepted as law;

c. the general principles of law recognized by civilized nations;

d. subject to the provisions of Article 59, judicial decisions and the teachings of the most highly qualified publicists of the various nations, as subsidiary means for the determination of rules of law.

2. This provision shall not prejudice the power of the Court to decide a case *ex aequo et bono*, if the parties agree thereto.

CHAPTER III
PROCEDURE

Article 39

1. The official languages of the Court shall be French and English. If the parties agree that the case shall be conducted in French, the judgment shall be delivered in French. If the parties agree that the case shall be conducted in English, the judgment shall be delivered in English.

2. In the absence of an agreement as to which language shall be employed, each party may, in the pleadings, use the language which it prefers; the decision of the Court shall be given in French and English. In this case the Court shall at the same time determine which of the two texts shall be considered as authoritative.

3. The Court shall, at the request of any party, authorize a language other than French or English to be used by that party.

Article 40

1. Cases are brought before the Court, as the case may be, either by the notification of the special agreement or by a written application addressed to the Registrar. In either case the subject of the dispute and the parties shall be indicated.

2. The Registrar shall forthwith communicate the application to all concerned.

3. He shall also notify the Members of the United Nations through the Secretary-General, and also any other states entitled to appear before the Court.

Article 41

1. The Court shall have the power to indicate, if it considers that circumstances so require, any provisional measures which ought to be taken to preserve the respective rights of either party.
2. Pending the final decision, notice of the measures suggested shall forthwith be given to the parties and to the Security Council.

Article 42

1. The parties shall be represented by agents.
2. They may have the assistance of counsel or advocates before the Court.
3. The agents, counsel, and advocates of parties before the Court shall enjoy the privileges and immunities necessary to the independent exercise of their duties.

Article 43

1. The procedure shall consist of two parts: written and oral.
2. The written proceedings shall consist of the communication to the Court and to the parties of memorials, counter-memorials and, if necessary, replies; also all papers and documents in support.
3. These communications shall be made through the Registrar, in the order and within the time fixed by the Court.
4. A certified copy of every document produced by one party shall be communicated to the other party.
5. The oral proceedings shall consist of the hearing by the Court of witnesses, experts, agents, counsel, and advocates.

Article 44

1. For the service of all notices upon persons other than the agents, counsel, and advocates, the Court shall apply direct to the government of the state upon whose territory the notice has to be served.
2. The same provision shall apply whenever steps are to be taken to procure evidence on the spot.

Article 45

The hearing shall be under the control of the President or, if he is unable to preside, of the Vice-President; if neither is able to preside, the senior judge present shall preside.

Article 46

The hearing in Court shall be public, unless the Court shall decide otherwise, or unless the parties demand that the public be not admitted.

Article 47

1. Minutes shall be made at each hearing and signed by the Registrar and the President.
2. These minutes alone shall be authentic.

Article 48

The Court shall make orders for the conduct of the case, shall decide the form and time in which each party must conclude its arguments, and make all arrangements connected with the taking of evidence.

Article 49

The Court may, even before the hearing begins, call upon the agents to produce any document or to supply any explanations. Formal note shall be taken of any refusal.

Article 50

The Court may, at any time, entrust any individual, body, bureau, commission, or other organization that it may select, with the task of carrying out an enquiry or giving an expert opinion.

Article 51

During the hearing any relevant questions are to be put to the witnesses and experts under the conditions laid down by the Court in the rules of procedure referred to in Article 30.

Article 52

After the Court has received the proofs and evidence within the time specified for the purpose, it may refuse to accept any further oral or written evidence that one party may desire to present unless the other side consents.

Article 53

1. Whenever one of the parties does not appear before the Court, or fails to defend its case, the other party may call upon the Court to decide in favour of its claim.
2. The Court must, before doing so, satisfy itself, not only that it has jurisdiction in accordance with Articles 36 and 37, but also that the claim is well founded in fact and law.

Article 54

1. When, subject to the control of the Court, the agents, counsel, and advocates have completed their presentation of the case, the President shall declare the hearing closed.
2. The Court shall withdraw to consider the judgment.
3. The deliberations of the Court shall take place in private and remain secret.

Article 55

1. All questions shall be decided by a majority of the judges present.
2. In the event of an equality of votes, the President or the judge who acts in his place shall have a casting vote.

Article 56

1. The judgment shall state the reasons on which it is based.
2. It shall contain the names of the judges who have taken part in the decision.

Article 57

If the judgment does not represent in whole or in part the unanimous opinion of the judges, any judge shall be entitled to deliver a separate opinion.

Article 58

The judgment shall be signed by the President and by the Registrar. It shall be read in open court, due notice having been given to the agents.

Article 59

The decision of the Court has no binding force except between the parties and in respect of that particular case.

Article 60

The judgment is final and without appeal. In the event of dispute as to the meaning or scope of the judgment, the Court shall construe it upon the request of any party.

Article 61

1. An application for revision of a judgment may be made only when it is based upon the discovery of some fact of such a nature as to be a decisive factor, which fact was, when the judgment was given, unknown to the Court and also to the party claiming revision, always provided that such ignorance was not due to negligence.
2. The proceedings for revision shall be opened by a judgment of the Court expressly recording the existence of the new fact, recognizing that it has such a character as to lay the case open to revision, and declaring the application admissible on this ground.
3. The Court may require previous compliance with the terms of the judgment before it admits proceedings in revision.
4. The application for revision must be made at latest within six months of the discovery of the new fact.
5. No application for revision may be made after the lapse of ten years from the date of the judgment.

Article 62

1. Should a state consider that it has an interest of a legal nature which may be affected by the decision in the case, it may submit a request to the Court to be permitted to intervene.
2. It shall be for the Court to decide upon this request.

Article 63

1. Whenever the construction of a convention to which states other than those concerned in the case are parties is in question, the Registrar shall notify all such states forthwith.
2. Every state so notified has the right to intervene in the proceedings; but if it uses this right, the construction given by the judgment will be equally binding upon it.

Article 64

Unless otherwise decided by the Court, each party shall bear its own costs.

CHAPTER IV
ADVISORY OPINIONS

Article 65

1. The Court may give an advisory opinion on any legal question at the request of whatever body may be authorized by or in accordance with the Charter of the United Nations to make such a request.

2. Questions upon which the advisory opinion of the Court is asked shall be laid before the Court by means of a written request containing an exact statement of the question upon which an opinion is required, and accompanied by all documents likely to throw light upon the question.

Article 66

1. The Registrar shall forthwith give notice of the request for an advisory opinion to all states entitled to appear before the Court.

2. The Registrar shall also, by means of a special and direct communication, notify any state entitled to appear before the Court or international organization considered by the Court, or, should it not be sitting, by the President, as likely to be able to furnish information on the question, that the Court will be prepared to receive, within a time limit to be fixed by the President, written statements, or to hear, at a public sitting to be held for the purpose, oral statements relating to the question.

3. Should any such state entitled to appear before the Court have failed to receive the special communication referred to in paragraph 2 of this Article, such state may express a desire to submit a written statement or to be heard; and the Court will decide.

4. States and organizations having presented written or oral statements or both shall be permitted to comment on the statements made by other states or organizations in the form, to the extent, and within the time limits which the Court, or, should it not be sitting, the President, shall decide in each particular case. Accordingly, the Registrar shall in due time communicate any such written statements to states and organizations having submitted similar statements.

Article 67

The Court shall deliver its advisory opinions in open court, notice having been given to the Secretary-General and to the representatives of Members of the United Nations, of other states and of international organizations immediately concerned.

Article 68

In the exercise of its advisory functions the Court shall further be guided by the provisions of the present Statute which apply in contentious cases to the extent to which it recognizes them to be applicable.

CHAPTER V
AMENDMENT

Article 69

Amendments to the present Statute shall be effected by the same procedure as is provided by the Charter of the United Nations for amendments to that Charter, subject however to any provisions which the General Assembly upon recommendation of the Security Council may adopt concerning the participation of states which are parties to the present Statute but are not Members of the United Nations.

Article 70

The Court shall have power to propose such amendments to the present Statute as it may deem necessary, through written communications to the Secretary-General, for consideration in conformity with the provisions of Article 69.

APPENDIX 7. RULES OF THE INTERNATIONAL COURT OF JUSTICE

RULES OF COURT

ADOPTED ON 14 APRIL 1978

[PREAMBLE]

The Court,

Having regard to Chapter XIV of the Charter of the United Nations;

Having regard to the Statute of the Court annexed thereto:

Acting in pursuance of Article 30 of the Statute;

Adopts the following revised Rules of Court, approved on 14 April 1978, which shall come into force on 1 July 1978, and shall as from that date replace the Rules adopted by the Court on 6 May 1946 and amended on 10 May 1972, save in respect of any case submitted to the Court before 1 July 1978, or any phase of such a case, which shall continue to be governed by the Rules in force before that date.

[PART I]

THE COURT

SECTION A. JUDGES AND ASSESSORS

Subsection 1. The Members of the Court

Article 1

1. The Members of the Court are the judges elected in accordance with Articles 2 to 15 of the Statute.

2. For the purposes of a particular case, the Court may also include upon the Bench one or more persons chosen under Article 31 of the Statute to sit as judges *ad hoc*.

3. In the following Rules, the term 'Member of the Court' denotes any elected judge; the term 'judge' denotes any Member of the Court, and any judge *ad hoc*.

Article 2

1. The term of office of Members of the Court elected at a triennial election shall begin to run from the sixth of February[1] in the year in which the vacancies to which they are elected occur.

2. The term of office of a Member of the Court elected to replace a Member whose term of office has not expired shall begin to run from the date of the election.

---

[1] This is the date on which the terms of office of the Members of the Court elected at the first election began in 1946.

Article 3

1. The Members of the Court, in the exercise of their functions, are of equal status, irrespective of age, priority of election or length of service.

2. The Members of the Court shall, except as provided in paragraphs 4 and 5 of this Article, take precedence according to the date on which their terms of office respectively began, as provided for by Article 2 of these Rules.

3. Members of the Court whose terms of office began on the same date shall take precedence in relation to one another according to seniority of age.

4. A Member of the Court who is re-elected to a new term of office which is continuous with his previous term shall retain his precedence.

5. The President and the Vice-President of the Court, while holding these offices, shall take precedence before all other Members of the Court.

6. The Member of the Court who, in accordance with the foregoing paragraphs, takes precedence next after the President and the Vice-President is in these Rules designated the 'senior judge'. If that Member is unable to act, the Member of the Court who is next after him in precedence and able to act is considered as senior judge.

Article 4

1. The declaration to be made by every Member of the Court in accordance with Article 20 of the Statute shall be as follows:

I solemnly declare that I will perform my duties and exercise my powers as judge honourably, faithfully, impartially and conscientiously.

2. This declaration shall be made at the first public sitting at which the Member of the Court is present. Such sitting shall be held as soon as practicable after his term of office begins and, if necessary, a special sitting shall be held for the purpose.

3. A Member of the Court who is re-elected shall make a new declaration only if his new term is not continuous with his previous one.

Article 5

1. A Member of the Court deciding to resign shall communicate his decision to the President, and the resignation shall take effect as provided in Article 13, paragraph 4, of the Statute.

2. If the Member of the Court deciding to resign from the Court is the President, he shall communicate his decision to the Court, and the resignation shall take effect as provided in Article 13, paragraph 4, of the Statute.

Article 6

In any case in which the application of Article 18 of the Statute is under consideration, the Member of the Court concerned shall be so informed by the President or, if the circumstances so require, by the Vice-President, in a written statement which shall include the grounds therefor and any relevant evidence. He shall subsequently, at a private meeting of the Court specially convened for the purpose, be afforded an opportunity of making a statement, of furnishing any information or explanations he wishes to give, and of supplying answers, orally or in writing, to any questions put to him. At a further private meeting, at which the Member of the Court concerned shall not be present, the matter shall be discussed; each Member of the Court shall state his opinion, and if requested a vote shall be taken.

Subsection 2. *Judges* ad hoc

Article 7

1. Judges *ad hoc*, chosen under Article 31 of the Statute for the purposes of particular cases, shall be admitted to sit on the Bench of the Court in the circumstances and according to the procedure indicated in Article 17, paragraph 2, Articles 35, 36, 37, Article 91, paragraph 2, and Article 102, paragraph 3, of these Rules.

2. They shall participate in the case in which they sit on terms of complete equality with the other judges on the Bench.

3. Judges *ad hoc* shall take precedence after the Members of the Court and in order of seniority of age.

Article 8

1. The solemn declaration to be made by every judge *ad hoc* in accordance with Articles 20 and 31, paragraph 6, of the Statute shall be as set out in Article 4, paragraph 1, of these Rules.

2. This declaration shall be made at a public sitting in the case in which the judge *ad hoc* is participating. If the case is being dealt with by a chamber of the Court, the declaration shall be made in the same manner in that chamber.

3. Judges *ad hoc* shall make the declaration in relation to any case in which they are participating, even if they have already done so in a previous case, but shall not make a new declaration for a later phase of the same case.

Subsection 3. *Assessors*

Article 9

1. The Court may, either *proprio motu* or upon a request made not later than the closure of the written proceedings, decide, for the purpose of a contentious case or request for advisory opinion, to appoint assessors to sit with it without the right to vote.

2. When the Court so decides, the President shall take steps to obtain all the information relevant to the choice of the assessors.

3. The assessors shall be appointed by secret ballot and by a majority of the votes of the judges composing the Court for the case.

4. The same powers shall belong to the chambers provided for by Articles 26 and 29 of the Statute and to the presidents thereof, and may be exercised in the same manner.

5. Before entering upon their duties, assessors shall make the following declaration at a public sitting:

> I solemnly declare that I will perform my duties as an assessor honourably, impartially and conscientiously, and that I will faithfully observe all the provisions of the Statute and of the Rules of the Court.

SECTION B. THE PRESIDENCY

Article 10

1. The term of office of the President and that of the Vice-President shall begin to run from the date on which the terms of office of the Members of the Court elected at a triennial election begin in accordance with Article 2 of these Rules.

2. The elections to the presidency and vice-presidency shall be held on that date or shortly thereafter. The former President, if still a Member of the Court, shall continue to exercise his functions until the election to the presidency has taken place.

Article 11

1. If, on the date of the election to the presidency, the former President is still a Member of the Court, he shall conduct the election. If he has ceased to be a Member of the Court, or is unable to act, the election shall be conducted by the Member of the Court exercising the functions of the presidency by virtue of Article 13, paragraph 1, of these Rules.

2. The election shall take place by secret ballot, after the presiding Member of the Court has declared the number of affirmative votes necessary for election; there shall be no nominations. The Member of the Court obtaining the votes of a majority of the Members composing it at the time of the election shall be declared elected, and shall enter forthwith upon his functions.

3. The new President shall conduct the election of the Vice-President either at the same or at the following meeting. The provisions of paragraph 2 of this Article shall apply equally to this election.

Article 12

The President shall preside at all meetings of the Court; he shall direct the work and supervise the administration of the Court.

Article 13

1. In the event of a vacancy in the presidency or of the inability of the President to exercise the functions of the presidency, these shall be exercised by the Vice-President, or failing him, by the senior judge.

2. When the President is precluded by a provision of the Statute or of these Rules either from sitting or from presiding in a particular case, he shall continue to exercise the functions of the presidency for all purposes save in respect of that case.

3. The President shall take the measures necessary in order to ensure the continuous exercise of the functions of the presidency at the seat of the Court. In the event of his absence, he may, so far as is compatible with the Statute and these Rules, arrange for these functions to be exercised by the Vice-President, or failing him, by the senior judge.

4. If the President decides to resign the presidency, he shall communicate his decision in writing to the Court through the Vice-President, or failing him, the senior judge. If the Vice-President decides to resign his office, he shall communicate his decision to the President.

Article 14

If a vacancy in the presidency or the vice-presidency occurs before the date when the current term is due to expire under Article 21, paragraph 1, of the Statute and Article 10, paragraph 1, of these Rules, the Court shall decide whether or not the vacancy shall be filled during the remainder of the term.

SECTION C. THE CHAMBERS

Article 15

1. The Chamber of Summary Procedure to be formed annually under Article 29 of the Statute shall be composed of five Members of the Court, comprising the President and Vice-President of the Court, acting *ex officio*, and three other members elected in accordance with Article 18, paragraph 1, of these Rules. In addition, two Members of the Court shall be elected annually to act as substitutes.

2. The election referred to in paragraph 1 of this Article shall be held as soon as possible after the sixth of February in each year. The members of the Chamber shall enter upon their functions on election and continue to serve until the next election; they may be re-elected.

3. If a member of the Chamber is unable, for whatever reason, to sit in a given case, he shall be replaced for the purposes of that case by the senior in precedence of the two substitutes.

4. If a member of the Chamber resigns or otherwise ceases to be a member, his place shall be taken by the senior in precedence of the two substitutes, who shall thereupon become a full member of the Chamber and be replaced by the election of another substitute. Should vacancies exceed the number of available substitutes, elections shall be held as soon as possible in respect of the vacancies still existing after the substitutes have assumed full membership and in respect of the vacancies in the substitutes.

Article 16

1. When the Court decides to form one or more of the chambers provided for in Article 26, paragraph 1, of the Statute, it shall determine the particular category of cases for which each chamber is formed, the number of its members, the period for which they will serve, and the date at which they will enter upon their duties.

2. The members of the chamber shall be elected in accordance with Article 18, paragraph 1, of these Rules from among the Members of the Court, having regard to any special knowledge, expertise or previous experience which any of the Members of the Court may have in relation to the category of case the chamber is being formed to deal with.

3. The Court may decide upon the dissolution of a chamber, but without prejudice to the duty of the chamber concerned to finish any cases pending before it.

Article 17

1. A request for the formation of a chamber to deal with a particular case, as provided for in Article 26, paragraph 2, of the Statute, may be filed at any time until the closure of the written proceedings. Upon receipt of a request made by one party, the President shall ascertain whether the other party assents.

2. When the parties have agreed, the President shall ascertain their views regarding the composition of the chamber, and shall report to the Court accordingly. He shall also take such steps as may be necessary to give effect to the provisions of Article 31, paragraph 4, of the Statute.

3. When the Court has determined, with the approval of the parties, the number of its Members who are to constitute the chamber, it shall proceed to their election, in accordance with the provisions of Article 18, paragraph 1, of these Rules. The same procedure shall be followed as regards the filling of any vacancy that may occur on the chamber.

4. Members of a chamber formed under this Article who have been replaced, in accordance with Article 13 of the Statute following the expiration of their terms of office, shall continue to sit in all phases of the case, whatever the stage it has then reached.

Article 18

1. Elections to all chambers shall take place by secret ballot. The Members of the Court obtaining the largest number of votes constituting a majority of the Members of the Court composing it at the time of the election shall be declared elected. If necessary to fill vacancies, more than one ballot shall take place, such ballot being limited to the number of vacancies that remain to be filled.

2. If a chamber when formed includes the President or Vice-President of the Court, or both of them, the President or Vice-President, as the case may be, shall preside over that chamber. In any other event, the chamber shall elect its own president by secret ballot and by a majority of votes of its members. The Member of the Court who, under this paragraph, presides over the chamber at the time of its formation shall continue to preside so long as he remains a member of that chamber.

3. The president of a chamber shall exercise, in relation to cases being dealt with by that chamber, all the functions of the President of the Court in relation to cases before the Court.

4. If the president of a chamber is prevented from sitting or from acting as president, the functions of the presidency shall be assumed by the member of the chamber who is the senior in precedence and able to act.

SECTION D. INTERNAL FUNCTIONING OF THE COURT

Article 19

The internal judicial practice of the Court shall, subject to the provisions of the Statute and these Rules, be governed by any resolutions on the subject adopted by the Court.[2]

Article 20

1. The quorum specified by Article 25, paragraph 3, of the Statute applies to all meetings of the Court.

2. The obligation of Members of the Court under Article 23, paragraph 3, of the Statute, to hold themselves permanently at the disposal of the Court, entails attendance at all such meetings, unless they are prevented from attending by illness or for other serious reasons duly explained to the President, who shall inform the Court.

---

2 The resolution now in force was adopted on 12 April 1976.

3. Judges *ad hoc* are likewise bound to hold themselves at the disposal of the Court and to attend all meetings held in the case in which they are participating. They shall not be taken into account for the calculation of the quorum.

4. The Court shall fix the dates and duration of the judicial vacations and the periods and conditions of leave to be accorded to individual Members of the Court under Article 23, paragraph 2, of the Statute, having regard in both cases to the state of its General List and to the requirements of its current work.

5. Subject to the same considerations, the Court shall observe the public holidays customary at the place where the Court is sitting.

6. In case of urgency the President may convene the Court at any time.

Article 21

1. The deliberations of the Court shall take place in private and remain secret. The Court may however at any time decide in respect of its deliberations on other than judicial matters to publish or allow publication of any part of them.

2. Only judges, and the assessors, if any, take part in the Court's judicial deliberations. The Registrar, or his deputy, and other members of the staff of the Registry as may be required shall be present. No other person shall be present except by permission of the Court.

3. The minutes of the Court's judicial deliberations shall record only the title or nature of the subjects or matters discussed, and the results of any vote taken. They shall not record any details of the discussions nor the views expressed, provided however that any judge is entitled to require that a statement made by him be inserted in the minutes.

[PART II]

THE REGISTRY

Article 22

1. The Court shall elect its Registrar by secret ballot from amongst candidates proposed by Members of the Court. The Registrar shall be elected for a term of seven years. He may be re-elected.

2. The President shall give notice of a vacancy or impending vacancy to Members of the Court, either forthwith upon the vacancy arising, or, where the vacancy will arise on the expiration of the term of office of the Registrar, not less than three months prior thereto. The President shall fix a date for the closure of the list of candidates so as to enable nominations and information concerning the candidates to be received in sufficient time.

3. Nominations shall indicate the relevant information concerning the candidate, and in particular information as to his age, nationality, and present occupation, university qualifications, knowledge of languages, and any previous experience in law, diplomacy or the work of international organizations.

4. The candidate obtaining the votes of the majority of the Members of the Court composing it at the time of the election shall be declared elected.

Article 23

The Court shall elect a Deputy-Registrar: the provisions of Article 22 of these Rules shall apply to his election and term of office.

Article 24

1. Before taking up his duties, the Registrar shall make the following declaration at a meeting of the Court:

I solemnly declare that I will perform the duties incumbent upon me as Registrar of the International Court of Justice in all loyalty, discretion and good conscience, and that I will faithfully observe all the provisions of the Statute and of the Rules of the Court.

2. The Deputy-Registrar shall make a similar declaration at a meeting of the Court before taking up his duties.

Article 25

1. The staff members of the Registry shall be appointed by the Court on proposals submitted by the Registrar. Appointments to such posts as the Court shall determine may however be made by the Registrar with the approval of the President.

2. Before taking up his duties, every staff member shall make the following declaration before the President, the Registrar being present:

I solemnly declare that I will perform the duties incumbent upon me as an official of the International Court of Justice in all loyalty, discretion and good conscience, and that I will faithfully observe all the provisions of the Statute and of the Rules of the Court.

Article 26

1. The Registrar, in the discharge of his function, shall:

(a) be the regular channel of communications to and from the Court, and in particular shall effect all communications, notifications and transmission of documents required by the Statute or by these Rules and ensure that the date of despatch and receipt thereof may be readily verified;

(b) keep, under the supervision of the President, and in such form as may be laid down by the Court, a General List of all cases, entered and numbered in the order in which the documents instituting proceedings or requesting an advisory opinion are received in the Registry;

(c) have the custody of the declarations accepting the jurisdiction of the Court made by States not parties to the Statute in accordance with any resolution adopted by the Security Council under Article 35, paragraph 2, of the Statute, and transmit certified copies thereof to all States parties to the Statute, to such other States as shall have deposited declarations, and to the Secretary-General of the United Nations;

(d) transmit to the parties copies of all pleadings and documents annexed upon receipt thereof in the Registry;

(e) communicate to the government of the country in which the Court or a chamber is sitting, and any other governments which may be concerned, the necessary information as to the persons from time to time entitled, under the Statute and relevant agreements, to privileges, immunities, or facilities;

(f) be present, in person or by his deputy, at meetings of the Court, and of the chambers, and be responsible for the preparation of minutes of such meetings;

(g) make arrangements for such provision or verification of translations and interpretations into the Court's official languages as the Court may require;

(h) sign all judgments, advisory opinions and orders of the Court, and the minutes referred to in subparagraph *(f)*;

(i) be responsible for the printing and publication of the Court's judgments, advisory opinions and orders, the pleadings and statements, and minutes of public sittings in cases, and of such other documents as the Court may direct to be published;

(j) be responsible for all administrative work and in particular for the accounts and financial administration in accordance with the financial procedures of the United Nations;

(k) deal with enquiries concerning the Court and its work;

(l) assist in maintaining relations between the Court and other organs of the United Nations, the specialized agencies, and international bodies and conferences concerned with the codification and progressive development of international law;

(m) ensure that information concerning the Court and its activities is made accessible to governments, the highest national courts of justice, professional and learned societies, legal faculties and schools of law, and public information media;

(n) have custody of the seals and stamps of the Court, of the archives of the Court, and of such other archives as may be entrusted to the Court.[3]

2. The Court may at any time entrust additional functions to the Registrar.

3. In the discharge of his functions the Registrar shall be responsible to the Court.

Article 27

1. The Deputy-Registrar shall assist the Registrar, act as Registrar in the latter's absence and, in the event of the office becoming vacant, exercise the functions of Registrar until the office has been filled.

2. If both the Registrar and the Deputy-Registrar are unable to carry out the duties of Registrar, the President shall appoint an official of the Registry to discharge those duties for such time as may be necessary. If both offices are vacant at the same time, the President, after consulting the Members of the Court, shall appoint an official of the Registry to discharge the duties of Registrar pending an election to that office.

Article 28

1. The Registry shall comprise the Registrar, the Deputy-Registrar, and such other staff as the Registrar shall require for the efficient discharge of his functions.

2. The Court shall prescribe the organization of the Registry, and shall for this purpose request the Registrar to make proposals.

---

[3] The Registrar also keeps the Archives of the Permanent Court of International Justice, entrusted to the present Court by decision of the Permanent Court of October 1945 (*ICJ Yearbook 1946–1947*, 26), and the Archives of the Trial of the Major War Criminals before the International Military Tribunal at Nuremburg (1945–1946), entrusted to the Court by decision of that Tribunal of 1 October 1946; the Court authorized the Registrar to accept the latter Archives by decision of 19 November 1949.

3. Instructions for the Registry shall be drawn up by the Registrar and approved by the Court.

4. The staff of the Registry shall be subject to Staff Regulations drawn up by the Registrar, so far as possible in conformity with the United Nations Staff Regulations and Staff Rules, and approved by the Court.

Article 29

1. The Registrar may be removed from office only if, in the opinion of two-thirds of the Members of the Court, he has either become permanently incapacitated from exercising his functions, or has committed a serious breach of his duties.

2. Before a decision is taken under this Article, the Registrar shall be informed by the President of the action contemplated, in a written statement which shall include the grounds therefor and any relevant evidence. He shall subsequently, at a private meeting of the Court, be afforded an opportunity of making a statement, of furnishing any information or explanations he wishes to give, and of supplying answers, orally or in writing, to any questions put to him.

3. The Deputy-Registrar may be removed from office only on the same grounds and by the same procedure.

[PART III]

PROCEEDINGS IN CONTENTIOUS CASES

SECTION A. COMMUNICATIONS TO THE COURT AND CONSULTATIONS

Article 30

All communications to the Court under these Rules shall be addressed to the Registrar unless otherwise stated. Any request made by a party shall likewise be addressed to the Registrar unless made in open Court in the course of the oral proceedings.

Article 31

In every case submitted to the Court, the President shall ascertain the views of the parties with regard to questions of procedure. For this purpose he shall summon the agents of the parties to meet him as soon as possible after their appointment, and whenever necessary thereafter.

SECTION B. THE COMPOSITION OF THE COURT FOR PARTICULAR CASES

Article 32

1. If the President of the Court is a national of one of the parties in a case he shall not exercise the functions of the presidency in respect of that case. The same rule applies to the Vice-President, or to the senior judge, when called on to act as President.

2. The Member of the Court who is presiding in a case on the date on which the Court convenes for the oral proceedings shall continue to preside in that case until completion

of the current phase of the case, notwithstanding the election in the meantime of a new President or Vice-President. If he should become unable to act, the presidency for the case shall be determined in accordance with Article 13 of these Rules, and on the basis of the composition of the Court on the date on which it convened for the oral proceedings.

Article 33

Except as provided in Article 17 of these Rules, Members of the Court who have been replaced, in accordance with Article 13, paragraph 3, of the Statute following the expiration of their terms of office, shall discharge the duty imposed upon them by that paragraph by continuing to sit until the completion of any phase of a case in respect of which the Court convenes for the oral proceedings prior to the date of such replacement.

Article 34

1. In case of any doubt arising as to the application of Article 17, paragraph 2, of the Statute or in case of disagreement as to the application of Article 24 of the Statute, the President shall inform the Members of the Court, with whom the decision lies.

2. If a party desires to bring to the attention of the Court facts which it considers to be of possible relevance to the application of the provisions of the Statute mentioned in the previous paragraph, but which it believes may not be known to the Court, that party shall communicate confidentially such facts to the President in writing.

Article 35

1. If a party proposes to exercise the power conferred by Article 31 of the Statute to choose a judge *ad hoc* in a case, it shall notify the Court of its intention as soon as possible. If the name and nationality of the judge selected are not indicated at the same time, the party shall, not later than two months before the time-limit fixed for the filing of the Counter-Memorial, inform the Court of the name and nationality of the person chosen and supply brief biographical details. The judge *ad hoc* may be of a nationality other than that of the party which chooses him.

2. If a party proposes to abstain from choosing a judge *ad hoc*, on condition of a like abstention by the other party, it shall so notify the Court which shall inform the other party. If the other party thereafter gives notice of its intention to choose, or chooses, a judge *ad hoc*, the time-limit for the party which has previously abstained from choosing a judge may be extended by the President.

3. A copy of any notification relating to the choice of a judge *ad hoc* shall be communicated by the Registrar to the other party, which shall be requested to furnish, within a time-limit to be fixed by the President, such observations as it may wish to make. If within the said time-limit no objection is raised by the other party, and if none appears to the Court itself, the parties shall be so informed.

4. In the event of any objection or doubt, the matter shall be decided by the Court, if necessary after hearing the parties.

5. A judge *ad hoc* who has accepted appointment but who becomes unable to sit may be replaced.

6. If and when the reasons for the participation of a judge *ad hoc* are found no longer to exist, he shall cease to sit on the Bench.

Article 36

1. If the Court finds that two or more parties are in the same interest, and therefore are to be reckoned as one party only, and that there is no Member of the Court of the nationality of any one of those parties upon the Bench, the Court shall fix a time-limit within which they may jointly choose a judge *ad hoc.*

2. Should any party amongst those found by the Court to be in the same interest allege the existence of a separate interest of its own, or put forward any other objection, the matter shall be decided by the Court, if necessary after hearing the parties.

Article 37

1. If a Member of the Court having the nationality of one of the parties is or becomes unable to sit in any phase of a case, that party shall thereupon become entitled to choose a judge *ad hoc* within a time-limit to be fixed by the Court, or by the President if the Court is not sitting.

2. Parties in the same interest shall be deemed not to have a judge of one of their nationalities upon the Bench if the Member of the Court having one of their nationalities is or becomes unable to sit in any phase of the case.

3. If the Member of the Court having the nationality of a party becomes able to sit not later than the closure of the written proceedings in that phase of the case, that Member of the Court shall resume his seat on the Bench in the case.

SECTION C. PROCEEDINGS BEFORE THE COURT

Subsection 1. Institution of Proceedings

Article 38

1. When proceedings before the Court are instituted by means of an application addressed as specified in Article 40, paragraph 1, of the Statute, the application shall indicate the party making it, the State against which the claim is brought, and the subject of the dispute.

2. The application shall specify as far as possible the legal grounds upon which the jurisdiction of the Court is said to be based; it shall also specify the precise nature of the claim, together with a succinct statement of the facts and grounds on which the claim is based.

3. The original of the application shall be signed either by the agent of the party submitting it, or by the diplomatic representative of that party in the country in which the Court has its seat, or by some other duly authorized person. If the application bears the signature of someone other than such diplomatic representative, the signature must be authenticated by the latter or by the competent authority of the applicant's foreign ministry.

4. The Registrar shall forthwith transmit to the respondent a certified copy of the application.

5. When the applicant State proposes to found the jurisdiction of the Court upon a consent thereto yet to be given or manifested by the State against which such application is made, the application shall be transmitted to that State. It shall not however be entered in the General List, nor any action be taken in the proceedings, unless and until the State

against which such application is made consents to the Court's jurisdiction for the purposes of the case.

Article 39

1. When proceedings are brought before the Court by the notification of a special agreement, in conformity with Article 40, paragraph 1, of the Statute, the notification may be effected by the parties jointly or by any one or more of them. If the notification is not a joint one, a certified copy of it shall forthwith be communicated by the Registrar to the other party.

2. In each case the notification shall be accompanied by an original or certified copy of the special agreement. The notification shall also, in so far as this is not already apparent from the agreement, indicate the precise subject of the dispute and identify the parties to it.

Article 40

1. Except in the circumstances contemplated by Article 38, paragraph 5, of these Rules, all steps on behalf of the parties after proceedings have been instituted shall be taken by agents. Agents shall have an address for service at the seat of the Court to which all communications concerning the cases are to be sent. Communications addressed to the agents of the parties shall be considered as having been addressed to the parties themselves.

2. When proceedings are instituted by means of an application, the name of the agent for the applicant shall be stated. The respondent, upon receipt of the certified copy of the application, or as soon as possible thereafter, shall inform the Court of the name of its agent.

3. When proceedings are brought by notification of a special agreement, the party making the notification shall state the name of its agent. Any other party to the special agreement, upon receiving from the Registrar a certified copy of such notification, or as soon as possible thereafter, shall inform the Court of the name of its agent if it has not already done so.

Article 41

The institution of proceedings by a State which is not a party to the Statute but which, under Article 35, paragraph 2, thereof, has accepted the jurisdiction of the Court by a declaration made in accordance with any resolution adopted by the Security Council under that Article,[4] shall be accompanied by a deposit of the declaration in question, unless the latter has previously been deposited with the Registrar. If any question of the validity or effect of such declaration arises, the Court shall decide.

Article 42

The Registrar shall transmit copies of any application or notification of a special agreement instituting proceedings before the Court to: *(a)* the Secretary-General of the United Nations; *(b)* the Members of the United Nations; *(c)* other States entitled to appear before the Court.

---

[4] The resolution now in force was adopted on 15 October 1946.

Article 43

Whenever the construction of a convention to which States other than those concerned in the case are parties may be in question within the meaning of Article 63, paragraph 1, of the Statute, the Court shall consider what directions shall be given to the Registrar in the matter.

Subsection 2. The Written Proceedings

Article 44

1. In the light of the information obtained by the President under Article 31 of these Rules, the Court shall make the necessary orders to determine, *inter alia*, the number and the order of filing of the pleadings and the time-limits within which they must be filed.

2. In making an order under paragraph 1 of this Article, any agreement between the parties which does not cause unjustified delay shall be taken into account.

3. The Court may, at the request of the party concerned, extend any time-limit, or decide that any step taken after the expiration of the time-limit fixed therefor shall be considered as valid, if it is satisfied that there is adequate justification for the request. In either case the other party shall be given an opportunity to state its views.

4. If the Court is not sitting, its powers under this Article shall be exercised by the President, but without prejudice to any subsequent decision of the Court. If the consultation referred to in Article 31 reveals persistent disagreement between the parties as to the application of Article 45, paragraph 2, or Article 46, paragraph 2, of these Rules, the Court shall be convened to decide the matter.

Article 45

1. The pleadings in a case begun by means of an application shall consist, in the following order, of: a Memorial by the applicant; a Counter-Memorial by the respondent.

2. The Court may authorize or direct that there shall be a Reply by the applicant and a Rejoinder by the respondent if the parties are so agreed, or if the Court decides, *proprio motu* or at the request of one of the parties, that these pleadings are necessary.

Article 46

1. In a case begun by the notification of a special agreement, the number and order of the pleadings shall be governed by the provisions of the agreement, unless the Court, after ascertaining the views of the parties, decides otherwise.

2. If the special agreement contains no such provision, and if the parties have not subsequently agreed on the number and order of pleadings, they shall each file a Memorial and Counter-Memorial, within the same time-limits. The Court shall not authorize the presentation of Replies unless it finds them to be necessary.

Article 47

The Court may at any time direct that the proceedings in two or more cases be joined. It may also direct that the written or oral proceedings, including the calling of witnesses, be in common; or the Court may, without effecting any formal joinder, direct common action in any of these respects.

Article 48

Time-limits for the completion of steps in the proceedings may be fixed by assigning a specified period but shall always indicate definite dates. Such time-limits shall be as short as the character of the case permits.

Article 49

1. A Memorial shall contain a statement of the relevant facts, a statement of law, and the submissions.

2. A Counter-Memorial shall contain: an admission or denial of the facts stated in the Memorial; any additional facts, if necessary; observations concerning the statement of law in the Memorial; a statement of law in answer thereto; and the submissions.

3. The Reply and Rejoinder, whenever authorized by the Court, shall not merely repeat the parties' contentions, but shall be directed to bringing out the issues that still divide them.

4. Every pleading shall set out the party's submissions at the relevant stage of the case, distinctly from the arguments presented, or shall confirm the submissions previously made.

Article 50

1. There shall be annexed to the original of every pleading certified copies of any relevant documents adduced in support of the contentions contained in the pleading.

2. If only parts of a document are relevant, only such extracts as are necessary for the purpose of the pleading in question need be annexed. A copy of the whole document shall be deposited in the Registry, unless it has been published and is readily available.

3. A list of all documents annexed to a pleading shall be furnished at the time the pleading is filed.

Article 51

1. If the parties are agreed that the written proceedings shall be conducted wholly in one of the two official languages of the Court, the pleadings shall be submitted only in that language. If the parties are not so agreed, any pleading or any part of a pleading shall be submitted in one or other of the official languages.

2. If in pursuance of Article 39, paragraph 3, of the Statute a language other than French or English is used, a translation into French or English certified as accurate by the party submitting it, shall be attached to the original of each pleading.

3. When a document annexed to a pleading is not in one of the official languages of the Court, it shall be accompanied by a translation into one of these languages certified by the party submitting it as accurate. The translation may be confined to part of an annex, or to extracts therefrom, but in this case it must be accompanied by an explanatory note indicating what passages are translated. The Court may however require a more extensive or a complete translation to be furnished.

Article 52[5]

1. The original of every pleading shall be signed by the agent and filed in the Registry. It shall be accompanied by a certified copy of the pleading, documents annexed, and any translation, for communication to the other party in accordance with Article 43, paragraph 4, of the Statute, and by the number of additional copies required by the Registry, but without prejudice to an increase in that number should the need arise later.

2. All pleadings shall be dated. When a pleading has to be filed by a certain date, it is the date of the receipt of the pleading in the Registry which will be regarded by the Court as the material date.

3. If the Registrar arranges for the printing of a pleading at the request of a party, the text must be supplied in sufficient time to enable the printed pleading to be filed in the Registry before the expiration of any time-limit which may apply to it. The printing is done under the responsibility of the party in question.

4. The correction of a slip or error in any document which has been filed may be made at any time with the consent of the other party or by leave of the President. Any correction so effected shall be notified to the other party in the same manner as the pleading to which it relates.

Article 53

1. The Court, or the President if the Court is not sitting, may at any time decide, after ascertaining the views of the parties, that copies of the pleadings and documents annexed shall be made available to a State entitled to appear before it which has asked to be furnished with such copies.

2. The Court may, after ascertaining the views of the parties, decide that copies of the pleadings and documents annexed shall be made accessible to the public on or after the opening of the oral proceedings.

Subsection 3. The Oral Proceedings

Article 54

1. Upon the closure of the written proceedings, the case is ready for hearing. The date for the opening of the oral proceedings shall be fixed by the Court, which may also decide, if occasion should arise, that the opening or the continuance of the oral proceedings be postponed.

2. When fixing the date for, or postponing, the opening of the oral proceedings the Court shall have regard to the priority required by Article 74 of these Rules and to any other special circumstances, including the urgency of a particular case.

3. When the Court is not sitting, its powers under this Article shall be exercised by the President.

---

[5] The agents of the parties are requested to ascertain from the Registry the usual format of the pleadings, and the conditions on which the Court may bear part of the cost of printing.

Article 55

The Court may, if it considers it desirable, decide pursuant to Article 22, paragraph 1, of the Statute that all or part of the further proceedings in a case shall be held at a place other than the seat of the Court. Before so deciding, it shall ascertain the views of the parties.

Article 56

1. After the closure of the written proceedings, no further documents may be submitted to the Court by either party except with the consent of the other party or as provided in paragraph 2 of this Article. The party desiring to produce a new document shall file the original or a certified copy thereof, together with the number of copies required by the Registry, which shall be responsible for communicating it to the other party and shall inform the Court. The other party shall be held to have given its consent if it does not lodge an objection to the production of the document.

2. In the absence of consent, the Court, after hearing the parties, may, if it considers the document necessary, authorize its production.

3. If a new document is produced under paragraph 1 or paragraph 2 of this Article, the other party shall have an opportunity of commenting upon it and of submitting documents in support of its comments.

4. No reference may be made during the oral proceedings to the contents of any document which has not been produced in accordance with Article 43 of the Statute or this Article, unless the document is part of a publication readily available.

5. The application of the provisions of this Article shall not in itself constitute a ground for delaying the opening or the course of the oral proceedings.

Article 57

Without prejudice to the provisions of the Rules concerning the production of documents, each party shall communicate to the Registrar, in sufficient time before the opening of the oral proceedings, information regarding any evidence which it intends to produce or which it intends to request the Court to obtain. This communication shall contain a list of the surnames, first names, nationalities, descriptions and places of residence of the witnesses and experts whom the party intends to call, with indications in general terms of the point or points to which their evidence will be directed. A copy of the communication shall also be furnished for transmission to the other party.

Article 58

1. The Court shall determine whether the parties should present their arguments before or after the production of the evidence; the parties shall, however, retain the right to comment on the evidence given.

2. The order in which the parties will be heard, the method of handling the evidence and of examining any witnesses and experts, and the number of counsel and advocates to be heard on behalf of each party, shall be settled by the Court after the views of the parties have been ascertained in accordance with Article 31 of these Rules.

Article 59

The hearing in Court shall be public, unless the Court shall decide otherwise, or unless the parties demand that the public be not admitted. Such a decision or demand may concern either the whole or part of the hearing, and may be made at any time.

Article 60

1. The oral statements made on behalf of each party shall be as succinct as possible within the limits of what is requisite for the adequate presentation of that party's contentions at the hearing. Accordingly, they shall be directed to the issues that still divide the parties, and shall not go over the whole ground covered by the pleadings, or merely repeat the facts and arguments these contain.

2. At the conclusion of the last statement made by a party at the hearing, its agent, without recapitulation of the arguments, shall read that party's final submissions. A copy of the written text of these, signed by the agent, shall be communicated to the Court and transmitted to the other party.

Article 61

1. The Court may at any time prior to or during the hearing indicate any points or issues to which it would like the parties specially to address themselves, or on which it considers that there has been sufficient argument.

2. The Court may, during the hearing, put questions to the agents, counsel and advocates, and may ask them for explanations.

3. Each judge has a similar right to put questions, but before exercising it he should make his intention known to the President, who is made responsible by Article 45 of the Statute for the control of the hearing.

4. The agents, counsel and advocates may answer either immediately or within a time-limit fixed by the President.

Article 62

1. The Court may at any time call upon the parties to produce such evidence or to give such explanations as the Court may consider to be necessary for the elucidation of any aspect of the matters in issue, or may itself seek other information for this purpose.

2. The Court may, if necessary, arrange for the attendance of a witness or expert to give evidence in the proceedings.

Article 63

1. The parties may call any witnesses or experts appearing on the list communicated to the Court pursuant to Article 57 of these Rules. If at any time during the hearing a party wishes to call a witness or expert whose name was not included in that list, it shall so inform the Court and the other party, and shall supply the information required by Article 57. The witness or expert may be called either if the other party makes no objection or if the Court is satisfied that his evidence seems likely to prove relevant.

2. The Court, or the President if the Court is not sitting, shall, at the request of one of the parties or *proprio motu*, take the necessary steps for the examination of witnesses otherwise than before the Court itself.

Article 64

Unless on account of special circumstances the Court decides on a different form of words,

(*a*) every witness shall make the following declaration before giving any evidence:

I solemnly declare upon my honour and conscience that I will speak the truth, the whole truth and nothing but the truth;

(*b*) every expert shall make the following declaration before making any statement:

I solemnly declare upon my honour and conscience that I will speak the truth, the whole truth and nothing but the truth and that my statement will be in accordance with my sincere belief.

Article 65

Witnesses and experts shall be examined by the agents, counsel or advocates of the parties under the control of the President. Questions may be put to them by the President and by the judges. Before testifying, witnesses shall remain out of court.

Article 66

The Court may at any time decide, either *proprio motu* or at the request of a party, to exercise its functions with regard to the obtaining of evidence at a place or locality to which the case relates, subject to such conditions as the Court may decide upon after ascertaining the views of the parties. The necessary arrangements shall be made in accordance with Article 44 of the Statute.

Article 67

1. If the Court considers it necessary to arrange for an enquiry or an expert opinion, it shall, after hearing the parties, issue an order to this effect, defining the subject of the enquiry or expert opinion, stating the number and mode of appointment of the persons to hold the enquiry or of the experts, and laying down the procedure to be followed. Where appropriate, the Court shall require persons appointed to carry out an enquiry, or to give an expert opinion, to make a solemn declaration.

2. Every report or record of an enquiry and every expert opinion shall be communicated to the parties, which shall be given the opportunity of commenting upon it.

Article 68

Witnesses and experts who appear at the instance of the Court under Article 62, paragraph 2, and persons appointed under Article 67, paragraph 1, of these Rules, to carry out an enquiry or to give an expert opinion, shall, where appropriate, be paid out of the funds of the Court.

Article 69

1. The Court may, at any time prior to the closure of the oral proceedings, either *proprio motu* or at the request of one of the parties communicated as provided in Article 57 of these Rules, request a public international organization, pursuant to Article 34 of the Statute, to furnish information relevant to a case before it. The Court, after consulting the

chief administrative officer of the organization concerned, shall decide whether such information shall be presented to it orally or in writing, and the time-limits for its presentation.

2. When a public international organization sees fit to furnish, on its own initiative, information relevant to a case before the Court, it shall do so in the form of a Memorial to be filed in the Registry before the closure of the written proceedings. The Court shall retain the right to require such information to be supplemented, either orally or in writing, in the form of answers to any questions which it may see fit to formulate, and also to authorize the parties to comment, either orally or in writing, on the information thus furnished.

3. In the circumstances contemplated by Article 34, paragraph 3, of the Statute, the Registrar, on the instructions of the Court, or of the President if the Court is not sitting, shall proceed as prescribed in that paragraph. The Court, or the President if the Court is not sitting, may, as from the date on which the Registrar has communicated copies of the written proceedings and after consulting the chief administrative officer of the public international organization concerned, fix a time-limit within which the organization may submit to the Court its observations in writing. These observations shall be communicated to the parties and may be discussed by them and by the representative of the said organization during the oral proceedings.

4. In the foregoing paragraph, the term 'public international organization' denotes an international organization of States.

Article 70

1. In the absence of any decision to the contrary by the Court, all speeches and statements made and evidence given at the hearing in one of the official languages of the Court shall be interpreted into the other official language. If they are made or given in any other language, they shall be interpreted into the two official languages of the Court.

2. Whenever, in accordance with Article 39, paragraph 3, of the Statute, a language other than French or English is used, the necessary arrangements for interpretation into one of the two official languages shall be made by the party concerned; however, the Registrar shall make arrangements for the verification of the interpretation provided by a party of evidence given on the party's behalf. In the case of witnesses or experts who appear at the instance of the Court, arrangements for interpretation shall be made by the Registry.

3. A party on behalf of which speeches or statements are to be made, or evidence given, in a language which is not one of the official languages of the Court, shall so notify the Registrar in sufficient time for him to make the necessary arrangements.

4. Before first interpreting in the case, interpreters provided by a party shall make the following declaration in open court:

> I solemnly declare upon my honour and conscience that my interpretation will be faithful and complete.

Article 71

1. A verbatim record shall be made by the Registrar of every hearing, in the official language of the Court which has been used. When the language used is not one of the two

official languages of the Court, the verbatim record shall be prepared in one of the Court's official languages.

2. When speeches or statements are made in a language which is not one of the official languages of the Court, the party on behalf of which they are made shall supply to the Registry in advance a text thereof in one of the official languages, and this text shall constitute the relevant part of the verbatim record.

3. The transcript of the verbatim record shall be preceded by the names of the judges present, and those of the agents, counsel and advocates of the parties.

4. Copies of the transcript shall be circulated to the judges sitting in the case, and to the parties. The latter may, under the supervision of the Court, correct the transcripts of speeches and statements made on their behalf, but in no case may such corrections affect the sense and bearing thereof. The judges may likewise make corrections in the transcript of anything they may have said.

5. Witnesses and experts shall be shown that part of the transcript which relates to the evidence given, or the statements made by them, and may correct it in like manner as the parties.

6. One certified true copy of the eventual corrected transcript, signed by the President and the Registrar, shall constitute the authentic minutes of the sitting for the purpose of Article 47 of the Statute. The minutes of public hearings shall be printed and published by the Court.

Article 72

Any written reply by a party to a question put under Article 61, or any evidence or explanation supplied by a party under Article 62 of these Rules, received by the Court after the closure of the oral proceedings, shall be communicated to the other party, which shall be given the opportunity of commenting upon it. If necessary the oral proceedings may be reopened for that purpose.

SECTION D. INCIDENTAL PROCEEDINGS

Subsection 1. Interim Protection

Article 73

1. A written request for the indication of provisional measures may be made by a party at any time during the course of the proceedings in the case in connection with which the request is made.

2. The request shall specify the reasons therefor, the possible consequences if it is not granted, and the measures requested. A certified copy shall forthwith be transmitted by the Registrar to the other party.

Article 74

1. A request for the indication of provisional measures shall have priority over all other cases.

2. The Court, if it is not sitting when the request is made, shall be convened forthwith for the purpose of proceeding to a decision on the request as a matter of urgency.

3. The Court, or the President if the Court is not sitting, shall fix a date for a hearing

which will afford the parties an opportunity of being represented at it. The Court shall receive and take into account any observations that may be presented to it before the closure of the oral proceedings.

4. Pending the meeting of the Court, the President may call upon the parties to act in such a way as will enable any order the Court may make on the request for provisional measures to have its appropriate effects.

Article 75

1. The Court may at any time decide to examine *proprio motu* whether the circumstances of the case require the indication of provisional measures which ought to be taken or complied with by any or all of the parties.

2. When a request for provisional measures has been made, the Court may indicate measures that are in whole or in part other than those requested, or that ought to be taken or complied with by the party which has itself made the request.

3. The rejection of a request for the indication of provisional measures shall not prevent the party which made it from making a fresh request in the same case based on new facts.

Article 76

1. At the request of a party the Court may, at any time before the final judgment in the case, revoke or modify any decision concerning provisional measures if, in its opinion, some change in the situation justifies such revocation or modification.

2. Any application by a party proposing such a revocation or modification shall specify the change in the situation considered to be relevant.

3. Before taking any decision under paragraph 1 of this Article the Court shall afford the parties an opportunity of presenting their observations on the subject.

Article 77

Any measures indicated by the Court under Articles 73 and 75 of these Rules, and any decision taken by the Court under Article 76, paragraph 1, of these Rules, shall forthwith be communicated to the Secretary-General of the United Nations for transmission to the Security Council in pursuance of Article 41, paragraph 2, of the Statute.

Article 78

The Court may request information from the parties on any matter connected with the implementation of any provisional measures it has indicated.

Subsection 2. Preliminary Objections

Article 79

1. Any objection by the respondent to the jurisdiction of the Court or to the admissibility of the application, or other objection the decision upon which is requested before any further proceedings on the merits, shall be made in writing within the time-limit fixed for the delivery of the Counter-Memorial. Any such objection made by a party other than the respondent shall be filed within the time-limit fixed for the delivery of that party's first pleading.

2. The preliminary objection shall set out the facts and the law on which the objection is based, the submissions and a list of the documents in support; it shall mention any evidence which the party may desire to produce. Copies of the supporting documents shall be attached.

3. Upon receipt by the Registry of a preliminary objection, the proceedings on the merits shall be suspended and the Court, or the President if the Court is not sitting, shall fix the time-limit within which the other party may present a written statement of its observations and submissions; documents in support shall be attached and evidence which it is proposed to produce shall be mentioned.

4. Unless otherwise decided by the Court, the further proceedings shall be oral.

5. The statements of facts and law in the pleadings referred to in paragraphs 2 and 3 of this Article, and the statements and evidence presented at the hearings contemplated by paragraph 4, shall be confined to those matters that are relevant to the objection.

6. In order to enable the Court to determine its jurisdiction at the preliminary stage of the proceedings, the Court, whenever necessary, may request the parties to argue all questions of law and fact, and to adduce all evidence, which bear on the issue.

7. After hearing the parties, the Court shall give its decision in the form of a judgment, by which it shall either uphold the objection, reject it, or declare that the objection does not possess, in the circumstances of the case, an exclusively preliminary character. If the Court rejects the objection or declares that it does not possess an exclusively preliminary character, it shall fix time-limits for the further proceedings.

8. Any agreement between the parties that an objection submitted under paragraph 1 of this Article be heard and determined within the framework of the merits shall be given effect by the Court.

Subsection 3. Counter-Claims

Article 80

1. A counter-claim may be presented provided that it is directly connected with the subject-matter of the claim of the other party and that it comes within the jurisdiction of the Court.

2. A counter-claim shall be made in the Counter-Memorial of the party presenting it, and shall appear as part of the submissions of that party.

3. In the event of doubt as to the connection between the question presented by way of counter-claim and the subject-matter of the claim of the other party the Court shall, after hearing the parties, decide whether or not the question thus presented shall be joined to the original proceedings.

Subsection 4. Intervention

Article 81

1. An application for permission to intervene under the terms of Article 62 of the Statute, signed in the manner provided for in Article 38, paragraph 3, of these Rules, shall be filed as soon as possible, and not later than the closure of the written proceedings. In exceptional circumstances, an application submitted at a later stage may however be admitted.

2. The application shall state the name of an agent. It shall specify the case to which it relates, and shall set out:

(*a*) the interest of a legal nature which the State applying to intervene considers may be affected by the decision in that case;

(*b*) the precise object of the intervention;

(*c*) any basis of jurisdiction which is claimed to exist as between the State applying to intervene and the parties to the case.

3. The application shall contain a list of the documents in support, which documents shall be attached.

Article 82

1. A State which desires to avail itself of the right of intervention conferred upon it by Article 63 of the Statute shall file a declaration to that effect, signed in the manner provided for in Article 38, paragraph 3, of these Rules. Such a declaration shall be filed as soon as possible, and not later than the date fixed for the opening of the oral proceedings. In exceptional circumstances a declaration submitted at a later stage may however be admitted.

2. The declaration shall state the name of an agent. It shall specify the case and the convention to which it relates and shall contain:

(*a*) particulars of the basis on which the declarant State considers itself a party to the convention;

(*b*) identification of the particular provisions of the convention the construction of which it considers to be in question;

(*c*) a statement of the construction of those provisions for which it contends;

(*d*) a list of the documents in support, which documents shall be attached.

3. Such a declaration may be filed by a State that considers itself a party to the convention the construction of which is in question but has not received the notification referred to in Article 63 of the Statute.

Article 83

1. Certified copies of the application for permission to intervene under Article 62 of the Statute, or of the declaration of intervention under Article 63 of the Statute, shall be communicated forthwith to the parties to the case, which shall be invited to furnish their written observations within a time-limit to be fixed by the Court or by the President if the Court is not sitting.

2. The Registrar shall also transmit copies to: (*a*) the Secretary-General of the United Nations; (*b*) the Members of the United Nations; (*c*) other States entitled to appear before the Court; (*d*) any other States which have been notified under Article 63 of the Statute.

Article 84

1. The Court shall decide whether an application for permission to intervene under Article 62 of the Statute should be granted, and whether an intervention under Article 63 of the Statute is admissible, as a matter of priority unless in view of the circumstances of the case the Court shall otherwise determine.

2. If, within the time-limit fixed under Article 83 of these Rules, an objection is filed to an application for permission to intervene, or to the admissibility of a declaration of intervention, the Court shall hear the State seeking to intervene and the parties before deciding.

Article 85

1. If an application for permission to intervene under Article 62 of the Statute is granted, the intervening State shall be supplied with copies of the pleadings and documents annexed and shall be entitled to submit a written statement within a time-limit to be fixed by the Court. A further time-limit shall be fixed within which the parties may, if they so desire, furnish their written observations on that statement prior to the oral proceedings. If the Court is not sitting, these time-limits shall be fixed by the President.

2. The time-limits fixed according to the preceding paragraph shall, so far as possible, coincide with those already fixed for the pleadings in the case.

3. The intervening State shall be entitled, in the course of the oral proceedings, to submit its observations with respect to the subject-matter of the intervention.

Article 86

1. If an intervention under Article 63 of the Statute is admitted, the intervening State shall be furnished with copies of the pleadings and documents annexed, and shall be entitled, within a time-limit to be fixed by the Court, or by the President if the Court is not sitting, to submit its written observations on the subject-matter of the intervention.

2. These observations shall be communicated to the parties and to any other State admitted to intervene. The intervening State shall be entitled, in the course of the oral proceedings, to submit its observations with respect to the subject-matter of the intervention.

Subsection 5. Special Reference to the Court

Article 87

1. When in accordance with a treaty or convention in force a contentious case is brought before the Court concerning a matter which has been the subject of proceedings before some other international body, the provisions of the Statute and of the Rules governing contentious cases shall apply.

2. The application instituting proceedings shall identify the decision or other act of the international body concerned and a copy thereof shall be annexed; it shall contain a precise statement of the questions raised in regard to that decision or act, which constitute the subject of the dispute referred to the Court.

Subsection 6. Discontinuance

Article 88

1. If at any time before the final judgment on the merits has been delivered the parties, either jointly or separately, notify the Court in writing that they have agreed to discontinue the proceedings, the Court shall make an order recording the discontinuance and directing that the case be removed from the list.

2. If the parties have agreed to discontinue the proceedings in consequence of having

reached a settlement of the dispute and if they so desire, the Court may record this fact in the order for the removal of the case from the list, or indicate in, or annex to, the order, the terms of the settlement.

3. If the Court is not sitting, any order under this Article may be made by the President.

Article 89

1. If in the course of proceedings instituted by means of an application, the applicant informs the Court in writing that it is not going on with the proceedings, and if, at the date on which this communication is received by the Registry, the respondent has not yet taken any step in the proceedings, the Court shall make an order officially recording the discontinuance of the proceedings and directing the removal of the case from the list. A copy of this order shall be sent by the Registrar to the respondent.

2. If, at the time when the notice of discontinuance is received, the respondent has already taken some step in the proceedings, the Court shall fix a time-limit within which the respondent may state whether it opposes the discontinuance of the proceedings. If no objection is made to the discontinuance before the expiration of the time-limit, acquiescence will be presumed and the Court shall make an order officially recording the discontinuance of the proceedings and directing the removal of the case from the list. If objection is made, the proceedings shall continue.

3. If the Court is not sitting, its powers under this Article may be exercised by the President.

SECTION E. PROCEEDINGS BEFORE THE CHAMBERS

Article 90

Proceedings before the chambers mentioned in Articles 26 and 29 of the Statute shall, subject to the provisions of the Statute and of these Rules relating specifically to the chambers, be governed by the provisions of Parts I to III of these Rules applicable in contentious cases before the Court.

Article 91

1. When it is desired that a case should be dealt with by one of the chambers which has been formed in pursuance of Article 26, paragraph 1, or Article 29 of the Statute, a request to this effect shall either be made in the document instituting the proceedings or accompany it. Effect will be given to the request if the parties are in agreement.

2. Upon receipt by the Registry of this request, the President of the Court shall communicate it to the members of the chamber concerned. He shall take such steps as may be necessary to give effect to the provisions of Article 31, paragraph 4, of the Statute.

3. The President of the Court shall convene the chamber at the earliest date compatible with the requirements of the procedure.

Article 92

1. Written proceedings in a case before a chamber shall consist of a single pleading by each side. In proceedings begun by means of an application, the pleadings shall be deliv-

ered within successive time-limits. In proceedings begun by the notification of a special agreement, the pleadings shall be delivered within the same time-limits, unless the parties have agreed on successive delivery of their pleadings. The time-limits referred to in this paragraph shall be fixed by the Court, or by the President if the Court is not sitting, in consultation with the chamber concerned if it is already constituted.

2. The chamber may authorize or direct that further pleadings be filed if the parties are so agreed, or if the chamber decides, *proprio motu* or at the request of one of the parties, that such pleadings are necessary.

3. Oral proceedings shall take place unless the parties agree to dispense with them, and the chamber consents. Even when no oral proceedings take place, the chamber may call upon the parties to supply information or furnish explanations orally.

Article 93

Judgments given by a chamber shall be read at a public sitting of that chamber.

SECTION F. JUDGMENTS, INTERPRETATION AND REVISION

Subsection 1. *Judgments*

Article 94

1. When the Court has completed its deliberations and adopted its judgment, the parties shall be notified of the date on which it will be read.

2. The judgment shall be read at a public sitting of the Court and shall become binding on the parties on the day of the reading.

Article 95

1. The judgment, which shall state whether it is given by the Court or by a chamber, shall contain:

the date on which it is read;
the names of the judges participating in it;
the names of the parties;
the names of the agents, counsel and advocates of the parties;
a summary of the proceedings;
the submissions of the parties;
a statement of the facts;
the reasons in point of law;
the operative provisions of the judgment;
the decision, if any, in regard to costs;
the number and names of the judges constituting the majority;
a statement as to the text of the judgment which is authoritative.

2. Any judge may, if he so desires, attach his individual opinion to the judgment, whether he dissents from the majority or not; a judge who wishes to record his concurrence or dissent without stating his reasons may do so in the form of a declaration. The same shall also apply to orders made by the Court.

3. One copy of the judgment duly signed and sealed, shall be placed in the archives of the Court and another shall be transmitted to each of the parties. Copies shall be sent by the Registrar to: *(a)* the Secretary-General of the United Nations; *(b)* the Members of the United Nations; *(c)* other States entitled to appear before the Court.

Article 96

When by reason of an agreement reached between the parties, the written and oral proceedings have been conducted in one of the Court's two official languages, and pursuant to Article 39, paragraph 1, of the Statute the judgment is to be delivered in that language, the text of the judgment in that language shall be the authoritative text.

Article 97

If the Court, under Article 64 of the Statute, decides that all or part of a party's costs shall be paid by the other party, it may make an order for the purpose of giving effect to that decision.

Subsection 2. *Requests for the Interpretation or Revision of a Judgment*

Article 98

1. In the event of dispute as to the meaning or scope of a judgment any party may make a request for its interpretation, whether the original proceedings were begun by an application or by the notification of a special agreement.

2. A request for the interpretation of a judgment may be made either by an application or by the notification of a special agreement to that effect between the parties; the precise point or points in dispute as to the meaning or scope of the judgment shall be indicated.

3. If the request for interpretation is made by an application, the requesting party's contentions shall be set out therein, and the other party shall be entitled to file written observations thereon within a time-limit fixed by the Court, or by the President if the Court is not sitting.

4. Whether the request is made by an application or by notification of a special agreement, the Court may, if necessary, afford the parties the opportunity of furnishing further written or oral explanations.

Article 99

1. A request for the revision of a judgment shall be made by an application containing the particulars necessary to show that the conditions specified in Article 61 of the Statute are fulfilled. Any documents in support of the application shall be annexed to it.

2. The other party shall be entitled to file written observations on the admissibility of the application within a time-limit fixed by the Court, or by the President if the Court is not sitting. These observations shall be communicated to the party making the application.

3. The Court, before giving its judgment on the admissibility of the application may afford the parties a further opportunity of presenting their views thereon.

4. If the Court finds that the application is admissible it shall fix time-limits for such further proceedings on the merits of the application as, after ascertaining the views of the parties, it considers necessary.

5. If the Court decides to make the admission of the proceedings in revision conditional on previous compliance with the judgment, it shall make an order accordingly.

Article 100

1. If the judgment to be revised or to be interpreted was given by the Court, the request for its revision or interpretation shall be dealt with by the Court. If the judgment was given by a chamber, the request for its revision or interpretation shall be dealt with by that chamber.

2. The decision of the Court, or of the chamber, on a request for interpretation or revision of a judgment shall itself be given in the form of a judgment.

SECTION G. MODIFICATIONS PROPOSED BY THE PARTIES

Article 101

The parties to a case may jointly propose particular modifications or additions to the rules contained in the present Part (with the exception of Articles 93 to 97 inclusive), which may be applied by the Court or by a chamber if the Court or the chamber considers them appropriate in the circumstances of the case.

[PART IV]

ADVISORY PROCEEDINGS

Article 102

1. In the exercise of its advisory functions under Article 65 of the Statute, the Court shall apply, in addition to the provisions of Article 96 of the Charter and Chapter IV of the Statute, the provisions of the present Part of the Rules.

2. The Court shall also be guided by the provisions of the Statute and of these Rules which apply in contentious cases to the extent to which it recognizes them to be applicable. For this purpose, it shall above all consider whether the request for the advisory opinion relates to a legal question actually pending between two or more States.

3. When an advisory opinion is requested upon a legal question actually pending between two or more States, Article 31 of the Statute shall apply, as also the provisions of these Rules concerning the application of that Article.

Article 103

When the body authorized by or in accordance with the Charter of the United Nations to request an advisory opinion informs the Court that its request necessitates an urgent answer, or the Court finds that an early answer would be desirable, the Court shall take all necessary steps to accelerate the procedure, and it shall convene as early as possible for the purpose of proceeding to a hearing and deliberation on the request.

Article 104

All requests for advisory opinions shall be transmitted to the Court by the Secretary-General of the United Nations or, as the case may be, the chief administrative officer of the body authorized to make the request. The documents referred to in Article 65, paragraph 2, of the Statute shall be transmitted to the Court at the same time as the request or as soon as possible thereafter, in the number of copies required by the Registry.

Article 105

1. Written statements submitted to the Court shall be communicated by the Registrar to any States and organizations which have submitted such statements.

2. The Court, or the President if the Court is not sitting, shall:

(a) determine the form in which, and the extent to which, comments permitted under Article 66, paragraph 4, of the Statute shall be received, and fix the time-limit for the submission of any such comments in writing;

(b) decide whether oral proceedings shall take place at which statements and comments may be submitted to the Court under the provisions of Article 66 of the Statute, and fix the date for the opening of such oral proceedings.

Article 106

The Court, or the President if the Court is not sitting, may decide that the written statements and annexed documents shall be made accessible to the public on or after the opening of the oral proceedings. If the request for advisory opinion relates to a legal question actually pending between two or more States, the views of those States shall first be ascertained.

Article 107

1. When the Court has completed its deliberations and adopted its advisory opinion, the opinion shall be read at a public sitting of the Court.

2. The advisory opinion shall contain:

the date on which it is delivered;
the names of the judges participating;
a summary of the proceedings;
a statement of the facts;
the reasons in point of law;
the reply to the question put to the Court;
the number and names of the judges constituting the majority;
a statement as to the text of the opinion which is authoritative.

3. Any judge may, if he so desires, attach his individual opinion to the advisory opinion of the Court, whether he dissents from the majority or not; a judge who wishes to record his concurrence or dissent without stating his reasons may do so in the form of a declaration.

Article 108

The Registrar shall inform the Secretary-General of the United Nations, and, where appropriate, the chief administrative officer of the body which requested the advisory opinion, as to the date and the hour fixed for the public sitting to be held for the reading of the opinion. He shall also inform the representatives of the Members of the United Nations and other States, specialized agencies and public international organizations immediately concerned.

Article 109

One copy of the advisory opinion, duly signed and sealed, shall be placed in the archives of the Court, another shall be sent to the Secretary-General of the United Nations and, where appropriate, a third to the chief administrative officer of the body which requested the opinion of the Court. Copies shall be sent by the Registrar to the Members of the United Nations and to any other States, specialized agencies and public international organizations immediately concerned.

INDEX

admissibility 191–8
  exhaustion of local remedies, *see under* exhaustion
    of local remedies
  nationality of claims, *see under* nationality of
    claims
African regional economic organisations 110–11
Algiers Accords 75–6
applicable law 239–48
  choice in arbitration agreement 245–6
  choice by parties 240; evasion of mandatory rules
    241; 'insulating' contract 244; limitations
    241; national law 242; reasons for 243; time
    for 242
  choice of tribunal 239
  and conflict of law rules 247–8
  economic development agreements 246
  examples of clauses 246–7
  general principles of law, choice of 245
  ICSID Convention 245–6
  implied choice 246
  lex mercatoria 244–5
  and treaty 239–40
appointment of arbitrators 219–22
  default procedure 220–1
  multi-party arbitrations 221
  procedure in agreement 219
arbitrability 202–4
  and national laws 203
arbitral process 190–273
arbitral tribunals 218–23
  challenges to jurisdiction 227–9; mechanisms 227
  delocalisation of, *see under* delocalisation
  establishment 218–23
  lex arbitri, see under *lex arbitri*
  procedure 218–23
  time limits 218–19; excessive delay 219; treaty
    provisions 218–19
  truncated, authority of 225–7; final award of
    226
arbitration 31–9
  agreement 33
  dispute between company and state 38–9
  Geneva Convention on the Execution of Foreign
    Arbitral Awards (1927) 55
  Geneva Protocol (1923) 55
  history 32–3
  ICSID 69–73, *see also under* ICSID
  ILC draft Convention 34–5
  international agreements on 54–7
  and judicial settlement 33
  and *lex arbitri* 51–2
  meaning 31–2
  mixed 38–9

Model Rules 34–5
national laws 51–4
New York Convention (1958) 56–7
origins 32
Permanent Court of Arbitration 35–8; *see also
  under* Permanent Court of Arbitration
procedure 34–5
use in recent times 38–9
arbitration agreement 215
  constitution of tribunal 210–11
  contents 210–12
  default procedures 211
  lex loci arbitri 211
  parties 207–8
  signature by government agency 207
  succession to rights and duties under 207
  validity 206
arbitration clauses 212–16
  autonomy 212–16
  and annulment of agreement 215–16; ICC Rules
    215
  and competence of tribunal 213
  and submission agreements 212
arbitrators:
  appointment 219–22; *see also* appointment of
    arbitrators
  challenge to 222–3
  control of proceedings 223–4
  disqualification 222–3
  duties 223–5; and agreement 225
  interim measures of protection 224–5
  organisational guidelines 224
  powers 223–5
  rendering of award 223–4
award 253–7
  annulment 257
  challenges to 257–61; consequences 261
  default 255
  dissenting opinion 254
  effects 261–3
  enforcement 256
  errors in 256
  interim 254
  interpretation of 256
  procedure 253–7
  recourse in municipal courts against 259
  res judicata, as 261–2
  review 258–9; UNCITRAL Model Law 259–60
  and settlement 255–6
  and *stare decisis* 262

capacity 204–6
  corporations 205

capacity (*cont.*):
  natural persons 205
  States 205
cessation of dispute:
  and justiciability 13–14
COMESA 107–9
  aim 107–8
  jurisdiction of court 108–9
compromis 235–6
  settling terms of 235
conciliation 29–31
  commissions 30
  and General Assembly 31
  ICSID 68
  meaning 29
  multilateral treaties 29–30
  OSCE 39
conflict:
  disputes and the law 1–5
  meaning 1–2
consultation, *see* negotiation
corporations:
  capacity 205
  nationality 193–5
costs 253

delocalisation 232–5
  arguments against 233
  arguments in favour 233–4
  and choice of parties 234–5
  inter-State arbitrations 235
  support for theory 232–3
  see also lex arbitri
dispute:
  existence of 10–13
  legal 14–16
  meaning 1–2
  optional recourse to legal processes 3–4
  separation of legal and non-legal issues 14–16
dispute settlement in the law of the sea 84–95
  Annex VII arbitral tribunals 90–1
  Annex VIII special arbitral tribunals 91–2
  International Court of Justice 90
  International Tribunal for the Law of the Sea
    87–90; *see also* International Tribunal for the
    Law of the Sea
  United Nations Convention on the Law of
    the Sea 84–7; basic principles for operation
    of tribunals 94; corporations 85–6; and
    discretion of states 86–7; exhaustion of
    local remedies rule 95; limitations on jurisdic-
    tion of tribunals 92–3; practice in choice of
    tribunal 94
dispute settlement mechanisms 39–40
dispute settlement procedures 5–10
  alternatives 8
  commercial disputes 7
  and contract 7
  and governments 8–9
  range of 5–10
  'satisfactory' result 8

ECOWAS 109–10
  aims 109
enforcement of judgments and awards 263–73
  mixed arbitrations 264
  municipal legislation 265–6
  and national courts 263–4
  negotiations 264–5
  New York Convention 266–70; controls by
    courts 269–70; grounds for refusal 267–9;
    and integrity of court 269; and procedural
    defects in arbitration 268
  recognition 265
  state immunity 270–3; *see also under* state
    immunity
European Community 105–7
  integration of law into municipal legal orders of
    Member States 107
European Court 105–7
  composition 105
  Court of First Instance 106–7
  jurisdiction 105–6
  preliminary rulings 106
  role 105
exchanges of views, *see* negotiation
exhaustion of local remedies 195–8
  burden of proof 196–7
  modification of rule 197
  preliminary objection 196
  waiver of rule 197–8
existence of dispute:
  and justiciability 10–13

fact finding 24–7
  and international organisations 26
  meaning 26–7
  and treaties 25–6
  and UN General Assembly 26–7
  see also inquiry
forum prorogatum 200

GATT system 96–9
  aim 97
  consultation 97–8
  notification 97–8
  'nullification or impairment' 98–9
  panel proceedings 98
General Assembly:
  and conciliation 31
  and fact finding 26–7
  Model Rules on Arbitral Procedure 34–5
good offices 27–9
  meaning 27–8
  and treaties 28
  and United Nations 28–9
  see also mediation
governments
  and dispute settlement procedures 8–9

Hague Convention on the Pacific Settlement of
  Disputes (1899) 35–6
Hague Convention on the Pacific Settlement of
  Disputes (1907) 35–6
  text 285–301

ICC Arbitration Rules 47–9
  agreement of parties 47
  choice of tribunal 47–8
  International Court of Arbitration 47–9
  rules governing proceedings 48–9
  submission of draft award to Court 49
  and UNCITRAL Arbitration Rules 50
  work of tribunal 47–8
inquiry 24–7,
  function 24–5
  international commissions 25
  and international organisations 26
  and treaties 25–6
  see also fact finding
interim measures 248–50
  and national courts 249
  and third parties 249
International Centre for the Settlement of
    Investment Disputes (ICSID) 59–73
  Additional Facility 62
  arbitration 69–73; annulment of awards 71–2;
    competence of tribunal 70; non-frustration 70;
    questioning awards 70–1
  conciliation 68
  enforcement of awards 73
  framework 60–8
  jurisdiction 61–2
  organs 60–1
  origin 59–60
  parties to dispute 64–8; 'foreign control' clause
    66–8; individual nationals 65; nationality of
    companies 65–6
  procedure 68–73
  submission to jurisdiction 62–4; bilateral
    investment protection treaty 63–4; first
    level 62–3; multilateral treaty practice 64;
    second level 63
ICSID Convention text 302–18
international commercial arbitration 45–58
  development 45–6
  history 45–6
  ICC rules 46–51
International Court of Justice 124–85
  admissibility 155–62; case has become 'moot'
    157; examples 161–2; hypothetical nature of
    case 156; jurisdiction compared 155–6; lack
    of interest in subject-matter 157–8; legal inter-
    est of third state 158–61; *Monetary Gold* prin-
    ciple 158–61, 167
  Advisory Opinions 131, 182–5; bodies which
    may request 182; and consent 183–5; legal
    question, on 185; legal questions at heart of dis-
    putes 183
  application 175
  Chambers 127–9
  competence and jurisdiction in contentious cases
    132–55; cases which parties refer 133–5;
    forum prorogatum 136; General Act for the
    Pacific Settlement of Disputes (1928) 137–8;
    international organisations 132–3; interpreta-
    tion of agreements for reference 134–5; mat-
    ters specially provided for in UN Charter

135–6; Optional Clause 137–8; States 132;
    'transferred' jurisdiction 139–40; treaties or
    conventions in force 137–9; treaty no longer in
    force 138–9
  composition 126–7
  counter-memorial 176
  interim measures of protection 168–75; clearly
    established jurisdiction 169; discretion exercise
    of 171–3; enforcement 174–5 jurisdiction
    169–71; relationship to claim on merits 174;
    scope 173–4
  interpretation of judgments 179–80
  intervention 162–8; construction of convention
    163–4; interest of legal nature 164–8; jurisdic-
    tional link 164–8; *Monetary Gold* principle
  judges 126–7; *ad hoc* 130–1; dismissal 127; dis-
    qualification 129–30; election 127
  judgments, effect of 177; enforcement of 178–9,
    263–4
  memorial 175–6
  non-appearance 180–1
  Optional Clause 137–8, 140–55; automatic
    reservations 143–6; 'Belgian' formula 147–8;
    character of relationships created by declaration
    140–1; Connolly amendment 143; domestic
    jurisdiction 143; limited success of system
    154–5; limitation of jurisdiction to certain cat-
    egories of case 146; multilateral treaty reserva-
    tions 148–9; past disputes reservations 151;
    reciprocity 141–2, 150–1; reservations
    141–50; resort to other means of peaceful
    settlement 149–50; self-judging reservations
    143–6; termination of declaration 152; time
    limitations 146–8, 151; transferred declara-
    tions 153–4; Vandenberg amendment 148–9;
    variation of terms of declaration 153; with-
    drawal of declaration 152
  participation 125–6
  parties to statute 125–6
  President 131–2
  procedure 175–6
  provisional measures of protection 168–75
  reciprocity 150–1
  Registrar 131–2
  rejoinder 176
  reply 176
  revision of judgments 179–80
  Rules: text 359–89
  seat 131–2
  sittings 127–9
  Statute: text 346–58
  Vice-President 131–2
  withdrawal of party 181
international economic disputes 96–123
international financial disputes 117–23
international law
  national law distinguished 4
  nature of 2–3
International Law Commission:
  and arbitral procedure 34–5
International Monetary Fund 117–19
  disputes procedure 118

International Tribunal for the Law of the Sea 87–90
  composition 87–8
  procedure 88–9
  quorum 88
  Sea-Bed Disputes Chamber 89
intervention 208–10
Iran-US Claims Tribunal 73–83
  Algiers Accords 75–6
  applicable law 82
  claims of nationals 77–81
  enforcement of awards 82–3
  excluded claims 78–80
  and Hostages Crisis 74
  interpretative cases 81
  jurisdiction 77–81
  membership 76
  and municipal courts 82–3
  'nationals', meaning 80
  official claims 81
  submission of cases to 77
Iraq:
  UN Compensation Commission, and 41–4

joinder 208–10
justiciability 10–16
  and cessation of dispute 13–14
  existence of dispute 10–13
  legal dispute 14–16

language:
  control of 4–5
legal dispute:
  and justiciability 14–16
lex arbitri 229–32
  and applicable law 230
  autonomy theory 231
  contractual theory 230–1
  importance 229
  jurisdictional theory 230
  scope 229–30
  seat of arbitration 230
  seat theory 231–2
  see also delocalisation
lex mercatoria 244–5
lump sum settlement 23–4

Manila Declaration on the Peaceful Settlement of
  International Disputes 20
  text 279–84
mediation 27–9,
  meaning 27–8
  and mixed disputes 29
  and treaties 28
  and United Nations 28–9
  see also good offices
Mercosur Agreement (1991) 116–17
methods of settlement of disputes 19–44
mixed arbitrations 59–83
Multilateral Investment Guarantee Agency 121–3
  disputes as to interpretation of Convention
    122–3
  and ICSID Convention rules 122

NAFTA 111–17
  antidumping disputes 113
  bi-national panel procedures 113
  consultation 111
  countervailing duty obligations 113
  Emergency Action Proceedings 115
  Free Trade Commission 111, 116
  interpretations of Treaty 115
  'mixed arbitrations' 113–14
  objects 111
  panel 112
national law:
  international law distinguished 4
nationality of claims 191–5
  corporations 193–4
  dual nationality 192
  ICSID 193
  Iran-US Claims Tribunal 80–1, 194–5
negotiation 20–4
  bilateral 22
  formalised 22
  imposition by judicial decision 22
  lump sum settlement 23–4
  mechanisms 23
  multilateral 22
  refusal of one party 23
  as subject of treaty 21
New York Convention on the Recognition and
    Enforcement of Foreign Arbitral Awards 1958
    56–7, 266–70

Organization of African Unity:
  dispute settlement mechanism 40
Organisation on Security and Co-operation in
    Europe (OSCE)
  Conciliation Commission 40
  Valetta principles 39–40

Permanent Court of Arbitration 35–8
  creation 35
  heyday 36–7
  importance 37–8
  revival, proposals for 37
  seat 36
procedural fairness 237–8
  audi alteram partem 237
  and natural justice 238
  and nullification of award 238
  proper deliberation by duly constituted tribunal 237
  reasoned award 238
procedure of arbitration 235–8

refusal to arbitrate 216–17
  and denial of justice 216–17
  and State immunity 217
remedies 248–53
  compensation 250–3; interest on 252
  declaratory judgment 250–3
  final 250–3
  interim measures, *see* interim measures
representation of parties 236
res judicata:
  awards as 261–2

sea, law of, *see* dispute settlement in the law of the sea
stare decisis
  and awards 262
state immunity 217, 270–3
  limitation 272
  waiver 271–2
submission to jurisdiction 198–206
  arbitrability 202–4
  capacity 204–6
  defined legal relationship 202
  existing disputes 199
  existing or future differences 201
  future disputes 199
  New York Convention (1958) 199–200
  validity 206
  written agreement 200–1; *forum prorogatum*
    200; model clause 201

third parties 208–10
  intervention 208–10
  joinder 208–10

UNCITRAL Arbitration Rules 50–1
  and ICC Rules 50
  text 319
UNCITRAL Model Law 53–4
  aim 53–4
  and intervention of national courts 54
  text 334–5
United Nations
  General Assembly, *see under* General Assembly
  and good offices 28–9

  and mediation 28–9
  settlement of disputes 19–20
UN Charter 19–20
  disputes to be referred to International Court of
    Justice 135–6
UN Compensation Commission 41–4
  approach to claims 43–4
  and Iraq 41–4
  nature of 42
  number of claims 42–3
  Provisional Rules 43
UN Compensation Fund 41–2

Valletta Principles 39–40

World Bank 119–21
  Board of Executive Directors 121
  Inspection Panel 120–1
  loan agreements 119
WTO system 99–104
  Appellate Body 102–3
  consultation 100–1
  Dispute Settlement Body 100
  Dispute Settlement Understanding 99–100
  implementation of obligations 103–4
  normal working procedures of panels 102
  notification 100–1
  panels 101
  success of 104
  third party interests 101–2
  time limits 103